2d edition

Investment & Analysis Portfolio Selection

Herbert E. Phillips, Ph.D.
Professor of Finance
Department of Finance
School of Business Administration
Temple University

John C. Ritchie, Jr., Ph.D.
Chairman, Department of Finance
School of Business Administration
Temple University

Published by

F44 **SOUTH-WESTERN PUBLISHING CO.**

CINCINNATI   WEST CHICAGO, ILL.   DALLAS   PELHAM MANOR, N.Y.   PALO ALTO, CALIF.

ISBN: 0-538-06440-4

Library of Congress Catalog Card Number: 82-50027

1 2 3 4 5 6 7 8 D 9 8 7 6 5 4 3 2

Printed in the United States of America

Preface

The second edition of this book continues the emphasis of the first edition on the presentation of modern theories and approaches in the area of portfolio selection and security analysis. Recognizing that the building blocks of portfolios are individual securities, particular emphasis is placed on integrating modern portfolio selection models with traditional valuation theory and analysis. The two approaches should not be viewed as competitive but rather as supportive of one another. Chapter 11 is a new chapter that presents a systematically developed approach for selecting portfolios of financial securities through integration of the work of the traditional financial analyst within the framework of a modern portfolio selection model.

Portfolio selection models and security analysis techniques are presented in a rigorous and comprehensive way. Where limiting or restrictive assumptions are necessary, such assumptions are placed in full view of the reader and carefully explained. The logical and practical shortcomings of the various approaches developed are pointed out. An entire chapter is devoted to current issues and controversies that arise in the investment field. Some issues are raised and left unresolved. This is not a shortcoming of this text but of the current state of the art.

An elementary knowledge of accounting, statistics, and micro- and macroeconomics is assumed on the part of the reader. Needless to say, various modern analytical models cannot be presented in a meaningful way without resorting to elementary mathematics and statistics.

Section I, Part I, of the book develops the nature of the securities traded in financial markets, the structure and operation of these markets, and the tax environment as it relates to investment decisions. This material, while basically descriptive in nature, provides the necessary background for effective application of the portfolio selection and security analysis techniques developed in the rest of the book. In addition, such a background can also help one recognize limitations in the approaches covered. Taxes play such an important role in financial decisions that a new chapter has been devoted to a rather detailed outline of current tax law and implications for the investor. Believing this chapter is an important addition to the book, we have developed the topic in greater depth than is done in the typical investment text. Stock and bond valuation material in Part 2 of Section I is expanded, although the section still aims at building the basic analytical foundations that underlie security analysis and modern portfolio selection approaches.

Section II has been reorganized to improve readability and extended. Section III introduces a new chapter dealing with pension funds. The inflation issue is highlighted in this chapter and illustrated by means of its impact on pension funds, thereby creating a better understanding of its impact on investment decisions.

In most books, security analysis is presented from the standpoint of analyzing industrial securities only. Part 8 of the book recognizes special analytical considerations that should be understood when dealing with the special classes of securities. These chapters have been updated and substantially rewritten.

Student involvement materials in the form of questions and work-study problems are presented at the end of each chapter. A comprehensive instructor's manual that provides suggested answers to questions and work-study problems and a bank of multiple-choice test questions is available to adoptors of the book.

The authors take full responsibility for all errors and omissions but are indebted to their colleagues and students for helpful comments and suggestions. A special debt is owed to Dr. Douglas H. Bellemore, a former co-author. His influence is present throughout the book, although this revision is entirely the work of the present authors. Appreciation is also expressed to our secretaries, Lynell Burke and Mae Renshaw, for their patience and assistance.

Contents

PART 1
The Investment Setting

1.

Investments: An Introduction

This book is about investing in marketable securities—that is, investing in financial instruments such as bonds, private placement notes, equipment trust obligations, preferred stocks, common stocks, and stock options. While the nature of the instruments and the markets in which they trade will be developed, the primary concern of this text is with the decision process that leads to the selection of a collection of financial assets.

Investment in its broadest sense involves the commitment of certain present values for the possibility of receiving uncertain future values. The focus of this text is limited to *marketable securities*—that is, financial instruments that are bought and sold regularly in the securities market. Security investment aims at increasing wealth through generating pecuniary gain in the form of interest income, dividend income, and/or capital gain. Of course, other kinds of investment, such as savings accounts, insurance policies, and real estate, have the same purpose. These alternatives, however, will not be covered in this book.

INVESTMENTS: A WORLD OF CHANGING CONCEPTS

Empirical and theoretical studies during the past two decades have raised questions regarding the philosophical basis of the traditional approach to investment decisions. That approach concentrates on selecting the "best" stock. However, it overlooks the interrelationships that exist between rates of return on financial assets and the possibility of reducing risk through diversification. Modern portfolio theory concentrates on exploiting these interrelationships through the use of mathematical models, wherein the basic inputs are return data and the volatility of these returns.

Investment constraints faced by investors and data limitations create problems in the utilization of existing portfolio models. Moreover, existing models that can handle financial assets other than common stocks have not really been developed, although the theoretical framework of modern theory is general. When dealing with uncertainty, judgment is still an important factor. According to Markowitz, the development of dependable estimates of risk and return "should combine statistical techniques and the judgment of practical men."[1] Fundamental analysis, modified to recognize its many shortcomings, offers a framework for utilizing statistical techniques and mathematical approaches to handling uncertainty and judgment. What is needed is an integration of portfolio selection approaches and fundamental analysis. In this book fundamental analysis is developed with the thought of integration with portfolio selection approaches always in mind.

THE INVESTMENT ENVIRONMENT

A *securities market* is a place where supply and demand for financial assets meet. The primary function of any market is to provide for the orderly transfer of both product and information between buyer and seller. Thus the price of a security reflects the interaction of suppliers of funds (who purchase financial assets) and demanders of funds. The supply of funds brought to a given segment of the securities market will reflect the expectations of investors, alternative possible uses of funds, and investor objectives and risk profiles. Instruments traded in the various segments of the securities market are discussed in Chapters 2, 3, 4, and 5. Tax considerations, including their implications for investment decisions, are developed in Chapter 6. A framework for portfolio selection and valuation considerations is then developed in Chapters 7 through 13 before returning to a consideration of the historical behavior, operations, structure, and regulation of securities markets in Chapters 14 and 15. The remainder of the book develops the fundamental considerations and analysis that underlie the selection of particular bonds or stocks.

Economic Importance of Investment

Capital goods are assets whose life expectancies are greater than one year and whose function is to produce actual products or to participate in economic production. Labor needs buildings, equipment, and other capital goods to produce the great and varied quantity of goods and services modern societies desire. Modern factories and machines incorporating current technology were created only to the extent that people were, and still are, willing to sacrifice present con-

---

[1] Harry M. Markowitz, "Portfolio Selection," *Journal of Finance*, Vol. 7, No. 1 (March, 1952), p. 91.

sumption to save and invest. Thus, real savings and investment promote economic growth through their allocation of income to long-term assets (capital goods) for future production rather than current consumption.

The economic function of all capital markets is to serve as intermediaries that will channel savings into productive uses. *Savings* represent claims by individuals to real resources to be delivered at a future date. Investment, by contrast, refers to the creation of new capital goods. If the claims represented by savings are not invested by those with productive ideas, total output may well fall below the potential for a society. Of course, the entrepreneur who raises the funds is left to employ them in a productive manner. Thus the funds raised in the capital market may not always be used for purposes that increase the productive capacity of the economy. For example, the government may utilize borrowed funds to produce bombs, or business may replenish working capital or retire debt rather than invest in capital goods.

The purchase of a stock or bond—whether a new or existing issue— does not in itself create a new capital good. However, the funds of the seller are freed by such a transaction and can be invested in a new venture or new issue. The availability of efficient markets to facilitate conversion from less to more liquid assets enhances the willingness of investors to commit funds to long-term instruments and thus helps to promote economic growth. If investors could not regain liquidity after an investment was made, they would hesitate to commit their savings to others. The important point to recognize here is that decisions made in the capital markets influence the future course of society; these decisions affect everyone.

Because savings and investment are interrelated, investors should examine and interpret trends in the flow of savings through the capital markets. The changing importance of various sectors of the markets represents changing supply and demand situations that have implications for yields and prices of securities. A historical overview of the flow of savings and an accompanying analysis of such flows is presented in Chapter 14.

Risk and Return

According to Webster's dictionary, risk is "the chance of injury, damage, or loss."[2] Risk is an important concept to the investor. Most investors are *risk averse* in that they prefer a low degree of risk with as high a rate of return as possible. A prime determinant of most investment decisions is the degree of risk an investor is willing to accept for a given rate of return or the probability of a given rate of return.

---

[2] *Webster's New World Dictionary,* College Edition (New York: The New World Pub. Co., 1968), p. 1,257.

Financial Investment Risk

Risk is a part of any financial investment decision and must be analyzed along with other facets of a potential investment. Various types of risk can affect an investment decision. Thus, a comprehensive analysis of risk for investment decisions is one that attacks the problem simultaneously from various points of view.

Expectations Concept of Risk. Decisions made under conditions of certainty should turn out after the fact to be correct. When these conditions apply, there is no variation of outcomes relative to one's expectations and there is no risk. In a reasonably efficient capital market, the reward for investing in a riskless asset should approach a limit that we refer to as the *riskless rate of return*. For example, the purchaser of a short-term treasury bill is practically certain of realizing the calculated rate of return based on the purchase price. Such a purchase is riskless in the sense discussed above. The purchase of treasury bills, however, is not truly a riskless investment when one considers opportunity costs, changing yield patterns over time, and inflation.

Because the outcome of an investment decision is determined at least in part by chance events, the environment of investment decision is called *uncertain*. A financial asset purchased on the basis of imperfect knowledge about future events is called a *risky asset*. The degree of risk differs for different financial assets, but all financial assets are risky assets, at least in the opportunity sense. For example, uncertainty exists over whether the issuer of a bond will make all promised payments, what the price will be at various times prior to maturity if liquidity is desired, and what the impact of inflation will be over a relatively long investment horizon. Predicting the future cash flows to be generated through investment in a common stock and the impact of inflation on the returns from such an investment could well be considered even more uncertain since no contractual promises have been made. The purchase of a risky financial asset is tantamount to the purchase of a financial lottery, and is so treated by this text.

Traditional Risk Concepts. Traditional analysis discusses specific types of risk that could lead to an investor's not realizing the anticipated return that led to a specific investment decision.

1. *Purchasing Power Risk*. Table 1–1 shows the consumer price index for the years 1967 through 1980. The value of a dollar relative to the base year 1967 is also shown. The effect of inflation on the purchasing power of payments received under a fixed-income contract, such as a bond or a nonparticipating, nonconvertible preferred stock, is fairly obvious.

TABLE 1-1. Consumer Price Index, 1967-1980

Year	CPI	Price Relative	Year	CPI	Price Relative
1967	100.0	1.00	1974	147.7	.68
1968	104.2	.96	1975	161.2	.62
1969	109.8	.91	1976	170.5	.59
1970	116.3	.86	1977	181.5	.55
1971	121.3	.82	1978	195.4	.51
1972	125.3	.80	1979	217.4	.46
1973	133.1	.75	1980	261.5	.38

To illustrate the impact that purchasing power risk can have, assume that a savings account was opened on January 1, 1967, with a deposit of $1,000 and that a 5 percent interest rate, compounded annually, was paid from then until the end of 1980. By December 31, 1980, the dollar value of the account would have grown to $1,000 $(1.05)^{14}$ = $1,979.93. By year-end 1980, however, the value of a dollar would have shrunk to just $.38 in terms of 1967 purchasing power. Therefore, $1,979.93 spent at year-end 1980 would not purchase as much as $1,000 spent in 1967:

$$1967 \text{ purchasing power} = \$1,979.93 \ (.38)$$

$$= \$752.37.$$

In other words, the holder of the savings account lost $247.63 in terms of 1967 purchasing power because of inflation. The compound interest payments on commercial bank passbook savings accounts (typically paying a 5 percent interest rate) were not sufficient to maintain the purchasing power of the funds originally deposited over the period 1967-1980.

2. *Interest Rate Risk.* Interest rate risk comes about as a result of unanticipated changes in interest rates. To the extent that future changes in the interest rate are anticipated, such changes will be reflected in the current period prices of fixed-income securities. The double-digit inflation of 1973 and 1974 was not anticipated by the market, and thus its impact was not properly reflected in the prices of fixed-income securities before the fact. For example, investors who purchased investment quality corporate bonds late in 1973 would (in horror) have seen market prices drop by as much as 20 percent from 1973 highs to 1974 lows. With the tapering off of the rate of inflation in 1975 and an easing of monetary policy by the Federal Reserve, the

average price of investment quality corporate bonds came back up to a point approaching their 1973 highs. Many bondholders were forced to take substantial losses during the period. Interest rates reached historic highs in August 1981, again causing serious losses for many earlier purchasers of bonds. Such outcomes are evidence that substantial interest rate risk is taken by participants in the bond market and that so-called efficient markets are able to predict the future only imperfectly.

Further evidence of the high degree of interest rate risk present in bond markets is offered in Table 1-2. Interest rates over the period have been rising, and as a result bond prices have been falling throughout the period.

TABLE 1-2. Bond Yields and Prices

Year	Yields			Related Bond Prices		
	U.S. Gov't Long-Term	Corporate High Grade (Aaa)	Municipal High Grade (Aaa)	U.S. Gov't Long-Term	Corporate High Grade (Aaa)	Municipal High Grade (Aaa)
1946	2.08%	2.44%	1.45%	111.80	124.6	141.6
1960	4.47	4.62	4.13	84.07	92.0	98.3
1967	4.85	5.51	3.74	76.55	81.8	100.5
1968	5.25	6.18	4.20	72.33	76.4	93.5
1970	6.59	8.04	6.12	60.52	61.6	72.3
1973	6.30	8.44	4.99	62.80	63.7	85.4
1974	6.99	8.57	5.89	57.45	58.8	76.3
1975	7.17	8.79	6.50	56.03	56.1	67.4
1976	6.78	8.43	5.66	74.33	58.3	72.6
1980	12.21	12.79	10.09	37.30	37.2	48.11

Source: Various issues of the *Federal Reserve Bulletin.* The April 1976 and January 1960 data are based on Standard & Poor Indexes.

3. *Business Risk and Financial Risk.* When purchasing a fixed-income security, an investor enters into a contract that provides for a guaranteed periodic cash flow over the life of the contract and the return of the principal amount on maturity of the instrument. A common or preferred stock, on the other hand, offers no certain future cash flows but is bought on the expectation of realizing some minimum in terms of future cash flows. In the event of default or temporary disruptions in the cash flows received by a business, the promised or expected future cash flows may not be received (or only received in part) by an investor.

Business risk is risk that is intrinsic in the firm's operations. This type of risk is defined in terms of the ratio of fixed to variable costs and the resultant implications for the variability of the firm's net cash flows under changing business conditions and sales levels. *Financial risk* is risk that stems from the firm's capital structure decisions. The higher the proportion of capital raised through the issuance of fixed-income contracts (debt and preferred stocks), the greater the variability of the firm's net cash flows under changing business conditions and sales levels.

The two types of risk are closely related and sometimes referred to as the *default risk*. In each case the underlying risk concept is difficult to represent analytically; whether the concepts can be usefully separated for analytical purposes is questionable. The calculations of the degree of operating and the degree of financial leverage are discussed as leverage measures in most business finance texts.[3] Much controversy surrounds the use of various accounting data in making such calculations. Moreover, the static assumptions underlying these measures limit their usefulness.

Investment vs. Speculation

Unknowns and uncertainties surround any investment decision. Furthermore, an asset that might seem quite risky in isolation could actually reduce risk when combined in a portfolio of assets if the pattern of its returns was not highly correlated with other assets in the portfolio. For these reasons, creating a useful dichotomy for decision purposes between the terms *investment* and *speculation* is difficult.

Still, many professionals in the investment field and the legal system distinguish between investment and speculative situations in terms of the time horizon involved, the degree of information available, and the degree of risk they see in the asset as an individual asset. The "speculator," as contrasted to the "investor," is generally assumed to concentrate on opportunities that suggest relatively large returns over a short period of time, where the information available for an analysis tends to be quite limited and where default risk is higher than a person with more conservatively oriented investment goals would be willing to accept. Such distinctions can have significance when attempting to decide if the results of asset selection properly reflect the goals and degree of risk aversion the investor is willing to accept.

---

[3] For example, see J. Fred Weston and Eugene F. Brigham, *Essentials of Managerial Finance* (Hinsdale, Ill.: The Dryden Press, 1979), chapter 15; especially pages 395–399.

SECURITY ANALYSIS, PORTFOLIO SELECTION, AND CAPITAL MARKET THEORY

An analysis for investment decision must be comprehensive. The investor's specific investment goals must be considered, and these goals must be contrasted with the investor's willingness and ability to bear risk. Since the environment of investment decision is complex, a truly rational approach for investment decision will embrace information from whatever sources are available. Such an approach is comprehensive and calls for a blend of both art and science.

Diversification Analysis

In portfolio selection the emphasis is on a collection, and on how each part of a collection relates to the whole. When building an investment portfolio, therefore, one does not merely "purchase the best stocks and bonds."

The object of financial diversification is risk reduction. When the rates of return on various financial assets are perfectly correlated, risk reduction through diversification cannot be achieved. Whatever advantage is gained through financial diversification is due to the covariance effects—that is, to the interrelationships that exist between rates of return on financial assets. Effective risk reduction can only be achieved by exploiting such interrelationships. This is not at all the same thing as purchasing stock averages or indexing. The logical and practical shortcomings of such approaches are discussed more fully later in the text.

Portfolio Selection

Modern portfolio theory is based on the pioneering work of Harry M. Markowitz.[4] Markowitz was the first to give rigorous content to the concept of portfolio diversification and to propose a quantitative procedure by which it might be brought about. The Markowitz procedure, which is presented in detail in Chapters 7 and 8, provides a method for identifying portfolios that are efficient in the sense that they satisfy certain efficiency criteria and various preconditions that may be imposed by a portfolio manager. A portfolio is efficient if it (1) offers a higher expected rate of return than any other portfolio having the same level of risk and (2) offers a lower level of risk than any other portfolio having the same expected rate of return. These efficiency criteria are appropriate for use by any investor who (1) is risk averse in the sense

---

[4] Harry M. Markowitz, "Portfolio Selection," *Journal of Finance*, Vol. 7, No. 1 (March, 1952), pp. 77-91.

that the investor is made happy by anticipation of financial gain but is vexed by uncertainty about future rates of return; and (2) is willing to base investment decisions about risky financial assets on probabilistic estimates about future events.

Realistic application of the Markowitz variance-covariance model is laborious. To facilitate practical application of his portfolio selection approach, Markowitz first suggested,[5] and Sharpe later developed, a computational alternative. This modification, which provides a number of important insights of its own, assumes that "the returns on various securities are related only through common relationships with some basic underlying factor,"[6] or market index. Sharpe's "simplified" market model is presented in Chapter 10.

Capital Market Theory

Portfolio selection models are normative models. A normative model serves as a guide for action. Capital market theory, by contrast, is positive. Positive theory is not intended or designed to serve as a guide for action. The purpose of positive theory is to simplify and explain, to serve as a guide for drawing meaningful inferences about the economic environment in which action takes place. Capital market theory seeks to explain what would be the positive implications of normative portfolio theory if all investors were to behave in the manner prescribed by normative portfolio theory. This capital market theory is presented in Chapter 12.

Issues and Controversy

As with any field of study, the theory of investment has its own repertoire of pleasing generalities. If this theory is to serve any useful purpose, however, what matters are specifics and not generalities. Chapters 11 and 13 deal with specifics. Various shortcomings of both traditional and modern theory are exposed and inconsistencies are explored.

Security Analysis

Fundamental security analysis attempts to identify undervalued and overvalued securities. The analyst proceeds from an in-depth study of the economy and its implications for industries and companies to a valuation of a security based on its future earning power and dividend-

---

[5] Harry M. Markowitz, *Portfolio Selection* (New Haven: Yale University Press, 1959), pp. 96-99.
[6] William F. Sharpe, "A Simplified Model of Portfolio Analysis," *Management Science,* Vol. 9, No. 2 (January, 1963), p. 280.

paying expectations. Theories of security valuations and their short-comings are discussed in Chapter 7.

There is substantial statistical evidence supporting the contention that fundamental analysis has not been able to produce the superior rates of return that a search for undervalued and overvalued situations would suggest. Furthermore, capital market theory, especially the efficient market hypothesis, suggests that new information is so quickly integrated into current prices that such superior returns are not likely. This literature is developed in Parts 3 and 4 of Section 1, and the appropriate role for fundamental analysis is suggested in Chapter 17. While security analysts may find that demonstrating consistently above-average market performance is extremely difficult, they can usefully estimate return expectations, the riskiness of investment in different securities, and the impact of changing market conditions. The framework of security analysis is developed in Section 4, Parts 6 and 7.

The fundamental analyst considers the timing problem solved once appropriate security and portfolio analysis has been accomplished. However, relationships between economic indicators and stock prices and patterns observed in stock prices over time have led some to suggest that these patterns may be used to predict turning points in stock prices. The ideas of this group and the criticisms that can be levied against this approach are discussed in Chapter 14.

Questions

1. Distinguish between real investment and security investment.
2. Discuss the crucial role played by investment in the American economy.
3. Is a U.S. government long-term bond a risky asset? Explain.
4. Is risk reduction effectively gained through the purchase of a large number of different securities? Discuss carefully.
5. Define an efficient portfolio.
6. (a) Distinguish between normative and positive theory.
   (b) Is capital market theory normative or positive theory?

2.

Equity Securities

An investor is confronted with a variety of investment alternatives, such as stocks, bonds, warrants, options, works of art, real estate, antique cars, and so on. These alternatives offer markedly different contractual arrangements and suggest widely varying combinations of potential risk and return. Our concern in this book is with investment in marketable securities, mainly corporate stocks and bonds.

There are many ways of classifying alternative securities for discussion purposes. Possibly the most fundamental distinction to be made is between securities of private business enterprise and those of governmental bodies and/or agencies of government. Private business securities, of general interest to investors, are almost always issued by corporations. They can be usefully divided into two major classes: equity securities (stocks) and debt securities (bonds and notes).

Prospective investors in corporate securities should understand the corporate form of organization and the rights and privileges attached to the various types of corporate securities that may be purchased. This chapter explains the nature of the corporation and the equity securities a corporation issues. It also briefly discusses the potential advantages and disadvantages of equity securities for investors. Corporate debt securities will be discussed in Chapter 3 and U.S. government and municipal securities in Chapter 4.

The total market value of the outstanding common stock of all publicly held companies reached a peak of $1.198 trillion in 1972, fell back to about $676 billion in 1974, and rose again to $1.086 trillion by the end of 1978.[1] Table 2-1 suggests the relative importance of various investment alternatives to individual investors for selected years. The

---

[1] *Flow of Funds Accounts: Assets and Liabilities Outstanding, 1968–1978,* Board of Governors of the Federal Reserve System (Washington, D.C.), September, 1979, p. 2.

TABLE 2-1. Financial Assets Held by Households, Selected Dates (billions of dollars)

	1970		1975		1978	
	$	%	$	%	$	%
1. Currency, Deposits and Money Market Funds	544.5	28.3	943.2	37.0	1,329.1	38.8
2. U.S. Government Securities	107.2	5.6	152.8	6.0	203.8	6.0
3. State and Local Obligations	46.0	2.4	68.1	2.7	75.0	2.2
4. Corporate and Foreign Bonds	34.3	1.8	63.5	2.5	64.8	1.9
5. Mortgages	52.9	2.7	71.9	2.8	106.2	3.1
6. Open Market Paper	11.7	0.6	15.1	0.6	36.1	1.1
7. Corporate Equities and Investment Co. Shares	729.4	37.9	659.7	25.9	808.5	23.6
8. Life Insurance Reserves	130.5	6.8	166.6	6.5	198.5	5.8
9. Pension Fund Reserves	239.4	12.4	365.7	14.3	530.5	15.5
10. Miscellaneous Assets and Security Credit	30.7	1.6	45.1	1.8	69.3	2.0
Total Financial Assets	1,926.6	100.0	2,551.7	100.0	3,421.8	100.0

Source: *Flow of Funds Accounts: Assets and Liabilities Outstanding, 1968–1978*, Board of Governors of the Federal Reserve System (Washington, D.C.), September, 1979, p. 2.

sharp break in the market prices of common stocks that had occurred by the end of 1974 no doubt explains part of the drop in relative importance of common stocks in individual portfolios by 1975. Disappointment with the performance of equity securities and rising rates of interest offered by short-term alternatives, such as money market funds, probably are the major causes of the shift from equity securities, which also seems to have occurred.

CORPORATIONS

A corporation has been defined as "an artificial being, invisible, intangible and existing only in contemplation of the law. Being the mere creation of law it possesses only those properties which the charter of its creation confers upon it."[2] In other words, a corporation is created

_____

[2] *Trustees of Dartmouth College* v. *Woodward*, 4 Wheat (U.S.) 518, 643, and 659 (1819).

by governmental authority and has only those powers, privileges, and limitations that are stipulated by that authority.

The Nature of the Corporation

A corporation is an individual in the eyes of the law and can own property, conduct business, borrow, sue, and be sued in its own name. Because of this independent legal existence, stockholders are liable for the debts of the corporation only for the amount of unpaid subscriptions for capital stock and for any difference in subscription price and par value in the event the former is lower. Stockholders are, in general, liable for wages due, but this liability is subject to limitations as specified by law. Corporate laws vary from state to state, despite the efforts of the American Bar Association to interest states in the creation of a uniform "model" code. State statutes govern stockholders' rights.

A corporation comes into being when its articles of incorporation are accepted by a state. These articles of incorporation become the charter of the corporation. A corporate charter represents the basic contract between the issuing state, the corporation, and its shareholders. The founders of a corporation write a set of articles pursuant to their own ends and subject only to broad limitations of law; an investor who subsequently purchases stock automatically accepts the articles of incorporation.

Because the powers of a corporation are limited by its charter, there is a tendency to construct the articles in such a way as to convey broad powers. Any activities outside the express and implied powers conveyed by the charter are *ultra vires*. When ultra vires activities are undertaken, the directors who approved such acts are personally responsible for any losses incurred by the corporation in the event of a successful stockholder suit. A stockholder, moreover, may seek an injunction to prevent such an act from being undertaken. Except for illegal acts, however, the broad purpose clauses written into most modern charters have made this right of a stockholder somewhat academic.

Control of the Corporation

Theoretically, stockholders control the corporation through their right to elect the board of directors; the board sets corporate policy and appoints management. However, widespread diffusion of stock ownership among many small stockholders is not uncommon. Questions concerning the effectiveness of such control therefore arise. Management often sends proxy statements to stockholders requesting that they assign to management the voting privilege that attaches to common stock. While stockholders can refuse to grant their proxy, and even form dissident groups in an effort to change management, they rarely do. In the event a stockholder decides to undertake a proxy fight, a list of stockholders can be obtained from the corporation so that communications can be sent to them. Only a small number of stockholders typically attend annual meetings; management therefore, through the proxies granted them, usually chooses the board of directors and thus controls the corporation.

Nature of Corporate Stock

Ownership of a corporation is represented by shares of stock. Each share represents a proportional claim on corporate assets, exercisable only after settlement of all creditors' claims in the event of liquidation. Each share has the same rights and limitations as every other share of the same class. The number of classes of stock and the total number of shares of each class that may be issued are specified in the original or an amended corporate charter.

Corporations issue securities for the purpose of raising large amounts of capital that would be unavailable from a single source. An issue is broken into relatively small units of marketable securities (shares in the case of corporate stock) that can be offered for sale to many individuals and institutions through organized financial markets. Such markets allow investors to acquire the securities of different corporations and different types of securities whose returns are not highly correlated. Investors are thus offered the possibility of lessening the risk accepted by means of diversification. As we will show in a later chapter, close to maximum risk reduction through diversification may be obtained with as few as eight to ten equity securities.

Transfer of Stock

Stockholders who wish to sell stock that is registered in their names may assign it to a purchaser by endorsing the back of the stock certificate. Alternatively, the stockholder may attach a signed stock power of attorney or assignment to the certificate. If a stockholder wishes to maintain ownership of a stock but use it as collateral for a loan, a stock power of attorney can be attached to the certificate, which will then be accepted as collateral. If a stockholder wishes to sell only a portion of the holdings, this must be indicated on the assignment. Two new certificates would then be issued, one to the former owner and one to the new owner.

The actual transfer work is usually completed by a trust company. A transfer agent and an independent registrar are usually required to effect a transfer of ownership of stock. The registrar checks to make certain that no more than the authorized stock is issued. Then the certificate is received by the transfer agent, who will cancel the old certificate, revise the records to show the correct owner, and issue the new certificate.

In some instances stock may be recorded in a broker's name rather than the stockholder's name to facilitate future transfers when sold or to offer security when a stock is purchased on margin. Such a stock is called a *street certificate*. When the stockholder sells a street certificate, the broker endorses it and sends it for transfer.

If a stock certificate is lost or stolen, the corporation will issue a new certificate, but the stockholder must post a surety bond. This is done to protect the corporation in the event that the "lost or stolen" certificate is presented to it by a person who can prove true and rightful ownership of the certificate.

Subscription Rights to New Stock Issues

When a corporation wishes to sell additional stock, the directors must approve the issue and the corporation must have sufficient authorized and unissued stock available to cover the requirements of the new issue. If sufficient authorized stock is not available, stockholders must vote to approve an increase in the number of authorized shares.

New stock issues are often offered to existing stockholders by means of subscription rights. If the additional shares were sold directly to the public, the proportionate interest of each original stockholder would be reduced. A *subscription right* gives the stockholder the privilege of purchasing new securities at a stipulated price within a specified time. The subscription price is usually sufficiently below the current market price to induce the stockholders to buy the additional shares. Because subscription rights expire in a few weeks, they have no value if the market price falls to or below the subscription price.

The right of a stockholder to subscribe to a new issue of stock is sometimes called the *preemptive right*. The preemptive right is a matter of common law doctrine rather than of statutory law. Some states, such as Delaware, Indiana, and California, set aside the common law doctrine by providing specifically that no stockholder shall have a preemptive right unless such a right is reserved in the corporate charter. When the preemptive right is recognized, it is usually denied to preferred stock and reserved solely for common stock.

The Value of a Stock Right. An announcement of a rights offering by a corporation will specify the record date, the subscription price, and the expiration date of the stock right. Stockholders who are listed in the corporate records on the stated record date will receive the stock rights when they are issued. One right is typically issued for each outstanding share of stock.

The market price of outstanding shares of stock could logically be expected to rise, all other things being equal, on the date of announcement of a rights offering to reflect whatever value the market attached to receiving the rights. A purchaser of an outstanding share during the period between the date of announcement and the date that will allow a purchaser to be recorded as an owner on the corporate books by the record date (the "cum" rights or "rights-on" period) will, after all, receive the stock right as soon as it is issued. After the record date (the "ex-rights" period, which ends with the expiration of the right), all other things being equal, one could expect a share of stock to drop in price by the value of a stock right since the rights now trade in the market separate from the stock. The assumption of "all other things equal" is, of course, a rather heroic assumption.

The value of a right during the "cum-rights" period can be estimated by using the following equation:

$$X = \frac{MPOS - SPNS}{N + 1}, \qquad (2.1)$$

where

MPOS = the market price per share of the already outstanding stock;
SPNS = the subscription price to purchase a new share by a holder of a sufficient number of rights;
N = the number of rights required to purchase one new share;
X = the estimated value of a right.

For example, assume that the subscription price was fixed at $44 per share, and ten rights were required to purchase one new share. If the outstanding stock were selling at $66 per share, the market would then be valuing a right at $2, calculated as follows:

$$X = \frac{66 - 44}{10 + 1} = \$2.$$

One can possibly better understand the logic of the above calculation by considering that an individual who wished to purchase eleven shares of the above stock could do so by paying $726 (66 X 11), ignoring commissions. Alternately, one could purchase ten shares at a cost of $660 and wait until the rights were issued. With the ten rights such a purchaser would receive, the person would purchase the eleventh share for $44. The total cost of purchasing the eleven shares would then be only $704 (660 + 44). Although able to save $22, the purchaser must deal in a block of eleven shares to realize that saving. The average saving per share was, therefore, $2.

Equation (2.1) can be adjusted to estimate consistently the value of a right during the "ex-rights" period by not adding one to the number of rights required (N) in the denominator. The market value of a share of stock would logically drop by the value of a right after the record date since the rights can no longer be attained through purchasing the stock. In the example above, notice that the value of a right would be consistently estimated at $2:

$$X = \frac{64 - 44}{10} = \$2.$$

Discussion of an estimated value for a right during the "ex-rights" period, however, seems purely academic since the rights will then be issued and traded in the marketplace at a known price.

COMMON STOCK

A *common stock* is an equity security representing a residual interest in a corporation. Common stockholders are residual claimants, entitled to what is left after all expenses and all claims of creditors, as well as the preferences of preferred stockholders, are met. Creditors, such as bondholders, can sue if their claims for interest and principal are not met when due. But stockholders, common or preferred, are entitled to dividends only when they are legally declared by the corporation's board of directors.

The rate of return realized from an investment in common stock depends primarily on corporate profitability. Since creditors and preferred stockholders have a prior claim against corporate assets, the common stockholder is most directly exposed to the risk of business failure. On the other hand, profit growth benefits the common stockholders since creditors and preferred stockholders receive only their stipulated payments, while only the profits of the corporation limit the common stock dividend that may be declared.

Par Value

A corporation's charter authorizes the corporation to issue up to a stated number of shares of common stock. It may also specify a par value for each share. Par value, when it exists, is arbitrarily established by the incorporators. Market value per share, on the other hand, is determined by forces of supply and demand and has little or no relationship to par value. Par value has little significance for the common stockholder.

In most states a corporation is precluded from making payments to common stockholders (basically dividends) that would reduce the stated value of the common stock equity in the balance sheet below the amount represented by par value of all outstanding stock. This restriction has led to the setting of low par values in corporate charters and the issuance of no-par stock. State and local taxes tend to make low par issues more advantageous than no-par, and common stocks usually will, therefore, carry a low par value.

Book Value

Book value per share is defined as the net accounting value of all assets owned by the corporation (as shown in the balance sheet), less the sum of all outstanding debt plus preferred stock, divided by the number of outstanding shares of common stock. Book value must be clearly distinguished from other concepts of value such as market value or liquidating value of a firm. Book value is not analogous with current worth; it refers to specific accounting valuations of assets. Such values are not considered useful when valuing common stock for two reasons:

1. Asset figures on a balance sheet represent only cost (adjusted to market value if lower than cost) for current assets and cost less amortization or depreciation for fixed assets and intangibles. There is no reason to assume that the price at which an asset was acquired in the past represents a sound basis for determining the market or liquidation value of that asset at a future time.
2. As we will learn, the value of most assets is represented by their expected earning power, not book figures.

Stock Market Quotations

Market price quotations for stocks are reported daily in *The Wall Street Journal* and many other newspapers. Share prices are quoted in points and eighths of a point. A point is equal to one dollar, and an eighth of a point equals 12.5 cents. Because the quotation system is different for listed and over-the-counter stocks, the two are therefore discussed separately.

Listed Stocks. Figure 2–1 shows the quotation information carried in *The Wall Street Journal* for a few selected stocks. The total number of shares traded on Tuesday, April 27, by exchange and in total is presented first, followed by price quotations for the ten most active stocks on that day. Last is the price and volume data for individual companies traded on the New York Stock Exchange.

The high and low prices for the individual stock during the past 52 weeks are read in the far left-hand columns. The name of the company follows in abbreviated form. Abbott Laboratories (abbreviated AbtLb), for example, sold at a high of $32\frac{1}{4}$ ($32.25) and a low of $23\frac{5}{8}$ ($23.625) during the preceding 52 weeks. Next is the annual dollar dividend payment per share currently being paid by the company. A letter following the dividend rate would refer to a qualifying footnote that can be found at the end of the stock price listing under the heading Ex-

54 THE WALL STREET JOURNAL, Tuesday, April 27, 1982

Monday's Volume
69,819,010 Shares; 159,250 Warrants

TRADING BY MARKETS

	Shares	Warrants
New York Exchange	60,500,000	159,000
American Exchange	....	....
Midwest Exchange	4,109,500	....
Pacific Exchange	2,227,300	....
Nat'l Assoc. of Securities Dealers	1,467,910	250
Philadelphia Exchange	801,000	....
Boston Exchange	462,400	....
Cincinnati Exchange	197,300	....
Instinet System	53,600	....

NYSE – Composite

Volume since Jan. 1:	1982	1981	1980
Total shares	4,812,765,076	4,408,793,873	3,971,216,467
Total warrants	12,793,650	15,375,700	22,268,100

New York Stock Exchange

Volume since Jan. 1:	1982	1981	1980
Total shares	4,140,887,686	3,859,360,813	3,511,746,487
Total warrants	12,770,400	15,305,200	22,261,900

MOST ACTIVE STOCKS

	Open	High	Low	Close	Chg.	Volume
Schlitz Brw	16½	16⅝	16⅜	16½	+ ⅛	1,174,400
IBM	65½	66⅛	65	66	+ ¼	911,700
CPC Intl	37¼	37⅞	37	37⅞	+ ⅝	883,100
SearsRoeb	20	20	19⅝	19⅞	– ⅛	809,200
Exxon s	28¾	28¾	28⅜	28½	– ¼	689,600
Schlumbrg s	47⅜	48⅞	46¾	48	+1	617,000
Soeast Bkg	15½	15⅞	15½	15¾	+ ¼	611,800
Amer T&T	56	56	55⅜	55⅝	– ⅝	598,300
Camp Soup	35¼	35⅞	34⅞	35⅜	+ ⅜	585,800
NorInd PS	11¼	11¼	11⅛	11⅛	– ½	581,800
RalstnPur	12⅞	13⅛	12⅞	13	+ ⅛	531,800
K mart	19¾	19¾	19¼	19⅝	– ¼	515,600
Southern Co	13½	13½	13¼	13½	....	448,500
Comw Edis	22¼	22⅝	22¼	22⅝	+ ⅜	438,800
PhilipMorr	52⅞	53⅛	52¼	53⅛	+ ¾	426,100

52 Weeks High	Low	Stock	Div.	Yld %	P-E Ratio	Sales 100s	High	low	Close	Net Chg.
		– A–A–A –								
12⅜	6	AAR	.44	6.1	16	382	7¼	7⅛	7¼	+ ⅜
49½	31½	ACF	2.76	7.3	7	104	38	37	37⅝	+ ⅝
28½	16⅝	AMF	1.36	7.4	10	1311	18½	18¼	18½	....
15½	1	vjAMIn		..	..	359	1¼	1⅛	1¼	+ ⅛
7	3¾	APL		..	..	8	4	4	4	– ⅛
37¼	23½	ARA	2	7.8	7	440	25⅞	25½	25½	– ⅛
56½	26¾	ASA	4a	12.	..	164	35½	34½	34⅝	– ½
36⅝	11½	AVX	.32	1.6	..	77	19⅞	19½	19⅝	– ⅛
32¼	23⅝	AbtLb s	.84	2.7	15	579	31⅛	30⅝	31⅛	+ ¼

Source: Reprinted by permission of *The Wall Street Journal,* © Dow Jones & Company, Inc., April 27, 1982. All rights reserved.

FIGURE 2-1. Regularly Published Stock Data for New York Stock Exchange Listed Stocks

planatory Notes. The yield percent column represents the dividend return an investor can expect during the current year, which is calculated by dividing the annual cash dividend by the current market price.

The price-earnings ratio appears next. A price-earnings ratio, computed by dividing a stock's selling price by the company's per share earnings for the most recent four quarters, represents the price paid that day for one dollar of the firm's current earnings. One can observe that Abbott Labs is more "expensive" than ARA Corporation, but not too much should be made of this comparison as it represents only one criterion for judging a stock's value. Price-earnings ratios will be discussed in more detail in Chapter 7 and Section 5 of this book.

The next four columns show the number of shares traded in multiples of 100, and the high, low, and closing price (price of the last trade) achieved that day. The net change, reported next, is the difference between the closing price of the preceding day and today's closing price.

Over-the-Counter Stocks. Sample over-the-counter quotations are shown in Figure 2-2. Again, information concerning the market in general and the ten most active stocks precedes data for individual com-

50 THE WALL STREET JOURNAL, Tuesday, April 27, 1982

Over-the-Counter Markets

Quotations From the Nasdaq System

4:00 p.m. Eastern Time Prices, Monday, April 26, 1982

Volume, All Issues 27,469,100

SINCE JANUARY 1

	1982	1981	1980
Total sales	2,147,521,249	2,529,434,496	1,783,193,593

MARKET DIARY

	Mon	Fri	Thur	Wed	Tues
Issues traded	3,369	3,370	3,370	3,369	3,367
Advances	668	784	760	554	457
Declines	420	300	275	410	569
Unchanged	2,281	2,286	2,335	2,405	2,341
xNew highs	140	161	130	107	96
xNew lows	37	44	39	59	70

x-Based on 4 p.m. Eastern time bid quote.

ACTIVE STOCKS

	Dollar Volume	4:00 Bid	Chg.
MCI Communications	$30,976,000	36¾	– 2⅝
Pabst Brewing	6,930,000	19⅜	+ ¾
Intel Cp	6,064,000	32½	+ ½
Safeco Cp	5,461,000	39⅝	....
Pizza Time Theatre	4,852,000	28	+ ½
Tandem Computers	4,328,000	28	+ ¼
Apple Computer	4,072,000	15¾	+ ⅜
Service Merchandise Co	3,502,000	16½	+ 1⅛
U S Surgical Cp	3,343,000	19¾	– 1½
Farmers Group	3,081,000	35⅜	+ ⅛

Stock & Div.	Sales 100s	Bid	Asked	Net Chg.
--A A--				
Academy Insu	426	14⅝	14⅞	+ ⅛
Acapulco Rest	11	4¾	5	...
AcclrtnCp .05d	6	3½	4	+ ¼
Accuray .05d	210	10¼	10½	+ ⅜
AcetoChem 3i	5	14⅞	15¼	...
ACMAT Corp	2	4¾	5½	...
Adac Labs	251	18½	18⅝	– ¼
Adage Incorp	19	21½	22½	– ½
AddWesley .50	10	10½	10¾	...
Advance Circt	10	3	3½	...
Advance Ross	65	3¼	3½	+ ⅛
--C C--				
C Cor Electrn	385	23	23¾	+ 2
C 3 Inc	45	16¼	16¾	...
Cable TV Ind	5	7	7¼	+ ¼
CACI Inc	44	43¾	44¾	+ ¾
CADO System	177	10¼	10¾	– ½
CalFstBk 1.08	17	14⅞	15	...
Cal Mcrowave	630	10⅝	10¾	+ ⅝
CalWtrSv 4.10	10	35½	36½	...
Callon Petrol	35	6⅝	6¾	+ ⅛
CalpropCp .15f	12	4	4½	...
Cambex Corp	61	2¾	3	– ¼
DepInGr .05d	10	8⅝	9⅛	...
DepGuarn 1.90	z41	25	25½	...
Detection Syst	31	10¼	10½	...
Detector Elect	77	15½	16	– ¾
DetrexCh 1.80	z90	29½	31	...
DetBnkCorp 2	13	21¾	22	...
DetCdaTn 1.30	2	11	11¾	...
Diagnstc Rtrv	14	13½	14¼	...
DiamCrys 1.20	7	21¾	23	– ½
DicknsnMn B	12	1 5-16	1⅝	– 1-16
DickeyJhn .24	3	13¾	14½	...
Dicomed Corp	23	9½	10	...

Source: Reprinted by permission of *The Wall Street Journal,* © Dow Jones & Company, Inc., April 26, 1982. All rights reserved.

FIGURE 2-2. Regularly Published Stock Data for Over-the-Counter Markets

panies. The company name and indicated annual dividend rate appears at the far left, followed by the number of shares traded in hundreds, as for New York Stock Exchange listed stocks. The price quotations, however, are quite different. A bid price and an asked price are offered rather than the high, low, and closing price.

The prices quoted are wholesale prices, which are quotes by dealers who make a market in the given stock. An individual may or may not get the dealer-quoted price, even if purchasing at the moment it was quoted. The bid price represents the price at which the quoting dealer would be willing to buy the stock. The ask price represents the price at which the dealer is willing to sell the stock. These quotes form the basis for negotiation, not the actual price at which an issue has been bought or sold. The differential between the quoted bid and ask price is called the *spread* and represents the gross profit margin sought by the dealer. The net change column represents the change in bid price since the previous bid.

Corporate Dividend Policies

Dividends are most commonly disbursed in cash, but corporations may pay dividends in stock and occasionally in property. Corporate directors weigh many factors, which are often conflicting, in determining an appropriate dividend policy. Since stockholders are the legal owners of the corporation, management's decisions should reflect their interest.

Dividend policy and financing corporate needs by means of earnings retention are interdependent. The more a corporation pays out in dividends, the less is available in the form of retained earnings to finance corporate needs. Earnings should be retained by a corporation only when the anticipated growth in earnings and dividends will more than offset the advantage to the common stockholders of a current dividend. The firm is justified in retaining earnings when it can earn a rate of return on the funds retained that exceeds the rate that stockholders could earn by investing their dividends.

Major Factors Determining Dividend Policy. The major factors that enter into the formation of a firm's dividend policy are the following:

1. *Availability of Cash.* Cash flow provides the funds to pay dividends, to meet requirements for additional working capital as the volume of business expands, to pay for replacement of and additions to plant and equipment, to meet debt amortization and other repayment requirements, and to provide funds for the repurchase of outstanding securities. The sources and uses of funds statement, the cash budget, pro forma statements, and the capital budget offer the basic data and projections utilized in deciding how much cash is

available for paying dividends. The volatility, as well as the amount, of earnings and cash flow is important.

2. *Legal and Tax Factors.* Legally, under most statutes, the directors must charge cash dividends to the retained earnings account. This account, with the addition of earnings for the current fiscal period, must be sufficient to absorb the amount charged for dividends declared. Furthermore, many debt indentures restrict part or all of the retained earnings account, preventing the paying of dividends based on the restricted funds. Such restrictions should appear in notes to the financial statements in annual reports. Under the Internal Revenue Code, Sections 531-537, the Treasury Department may assess a penalty tax for the unreasonable retention of earnings. Directors must therefore review current working capital, cash budgets, and capital budgets, as well as any requirements for corporate securities to be reacquired at regular intervals. If such a review justifies the need of the business for the retention of earnings in terms of the planned level of operations, the directors can feel assured that the corporation will not later be assessed a penalty for unreasonable retention of earnings.

3. *Restrictions.* Any restrictions imposed by existing debt contracts or regulatory commissions affect dividend policy. For example, the ICC, under certain conditions, can impose constraints on dividend payments of railroads that fall under their regulatory control.

4. *Desires of the Stockholders for Dividends.* The attitude of stockholders in general toward current dividend policy is reflected in the market price of the company's stock. The corporation must bear this in mind. A stockholder in a high tax bracket, for example, would tend to favor earnings retention in the hope of stimulating profit growth and a rise in the price of the company's stock. Stockholders in lower tax brackets and those who depend on the income generated from investments to support current expenditures would have more interest in receiving higher current dividends. Clearly, directors must face conflicting factors and demands in determining dividend policy.

The choice regarding dividend policy is not necessarily a choice between paying dividends or meeting the corporation's need for funds to replace worn-out capital and support growth. Rather, it is a choice between utilizing internal and external sources of funds. The excess of corporate needs over retained earnings can be, and usually is, met from external sources.

Cash Dividends. The most frequently used dividend is the cash dividend, although dividends may also be paid in property or as additional shares of stock. Cash dividends are declared by the board of directors, who determine dividend policy, to be paid by check at a future date to stockholders of record as of a certain date (the *record date*). For example, a corporation may declare a dividend on November 15, payable on December 15 to stockholders of record on December 1. Corporations typically declare and pay cash dividends quarterly.

Cash dividends, preferred or common, are not a liability to the corporation until declared by the directors. Cash dividends are ordinarily paid out of earnings and are fully taxable to the recipient, except when the stockholder is notified that it is partly or totally a return of capital.

Stock Dividends. Stock dividends are simply payments of additional stock to shareholders. Legally a stock dividend may only be declared and paid when surplus accounts are available against which to charge the dividend. Stock splits also result in stockholders' receiving additional shares in proportion to their current holdings. There is no charge against the retained earnings account in the case of a stock split, however.

Assume, for example, that a corporation has the following capital structure before a stock dividend:

Common stock ($100 par, 10,000 shares)	$1,000,000
Capital surplus	1,000,000
Retained earnings	6,000,000
Owners' equity	$8,000,000

Assume, moreover, that the company pays a 100 percent stock dividend (each stockholder receives a share for each share presently held), and that the fair market value of the firm's common stock is currently $300 a share. Under most state laws a stock dividend must be charged to retained earnings.[3]

The owner's equity section of the balance sheet after such a stock dividend would be:

Common stock ($100 par, 20,000 shares)	$2,000,000
Capital surplus	3,000,000
Retained earnings	3,000,000
Owners' equity	$8,000,000

In this example, the retained earnings account is reduced by $3,000,000, representing the addition of 10,000 shares of stock at a fair market value of $300 per share. The common stock account is

_____
[3] The New York Stock Exchange requires for listed corporations that the minimum amount a company charges to retained earnings be equivalent to the pro rata market value of the stock dividend and that this be explained in a memorandum to stockholders. In some states a corporation may charge the stock dividend to a capital surplus account—this is an objectionable practice. Stock dividends are meant to represent the permanent capitalization of earnings that are being reinvested in the business with the expectation that the added capital will lead to increased future profits.

always kept at par, and is therefore credited for $1,000,000, with the remaining $2,000,000 being credited to the capital surplus account. Since dividends may only be paid out of retained earnings, the dividend-paying capacity of the corporation has been reduced by the $3 million. Stock dividends of between 2 percent and 10 percent are more commonly paid by American corporations than the 100 percent dividend illustrated above.

Stock Dividends versus Stock Splits. A *stock split* merely increases the number of shares outstanding without any change in the owners' equity section of the balance sheet. This results in a proportionate reduction in the par or stated value of each share of the firm's stock. Assume a 2-for-1 stock split, for example, with no stock dividends paid. The capital structure of the above corporation would then appear as follows:

Common stock ($50 par, 20,000 shares)	$1,000,000
Capital surplus	1,000,000
Retained earnings	6,000,000
Owners' equity	$8,000,000

There would be no transfer from retained earnings in this case, as was the case where a stock dividend was paid. Notice, however, that while the par value of the firm's stock is not affected by a stock dividend, it is reduced proportionally in a stock split. A reduction of par value would require a change in the corporate charter and the approval of the firm's stockholders. The declaration of a stock dividend, by contrast, is a discretionary right of the board of directors of a firm and requires no approval by the stockholders.

The purpose of a stock split is different from that of a stock dividend. Stock splits are typically used when the firm wishes to reduce the market price per share of its stock. A stock dividend, on the other hand, is used in recognition of earnings that are to be retained by the corporation. In the case of either a stock split or dividend, however, a shareholder's proportional ownership in the firm remains unchanged. The market price per share, therefore, other things being equal, should decline proportionally to the split or dividend. For example, assume that prior to a stock dividend or a stock split a share had a market value of $100. After a 100 percent stock dividend, or 2-for-1 stock split, the market value should fall to $50 per share. However, because many investors may be more willing to purchase a stock in the $50 range, for good or bad reasons, the stock may only fall to $52 per share, reflecting a greater demand and better marketability.

A Caveat: Sales, Share Value, and Increased Future Dividends. Stockholders should realize that when stock received as a dividend or through a split is sold, a part of one's share in the assets, voting power, and earning power of the firm is also sold. Unfortunately, some investors behave as if shares received through a stock dividend or split are a windfall gain. They do not seem to realize that the sale of such shares dilutes one's interest in a firm.

An increase in the cash dividend paid to each stockholder will often follow a large stock dividend or split, based on corporate profit growth. The expectation of such growth may result in a rising market value per share of stock. One should recognize that the increased market value stems from the growth expectation, not from the stock dividend or split. In fact, the corporation could have avoided the cost of issuing a stock dividend by merely retaining the earnings and increasing the cash dividend paid on each of the old shares. In many cases, this would seem to be more in accordance with stockholder interests than the payment of a stock dividend.

Stock Dividends of Less Than 100 Percent. Stock dividends of less than 100 percent may result in the issuance of rights representing fractional shares. For example, if a stock dividend of 2 percent is declared, the owner of 40 shares would be entitled to $\frac{8}{10}$ of a share of new stock. Corporations usually provide either for the stockholder to buy an additional fraction (in this case $\frac{2}{10}$ of a share) or for the corporation to sell, at the stockholder's request, the fractional shares.

Tax Position of the Stockholder. The tax law recognizes that the equity value of the stockholder would not change because of a stock dividend or a stock split. Therefore, such receipts of stock are not considered to represent taxable income to the recipient, unless the distribution of stock changes the equity position of the recipient. However, the stockholder must reduce the cost basis of the stock held in proportion to the split or dividend. For example, if the shareholder had purchased 100 shares at $100 per share and a 2-for-1 stock split occurred, the cost basis for each of the 200 shares would have to be reduced to $50 per share. If a share were then sold for $60, a taxable capital gain of $10 would result.

Property Dividends. Property dividends represent a distribution of the assets of the corporation. If these dividends take the form of a liquidating dividend, stockholders must approve the distribution. Property dividends may take one of three forms:

1. Payment in the form of securities of other corporations owned by the distributing company. One example would be the distribution to Du Pont stockholders several years ago of shares in General Motors Corporation. Such distributions of securities of corporations other than the one making the distribution are frequently described as spin-offs.
2. Payment in the form of merchandise. Such payments are unusual, but they may be made in products produced and sold by the corporation in lieu of cash dividends.
3. Payment in the form of other securities, such as preferred stocks or bonds, of the same corporation.

The tax treatment of property dividends may be complicated. In most cases the distributing corporation will obtain a tax ruling from federal income tax authorities and will then notify the stockholders of the ruling and the required tax accounting treatment on the stockholder's own records. If a property dividend is clearly a liquidating dividend (approved as such by the stockholders), the dividend is considered to be a return of capital to stockholders and as such is not taxable. However, nontaxable dividends which represent a return of capital to stockholders must be shown on the shareowner's own records as a deduction from original cost, thereby establishing a new cost basis for tax purposes.

Repurchasing Stock as an Alternative to Paying Dividends. When faced with a lack of profitable investment opportunities, stockholders' may benefit more if the firm repurchases shares of stock outstanding rather than if the firm pays a cash dividend. Stock repurchase results in fewer shares outstanding and therefore, other things being equal, in higher earnings per share and a higher market price per share for the remaining stock outstanding.

A shareholder who purchased stock at a price lower than that at which the corporation is reacquiring the stock would experience a tax advantage, as contrasted with the tax liability that would result if a cash dividend were paid. Dividends are taxed as ordinary income, but gains received through the sale of shares are taxed at a lower capital gains rate.

Management has tended in recent years to buy back stock when it believed the stock to be markedly undervalued. The record suggests, however, that management has also tended to be overly optimistic about future prospects when making such purchases,[4] and that the actual benefits to stockholders realized through such transactions are often negligible or nonexistent.

Empirical Evidence of Dividend Policies. Dividend policies vary widely among companies. However, a large percentage of companies would fall within the range of dividend payout ratios indicated in Table 2-2. Corporate dividend policies, during the time period covered in the table, are briefly reviewed in this section.

Dividend Policy in the Depressed 1930s. U.S. corporations paid aggregate dividends that exceeded reported net profits during the 1930s. Table 2-2 shows, however, that aggregate corporate cash flow income always exceeded the total dividend payments of U.S. corporations.

---

[4] See, for example, *Forbes*, April 15, 1973, p. 60, or *Business Week*, May 22, 1973, p. 1.

TABLE 2-2. Historical Record of Earnings, Dividends, Cash Flow, and Payout Ratios (All U.S. Corporations)

Year	Profits after Taxes	Capital Consumption Allowances	Cash Flow Net Profits after Taxes Plus Cap. Cons. Allowances	Dividends	Dividends as % of Net Profits (Payout Ratios)	Dividends as % of Cash Flow
	($ Bil.)	($ Bil.)	($ Bil.)	($ Bil.)	%	%
1930	2.9	4.3	7.2	5.5	190	76
1931	−.9	4.3	5.2	4.1	...	79
1932	−2.7	4.0	6.7	2.5	...	37
1933	.4	3.8	4.2	2.0	500	48
1934	1.6	3.6	5.2	2.6	163	50
1935	2.6	3.6	6.2	2.8	108	45
1936	4.9	3.6	8.5	4.5	92	53
1930–36	8.8	27.2	43.2	24.0	273	56
1937	5.3	3.6	8.9	4.7	89	53
1938	2.9	3.7	6.6	3.2	110	48
1939	5.6	3.7	9.3	3.8	68	41
1937–39	13.8	11.0	24.8	11.7	85	47
1940	7.2	3.8	11.0	4.0	56	36
1941	10.1	4.3	14.4	4.4	44	31
1942	10.1	5.0	15.1	4.3	43	28
1943	11.1	5.4	16.5	4.4	40	27
1944	11.2	6.1	17.3	4.6	41	27
1945	9.0	6.4	15.4	4.6	51	30
1940–45	58.7	31.0	89.7	26.3	45	29

Year						
1946	15.5	4.7	20.2	5.6	36	28
1947	20.2	5.8	26.0	6.3	31	24
1948	22.7	7.0	29.7	7.0	31	24
1949	18.5	7.9	26.4	7.2	39	27
1950	24.9	8.8	33.7	8.8	35	26
1946–50	101.8	34.2	136.0	34.9	34	26
1951	21.6	10.3	31.9	8.6	40	27
1952	19.6	11.5	31.1	8.6	44	28
1953	20.4	13.2	33.6	8.9	44	26
1954	20.6	15.0	35.6	9.3	45	26
1955	27.0	17.4	44.4	10.5	39	24
1956	27.2	18.9	46.1	11.3	42	25
1957	26.0	20.8	46.8	11.7	45	25
1958	22.3	22.0	44.3	11.6	52	26
1959	28.5	23.5	52.0	12.6	44	24
1951–59	213.2	152.6	365.8	93.1	44	25
1960	26.7	24.9	51.6	13.4	50	26
1961	27.2	26.2	53.5	13.8	51	26
1962	31.2	30.1	61.3	15.2	49	25
1963	33.1	31.8	64.8	16.5	50	25
1964	38.4	33.9	72.3	17.8	46	25
1965	46.5	36.4	82.9	19.8	43	24
1966	49.9	39.5	89.5	20.8	42	23
1960–66	253.0	222.8	475.9	117.3	46	24

TABLE 2-2. Historical Record of Earnings, Dividends, Cash Flow, and Payout Ratios (All U.S. Corporations) (continued)

Year	Profits after Taxes	Capital Consumption Allowances	Cash Flow Net Profits after Taxes Plus Cap. Cons. Allowances	Dividends	Dividends as % of Net Profits (Payout Ratios)	Dividends as % of Cash Flow
	($ Bil.)	($ Bil.)	($ Bil.)	($ Bil.)	%	%
1967	46.6	43.0	89.6	21.4	46	24
1968	47.8	46.8	94.6	23.6	49	25
1969	44.8	51.9	96.7	24.3	54	25
1970	39.3	56.0	95.3	24.7	63	26
1971	47.6	60.4	108.0	25.1	53	23
1972	55.4	65.9	121.3	26.0	47	21
1973	67.1	73.7	140.8	27.8	41	20
1974	75.2	81.6	156.8	30.8	41	20
1975	73.3	89.5	162.8	32.4	44	20
1976	92.2	97.2	189.4	35.8	39	19
1977	104.5	109.3	218.8	42.1	40	20
1967–77	693.8	775.3	1469.1	314.0	45	21
1978	140.3	122.9	241.3	44.6	32	18
1979	167.7	139.5	275.1	50.2	30	18
1980	163.1	158.3	311.4	56.0	34	18

Source: Various issues of the Federal Reserve Bulletin; calculations by the authors.

The data give strong support to the argument that corporate directors try to avoid reducing the level of dividends below a previously established norm. Investment opportunities for corporations during the 1930s would not have appeared promising, so there would have been little incentive to retain earnings. Clearly, however, dividend payments in excess of earnings constitute a capital divestiture that could adversely affect the future earnings of a firm.

Dividend Policy Since World War II. Since World War II, dividend payout ratios have ranged from a low of 30 percent of reported profits to a high of 63 percent, most typically ranging from 45 to 50 percent of reported profits until 1973. After 1973, the proportion of profits paid out has exceeded 41 percent in only one year (1975). The ratio of dividends to cash flow earnings ranged between 18 and 28 percent since 1950, with a declining trend since 1969. This ratio has consistently stayed in the range of 18 to 20 percent since 1972. The relatively low payout since 1973 would seem to suggest that corporate directors considered opportunities for reinvestment of earnings especially profitable, or such reinvestment may have been necessary to meet changing social obligations and/or the ravages of inflation. The possibility exists that the proportion of earnings paid out by U.S. corporations could rise a bit in future years, especially if inflation is curbed so that reported profits more closely represent economic profits.

Dividend Growth

Table 2–3 shows that growth in dollar dividends paid for all U.S. corporations has exceeded the rate of inflation since 1950, whenever long periods of time are considered. The rate of growth in dividends paid relative to the rate of growth in the consumer price index is less impressive since 1967. Individual investors, moreover, hold the stocks of particular corporations and may well have experienced a lower rate of growth in dividend payments than has occurred in the consumer price index since 1967. The important question is whether future experience for common stock investors will parallel that of the 1950s and early 1960s or the experience since 1967.

The yield to maturity for seasoned corporate bonds, all industries, reached 14.44 percent during March 1981,[5] while dividend yields on common stocks (based on Standard & Poor's 500 Stock Index) averaged between 5.5 and 6 percent. Growth in market value of common stocks must be adequate to offset the above-noted yield difference to justify the purchase of common stocks. Prior to 1967, common stock

---

[5] *Federal Reserve Bulletin* (April, 1981), p. A25.

TABLE 2-3. Growth in Profits and Cash Dividends for U.S. Corporations Contrasted with Inflation Experience, Selected Periods, 1933-1979

Years	Percentage Increase in Dividends Paid	Percentage Increase in Consumer Price Index	Percentage Increase in Profits after Taxes	Percentage Increase in Cash Flow Net Profits after Taxes Plus Cap. Cons. Allowances
1933-1979	2535.0	460.3	35,925.0	6450.0
1933-1966	940.0	150.5	12,375.0	2031.0
1933-1947	215.0	72.4	4,950.0	381.0
1950-1961	56.8	24.3	9.2	58.8
1950-1966	136.4	34.8	100.4	165.6
1960-1979	293.3	145.1	439.7	433.1
1967-1979	146.3	117.4	209.2	207.0

Source: Economic Report of the President, January, 1981, p. 289, and Table 2-2. Calculations by the authors.

portfolios consistently tended to outperform bonds on a total return basis, but this has not necessarily been true since then.

PREFERRED STOCK

A *preferred stock*, as the name suggests, is an equity security that enjoys certain preferences or priorities relative to common stock. Specifically, those preferences are (1) preferences as to dividends and (2) usually preferences as to corporate assets in the case of liquidation of the firm. No dividend may be paid on common stock in any period before required dividends are paid on the preferred stock for that period. In liquidation, assets equal to an amount stated in the preferred stock contract must, in most cases, be distributed to the preferred stockholders before any distribution is made to the common stockholders. Very few preferred stocks are granted the privilege of participation in income beyond their stated dividend.

Preferred Stock Versus a Creditor Security

Preferred stock is like a creditor security in that the rate of return paid is strictly limited to the amount of the contract, regardless of the prosperity of the issuer. But it is distinctly unlike a creditor security in that the dividend is not a liability to the firm and is not "owed" until it is declared by the board of directors. The interest on a debt contract is a legal claim that when due is enforceable in the courts. A preferred stock contract is distinctly inferior to a creditor of a bond or other debt instrument. A preferred stock never matures, but a bond does; the principal amount stated in the bond contract must be paid on maturity.

Preferred Stock Versus Common Stock

Preferred stock is like a common stock in that it is an equity security, and dividends are paid at the discretion of the board of directors of the firm. Preferred stock is unlike common stock, on the other hand, in that it does not usually participate in earnings beyond the stated dividend in the preferred contract. Thus, the benefits of corporate growth accrue to the common stockholder. The corporation may have several issues of preferred stock outstanding, each with its own order of priority, indicated by a designation such as first, second, or third preferred stock issue.

Preferred Stock Contractual Provisions

The exact priorities enjoyed by a preferred stock vary considerably by issue, and the investor can be sure of the nature of the preference only upon examination of the articles of incorporation. Because the articles of incorporation are not easily accessible, investors and financial analysts usually rely on the summary of the contractual provisions contained in the stock certificates and in the material furnished by services such as Standard & Poor's and Moody's. Preferred issues may or may not have provisions for voting, cumulative, callable, participating, convertible, and sinking fund privileges.

Voting Provisions. Practically all preferred contracts specify that the preferred stockholder has given up voting rights in consideration of preference as to dividends at a stipulated rate. If nothing were said in the contract about voting rights, the preferred stock would vote equally with the common. However, many preferred stock contracts call for automatic voting power if dividends are in arrears for a stated period. The New York Stock Exchange requires that this provision be met for preferred stocks of listed companies.

Actually, the number of preferred shares is usually so small in comparison with common shares that even when they have the right to vote, they have relatively little power. As long as there is adequate earnings coverage of dividends, preferred stockholders need not be concerned with their limited control powers.

Cumulative and Noncumulative Provisions. Preferred stock may be cumulative or noncumulative. If it is *cumulative*, any dividends not paid when due are in arrears and no dividends may be paid on the common stock until all past arrears and the current required dividend have been paid.

Noncumulative preferred stock invites an obvious abuse in that directors could refuse to pay dividends on the preferred stock for a number of years, even if earned. Then they might pay one dividend on the preferred and pay the rest of the accumulated earnings to the common stockholders if funds were available. The U.S. Supreme Court has held that if the preferred contract states that the stock is noncumulative, there is no requirement to pay past preferred dividends regardless of the amount of the corporation's profits during the years when dividends were not declared.

Callable Provisions. Most preferred contracts provide that the issuer may, on proper notice, call in the preferred stock. The *call price* stated in the contract is usually at a premium stated at $5 to $10 above par, but may be as high as $25 above par. The call feature must be considered a disadvantage or negative feature by investors, as it will usually be exercised by the issuer in a manner that is not to the advantage of the preferred stockholder. When a call is exercised for the purpose of refunding, for example, the corporate objective is to take advantage of the fact that current yields on preferred stocks or bonds are lower than the contractual rates on the outstanding issue being called. Conversely, investors lose income if they reinvest the payment received in an issue of the same quality at the current market yields.

Participating Provisions. Earlier we pointed out that a preferred stock receives a stated dividend before the common stock receives any dividend. Usually the common stock will receive a matching dividend based on proportional book values, or some other agreed amount, before any further payments to preferred stock. If, however, the common stock is to receive any excess over this amount, *participating* preferred stock would share with the common stock in the excess earnings in proportion to the book value of the two classes of stock. Most preferred stocks are nonparticipating, however.

Convertible Provisions. Numerous preferred stocks enjoy *convertible* provisions that permit their holders to convert into common stock at a stated number of common shares for each preferred share. Calculations pertinent to the appraisal of convertible securities are covered in relation to bonds in Chapter 24. Many of these calculations are also useful in appraising convertible preferred stock.

An issuer can usually sell a convertible preferred stock at a lower yield than a straight preferred stock, and frequently at a lower cost than if common stock were sold. But an issuer can also assume that over the years much or all of the preferred stock will be converted into common stock. Dividends will rise to a point where the dividend received through the common stock that would be received on conversion will exceed the dividend paid by the preferred stock.[6]

A considerable amount of convertible preferred has been issued over the past 30 years, especially in periods when investors were particularly inflation-conscious but still desired the protection of a limited-income security. Many were issued in mergers in the 1960s. If earnings of a corporation rise along with inflation (which is by no means certain), the common shares rise in price and therefore the preferred stock, which is convertible into common stock, will also rise in market value.

Some corporations, instead of issuing convertible preferred, have sold preferred with purchase option warrants attached. The warrant may be detached and, together with a stipulated amount of cash, exchanged for a given number of shares of common stock.

Sinking Fund Provisions. Under a sinking fund agreement, the issuer is obligated to retire an amount of preferred stock annually. The annual dollar amount to be used to retire the shares may be fixed (as is the case under many bond-sinking fund agreements) or it may fluctuate with earnings or with sales (as is also the case under some bond-sinking fund agreements). As the amount of shares outstanding is progressively reduced, the quality of the outstanding issues should improve.

Some investment people have sought, usually as a sales device, to designate preferred stocks with sinking fund provisions as "junior bonds." However, the inclusion of a sinking fund provision in a preferred contract in no way changes the equity nature of the preferred stock to a creditor relationship, even though it does strengthen the contract.

Other Protective Provisions. Preferred stock is frequently protected by certain restrictive covenants in the contract. In general these covenants parallel some of the restrictions used in bond and private placement note indentures to protect creditors. For instance, a protective provision may limit the payment of common stock dividends if earnings and working capital are below a certain level.

The preferred contract usually also contains a provision preventing the issue of certain new securities, such as secured obligations, that would have priority over the preferred stock. On the other hand, few preferred contracts contain provisions regarding the maintenance of net working capital at a certain minimum level, which in fact limits the amount of unsecured debt. Clearly, by excluding such provisions the corporation is given the latitude to undermine severely the position of the preferred stock.

---

[6] This occurred in early 1977 for the $4 convertible preferred stock of AT&T then outstanding.

Summary

The nature of a corporation and the equity securities it issues, both common and preferred stock, have been explained in this chapter. Each share of common stock represents a fractional share of ownership of a corporation. Common stock entitles the holder to

1. Share in corporate income (after prior claimants, including creditors and preferred stockholders, have been paid);
2. Participate in the election of the members of the board of directors and vote on changes in the corporate charter or bylaws;
3. In most cases, have a first opportunity to purchase new stock issued by the corporation before it may be sold to outsiders (the preemptive right);
4. Inspect the corporate books if information provided by the corporation is inadequate;
5. Freely transfer their shares;
6. Share in all assets remaining after settlement of creditors' and preferred stockholders' claims in the event of liquidation.

The liability of common stockholders is limited to the funds committed when purchasing the stock, except for possible and limited claims for wages by employees.

Common stockholders *do not have a right to dividends*. Directors have the sole authority to declare dividends. If earnings are not paid out in the form of dividends, common stockholders share in these earnings through the increase in the book value per share of their stock that results from the additions to the retained earnings account. Since common stockholders share equally in all earnings available after payment of creditors' and preferred stockholders' claims, the growth potential of common stock is limited only by the success enjoyed by the issuing corporation.

Preferred stock is a fixed income security and in this sense is like a bond. But it is an ownership rather than a debt instrument. The dividend mandated by a preferred stock is not a liability of the corporation until legally declared by the board of directors. The stipulated dividend must be paid to the preferred stockholders before dividend payments may be made to common stockholders. However, it is important to realize that if no dividend is paid on the common stock, there is no legal obligation to declare or pay a dividend to preferred stockholders even though earnings may be adequate to cover such a dividend. Also, preferred stock has no maturity date at which principal is repaid, as does a debt instrument.

Questions

1. Corporations are often described as "entities" or "personalities." What is meant by this? Of what significance is an understanding of this concept to investors?

2. What is meant by a "residual claim on income" and what advantages, if any, are associated with such a claim?

3. Discuss the basic rights of the common stockholder, noting any limitations that may be present in relation to these rights.

4. XYZ Corporation announced on May 1 that rights will be mailed on June 1 to stockholders of record as of May 15. May 12 was announced by the stock exchange as the final date, allowing sufficient time to become a stockholder of record on May 15, in the event one purchased a share of XYZ stock after May 1. The holder of five rights would be entitled to purchase one new share at a cost of $50. What would be the theoretical value of a right on May 9 if XYZ stock was then priced at $100 a share?

5. (a) What is the significance of the record date in relation to a declared dividend?
   (b) Distinguish between a stock dividend and a stock split and discuss the significance of each to stockholders.
   (c) What is the tax status of the recipient of a stock dividend? Of a property dividend?

6. Describe the conditions under which a corporation might prefer to issue a stock dividend rather than pay a cash dividend. Under what conditions would you as a stockholder prefer stock dividends to payment of cash dividends?

7. Assume the stock of Happytime Corporation was currently selling at $150 per share. What would you expect to happen to the price of the stock after a 3-for-1 stock split? Why?

8. How are the rights of the preferred stockholder determined? What rights are usually given to the preferred stockholder?

9. Define each of the following terms in relation to preferred stock: (a) Cumulative, (b) Callable, (c) Participating, (d) Convertible.

10. Explain the significance of a call feature in a preferred stock from the standpoint of both the issuing corporation and the investor.

11. (a) Distinguish between the two basic contractual forms of investment securities.
    (b) Explain the legal and investment position of common stockholders relative to holders of other classes of securities in a corporation.

Work-Study Problems

1. In early 1961 the American Telephone & Telegraph Company announced a rights offering. Each holder of 20 shares of AT&T common stock on February 23, 1961 (the date of announcement) would later receive sufficient rights to subscribe to one additional share at $86. The stock rights would expire on April 14, 1961.
   (a) Based on the closing price for AT&T stock on February 23, 1961, what value did the market place on the rights being is-

sued by AT&T? To answer this question, the student must determine the closing price of AT&T stock on February 23, 1961.

(b) Determine the price movements of the stock and the rights to the expiration date from published sources. How do they compare with the theoretical price calculated on February 23, 1961? Explain the differences you find.

2. Assume that a corporation reports earnings in the current fiscal year of $50,000. The following estimates of net profit after taxes are those that could be obtained in the long run by retaining various amounts of earnings. Assume that stockholders could earn 7 percent after taxes through alternative investments of equivalent risk.

Retained Earnings	Estimated Net Profit after Taxes
$10,000	$1,500
20,000	2,400
30,000	3,000
40,000	3,200
50,000	3,300

(a) Ignoring personal income taxes, what amount should be paid out in dividends if the stockholders wish to maximize the amount earned on their total investment?

(b) If the stockholders face a personal income tax rate of 25 percent on marginal income, how should this affect dividend policy?

3. Prepare a table covering a ten-year period showing the following data for AT&T Corporation and IBM Corporation:

Year	Earnings Per Share	Dividends Per Share	Price Range Common Stock	Percentage of Earnings in Dividends	Dividend Yield

On the basis of these data answer the following questions:

(a) What differences do you find in dividend policy?

(b) What explanations would you advance for these differences? Do you believe each policy is justified? Why?

(c) What effects do you believe changes in the current dividend policies of each company would have on current market prices of their stocks? Explain your answer.

3.

Corporate Debt Securities

Common stocks, which offer a potential return bounded only by company profit expectations, have generally appealed to individual investors more than bonds or other fixed-income securities. At the end of 1978, the total financial asset holdings of individuals were approximately $3.4 trillion. Their net equity in financial assets after deductions for mortgage debt, consumer debt, and security loans was $2.2 trillion. Of the total financial assets of $3.4 trillion, only $100.9 billion was in the form of corporate bonds, notes, and commercial paper. Thus, individual holdings of corporate debt issues represented only 3 percent of their total financial assets and 21 percent of their holdings of all debt securities.[1]

The interest of individual investors in bonds increased markedly in the late 1960s and early 1970s for two reasons. First, stock market prices behaved in an erratic fashion, and rates of return on stocks were often disappointing after 1966. Second, interest rates rose to levels that were high and relatively attractive when compared with previous periods in our history. High inflation rates and the historically high yields offered by highly liquid money market funds caused bonds to become unattractive again in the late 1970s and to remain in a seriously depressed market at the time of writing this book. While many individuals never purchase a bond or any other debt security, practically all individuals have an interest in some portfolio that includes corporate debt instruments through funds they have committed to financial institutions such as a bank or insurance company.

Contrary to popular opinion, fixed-income securities can and do undergo sizable price changes as the general level of interest rates changes, reflecting changing supply and demand conditions for loanable funds. Bonds can be acquired for income, emphasizing the relative sureness and attractiveness of periodic interest receipts, while tending

---

[1] *Flow of Funds Accounts 1968–1978,* Division of Research and Statistics (Washington, D.C.: Board of Governors of the Federal Reserve System), p. 27.

to ignore price fluctuations. On the other hand, fixed-income securities can be among the most speculative investment vehicles available when bought on margin or when a low-quality issue is purchased.

This chapter explores the general characteristics of corporate debt instruments and describes the many different types of debt instruments available in the market. Chapter 4 discusses U.S. government and municipal securities. Chapter 14 explores historical variations in bond prices and yields. Chapter 15 describes the markets in which both debt and equity instruments trade. Valuation of bonds is developed in Chapter 7. Discussion of the selection and analysis of corporate bonds is postponed until Chapters 23 and 24 after an appropriate framework for analyzing risk and portfolio selection has been developed.

The major forms of long-term debt instruments used by corporations are bonds, notes, equipment obligations, and commercial bank term loans. The major short-term debt instrument issued by corporations, which is available to individual investors, is commercial paper. Promissory notes, simply the IOU's of the issuer, are typically exchanged between institutions on the basis of personal agreement and are not generally available to individual investors.

BONDS: A LONG-TERM DEBT INSTRUMENT

A *corporate bond* is a long-term promissory note given under seal, usually as part of a mass borrowing arrangement. The essential features are relatively simple. The issuer promises to pay a specified percentage of par value on designated dates (known as *coupon payments*) and to return the par or face value (principal) of the bond at maturity.[2] Failure to pay either the principal or interest when due constitutes legal default, and court proceedings can be instituted to enforce the contract. Creditors have a prior legal claim over common and preferred stockholders as to both income and assets of the corporation for the principal and interest due them. In fact, default may result in creditors taking over ownership of the corporation in reorganization; stockholders, in contrast, may find their stock valueless. A superior legal status, however, would not prevent the bondholders from suffering financial loss when the ability of a corporation to generate cash flow adequate to pay its obligations is seriously eroded.

The main advantage of bonds relative to stocks is the assurance of a fixed and regular income payment and a higher current yield. As noted in the preceding chapter, all dividend payments on both common and preferred stock are at the discretion of the board of directors and may be cut or eliminated entirely during a recessionary period. The fixed

---

[2] While no such issues have been offered in the United States, the British Consuls have no maturity date. They contract to pay a stipulated interest rate forever.

nature of payments, however, is also a source of disadvantage for bonds. A bondholder receives the same annual dollar interest payment throughout the life of a contract, no matter how successful the corporation is in using the capital provided through the bonds. No adjustment is made to account for inflation, which can result in a negative real return over the life of a bond.[3] Finally, while they do not share in corporate success, bondholders still suffer the penalties of financial failure of the corporation.

Trading on the Equity and Leverage

When a corporation borrows (or issues preferred stock), it is trading on the common stockholders' equity position. When a corporation trades on stockholders' equity, leverage is introduced into the capitalization. If, as a result, the rate of return earned on total capitalization increases, the rate of return on the stockholders' equity will rise at a faster rate because of the fixed rate paid to creditors. Conversely, if the rate of return on total capitalization declines, the rate of return on stockholders' equity will decline by a multiple and may even disappear in order that creditors receive in full the amounts due them. The degree of leverage relative to the stability of cash flow has a direct bearing on the ability of a firm to meet its contractual debt obligations, which has a direct effect on the "quality" of the debt instruments that it issues.

Bond Contract or Indenture

A contract setting out the terms and conditions of the bond issue is an *indenture*. There are three parties to this contract: the issuer, the trustee for the bondholders, and the bondholders.[4] The indenture provisions include a promise of the borrower to pay principal and interest when due, to maintain the property adequately, and to operate the corporation judiciously. The borrower generally agrees not to change its business materially through merger or sale of property except under certain conditions, which are delineated in the indenture. Indentures usually include agreements to make sinking fund payments, to allow redemption prior to maturity, to provide for annual debt amortization in some instances, to limit indebtedness, and to subject dividend payments to certain restrictions.

A trustee is appointed to protect the interests of the bondholders under the indenture arrangement and to enforce its terms. The functions of a trustee are

---

[3] Holders of some issues of U.S. government savings bonds purchased during World War II and held to maturity actually suffered such an experience.

[4] Federal, state, and municipal general obligation bond issues do not use indentures, but revenue bonds do.

1. To authenticate the bonds by countersigning them at the time of issue to prevent the issue of bonds above the authorized limit.
2. To hold the mortgage on real property (real estate) or act as custodian of the personal property (stocks or bonds) in the case of collateral obligations.
3. To receive both interest and principal payments from the debtor when due and distribute them to the bondholders.
4. To ascertain that all provisions laid down in the indenture that are obligations of the debtor are complied with.
5. To take action against the debtor if the latter fails to fulfill obligations, especially if the debtor is in default either as to interest or to principal.

The Trust Indenture Act of 1939 was passed to provide protection for bondholders. The act prohibits any personal financial interest in the issue by the trustee and requires the issuer to send semiannual financial reports through the trustee to the bondholders. Other requirements provide that the trustee should receive lists of original bondholders, financial statements, and evidence that the provisions of the bond indenture are being fulfilled. These provisions must be complied with or registration under the Securities Act of 1933 will not be allowed.

Bond Ratings and Bond Quality

Several reporting services[5] compile and publish useful financial data for evaluating companies; they also rate bonds in terms of quality. Such ratings represent attempts to rank issues according to the probability of loss due to default. Bond quality ratings are not intended to serve as a guide to relative attractiveness in terms of the yield likely to be realized by an investor, though such ratings certainly affect market yields. The ratings published by these agencies and a brief summary of their meaning are shown in Table 3-1. Bonds rated A and above are considered investment quality bonds that expose the investor to minimal risk in terms of the probability of receiving promised payments.

The record suggests that in general, agency ratings have been good predictors of risk of default.[6] Agency ratings, however, have not been infallible. For example, the agencies failed to predict (that is, by lowered ratings) the difficulties experienced by holders of New York City obligations during the early 1970s. Various other standards and analytical techniques useful in judging the quality of bonds and preferred stocks will be discussed in much greater detail in Chapter 24. The ratings will serve as an indication of general market judgment concerning quality for purposes of this chapter, with the caveat that further analysis should be undertaken before selecting a given bond for purchase.

---

[5] The most widely used services are those offered by Standard & Poor's Corporation and Moody's Investor Service, Inc.

[6] For a thorough study of such ratings, see W. Braddock Hickman, *Corporate Bond Quality an Investor Experience*, National Bureau of Economic Research (Princeton, N.J.: Princeton University Press, 1958).

TABLE 3-1. Description of Agency Ratings

Moody's	Standard & Poor's	Quality Indication
Aaa	AAA	Highest quality
Aa	AA	High quality
A	A	Upper medium grade
Baa	BBB	Medium grade
Ba	BB	Contains speculative elements
B	B	Outright speculative
Caa	CCC & CC	Default definitely possible
Ca	C	Default, only partial recovery likely
C	DDD-D	Default, little recovery likely

Secured Bonds

Corporate bonds having specific assets of the corporation pledged as security are *secured bonds.* The most commonly issued secured bonds are mortgage bonds, leasehold mortgage bonds, collateral trust bonds and notes, guaranteed bonds, and equipment trust certificates and notes.

Mortgage Bonds. A *mortgage bond* is secured by the assets of the corporation. In case of bankruptcy, mortgage bondholders have first claim for repayment from either liquidation or reorganization proceeds. Mortgage bonds emerged from the practice of making secured loans on homes and business properties, with the loans secured by pledges of real estate. Mortgage bonds are widely used by utility and railroad corporations, but industrial corporations generally issue unsecured bonds, known as debentures (see pages 47–48), that share equally with all unsecured creditors in the event of financial insolvency. First-mortgage bonds are called *senior* or *underlying issues;* second-mortgage bonds are known as *junior issues.*

Mortgages may be either open, closed, open-end, or limited open-end. An *open mortgage,* which is the most liberal arrangement, allows a corporation to issue as many bonds as it wishes, all with an equal first-mortgage claim. This arrangement offers no protection to the original bondholders from the possibility that additional issues will seriously dilute their protection. The poor investment position of original holders could create marketing difficulties, and therefore such bonds are rarely issued. A *closed mortgage* requires that secondary issues maintain a junior position relative to the original issue. Rather than affording the investor maximum protection, rigidity of this provision could limit corporate expansion and the acquisition of needed funds in the future.

A compromise between extremes of liberality and rigidity is provided by an *open-end mortgage*. Under this arrangement the issuance of secondary issues on an equal status with the original issue is permissible, but certain protective investor provisions are included. For example, a corporation may issue additional bonds under the original mortgage up to x percent of the value of the assets acquired if the interest charges on the total indebtedness of the corporation (including the new issue) can be earned y times over. Provisions to be met under such an issue are varied in actual practice, and thus various combinations of ratios and numbers (i.e., x and y above) are found.

A *limited open-end mortgage* allows for financial growth by permitting bonds to be issued up to some authorized amount, considerably in excess of the amount of the initial issue. Such an arrangement, however, places a definite limit on the maximum amount of first-mortgage bonds that may be issued, thereby providing protection for the original bondholders. The mortgage indenture also typically contains safeguards similar to those in open-end mortgages, such as an earnings-coverage restriction.

Corporations issuing mortgage bonds pledge specific assets, which are listed in the indenture, as security against the payment of interest and principal. Assets so pledged may include not only all assets currently owned, but also assets that may be acquired in the future. Such a provision is called an *after-acquired clause*. This clause was frequently used prior to 1900, but went out of use subsequently. In recent years, however, corporations issuing open-end mortgage bonds have frequently included an after-acquired clause. As a result, collateral tends to increase with debt since the sale of new bonds brings additional assets to the corporation.

When a corporation defaults on its contract under a mortgage, it is the duty of the trustee to bring legal action in the courts to secure payment, which may take the form of foreclosure proceedings against pledged assets. Assets may be held under court supervision to satisfy the claims of different classes of creditors. The bankruptcy statutes, revised in the 1930s, emphasize reorganization rather than liquidation. In case of default in any part of the contract, the entire debt usually becomes due automatically and is in default (*acceleration clause*).

In case of reorganization or liquidation, the order of the creditors' priority of claim will determine the distribution of the new securities of the reorganized corporation or the liquidation payments. The U.S. Supreme Court has stated repeatedly the doctrine of absolute priority, whereby no claim junior in priority to a senior claim may be compensated until all senior claims are fully satisfied. Of course, the claimants with senior claims may waive wholly or partially their rights if they desire to do so. In case of financial difficulty, therefore, the value of a secured claim, relative to an unsecured claim, is important. In some cases the secured claimants receive all the value available in reorganization or liquidation and leave nothing to be paid to unsecured claimants.

Leasehold Mortgage Bonds. *Leasehold mortgage bonds* are issued to finance the construction of buildings (such as apartment houses, hotels, office buildings, or shopping centers) on leased land. Under such an arrangement a corporation issuing the bonds would previously have leased the land on which the buildings are to be erected. The lease will generally require that all taxes on the land be paid, plus a fixed annual rental. The lease and the buildings constructed are pledged as security for the leasehold mortgage bonds. Income from the buildings must be sufficient to meet all taxes, lease rental costs, and all operating and maintenance expenses before any part of the proceeds is available for payment to leasehold mortgage bondholders. These bonds were issued in rather large amounts in the 1920s; then, because of a poor record, they became rather uncommon until the post–World War II years.

Collateral Trust Bonds and Notes. *Collateral trust bonds* or notes are secured by stocks and bonds of other corporations[7] that are pledged with the trustee. Occasionally, the issuer pledges certain of its own senior issues as security. If the collateral trust bonds are issued by a parent holding company, as is usually the case, the pledged securities are generally securities of subsidiaries.

The most relevant factors determining the worth of a collateral trust bond are the strength and credit worthiness of the issuing corporation, apart from the value and nature of the pledged collateral. In some cases the only assets owned by a company issuing collateral trust bonds are securities pledged as collateral to secure the bond. In such a case, the credit of the issuing company is itself based on the value of the pledged securities. Before an investor purchases collateral trust securities, a careful analysis should be made of the pledged securities. If substitution of collateral is permitted, adequate safeguards should be present to ensure that quality of the collateral is maintained.

Guaranteed Bonds. *Guaranteed bonds* almost always have been railroad bonds. Sometimes a railroad company finds that guaranteeing the securities of another company when leasing its road is advantageous or necessary. The security holders of the leased road usually require some definite assurance of income in exchange for relinquishing control over

---

[7]Personal property, financial claims such as stocks and bonds, as opposed to real estate, the latter being legally designated as real property.

the railroad. Indeed, most guaranteed bonds that have been issued were issued for precisely this purpose.

Equipment Trust Certificates and Notes. *Equipment trust certificates* are issued principally to finance the purchase of railroad equipment, buses, trucks, and aircraft.[8] Such an instrument gives the holder a right to share in the pool of rents to be derived from leasing equipment and is not strictly a debt instrument, although the rights of investors are quite similar. Equipment trust certificates are retired annually, according to a specified time schedule, usually over a ten-year period. Investors can select certificates which are due at times that best fit their needs. Repayment is typically at a rate faster than the equipment depreciates, in order to maintain sufficient asset value behind outstanding certificates. Certificates are customarily issued to a maximum of 85 percent of the value of the new equipment, although in the last decade a few have been issued at nearly 100 percent.

Equipment trust certificates are issued under two plans: the Philadelphia (Lease) Plan, or the New York (Conditional Bill of Sale) Plan. From the investor's standpoint, which plan is followed does not make much difference. Under the Lease Plan, the trustees sell participation certificates against the equipment to investors and lease the equipment to the railroad. Under the Conditional Bill of Sale Plan, equipment is sold to the railroads under a conditional bill of sale with possession passing to the buyer but title remaining with the seller until payments have been completed.

The investment standing of such securities, as a class, is high because of their generally excellent record regarding ongoing situations and in litigation. Credit ratings vary depending on the credit standing of the issuing corporation.[9] This excellent experience is based on a number of factors:

1. An issuer, even in financial difficulty, wishes to keep its newest and most efficient equipment, which is essential to its operation, and this new equipment will be well maintained.
2. Even in reorganization, courts usually permit continued payment of interest in equipment trust securities, even when all other securities of the issuer may be in default.
3. The asset value behind equipment trust debt is constantly increasing because debt is paid off faster than the equipment depreciates.
4. Generally, there is a good secondhand market for mobile equipment if the trustees decide to repossess.

---

[8] Donald MacQueen Street, *Railroad Equipment Financing* (New York: Columbia University Press, 1959).
[9] However, even the equipment trust certificates of the New York, New Haven Railroad, in reorganization, were rated BBB in 1968, the lowest ratings of any such issues.

Commodity-Backed Bonds

Commodity-backed bonds, indexed to the price of silver, were issued during spring 1980 by Sunshine Mining Company. Similar issues by other companies could be linked to gold, other precious metals, or natural resources. In fact, such issues could be linked to anything that has the potential for rising in value at a faster rate than the general cost of living. *The Wall Street Journal* reported that "dozens of companies are now said to be studying the idea which might enable them to persuade investors to accept a lower interest rate on corporate borrowings in return for a chance to share in the appreciation of the underlying assets."[10]

Commodity bonds offer potential protection from a run-up in interest rates that would erode traditional bond values, depending on the price performance of the underlying collateral. Such bonds could also have a tax advantage over traditional bonds since appreciation of the collateral above face value of the bond would be a capital gain at maturity taxed at a maximum rate of 28 percent under current law, as opposed to a maximum rate of 70 percent for interest income. Moreover, the cost of storing and insuring the underlying asset is absorbed by the issuing company.

The Sunshine issue, however, offered an interest rate of only $8\frac{1}{2}$ percent at issue when AAA corporates were offering yields approaching 14 percent. A gold-linked issue in the European markets (not available to American residents) offered an interest yield of 4 to 5 percent. If substantial price appreciation is not realized in the underlying asset, direct investment in that asset might well be a better investment. Moreover, the investor would have been better off to buy traditional bonds.

Unsecured Bonds or Debentures

Unsecured bonds, or *debentures*, are secured only by the general credit standing of the issuer. Many unsecured industrial debenture issues enjoy high investment ratings and compare favorably in yield to high-grade first-mortgage bonds, since bond quality in the final analysis depends not on asset liens but on what the company can earn and its cash flow. The key to all investment value is earning power and cash flow.

In case of default, debenture bondholders hold no claim to specific assets and only share with other unsecured creditors in the event of reorganization or liquidation. A secured bond, on the other hand, is protected by a specific lien against either real or personal property, giving it a prior claim on the proceeds generated by such assets. A debenture is typically not preceded by any secured issue with prior claims; fre-

---

[10] *The Wall Street Journal*, February 2, 1981, p. 40.

quently the indenture contains a covenant that would place the debenture on a par with a new mortgage if one were subsequently placed on the property.

In recent years a considerable number of *subordinated debentures* have been issued. These bonds are subordinated to other debentures, and general creditors, as well as to secured bonds outstanding and in some cases to mortgage bonds that may later be issued, subject to stated restrictive measures. In the majority of cases, subordinated debentures are made acceptable to investors by inclusion of a conversion feature (into common stock). Standard & Poor's Corporation has typically rated these bonds as BBB, BB, or B. Some examples of such issues are given in Table 3-2.

TABLE 3-2. Subordinated Convertible Debentures

Issuer	Type	S&P Rating (1974)	
Air Reduction Co.	CV Sub Deb $3\frac{7}{8}$'s	'87	BBB
Aluminum Company of America	CV Sub Deb $5\frac{1}{4}$'s	'91	BBB
American Airlines, Inc.	CV Sub Deb $4\frac{1}{4}$'s	'92	BB
Celanese Corp.	CV Sub Deb 4's	'90	BB
General Telephone & Electronics Corp.	CV Sub Deb 4's	'90	BB
Grace (W. R.) & Co.	CV Sub Deb $4\frac{1}{4}$'s	'90	BB
Pan American World Airways, Inc.	CV Sub Deb $4\frac{1}{2}$'s	'86	CCC
Standard Packaging	CV Sub Deb $5\frac{1}{4}$'s	'90	B
Stevens (J. P.) & Company	CV Sub Deb 4's	'90	BB
United Air Lines, Inc.	CV Sub Deb 5's	'91	BB
United Merchants & Mfgs.	CV Sub Deb 4's	'90	BB

Special Features of Bonds

The issuing corporation determines which of the various features to include as part of its bond issue. Some of the most common features of bonds are described in the following paragraphs.

Coupon or Bearer Bonds. A *coupon bond* is one to which one coupon is attached for each interest payment due. The holder of such a bond clips the coupon on each interest date and deposits it at a bank for collection. The owner's name does not appear on the bond, and the issuer does not keep a record of owners. Since coupon bonds are transferred simply by delivery, they are also called *bearer bonds;* thus, whoever lawfully has possession of a bearer bond is the owner and is entitled to all interest payments and principal when due. Because transfer is made not by endorsement but by delivery, unusual care must be exercised to prevent coupon or bearer bonds from being lost or stolen. Bondholders should keep a record of the number appearing on each bond they hold. Most bonds outstanding are coupon bonds or bearer bonds; many may be exchanged at the holder's option for registered bonds.

Registered Bonds. A *registered bond* differs from a coupon or bearer bond in that the owner's name appears on the bond. The issuing corporation records the number and current owner of each bond, thereby making it transferable only by endorsement by an owner, as is the case with stock. There are two classes of registered bonds: (1) fully registered bonds and (2) bonds registered as to principal only. In the case of fully registered bonds, interest is paid by check on interest dates to the owner of record. Bonds that are registered as to principal only, however, have coupons attached for each interest payment; these are clipped and deposited for collection as is the case with unregistered coupon bonds.

For various reasons, registration is advantageous to both institutional and private holders (except for those interested in an illicit purpose, such as tax avoidance). In recent years, therefore, pressure has been put on corporations to issue registered bonds rather than coupon bonds.

Income Bonds. The distinguishing feature of *income bonds* is that interest must be paid only to the extent that it is earned. Furthermore, interest not paid usually accrues only for a limited number of payments missed. In some cases a portion of the interest payment is mandatory, and the remainder is contingent on earnings. Income bonds resemble stocks more than bonds in terms of the contingent nature of their claim, although they enjoy a priority relative to stocks of the same issuer in the event of default, and interest must be paid if it is earned.

Income bonds are often issued in exchange for other fixed-income securities in readjustments and reorganizations in order to reduce the burden of fixed charges. Many, and perhaps most, income bonds have been issued in reorganization of railroads or construction companies. Income bonds have in some instances been issued to replace preferred stocks because the interest on debt is tax deductible; thus the net cost is less than preferred dividends, which are not tax deductible. The tax advantage associated with debt issues has led recently to their being offered and sold as new financing.

Investors in income bonds should be sure that the contract under which the income bonds are issued specifies in great detail exactly how the income available to pay the interest is to be calculated. Without satisfactory provisions, the management would be able to manipulate expenses so as to avoid payment of interest on the bonds.

Sinking Fund Bonds. A *sinking fund provision* requires that the corporation set aside periodically a specific sum for the purpose of retiring all, or a substantial portion, of its outstanding bonds before or at maturity. Provisions vary widely, and the value of a sinking fund can be determined only by specific analysis of the actual sinking fund in question.

The fact that a bond is "protected" by a sinking fund provision does not change what would otherwise be a speculative bond into a high-grade investment. In any case, a bondholder would not wish annual sinking fund requirements to be so large as to cause financial difficulty for the corporation.

A sinking fund provision may call for payment of specific amounts annually, or a certain percentage on annual sales or earnings to allow flexibility in times of poor business. The purpose of a sinking fund is to provide for payment of the debt at maturity. In most cases payments into the sinking fund exceed the rate of depreciation of property securing the debt instrument. Some contracts permit the issuer to acquire new property, which acts as security for the bonds, as an alternative to reducing the debt by calling bonds. Most utility mortgage bond indentures include such a provision. A sinking fund provision is usually more flexible than serial bond requirements and not, therefore, so often the cause of defaults. If interest payments are made, bondholders often waive sinking fund requirements rather than force the issuer into reorganization or bankruptcy.

Serial Bonds. A corporation or government body may sell a large issue consisting of bonds that mature on successive dates (rather than on a single maturity date) as specified by the serial numbers on the bonds. Most *serial issues*, except for equipment trust issues, are the issues of municipalities. Many private placement issues (discussed in Chapter 15) include in the indenture an amortization requirement that makes the issue a serial issue in effect. The serial feature provides a means for paying off debt periodically in installments and is thus a substitute for a sinking fund provision, which accomplishes the same purpose. Interest rates are adjusted for the various maturities, from the shortest to the longest, by varying the coupon rate or by varying the selling price at the time of the issue. Many investors favor such securities as a convenient means of staggering the maturity dates of their investments over a predetermined time schedule.

Callable Bonds. Bond issues that may be redeemed before maturity at the option of the issuer are referred to as *callable* or *redeemable*. A call feature in a bond contract is undesirable from the investor's standpoint. The call feature can be exercised only at the option of the corporation and will be exercised only when it is advantageous to the corporation. The most frequent reason for calling bonds is to refund at a lower interest rate. Institutional investors therefore press for noncallable bonds when funds are relatively tight and interest rates are relatively high. Many call features cannot be exercised until a predetermined time period has elapsed after issue, such as five years.

The call price typically starts well above par and declines gradually by steps as the maturity date approaches. There are actually two call prices stated in most indentures: (1) the first (lower) price is for calls by lot in accordance with sinking fund provisions; (2) the second (higher) price is for the redemption of the entire issue upon call. The latter declines over time. The nearer to maturity, the less may be saved by refunding an issue at a lower interest rate and, conversely, the less an investor would stand to lose because of a call.

Convertible Bonds. Some bonds are *convertible* at the option of the holder into another type of security—usually common stock. Some convertibles must be converted on or before a given date and others are unrestricted in this sense. A detailed treatment of the analysis of convertible bonds is presented in Chapter 24.

The conversion feature offers the bondholder a combination of fixed income and an opportunity to share in earnings growth of the firm through the option to convert. As with any other sweetener, however, a conversion feature comes only at a price. The fixed income yield on a convertible bond is almost always less than the yield on an equivalent quality straight bond. Only when the conversion price is set at an unreasonably high level would the market fail to attach some value to the conversion feature.

A convertible bond indenture must specify the terms of conversion, the period in which conversion can take place if there is a time limit, the ratio at which each bond can be converted into stock (the conversion ratio), and the provisions protecting against dilution of the conversion privilege if additional stock is issued by the corporation. If there were no provisions protecting against dilution of the conversion privilege, a convertible bondholder might be put at a disadvantage by the issuance of additional stock. For example, if the corporation paid a 100 percent stock dividend or split its stock two for one, the value of the conversion privilege, if not protected, would be cut in half.

If the convertible bond has a call provision, as most do, the issuer can force conversion by calling the bond at a time when the investor will receive more in stock value than in accepting the call price. American Telephone and Telegraph Company has frequently followed this procedure.

Special-Purpose Bonds

Most bond titles in this category are self-explanatory. It is fairly obvious, for example, that the major portion of the proceeds from a bridge bond issue should be used to construct a bridge. A bond title often serves as a statement of intended purpose, although sometimes a title may be misleading. Special-purpose bonds are discussed in the following paragraphs.

Prior-Lien Bonds and Receivers' Certificates. A corporation may issue securities with a prior lien ahead of outstanding mortgage bonds in times of financial difficulties, such as receivership. When issued with the consent of the first-mortgage bondholders, such bonds are called *prior-lien bonds*. When issued by court decree during a receivership, on the other hand, they are called *receivers' certificates*.

Mortgage bondholders may subordinate their interests when the corporation is in financial difficulty in the hope that an injection of new funds will enable the corporation to operate successfully again. Without the injection of new funds, the corporation might be forced to liquidate its assets. The sacrifices that would be experienced by the bondholders in liquidation could well be greater than the loss of a prior lien.

Refunding Bonds. A *refunding bond* is issued to replace an outstanding issue that has come due or to replace a higher coupon rate bond with a lower coupon rate bond during a time of low market bond yields.

Adjustment Bonds. *Adjustment bonds* are issued during a reorganization of a corporation in exchange for securities outstanding.

Bond Denominations and Prices

Bond certificates are typically issued in denominations of $1,000, although some issues have denominations as high as $100,000 and some have a par of $100. U.S. government savings bonds are issued with par values as low as $25. Bonds of small denominations (under $1,000 par value) are frequently referred to as *baby bonds*. Many corporations regard the expense incidental to the issuance of a baby bond as prohibitive and believe that bond investors, as a class, have little interest in such issues.

The market price of a bond is usually expressed as a percentage of its par (face value), which is customarily $1,000. Corporate bonds are quoted to the nearest one-eighth of a percent, and a quote of $97\frac{1}{8}$ indicates a price of $971.25 or $97\frac{1}{8}$ percent of $1,000. U.S. government bonds are highly marketable and deal in such keenly competitive markets that they are quoted in thirty-seconds or sixty-fourths rather than eighths. Moreover, decimals are used, rather than fractions, in quoting prices. A quotation of 106.17 for a treasury bond indicates a price of $1,065.31 [$1,060 + ($\frac{17}{32}$ × $10)]. When a plus sign follows the quotation, the treasury bond is being quoted in sixty-fourths. One must double the number following the decimal point and add one to determine the fraction of $10 represented in the quote. For example, a quote of 95.16$^+$ indicates a price of $955.16 [$950 + ($\frac{33}{64}$ × $10)].

The difference between market price and the par value of a bond is called a *premium* when market price exceeds par value and a *discount* when market value is below par value. As will be demonstrated in Chapter 7, a change in the general level of interest rates is a major factor in determining price fluctuations relative to par value. The price of a bond reflects its risk and the supply and demand conditions in the market for loanable funds. The Federal Reserve affects the supply of loanable funds, and thus its actions have an important bearing on bond prices.

Bonds may be quoted "flat" or on an "and interest" basis. *Flat quotations* are normally used for bonds that are in default in the payment of interest and, in the case of income bonds, where the payment of interest is contingent upon earnings. When quoted on an *and interest* basis, the buyer pays the seller not only the agreed price, but also accrued interest. Since accrued interest for the full interest period will be paid to the buyer on the next interest date, or to whomever is the holder of the bond on that date, the buyer is expected to pay the seller the amount of interest earned while the seller owned the bond. Accrued interest on bonds is normally computed on the basis of a 30-day month and a 360-day year, except in the case of U.S. government securities where the actual number of days is used. The seller is entitled to accrued interest up to, but not including, the day of delivery.

To illustrate, assume that a 6 percent bond, par $1,000, with interest payment dates on January 1 and July 1, is sold to you on Monday, June 12, for delivery on Friday, June 16, at a quoted price of 105. On July 1, the buyer of the bond will receive six months' interest, or $30. However, the buyer is only entitled to interest covering the period June 16 through June 30, or fifteen days. Therefore, the buyer reimburses the seller for accrued interest covering the period January 1 through June 15, or 5 months and 15 days, at 6 percent (amounting to $27.50) by including this amount in the purchase price of the bond.

Bonds of Nonprofit Corporations

Nonprofit organizations comprise that portion of the capital market that supplies funds for churches, hospitals, colleges, and other non-profit institutions. Church bonds, which range in issue from several hundred thousand dollars to over $2 million, are rated highly by rating services, usually as AA or A. If the issuer is a public institution, such as a state university, the bonds will be revenue bonds with the tax-exempt advantage.

Most investors hold such bonds until maturity or until they are retired. Bonds issued by churches have had a favorable experience; for over a quarter of a century, there have been no defaults in such bonds, although a few issues were considered of questionable quality in recent years.

Under SEC regulations, registration is not required for offerings made by nonprofit organizations.

SHORT-TERM DEBT INSTRUMENTS

A short-term financial instrument is one having a maturity of less than one year from date of issue. The four main short-term investment instruments available to investors are U.S. treasury bills (and other short-term issues of governmental bodies both domestic and foreign), commercial paper, certificates of deposit, and bankers' acceptances. They are generally highly liquid and are typically used to employ temporarily idle cash balances when better long-term investment opportunities are anticipated in the near future. Long-term instruments typically offer a higher yield, but the more distant maturity date subjects the investor to a "price risk" (selling for less money than was committed to acquire the instrument) if interest rates rise after purchase and the funds are needed.

Treasury bills are offered with maturities ranging from 91 days to a full year. An investor, therefore, can choose from a wide variety of maturity dates. A treasury bill can be ordered through a commercial bank, which charges a fee for handling the order, or directly from a Federal Reserve bank for a new issue. At the time of this writing, the minimum purchase requirement was $10,000, with purchases over that amount available in multiples of $5,000. For new issues, an investor may submit either a competitive bid or a noncompetitive bid (accepting the average discount rate for all bills accepted during that auction). Bid prices for competitive bids are expressed as percentages of par to three decimal places.

Commercial paper consists of unsecured, short-term promissory notes sold by large, well-known corporations at a discount to investors and commercial paper dealer firms. The yield offered on such paper has typically been higher than that for treasury bills and other short-term money market instruments. In tight money periods, such as 1974, the yield may exceed that available on treasury bills by as much as 200 to 500 basis points.[11] Also, investors have great flexibility in choosing size and maturity date. Such paper is not usually available to a small investor, however. In practice, $25,000 is the smallest amount that can ordinarily be purchased, and a fee of about $25 is typically charged when such a small amount is sold. A common practice is for commercial paper to be sold in units of $100,000, $500,000, or $1 million.

A *banker's acceptance* is a time draft, usually arising in international trade, that has been accepted by a bank. The bank is responsible for payment at maturity, and the paper is also implicitly backed by the firm issuing the draft. Bankers' acceptances typically yield 50 basis points or more higher than treasury bills of comparable maturity and are available in a broad spectrum of maturity dates. A wide variety of principal amounts, ranging from $5,000 to $1 million or more, is typically available, but because of the relatively small amount available at any time it may be difficult to find the exact amount and maturity wanted by the investor.

A *certificate of deposit* is a receipt from a bank or savings and loan institution for a deposit of money at a specified rate of interest for a given period of time. Negotiable certificates of deposit are usually not issued in amounts under $25,000 and typically range from $100,000 to $1 million. Thus, they are not available to the small investor. One-month certificates of deposit in the secondary market offered a record high yield of 19.24 percent during December 1980.[12] Nonnegotiable certificates of deposit are available from banks and savings and loans in amounts as small as $500. They have offered yields approximating 12 percent during 1980–81 when money was committed for four to six years. Serious penalties are imposed, however, when an investor liquidates prior to maturity.

Summary

Various types of debt obligations are availabile to the investor. Debt securities, like preferred stocks, provide an investor with a fixed income flow and a prior position to equity securities in the event of liquidation. Fixed-income securities, however, do not provide the investor with an opportunity for growth in income payments or capital value stemming from corporate growth as do equity securities.

---

[12] *Federal Reserve Bulletin*, April, 1981, p. A25.

Short-term debt instruments offer higher liquidity and a place to temporarily employ idle cash balances until better long-term investment opportunities are anticipated. Long-term securities typically offer higher yields than short-term instruments, but the more distant maturity date subjects the investor to a "price risk." If interest rates rise after purchase, the price at which a long-term bond could be sold would fall below the amount committed to acquire the bond.

All debt instruments are fully exposed to purchasing power risk—that is, to the debilitating effects of inflation. Equity securities offer the possibility of offsetting the ravages of inflation through corporate growth, leading to increased dividend payments and rising prices for the stocks. Since 1967, however, stock investment has not, in general, been a very effective hedge against inflation.

Questions

1. (a) Define trading on the equity and illustrate the concept by means of assumed figures. Explain leverage.
   (b) Of what significance to investors is the degree of trading on the equity practiced by a corporation?
2. Would you be using financial leverage if you bought a car or a home on credit terms? Why or why not?
3. (a) Define a bond indenture and describe its usual provisions.
   (b) Discuss the importance to investors of the Trust Indenture Act of 1939.
4. (a) Why are most high-grade industrial bonds usually debenture bonds?
   (b) How should the safety of a bond be evaluated? Should a lien on assets receive major consideration from a bond analyst? Discuss.
   (c) What is a subordinated debenture?
5. (a) Why do financial intermediaries prefer registered bonds to coupon bonds?
   (b) Which type of bond do you believe is preferable for individual investors? Why?
6. (a) Are callable bonds desirable from the investor's standpoint?
   (b) What protection does a sinking fund offer the investor? What are its limitations?
7. (a) Distinguish between a convertible bond and a bond with detachable warrants.
   (b) How would one calculate the possible dilution effect of each type while the bond is outstanding?
8. Explain carefully each of the following terms used in describing a bond: A $7\frac{1}{2}\%$ convertible, subordinated debenture bond.
9. Is an equipment trust certificate a bond? Discuss.

Work-Study Problems

1. Select two investment grade bonds and determine the following information.
   (a) Exact name and description.
   (b) The current market quote for the bond and that quote translated into a current dollar price.
   (c) Whether or not the bond is callable and the terms of call.
   (d) The yield to maturity. (Calculation of a yield to maturity and the meaning of such a yield concept are discussed in Chapter 7.)
   (e) The nature of the security supporting the bond issue.
   (f) The Standard and Poor's rating for the bond.
   Briefly discuss the significance of each of the above pieces of information to an investor.

2. Assume $100,000 had been committed ten years ago to each of the following: (a) a savings account in a commercial bank; (b) a long-term U.S. government bond; (c) a mutual fund of your choice; (d) a high-grade portfolio of corporate bonds; (e) a high-grade portfolio of municipal bonds; and (f) a common stock portfolio represented by the S&P 400 Stock Index.
   (a) What would be the terminal wealth position of the investor in each case? Assume interest or dividends are reinvested in all cases, and that the investor was in a 45 percent income tax bracket.
   (b) Using the consumer price index to represent the degree of inflation experienced during the period, which portfolio offered the best purchasing power protection?

3. (a) Through discussion with brokers and the use of bond manuals (such as those published by Standard & Poor's Corporation), determine if any commodity-backed bonds, other than those issued by Sunshine Mining Company, have been issued.
   (b) Carefully explain the way payments to bondholders over the life of the bond will be determined. Be sure to clarify the following: (1) Are both interest and principal payments affected by changes in value of the underlying asset or only the principal payment? (2) How is the change in the value of the underlying asset determined for purposes of paying bondholders?
   (c) tional bonds? (Hint: consider the yield that would have been realized by a holder to date versus what such an investor could have earned by holding a traditional bond.)

4.

U.S. Government and Municipal Securities

Public securities include the obligations of the U.S. Treasury, the various federal government agencies, and the debt issues of states, cities, counties, and school districts. The U.S. government is, by a wide margin, the largest single issuer of securities in the world, and the market for such securities is, therefore, quite important. Municipal debt issues (those of states, cities, counties, and school districts) also form a large and important market.

Although many investors own a public security at some time, they are often not aware of the many types of securities issued by government bodies or of the different ways in which one can utilize such securities in a portfolio. This chapter discusses the different types of securities issued and suggests an approach to analyzing such securities.

For the typical investor, ownership of federal government securities is for a combination of liquidity and the highest quality reserves. On the other hand, one can speculate on interest rate changes through federal government securities, utilizing a high degree of leverage since the margins required to purchase such securities are relatively low. The main attraction of state and local securities is the exemption of interest received by the investor from federal income taxation, causing this class of securities to appeal mainly to high tax bracket investors.

FEDERAL GOVERNMENT SECURITIES

U.S. government securities are considered to be among the highest-quality investment vehicles in the world in the sense that there is virtually no risk of failure to pay interest and principal in accordance with the debt contract. The federal government has unlimited power to tax, power to borrow, and sufficient control over the banking system to assure demand for its securities. Imagining the circumstances that would result in default of federal securities is difficult. Such circumstances (possibly a hyperinflation) would cause most, if not all, other securities to default also. All debt instruments, however, including government bonds, are subject to the interest rate and purchasing power risk as already discussed in Chapter 1. Prices of government bonds have fallen sharply over the past decade as interest rates have risen to record highs. Inflation, moreover, has led to relatively low real yields and even negative real yields at times. A key question when purchasing any debt security is what will interest rates and inflation rates be in the future?

For discussion purposes, U.S. government securities can be separated into two main categories: nonmarketable and marketable securities.

Nonmarketable Government Debt

Nonmarketable government debt includes (1) securities that are not transferable and that are redeemable at fixed prices, such as savings bonds, and (2) "special issues" sold to government trust funds and holdings by foreign governments and central banks. Saving bonds are the nonmarketable instrument of interest to individual investors.

Two types of savings bonds were offered at the time of writing this book: series EE and series HH savings bonds. Series EE savings bonds are registered securities that provide a yield of 9 percent if held to maturity. The cash surrender value of the bond increases each six months in such a way that the maximum return of 9 percent is only realized if the bond is held to its eight-year maturity. A return of less than 9 percent is earned if the bond is cashed prior to maturity. These bonds are purchased at a price representing 50 percent of maturity value. They are issued in various denominations with a minimum denomination of $50. Interest, represented by the difference between surrender value and purchase price, may be accrued and reported annually for federal income tax purposes or reported in one lump sum at surrender. It is advisable to report the interest for tax purposes at surrender in most cases since the postponement of tax liability can be considered analogous to an interest-free loan in the amount of the tax liability that would be incurred through annual reporting of interest.

Series HH savings bonds are registered securities that mature in ten years and are redeemed at face value. They pay interest semiannually. A 5 percent rate is paid for the first six months, a $7\frac{1}{2}$ percent rate for the next four and a half years, and an $8\frac{1}{2}$ rate for the sixth through the tenth year. An average yield of a bit less than 8 percent is earned if the bond is held to maturity, and a still lower average yield is realized if the bond is cashed prior to maturity.[1] These bonds can be turned in for

---

[1] A yield to maturity would generally be considered a more useful concept than an average yield. The calculation of a yield to maturity is discussed in Chapter 7. Actually, the average yield is a reasonable approximation here.

full face value (the price paid to acquire them) any time after six months from the date of original purchase. The minimum amount in which they can be purchased is $500, and larger denominations are available. Series EE bonds can be exchanged into series HH bonds at the option of the holder at any time during their life.

The relatively small investment required, the fact that no commissions are charged when purchasing savings bonds, and the certainty of returns are advantages offered by these securities. Moreover, they offer a yield exceeding that offered by a passbook savings account. Finally, the interest earned is exempt from state and local taxes, but not the federal income tax, for all government securities. The main disadvantages of these securities are the relatively low yield offered and the fact that the investor is fully exposed to the purchasing power risk. There have been several periods since the 1950s, including the late 1970s, during which investors in such securities would have realized a negative real return. When the inflation rate exceeds the return offered by these bonds, there is no doubt that the real return is negative.

Marketable Government Debt

Marketable interest-bearing government debt issues consist of those originally offered for sale to the public and subsequently traded in the securities markets. New issues are usually sold through Federal Reserve banks, while almost all secondary trading takes place in the over-the-counter (OTC) market. Government security dealers usually do not charge a commission for buy or sell orders of round lots (security orders having a par value of $100,000 or multiples of $100,000), but charges are typically made for smaller purchases. One must realize that on small purchases, custody fees and odd-lot charges may significantly reduce the realized yield. Marketable securities are by far the larger part of total Treasury debt, as shown in Table 4-1.

TABLE 4-1. Gross Public Debt of U.S. Treasury by Type, March 1981

Type of Security	Amount (in billions)	Percentage
Nonmarketable	$302.1	31.3
Marketable	661.1	68.6
Treasury bills	235.3	24.4
Treasury notes	336.5	34.9
Treasury bonds	89.3	9.3
Noninterest-backing debt	1.3	0.1
Total gross public debt	$964.5	100.0

Source: Federal Reserve Bulletin (April, 1981), p. A30

Treasury Coupon Issues. Treasury notes (with a maturity between one and ten years) and treasury bonds (usually maturing in more than ten years) pay interest by the coupon method. Yields vary depending on the relative demand for and supply of loanable funds at a given moment, including the needs of the U.S. Treasury and Federal Reserve actions. Yields on government bonds have ranged from as low as 20 basis points lower to as much as 180 basis points lower than those offered on the highest-quality corporate bonds (AAA) over the last two decades.

Treasury notes and bonds may be issued in minimum denominations of $1,000 or $5,000. Notes of less than four years maturity are not issued in denominations of less than $5,000. Notes and bonds may also be issued in larger denominations of $10,000, $100,000, and $1,000,000. A forthcoming sale of notes or bonds is announced in daily newspapers and Treasury newsletters. An exchange offering by the U.S. Treasury, not often available, allows investors to exchange specifically announced outstanding securities for a new issue of notes and/or bonds. An additional payment may be required or a refund may be due when such an exchange is made.

Treasury bonds and notes can be acquired in bearer or registered form. Semiannual interest payments are mailed to registered bondholders, but coupons must be clipped and returned to a Federal Reserve or commercial bank to collect interest on bearer bonds. The greater safety of registered bonds, as discussed in the preceding chapter, suggests that they should be preferred except by very active traders.

Either a competitive or noncompetitive bid may be submitted for new issues of treasury bonds, notes, or bills. Bids in multiples of $1,000, and in accordance with the offering circular, are submitted by mail or in person at a Federal Reserve bank before the termination of the subscription period. Competitive price bids must be expressed to two decimal places on the basis of 100 percent of face value—for example, 96.40. A minimum tender price is often specified by the Treasury. Noncompetitive bidders usually agree to pay a weighted average price of the accepted competitive bids, but at times the Treasury will award all accepted competitive bids and the noncompetitive bids at the lowest accepted bid price (called the "Dutch Auction" method). In mid-1944 the Treasury introduced the yield-basis auction. When these auctions are used, bids are submitted in terms of required yield, carried out to two decimal places, rather than price. At maturity (or call) treasury bonds or notes should be endorsed and transmitted to a Federal Reserve bank or processed through a commercial bank for payment of face value.

Bond issues have been declining in importance relative to other treasury issues because of aversion by the Treasury to "locking-in" debt at the historically high interest rates prevailing since 1966. The result has been a thinner market for government bonds and, coupled with sharply rising interest rates, has lead to much greater price variability than was experienced from World War II through 1966.

Terms Bonds. A callable treasury bond (often referred to as a *term bond*) provides for redemption by the government, at its option, anytime after five years prior to maturity. For example, one treasury bond was described as follows in *The Wall Street Journal*:[2] $3\frac{1}{4}$'s 1978–83 June. The maturity date of this bond is June 15, 1983, but the Treasury has the right to redeem the bond at face value anytime between June 15, 1978, and June 15, 1983.

Flower Bonds. Certain issues of treasury bonds are particularly used in the settlement of estate taxes after death (often referred to as *flower bonds*). These bonds are appraised at market value in computing the total value of the estate for federal estate tax purposes but are accepted at their full face value for tax-paying purposes. A list of such bonds available at the writing of this book is contained in Table 4–2. In recent

TABLE 4–2. U.S. Government "Flower Bond" Issues as of Year-End, 1980

Issue	Issue
$3\frac{1}{4}$'s due June 15, 1983/78	$4\frac{1}{4}$'s due August 15, 1992/87
$3\frac{1}{4}$'s due May 15, 1985	4's due February 15, 1993/88
$3\frac{1}{4}$'s due May 15, 1985	$4\frac{1}{8}$'s due May 15, 1994/89
$4\frac{1}{4}$'s due May 15, 1985/75	3's due February 15, 1995
$3\frac{1}{2}$'s due February 15, 1990	$3\frac{1}{2}$'s due November 15, 1998

years market value has been substantially below face on many of these issues. Flower bonds should not be purchased after a person's death since they then are accepted for tax payments only at market value, not at face value.

Treasury Bills. Treasury bills are usually sold at auction each Monday and mature in less than one year. Maturity may be 13 weeks (91 days), 26 weeks, or 52 weeks. Bids can be placed directly through a Federal Reserve bank during the preceding week, thus saving commission charges and fees. The minimum quantity that can be purchased at

---

[2] *The Wall Street Journal*, June 8, 1981, p. 40.

the writing of this book is $10,000, and multiples of $5,000 for orders above the minimum. Guidelines for submitting bids can be obtained from any Federal Reserve bank. Alternatively, the order can be placed through a commercial bank, which will usually charge a fee.

Treasury bills are noninterest bearing and are purchased at a price below the face value. To approximate the yield that will be earned, divide the difference between face value and purchase price by the purchase price and multiply the result by the inverted fraction of a year represented to the bill's maturity. For example, if $9,875 were paid to acquire a 91-day bill with a face value of $10,000, the yield would be 5.01 percent calculated as follows:

$$\frac{125}{9,875} = .0126582$$

$$.0126582 \times \frac{360}{91} = .0500763 \text{ or } 5.01\%$$

Bills cannot be cashed prior to maturity, but an active secondary market exists in which they can be traded through a security broker or a commercial bank. The high degree of certainty of payment and their liquidity make them useful for purposes of building reserve funds that are almost as accessible as cash.

GOVERNMENT BOND MARKET

The government bond market is made up of a primary market and a secondary market. The former is the market for new issues, while the latter is the market for outstanding issues. Each monthly issue of the *Federal Reserve Bulletin* presents three pertinent tables: (1) dealer transactions, (2) dealer positions, and (3) dealer financing. More complete data appear monthly in the *Treasury Bulletin*.

Primary Market

New treasury issues come to market either to refund a maturing issue or to raise additional cash to meet increased operating expenses of the U.S. Treasury. The Treasury establishes a coupon and yield that it thinks will be attractive and clear the market. In many cases the Federal Reserve has helped condition the market for new issues by making reserves in the banking system readily available. New issues are offered on either an exchange basis or a cash basis. An exchange basis entitles holders of maturing issues preemptive rights in obtaining the new issue. This often leads to considerable speculation in "rights" and has on occasion led to rather chaotic market conditions. For example, in May of 1958 the $2\frac{5}{8}$ percents of 1965 were issued[3] during a recession when speculators were "certain" that interest rates were going to decline and bond prices rise.

When a cash refunding takes place, holders of maturing issues have no preemptive rights. They subscribe for new issues on the same basis as anyone else. Usually a cash offering results in oversubscriptions, so the Treasury must make allotments. In most cases, small subscriptions (up to $100,000 or $200,000) are allocated 100 percent. The problem for the larger buyer is to guess the allotment and then to oversubscribe to ensure getting the amount wanted. There are some hazards to this procedure, but investors are left with little choice if they want that issue.

Secondary Market

The secondary market involves outstanding bonds. Only a few investment dealers and a few commercial banks (dealer banks) make a market in government issues. The market is restricted to few participants because of large capital requirements, the need for very large credit lines, and the relatively low operating margins that necessitate enormous volume. To illustrate this last point, a government bond dealer might turn over capital in excess of 5,000 times in one year.

Dealers in government bonds take positions in or inventory the bonds they offer for sale. Also, they must maintain substantial inventories so that they can offer bonds for sale when called on to do so. Their risk, therefore, is considerable. Sizable losses have been registered by dealers in bear markets, sometimes even resulting in bankruptcy of a dealer.

Brief History of the Government Bond Market

Huge military expenditures brought on by World War II led to unusually large government borrowing needs and resulted in a phenomenal rise in government debt. Associated inflationary pressures were largely curbed by implementation of direct controls over the private economy, including price controls and rationing. To hold down the cost of government borrowing while assuring that funds needed to finance the war effort were readily available, interest rates on government securities were fixed at historically low levels. Long-term U.S. government bonds yielded only 2.08 percent during April 1946.

Interest rates were fixed by means of having the Federal Reserve (the Fed) announce its willingness to buy or sell government securities at par whenever the market wished. This fixed the price at par (the

---

[3] For a full treatment of this subject, see "Treasury-Federal Reserve Study of the Government Securities Market, 1959," issued in three parts in 1959 and 1960 by the secretary of the Treasury and the Board of Governors of the Federal Reserve System.

"peg"), and the Treasury established the low coupon rates offered. Moreover, the issuance of municipal and corporate securities was greatly curtailed during the war since the federal government acted directly to finance or facilitate the financing of war-related activities. The Fed also made sure the banks had adequate reserves to support new offerings.

The Fed, by agreeing to buy and sell at the whim of the market, accomplished the fixing of interest rates but made itself ineffective in terms of combating inflationary pressures that built during the war and were released when controls were removed at the end of the war. Open market operations are the main daily quantitative weapon available to the Fed for prosecuting monetary policy, but use of this tool requires that the Fed decide when it will buy or sell financial assets, not the market. Inflation pressures finally led to the famous 1951 "accord" with the Treasury, which stated that the Fed would no longer "peg" government bond prices but would act only to ensure orderly markets. The yields on government bonds quickly rose, and prices of government bonds dropped.

The federal debt has continued to expand, as seen in Table 4–3.

TABLE 4-3. Total Gross Public Debt of the U.S. Treasury, Selected Years (billions of dollars)

Year	Gross Public Debt	Year	Gross Public Debt
1965	270.3	1977	718.9
1970	309.1	1978	789.2
1975	576.6	1979	845.1
1976	653.5	1980	930.2
		Mar. 1981	964.5

Source: Federal Reserve Bulletins, various issues.

This expansion is due not only to military involvements and current world tensions but also to changing social and economic policies and priorities. Inflation continued to be a serious problem in 1981.

Inflation places upward pressure on interest rates since savers must be offered real incentives if they are to postpone current consumption and acquire financial assets. Ironically, at the very time of most rapid debt expansion and associated rising government borrowing requirements, anticipated losses in the purchasing power of dollars to be received in the future make all debt instruments, including government securities, less attractive as investment vehicles. Moreover, rising interest rates increase the cost of refinancing the federal debt, which, in turn, tends to result in higher future deficits and increasing expectations in terms of the inflation rates. Government security yields reached historic highs by August 1981, when a $4.25 billion issue of 39-month notes paid an average yield of 15.96 percent.

Several other factors also help explain the sharply rising yields on debt instruments experienced since the late 1950s. Competition for funds became more intense as inflation expectations grew and investors looked for inflation hedges. Because stocks, real estate, precious metals, and other real assets all received increasing attention (generally at different times), higher yields had to be offered to attract purchasers to debt instruments. Balance of payments problems that arose after 1957 also contributed to inflationary pressures. So did the need to keep interest rates high in the United States to attract capital inflows. The government's attempt to increase social welfare programs while financing the Vietnam war is another factor. Many of these problems were still with us in 1981 as interest rates reached historic highs, despite a changed government and Fed philosophy that emphasized the need to lessen inflationary pressures. Undoubtedly, these relatively high interest rates, by historic standards, will prevail during the remainder of the 1980s.

Ownership of Government Securities

Table 4–4 shows the changing ownership pattern of U.S. government securities, the major part of which is owned by government trust accounts, the Federal Reserve banks, and financial institutions. In 1946 government securities represented the largest segment of assets of financial institutions.

In the postwar years, despite the tremendous growth in their assets, all financial institutions except commercial banks and savings and loan associations showed a sharp decline in their dollar holdings of government securities. In all cases, including savings and loan associations and commercial banks, the proportion of government securities to total assets declined precipitously as the institutions shifted to higher-yielding investments. Government securities are currently held only to the extent of requirements for liquidity and other reserves of the highest quality.

Speculative Characteristics of Government Bonds

Government bonds behave in the same manner as any other high-grade bonds when interest rates change. In all cases the amplitude of price change is most pronounced in long-term issues, while yield fluctuations are greater in short-term issues. Because price variation is quite modest in short-term issues, even with wide swings in yields, such issues are used as a ready source of liquidity. For quite the opposite reason speculators choose long-term bonds as their vehicle to quick profits.

A modest yield change in the long-term market will result in a considerable change in price. Assuming that the speculator was precise in

TABLE 4-4. Ownership of Gross Public Debt of U.S. Treasury (billions of dollars)

Holder	Feb. 1946	1975	1980
Total gross public debt*	279.8	579.3	930.2
Held by government agencies:			
U.S. govt. trust accounts	28.0	145.3	192.5
Federal Reserve banks	22.9	84.7	121.3
State and local governments	6.7	34.2	74.7
Total	57.6	264.2	388.5
Held by private investors:			
Commercial banks	93.8	85.1	104.7
Mutual savings banks	11.1	4.5	5.8
Insurance companies	24.4	9.5	15.2
Other corporations	19.9	20.2	24.6
Individuals:			
Savings bonds	43.3	67.3	72.2
Other government securities	20.8	24.0	56.7
Foreign and international	2.4	66.5	134.3
Other miscellaneous investors	6.6	38.0	127.9
Total	222.2	315.1	541.4

*Totals were revised in accordance with revisions reported for internal data.
Source: Federal Reserve Bulletins, various issues.

timing purchases and sales in the long-term markets, handsome profits would accrue. Another advantage accruing to speculators in government bonds is the very high margins on which these bonds can be purchased. In most cases banks will advance up to 90 percent of the purchase price, and brokers may legally loan up to 95 percent.

Agency Issues

A chapter on government securities would not be complete without some consideration of securities issued by federal agencies. The term federal agencies includes government-sponsored enterprises and government agencies.[4] Both groups were organized under federal charters. They were originally capitalized by the U.S. Treasury, but their debt is

---

[4] For more complete details on federal agency bonds, see *Debt Characteristics of Federal Agencies* (New York: Moody's Investor's Service, Inc., 1972), or David M. Darst, *The Complete Bond Book* (New York: McGraw-Hill, 1975), chapter 7.

not always guaranteed by the federal government and is not included as part of federal debt. The distinguishing characteristic is that government agencies are those in which the public has no ownership interest. Agency issues outstanding in January 1981 are shown in Table 4-5.

TABLE 4-5. Interest-Bearing Securities Issued by Federal Agencies, January 1981 (billions of dollars)

Government-sponsored enterprises	
Banks for cooperatives	4,330
Federal Home Loan Banks and	
Federal Home Loan Mortgage Corporation	18,501
Federal Intermediate Credit Banks	10,494
Federal Land Banks	17,127
Federal National Mortgage Association	30,565
Other	412
Total	81,429
Government agencies	
Defense Department-family housing mortgages	600
Federal Housing Administration	476
Government National Mortgage Association	2,817
Export-Import Bank	11,239
Tennessee Valley Authority	11,375
United States Postal Service	1,770
United States Railway Association	492
Total	28,768

Source: Federal Reserve Bulletin (April, 1981), p. A33.

In many cases agency issues afford yields of $\frac{1}{8}$ percent to $\frac{1}{2}$ percent higher than direct treasury issues of comparable quality and maturity. Many investors have thus substituted federal agency issues for treasury issues, especially for short-term purposes.

STATE AND MUNICIPAL SECURITIES

Security issues of state and local governments are commonly referred to as municipal bonds. To simplify matters, they will be so called throughout this chapter, although there are major differences between the two groups. The state group is much more homogeneous than the local government group.

Municipal Bonds

The principal feature and attraction of *municipal bonds* is that interest income earned by holding this type of bond is not subject to federal income taxes. This condition derives from the rule of reciprocity established in 1819 in the well-known case of *McCulloch* v. *Maryland*. Under the rule of reciprocity, state and local governments could levy no taxes on obligations of the U.S. Treasury; the Treasury could reciprocate by not taxing the income earned by holding the obligations of state and local governments. The federal exemption privilege does not, however, apply to capital gains earned through the purchase and sale of municipal securities in the secondary market, as will be discussed further below.

The pressure to remove the tax-exempt feature of municipal bonds has been strong at various times, but a constitutional amendment would be required. Approval of such an amendment by the states seems unlikely unless there could be an agreement that the states would receive a federal subsidy equivalent to the higher cost of financing taxable issues. However, the tax-exempt feature was removed for issues of industrial revenue bonds issued after the 1968 amendments to the Internal Revenue Code for issues that exceed $5 million.

Aside from the tax-free feature, municipal bonds are essentially the same as other classes of bonds. They have indentures with the usual covenants pertaining to calls, defaults, security, additional bond provisions, and so forth. Good delivery of a municipal bond requires that it be accompanied by a legal opinion from qualified bond counsel stating that the bond has been issued for purposes within the powers of state or local officials and within corporate powers of the issuing body. In recent years legal opinions have been printed on the bond itself. Older issues, however, may be accompanied by a separate legal opinion. A buyer should make certain that a legal opinion is attached, if not printed, on the bond.

Tax Treatment of Capital Gains. Sale or maturity of a municipal bond may result in a taxable long- or short-term *capital gain* when the proceeds exceed the price paid to acquire the bond. The taxation of long- and short-term capital gains and losses is handled in Chapter 6. We are merely interested here in rules that determine whether or not a taxable gain or deductible loss has been realized.

When an original issue is purchased at a discount (a price below par), the buyer incurs no tax liability for the difference between purchase price and par if held to maturity. For example, if an original issue municipal bond with a par of $1,000 were purchased for $980, the $20 additional income received at maturity is considered interest income under current tax laws, and therefore, not taxable. The investor must, however, *accrete* the discount over the life of the bond when determining a possible taxable capital gain (or deductible capital loss) if the bond is sold prior to maturity.

To illustrate, assume an investor purchased a ten-year bond at $98 (par $1,000) when originally issued. Seven years later the bond is sold at $100\frac{1}{2}$. To determine the tax-adjusted purchase cost, the $20 discount must be added in equal amounts each year over the ten-year maturity period, or at $2 per year. The tax-adjusted purchase cost in the seventh year would be $994 (the original cost of $980 plus $2 a year for seven years). Since the bond has been held for more than one year, the investor would realize a long-term capital gain for tax purposes of $11, calculated as follows:

Receipts from sale of bond		$1,005.00
Initial purchase price	$980	
Plus accretion of discount	14	
Tax-adjusted cost after seven years		994.00
Taxable long-term capital gain		11.00

When a bond is purchased at a discount in the secondary market, the excess of proceeds received through sale or at maturity over the purchase price is fully taxable as a long- or short-term capital gain. For example, if a municipal bond were purchased at $98 in the secondary market and held to maturity, the investor would realize a taxable capital gain of $20. When a municipal bond is purchased at a premium and held to maturity, the holder does not realize a capital loss for tax purposes. Instead, the holder must amortize the premium over the remaining life of the bond and reduce the cost basis accordingly.

Tax Equivalent Yields. The before-tax yield that would have to be offered by a fully taxable instrument (such as a corporate bond) to produce the same after-tax yield as a tax-exempt municipal security is referred to as a *tax equivalent yield*. For example, a married couple with a taxable income of $30,000 would have incurred a marginal tax bracket rate of 39 percent in 1980 until taxable income exceeded $35,200. This couple must realize a before-tax yield of 11.48 percent on a corporate bond, assuming only interest income is involved, to equal the after-tax yield offered by a 7 percent coupon municipal bond purchased at par. The 11.48 percent is a tax equivalent yield, in terms of the federal income tax, and is calculated by dividing the yield offered by the municipal bond by one minus the marginal tax bracket rate of the investor (7.00 percent/1−.39 = 11.48 percent).

Brokerage houses will often provide tables showing the tax equivalent yield for several different tax-exempt yields and covering the range of possible marginal tax bracket rates. These calculations, however, are likely to estimate incorrectly the true tax equivalent yield. Most states exempt residents who own municipal bonds of that state, or one of its communities or authorities, from paying state income tax on the interest generated by such bonds. This exemption is an added tax advantage of municipals over corporates (though not over U.S. government securities) that is not recognized in tax equivalent yield calculations. Moreover, the tables, or the calculation illustrated above, do not reflect taxable capital gains that may be earned when investing in municipal bonds.

Margin Purchases and Taxes. The interest expense incurred when taxable securities are purchased on margin is fully deductible when determining taxable income. The tax rules, however, disallow the deduction of interest incurred to hold or avoid liquidating tax-exempt securities.[5] This limitation could be highly important to investors who buy securities on margin or incur debt as part of limited-partnership tax shelters.

Types of Municipal Bonds

State Bonds. *State bonds* are those issued by the fifty states. These bonds are secured by full faith and credit of the issuing state. State bonds are probably of uniformly higher quality than any other class of municipal bonds, although recent problems in New York suggest caution in choosing among the various issues of states.

Because of their high quality, state bonds are more marketable than other classes of municipal bonds. Moreover, marketability is aided by greater recognition of state names, larger volume, and also the fact that state bonds are acceptable for hypothecation while other classes are frequently not acceptable.

In event of default, an individual investor has no legal recourse and must be content to await the state's pleasure in meeting arrearages. The state is sovereign and therefore is in a legal position to refuse to pay its debts, even though legally incurred, simply if it is unwilling to do so. An individual has no standing in court against a state and therefore may not enter suit with the hope of accelerating or obtaining satisfaction of payment unless the state agrees to accept suit. However, as shown in the 1930s, if a state is in default, its credit in the capital markets is zero, so economic pressures are extremely strong to prevent default.

---

[5] Tax Code Section 265 (2).

General Obligation Bonds of Political Subdivisions of States. *General obligation bonds* of cities, counties, or other political subdivisions are secured by full faith and credit or, more succinctly, by taxing power. In most cases general obligation bonds with ratings of "A" or better enjoy broad markets and trade without much difficulty. In some cases, however, the investor could have trouble disposing of bonds, especially when the issue is of relatively small size. If sale prior to maturity is the intent or a good possibility, the investor should be certain to confine purchases to a well-known name and to avoid more obscure issues that may afford some yield concession because of limitations of marketability. Quantities of $5,000 or $10,000 of bonds can generally be sold, but the price received is likely to be below that quoted for larger lots.

Public Housing Bonds and Notes. *Public housing bonds* and *notes* are obligations of various housing agencies issued under the 1949 amendment to the U.S. Housing Act of 1937. Both principal and interest are guaranteed by the federal government. Therefore, these bonds carry "AAA" ratings and afford yields substantially below those of other classes of municipal bonds but higher than direct U.S. government obligations.

Revenue Bonds. *Revenue bonds* are those with principal and interest payments secured by revenue generated by specific projects such as water systems, sewer systems, electric utilities, toll roads, bridges, and parking facilities. By definition, principal and interest payments are made solely from revenues generated by the projects, just as in the case of a private corporate bond, which they resemble. Their only factor in common with other tax-exempt issues is their tax-exempt feature. Defaults of such bonds as the West Virginia Turnpike Bonds and Calumet Skyway Bonds highlight the risk factor in new issue, untested revenue bonds—that is, that revenues generated by the project are the sole source of interest and principal payments.

In some cases the state or municipality in which the revenue project is operating will pledge to make up any deficiencies in amounts needed to service the debt. When this condition occurs, the security is referred to as a "double barrel" obligation and should no longer be classed as a revenue bond but as a full faith obligation issue.

As a general rule, revenue bonds are not as marketable as full faith and credit general obligation issues. Investors usually consider revenue issues as a class to be of lower quality than full faith and credit bonds. Many revenue bonds, however, especially those of water and electric systems, are of good quality. They are frequently better than those of the municipality in which the system operates. Because analysis of revenue bonds is closely akin to appraisal of corporate issues, value is perhaps easier to identify in revenue issues than in general obligation issues in which analysis is somewhat more difficult.

Industrial Revenue Bonds. *Industrial revenue bonds* are issued by agencies or localities to finance capital expenditures for private industry. A typical arrangement would be for the authority to sell a bond issue, raise funds, and erect a plant. The plant would then be leased on a long-term basis to a company. In this manner the municipality attracts industry with its attendant advantages, and the company expands with low-cost funds made possible through the tax-free advantage available to municipalities.

Industrial revenue bonds were issued as early as 1936, but not until the mid-1960s did they gain prominence and increase appreciably in volume. However, a 1968 amendment to the Internal Revenue Code that eliminated the tax-exempt feature on subsequent issues of over $5 million greatly reduced the issuance of additional industrial revenue bonds. As concern over ecology began to grow in the early 1970s, industrial revenue bonds for pollution control in excess of the $5 million limitation were issued. Industrial revenue bond issuance was thus permitted to reach 1967–1968 levels again.

Authority Bonds. *Authorities* are established to carry out functions outside the scope of the municipality or to circumvent debt limitations established by outdated charters or constitutions. Authority-type financing has grown markedly since 1950, and, unless constitutional revisions make authorities unnecessary, they will undoubtedly continue to grow.

Authority bonds, as a class, are of good quality. However, the investor should exercise caution, especially among the toll road issues. Toll roads have experienced competition in many areas from free highways, and earnings often have suffered. Other authority issues have not met with competition, but in some cases the volume of debt outstanding has mounted to levels at which concern is warranted. Because payments on revenue bonds are made solely on the basis of receipts from the revenue project, they must be analyzed as corporate bonds. The government body that created the authority issue has no responsibility for payment.

Moral Obligation Bonds. *Moral obligation bonds* are primarily secured by project revenues but are also backed by the moral pledge of a state to make up any deficiency in the capital reserve fund of the issue in the event that revenues are insufficient to cover debt service. The pledge is not legally binding; it is only evidence of good intentions. The authors recommend judging these bonds pretty much as other revenue bonds are judged.

Market for Municipal Bonds

Since World War II, the market for municipal bonds has been among the fastest growing of all financial markets. There are three reasons for this growth:

1. Because expenditures by states and municipalities became practically non-existent during the depression and war years, there was much catching up to do after the war ended.
2. A greater demand for government services became evident in the postwar years.
3. The United States realized an appreciable gain in population in the postwar years.

Immediately after World War II, municipal bonds outstanding amounted to $15 billion. By the end of 1978, the outstanding amount of state and local government long-term debt issues had increased to about $276 billion.[6] Not only has volume grown but also the number of large issues. In 1960 only seven municipal bond issues of $100 million or more sold; in 1971, 45 issues in excess of this amount sold.

The substantial increase in volume of municipal bonds has made them more marketable. As volume has increased, ownership has become more widespread, and markets have broadened. Acceptance of municipal bonds has been enhanced by their impressive safety record and by continued high federal tax rates.

Ownership of Municipal Bonds

The principal holders of municipal securities are shown in Table 4-6. The data show that commercial banks are the largest purchasers and the largest holders of state and local government issues, except for 1977 and 1978 when fire and casualty insurance companies were the largest purchasers.

In the period 1960-1971 inclusive, commercial banks increased their holdings of municipals from $16.7 billion to $78.0 billion, a rise of 467 percent. This increase in their holdings was largely the result of the necessity of earning income sufficient, after taxes, to offset costs of the very substantial increase in total time deposits, including time certificates of deposit. The increase in time deposits was obtained by paying more competitive rates on time deposits after legislation was changed to permit the banks to be more competitive in this area. In 1967, for the first time, private time deposits of commercial banks exceeded private demand deposits. As recently as 1960, private time

---

[6] *Flow of Funds Accounts: Assets and Liabilities Outstanding, 1968-78,* Division of Research and Statistics, Board of Governors of the Federal Reserve System (Washington, D.C.), p. 18.

TABLE 4-6. State and Local Government Obligations (billions of dollars)

	1975	1976	1977	1978	1979	1980 (est.)	1981 (proj.)
Funds Raised							
Long-term debt							
New offerings:							
Industrial bonds	3.0	3.0	4.3	4.1	4.2	4.2	4.4
Other	26.3	30.8	40.7	42.1	38.0	42.1	40.4
Total	29.3	33.8	45.1	46.2	42.3	46.3	44.8
Less: retirements, refundings, and adjustments*	12.9	14.1	18.8	18.5	20.0	20.5	21.0
Net	16.4	19.7	26.3	27.7	22.3	25.8	23.8
Short-term debt**							
New offerings	29.0	21.9	21.3	21.6	20.9	26.4	28.0
Less: retirements and adjustments*	29.3	26.0	23.9	21.0	20.8	25.9	27.3
Net	−.3	−4.1	−2.6	.6	.1	.5	.7
Total	16.1	15.7	23.7	28.4	22.4	26.3	24.5
Funds Supplied							
Insurance companies and pension funds							
Life insurance companies	.8	1.1	.5	.4	- - - -	.1	.1
State and local retirement funds	1.9	1.4	.2	.4	−.1	.1	.1
Fire and casualty insurance companies	2.4	5.1	10.3	13.5	9.6	7.0	6.2
Total	5.2	7.5	11.0	14.2	9.6	7.2	6.4
Thrift Institutions							
Savings and loan associations	.6	- - - -	- - - -	.1	−.1	−.1	- - - -
Mutual savings banks	.6	.9	.4	.5	−.6	−.3	−.1
Total	1.2	.9	.4	.6	−.7	−.4	−.1

TABLE 4-6. State and Local Government Obligations (billions of dollars)
    (continued)

	1975	1976	1977	1978	1979	1980 (est.)	1981 (proj.)
Investment companies	2.2	3.0	3.9	3.1	4.0	7.3	6.8
Commercial banks	1.8	3.0	9.2	9.6	9.5	13.5	11.2
Business corporations	—.2	—1.1	- - - -	.2	- - - -	—.1	- - - -
State and local general funds	2.4	2.4	—.1	1.0	—.1	- - - -	.2
Individuals and others	3.5	- - - -	—.6	—.3	.2	—1.2	. . . .
Total	16.1	15.7	23.7	28.4	22.4	26.3	24.5
Memorandum							
Structures	34.7	32.3	31.0	37.5	40.3	45.3	51.0

*Residual; includes adjustments for issues offered in the calendar year before issuance.

**Includes tax-exempt commercial paper.

Source: Credit and Capital Markets 1981, Bankers Trust Company, Economics Division, New York, p. T9.

deposits were equal to only approximately 50 percent of private demand deposits of commercial banks. As a result of the tremendous increase in time deposits as well as the higher rates paid on such deposits, the total interest paid by commercial banks on time or savings deposits increased from $1.8 billion in 1960 to $10.5 billion in 1970. To meet these costs, the banks substantially increased their holdings of municipals and also of mortgages in the 1960s. Commercial banks continue to find municipal securities attractive.

Individuals have not been relatively large buyers of municipals. Individuals often seem to buy municipals and sell equities during high-yield, tight money conditions such as prevailed in 1973, 1974, and 1975. They tend to reverse the procedure during easy money periods. Although individuals have been large net sellers of stocks during the high-yield, tight money period 1977–1981, they have also been net sellers of municipal obligations. People have bought U.S. government securities and money market funds during this period.

In 1971 holdings of municipals by life insurance companies were only $3.4 billion, unchanged since 1960, and they reached only $6.4

billion by year-end 1978. Tax-exempt issues lost much of the advantages of the tax-exempt feature for life insurance companies as a result of the Supreme Court decision in the Atlas case.[7] On the other hand, municipal holdings of fire and casualty companies increased from $7.7 billion in 1960 to $20 billion in 1971 and $63 billion by year-end 1978. Municipal issues are attractive to fire and casualty insurance companies when their underwritings business is profitable and is subject to the corporate tax rates.

Corporations since 1976 have become large holders of municipal securities. The reason is that with relatively high, short-term interest rates, municipals are a productive use for otherwise temporarily idle cash. Virtually all municipal holdings of business corporations are short term.

Primary and Secondary Markets for Municipal Bonds

Like all marketable securities, municipal bonds have a primary market and a secondary market. The primary market is very similar to that of the corporate bond market. New issues must be sold at competitive bidding. Syndicates are formed to bid on forthcoming issues. The syndicate willing to purchase the issue at the lowest net interest cost is awarded the bonds. If the bond issue fails to sell, which, for example, happened to some issues in the erratic and difficult capital markets of 1966–1970, then the usual process of price concessions takes place until all the bonds are sold.

The marketing of municipal bonds in the secondary market can be accomplished in various ways, but one of the most effective methods is by listing in the Blue List. The Blue List is published daily and reflects the bonds that dealers own and would like to sell. The Blue List shows the bonds by state, the yield basis on which the dealers are offering to sell them, and the dealers who hold the particular bonds.

Activity in the municipal bond market is also conveyed to the potential investor through financial publications such as *The Wall Street Journal*, *The New York Times*, *Barron's*, the *Daily Bond Buyer*, and the *Weekly Bond Buyer*. Bond dealers also flood potential buyers of municipal bonds with information concerning the calendar of new issues coming to market, secondary market offerings, and pertinent statistics on the municipal market as a whole. Today there are more municipal bonds outstanding, more municipal bond dealers, more financial coverage of municipal markets, and more investors buying and selling municipal bonds than ever before. Municipal bonds are becoming an acceptable investment medium and a broadening market for tax-exempt securities has developed.

---

[7] See *The Wall Street Journal*, May 18, 1965, for a discussion of the Atlas Life Insurance Case.

Improved marketability is one reason why the municipal bond market has broadened so appreciably. Development of an active secondary market with breadth, depth, and resiliency has caused both individual and institutional buyers to substitute municipal bonds for other assets that were used primarily for liquidity purposes. This has been especially true among commercial bank buyers. With all due respect to municipal bonds, however, the investor should constantly be aware that for purposes of liquidity there is no replacement for short-term government bonds. The "credit crunch" of 1966, and especially the "liquidity crisis" of 1970, demonstrated how vulnerable even short-term municipal bonds can be to tight credit conditions. Sustained selling of municipal bonds by a few major commercial banks resulted in a dramatic decline in price and hence evaporation of any characteristics of liquidity.

Quality of Municipal Bonds

As a class, municipal bonds have a better safety record than any other type of security except U.S. government bonds. Municipal bonds fared poorly in the period of Reconstruction and were in large part responsible for the financial crisis of 1874. This period, however, was one in which irresponsibility and abuse were rampant in some state and local governments. In fact, some prejudice still lingers against southern bonds as a result of practices during the era of Reconstruction.

During the depression years of the 1930s, only one state bond defaulted, and this situation was remedied very quickly. There were, however, several thousand municipal bond defaults. Most municipal issues that proved troublesome were those issued for industrial purposes or those issued by municipalities heavily dependent on one or a few cyclical industries or located in largely recreational areas. General obligation issues and revenue issues for water, sewage, and electric facilities have had records of safety that are enviable.

Yields for municipal securities have risen sharply since 1975, reaching a peak of 9.8 percent for Moody-rated Aaa bonds during March 1981 (the latest data available at the time of writing this chapter). Inflationary pressure and expectations for continuing inflation would appear to be the main factors underlying sharply rising yields for all debt securities during this period. Also, the financial problems faced by large cities have raised serious questions about the quality of many municipal issues, no doubt heightened by the threat of default of New York City securities in the mid-1970s.

MUNICIPAL BOND ANALYSIS

As in the analysis of any securities, no formula can be followed blindly in the evaluation of municipal credit. Investors must use judgment in assessing the abundance of facts at their disposal. Safety in terms of municipalities' meeting the obligations they have incurred depends basically on the adequacy of tax or other revenues generated by the issuer to cover required expenditures.

Credit Analysis of Municipal Bonds

The investor must be ever alert to changes in various credits. For example, some major cities such as New York or Cleveland have been suffering an erosion of their socioeconomic bases and have experienced a lowering of their credit rating by the statistical agencies. Their debt burdens have grown, and their tax base with which to meet the burdens has declined. Extended far enough, this situation could lead to eventual problems and even a financial panic. History shows that U.S. recessions have tended to be short and relatively mild except when a financial collapse has also occurred. The investor should remember that no situation is static, even in the unromantic field of municipal finance.

Debt per Capita. Debt per capita is the most frequently used figure in appraising general obligation issues. This ratio is good as a first approximation, but it can be very misleading. It makes no allowance for the quality or the composition of the population or for the source or the nature of the income of the area. Neither does it provide for ability or willingness to pay, which are the two most important factors in any credit. Nevertheless, debt per capita is helpful because it is simple to calculate and can give the investor something to relate easily to other general obligation issues. As a rule of thumb, if debt per capita is in excess of $500 for a large city or $300 for a smaller unit, the investor should closely scrutinize the situation before investing.

Debt to Assessed Value and Market Value. Debt to assessed value and debt to market value are also commonly used ratios. Debt to assessed value is not too meaningful because assessments vary among municipalities and counties. In any event, their ability to carry debt burdens depends on the amount and the quality of income generated in the area. Any comparison of debt to assessed value is meaningless unless the basis of assessment is known. Debt to assessed value is important only as some indication of debt in relation to the tax base. Debt to the true market value is important in showing whether or not the overall level of debt is becoming burdensome. If debt exceeds 7 percent of true market value, the investor should investigate other factors thoroughly before investing.

Assessed value, in combination with millage (mils per dollar), gives some idea of latitude remaining to increase taxes to meet any increase in expenditures. If both assessments and millage are high, then little latitude remains; the reverse is true if either or both are low. This relationship bears close scrutiny, especially at present with debt levels of most major municipalities being at unprecedented levels.

Debt per Capita to Income per Capita. Debt per capita to income per capita is probably one of the most helpful indicators in quickly identifying the degree of burden of the debt. As a general rule, if debt per capita is in excess of 10 percent of income per capita, the issue should be avoided. If debt is too high in relation to income, meeting debt service may become impossible, and the issuance of additional debt may be seriously limited. Many issuers of general obligation debt have reached or will soon reach this level, especially big cities.

Competence of Administration. Knowing how well the municipality is administered is important, but this information is very difficult to ascertain. One indicator is tax collections. If tax collections are poor, one can assume that other areas of administration are also lacking. If tax collections are not at least 95 percent current, the investor has some cause for concern. Also, total debt service costs to total budget give some indication of administration as well as degree of burden of total debt. If debt service costs are in excess of 25 percent of total budget, the investor should be wary.

Other Factors in Analysis of Municipal Bonds. Many other factors in the analysis of municipal bonds could be considered, but in the interest of brevity only a few will be discussed here. The trend of debt is important and should be watched. If the rate of increase becomes too rapid, additional purchases should be stopped, and any holdings should be considered as candidates for sale. Attention should be given to the industrial and socioeconomic base. Ideally, industry should be diversified so that too great a reliance is not placed on one company or one industry. Erosion of the socioeconomic base has become commonplace in some cities as a result of high-income groups moving to suburban communities. These cities have experienced a reduction in tax base and an increase in welfare expenses. Taken to extremes, these problems could prove burdensome and should be an important item for consideration. Again, New York City is a case in point.

Analysis of Revenue Bonds

The credit of the government body is not pledged, and the government body accepts no responsibility for the payment of revenue bonds. Their payment depends entirely on revenues generated by the project they financed. Revenue bonds should therefore be analyzed in the same way as corporate bonds.[8] The important factor is size and stability of revenue and its adequacy in servicing outstanding debt. Revenue bonds are issued for purposes such as sewer and water systems, publicly owned electric systems, airports, tunnels, and highways.

---

[8] The analysis of corporate bonds is discussed in Chapter 17.

Of all revenue bonds, water and electric issues, as classes, are considered to be of highest quality. That the market recognizes this reputation is evident from good trading characteristics and lower yields afforded by this type of issue as compared with other revenue bonds. Both water and electric revenue bonds offer a stable stream of income derived from inelastic demand curves. The investor will thus accept much lower coverage of debt service by revenues from these types of issues than from other revenue bonds. To illustrate market sentiment for water and electric revenue issues, they frequently trade at lower yield levels than general obligation issues of the municipalities in which the systems operate.

Sewer issues also are highly acceptable and trade well in the marketplace. So too are highway issues that are supported by some special tax. Straight toll road issues, however, are different and should be recognized as such. Early toll roads, such as the New Jersey and Pennsylvania Turnpike systems, had several advantages and should be considered apart from the "average" toll road. Older toll roads were financed at lower interest rates and construction costs, which resulted in lower debt service requirements. More recent roads were more costly, and several have experienced serious competition from freeways financed largely by the federal government. Investors in toll road bonds should exercise caution, especially for new roads.

Airport, parking, and seaport revenue issues have grown in volume over the past several years. These issues can be erratic from an earnings point of view, and the investor should recognize that the range of quality is quite wide. In recognition of this, many municipalities have pledged to make up any deficiencies that may arise from inadequate earnings. If the full faith and credit of a municipality is pledged, such bonds are revenue bonds in name only and can be considered to be full faith and credit obligation municipal issues. Unless there are some unusual circumstances, the quality investor should confine purchases of airport, seaport, and parking revenue issues to those also having the backing of general taxing powers.

Municipal Bond Ratings

As implied throughout this chapter, there is considerable variation in the credit worthiness of municipal bonds. Because of this variation and the heterogeneous nature of this type of bond, two investor services assign quality ratings to municipal issues that are of a certain size: Moody's Investor Service and Standard & Poor's Investor Service.

The question is to what extent the investor should rely on ratings assigned by these agencies. Since both these services are objective sources of information and because they are well qualified to make judgments on municipal credits, the investor can rely on their quality ratings as general guides. However, there are wide variations within quality categories and neither rating service makes any guarantee concerning the permanence of a rating. Moreover, Moody's did upgrade the ratings of New York City from Baa to A in 1972, and Standard & Poor's awarded the investment quality A rating a year later. A year or two after this upgrading, New York City did face the possibility of bankruptcy. Accordingly, investors must make their own credit analyses. Ratings can be used to make broad judgments, but final decisions should be based on closer investigation.

MARKET BEHAVIOR OF MUNICIPAL BONDS

Municipal bonds in general behave in the same manner as any other class of fixed-income securities. When interest rates rise, prices of municipal bonds fall; when interest rates decline, prices of municipal bonds rise. There is, however, because of the heterogeneous nature of this market, some variation in the rapidity with which prices change among the various classes of municipal bonds. In the discussion here attention will be given to price patterns under varying market conditions for premium and discount issues, primary and secondary market issues, and high- and lower-quality bonds.

Premium and Discount Issues

There is usually some yield advantage to the buyer of premium or discount issues. The reason is that institutional investors, especially buyers for trust accounts, show a very strong preference for par or, as they are sometimes called, current coupon bonds. In the case of the trust buyer, this preference is entirely logical, since premium bonds would benefit the income beneficiary to the detriment of those entitled to the remainder, while discount issues would have the reverse effect. Other investors, however, have no logical basis to favor current coupon issues.

The discerning investor would be wise to consider using discount or premium bonds if their net yield is greater than that for par bonds of comparable quality and maturity. Aside from yield advantages, other factors have to be considered. In a rising bond market, discount bonds appreciate faster and by a larger percentage than other bonds.[9] For this reason speculators in the bond market most often use this medium to realize gains. Remember, however, that discount issues also react more quickly in a falling market. Also, discount issues by virtue of their low coupons are not as subject to call; therefore, the investor usually obtains automatic call protection.

Premium bonds, as a general rule, do not show as much apprecia-

---

[9] Bond price volatility and its causes are discussed further in Chapter 12.

tion as discount issues in a rising bond market. In a declining market, however, they afford greater protection against downside risk. As the price moves closer to par, the market actually broadens because the amount of the premium is becoming more palatable to those having some prejudice against premiums. This one small example shows how the astute investor can add to performance by capitalizing on prejudices of the market in general.

Market Patterns for Issues of Different Quality

Definite patterns evolve under varying market conditions for bonds of high and low quality. During strong markets, the yield spread (differential) between bonds of high and low quality becomes narrow. During weak markets, the spread becomes wider. Therefore, the careful investor will upgrade quality when buying into strong markets and will downgrade quality when taking advantage of a weak market.

Patterns on a quality basis are brought on by conditions peculiar to the large institutional investor. Large institutional investors attempt to maintain a given yield level. Since funds for investment are almost continually flowing in, these investors are obligated to buy securities almost without regard to market levels. Accordingly, in strong markets they will sacrifice quality to maintain the given yield level. In weak markets they will upgrade quality to compensate for lower quality bought earlier. An investor without the rigidities peculiar to many institutional investors can improve performance by knowing and making use of these patterns. During strong market conditions, emphasis should be placed on higher-quality issues because of little yield advantage in issues of lower quality. During periods of weakness in fixed-income markets, greater stress should be given to bonds of lower quality. In brief, better performance can be realized by following buying practices contrary to those of the vast majority of institutional investors.

Market for Municipals and Free Reserves of Banks

Of importance to note is that the level of the municipal market closely follows free reserves in the banking system. This is a reflection of commercial bank dominance in the municipal market. Table 4–7 gives some idea of the closeness of this correlation.

The year 1965 is atypical because of a large inflow of certificates of deposit into the banking system and considerable buying by commercial banks to offset the increased cost of money. In 1967 Federal Reserve monetary policy changed abruptly from ease in the first half of the year to tightness in the second half, but bank buying of municipals anticipated tighter money by several months. Despite occasional variation, the investor can use free reserves as a rough indicator of market direction and can adjust buying patterns accordingly.

TABLE 4-7. Changes in Free Reserves and Municipal Bond Prices

Year	No. of Months in Which Free Reserves Increased (Plus) or Decreased (Minus)		No. of Months in Which Municipals Increased (Plus) or Decreased (Minus)	
1971	Plus	7	Plus	7
	(Minus)	5	(Minus)	5
1970	Plus	8	Plus	7
	(Minus)	4	(Minus)	5
1969	Plus	5	Plus	3
	(Minus)	7	(Minus)	9
1968	Plus	5	Plus	5
	(Minus)	7	(Minus)	7
1967	Plus	7	Plus	3
	(Minus)	5	(Minus)	9
1966	(Minus)	12	Plus	6
1965	Plus	2	Plus	9
	(Minus)	10	(Minus)	3
1964	Plus	11	Plus	8
	(Minus)	1	(Minus)	4
1963	Plus	12	Plus	10
			(Minus)	2
1962	Plus	12	Plus	11
			(Minus)	1

Source: Survey of Current Business (January editions, 1963-1972).

Yield Patterns in Primary and Secondary Markets

Over the course of an interest rate cycle, some discernible yield patterns evolve in both primary and secondary markets. This being true, it follows logically that there must be a time to avoid one market and to concentrate on the other. In most cases the secondary market is more attractive in rising markets, while the primary market is more attractive in declining markets. This condition exists because rising prices are usually reflected first in new issues, while upward price adjustments lag in positioned bonds. In declining markets inventories of municipal bonds are usually mounting and often become burdensome. Therefore, new issues coming to market are priced to sell so that inventory levels do not become more burdensome with additional unsold bonds. At the same time, most dealer houses display some hesitancy in marking down inventoried bonds unless the market shows real evidence of further deterioration.

By using all of the patterns described above, the investor can realize significant yield advantages. The patterns are by no means regular or precise, but they are apparent enough to be highly useful.

Summary

U.S. government securities are considered to be of the highest investment quality. While there is no question concerning default, there are other risks incurred by investors in government bonds; namely, the interest rate risk and the purchasing power risk. Such securities are attractive to investors seeking a high degree of safety of principal, an assured stable income, and relatively high marketability. Speculators may also find long-term government securities attractive, depending on returns relative to other securities and interest rate expectations, because of the low margin requirements required of purchasers.

Government securities fall into two main categories: nonmarketable and marketable securities. Nonmarketable securities are not transferable and are redeemable at fixed prices. Savings bonds, both Series E and Series H, are the nonmarketable instruments of interest to investors. The relatively small investment required, the fact that no commissions are charged for purchase or when redeeming them, and the certainty of returns are the main advantages offered by nonmarketable securities. The main disadvantage is that the yields offered by nonmarketable government securities are among the lowest usually available.

Marketable interest-bearing government debt is composed of treasury bonds, notes, and bills. It is important to realize that on small purchases of such instruments ($100,000 or less), commissions, custody fees, and odd-lot charges may significantly reduce realized yield. Treasury bills are noninterest-bearing securities that have maturities up to one year and are purchased at a discount from redemption value. Treasury notes have maturities from one to seven years, and treasury bonds are usually issued with maturities of more than seven years. Marketable government securities are typically held only to the extent of requirements for liquidity and other reserves of the highest quality.

Government agencies have been established by the federal government to serve as intermediaries in channeling funds to particular sectors of the economy. Although their debt is not expressly guaranteed by the federal government, the issues of such agencies are considered to be of high quality. Agency issues typically offer yields of $\frac{1}{8}$ percent to $\frac{1}{2}$ percent higher than direct treasury issues.

Security issues of state and local governments are referred to as municipal securities. The principal attraction of such instruments is that income received from such issues is not subject to federal income tax, and most states do not tax interest on their own obligations. There has been strong pressure to remove the tax-exempt feature, but a constitutional amendment would be required to do so. Passage of such an amendment seems unlikely at this time.

Municipal bonds may be secured by the full faith and credit of the issuer, or only by revenues generated by specific projects or tax sources. Defaults have occurred and continue to cause difficulties for investors in certain revenue-type municipal bonds. As a general rule, revenue-type bonds are not as marketable as full faith and credit obligations, although those of water and electric systems have had a good record.

The analysis of municipal bonds is complex and involves an analysis of the underlying socioeconomic characteristics of the issuing state or local unit. Debt in relation to income and property value of the issuing governmental unit, the competence of administration, and the diversification of economic activity are among the most important factors to consider.

Questions

1. A friend is about to retire and suggests liquidating all investments now held and investing the total in U.S. government notes with maturities of three to five years. The friend desires stable income and minimum risk and feels this plan will assure both objectives. Comment on this plan.
2. Over the past three decades the government bond market has undergone considerable change.
   (a) In view of the large demand for funds by the federal government during World War II, how do you explain the relatively low interest rates that prevailed?
   (b) What was the significance and the effect of the Federal Reserve-Treasury "accord" of 1951?
   (c) What factors underlie the dramatic rise in interest rates that took place in the late 1950s and throughout most of the 1960s? Do you anticipate a return to interest rate levels that prevailed during the 1950s? Discuss.
3. The long-term market for treasury bonds is often spoken of as having been "quite thin" during the 1960s.
   (a) What does "quite thin" mean?
   (b) What brought about this condition?
4. (a) Define nonmarketable bonds.
   (b) Discuss the nature of nonmarketable bonds, their relative importance, and to whom they are sold.
5. A treasury bill has no interest coupon attached, nor does the instrument say anything about payment of interest. How does an investor get a return on such an instrument?
6. What special benefits may be derived from treasury issues in reference to settling of estates?

7. (a) Distinguish between the offering of new treasury issues on an exchange basis and on a cash basis.
   (b) Who are the dealers in the U.S. government securities market? Why is the market restricted to relatively few dealers?
8. (a) List the principal types of owners of U.S. government securities and indicate their relative importance. (Use the most current statistics available.)
   (b) Why are government securities so attractive to commercial banks?
9. (a) What are the major classifications of municipal bonds?
   (b) What are the major differences between them?
10. (a) Explain the meaning of state sovereignty.
    (b) What is its significance for investors?
11. (a) What is an industrial revenue bond?
    (b) What significant event occurred during 1968 that is of importance to investors considering purchase of industrial revenue bonds? Are any exceptions now available to the restriction imposed in 1968?
12. (a) What has led to the rapid growth experienced in the market for municipal bonds since World War II?
    (b) What explanation can you offer for the fact that commercial banks are the largest holders of municipal bonds?
13. What is the *Blue List?* What is its significance to investors?
14. What determines the investment quality of municipal bonds?
15. (a) Why is the ratio of debt to assessed valuation a rather unsatisfactory measure of the quality of state debts?
    (b) What other comparisons might be more useful?
16. Should an investor in the 70 percent marginal income tax bracket purchase a corporate bond yielding 8 percent or a municipal bond yielding 4 percent, assuming financial risk is negligible in both cases? Why?
17. (a) Why is there likely to be some yield advantage to the buyer of premium or discount issues of municipal bonds?
    (b) What other advantages might the investor gain by investing in discount issues?
18. (a) What market patterns evolve under varying market conditions between municipal bonds of high and low quality? Why?
    (b) What investment policies are suggested?
    (c) When should the investor in municipal bonds buy in the primary market and when should the investor buy in the secondary market? Why?

Work-Study Problems

1. Assume that an individual has a total portfolio of $250,000. Indicate the amount of U.S. government securities, including U.S. sav-

ings bonds if any, that should be in this portfolio, the exact type and issues that should be held, and the reasons for your selection.

2. Assume that a commercial bank has total assets of $100 million. Indicate the amount of U.S. government securities that should be held, the specific issues and their maturities, and the percentage distribution by maturities. Explain your reasons for the selection. (The student should read the chapter on bank stocks before trying to answer this problem.)

3. Assume that a wealthy customer advises a broker of information that the following bond is attractive:

    Miami, Water Revenue Bonds, Series 1953A, $2\frac{3}{4}$ Serial, due June 1, 1979.

    (a) As the broker, write a memorandum giving the customer, among other things, the following information:
        (1) Yield to maturity.
        (2) Size of the issue of which it is a part.
        (3) Call provisions.
        (4) Moody's rating and Standard & Poor's rating.
        (5) Collection record and comment.
        (6) Type of obligation.
        (7) Debt per capita compared with median.
        (8) Type of government.
        (9) Maturities.
        (10) Economic aspects:
            a. Industrial diversification.
            b. Growth of population.
        (11) Percent of debt to assessed value.

    (b) Assume that this individual has $500,000 in an investment portfolio and faces a 50 percent income tax rate. What is the tax-equivalent yield necessary on a common stock or a U.S. government bond to make one of these instruments attractive? Compare this yield to yields on the DJIA and S&P indexes.

    (c) Would you recommend that your customer buy the bond? Support your recommendation carefully.

4. (a) Take an actual commercial bank and determine the following:
        (1) The actual amount of tax-exempt issues in its portfolio.
        (2) The ratio of tax-exempts to total "other securities."
        (3) The ratio of tax-exempts to holdings of U.S. government securities.

    (b) Explain the reason for the amount and the ratio of tax-exempt securities in the portfolio of this particular bank.

5.

Stock Options

Two parties are involved in every option contract—a buyer and a seller (also known as the option writer). Anyone can buy an option and anyone can sell one, but only the buyer enjoys the privilege of *exercising* an option.

A stock option contract conveys to the buyer the right either to buy or to sell a specified number of shares of a particular security, called the *underlying security*, at a particular price on or before a particular date, called the expiration date. Most option contracts provide for the purchase or sale of 100 shares of the underlying security.

A *call option* gives the buyer the right to purchase 100 shares of the underlying security from the option writer at the agreed price, called the *exercise price*, and a *put option* gives the buyer the right to sell. In either case, the option contract may be *exercised* on or before the *expiration date* in the case of an *American option*, and only on the expiration date in the case of a *European option*.

The option buyer must pay a price to the option writer in exchange for the privilege bestowed by the option contract. The *option premium* is an amount paid by an option buyer to an option writer for the privilege to "put" or "call," as the case may be. A stock option premium is not a down payment or credit in the event that the option is exercised. The premium stays with the seller whether or not the option is exercised.

The expiration date is the last day on which an option holder may exercise an option to buy or sell 100 shares of the underlying security. According to present procedures of the exchanges, each class of options is assigned to one of three expiration month cycles. Each cycle consists of four expiration months, and trading in options of a particular expiration month normally begins approximately nine months earlier. Thus, at any point in time there may be trading in each class having three different expiration months. For a particular stock, moreover, there may be trading in as many as three puts and/or three calls having the same exercise price but different expiration dates.

Exercise prices are typically set at 5-point intervals for securities trading below 50, 10-point intervals for securities trading between 50 and 200, and 20-point intervals for securities trading above 200. If a significant change takes place in the market price of the underlying security after options of a particular expiration month cycle have been written against it, a new series of options may be opened for trading at a different price but having the same expiration month or months as options that are already the subject of trading. Thus, options on the same underlying security that have the same or different expiration dates can trade at different exercise prices.

An excerpt from *The Wall Street Journal* is shown in Figure 5-1. Three dates appear in the table heading for both calls and puts. Each date represents a different expiration month cycle. The underlying security is identified in column 1, along with the New York or American Exchange final price. Column 2 shows the exercise (strike) price of the option. The option premiums, labeled "last," are shown in the body of the table. An "a" in the body of the table indicates that the option was not traded on that day, and a "b" indicates that no option was offered.

STOCK OPTION TRANSACTIONS

A variety of different motives would seem to guide stock option transactions, among them the following three objectives:

1. To achieve a specific short-term investment objective or hedge.
2. To exploit an opportunity created by the systematic miscalculation of others.
3. To satisfy one's gambling instincts by speculating on a securities-based numbers game.

Four participants are involved in every stock option transaction: a writer, a buyer, a broker, and the IRS. Some tax implications of stock option transactions do exist, but they will be discussed later in the chapter. Brokerage fees are paid by both sides of an opening transaction, with more fees to be paid later in the relatively unlikely event that the option is exercised. According to our information at the time of this writing, fewer than 20 percent of all options written are ever exercised.

Some stock options trade on the over-the-counter market, where premiums are determined by negotiation and where expiration periods range from a few days to a year or more. Most stock options trades take place on organized exchanges, however, where matters are much more formal. We will confine our attention here to the activities that take place on these organized exchanges and to the rules and regulations that govern them. Investment strategies involving stock options will only be touched on in the present chapter but will be taken up at length in Chapter 11.

44 THE WALL STREET JOURNAL, Wednesday, February 24, 1982

Chicago Board

Option & NY Close	Strike Price	Calls—Last Mar	Calls—Last Jun	Calls—Last Sep	Puts—Last Mar	Puts—Last Jun	Puts—Last Sep
Apache	10	3¼	r	4½	r	r	5-16
13⅛	15	⅜	1⅛	2	1¾	2⅜	2½
13⅛	20	1-16	7-16	⅞	r	6⅞	r
13⅛	25	r	7-16	r	r	r	r
BrisMy	45	9¾	r	s	1-16	r	s
54⅝	50	5	7	r	¼	13-16	r
54⅝	55	1⅜	3½	4¾	1¼	2⅛	r
54⅝	60	3-16	1 5-16	r	5½	5¾	r
Bruns	15	9⅜	9⅜	r	⅛	½	r
24⅜	20	4¼	4⅜	4½	1⅝	2¾	3⅛
24⅜	25	⅝	1	1	5	7	7½
24⅜	30	⅛	5-16	r	9⅞	11	r
Chamln	10	s	r	r	s	¼	r
16	15	r	r	r	¼	1	r
16	20	1-16	⅜	¾	4	4	r
CompSc	10	r	4	r	r	r	r
13¾	15	¼	1 3-16	r	1⅞	r	r
13¾	20	r	¼	¾	r	r	r
CornGl	45	1¼	s	s	1¾	s	s
44½	50	⅛	s	s	5¾	s	s
44½	55	r	s	s	10½	s	s
Dow Ch	20	1⅜	2⅜	3¼	¼	15-16	1¼
21¼	25	1-16	½	1	4	4	4
21¼	30	1-16	3-16	r	r	9⅜	r
Esmark	45	3	5¼	r	¾	2⅛	3
48	50	11-16	r	3½	3¼	r	r
48	55	1-16	¾	r	r	r	r
Evans	15	2⅛	s	s	⅛	s	s
17	20	⅛	s	s	3	s	s
17	25	1-16	s	s	r	s	s
Ford	15	3¼	3⅝	4⅛	1-16	½	r
18⅛	20	3-16	15-16	1⅞	2	2½	2¾
18⅛	25	1-16	5-16	s	r	r	s
FptMcM	20	⅝	s	s	1⅝	s	s
19	25	⅛	s	s	6	s	s
19	30	1-16	s	s	r	s	s
19	15	r	s	s	⅛	s	s
Gen El	50	r	12	r	1-16	⅜	r
61	55	6	r	9¼	¼	15-16	r
61	60	1⅞	4	5¾	1⅛	2 9-16	3
61	65	5-16	1½	2¾	4¼	5¼	r
61	70	1-16	s	s	9½	s	s
G M	30	4⅞	6	r	⅛	⅝	1⅛
34⅞	35	1¼	2 13-16	4⅛	1¼	2 5-16	2⅞
34⅞	40	⅛	1	2	5¼	5¼	6
34⅞	45	1-16	⅜	13-16	10½	10⅝	r
34⅞	50	1-16	⅛	s	15½	r	s
Glf Wn	10	6	r	r	r	r	r
15¾	15	1⅛	1 13-16	2¼	¼	9-16	¾
15¾	20	1-16	5-16	9-16	4⅜	r	r
HughTl	25	6½	7½	s	1-16	½	s
31⅜	30	2½	4¼	5½	13-16	1¾	r
31⅜	35	⅜	2	3⅛	3¾	4⅝	4⅞
31⅜	40	1-16	13-16	1¾	r	8¾	r
31⅜	45	1-16	⅜	15-16	13¾	r	r
31⅜	50	1-16	s	s	r	s	s
I T T	25	1½	2½	2⅞	3-16	11-16	1⅛
26⅛	30	1-16	½	15-16	r	r	r
K mart	15	1 9-16	2 3-16	2½	⅛	½	r
16⅜	20	1-16	⅜	11-16	r	r	3¾
Litton	45	r	8	r	5-16	1½	r
50⅝	50	2¼	4⅞	r	1 7-16	3⅛	4¼
50⅝	55	½	2⅝	4¾	4¾	5⅞	6¾
50⅝	60	⅛	1⅜	2¾	9	9¼	r
50⅝	65	r	⅝	r	r	r	r
Lttn o	49	3	s	s	1⅛	s	s
50⅝	53⅞	15-16	s	s	r	s	s
50⅝	58⅞	5-16	s	s	9	s	s
50⅝	68⅝	1-16	s	s	r	s	s

Listed Options Quotations

Tuesday, February 23, 1982

Closing prices of all options. Sales unit usually is 100 shares. Security description includes exercise price. Stock close is New York or American exchange final price.

Most Active Options

Option		Vol.	Last	Chg.		Comp. Close
CHICAGO BOARD OPTIONS EXCHANGE						
Calls						
IBM	Apr60	4,650	3⅜	+	⅛	60⅞
IBM	Apr65	4,523	1 1/16		....	60⅞
Rayth	May35	3,503	1¼	−	¼	31⅞
Pennz	Apr60	3,353	1⅜		....	42
NWInd	Mar70	3,200	¾	+	⅛	62⅝
Total volume: 169,406 contracts.						
Puts						
IBM	Apr60	5,715	1 9/16	−	¼	60⅞
NWInd	Mar60	2,840	2¾	−	¼	62⅝
Teldyn	Apr120	2,826	3¼	−	⅜	125
IBM	Apr55	2,630	7/16	−	1/16	60⅞
EsKod	Apr70	2,453	4⅜	+	⅛	66
Total volume: 119,485 contracts.						
AMERICAN STOCK EXCHANGE						
Calls						
PhilP	May50	4,508	1	+	¼	33¼
PhilP	May35	4,154	3¼	+	1⅛	33¼
PhilP	May40	3,759	2⅛	+	¾	33¼
Tandy	Apr35	3,722	1⅜	+	⅛	31⅜
Tandy	Apr30	3,241	3⅝	+	¼	31⅜
Total volume: 109,893 contracts.						
Puts						
Tandy	Apr30	3,759	1½	−	⅛	31⅜
DigEq	Apr80	2,424	2⅜	−	¼	83⅝
Tandy	Apr35	2,114	4¼		....	31⅜
ASA	May35	1,610	2⅞	−	⅜	33⅝
MarOil	Jun70	1,452	1⅜	−	⅜	73⅝
Total volume: 54,331 contracts.						
PHILADELPHIA STOCK EXCHANGE						
Calls						
CitiSvc	Jun30	1,099	2⅝	+	1/16	27⅜
Cmptvsn	May30	910	2 9/16	−	3/16	28⅜
LouLndx	May25	778	2½	+	¼	25⅛
LouLndx	May30	776	⅞	+	⅛	25⅛
CitiSvc	Mar35	683	7/16	−	1/16	27⅜
Total volume: 25,530 contracts.						
Puts						
GenInst	Mar35	1,090	1 1/16	−	3/16	37
Cmptvsn	May30	924	3¾	+	⅛	28⅜
Cmptvsn	May25	903	1½	+	1/16	28⅜
TexOil	Mar30	479	5⅝	+	½	24
LouLndx	May25	445	1 9/16	−	3/16	25⅛
Total volume: 13,435 contracts.						
PACIFIC STOCK EXCHANGE						
Calls						

FIGURE 5-1. Stock Quotations from *The Wall Street Journal*

Covered and Uncovered Option Writing

The writer of a *call option* may or may not own shares of the underlying security. A call option is *covered* when the required number of shares of the underlying security are on deposit with the broker, or when the writer holds another call on the same underlying security whose expiration date is no sooner and whose exercise price is no higher than on the option in question. The option is otherwise referred to as *uncovered* or *naked*.

The writer of a *put option*, by contrast, delivers cash to the buyer when the option is exercised and receives shares of the underlying security. The situation is just the reverse of that outlined in the preceding paragraph. Thus the writer of a put option cannot *cover* by purchasing shares of the underlying security but only by purchasing a put on the same underlying security whose expiration date is no further away and whose exercise price is no lower than on the option in question. The purchase of such an option by a put option writer is tantamount to liquidating his or her obligation.

Uncovered option writing must be done on margin account. Such accounts are subject to regulation by the exchanges, the Options Clearing Corporation, the Securities and Exchange Commission, and other regulatory agencies.[1]

Stock Option Transactions and Games of Chance

A stock option transaction may be analyzed best by means of an analogy: as a game of chance.[2] Thought of in this way, the option buyer antes a predetermined amount in the form of a premium plus a modest brokerage fee. The option writer, by contrast, covers the buyer's bet and pockets the option premiums (less a brokerage fee) regardless of the outcome of the game.

A stock option is a *wasting asset* in that its value becomes zero on expiration if not exercised by then. Thus, not only does an option in effect bet buyer against the writer but also against the clock. Time acts to the benefit of the option writer and pretty much serves to stack the deck in his or her favor. An option buyer, by contrast, is subject to a variant form of gambler's ruin; when the clock runs its course, the game ends and the players part.

---

[1] For further detail see the *Prospectus of the Options Clearing Corporation— Exchange Traded Put and Call Options*. This prospectus is available by writing to any of the organized exchanges or from any options broker who is registered with an organized exchange.

[2] The concept of a game of chance will be discussed in detail in Chapter 8. The salient feature of such a game, or lottery, however, is that the outcome cannot be known for certain before the event. Such an outcome, which is governed by some probability distribution, is called uncertain.

Simple Call Options

An unhedged option buyer, or an uncovered option writer, is speculating on the future price of the underlying security. The same is true of the option buyer. The writer of a covered call option, on the other hand, may not know or believe anything about the future price of the underlying security but may have the best calculated justification of all for participating in a stock option game.

Suppose that a call option is actually exercised to the advantage of the buyer and thus to the disadvantage of the writer. What then? The writer of a covered call option, in this event, will suffer an *opportunity loss*, which is partly offset by the option premium. The amount of this opportunity loss, which should be clearly distinguished from out-of-pocket loss, however, is necessarily less than what the opportunity loss would have been had the option writer sold his or her stock outright on the day of the opening transaction rather than write the option.

Only one set of circumstances could result in out-of-pocket losses for the writer of a covered call option. Should the price of the underlying security plummet and should the writer not liquidate his or her commitment or be hesitant to sell the security because of that commitment, then both buyer and seller would realize actual out-of-pocket losses. When the market price of the underlying security is on the decline, however, a writer shouldn't have any trouble finding another call option of the same series to buy in order to liquidate his or her commitment, thereby limiting the out-of-pocket loss.

Simple Put Options

Turning from a discussion of simple call option contracts to a discussion of puts requires adjusting one's logic. Whereas a call option gives the buyer the right to purchase 100 shares of the underlying security at a fixed price, a put option contract gives the buyer the right to sell. As with a call option, the outcome of a put option contract is determined by the outcome of the random process that governs change in the market price of the underlying security on or before expiration. The implication of such price changes, and/or of execution, however, is not the same as before.

Buying a Put. If the market price of a security is expected to fall, the situation may be exploited either by selling the stock short or by purchasing a put option.[3] The potential for out-of-pocket loss is un-

---

[3] A *short sale* is accomplished by selling shares of an underlying security that one does not own; the certificates required to execute the trade are *borrowed*, to be replaced at a later date. If the market price of the security goes down as *expected*, the short seller realizes a profit. Should the market price go up, however, the short seller may realize very heavy losses.

limited in the case of a short sale but is limited to the premium plus brokerage fee when purchasing a put option. The use of a put option, therefore, has advantages over a short sale.

Hedging Motive. The purchase of a put option is sometimes recommended as a hedge. That is, one may "purchase puts as protection against a possible decline in the price of the stock."[4] Unfortunately, the logic that underlies such hedging strategies is somewhat suspect. One might insure, for example, by selling the stock outright and replacing it with an investment substitute. When account is taken of the impact of repeated put option premiums and brokerage fees on rate of return, moreover, then the probability that one attaches to the upside potential would have to be sufficiently great to beg the question—why insure? The situation seems analogous to purchasing a succession of renewable term life insurance policies and then naming one's friendly insurance salesperson as primary beneficiary. One can concoct numerous examples to demonstrate the advantage of such a strategy after the fact, of course, but based on one's alternatives at the time of decision, the purchase of a put to effect a hedge is often irrational. Some useful applications, however, will be discussed in Chapter 11.

Selling a Put. The writer of a call option agrees to deliver 100 shares of the underlying security if the option is exercised. The writer of a put option, by contrast, agrees to deliver cash. By way of further contrast, the writer of a put option is subject to at least three identifiable sources of disadvantage relative to a colleague who writes a call option.

The first disadvantage results from an institutional restriction. A covered call option writer locks into an income-earning asset (that is, the underlying security) for the life of the commitment. A call option writer, on the other hand, ties up an amount of cash—sometimes in a noninterest-bearing account managed by an option broker—that is sufficient to cover the commitment. The resulting opportunity loss should be regarded as a reduction from the option premium, which will be taxed in its entirety as income if the option is not exercised.

A second disadvantage is that a call option is not always exercised when the market price of the underlying security rises above the exercise price, but a put option is virtually certain to be exercised when the market price of the underlying security falls to a price, or is at a price, which is below the exercise price of the option. Put options, for example, are sometimes written on an *"in-the-money"* basis.[5] Such a put

---

[4] *Understanding Options: A Guide to Puts and Calls*, The Chicago Board Options Exchange (Chicago), p. 31.

[5] A put option is said to be *"in-the-money"* when its exercise price is *above* the current market price. A call option, by contrast, is "in-the-money" when its exercise price is *below* the current market price. An option, put or call, is said to be *"at-*

option is almost always exercised unless the market price of the under-lying security *goes up* by enough to surpass the exercise price.

A third disadvantage to which a put option writer is exposed, rela-tive to a call option writer, has to do with the consequence of an ad-verse event. An adverse event from the point of view of a call option writer is one that produces an opportunity loss. An adverse event from the point of view of a put option writer, on the other hand, is one that results in the purchase of an unwanted security at an exercise price that is greater than the current market price. The result of such an outcome is not opportunity loss but out-of-pocket loss.

Strategies for writing put options are more difficult to justify than strategies for writing call option contracts. Nevertheless, an investor who wishes to own (as opposed to speculating on) an underlying se-curity may under certain conditions benefit by writing a put option on that security.

When a put option contract is written against an underlying security, the option writer not only establishes the possibility of being able to acquire the desired security at a lower future price, but also pockets the option premium as an extra and certain income regardless of what hap-pens to the future price of the security. If the market price of the underlying security should increase, the option writer's only loss would be the opportunity foregone by not having purchased the security at the outset. Provided only, therefore, that one actually wishes to own the underlying security, acquisition by the exercise of a put option (that is, by the option buyer) offers the option writer the potential for gain and not loss. We will see in Chapter 11 that this logic accords well with the logic of portfolio diversification.

More Complex Option Transactions

Rather than purchase or sell a simple put or call, one may (to the delight of the stock option broker) enter into a transaction that in-volves both puts and calls. The logic underlying such a transaction is necessarily speculative and usually inconsistent. As our concern in this text is with investment and not speculation, we will limit our coverage here to defining some commonly used terms. In the interest of fairness, the present authors confess to having a very dim view of such transactions.

Straddle. A straddle is an option strategy that calls for the simul-taneous purchase (or sale) of a put and a call option. The put and call are for the same number of the same underlying security. The two

---

the-*money*" when the exercise price is precisely equal to the market price of the underlying security. A call option is *"out-of-the-money"* when its exercise price is *above*—and a put option when its exercise price is *below*—the market price of the underlying security.

option contracts, moreover, sport the same exercise price and the same expiration date.

Spread. Like a straddle, a spread option transaction calls for the simultaneous purchase (or sale) of a put and a call option. In its most common configuration, however, the execution price of the put is set below (and the execution price of the call is set above) the current market price of the underlying security.

Strip and Strap. Strips and straps are variations on a single theme. A strip is a transaction in two puts and one call. A strap is a transaction in two calls and one put.

Combinations. A straddle, spread, strip, and strap are but four examples of stock option combinations. Clearly, the list goes on and on. Combinations are typically written against stocks that are subject to considerable price fluctuation. The buyer, in such a stock option transaction, is, in effect, playing the variance and leverage effects. The seller, by contrast, plays the odds. As with any game of chance, such a game may be played in accordance with a set of rules that resembles a real strategy. To describe the participants in such a game as "astute investors," however, seems a bit farfetched.[6]

Risk in Stock Option Transactions

As pointed out in Chapter 8, various concepts of risk can be devised—some useful and others not. One can argue, for example, that stock options offer an investor "a potentially large profit from a relatively small investment with known and predetermined risk." That is, the option buyer knows in advance the most that he or she can lose. When one takes account of the probability of realizing a loss, however, then the situation may be conceived as quite risky. We shall have more to say on the subject of risk in Chapter 8. Some option strategies and valuation methods will be taken up in Chapter 11.

WARRANTS AND RIGHTS

A warrant is similar to a call option in that it conveys to the holder the privilege of buying a specified number of shares of the underlying security at the exercise price at any time on or before an expiration date. A warrant differs from a call option in a number of important respects, however. The writer of a warrant (that is, the issuer) is the

---

[6] *Understanding Options: A Guide to Puts and Calls*, The Chicago Board Options Exchange (Chicago), p. 2.

corporation that issues the underlying security. Strictly speaking, therefore, a warrant is always covered. Most warrants sport original maturities of several years, while the typical stock option is written for from three to nine months. The issuer does not charge a premium as such for the privilege conveyed by a warrant; the typical warrant originates by attachment to a bond or a preferred stock issue, which is done to make such an issue more attractive to investors and to improve its market. A warrant that is *attached* to a bond or preferred stock can only be exercised by the holder of that financial instrument. A warrant may be *detached* as of a particular date, however, and subsequently traded on its own merits. A number of warrants are now listed by the New York Stock Exchange, and trading in warrants can be expected to increase in volume in the years ahead.[7]

Stock purchase rights are created by corporations that issue them to existing common stockholders when making a privileged subscription offering. A stockholder who does not wish to exercise stock purchase rights may sell them—hence there is a market for stock purchase rights. Unlike a warrant, the privilege conveyed under a stock purchase right is typically in effect for only a few weeks.

ORGANIZED STOCK OPTIONS EXCHANGES

The five organized options exchanges are the Chicago Board Options Exchange, the American Stock Exchange, The Philadelphia Stock Exchange, the Midwest Stock Exchange, and the Pacific Stock Exchange. With the single exception of the Chicago Board Options Exchange, every organized options exchange is a part of a larger exchange on which stocks are traded.

Stock options are written against only those securities that are widely held, actively traded, and listed on an organized exchange. In the context of a stock option transaction, however, the term "listed" refers to the option itself and not to the underlying security.

For any security against which an option may be written, the number of available shares is fixed, but there is no limitation on the number of options that may be written against an underlying security. The relationship between buyer and seller is never face to face. A buyer and seller are paired by the exchange. Once the premium is paid, moreover, the relationship between buyer and seller is severed completely by activities of the Options Clearing Corporation.

---

[7] The first warrant to be listed on the NYSE was an AT&T warrant that expired April 1975. Other warrants have since been listed there. Most existing warrants are listed on the American or Pacific Coast Stock Exchanges, however, or are traded over the counter; these include warrants on common stocks that are listed on the NYSE.

The Options Clearing Corporation

The Options Clearing Corporation is jointly owned by the five organized options exchanges. Information about the corporation is given in its prospectus, which option brokers who transact business on any of the exchanges must provide. Once a premium is delivered to a seller, the Options Clearing Corporation steps in and acts as seller to the buyer and buyer to the seller, leaving each free to act independently of the other.

A seller, for example, may *cover* (that is, terminate) his or her obligation at any time by buying an identical option from a different seller. Similarly, a buyer may liquidate his or her position by writing an identical option and thus acting as seller to a different buyer. Such a liquidating transaction by either party in no way affects the rights, privileges, or obligations of an opposite party.

Opening and Closing Transactions

Under the rules of each exchange, before one can be a party to a stock option transaction, his or her account must first be approved by the exchange. All business, moreover, must be conducted through options brokers who are members of the exchange. Options writers and buyers must agree to act in accord with the rules of the Options Clearing Corporation and to adhere to the position and limits established by the exchange.

An option may be purchased or written by placing an order with a broker. An order would specify whether it be for a put or call, to be purchased or written, and whether the transaction is an *opening* or a *closing transaction.* An *opening transaction* is one in which a writer establishes an obligation or a buyer establishes a position. A *closing transaction* is one in which an obligation is terminated or a position is liquidated.

Exercising an Option

When a buyer elects to exercise an option, the Options Clearing Corporation randomly assigns the exercise notice to a brokerage firm whose customers have written the same class of option. In turn, the brokerage firm must allocate the exercise notice to a customer who is still obligated as an option writer. Once an exercise notice is presented to a writer, that person must honor the commitment imposed by the option contract—it is too late to cover. In addition to its other vital functions in establishing a market for put and call options, the Options Clearing Corporation acts as guarantor to the buyer in the event of default by the seller.

Over-the-Counter Options

Unlisted option contracts may be obtained through OTC brokers who pair buyers and sellers. OTC contracts are unique (that is, not interchangeable). Relationships are virtually face to face; there is no guarantor in the event of default, and virtually no secondary market exists. For these and other reasons, few OTC options are written.

Questions

1. What is the difference between a European and an American stock option?
2. Explain the difference between a put and a call.
3. Explain the following terms: (a) option premium, (b) exercise price, (c) expiration date.
4. Explain the meaning of each of the following transactions: (a) an opening transaction, (b) a closing transaction, (c) exercising an option, (d) covering a position, (e) terminating a commitment.
5. What is the difference between a covered and an uncovered call option?
6. What are some functions of the Options Clearing Corporation?
7. What is an expiration month cycle?
8. What is the difference between a stock option, a warrant, and a stock purchase right?
9. What are some implications of the federal tax laws for options transactions?
10. Outline some stock option strategies. Explain what justifications (if any) exist for each, and how the participants on either side of a transaction would approach the question of risk under each strategy. (Note that there can be many different answers to this question.)

6.

Tax Considerations

Taxes play an important role in investment decisions in that they affect both the profitability of particular security investments and investment timing decisions. Tax laws and the supporting court decisions are so complex and voluminous, however, that an analyst or investor can hardly expect to have the time and training necessary to become a tax expert. Still, an investor should be familiar with certain basic rules and their impact on investment decisions. An informed investor can make many decisions involving taxes without professional help. Of course, complex problems should be reviewed with a qualified tax lawyer and/or accountant.

This chapter highlights major tax considerations that affect most investors, often on a recurring basis. Federal income taxes, gift and estate taxes, and Keogh and IRA plans are discussed. The information provided in this chapter is current as of the date of this writing. Tax rules and regulations often change, however, and details should be checked from time to time.

FEDERAL INCOME TAXES AND THE INDIVIDUAL INVESTOR

Securities may generate two types of return that are subject to the federal income tax: (1) periodic cash flows in the form of interest or dividends and (2) realized increases in the market value of the securities purchased, which are classified as short-term or long-term capital gains.

Tax Rate Structure and Determining Taxable Income

The 1981 Economic Recovery Tax Act reduced individual income taxes in four ways:

1. Mandated across-the-board rate reductions.
2. Reduced the maximum tax rate applicable to investment income from the 70 percent rate applicable through 1981 to a maximum of 50 percent, beginning with the 1982 tax year.

3. Reduced the so-called marriage penalty.
4. Arranged for the eventual indexation of taxes to mitigate the effects of inflation.

Prior to the passage of this act, tax rates ranged from 14 to 70 percent, as illustrated in Table 6-1, with a maximum rate charged on earned income of 50 percent. Earned income includes items such as salaries, wages, and net income from producing and selling a service or product. The federal income tax rate schedules for taxable years beginning in 1982 are presented in Table 6-2. On October 1, 1981, a 5 percent rate reduction took effect. Since the reduction applied only to the last quarter of the year, the analyzed rate decrease for 1981 was $1\frac{1}{4}$ percent. This reduction has been incorporated in new tax tables that were issued for 1981 by the Internal Revenue Service.

Two points are worth noting. First, tax rates rise as income rises— that is, increases in taxable income that place a taxpayer in a higher bracket are taxed at the higher rate corresponding to that higher bracket income. Second, the tax rate applicable to the level of income for each given income bracket always is applied to that bracket income. When making investment decisions, the marginal rate (that rate applicable to the highest bracket income reached by the investor) is important. Note that one can lower the effective tax rate over a two-year period if income can be shifted from a year in which total taxable income is high to a year in which a lower total taxable income would be reported (including investment income), since that income would then be taxed at a lower bracket rate. Investors do, at times, have opportunities to change the period in which income is recognized for tax purposes, as will be illustrated later.

Tax Planning and the 1981 Act. Investors in the higher tax brackets would have been well advised to postpone tax recognition of income taxed at up to 70 percent in 1981 until 1982 when the maximum rate dropped to 50 percent and to accelerate deductions into the 1981 tax year, where possible. For example, one could have considered postponing sale of a stock until 1982, so as to realize a long-term capital gain in that year rather than during 1981. One could also have accelerated planned charitable donations into 1981, since a $1,000 donation in 1981 for a person in the 70 percent bracket saved $700 in taxes versus only $500 in 1982 when the maximum tax rate drops to 50 percent. In the event an individual had a short-term gain in a stock during 1981 and feared the price would drop in the future, he or she could have sold the stock short against the box and delivered stock presently held to complete the short sale in 1982. Short sales against the box are explained more fully on page 359. The reader can no doubt offer additional examples. The intent here is merely to be illustrative.

TABLE 6-1. Income Tax Rates—Individuals, 1979 and 1980

SCHEDULE X—Single Taxpayers

Use this schedule if you checked Filing Status Box 1 on Form 1040—

If the amount on Schedule TC, Part I, line 3, is:

Not over $2,300......Enter on Schedule TC, Part I, line 4: —0—

Over—	But not over—		of the amount over—
$2,300	$3,400	14%	$2,300
$3,400	$4,400	$154+16%	$3,400
$4,400	$6,500	$314+18%	$4,400
$6,500	$8,500	$692+19%	$6,500
$8,500	$10,800	$1,072+21%	$8,500
$10,800	$12,900	$1,555+24%	$10,800
$12,900	$15,000	$2,059+26%	$12,900
$15,000	$18,200	$2,605+30%	$15,000
$18,200	$23,500	$3,565+34%	$18,200
$23,500	$28,800	$5,367+39%	$23,500
$28,800	$34,100	$7,434+44%	$28,800
$34,100	$41,500	$9,766+49%	$34,100
$41,500	$55,300	$13,392+55%	$41,500
$55,300	$81,800	$20,982+63%	$55,300
$81,800	$108,300	$37,677+68%	$81,800
$108,300	....	$55,697+70%	$108,300

SCHEDULE Y—Married Taxpayers and Qualifying Widows and Widowers

Married Filing Joint Returns and Qualifying Widows and Widowers

Use this schedule if you checked Filing Status Box 2 or 5 on Form 1040—

If the amount on Schedule TC, Part I, line 3, is:

Not over $3,400......Enter on Schedule TC, Part I, line 4: —0—

Over—	But not over—		of the amount over—
$3,400	$5,500	14%	$3,400
$5,500	$7,600	$294+16%	$5,500
$7,600	$11,900	$630+18%	$7,600
$11,900	$16,000	$1,404+21%	$11,900
$16,000	$20,200	$2,265+24%	$16,000
$20,200	$24,600	$3,273+28%	$20,200
$24,600	$29,900	$4,505+32%	$24,600
$29,900	$35,200	$6,201+37%	$29,900
$35,200	$45,800	$8,162+43%	$35,200
$45,800	$60,000	$12,720+49%	$45,800
$60,000	$85,600	$19,678+54%	$60,000
$85,600	$109,400	$33,502+59%	$85,600
$109,400	$162,400	$47,544+64%	$109,400
$162,400	$215,400	$81,464+68%	$162,400
$215,400	....	$117,504+70%	$215,400

Married Filing Separate Returns

Use this schedule if you checked Filing Status Box 3 on Form 1040—

If the amount on Schedule TC, Part I, line 3, is:

Not over $1,700......Enter on Schedule TC, Part I, line 4: —0—

Over—	But not over—		of the amount over—
$1,700	$2,750	14%	$1,700
$2,750	$3,800	$147.00+16%	$2,750
$3,800	$5,950	$315.00+18%	$3,800
$5,950	$8,000	$702.00+21%	$5,950
$8,000	$10,100	$1,132.50+24%	$8,000
$10,100	$12,300	$1,636.50+28%	$10,100
$12,300	$14,950	$2,252.50+32%	$12,300
$14,950	$17,600	$3,100.50+37%	$14,950
$17,600	$22,900	$4,081.00+43%	$17,600
$22,900	$30,000	$6,360.00+49%	$22,900
$30,000	$42,800	$9,839.00+54%	$30,000
$42,800	$54,700	$16,751.00+59%	$42,800
$54,700	$81,200	$23,772.00+64%	$54,700
$81,200	$107,700	$40,732.00+68%	$81,200
$107,700	....	$58,752.00+70%	$107,700

SCHEDULE Z—Heads of Household (including certain married persons who live apart (and abandoned spouses)—see page 7 of the Instructions)

Use this schedule if you checked Filing Status Box 4 on Form 1040—

If the amount on Schedule TC, Part I, line 3, is:

Not over $2,300......Enter on Schedule TC, Part I, line 4: —0—

Over—	But not over—		of the amount over—
$2,300	$4,400	14%	$2,300
$4,400	$6,500	$294+16%	$4,400
$6,500	$8,700	$630+18%	$6,500
$8,700	$11,800	$1,026+22%	$8,700
$11,800	$15,000	$1,708+24%	$11,800
$15,000	$18,200	$2,476+26%	$15,000
$18,200	$23,500	$3,308+31%	$18,200
$23,500	$28,800	$4,951+36%	$23,500
$28,800	$34,100	$6,859+42%	$28,800
$34,100	$44,700	$9,085+46%	$34,100
$44,700	$60,600	$13,961+54%	$44,700
$60,600	$81,800	$22,547+59%	$60,600
$81,800	$108,300	$35,055+63%	$81,800
$108,300	$161,300	$51,750+68%	$108,300
$161,300	....	$87,790+70%	$161,300

TABLE 6-2. Individual Income Tax Rate Schedules, 1982 and Succeeding Years

Category	Taxable Income	Tax
Married individuals filing joint returns and surviving spouses	Not over $3,400	No tax
	Over $3,400 but not over $5,500	12% of the excess over $3,400
	Over $5,500 but not over $7,600	$252, plus 14% of the excess over $5,500
	Over $7,600 but not over $11,900	$546, plus 16% of the excess over $7,600
	Over $11,900 but not over $16,000	$1,234, plus 19% of the excess over $11,900
	Over $16,000 but not over $20,200	$2,013, plus 22% of the excess over $16,000
	Over $20,200 but not over $24,600	$2,937, plus 25% of the excess over $20,200
	Over $24,600 but not over $29,900	$4,037, plus 29% of the excess over $24,600
	Over $29,900 but not over $35,200	$5,574, plus 33% of the excess over $29,900
	Over $35,200 but not over $45,800	$7,323, plus 39% of the excess over $35,200
	Over $45,800 but not over $60,000	$11,457, plus 44% of the excess over $45,800
	Over $60,000 but not over $85,600	$17,705, plus 49% of the excess over $60,000
	Over $85,600	$30,249, plus 50% of the excess over $85,600
Heads of household	Not over $2,300	No tax
	Over $2,300 but not over $4,400	12% of the excess over $2,300
	Over $4,400 but not over $6,500	$252, plus 14% of the excess over $4,400
	Over $6,500 but not over $8,700	$546, plus 16% of the excess over $6,500
	Over $8,700 but not over $11,800	$898, plus 20% of the excess over $8,700
	Over $11,800 but not over $15,000	$1,518, plus 22% of the excess over $11,800
	Over $15,000 but not over $18,200	$2,222, plus 23% of the excess over $15,000

TABLE 6-2. Individual Income Tax Rate Schedules, 1982 and Succeeding Years
    (continued)

Category	Taxable Income	Tax
	Over $18,200 but not over $23,500	$2,958, plus 28% of the excess over $18,200
	Over $23,500 but not over $28,800	$4,442, plus 32% of the excess over $23,500
	Over $28,800 but not over $34,100	$6,138, plus 38% of the excess over $28,800
	Over $34,100 but not over $44,700	$8,152, plus 41% of the excess over $34,100
	Over $44,700 but not over $60,000	$12,498, plus 49% of the excess over $44,700
	Over $60,600	$20,289, plus 50% of the excess over $60,600
Unmarried individuals	Not over $2,300	No tax
	Over $2,300 but not over $3,400	12% of the excess over $2,300
	Over $3,400 but not over $4,400	$132, plus 14% of the excess over $3,400
	Over $4,400 but not over $6,500	$272, plus 16% of the excess over $4,400
	Over $6,500 but not over $8,500	$608, plus 17% of the excess over $6,500
	Over $8,500 but not over $10,800	$948, plus 19% of the excess over $8,500
	Over $10,800 but not over $12,900	$1,385, plus 22% of the excess over $10,800
	Over $12,900 but not over $15,000	$1,847, plus 23% of the excess over $12,900
	Over $15,000 but not over $18,200	$2,330, plus 27% of the excess over $15,000
	Over $18,200 but not over $23,500	$3,194, plus 31% of the excess over $18,200
	Over $23,500 but not over $28,800	$4,837, plus 35% of the excess over $23,500
	Over $28,800 but not over $34,100	$6,692, plus 40% of the excess over $28,800
	Over $34,100 but not over $41,500	$8,812, plus 44% of the excess over $34,100

TABLE 6-2. Individual Income Tax Rate Schedules, 1982 and Succeeding Years
   (continued)

Category	Taxable Income	Tax
	Over $41,500	$12,068, plus 50% of the excess over $41,500
Married individual filing separately	Not over $1,700	No tax
	Over $1,700 but not over $2,750	12% of the excess over $1,700
	Over $2,750 but not over $3,800	$126, plus 14% of the excess over $2,750
	Over $3,800 but not over $5,950	$273, plus 16% of the excess over $3,800
	Over $5,950 but not over $8,000	$617, plus 19% of the excess over $5,950
	Over $8,000 but not over $10,100	$1,006, plus 22% of the excess over $8,000
	Over $10,100 but not over $12,300	$1,468, plus 25% of the excess over $10,100
	Over $12,300 but not over $14,950	$2,018, plus 29% of the excess over $12,300
	Over $14,950 but not over $17,600	$2,787, plus 33% of the excess over $14,950
	Over $17,600 but not over $22,900	$3,661, plus 39% of the excess over $17,600
	Over $22,900 but not over $30,000	$5,728, plus 44% of the excess over $22,900
	Over $30,000 but not over $42,800	$8,852, plus 49% of the excess over $30,000
	Over $42,800	$15,124, plus 50% of the excess over $42,800
Estates and Trusts	Not over $1,050	12% of taxable income
	Over $1,050 but not over $2,100	$126, plus 14% of the excess over $1,050
	Over $2,100 but not over $4,250	$273, plus 16% of the excess over $2,100
	Over $4,250 but not over $6,300	$617, plus 19% of the excess over $4,250
	Over $6,300 but not over $8,400	$1,006, plus 22% of the excess over $6,300

TABLE 6-2. Individual Income Tax Rate Schedules, 1982 and Succeeding Years *(continued)*

Category	Taxable Income	Tax
	Over $8,400 but not over $10,600	$1,468, plus 25% of the excess over $8,400
	Over $10,600 but not over $13,250	$2,018, plus 29% of the excess over $10,600
	Over $13,250 but not over $15,900	$2,787, plus 33% of the excess over $13,250
	Over $15,900 but not over $21,200	$3,661, plus 39% of the excess over $15,900
	Over $21,200 but not over $28,300	$5,728, plus 44% of the excess over $21,200
	Over $28,300 but not over $41,100	$8,852, plus 49% of the excess over $28,300
	Over $41,100	$15,124, plus 50% of the excess over $41,100

Source: 1981 Economic Recovery Tax Act, Supplement to Accompany the 1982 Edition of *West's Federal Taxation*, Vol. 1, *Individual Income Taxes* (St. Paul, Minn.: West Publishing Company, 1981), pp. 3–6.

Calculating Taxable Income. Taxpayers are allowed many deductions from gross income for purposes of determining taxable income. Among the deductions allowed are

1. Ordinary and necessary expenses of operating a personally owned business;
2. Certain gifts to charitable organizations;
3. Interest expense, including any interest penalty on early withdrawal of savings;
4. State and local income, sales, and real estate taxes;
5. Payments to an IRA or Keogh retirement plan;
6. Medical and dental payments exceeding 1 percent of adjusted gross income for medicine and drugs and 3 percent of adjusted gross income for payments to doctors, dentists, nurses, and hospitals;
7. Casualty losses;
8. Alimony paid.

Of course, many other deductions are allowed; this list merely presents the most common ones. Capital gains and losses receive special treatment under the tax code and will be discussed separately.

Constructive Receipt of Income. Ordinary income (other than capital gains and losses) arising from security transactions must generally be reported under the federal income tax code once ownership of such taxable cash flow is established. For example, the interest payable on December 31, 1980, for a bond is taxable income for the year 1980 even though the interest coupon was not cashed until January 15, 1981. Interest earned on savings accounts during a given year is also taxable income of that year even though the interest has not yet been posted to the depositor's passbook. In other words, the cash flow itself doesn't necessarily determine receipt of taxable income, but rather whether or not the taxpayer has earned full right to that receipt.

U.S. government savings bonds are an exception to the rule. Increments in the value of such a bond that occur regularly over its life are considered interest income for tax purposes (not capital gains), but a taxpayer reporting on a cash basis can and should choose to report the total increase in value at maturity of the savings bond. There is a present value advantage in doing this in the sense that capital not diminished by tax payments during the life of the bond can continue to earn a return. The present value advantage could possibly be offset by a shift to a higher bracket in the year the savings bond matures, but this rarely happens.

The closing of a security position (date of sale or maturity of a bond) fixes accountability for a capital transaction in that year. Capital gains and losses are treated differently, however. The trade date (the date on which the investor instructs the broker to make the purchase or sale) determines when a capital loss must be reported. A capital loss must be reported in the year in which the trade date occurs. Capital gains, on the other hand, must be reported in the year in which the settlement date occurs. The settlement date is the date on which the seller must deliver the securities to the buyer and the buyer must make payment; this date typically occurs five days after the trade date. The gain from a profitable sale of a stock on December 30 (the trade date), therefore, is reported in the following year, but a loss would have to be reported in that year.

In the event a taxpayer preferred that a gain be included in the current year when making a sale during the last five days of that year, he or she should instruct the broker to sell the securities for "cash" or "next day settlement" rather than in the usual way where delivery of the securities and payment are not required until five days after the trade date.

Year-end transactions that result in taxable gains are desirable taxwise since payment of the resulting tax is postponed for one year. Where the transactions result in losses, however, one might prefer to postpone the trade until January of the next year, especially if there were no realized short-term gains available in the current year against which the loss could be applied.

Interest Receipts and Dividend Income

Interest receipts and cash dividends are both taxed as ordinary income (that is, at full bracket rates). An individual taxpayer may exclude the differing amounts of interest and/or dividend income from taxable income as follows:

Year	Amount on Exclusion	Type of Income Excluded
1980 and before	$100 ($200 on a joint return)	Dividends only
1981	$200 ($400 on a joint return)	Dividends and/or interest
1982 and thereafter	$100 ($200 on a joint return)	Dividends only

Where the securities are jointly owned, a husband and wife enjoyed a $400 annual exclusion in 1981. This favors joint ownership of securities by married couples, at least in terms of tax considerations. To illustrate, assume that Bill and Martha, who file a joint return, receive dividends from stock registered as follows:

From stock registered in Bill's name: $550
From stock registered in Martha's name: $60.

Bill and Martha could only exclude $260 from taxable income on their joint return; the $200 dividend exclusion available to each individual can only be used by that individual if they file a separate return. On the other hand, they could have excluded $400 from taxable income if the securities were jointly owned (rather than individually) and a joint return were filed. Incidentally, the interest and dividend exclusion cannot be applied to distributions by real estate investment trusts (REITs), because a REIT that distributes 90 percent of its income to shareholders is not subject to taxation.

Dividends received from foreign or U.S. corporations that do not pay federal income taxes may not be excluded from taxable income under the dividend exclusion rule discussed above. This could be significant when considering purchase of the shares of a foreign corporation by an investor who does not have sufficient dividends and/or interest income from taxable U.S. corporations to utilize the exclusion fully.

Corporations are entitled to exclude 85 percent of dividends received (except for certain dividends paid by utilities and foreign corporations) from taxable income, although this exclusion is not available to subchapter S corporations.[1] The yields on preferred stocks have often been below those offered by high-quality bonds because of this tax exclusion, as developed in Chapter 2.

Capital Returned in the Form of Dividends. Dividends not paid out of current or accumulated earnings or profits of a corporation are considered a return of capital for tax purposes, not taxable dividend income to the recipient. Utilities have frequently paid such dividends. The paying corporation must advise the recipient at payment that the dividend is a return of capital. The investor receiving such a dividend reduces the cost basis of the underlying security by the amount of such dividends received. For example, assume an investor purchased 100 shares of Philadelphia Electric common stock at $15 per share and received during the next year a dividend of which the utility advised $1 per share was considered a return of capital. If the stock were sold at the end of the year in which the $1 was paid at the same price at which it was purchased, the investor would have a reportable capital gain of $100 ($1 times 100 shares) for income tax purposes. We will see shortly that capital gains are taxed at more favorable rates than dividend income. For this reason, dividends considered a return of capital must be properly reported as such, and not as dividend income.

Stock Dividends and Stock Splits. The tax law recognizes that the value of the total ownership position in a corporation has not changed when additional shares are received because of a stock dividend or stock split.[2] Such receipts of stock, therefore, are not generally considered taxable income unless the investor has a choice between payment in cash or stock. Even though the investor chooses to receive the stock, when such a choice is offered, the distribution is then taxable as dividend income as though the investor had chosen to receive the cash.

When additional stock is received through a stock dividend or stock split, the recipient must adjust the cost price of each original share proportional to the receipt of additional shares. To illustrate, assume a share of stock had been purchased for $100, and an additional share was received as a stock dividend. The cost per share, for purposes of determining a taxable capital gain or loss at disposal, would then be $50 per share. If a share were then sold for $60, the investor would realize a $10 taxable capital gain.

_____

[1] A subchapter S corporation (also referred to as a tax-option corporation) is one that has elected (by unanimous consent of its shareholders) not to pay any corporate income tax, choosing instead to have the shareholders pay taxes as individuals on their proportional share of earnings, even though earnings are not distributed.
[2] See the previous discussion of stock dividends and stock splits in Chapter 2 for clarification of this point.

Capital Transactions

A capital gain or loss is realized for tax purposes only when there is a sale or exchange of a capital asset. Stocks, bonds, options,[3] warrants, commodity contracts, real estate, and other long-life assets held for investment purposes are capital assets. A taxable gain is realized when a capital asset is sold for more than original cost; a capital loss results when a capital asset is sold for less than original cost.

The length of time the investor has held a capital asset before selling it determines whether a capital gain is long term or short term. The holding period begins the day after the trade date of a purchase and ends on the trade date of a sale. If the asset was held for more than one year, the realized loss or gain is long term. If the asset was held for one year or less, the transaction results in a short-term capital gain or loss. Long-term capital gains are treated more favorably in the tax law than short-term gains, while long-term losses are treated less favorably.

Capital Gains Tax Computation. Long-term gains must first be matched against long-term losses and short-term gains against short-term losses to determine the net long-term and short-term gain or loss. The net gain or loss figures include transactions expenses, such as commissions and service charges paid to brokers, which are added to cost. State transfer taxes, however, are deductible (as a tax) against ordinary income if the taxpayer itemizes deductions. This is preferable to including them in calculating long-term gains or losses, both because deductions against ordinary income are preferable to long-term losses (as will be made clear next) and on the basis of present value. The resultant net short-term capital gains and losses and net long-term capital gains and losses must then be paired off to arrive at one overall net figure. The following various situations can develop:

1. A net short-term gain, assuming no long-term losses, is simply added to ordinary income and taxed at the appropriate tax bracket rate.
2. Only 40 percent of net long-term gains is added to ordinary income to determine total taxable income. This rule also applies to the portion of net long-term gains in excess of net short-term losses. For example, if an investor sold a stock held for more than one year, thereby realizing a $5,000 long-term capital gain, $2,000 (40 percent) of the gain would be taxable at the ordinary bracket rate. The remaining $3,000 does not result in taxable income, though it may result in the imposition of the so-called minimum tax that will be discussed later. To add a complication, assume the same investor had also incurred a $2,000 loss on sale of another capital asset. Forty

---

[3] Premiums earned from unexercised puts and calls, however, are considered ordinary income taxable at full bracket rates.

percent of the resulting net long-term gain, whether the capital asset from which the loss resulted was held for more or less than a year, or $1,200 (.4 × $3,000) would then be added to ordinary income and taxed at ordinary bracket rates.

3. All net short-term capital losses must first be used to offset net long-term gains. In the event that the net short-term loss exceeds the net long-term gain, the difference, up to $3,000 in any one year, may be deducted from other taxable income to determine taxable income. Net short-term capital losses in excess of the $3,000 annual limitation may be carried forward to succeeding years until the loss is exhausted.

4. A net long-term capital loss can be fully used to offset a net short-term capital gain; that is, $1 of long-term capital loss can offset $1 of short-term capital gain in a given year. In the event the long-term capital loss exceeds the net short-term gain of that year, only one-half of the difference, to a maximum of $3,000, may be used to offset other taxable income in that year. Net long-term losses exceeding $3,000 (not including the disallowed one-half) may be carried forward indefinitely until exhausted as discussed in (3) above. An investor who has unrealized losses in securities, which are not likely to later become gains, would be well advised to realize those losses in years when there are net short-term capital gains to offset, so as to realize fully the loss incurred for tax purposes.

5. If an investor incurs both a net short-term and a net long-term capital loss in a given year, the gain and loss may not be netted. Each type of loss retains its own character. The investor may deduct 100 percent of the net short-term loss against other taxable income, but only 50 percent of the long-term loss may be deducted. Short-term capital losses must be used before long-term capital losses, and any excess over the annual $3,000 deduction limit may be carried forward indefinitely. To illustrate, assume an investor experienced the following losses during 1981:

Net Short-term Capital Loss: $1,500;
Net Long-term Capital Loss: $5,000.

The investor can deduct the full $1,500 of net short-term capital loss against ordinary income. The investor is entitled to a total deduction of $2,500 (50 percent of the realized net long-term capital loss), but can use only $1,500 in 1981 because of the annual $3,000 limitation on deduction of capital losses. The remaining $1,000 ($2,000 of net long-term loss) can be carried forward and deducted against income in future years.

The 30-Day Wash Rule. One further special aspect of the tax code must be kept in mind when dealing with capital losses. A position established in a security within 30 days before or after a completed transaction in that issue will disqualify a resulting loss from deductability for tax purposes. Instead, when such a transaction occurs, the investor must increase the cost figure for acquisition of the securities within the sixty-one-day period by the amount of the disallowed loss. The loss will, in effect, be realized when the new position is sold, but this postponement of realization of the loss for tax purposes can be disadvantageous to a taxpayer in present value terms. It is, therefore, preferable to replace an issue sold with one of similar characteristics (rather than the same stock as the one sold) during the sixty-one-day period if the investor wishes to retain a position in that area. For example, if Exxon were sold, and one wished to maintain a position in the oil industry, Texaco might be purchased during the sixty-one-day period.

Stock Rights

The receipt of stock rights (unless such receipt was in lieu of money) again does not create taxable income, but the sale of such rights will typically result in taxable income.

The receipt of a right lowers the cost basis of the underlying stock and allocates a portion of that cost to the right. To illustrate, assume that an investor received one right for each of the 100 shares of ABC stock that he or she had previously purchased at $60 per share. Further assume that ABC stock had a market value of $63 a share at the time the rights were distributed, and the rights later had a market value of $3 each. The investor would determine the cost basis for a share of stock and a right for purposes of determining a gain or loss at disposal (using the allocation method) as follows:

Market value of ABC stock at distribution (100 shares @ $63/share):	$6,300
Market value of the rights (100 rights @ $3/right):	300
Total Market Value:	$6,600

Basis allocable to original stock:

$$\frac{6,300}{6,600} \times 6,000 = \$5,727.27 \text{ or } \$57.27 \text{ per share}$$

Basis allocable to rights:

$$\frac{300}{6,600} \times 6,000 = \$272.73 \text{ or } \$2.73 \text{ per right.}$$

If rights were then sold for $3 per right, there would be a taxable gain of $0.27 per right ($3 – $2.73). If the stock were sold for $63 per share, there would be a taxable capital gain of $5.73 per share ($63.00 – $57.27).

Alternatively, let us assume that the above stockholder chose to exercise his or her rights, and that one new share of ABC stock could be acquired for four rights and $50 in cash. The cost basis for tax purposes of each new share of stock would then be determined as follows:

Cost basis of rights, as determined above:	$ 272.73
Subscription price of new shares	
(25 shares X $50/share):	$1,250.00
Total cost basis for new stock:	$1,522.73
Cost basis of each new share:	
($1,522.73 ÷ 25)	$ 60.91

Notice that the cost basis of an original share ($57.27) and the cost basis of a new share ($60.91) are now different. To determine the capital gain or loss when a share of ABC stock is sold, the investor can assume that the original lower-priced shares are sold first and then the new shares.

In the event that rights are received because the investor chose them rather than a cash distribution alternatively offered, the rights represent taxable income at the fair market value per right.

Short Sales

A short sale is the selling of a borrowed security, usually with the anticipation that the price of that security will fall, allowing purchase at that lower price and therefore return of the stock with a profit.[4] Gains from short sales are always classified as short term, regardless of how long the loan was outstanding. Since the holding period for a capital asset begins with the acquisition of that asset, and a short seller has never acquired the stock he or she short sold, a short sale does not start the holding period. Interestingly, a loss on a short transaction, however, is classified as a long-term or short-term capital loss according to the time involved between the short sale and a repurchase to cover. This seems inconsistent and can penalize a taxpayer in the sense that only 50 percent of long-term losses are deductible for tax purposes, but it is the law.

Selling Short Against the Box. A short sale against the box refers to an investor's borrowing and selling short a security at a time when he

---

[4] Short sales are discussed in greater detail in Chapter 15. We are interested only in tax considerations here.

or she owned and held that security. This is usually done to transfer the tax liability resulting from a given trade from the year in which that trade occurred to the next year because the taxpayer expects that taxable income will be significantly lower in the succeeding year. For example, assume that AT&T stock was selling for $57 a share in December 1981, while an investor had acquired 100 shares of that stock at $45 per share in 1977. Further assume that the investor anticipates being in a lower tax bracket rate category in 1982 than in 1981 but fears that AT&T will fall in price in the future. The investor might well borrow and short sell 100 shares of AT&T at $57 per share during December 1981 to lock in the profit of $12 per share.

A short sale does not, however, close a position. No taxable event, therefore, occurs until the stock that was sold short is repurchased and returned to the lender. The investor could deliver the 100 shares he or she owned at the time of the short sale during January 1982 to close the loan, thereby realizing the profit of $12 a share, less commissions on the short sale and possible interest charges on the loan. Forty percent of the resulting long-term capital gain would be taxed in 1982, not 1981. The holding period is determined by the date at which the shares of AT&T that were owned were acquired.

Of importance to note is that one cannot turn a short-term capital gain into a long-term capital gain by means of a short sale against the box and a repurchase of the stock to cover the short sale. Once a short sale against the box is made, the holding period of the stock held long is destroyed, and a new holding period begins only after the short position is covered. For example, assume an investor was involved in the following transactions:

1. The investor purchased 100 shares of Du Pont on March 1, 1980, at $40 per share.
2. On August 1, 1980, 100 shares of Du Pont were sold short against the box at $50 per share.
3. On March 20, 1981, the investor purchased 100 shares of Du Pont at $47 a share to cover the short position.
4. On June 1, 1981, the 100 shares of Du Pont acquired March 1, 1980, were sold at $55 a share.

The tax consequences of the above transactions, ignoring commission and interest costs, are as follows:

1. The short sale against the box on August 1, 1980, destroyed the holding period that had been built up on the Du Pont stock acquired on March 1, 1980.
2. The holding period for that 100 shares began again when the short position was closed on March 20, 1981. The short sale on August 1, 1980, and the repurchase to cover that short sale on March 20, 1981, result in a taxable short-term capital gain of $3 per share ($50 - $47 per share). The sale of the

100 shares originally acquired on March 1, 1980, results in a short-term capital gain of $15 a share ($55 - $40). The holding period for these shares started over again when the short-sale position was closed on March 20, 1981, so that the 100 shares acquired on March 1, 1980, had been held less than three months for tax purposes.

The rules determining the holding period for the stock held long when a short sale against the box is covered by purchase do tend to be disadvantageous to the investor. If the above investor had not made the short sale against the box, only 40 percent of the $15 per share profit realized through the sale on June 1, 1981, would have been taxable as a long-term gain rather than the entire $15 per share. Of course, if the short sale had not been made, the stock could have continued falling from the $50 price realized on August 1, 1980, possibly falling even below the $40 a share acquisition price.

The Minimum Tax

In addition to the regular federal income tax due, a taxpayer may be subject to a 15 percent tax on certain tax preference items or an alternative minimum tax. The purpose of this tax is to ensure that wealthy individuals, who are most likely to be in a position to claim tax preference deductions, do not escape all taxation or are necessarily able to pay a lower effective tax rate on economic income than other taxpayers. Noncorporate and corporate taxpayers face different minimum tax rules.

The rules are somewhat complex. Both corporate and noncorporate taxpayers are subject to a 15 percent add-on minimum tax (in addition to regular income taxes) that is imposed on the following list of "tax preference items":

1. Certain tax preference items resulting from realization of long-term capital gains.
2. The excess of accelerated depreciation deductions over allowable straight-line depreciation.
3. The excess of rapid amortization of pollution control facilities, child-care facilities, and railroad rolling stock over regular allowed deductions.
4. Specified portions of the bad debt deductions of financial institutions.
5. The excess of allowable percentage depletion over the adjusted basis of a property at the end of a taxable year.
6. Intangible drilling costs deductions of a given tax year that exceed the taxpayer's net income from oil, gas, and geothermal properties during that year.
7. Itemized deductions that exceed 60 percent of a taxpayer's adjusted gross income.
8. The excess of the fair market value of the underlying stock over the option price when a qualified stock option is exercised.

In the event an investor (corporate or individual) has utilized any of the above-listed tax preference items in a given year, he or she should calculate the regular and alternative methods for determining tax liability under provisions for the minimum tax as explained in the instructions accompanying tax form 4625 and/or check with his or her tax advisers.

Income Averaging

A taxpayer with substantially higher than average income in a given year may be able to reduce federal income tax liability by utilizing the income-averaging provisions of the tax code. Schedule G, used in computing the tax when income averaging is used, and a special set of instructions may be obtained directly from the Internal Revenue Service. The taxpayer should, however, carefully consider both benefits and possible disadvantages before deciding to income average when filing tax returns. The advisability of income averaging should be seriously discussed with one's tax adviser when income is highly variable from year to year.

KEOGH PLANS

A law passed in 1962 and amended by the Employment Retirement Income Security Act of 1974 (ERISA) offers the self-employed and certain other people[5] an opportunity to set up tax-sheltered retirement plans. ERISA will be further discussed in Chapter 16. A Keogh plan[6] retirement program can be created by establishing a legal trust, annuity, pension, or profit-sharing plan under the custodianship of a bank, savings and loan association, mutual fund, stockbroker, or other qualified trustee. The assets committed to a Keogh plan may be invested in stocks, bonds, mutual funds, life insurance, variable annuities, real estate mortgages, or any combination of these investments.

Determining the Contribution Level

All individuals covered by a Keogh plan may contribute the lesser of 15 percent of earned income or $7,500 through 1981. Starting in 1982, the dollar limitation rose to $15,000 in any one year. A participant may choose to invest $750 or 100 percent of earnings from self-employed activity in a Keogh retirement program in which the 15 percent contribution rule would result in a lower contribution.

---

[5] Professional people operating their own businesses (such as accountants, doctors, lawyers, and dentists) as well as salaried individuals who operate a profitable sideline business (such as a university professor who engages in consulting activities) are included.

[6] Named after Congressman Eugene J. Keogh, who sponsored the 1962 law.

Contributions to a plan established by a self-employed person who hires other individuals (or benefits derived from the plan) may not discriminate against the hired people. An amount must be deposited for each employee that when related to the income of that employee equals the percentage of self-employed income deposited for the owner-employer's personal benefit, based on the first $100,000 of earned income for the owner-employer for years prior to 1982. For example, if an owner-employer contributed the maximum allowable ($7,500) to a Keogh plan for a given year, the percentage rate of contribution for employees on their salaries would be 7.5 percent, whether that owner-employer earned $100,000 or $200,000 of self-employed income in that year. The amount of compensation upon which the percentage that must be paid employees is calculated has been increased to $200,000 for 1982 and succeeding years. If the contribution rate is based on compensation in excess of $100,000, however, the employee's rate cannot be less than 7.5 percent. In the unusual event that an employee's earnings exceed the owner-employer's income in a given year, the contribution on behalf of the employee could not only exceed that of the owner but could also exceed the limitation per owner-contributor for that year.

Vesting Rights

An individual's rights under a pension plan are fully vested when the accrued benefits derived from contributions to the plan, both by the individual and the employer, are 100 percent nonforfeitable at all times, even if the individual chooses to accept employment elsewhere. Workers participating in an employer's Keogh plan enjoy a benefit, in terms of vesting rights, not usually available to employees participating in corporation-sponsored qualified pension plans. Contributions to a Keogh plan for employees become fully vested when made in the individual employee's name; employees have an immediate right to all such contributions in terms of the scheduled retirement benefits if they decide to leave their current position. Full vesting rights, in the case of a typical corporate retirement plan, are typically not granted until ten years of employment have expired. Employees who decide to leave the firm before the ten-year employment period has expired usually have to forfeit some or all of the monies built up through contributions in their names to the typical corporate qualified plan.

Distributions from a Keogh Plan

Withdrawal of funds contributed to a Keogh plan generally may not begin before the plan participant reaches $59\frac{1}{2}$ years of age and must begin before the participant reaches $70\frac{1}{2}$ years of age. All assets accumulated in the plan by the time a participant reaches $70\frac{1}{2}$ years of age must be distributed within five years of death of the plan holder or spouse, whichever occurs later. All distributions are taxed as ordinary income in the year received.

The amount that must be withdrawn periodically depends on the type of plan adopted and the life expectancy of the beneficiary and the spouse. An individual's accountant and/or lawyer can help set up a proper plan of distribution.

Premature distributions—that is, withdrawals occurring before the participant reaches $59\frac{1}{2}$ years of age—are subject to a penalty tax of 10 percent of the money withdrawn. If $10,000 was withdrawn prematurely, for example, the recipient would incur a penalty tax of $1,000, in addition to being obligated to pay regular federal income tax due on the $10,000 receipt of income (calculated at the ordinary bracket rate applicable in the year of withdrawal). The moral: do not commit funds to a Keogh plan unless you are confident the money contributed will not be required before you reach an age of $59\frac{1}{2}$ years.

The penalty tax on premature distributions is not applicable in the event of death or disability of the participant. In the event of the participant's death, or a medically determined disability that prevents gainful activity, a distribution may be made at that time without penalty. The participant's interest in the plan must then be (1) distributed to his or her named beneficiaries within five years of the date of death, unless a spouse is involved and the distribution is postponed to the date of death of the spouse, or (2) used within that five-year period to purchase an annuity payable over a period not exceeding the beneficiaries' life expectancy, or (3) paid out in a plan of distribution already commenced over a period no longer than had been the life expectancy of the participant and the spouse.

IRA PLANS

Prior to the 1981 act, individuals who were not active participants in a tax-qualified retirement plan or governmental retirement plan during a given year were permitted to set up an individual retirement plan (IRA). As of January 1, 1982, individuals already covered by corporate or government pension plans and Keogh plans may also set up an IRA plan. Some have called this change the "first riskless tax shelter for the common man."

IRA plans and Keogh plans differ basically in terms of the amount of tax-deductible income that can be contributed to the fund, and because IRAs are not limited to self-employed income as a basis for determining the maximum annual contribution. Prior to the 1981 act, an individual could contribute up to 15 percent of gross earned income, or $1,500, whichever was less, to an IRA plan in a given year. The maximum tax-deductible contribution to a Keogh plan at that time was $7,500. The new law raises the maximum contribution for an individual to $2,000, and this amount may equal 100 percent of pay.

The Contribution of a Spouse

In the event that both a husband and wife separately earn income during a given year, both can set up a separate IRA plan and take an IRA deduction against taxable income to the maximum allowed. A married individual, moreover, may set aside tax-deductible retirement savings for the benefit of a spouse who was not gainfully employed. The deductible maximum was raised from $1,750 to $2,250 as of January 1, 1982.

Simplified Employee Pension Plans

A "simplified employee pension plan" allows an increased deduction for contributions to an employee's IRA by an employer who does not otherwise provide a pension plan. The maximum deduction allowed is the lesser of 15 percent of the employee's includable compensation or $7,500. All employer contributions to an employee's IRA plan are includable in the employee's taxable income, even if a pension deduction is not permitted.

To participate in such a plan an employee must have (1) attained an age of 25 and (2) performed work for the employer in at least three of the preceding five calendar years. The possibility of employer participation in a simplified employee pension plan offers a possibly attractive way for smaller businesses to set up a pension program for their employees that is superior to individual savings efforts by those employees.

Tax-Free Rollover

Special rules permit a "tax-free rollover" when switching investment mediums utilized by a given IRA plan and also permit the transfer of assets from a qualified retirement plan or tax-sheltered annuity plan (such as a Keogh plan) to an IRA plan if two conditions are met:

1. The amount distributed to an individual from an old account must be transferred to the IRA plan within 60 days of being received.
2. A tax-free rollover from one type of IRA plan to another is not permitted if an earlier rollover of this type occurred within the preceding year. In the event an earlier rollover had occurred within the one-year period, the present rollover is a taxable distribution.

Taxation of Benefits

Benefits received from an IRA plan are taxed as ordinary income in the year received at appropriate federal income tax bracket rates. When an annuity contract is received as a distribution of the assets of an IRA plan, however, its value will not be included in gross taxable income of that year. Instead, the annual annuity payments received under that contract are included as taxable income in the year received.

Premature Distributions of Benefits

Benefit distributions from an IRA account, other than for disabled individuals or at death of the participant, received before reaching $59\frac{1}{2}$ years of age are subject to a 10 percent penalty tax as well as being taxed as ordinary income from an IRA account. Moreover, loans will be treated as though they are distributions; if premature, they are subject to the 10 percent penalty tax. As with a Keogh plan, a person should not contribute funds to an IRA plan unless the individual is confident that the money contributed will not be required before that individual reaches an age of $59\frac{1}{2}$ years.

EMPLOYEE STOCK OWNERSHIP PLANS

The tax laws provide a strong incentive for, and have led to the growth of, employee stock ownership plans (ESOPs) by permitting extra investment tax credits (up to 1 percent of contributions) for employer contributions to an ESOP. Such a plan is really a defined contribution pension plan in which the assets of the plan are invested in the employer's own securities.

Allocation of Employer Securities

Amounts allocated to participants in an ESOP must be substantially in the same proportion as the ratio between the amount of compensation paid a participant during the plan year and the total compensation paid all participants during that year. This can be stated in equation form as follows:

$$\begin{matrix} \text{Allocation to} \\ \text{a participant's} \\ \text{account} \end{matrix} = \begin{matrix} \text{Total dollar amount} \\ \text{of employer} \\ \text{securities acquired} \\ \text{by an ESOP} \end{matrix} \times \frac{\text{Compensation paid participant}}{\text{Total compensation paid all participants}}$$

Employer securities (plan assets) may not be transferred to a participant before the end of the eighty-fourth month, beginning after the month in which the securities were allocated to the participant's account. The plan may provide, however, for earlier distributions in the event of separation from employer service, death, or disability.

Rights of Participants

An ESOP participant has a nonforfeitable right to employer securities allocated to his or her account; in other words, he or she is fully vested when the securities are allocated. The employee-participant, moreover, is entitled to direct the manner in which securities allocated to his or her account are voted by the plan. An ESOP, therefore, provides a systematic approach for granting partial ownership of a business to its employees while helping provide future pension benefits for those employees.

ESTATE AND GIFT TAXES

The Tax Reform Act of 1976 made a comprehensive overhaul of federal estate and gift tax laws. The 1981 act made further major changes, intended primarily to lessen the tax burden on smaller estates and to recognize the significant impact of inflation in recent years.

A single unified estate and gift tax rate schedule, with progressive rates on the basis of cumulative lifetime and at-death transfers, was adopted in 1976. Also, a simple unified credit, to be discussed later, replaced both the $60,000-estate tax exemption and the $30,000-once-during-a-lifetime-gift tax exemption.

Prior to 1982, estate and gift tax rates ranged from 18 percent to a maximum rate of 70 percent, as shown in Table 6–3. The 1981 act sig-

TABLE 6–3. Unified Transfer Tax Rate Schedule

Amount with Respect to Which the Tentative Tax Is to Be Computed	Tentative Tax
Not over $10,000	18 percent of such amount
Over $10,000 but not over $20,000	$1,800, plus 20 percent of the excess of such amount over $10,000
Over $20,000 but not over $40,000	$3,800, plus 22 percent of the excess of such amount over $20,000
Over $40,000 but not over $60,000	$8,200, plus 24 percent of the excess of such amount over $40,000
Over $60,000 but not over $80,000	$13,000, plus 26 percent of the excess of such amount over $60,000
Over $80,000 but not over $100,000	$18,200, plus 28 percent of the excess of such amount over $80,000
Over $100,000 but not over $150,000	$23,800 plus 30 percent of the excess of such amount over $100,000
Over $150,000 but not over $250,000	$38,800, plus 32 percent of the excess of such amount over $150,000
Over $250,000 but not over $500,000	$70,800 plus 34 percent of the excess of such amount over $250,000
Over $500,000 but not over $750,000	$155,800, plus 37 percent of the excess of such amount over $500,000
Over $750,000 but not over $1,000,000	$248,300, plus 39 percent of the excess of such amount over $750,000
Over $1,000,000 but not over $1,250,000	$345,800, plus 41 percent of the excess of such amount over $1,000,000

TABLE 6-3. Unified Transfer Tax Rate Schedule *(continued)*

Amount with Respect to Which the Tentative Tax Is to Be Computed	Tentative Tax
Over $1,250,000 but not over $1,500,000	$448,300, plus 43 percent of the excess of such amount over $1,250,000
Over $1,500,000 but not over $2,000,000	$555,800, plus 45 percent of the excess of such amount over $1,500,000
Over $2,000,000 but not over $2,500,000	$780,800, plus 49 percent of the excess of such amount over $2,000,000
Over $2,500,000 but not over $3,000,000	$1,025,800 plus 53 percent of the excess of such amount over $2,500,000
Over $3,000,000 but not over $3,500,000	$1,290,800, plus 57 percent of the excess of such amount over $3,000,000
Over $3,500,000 but not over $4,000,000	$1,575,800, plus 61 percent of the excess of such amount over $3,500,000
Over $4,000,000 but not over $4,500,000	$1,880,800, plus 65 percent over the excess of such amount over $4,000,000
Over $4,500,000 but not over $5,000,000	$2,205,800, plus 69 percent of the excess of such amount over $4,500,000
Over $5,000,000	$2,550,800, plus 70 percent of the excess of such amount over $5,000,000

nificantly reduced the tax rate on transfers over $2,500,000 during a four-year transitional period beginning in 1982. The new rates, applicable to transfers after December 31, 1981, are summarized and compared to prior rates in Table 6-4.

Taxation of Estates

The federal estate tax is levied on the transfer of a person's property at his or her death. The estate of decedents who were neither citizens nor residents of the United States at the time of death are subject to tax only on property situated within the United States. States also impose inheritance taxes on the assets of deceased persons. The amount of the state tax is typically quite small in comparison with the federal estate tax liability, although significant, and rules and tax rates vary from state to state. Only the federal estate tax will be discussed in this chapter.

TABLE 6-4. Changes in the Unified Transfer Rate Schedule Imposed by the 1981 Tax Reform Act

		Rates			
	Prior			New Rates	
Taxable Transfer	Law	1982	1983	1984	1985
$2,500,000 to $3,000,000	53%	53%	53%	53%	50%
$3,000,000 to $3,500,000	57	57	57	55	50
$3,500,000 to $4,000,000	61	61	60	55	50
$4,000,000 to $4,500,000	65	65	60	55	50
$4,500,000 to $5,000,000	69	65	60	55	50
$5,000,000 and over	70	65	60	55	50

Source: *Economic Recovery Act of 1981*, Arthur Anderson & Company, p. 12.

Determining the Taxable Estate. The value of all property in which the decedent has an interest at death comprises the gross estate. Property included in a decedent's estate is valued at "fair market" value determined either by (1) the price of the asset at the date of death or (2) the price six months to the day after death. The cost basis of assets has no bearing on the value of property included in an estate or the amount of estate taxes payable, although it does have importance for the filing of federal income taxes on behalf of the decedent.

The taxable estate is determined by subtracting from the gross estate the following deductions:

1. *Funeral expenses* that were paid out of the decedent's estate, including the cost of a grave marker and burial lot or vault.
2. *Administration expenses* limited to those that are actually and necessarily incurred in the administration of the decedent's estate. Included are expenses incurred in (a) collection of estate assets, (b) payment of debts, and (c) distribution of property.
3. *Personal obligations* and debts of the decedent existing at the time of death, whether or not they have matured and must be paid at the time of death.
4. *Medical expenses* incurred while the decedent lived and paid within one year after death if they have not been claimed as an income tax deduction on the decedent's final return.
5. *Property taxes* when the personal liability arose prior to the decedent's death. Inheritance and estate taxes paid are not generally deductible. Payments of state and foreign death taxes, however, may result in deductions.
6. *Casualty losses* arising during the period of administration of the estate that are not compensated for by insurance or otherwise.
7. *A marital deduction,* discussed separately below.
8. *The value of property donated* to charitable institutions.
9. *Various other expenses* that are specifically identified and ordered by a will.

The Marital Deduction. When any part of a deceased person's estate passes to a surviving spouse, a *marital deduction* is allowed. The 1981 act eliminated all previous quantitative limitations on this deduction. All qualifying transfers between spouses are allowed to pass free of gift and estate taxes, beginning in January 1982. Prior to 1982, a marital deduction of $250,000 or one-half of the decedent's gross estate was allowed. The act also provides for a 100 percent gift tax marital deduction for gifts to spouses made on or after January 1, 1982.

Computation of the Tax. Steps to calculate the estate tax due are briefly summarized as follows:

1. *Determine the taxable estate* as discussed above.
2. *Compute the "adjusted taxable gifts"* and add the total to the taxable estate. "Adjustable taxable gifts" include all taxable transfers made by the decedent after December 31, 1976, except post-1976 gifts, which are included in the gross estate.
3. Apply the rate from the uniform rate schedule (see Tables 6–3 and 6–4) to the total of steps 1 and 2.
4. Subtract all gift taxes paid on gifts made after 1976.
5. Subtract the following credits allowed against the estate tax itself: (a) the portion of the unified credit not consumed on lifetime gifts, (b) credit for state death taxes paid, (c) credit for federal gift taxes paid on pre-1977 gifts that were included in the decedent's estate, (d) credit for prior transfer taxes, and (e) credit for foreign death taxes.

Final Income Tax Return of the Decedent. The estate representative must file a final income tax return for the decedent and an income tax return for each taxable year until the administration of the estate is ended and the decedent's assets are distributed to the proper beneficiaries.

Transfers Within Three Years of Death. Prior to the 1981 act, transfers of property made within a three-year period ending on the date of the decedent's death, on which full and adequate consideration was not received, were included in the gross estate. Moreover, gift taxes paid on such transfers were also included in the donor's gross estate, on the grounds the assets so expended would have been there if the gifts were not made.

The 1981 act completely reversed this policy. Practically all gifts are now excluded in the computation of the taxable estate—even those made within three years of death. A gift during life, however, made within three years of death will still be included in the gross estate. Moreover, those transfers that are excluded from the taxable estate under the new rules are included in the gross estate for purposes of determining the estate's eligibility for certain benefits, such as deferred payment of estate taxes and special use valuation.

Estate Planning. Careful estate planning can result in substantial savings in estate taxes. For example, trusts may be created that help reduce an individual's tax burden, not only in terms of estate and inheritance taxes but also in terms of the federal income tax. Written material concerning this complex subject is voluminous. Such planning is best done with the help of a knowledgeable lawyer and/or accountant who specializes in tax matters.

Gift Taxes

The federal gift tax is an excise tax imposed on the transfer of property made without adequate and full consideration while the individual transferring the property is living. Gift taxes paid by a decedent on lifetime transfers of property before 1977 are allowable deductions against the estate tax. The deduction is limited to the smaller of (1) the amount of gift tax paid when the gift was made or (2) the amount of estate tax attributable to inclusion of the same property. Gift taxes, on the other hand, are not deductible for federal income tax purposes.

Exclusions and Deductions. The first $3,000 of gifts made during a calendar year *to each separate donee* were not subject to the gift tax through 1981. An individual could, therefore, make a gift of $3,000 to each of four children during a given year, and the $12,000 total of gifts would not be taxable. If a donor and his spouse, moreover, elect to treat gifts to third persons as being one-half from each, then $6,000 may be given to each donee in a given year without incurring a gift tax liability. Married couples can effectively utilize this "gift splitting" option. Note, however, that the recipient of a gift must realize unqualified ownership of the property or the gift inclusion will be disallowed; in other words, gifts may not have strings attached that return control to the donor if one is to take advantage of the annual gift exclusion. For gifts made after 1981, the act raises the basic exclusion to $10,000 ($20,000 for consenting spouse gifts).

Gifts to charitable, religious, educational, and public institutions must be reported, but the $3,000 or greater exclusion is then taken and the balance excluded as nontaxable gifts by deduction. Such gifts are not taxable under the gift tax and are deductible when determining taxable income for federal income tax purposes. The idea is to encourage the giving of gifts to charitable organizations.

The gift tax law, prior to the 1981 act, provided a *marital deduction* of 100 percent on the first $100,000 of lifetime gifts to a spouse,

with no deduction for the second $100,000 of such gifts, and a 50 per-
cent deduction for interspousal transfers exceeding $200,000. The
1981 act provides for a 100 percent gift tax marital deduction for gifts
to spouses made after January 1, 1982, as well as an unlimited estate
tax marital deduction.

The Unified Credit. Under the 1976 act, an individual is entitled to
a single unified lifetime credit of $47,000, which may be used in whole
or in part to reduce gift tax or estate tax liabilities. Beginning in 1982,
the unified credit increases annually until 1987, as shown in Table 6-5.

TABLE 6-5. The Unified Credit and Taxable Transfer Exemption Equivalent

Year	1982–1987 Unified Credit	Taxable Transfer Exemption Equivalent
1982	$ 62,800	$225,000
1983	79,300	275,000
1984	96,300	325,000
1985	121,800	400,000
1986	155,800	500,000
1987	192,800	600,000

To illustrate the use of the unified credit in 1981 or before, assume an
unmarried individual who had never before made a taxable gift decided
to give $30,000 to his daughter to help finance the purchase of a house.
The tax treatment of this gift would be as follows:

Taxable gift	$30,000
Less annual exclusion	3,000
Taxable gift	$27,000
Gift tax from Table 6-3	$ 5,340
Less unified credit used	$ 5,340
Tax liability	0
Total unified credit	$47,000
Less amount used	$ 5,340
Available unified credit	$41,660

Note that use of $5,340 of the unified credit offset a taxable gift of
$30,000, explaining the taxable transfer exemption equivalent column
in Table 6-5.

When Must a Gift Tax Return Be Filed? Gifts made after 1976 require filing a return on a quarterly basis when the taxable gifts for a

given quarter, plus all other taxable gifts for the calendar year for which an annually required tax return has not been filed, exceed $25,000. The return is due one and a half months after the end of the quarter.

Tax Basis of Gift for Donee. Property acquired through gift generally keeps the same holding period and tax basis for purposes of determining capital gains or losses on sale as it had in the hands of the donor. The rules are complicated, however, and competent tax counsel should be sought when deciding on the tax basis and holding period for property being sold that was acquired through gift or because of death of the donor.

Gifts to Minors. A security cannot normally be registered in a minor's name because the minor lacks legal status. Gifts of securities can be made to a minor, however, under the Uniform Gifts to Minors Act, now adopted by all fifty states. A custodian who is of legal age must be appointed for the property.

The custodian is responsible for prudently managing the assets donated to the minor. Custodians may not use margin accounts when supervising the investment account of a minor. Custodians can also be held personally liable for losses incurred through speculation. A donor of assets to a minor should not appoint himself or herself as custodian of the investment account. If a donor is named as custodian and dies before the minor reaches legal age, the current value of the securities given to the minor will be considered part of the donor's estate.

A gift to a minor, under the Uniform Gift to Minor's Act, is irrevocable—that is, the assets are permanently removed from the donor's control. Income earned on the donated property accrues to and is taxable as income of the minor, thereby offering the possibility for substantial federal income tax savings through the usually lower applicable bracket rate. Estate tax savings may also result.

When the minor reaches majority (age 21), the custodial security certificate and proof of age are presented to the appropriate corporate transfer agents, who then issue new securities in the name of the minor.

TAXATION OF CORPORATIONS

The rules governing the taxation of corporations differ in several respects from those applicable to individuals. Our purpose here is merely to highlight briefly the most important of these differences from the standpoint of an investor.

As for an individual investor, a corporate investor should aim at maximizing after-tax cash flows for the level of risk accepted. This implies structuring any portfolio so as to maximize available tax deductions, unless resulting tax advantages would be more than offset by adverse effects on cash flow or risk.

The Rate Structure

The federal corporate income tax rate structure is simpler and quite different than the rate structure applicable to individuals. Rates rise from a minimum to a maximum of 46 percent in five equal $25,000 steps. Moreover, the 1981 act reduces the rates applicable to the two lowest brackets only in 1982 and 1983, as shown in Table 6-6.

Table 6-6. Corporate Tax Rate Structure

Taxable Income	1981	1982	1983
$0 to $25,000	17%	16%	15%
$25,000 to $50,000	20	19	18
$50,000 to $75,000	30	30	30
$75,000 to $100,000	40	40	40
Over $100,000	46	46	46

A corporation that earned a taxable income of $82,500 in 1981, therefore, would incur a tax liability of $19,750, calculated as follows:

First $25,000 @ 17%	= $ 4,250
Next 25,000 @ 20%	= 5,000
Next 25,000 @ 30%	= 7,500
Remaining $7,500 @ 40%	= 3,000
	$19,750

For large corporations, a federal income tax rate of 46 percent is typically assumed when projecting after-tax profits since that rate is applicable to such a large portion of the earnings. Considering the state income liability of such corporations, an effective income tax rate of 50 percent is a reasonable estimate for a large corporation.

Capital Gains and Losses

Short-term and long-term capital gains and losses arising from corporate trading activities are defined as they were earlier for an individual. The rates applicable to such gains and the treatment of capital losses do, however, differ. A net short-term gain realized by a corporation is added to other corporate taxable income and taxed at the proper bracket rate specified above. A long-term capital gain receives more favorable treatment since it is usually taxed at a rate equal to 28 percent of the net long-term gain realized; no portion of the long-term gain is excludable from taxable income as it is for an individual.

Corporations, moreover, may not deduct any part of the excess of capital losses over capital gains in a given year. Capital losses may only be used to offset capital gains. An excess of capital losses over capital gains in a given year, however, may be carried back for three years and/or carried forward for five successive years to reduce taxable income.

Intercorporate Dividend Payments

The same corporate income is already subject to a double layer of taxation: (1) the corporate income tax is applied to corporate earnings and (2) dividends paid to shareholders out of these already taxed earnings are taxed again as income to the shareholders. To avoid imposing a third layer of taxation, a corporation can exclude 85 percent of all dividends received from taxable income. Assuming an effective tax rate of 46 percent (the maximum corporate rate), corporations pay only an effective rate of about 6.9 percent on dividend income (46 percent times 15 percent). Dividend-paying instruments (such as preferred stocks) can, therefore, be quite attractive to a corporation in terms of after-tax yield even though their before-tax yield is lower than that offered by debt instruments (such as bonds). Remember, debt instruments pay interest, and all interest income is taxable to the corporation. For example, a corporate investor had a strong incentive during March 1981 for purchasing a straight preferred stock, then yielding about 10 percent, rather than an AA corporate bond offering a yield of 13.9 percent. The corporate investor would realize an after-tax yield of 9.31 percent $[.10 - (.10 \times .15 \times .46)]$ by investing in the preferred stock, while realizing only a 7.50 percent after-tax yield $[.139 \times (.139 \times .46)]$ if the bond were chosen instead.

The corporate dividend exclusion cannot, however, be applied to dividends received from nontaxpaying (in the United States) foreign corporations.

Operating Losses

A corporation may carry a business-incurred operating loss, as may an individual, back three years or forward seven years to offset taxable income. The sequence of years in which such a loss must be applied is as follows:

1. The loss must first be carried back and applied to the third year preceding the year in which it occurred, then to the second year, and the first year.
2. Any part of the loss not used by carrying it back may then be carried forward beginning with the year following the loss for seven years, unless fully used before then.

The carry-back and carry-forward provisions with respect to losses help avoid what could otherwise result in a penalty to a corporation that experiences marked fluctuations in income, causing profits in some years and losses in others.

A corporation that was attractive as a merger candidate because the prediction was that proper management could convert losses now being experienced into future profits would become even more attractive since the acquiring firm can typically carry the past losses incurred back or forward to offset its own taxable income. The resultant tax savings heighten the attractiveness of an already attractive candidate. Note, however, that several restrictions may apply, thus limiting the ability of an acquiring corporation to utilize such losses to offset its income for tax purposes.

Summary

The aim of this chapter was to discuss those tax laws of particular interest to investors. A reader should be able to handle many relatively simple tax questions as they arise while recognizing the need for expert tax counsel when such counsel is necessary. The tax code is voluminous; no pretense is made that definitive and complete explanation of that code is offered here.

Many feel that our current tax laws are inequitable, but they are the law. Special-interest groups have had a marked effect on the development of our tax laws and are likely to continue to have such effects in the future. The result has been what many describe as a patchwork of laws rather than a cohesive code. Loopholes do exist in our tax laws, and sound analysis and planning can lower the effective tax rate incurred. A competent tax adviser may well be able to save a client more in terms of tax liability than the fee charged for such services.

Questions

1. The federal income tax is said to have a progressive rate structure. What does this mean? Of what significance is an understanding of this structure to an investor?
2. In what way do U.S. government savings bonds represent an exception to the usual rule for reporting interest income earned through holding bonds? Is this exception an advantage or disadvantage to the investor? Explain.
3. What tax considerations could lead an investor to instruct his or her broker to sell securities for "cash" or "next day settlement"? Explain carefully.
4. Tax considerations are said to favor joint ownership of securities by married couples. Explain why this is so. Discuss considerations

other than taxes that lead a married couple to prefer individual ownership of securities.

5. Several utilities have paid dividends that exceed their reported earnings and were not charged against retained earnings in recent years. What is the tax status of such a dividend?

6. Does the receipt of added shares of a corporation through a stock dividend or stock split by an investor result in taxable income? Answer carefully.

7. Janet Jones purchased 200 shares of ABC stock on January 1, 1980, at $50 a share. She sold the securities "regular way" on December 28, 1980, at $60 a share.
   (a) Would the tax obligation resulting from the gain fall in 1980? Explain.
   (b) If a capital loss rather than a capital gain had been realized, would your answer have been different? Explain.
   (c) Did Janet earn a short-term or long-term capital gain? Explain.

8. What is a short sale against the box? What tax purpose can such a transaction fulfill? Illustrate a short sale against the box and explain the tax effects.

9. Bill and Anne Williams filed a joint tax return for the tax year 1981. During that year Bill received $374 in dividends on stocks that are registered in his name. Anne received $97 in dividends on stocks that are registered in her name. How much of this dividend income can be excluded from tax liability by Bill and Anne? How could they have increased the amount that could have been excluded?

10. Robert Barrett is a college professor. He is paid a salary of $35,000 a year by the college. In addition, he earns $18,000 during the year from consulting activities. Can he establish a Keogh plan? If so, what is the maximum federal income tax-deductible amount he can contribute to that plan?

11. Dorothy Lott is a dentist. She earned $71,500 in taxable income during 1980. What is the maximum tax-deductible amount she can contribute to a Keogh plan during that year?

12. Assume a college professor earned $1,200 as a consultant during a given tax year. What is the maximum tax-deductible amount that he or she can contribute to a Keogh plan during that year?

13. How does an IRA retirement plan differ from a Keogh plan?

14. (a) What is the maximum gift that may be made to any one individual in a given year wthout incurring a gift tax liability? Consider both a single individual and a married couple in your answer.
    (b) Why might the stock of a growth company make an excellent gift on the part of parents to their children?

15. What is the "unified credit" and how may it be used by a taxpayer?

16. How do the tax laws differ in terms of the treatment of capital gains and losses by corporations as opposed to individuals?

Work-Study Problems

1. Jim Smith received one stock right for each of the 200 shares of ABC stock that he had previously purchased at $50 per share. ABC stock had a market value of $54 per share at the time the rights were distributed. The rights had a market value of $3 each when they sold separately in the market.
   (a) Determine the cost basis for a share of the stock and for a right using the allocation method.
   (b) Assume that thirteen months after the distribution of stock rights, Jim Smith sold the 200 shares of ABC stock at $50 a share. Determine the total capital gain or loss he realized (ignoring commissions) for tax purposes. Was the gain or loss long term or short term?
   (c) Assume that Mr. Smith had no other capital transactions during the year, and that a 40 percent tax rate would be applicable to this transaction. What additional tax liability would he incur because of this transaction and what would the after-tax gain on the sale of stock be?
   (d) Assume Mr. Smith sold the 200 rights at $3 per right when he received them. Determine the taxable capital gain or loss incurred and note whether it was a long-term or short-term gain or loss. Ignore commissions.

2. Assume Jane Rodgers had the following short-term and long-term capital gains and losses during a given year:

Short-Term Gains	
Gain on Sale of Du Pont Stock	$2,500
Gain on Sale of Texas Stock	3,000
Gain on Sale of IBM Stock	6,000
Short-Term Losses	
Loss on Sale of First Pennsylvania Bank Stock	$2,000
Long-Term Gains	
Gain on Sale of Reynolds Ind's Stock	$8,200
Gain on Sale of Continental Corp. Stock	$7,600
Long-Term Loss	
Loss on Sale of Exxon Stock	$1,800

   (a) Specify whether Ms. Rodgers has incurred a long-term or short-term capital gain or loss for tax purposes and determine the amount or amounts involved.
   (b) Assuming a 45 percent federal income tax rate is applicable, what total liability would Ms. Rodgers incur because of the above capital transactions?

PART 2
The Analytic Foundations
of Investment Theory

Chapter 7
Stock and Bond Valuation

Chapter 8
Uncertainty Analysis: The Theory of Chance Events

7.

Stock and Bond Valuation

The greatest gift of all gifts is the power to estimate things at their true worth.

La Rochefoucauld, *Reflections, on sentences et maximimes morales.*

Part 1 described the characteristics of the various debt and equity securities available to an investor and the tax environment affecting investor decisions. The chapters in Part I were primarily descriptive in nature. In Part II we now turn to the task of building an analytical framework for making investment decisions.

One of the major decisions facing an investor is whether to buy, hold, or sell particular securities. Such decisions must be made in terms of their impact on portfolio risk and rate of return.[1] The basic building blocks of a portfolio, after all, are the individual assets it contains.

Any valuation approach is aimed at determining an *intrinsic value* of an asset that reflects investors' expectations about future cash flows that will be generated by means of acquisition of that asset. In effect, an intrinsic value is a forecasted value that could be quite different from current market price. Intrinsic value estimates for a given security could differ among individuals since the personal projection of future cash flows and risk could differ.

An important point to recognize is that under conditions of uncertainty intrinsic value estimates can never be precise. They merely provide a yardstick against which to measure current prices on the basis of expectations for future economic and other events. Such estimates are no more accurate than the expectations underlying them. Still, a standard is necessary and useful, even if only a loose one, to serve as a check on the reasonableness of estimations that underlie the selection of portfolios.

---

[1] Portfolio theory is introduced in Section 2, Part 3 of the text.

EXPECTATION, UNCERTAINTY, AND VALUATION THEORY

Investors, acting individually or with others through institutions, invest in order to increase wealth. We assume that the investor seeks the highest level of expected return for any level of risk. However, expectations about future events can be based only in part on known facts, and in part on forecasts that are subject to uncertainty. The interest payments that are supposed to be made on a corporate or municipal bond, for example, may be counted among the known facts, but whether or not such future commitments will be met will be determined, at least in part, by chance factors.

Decisions regarding the purchase or sale of a risky financial security are necessarily based on expectations about the outcome of future chance events. Such events are continually reassessed, whether implicitly or explicitly, and securities that trade in organized markets are "revalued" accordingly. It would be a mistake to suppose that in the aggregate, investors are less uncertain than they are as individuals. According to Keynes, "Our knowledge of the factors which govern the yield of an investment some years hence is usually very slight and often negligible."[2] Valuation theory, therefore, must deal with the evaluation of uncertain future events. In this regard, the assumption of perfect certainty, seemingly implicit in many valuation approaches, is clearly a shortcoming.

The behavior of a financial market is an expectations phenomenon. Investors, individually and collectively, react and often overreact to information as it becomes available. The losses brought about by the following well-documented financial fiascos are examples:[3]

1. *The tulip bulb craze of the 17th century.* Tulip bulb prices were high relative to other flowers in the early 1600s, but the tulip became a much sought after fad by 1630. Dutch merchants began to stockpile tulip bulbs, based on their predictions as to what would be the most sought after color in the coming year. The price of tulip bulbs began to rise wildly as people became aware of the large profits some had already realized. During the final years of the speculative orgy (1634-1638), a single bulb was said to have been exchanged for twelve acres of building ground. A bulb of the Viceroy species commanded all the following in exchange: 17 bushels of wheat, 34 bushels of rye, four fat oxen, 8 fat swine, 12 fat sheep, 2 hogshead of wine, 4 tuns of beer, two tons of butter, 1,000

---

[2] John M. Keynes, *The General Theory of Employment, Interest and Money* (New York: Harcourt Brace, 1936).

[3] The affairs briefly described here are developed more fully in a thought-provoking discussion in Burton G. Malkiel, *A Random Walk Down Wall Street* (New York: W. W. Norton, 1975), Chapters 2 and 3.

pounds of cheese, a bed, a suit of clothes and a silver drinking cup. Prices rose to the equivalent of thousands of dollars for a single tulip bulb of an "in" species.

Some cooler-headed speculators finally began questioning such prices; prices then began to plummet, and panic reigned. Tulip bulbs became practically worthless; the resulting shock has been cited as a major cause of a prolonged depression that then began.

2. *The South Sea bubble of the early 1700s.* The South Sea Company, which was founded in 1711, gave the English government a prommissory note for £ 10 million in exchange for a monopoly over all trade to the South Seas. At that time such trade was thought to yield great riches. The company sold stock, the price of which soon rose from £ 130 to £ 300 per share.

The directors of the company spread favorable rumors. For example, they said that Mexico would empty its gold mines in return for England's abundant supply of cotton and woolen goods. Investors fought to buy a new stock issue by the company at £ 300 per share on April 12, 1720. South Sea Company stock rose to £ 340 per share within a few days. A further issue was soon sold by the company at £ 400 per share, and within a month a still further issue was sold at £ 500 per share. At the height of the speculative craze for this company's stock, the price per share rose from £ 550 to £ 890 in one day. The price of the stock briefly fell during June 1720 from a high of £ 890 to £ 640 per share. Directors bought sufficient shares to stabilize the price and then drive the price to £ 1,000 per share. Other new companies were being formed during this period to take advantage of the speculative fever that gripped the market. Things reached such a degree of absurdity that one company stated it was founded "for carrying on an undertaking of great advantage, but nobody to know what it is." The idea conveyed was that if the venture the company intended to undertake were revealed, it would attract others, thereby lessening its great profit potential. Even in the face of such a complete lack of information, investors fought to subscribe.

The directors of the South Sea Company began selling their shares during the summer of 1720 as prices peaked, and prices fell from £ 1,000 to £ 700 by September 1720. Prices then continued to fall and were soon at £ 150 per share. Many investors suffered very large losses.

3. *The market crash of 1929.* Booming economic conditions during the 1920s made the businessman a favorite of the American public. Growing business profits and faith in the future of the American economy led to a rising stock market and growing enthusiasm by the public concerning stock market prospects. Malkiel and others have noted that much of the increase in stock prices during the period

1923 through 1927 could be explained in terms of fundamentals; dividend payments and earnings per share increased markedly. Speculation then began and accelerated throughout 1928, leading to stock prices that appear to go well beyond levels supportable in terms of fundamentals. Stock prices reached a high during September 1929 and began to fall sharply thereafter, as illustrated in Table 7-1.

TABLE 7-1. Selected Stock Prices, 1928-1932

Security	Opening Price 3/3/28	High Price 9/3/29	Low Price 11/13/29	Low Price 1932
AT&T	$179\frac{1}{2}$	$335\frac{5}{8}$	$197\frac{1}{4}$	$70\frac{1}{4}$
Bethlehem Steel	$56\frac{7}{8}$	$140\frac{3}{8}$	$78\frac{1}{4}$	$7\frac{1}{4}$
General Electric	$128\frac{3}{4}$	$396\frac{1}{4}$	$168\frac{1}{8}$	$8\frac{1}{2}$
Montgomery Ward	$132\frac{3}{4}$	$466\frac{1}{2}$*	$49\frac{1}{4}$	$3\frac{1}{2}$
National Cash Register	$50\frac{3}{4}$	$127\frac{1}{2}$	59	$6\frac{1}{4}$
RCA	$94\frac{1}{2}$	505*	28	$2\frac{1}{2}$

*Adjusted for stock splits.

Source: Burton G. Malkiel, *A Random Walk Down Wall Street* (New York: W. W. Norton, 1975), pp. 38 and 43.

4. *The growth stock craze of 1961.* In 1961 price-earnings ratios for several stocks rose above 50 only to fall sharply in 1962. Table 7-2 illustrates this process for some selected stocks.
5. *The new issue phenomenon of the 1960s.* Companies whose names suggest association with newer technological advances seemed able to sell at high prices unrelated to any performance record. For example, Geophysics Corporation of America was offered on December 8, 1960, at a price of $14 per share. It rose to a bid price of $27 per share on the first day of trading, and reached a high of $58 per share before falling to a price of $9 per share in 1962.
6. *The play on conglomerates and/or "growth companies" during the late 1960s,* illustrated in Table 7-3.
7. *The repeat of the popularity of "growth" stocks in the early 1970s.* "Growth" stocks became popular again in the early 1970s but were shattered by the 1973-74 bear market. Avon was still down 71 percent from its 1972 year-end price; Xerox, 63 percent; Kodak, 48

TABLE 7-2. Price Performance of a Few Selected "Growth" Stocks, 1961–1962

	1961		1962	
Security	High Price	Price-Earnings Ratio	Low Price	Price-Earnings Ratio
IBM	607	80.7	300	34.4
Texas Instruments	$206\frac{3}{4}$	87.6	49	23.0
Microwave Associates	$60\frac{3}{8}$	85.0	8	12.7
Fairchild Camera	$88\frac{1}{4}$	42.0	31	13.1
Perkin-Elmer	$83\frac{1}{2}$	67.3	25	16.7

Source: Burton G. Malkiel, *A Random Walk Down Wall Street* (New York: W. W. Norton, 1975), p. 49.

TABLE 7-3. Price Performance of Selected Conglomerates, 1967–1969

	1967		1969	
Security	High Price	Price-Earnings Ratio	Low Price	Price-Earnings Ratio
Automatic Sprinkler	$73\frac{5}{8}$	51.0	$10\frac{7}{8}$	13.4
Litton Industries	$120\frac{3}{8}$	44.1	35	14.4
Teldynamics	$71\frac{1}{2}$	53.8	$28\frac{1}{4}$	14.2
Textron, Inc.	55	24.9	$23\frac{1}{4}$	10.1

Source: Burton G. Malkiel, *A Random Walk Down Wall Street* (New York: W. W. Norton, 1975), p. 63.

percent; International Flavors, 51 percent; and Coca-Cola, 53 percent in early July 1981.[4]

What is most truly "efficient" about financial markets, therefore, is that the changing waves of optimism and pessimism tend to be *self-fulfilling*, at least in the short run, regardless of how capricious may be the motivation that underlies market expectations.

The systematic use of valuation techniques in concert with modern

---

[4] Charles J. Elia, "Growth Stocks Today Are As Extended in Price As Those of 1972," *The Wall Street Journal*, Monday, July 6, 1981, p. 29.

portfolio selection approaches should reduce the likelihood of including seriously overvalued securities in an investment portfolio.

THE TIME VALUE OF MONEY

The time value of money is a phenomenon common to all valuation approaches. This concept will therefore be developed at the outset. An investor commits a given sum of money, foregoing present consumption, in exchange for the promise of a future stream of benefits. A dollar to be received today, however, is worth more than one to be received at some future date because

1. The risk that a dollar due to be received at a future date may not be received would be avoided were it forthcoming immediately.
2. A dollar in hand could earn a return in each period it is available, leading to an increase in investor wealth.

The timing of cash flows, therefore, is highly important in determining the expected return from an investment.

Future Values and Compound Interest

The process by which interest earns interest upon itself is called *compounding*. Table 7–4 shows the effect of interest compounding at an annual rate of 8 percent on an initial balance of $1,000 over a five-year period. Note the growing importance of interest earned on interest

TABLE 7–4. The Annual Effect of Compounding at 8 Percent over a Five-Year Period

Year	Initial Balance	Interest on Principal	Interest Earned on Reinvested Interest	Total Interest Earned	Year-End Balance
1	$1,000.00	$80.00	0	$ 80.00	$1,080.00
2	1,080.00	80.00	$ 6.40	86.40	1,166.40
3	1,166.40	80.00	13.31	93.31	1,259.71
4	1,259.71	80.00	20.78	100.78	1,360.49
5	1,360.49	80.00	28.84	108.84	1,469.93

through reinvestment. For long-term bonds, for example, the interest-on-interest component may amount to over half the total return received by an investor, depending on the reinvestment assumptions that are made.[5]

_____
[5] Sidney Homer and Martin L. Leibowitz, *Inside the Yield Book*, New York Institute of Finance (Englewood Cliffs, N.J.: 1972), pp. 21-22.

The process of interest compounding may be represented compactly in equation form as follows:

$$TV_t = A_0(1 + r)^t, \tag{7.1}$$

where

TV_t = the terminal value at time t,

A_0 = the cash flow at time $t = 0$, or the invested principal,

r = the periodic interest rate,

t = the number of interest periods for which compounding takes place.

Thus, where $1,000 was placed in an 8 percent interest-bearing account compounded annually, assuming no withdrawals were made during the period, balances for the first and second years corresponding with those shown in Table 7–4 may be calculated as follows:

$$TV_1 = \$1,000(1 + .08)^1 = \$1,080.00;$$
$$TV_2 = \$1,000(1 + .08)^2 = \$1,166.40.$$

Compound return is a more potent growth force than investors sometimes realize. At a compound growth rate of 8 percent, for example, a $1,000 principal would double approximately every nine years. Thus, $1,000 would grow to $8,000 in about 27 years, $50,540 in about 50 years, and $2,550,749 in 100 years. As one wit has said, "Thrift is a marvelous virtue in one's ancestors." The annual rate available on high-quality bonds has generally exceeded 8 percent during the 1970s, surpassing 15 percent in 1981. This high rate has tended to attract funds to debt instruments that would previously (when interest rates were lower) have been invested in stocks.

Present Value

Suppose that a security whose par value is $1,000 is retired at the end of one year with a single lump-sum payment of $1,080 and that there are no payments on the security in the interim. Suppose, moreover, that the actual per annum yield on an ordinary passbook account in a bank is 8 percent. Let us disregard the tax implications for the moment. If the market price of the security were $1,000 or more, the investor would be at least as well off putting the money in the bank at

8 percent. The present value of a single payment to be received at some future point in time, t, may be obtained as follows:

$$PV_t = A_t \left[\frac{1}{(1 + r)^t} \right],$$ (7.2)

where

A_t = cash flow at time t,
r = the discount rate or opportunity cost.

Present value, in the sense of Equation (7.2), is an amount of money, A_0, which, if deposited in an ordinary passbook account whose effective annual yield is r percent, would result in a terminal value TV_t that is precisely equal to the cash flow A_t. For example, substituting into Equation (7.2):

$$PV_t = A_t \left[\frac{1}{(1 + r)^t} \right]$$

$$= \frac{\$1,080}{(1 + .08)^1}$$

$$= \$1,000.$$

Given the alternative provided by an ordinary passbook account whose effective yield is 8 percent, one should not pay more than $1,000 for this security.

Present value tables are presented at the end of this chapter. In Equation (7.2) the present value of the cash flow A_t is obtained by multiplying that cash flow by the quantity:

$$PV_\$ = \frac{1}{(1 + r)^t} .$$ (7.3)

This quantity is the present value of *one dollar* forthcoming at time t. The present value of a one-dollar cash flow, $PV_\$$, will vary, depending on the discount rate r and the timing of that cash flow t. The present value table shows the present value of $1 for various combinations of the discount rate and the timing of cash flow.

Contracts and Annuities. Suppose that a contract involves a stream of cash flows, A_t, t = 1, 2, . . . , T (the number of years to maturity), which represent payments of various amounts for T periods beginning at time, $t = 1$. The present value of a series of cash flows is simply the sum of the present values associated with each cash flow:

$$PV = \sum_{t=1}^{T} A_t \left[\frac{1}{(1+r)^t} \right] \qquad (7.4)$$

An *annuity* is a special form of contract whose payment stream, A_t, $t = 1, 2, \ldots, T$, consists of payments, A_c, which are the same from one period to the next. If we substitute the constant A_c for the variable A_t in Equation (7.4), the constant factors out, and the result simplifies as follows:

$$PV = A_c \left[\sum_{t=1}^{T} \frac{1}{(1+r)^t} \right]. \qquad (7.5)$$

Equation (7.5) defines the present value of an annuity which offers a constant payment, A_c, where the appropriate discount rate is r. In the special case where the constant payment is $A_c = \$1.00$, the constant A_c drops out of Equation (7.5) and we obtain:

$$PV_\$ = \left[\sum_{t=1}^{T} \frac{1}{(1+r)^t} \right]. \qquad (7.6)$$

Equation (7.6) defines the present value of a one-dollar annuity to be received for T periods, beginning at the end of period $t = 1$, where the discount rate is r. The present value of *any* annuity, of course, will vary, depending on the variables A_c, T, and r.

An annuity table is presented in the chapter appendix, which sets out the present value of a one-dollar annuity for various combinations of the discount rate r and time periods T. For example, suppose an investor wished to know the present value of $1 to be received one year from today, assuming 8 percent compounded annually could be earned in alternative uses of the money. Using Equation (7.3) the present value is:

$$PV_\$ = \frac{1}{(1+r)^t} = \frac{1}{(1 + .08)} = .92593.$$

The present value of $1 to be received each year for the next three years, assuming 8 percent can be earned in alternative uses of the funds, is determined by adding the present values of each individual receipt, as determined from Table 7-A in the chapter appendix:

$$PV_1 = .926$$
$$PV_2 = .857$$
$$PV_3 = \underline{.794}$$

Present value of series = $2.577

If $850 is expected each year for three years rather than $1, the present value of such a series can be calculated by multiplying $850 × 2.577, or the present value is $2,190.45.

Perpetuities. While all bonds in the United States have a maturity date, the British Consuls are perpetual bonds. A consul pays interest to perpetuity to whoever happens to own it, but the principal is never repaid.

The present value of a consul at any moment in time is equal to the net present value of all interest payments due into perpetuity and may be expressed as follows:

$$PV = A_c \left[\sum_{t=1}^{\infty} \frac{1}{(1+r)^t} \right], \tag{7.7}$$

where A_c is the constant interest payment and r is the discount rate.

The calculation of this present value is simplified by exploiting the fact that the summation in Equation (7.7) has a limit:

$$PV = \frac{A_c}{r} \tag{7.7a}$$

Equation (7.7a) may be used in actual computations. For example, the maximum price an investor, who could earn 9 percent on alternative investments of equivalent risk, would pay for at 6 percent, $1,000 par Consul would be $666.67 ($60/.09).

BOND VALUATION

The basic idea underlying all valuation approaches is the present value concept. The value of a bond, therefore, can be defined as the total present value of all interest payments plus the present value of the return of principal upon maturity. The amount of each interest payment, the time pattern in which they will be paid, and the face value of the bond are specified in a bond contract.

It is important to understand that investors seek a yield when purchasing bonds that is commensurate with alternative possible uses of funds. The yields desired by investors change over time as the supply of and the demand for loanable funds change. Bond prices also change over time, reflecting changing desired yields and other market phenomena.

Yield to Maturity

The yield to maturity on a bond is that discount rate which equates the purchase price of a bond to the present value of the cash inflows. This is merely the internal rate of return, r^*, which is defined in the following identity:

$$\sum_{t=0}^{T} \frac{A_t}{(1 + r^*)^t} = 0, \tag{7.8}$$

where A_t is the cash flow for period t, whether it be a net cash outflow or inflow, and T is the last period in which a cash flow is expected.

To illustrate, suppose that a $1,000 par bond has five years remaining to maturity, a 4 percent coupon rate, and interest that is payable semiannually. If market conditions are such as to require a 6 percent yield to maturity, we see from Table 7-5 that the bond would sell for

TABLE 7-5. Determination of Present Value of a 4 Percent Coupon, $1,000 Par, Five-Year Bond When 6 Percent Yield to Maturity Is Desired

Period	Cash Flow	Present Value Factor @ 3%	Present Value of Cash Flow
1	$ 20	.970874	$ 19.418
2	20	.942596	18.852
3	20	.915142	18.303
4	20	.888487	17.770
5	20	.862609	17.252
6	20	.837484	16.750
7	20	.813092	16.262
8	20	.789409	15.788
9	20	.766417	15.328
10	1,020	.744094	758.976
Sum of present values			$914.699

Note: Three-place present value tables, both for the present value of $1 received at the end of year and for $1 received annually at the end of each year for n years, are presented in an appendix at the end of this chapter. Six-place accuracy for discount factors was used in the example to minimize rounding error.

$914.70 (which is the present value of the future cash inflows). Since cash flows are received semiannually, they are not discounted at the 6 percent annual rate, but at one-half the annual rate.

Bond yield tables eliminate the necessity of performing laborious calculations such as that illustrated in Table 7–5. Table 7–6 shows the various prices required to offer given yields to maturity for a 4 percent coupon bond maturing in five years. The numbers in the body of the table represent a percentage of par value. For example, a five-year, 4 percent coupon bond should sell at 91.47 percent of par value to yield 6 percent to maturity, or at a price of $914.70 for a $1,000 par bond.

TABLE 7-6. Coupon Yield Tables, 4 Percent Coupon

	Years and Months							
Yield	4–9	4–10	4–11	5–0	5–3	5–6	5–9	6–0
2.00	109.02	109.17	109.32	109.47	109.92	110.37	110.81	111.26
2.20	108.07	108.21	108.34	108.48	108.88	109.28	109.67	110.07
2.40	107.14	107.26	107.38	107.50	107.85	108.20	108.54	108.89
2.60	106.21	106.32	106.42	106.52	106.83	107.13	107.43	107.73
2.80	105.30	105.39	105.47	105.56	105.82	106.08	106.33	106.59
3.00	104.39	104.46	104.54	104.61	104.82	105.04	105.24	105.45
3.20	103.50	103.55	103.61	103.67	103.83	104.01	104.17	104.34
3.40	102.61	102.65	102.69	102.74	102.86	102.99	103.11	103.23
3.60	101.73	101.76	101.79	101.82	101.89	101.98	102.06	102.14
3.80	100.86	100.87	100.89	100.90	100.94	100.98	101.02	101.06
4.00	100.00	100.00	100.00	100.00	100.00	100.00	100.00	100.00
4.20	99.14	99.13	99.12	99.11	99.06	99.03	98.98	98.95
4.40	98.30	98.27	98.25	98.22	98.14	98.06	97.98	97.91
4.60	97.46	97.42	97.38	97.35	97.22	97.11	96.99	96.89
4.80	96.63	96.58	96.53	96.48	96.32	96.17	96.02	95.87
5.00	95.81	95.75	95.68	95.62	95.43	95.24	95.05	94.87
5.10	95.40	95.33	95.27	95.20	94.98	94.78	94.57	94.38
5.20	95.00	94.92	94.85	94.78	94.54	94.32	94.10	93.88
5.30	94.60	94.51	94.43	94.36	94.10	93.87	93.62	93.39
5.40	94.20	94.11	94.02	93.94	93.67	93.41	93.15	92.91
5.50	93.80	93.70	93.61	93.52	93.23	92.96	92.68	92.42
5.60	93.40	93.30	93.20	93.11	92.80	92.52	92.22	91.94
5.70	93.01	92.90	92.80	92.69	92.37	92.07	91.76	91.46
5.80	92.61	92.50	92.39	92.28	91.95	91.63	91.30	90.99
5.90	92.22	92.10	91.99	91.88	91.52	91.19	90.84	90.52
6.00	91.83	91.71	91.59	91.47	91.10	90.75	90.39	90.05
6.10	91.44	91.32	91.19	91.07	90.68	90.31	89.94	89.58
6.20	91.06	90.93	90.79	90.66	90.26	89.88	89.49	89.12
6.30	90.68	90.54	90.40	90.26	89.85	89.45	89.04	88.65
6.40	90.29	90.15	90.01	89.87	89.43	89.02	88.60	88.20
6.50	89.91	89.76	89.62	89.47	89.02	88.59	88.16	87.74
6.60	89.54	89.38	89.23	89.08	88.61	88.17	87.72	87.29
6.70	89.16	89.00	88.84	88.69	88.21	87.75	87.28	86.84
6.80	88.79	88.62	88.46	88.30	87.80	87.33	86.85	86.39
6.90	88.41	88.24	88.08	87.91	87.40	86.91	86.42	85.95
7.00	88.04	87.87	87.70	87.53	87.00	86.50	85.99	85.50
7.10	87.67	87.49	87.32	87.14	86.60	86.09	85.56	85.07
7.20	87.31	87.12	86.94	86.76	86.20	85.68	85.14	84.63
7.30	86.94	86.75	86.57	86.38	85.81	85.27	84.72	84.20
7.40	86.58	86.38	86.19	86.00	85.42	84.86	84.30	83.76
7.50	86.22	86.02	85.82	85.63	85.03	84.46	83.88	83.34
7.60	85.86	85.65	85.45	85.25	84.64	84.06	83.47	82.91

TABLE 7–6. Coupon Yield Tables, 4 Percent Coupon (*continued*)

Yield	Years and Months

Yield	4–9	4–10	4–11	5–0	5–3	5–6	5–9	6–0
7.70	85.50	85.29	85.08	84.88	84.26	83.66	83.06	82.49
7.80	85.14	84.93	84.72	84.51	83.87	83.26	82.65	82.06
7.90	84.79	84.57	84.36	84.14	83.49	82.87	82.24	81.65
8.00	84.44	84.21	83.99	83.78	83.11	82.48	81.84	81.23
8.10	84.09	83.86	83.63	83.41	82.74	82.09	81.44	80.82
8.20	83.74	83.50	83.28	83.05	82.36	81.70	81.04	80.41
8.30	83.39	83.15	82.69	82.69	81.99	81.32	80.64	80.00
8.40	83.04	82.80	82.57	82.33	81.62	80.93	80.24	79.59
8.50	82.70	82.45	82.21	81.98	81.25	80.55	79.85	79.19
8.60	82.36	82.11	81.86	81.62	80.88	80.17	79.46	78.79
8.70	82.02	81.76	81.51	81.27	80.51	79.80	79.07	78.39
8.80	81.68	81.42	81.17	80.92	80.15	79.42	78.69	77.99
8.90	81.34	81.08	80.82	80.57	79.79	79.05	78.30	77.60
9.00	81.00	80.74	80.48	80.22	79.43	78.68	77.92	77.20
9.20	80.34	80.06	79.79	79.53	78.71	77.94	77.16	76.43
9.40	79.68	79.39	79.12	78.84	78.01	77.22	76.42	75.66
9.60	79.02	78.73	78.45	78.17	77.31	76.50	75.68	74.90
9.80	78.37	78.08	77.78	77.50	76.62	75.78	74.95	74.15
10.00	77.73	77.43	77.13	76.83	75.93	75.08	74.22	73.41

Source: Reproduced from *Expanded Bond Values Table,* Publication #83, p. 299. Copyright 1970, Financial Publishing Company, Boston Massachusetts.

The Reinvestment Assumption. Yield to maturity calculations assume that all interim cash flows are reinvested at the yield to maturity rate. This can be illustrated by noting that if $914.70 were invested at a 6 percent rate compounded semiannually for five years, it would grow to $1,229.28. Alternatively, a receipt of $20 every six months for five years, assuming receipts are reinvested at 6 percent compounded semiannually over the five-year period, plus $1,000 at the end of the fifth year, would also result in a wealth position of $1,229.28 at the end of the period, as shown in Table 7–7.

The realized yield on a bond held to maturity will in most instances be quite different from the yield to maturity calculated at purchase due to changing money market conditions and reinvestment rates over the life of the bond. If the $20-semiannual interest payments in the previous illustration were reinvested at less than the assumed 6 percent annualized rate, the realized yield would be less than 6 percent upon maturity. Of course, if interest payments were reinvested at a rate higher than 6 percent, realized yield would exceed 6 percent upon maturity. If a bond is not held to maturity, of course, the realized yield may again be quite different since the reinvestment period has changed and the price at which the bond was sold could be quite different from face value.

Rising interest rates after purchase of a bond would allow reinvestment at higher rates than assumed by the yield to maturity calculation but would cause the price of the bond to fall, resulting in a lower

TABLE 7-7. An Illustration of the Reinvestment Assumption

Period	Cash Received and Reinvested	Terminal Value of $1 Invested for T Years	Terminal Value
1	$ 20	$(1.03)^9$	$ 26.097
2	20	$(1.03)^8$	25.337
3	20	$(1.03)^7$	24.599
4	20	$(1.03)^6$	23.882
5	20	$(1.03)^5$	23.186
6	20	$(1.03)^4$	22.511
7	20	$(1.03)^3$	21.855
8	20	$(1.03)^2$	21.218
9	20	$(1.03)^1$	20.600
10	1,020	1	1,020.000
Total			$1,229.285

terminal value if sold before maturity. A decline in quality (as perceived in the market) after purchase would also result in a fall in price, other things being equal. Therefore, an investor is subject to "price risk" when interest rates rise after purchase or quality of the bond declines. If interest rates fell after purchase or quality improved, of course, the result would be precisely the opposite.

The reinvestment assumption has other important implications, as when selecting among discount, par, and premium bonds. When rising interest rates are anticipated, an investor should prefer premium or par bonds since their coupon rates will be higher than those on discount bonds of equivalent quality. Under these conditions, an investor seeks to maximize the current interest receipts so as to obtain more to reinvest at rising rates. On the other hand, when interest rates are expected to decline, deep discount bonds would be attractive. A large part of the total yield for a deep discount bond is represented by the accumulation (excess of face value over purchase price) received upon maturity, which will not have to be reinvested at falling rates.

Tax-Adjusted Yield to Maturity. For tax purposes, a bond bought at a discount receives a portion of its return in the form of a capital gain. The effective tax rate on long-term capital gains is less than one-half the ordinary income rate, which is applicable to interest income for most taxpayers.[6] Any comparison of expected return should therefore be made on an after-tax basis.

[6] See Chapter 6 for a discussion of the taxation of capital gains.

For example, an individual in the 50 percent tax bracket should prefer a municipal bond yielding 7 percent to maturity and purchased at par to a corporate bond yielding 10 percent if the risk of the two is assumed to be equal and the return on the corporate bond is half in the form of interest income and half in the form of long-term capital gain. The 7 percent income on the municipal is not taxed, while half of the 5 percent interest income on the corporate bond is taxed away and 40 percent of the capital gain is taxed at the 50 percent rate, leaving an after-tax return of 6.50 percent. By contrast, an investor in a 20 percent tax bracket would logically prefer the corporate bond since the after-tax return would be 8.6 percent. When selecting securities, investors should compare after-tax returns that represent their individual tax situation.

Yield to Call. A call clause gives the issuing corporation the right, at its discretion, to require that the bonds be submitted for payment prior to maturity at some designated price. A corporation would only exercise the call privilege when an opportunity existed to refinance an issue at a lower interest cost. When a call clause is exercised, the bondholder receives a return significantly different from that suggested by yield to maturity. For this reason, the yield to call, rather than the yield to maturity, should be used when one expects a bond to be called prior to maturity.

The date at which a bond will be called is uncertain. In fact, a call clause may never be exercised, depending on whether or not interest rates fall sufficiently after issue to make refinancing a practical alternative. In view of this uncertainty, a yield to call is typically calculated in either of two ways:

1. Yield to call may be calculated so as to reflect the lowest assured yield.
2. Relative probabilities may be assigned to the possibility of call at various dates, and used as weights to determine a weighted average yield to maturity.

To illustrate, assume that 10 percent bonds issued by Corporation X are callable after five years at $1,050 per bond. The bonds currently sell at par and thus yield 10 percent to maturity, which is ten years hence. Assume, moreover, that interest rate expectations are such that one assigns a 20 percent chance that the bonds will not be called and an 80 percent chance that they will be called in five years. If called, further assume the investor would be forced to reinvest at 8 percent. Corporation X bonds, if called, would therefore pay $50 semiannually for the first five years and $42 ($1,050 × .08/2) semiannually for the next five years, plus $1,050 at the end of the tenth year.

The bonds will yield precisely 10 percent if they are not called, and approximately 9.1 percent if they are called. The weighted average yield is calculated as follows:

Assumption	Possibility	× Yield	= Weighted Yield
Not called	.20	.10	.0200
Called	.80	.091	.0728
	Weighted average yield		.0928

The weighted average yield will never actually materialize; the bond will be called or not called. The weighted average of 9.28 percent is a mathematical expectation (to be developed more completely in the next chapter), while the 9.1 percent yield to call is the minimum yield that might be realized according to the stated assumptions.

Approximating Net Yield to Maturity. When bond yield tables and present value tables are not readily available, an approximation of the net yield to maturity is provided by

$$YTM = \frac{C + \dfrac{F - P}{T}}{\dfrac{F + P}{2}}, \qquad (7.9)$$

where

YTM = net yield maturity,
C = annual dollars paid in interest,
F = face or par value of the bond,
P = selling price of the bond,
T = number of years to maturity.

For a 4 percent, $1,000 bond purchased at $914.70, with five years remaining to maturity, we obtain

$$YTM = \frac{40 + \dfrac{1000 - 914.70}{5}}{\dfrac{100 + 914.70}{2}} = \frac{57.06}{957.35} = 0.59602,$$

according to this approximation.

Current Yield

Current yield on a bond is calculated by dividing the annual interest received in dollars by the cash price of the bond. For a 4 percent bond selling at $914.70, for example, the current yield would be 4.37 percent. This yield concept becomes significant when cash flow is highly important. The current yield measures the annual cash rate of return on the bond.

Bonds bought at a discount might offer attractive net yields to maturity; but if maturity will not occur for 20 years, an individual dependent on current income could suffer markedly waiting for that far distant cash flow at maturity that makes up a large part of the return that will be realized. Current yield rather than net yield to maturity, moreover, is often quoted on very speculative bonds. The yield to maturity is less meaningful the more uncertain the flow of future payments. Where the emphasis is on cash flow, the appropriate measure is current yield.

The current yield on a bond is sometimes referred to as the "stock yield." This terminology confuses the issue since the interest payments on a bond are a contractual obligation of the corporation, while dividend payments are discretionary. Corporations, even large, well-known corporations such as General Motors and U.S. Steel, have cut dividend payments during recession periods. Also, dividends may increase over time. The two concepts are quite different.

Conclusions Concerning Bond Yields and Prices

Under conditions of perfect certainty, the value of a bond (or any other investment asset) is the present value of all anticipated cash flows. Bond prices change from time to time, reflecting changing market conditions and quality ratings for individual bonds. Bond prices vary inversely, moreover, with each change in minimum required yield.

Yield to maturity calculations assume reinvestment of all cash flows at the yield to maturity rate. This explains the advantage of discount over par or premium bonds for an investor who expects interest rates to decline over the time the bond will be held, as a part of the return on a discount bond is fixed and thus would not be subject to reinvestment at a lower interest rate. If interest rates are expected to increase over time, by contrast, premium bonds would have an advantage. One's expectation concerning future interest rates, therefore, is an important consideration when purchasing bonds.

STOCK VALUATION

Under conditions of certainty, a stock's intrinsic value, as with a bond, would be the discounted present value of all future cash flows. Stocks (preferred or common), however, offer no legal commitment to pay dividends or return principal as bonds do, and thus the valuation of future cash flows is more complicated. The stream of income that will flow to stockholders is highly uncertain and depends on corporate success and the outcome of other chance events. As noted earlier, an intrinsic value can never be precisely determined. The systematic use of valuation theory, however, should serve an important purpose as a check on the reasonableness of current market price and the inputs that enter into portfolio selection approaches introduced in Part 3 of this book.

Traditional valuation theory treats all future cash flows as known certainties, which, of course, they can never be in the real world. Current writers on the subject are more thoughtful. A formal introduction to uncertainty and risk is presented in Chapter 8. The literature of uncertainty analysis has much to contribute to useful applications of valuation techniques.

Historical Background

The stock market crash in 1929, which by 1932 culminated in a 90 percent decline in the Dow Jones Index, stimulated efforts to develop a theory of stock valuation. The development of formal stock valuation approaches seems to have begun in 1930 when Robert F. Weiss stated that "the proper price of any security, whether a stock or a bond, is the sum of all the future income payments discounted at the current rate of interest in order to arrive at present value."[7]

Samuel Elliot Guild[8] was the first to present a series of tables based on the present value approach for the purpose of measuring intrinsic value. Guild's approach was an ad hoc approach that assumed the following:

1. The average rate at which company earnings would grow over the time period in question.
2. The dividend-earnings ratio of the corporation over the time period in question.
3. The price-earnings ratio that would prevail for the stock at the end of the holding period selected.
4. The internal rate of return or yield required by the investor.

Guild's objective was to provide an investor with a simple procedure for calculating the maximum price, given a set of known parameters, that would be commensurate with a specified rate of return.[9]

---

[7] R. F. Weiss, "Investing for True Value," *Barron's*, September 8, 1930.

[8] S. E. Guild, *Stock Growth and Discount Tables* (Boston: Financial Publishing Co., 1931).

[9] For expansions of the Guild tables utilizing a present value approach and incorporating more sophisticated assumptions, see R. M. Soldofsky and J. T. Murphy, *Growth Yields on Common Stocks: Theories and Tables*, Rev. ed. (Iowa City: Bureau of Business and Economic Research, State University of Iowa, 1964); W. Scott Bauman, *Estimating the Present Value of Common Stocks by the Variable Rate Method*, Monograph (Ann Arbor: Bureau of Business Research, The University of Michigan, 1963); and N. Molodovsky, C. May, and S. Chottiner, "Common Stock Valuation: Theory and Tables," *Financial Analysts Journal* (March–April, 1965), pp. 104–112.

John Burr Williams[10] was the first to provide a comprehensive and rigorous foundation on which the intrinsic value of a stock could be defined. While Williams's contribution was singularly important in the development of a modern theory of security valuation, it suffered from at least one serious shortcoming: Williams, as was the fashion among academics in his day,[11] treated all cash flows as known certainties. No account was taken by Williams of uncertainty regarding either future cash flows, one's knowledge about these flows, or the likelihood that the appropriate discount rate would not remain constant over the holding period assumed for the stock. These shortcomings, unfortunately, have not yet been fully corrected and are a serious deficiency of both existing stock valuation and portfolio selection approaches. This point is taken up at length in Chapter 13.

Present Value Approaches

Asset values, as recorded on a balance sheet, are not utilized in stock valuation theory. Accounting values (original cost less accumulated depreciation) tell us little about the current worth of a company. The liquidation value of a firm's assets is also of little significance since liquidation will usually occur only when serious financial difficulties have been encountered.

An investment asset has *value* because an owner anticipates receiving future cash flows from it. The value of an asset, therefore, depends on the size of the future cash flows generated, the time pattern over which they are to be received, the risk involved, and the rate that could be earned in alternative uses of the funds. What is important, therefore, is current expectation concerning the cash flows, and not what was paid to acquire an asset at some time in the past.

Dividend-Capitalization Models. A corporation is granted a charter into perpetuity, and the presumption is made that it will be in existence for an infinite period. Williams held, therefore, that the current value of a stock should represent the discounted present value of the dividend payments that would be forthcoming over that infinite time horizon. This relationship is expressed by the equation:

$$PV = \sum_{t=1}^{\infty} D_t \left[\frac{1}{(1 + k)^t} \right],$$ (7.10)

---

[10] J. B. Williams, *The Theory of Investment Value* (1938; reprint ed., Amsterdam, The Netherlands: North Holland Publishing Co., 1964).
[11] See F. H. Knight, *Risk, Uncertainty and Profit* (London School of Economics and Political Science, Series of Reprints of Scarce Tracts, No. 16, 1933).

where

D_t = the dividend per share in period t,
k = the market return appropriate to a pure equity stream, or the discount rate.

Where the dividend payment is to be made into perpetuity at a constant rate (the no-growth case), Equation (7.10) simplifies to

$$PV = \frac{D}{k}, \tag{7.10a}$$

which defines the present value of a perpetuity.

Book Value versus Intrinsic Value. The no-growth assumption would apply to a firm whose capital (C) and the rate of return earned on that capital (r) remained constant, further assuming that the firm paid all profits as dividends in the year earned. Total profits of the firm could be defined as (rC), and total dividend payments would also equal (rC). The value of the firm's stock would then equal

$$V_0 = \frac{rC0}{(1 + k)} + \frac{rC0}{(1 + k)^2} + \ldots + \frac{rC0}{(1 + k)^\infty}$$

$$V_0 = \frac{rC0}{k}.$$

Although this model is unrealistic, it does provide interesting insight into the relation between book value of the firm (C_0) and intrinsic value (V_0). If $r = k$, then book value (C_0) equals intrinsic value (V_0). If r is greater than k, however, intrinsic value (V_0) will exceed book value. This conclusion is quite reasonable since the firm is assumed to earn a higher rate on new investment than that required by the market. On the other hand, if r is less than k, intrinsic value (and, therefore, market value) will be less than book value.

Not surprisingly, therefore, stocks typically sell at a price different from book value. A firm is not likely to earn a return on new investment exactly equal to the market-required return for investment in its stock over any extended period of time.

A growth firm, in terms of the above logic, can be defined as a firm earning a higher rate of return on new investments (r) than market-required return for investment in its stock (k). A declining firm would be one where $k > r$.

Growth Models. To assume that dividend payments could be constant into perpetuity is unrealistic. Dividends do change over time, reflecting corporate success or failure and market factors. Stocks are usually purchased with the anticipation of corporate success and dividend growth, and models have been developed by Gordon[12] and Lerner and Carleton[13] which incorporate a constant growth assumption. The constant growth assumption, as we shall see, does little to overcome the deficiencies that are inherent in dividend capitalization models.

Let the dividend received on a particular stock at time $t = 0$ be D_0 (the current dividend). Suppose that dividends will grow at a constant rate, g, forever. The dividend at any future point in time, t, therefore, is simply:

$$D_t = D_0(1 + g)^t. \tag{7.11}$$

Substituting Equation (7.11) into Equation (7.10) and simplifying we obtain

$$PV = D_0 \left[\sum_{t=1}^{\infty} \frac{(1+g)^t}{(1+k)^t} \right]. \tag{7.12}$$

Provided that the discount rate, k, is larger than the growth rate, g, it can be shown that Equation (7.12) is mathematically equivalent to[14]

$$PV = \frac{D_1}{k - g}, \tag{7.13}$$

where D_1 is the dividend to be received at time $t = 1$.

Discounting Dividends Rather Than Earnings. Earnings not paid out in dividends are retained. When retained earnings are invested in profitable projects, the added earnings produce opportunities for higher future dividends. A present value approach, therefore, considers the earnings potential that results from the reinvested earnings by taking account of the future dividends generated. It would be double counting to discount both present earnings and future dividends that result from earnings retention.

Implicit Consideration of Capital Gains. A shareholder who sells his or her stock might well realize a capital gain as well as receiving divi-

---

[12] M. J. Gordon, *The Investment, Financing and Valuation of the Corporation* (Homewood, Ill.: Richard D. Irwin, 1962).
[13] Eugene M. Lerner and Willard T. Carleton, *A Theory of Financial Analysis* (New York: Harcourt, Brace & World, 1966).
[14] For proof see Lerner and Carleton, ibid., pp. 105–108.

dends. Capital gains are considered in the above growth model, consistent with the assumed dividend growth rate and constant discount rate. To illustrate, assume Firm A pays a $1 dividend at the end of the first year of holding the stock (D_1), and dividends are expected to grow at a constant rate of 8 percent. Further assume that opportunity cost of a particular investor is 14 percent. The intrinsic value of Firm A stock at this moment according to equation (7.13) is

$$PV_a = \frac{D_1}{k - g} = \frac{1}{.14 - .08} = \frac{1}{.06} = \$16.67.$$

Let us now determine the present value of the stock five years from now, utilizing the same growth and discount rate assumptions:

$$PV_{a_5} = \frac{D_6}{k - g}.$$

The expected dividend at the end of year five (D_6) is

$$D_6 = \$1 \ (1 + g)^5 = \$1 \ (1.08)^5 = \$1 \ (1.46933) = \$1.46933.$$

The value of Firm A stock at the end of year five would, therefore, be

$$PV_{a_5} = \frac{D_6}{k - g} = \frac{\$1.46933}{14 - .08} = 24.488.$$

Discounting the expected cash flows generated by holding the stock for five years, we arrive at a consistent present value of $16.67, as calculated below:

End of Period	Cash Flow Dividend	Cash Flow Sales Price	Discount Factor	
1	1.0000	—	.87719	0.87719
2	1.0800	—	.76947	0.83103
3	1.1664	—	.67497	0.78729
4	1.2597	—	.59208	0.74584
5	1.3605	24.4888	.51937	13.42535
Total Present Value				16.66667

We have ignored the impact of taxes in the above calculations, which will be introduced in our discussion of a finite holding period below.

Dividend Policy and Stock Valuation. Miller and Modigliani argued that the value of a firm is not affected by the dividend policy of that firm in a world without taxes or transaction costs.[15] Let us illustrate this argument in terms of a dividend growth valuation model.

Consider a firm that expands its capital (C) each year by retaining a portion of earnings (b). Profit for this firm can be defined in terms of the rate earned on capital (r) or as rC_0. Retained earnings would then equal brC_0. Capital one year hence would equal capital at the beginning of the year (C_0) plus retained earnings brC_0. The rate of growth in capital can then be expressed as

$$g = \frac{C_1 - C_0}{C_0} = \frac{[C_0 + brC_0] - C_0}{C_0} = \frac{brC_0}{C_0} = br. \qquad (7.14)$$

The rate of growth in dividends, in accordance with the above assumptions, also equals br:

$$g = \frac{D_1 - D_0}{D_0} = \frac{[(1 - b)r(C_0 + brC_0)] - [(1 - b)rC_0]}{(1 - b)rC_0} \qquad (7.15)$$

$$= (1 + br) - 1 = br.$$

Now, we restate equation (7.13) in terms of earnings per share (e) and an assumed dividend payout ratio ($1 - b$).

$$V_0 = \frac{e_1(1 - b)}{k - br}, \qquad \text{since } g = br. \qquad (7.16)$$

If one further assumes that the firm exactly earns the rate required by the market on new investments in accordance with capital budgeting literature ($k = r$), the valuation equation can be restated as follows:

$$V_0 = \frac{e_1(1 - b)}{k - bk} = \frac{e_1(1 - b)}{k(1 - b)} = \frac{e_1}{k}. \qquad (7.16a)$$

Under these assumptions, dividend policy is irrelevant (it has no effect on the valuation of the firm) since b cancels out.

The above conclusion obviously does not follow when r and k differ or when taxes and transaction costs are considered. Ross, moreover,

_____
[15] M. Miller and F. Modigliani, "Dividend Policy, Growth and the Valuation of Shares," *The Journal of Business* (October, 1961), pp. 411–433.

points out that a firm is valued on the basis of the *perceived* stream of cash flows that an investment in that firm will generate, and that changes in dividend policy could well alter the market's perceptions[16] and thus affect the firm's valuation. For example, if the dividend were reduced, the market might well interpret this reduction as implying a reduction in future profitability, resulting in the sale of shares and downward pressure on market price and intrinsic value estimations. The relation between k and r does appear to be the critical variable when trying to assess the likely impact of dividend policy changes on stock values.

Finite Horizons and Valuation. Investors have the opportunity to sell their stock at any time and likely perceive of their investment horizons as limited to some finite period. A model that assumes an infinite horizon would not serve as a very useful basis for stock selection or as a check on the reasonableness of estimations that enter into application of a portfolio selection model.

A limited holding period model, by contrast, assumes a sale of the stock being valued at the end of an assumed holding period. The present value, in this context, is the sum of the present values associated with the dividends received during a holding period, plus the present value of the sales price at the end of the holding period:

$$PV = \sum_{t=1}^{T} \left[\frac{D_t}{(1+k)^t} \right] + \frac{P_T}{(1+k)^T}, \qquad (7.17)$$

where P_T is the expected sales price. Equation (7.17) can be rewritten in terms of earnings per share as follows:

$$PV = C_0 l \sum_{t=1}^{T} \frac{(1+g)^t}{(1+k)^t} + \frac{C_0 M_c (1+g)^T}{(1+k)^T}, \qquad (7.17a)$$

where

C_0 = current earnings per share,
g = the anticipated compound annual growth rate of earnings per share,
l = the proportion of earnings paid out as dividends in each holding period,
M_c = the multiplier applied to earnings per share in the terminal year to determine selling price,
k = the appropriate discount rate.

---

[16] S. A. Ross, "The Determination of Financial Structure: The Incentive-Signaling Approach," *The Bell Journal of Economics* (Spring, 1977), pp. 23–40.

Equations (7.17) and (7.17a) can be modified to account for the effects of taxation. To illustrate, suppose that

1. A stock is purchased at year-end 1978 at $95 per share;
2. Dividend income is taxed at a 50 percent rate and capital gains at an effective rate of 20 percent (in accordance with current capital gains tax law);
3. Earnings per share at the time of purchase are $9.50, and are expected to grow at a compound annual rate of 6 percent;
4. The company pays out 55 percent of earnings in the form of dividends each year;
5. The stock will be sold at the end of the third year, and a price-earnings ratio of 15 is expected to apply to the stock at the time of sale;
6. A rate of 8 percent is available in alternative investment opportunities felt to be of equivalent risk.

Based on these assumptions, the present value of the stock is found to be $127.44, by means of the following sample calculation:

Year	EPS	Dividends	After-Tax Dividend	After-Tax Proceed from Sale	Present Value Factor @ 8%	Present Value of Cash Flow
1978	9.50					
1979	10.07	5.54	2.77		.926	2.565
1980	10.67	5.87	2.94		.857	2.520
1981	11.31	6.22	3.11	154.72*	.794	125.317
Present Value of Stock						130.402

*The expected selling price of $169.65 (15 $\times$ 11.31) less the capital gains tax of $14.93 ([74.65 (capital gain) $\times$ .4 $\times$ .5]).

The model described by Equation (7.17a) may be used in sensitivity analysis; that is, the estimates of C_0, P, g, k, and T can be varied one at a time, or in combination, to determine the sensitivity of the valuation estimate to changes in these parameters. The model does not require a constant growth rate or discount rate assumption, and to this extent is more realistic.

Growth Duration. The longer one projects an above-average growth rate for dividends and earnings, the higher will be the present value of the stock as calculated by any of the models discussed above. There is always some combination of growth rate and growth period that will justify any current market price. This point is made nicely by an illustrative valuation of IBM stock by Williamson.[17] In 1968 IBM sold at about

---

[17] J. Peter Williamson, *Investments: New Analytic Techniques* (New York: Praeger, 1971), pp. 155–159.

$320 per share; 1967 earnings were $5.80 per share, and dividends were $2.17 per share. Consistent with recent growth, Williamson predicted earnings per share of $7 for 1968. He initially forecast a 16 percent earnings growth rate for ten years, followed by indefinite growth of 2 percent and a dividend payout rate of 40 percent, which were in line with experience for IBM over the previous ten years. Using a discount rate of 7 percent, he calculated an intrinsic value of $172.94. Noting that this represented about one-half of the current market value, Williamson said, "It does not seem sensible to predict only ten years of above-average growth for IBM, so I extended my growth forecast to twenty years." Now the intrinsic value came to $432.66—well above the market. When a 10 percent discount rate was substituted for the 7 percent rate, and a growth rate of 16 percent for twenty years, however, Williamson found an intrinsic value of only $205.73.

Clearly, a growth model is quite sensitive to changes in the parameters included. The illustration shows the importance of not being carried away by enthusiasm that may prevail from time to time in the market and the tenuous nature of intrinsic value estimates.

Limitations of Dividend Valuation Models. The models discussed to this point are all subject to a number of simplifying assumptions that severely limit the accuracy of intrinsic value estimates. These limitations are briefly summarized as follows:

1. The intrinsic value estimate is no more accurate than the estimates of earnings and dividends underlying that valuation. The tendency has been to assume that earnings grow at a constant rate and that dividends also grow at a constant rate or the dividend payout ratio is constant. Experience suggests that earnings growth rates can vary markedly over time, and firms do change their dividend policies. The problem of forecasting earnings and dividends will be discussed in more depth in Part 5 of this book.

2. The discount rate (k) is typically held constant for the time period covered by the model. In actuality, required market rates change over time, and the risk-class of a given firm may also change. In either situation, the assumption of a constant (k) would not be valid.

3. Either earnings growth is assumed into perpetuity, or a terminal value representing the expected sales price of the stock at some predetermined time is made. The declining present value of far distant streams does lessen the importance of errors in the estimation of such streams when a hold into infinity is assumed. However, the difficulty lies in imagining how accurate estimates can be made over such long horizons. When a finite holding period is assumed, the question arises as to how one determines that holding period in advance. Even if the holding period could be estimated accurately, one still faces the difficult problem of estimating the market value of the stock at the end of the holding period.

4. Growth is assumed to be financed through retained earnings. This assumption ignores the possible use of debt, new stock issues, and other sources of funds that could finance growth in assets and earnings.

5. After-tax cash flows could be estimated by assuming the tax bracket rate that will be applicable to the investor for each annual holding period. The appropriate tax bracket rate will depend, however, on the total income of the investor and tax deductions available, not just investment income. Such estimates are, of course, subject to error.

One would not anticipate a high degree of accuracy in intrinsic value estimates when the inherent limitations of the valuation models are considered. The models do serve to clarify the relationship between the key factors that affect stock valuation, however. The also offer a way of studying the reasonableness of the assumptions that seem to underlie market values at a given point in time. In this backward induction sense the models are useful, especially as a valuable teaching tool.

Price-Earnings Ratios

Another approach to the determination of intrinsic value is provided by the use of price-earnings ratios. Like its predecessors, this approach to stock valuation is essentially deterministic in nature but is felt to be more easily modified for application to real-world investment decision problems by its advocates.

Let the normalized earnings for a particular firm be defined as the "level of net income which would prevail currently if the economy were experiencing mid-cyclical business conditions,"[18] which is an average of sorts. The evaluation of a normalized earnings statistic (e_n) therefore involves a consideration of the earnings experience of a firm over a previous business cycle and an evaluation of current market conditions.

The intrinsic value of a share of stock (V_0) has been defined as the discounted present value of the stream of future dividends to be realized from the stock. This present value may be approximated by use of various procedures that employ price-earnings ratios. For example, the "true" intrinsic value of a share of stock is sometimes estimated by multiplying normalized earnings per share by an *adjusted* price-earnings ratio, p/e_n', which reflects the analyst's subjective judgment about future growth prospects for the firm and dividend policy, as well as uncertainty about the prospects.

Formally, an estimate is provided by

$$V_0' = e_n [p/e_n']. \tag{7.18}$$

Notice that the price-earnings multiplier in Equation (7.18) is *not* the

_____
[18] Volkert S. Whitbeck and Manown Kisor, Jr., "A New Tool in Investment Decision Making," *Financial Analysts Journal*, Vol. 19, No. 3 (May-June, 1963), p. 57.

same price-earnings ratio that one would find reported in the newspaper. Many factors enter into the determination of an adjusted price-earnings ratio, not the least of which is subjectivity. A detailed discussion of this type of analysis is reserved for Section 2 of the book.

Price-earnings ratios of the sort reported in the newspaper or trade publications can give a distorted view of relative value due to different accounting techniques and definitions that may be employed by various firms or by the same firm in transition (voluntarily or otherwise) from one accounting system to the next. Recent governmental and Financial Accounting Standards Board actions, which mandate a change in accounting standards, for example, will have an important bearing on interpreting price-earnings ratios. These issues are taken up in Section 2 of the text. What is important here is that a price-earnings ratio provides only a crude indication of the relative merit of one's investment alternatives and must be used with discretion.

Summary

The theory of stock valuation represents an attempt to uncover the relationships that exist among the variables that affect the intrinsic value of individual financial assets. Intrinsic value, of course, is an abstraction; it can be defined by theory but can never be known for certain in practice.

Early contributions to the literature of valuation, following a tradition that existed in various allied fields at the time, assumed a world of perfect certainty. Attempts have since been made to relax this assumption and its implications, as will be made clear in Section 2 of the book. The remainder of Section 1 of the text, however, is devoted to a different approach to uncertainty analysis, in which emphasis is placed on discovering the relationships that exist among rates of return on various financial assets and not on the intrinsic value of individual financial assets.

Questions

1. (a) What rate would you earn on your money if you paid $624 and received $656 nine months later? If you paid $9.68 immediately and received a single payment of $15 ninety months later?
   (b) What amount of money should one invest today:
      (1) at 8 percent to receive $10,000 two years from now?
      (2) at 3 percent to receive $9,750 two years from now?
      (3) at 8 percent to receive $10 annually each year for five years?

2. (a) What price is indicated for a 5 percent, $1,000 par, corporate bond quoted at $97\frac{3}{8}$?
   (b) If the above bond was quoted "and interest," with interest payment dates on January 1 and July 1, for delivery on May 10, what would be the total cost to the buyer of such a bond? (Ignore commissions.)

3. Is yield for a bond usually quoted on the same basis as yield for a stock? Are they equally significant to an investor? Discuss.

4. (a) Calculate the current yield and net yield to maturity by the approximate method for each of the following bonds:
   (1) a 20-year, $8\frac{1}{4}$ percent bond offered at $1,020, par $1,000.
   (2) a 30-year, $4\frac{1}{2}$ percent bond offered at $700, par $1,000.
   (b) Based on the above information only, which of these bonds appears to be of higher quality? Explain.

5. What kind of change in the general level of interest rates would have a similar effect as deterioration in quality on the price of a bond? Explain.

6. (a) What reinvestment assumption is inherent in the calculation of a net yield to maturity for a bond?
   (b) "For the compounding investor who expects interest rates to average lower than at time of purchase, over a long period of time, there is a structural advantage in discount bonds over par (or premium) bonds because that part of his return represented by the discount is fixed and cannot decline with interest rates." [Sidney Homer and Martin L. Leibowitz, *Inside the Yield Book* (Englewood Cliffs, N.J.: Prentice-Hall, 1972), p. 28.] Explain this statement.

7. Should an investor who is in a 40 percent tax bracket prefer a municipal bond yielding 6 percent to maturity or a corporate bond yielding 9.5 percent to maturity? Assume whichever bond is selected will be held to maturity and that the risk involved for the two bonds is equal. Support your answer with calculations.

8. (a) What is meant by the phrase, "intrinsic value of a security"?
   (b) Can the intrinsic value of a stock be calculated? Discuss.

9. Valuation theory suggests that the value of a common stock is dependent either on earnings or on dividends paid. How would you reconcile this with the fact that common stocks of companies currently reporting losses and paying no dividends have had market values?

10. Should dividends or earnings be used as the basis for estimating the value of a common stock? Discuss.

11. Outline the conditions under which dividend policy of a firm would not affect the intrinsic value of the common stock of that firm. Are these conditions met in the real world?

12. What practical difficulties does one encounter in applying present value theory to stock valuation?

13. Is the price-earnings ratio approach to valuing stock consistent with a present value approach? Discuss.

Work-Study Problems

1. Prove by use of present value tables that a $1,000 par bond with a $4\frac{1}{2}$ percent coupon rate, 18 years to go until maturity, and currently quoted at 83.6258, will yield 6 percent to maturity. Assume interest is paid annually on this bond.

2. (a) What yield would you earn if you paid $1,940 to acquire treasury bills that will have a maturity value of $2,000 in six months?

   (b) Check the sensitivity of treasury bill yields to given price changes by assuming a price of $1,900 and a price of $1,960.

3. Assume that you consider the bonds of Happy Hour Brewery Co. and Bavarian Brewery as equal in quality. Also assume that the asset size and earnings potential of the two breweries are equal. Further assume that Happy Hour Brewery 9 percent bonds, par $1,000, mature in 20 years, sell at 120, and are callable at 105 at any time. The Bavarian Brewery $4\frac{1}{2}$ percent bonds, par $1,000, sell at 68, mature in 15 years, and are also callable at 105 at any time. Interest is payable annually on both bonds.

   (a) Which bond would be preferable in terms of the suggested yield to maturity?

   (b) How would your answer above be affected if interest were paid semiannually instead of annually?

   (c) If there was a 50 percent chance that interest rates would fall to 6 percent in ten years with reinvestment to maturity at 6 percent, would your answer change? Discuss.

4. (a) If one assumes a growth rate to perpetuity of 4 percent and a discount rate of 8 percent, what is the present value of $1 of current dividends?

   (b) What considerations are important in choosing an appropriate discount rate in present value calculations?

5. Assume that Corporation A presently earns $7 per share and pays a $4 dividend per share. Further assume that earnings per share and dividends are expected to grow at a 5 percent annual compounded rate for the next five years, that the stock is expected to sell at a price-earnings ratio of 16 after five years, and that the risk associated with the stock justifies a before-tax discount factor of 8 percent. According to present value theory, what is the intrinsic value of this stock?

6. (a) Compute the intrinsic value for a share of common stock, utilizing present value techniques and the following assumptions:
   (1) The investor is taxed at 50 percent on ordinary income and 25 percent on capital gains;
   (2) The stock is expected to pay a $2 dividend at the end of the first annual holding period, and dividends are expected to grow at a 10 percent compound annual rate thereafter;
   (3) Earnings per share are currently $4.50 and are expected to grow at a compound annual rate of 20 percent for each year during which the investor holds the stock;
   (4) The investor expects to sell the stock at the end of the third holding period, and expects a P/E ratio of 25 to apply to the stock at that time;
   (5) The investor believes that 8 percent after taxes can be earned on investments of equivalent risk;
   (6) The stock is currently selling for $81.00 per share.
   (b) Would the above appear to be an attractive investment opportunity? Explain your answer in terms of the percentage margin available to cover forecasting errors.
   (c) What limitations are inherent in the model used to calculate an intrinsic value for the above stock?
7. (a) Forecast the sales, profits, and earnings per share for a company, selected by you, for the next five years. Carefully identify the assumptions underlying your forecast for both the industry and the company.
   (b) Using the above forecast as a basis, value the stock by means of the present value approach. Explain your choice of a discount rate. Assume that at the end of the fifth year you sold the stock at a price equal to expected EPS at that time multiplied by the expected price-earnings ratio at that time.
   (c) Value your stock by means of the P/E ratio approach. Justify your choice of P/E ratio and the earnings per share figure you use.

APPENDIX TABLE 7-A. Present Value of $1 Received at the End of Year

Years Hence	1%	2%	4%	6%	8%	10%	12%	14%	15%	16%	18%
1	0.990	0.980	0.962	0.943	0.926	0.909	0.893	0.877	0.870	0.862	0.847
2	0.980	0.961	0.925	0.890	0.857	0.826	0.797	0.769	0.756	0.743	0.718
3	0.971	0.942	0.889	0.840	0.794	0.751	0.712	0.675	0.658	0.641	0.609
4	0.961	0.924	0.855	0.792	0.735	0.683	0.636	0.592	0.572	0.552	0.516
5	0.951	0.906	0.822	0.747	0.681	0.621	0.567	0.519	0.497	0.476	0.437
6	0.942	0.888	0.790	0.705	0.630	0.564	0.507	0.456	0.432	0.410	0.370
7	0.933	0.871	0.760	0.665	0.583	0.513	0.452	0.400	0.376	0.354	0.314
8	0.923	0.853	0.731	0.627	0.540	0.467	0.404	0.351	0.327	0.305	0.266
9	0.914	0.837	0.703	0.592	0.500	0.424	0.361	0.308	0.284	0.263	0.225
10	0.905	0.820	0.676	0.558	0.463	0.386	0.322	0.270	0.247	0.227	0.191
11	0.896	0.804	0.650	0.527	0.429	0.350	0.287	0.237	0.215	0.195	0.162
12	0.887	0.788	0.625	0.497	0.397	0.319	0.257	0.208	0.187	0.168	0.137
13	0.879	0.773	0.601	0.469	0.368	0.290	0.229	0.182	0.163	0.145	0.116
14	0.870	0.758	0.577	0.442	0.340	0.263	0.205	0.160	0.141	0.125	0.099
15	0.861	0.743	0.555	0.417	0.315	0.239	0.183	0.140	0.123	0.108	0.084
16	0.853	0.728	0.534	0.394	0.292	0.218	0.163	0.123	0.107	0.093	0.071
17	0.844	0.714	0.513	0.371	0.270	0.198	0.146	0.108	0.093	0.080	0.060
18	0.836	0.700	0.494	0.350	0.250	0.180	0.130	0.095	0.081	0.069	0.051
19	0.828	0.686	0.475	0.331	0.232	0.164	0.116	0.083	0.070	0.060	0.043
20	0.820	0.673	0.456	0.312	0.215	0.149	0.104	0.073	0.061	0.051	0.037
21	0.811	0.660	0.439	0.294	0.199	0.135	0.093	0.064	0.053	0.044	0.031
22	0.803	0.647	0.422	0.278	0.184	0.123	0.083	0.056	0.046	0.038	0.026
23	0.795	0.634	0.406	0.262	0.170	0.112	0.074	0.049	0.040	0.033	0.022
24	0.788	0.622	0.390	0.247	0.158	0.102	0.066	0.043	0.035	0.028	0.019
25	0.780	0.610	0.375	0.233	0.146	0.092	0.059	0.038	0.030	0.024	0.016
26	0.772	0.598	0.361	0.220	0.135	0.084	0.053	0.033	0.026	0.021	0.014
27	0.764	0.586	0.347	0.207	0.125	0.076	0.047	0.029	0.023	0.018	0.011
28	0.757	0.574	0.333	0.196	0.116	0.069	0.042	0.026	0.020	0.016	0.010
29	0.749	0.563	0.321	0.185	0.107	0.063	0.037	0.022	0.017	0.014	0.008
30	0.742	0.552	0.308	0.174	0.099	0.057	0.033	0.020	0.015	0.012	0.007
40	0.672	0.453	0.208	0.097	0.046	0.022	0.011	0.005	0.004	0.003	0.001
50	0.608	0.372	0.141	0.054	0.021	0.009	0.003	0.001	0.001	0.001	

Years Hence	20%	22%	24%	25%	26%	28%	30%	35%	40%	45%	50%
1	0.833	0.820	0.806	0.800	0.794	0.781	0.769	0.741	0.714	0.690	0.607
2	0.694	0.672	0.650	0.640	0.630	0.610	0.592	0.549	0.510	0.476	0.444
3	0.579	0.551	0.524	0.512	0.500	0.477	0.455	0.406	0.364	0.328	0.290
4	0.482	0.451	0.423	0.410	0.397	0.373	0.350	0.301	0.260	0.226	0.198
5	0.402	0.370	0.341	0.328	0.315	0.291	0.269	0.223	0.186	0.156	0.132
6	0.335	0.303	0.275	0.262	0.250	0.227	0.207	0.165	0.133	0.108	0.088
7	0.279	0.249	0.222	0.210	0.198	0.178	0.159	0.122	0.095	0.074	0.059
8	0.233	0.204	0.179	0.168	0.157	0.139	0.123	0.091	0.068	0.051	0.039
9	0.194	0.167	0.144	0.134	0.125	0.108	0.094	0.067	0.048	0.035	0.026
10	0.162	0.137	0.116	0.107	0.099	0.085	0.073	0.050	0.035	0.024	0.017
11	0.135	0.112	0.094	0.086	0.079	0.066	0.056	0.037	0.025	0.017	0.012
12	0.112	0.092	0.076	0.069	0.062	0.052	0.043	0.027	0.018	0.012	0.008
13	0.093	0.075	0.061	0.055	0.050	0.040	0.033	0.020	0.013	0.008	0.005
14	0.078	0.062	0.049	0.044	0.039	0.032	0.025	0.015	0.009	0.006	0.003
15	0.065	0.051	0.040	0.035	0.031	0.025	0.020	0.011	0.006	0.004	0.002
16	0.054	0.042	0.032	0.028	0.025	0.019	0.015	0.008	0.005	0.003	0.002
17	0.045	0.034	0.026	0.023	0.020	0.015	0.012	0.006	0.003	0.002	0.001
18	0.038	0.028	0.021	0.018	0.016	0.012	0.009	0.005	0.002	0.001	0.001

APPENDIX TABLE 7-A. *(continued)*

Years Hence	20%	22%	24%	25%	26%	28%	30%	35%	40%	45%	50%
19	0.031	0.023	0.017	0.014	0.012	0.009	0.007	0.003	0.002	0.001	
20	0.026	0.019	0.014	0.012	0.010	0.007	0.005	0.002	0.001	0.001	
21	0.022	0.015	0.011	0.009	0.008	0.006	0.004	0.002	0.001		
22	0.018	0.013	0.009	0.007	0.006	0.004	0.003	0.001	0.001		
23	0.015	0.010	0.007	0.006	0.005	0.003	0.002	0.001			
24	0.013	0.008	0.006	0.005	0.004	0.003	0.002	0.001			
25	0.010	0.007	0.005	0.004	0.003	0.002	0.001	0.001			
26	0.009	0.006	0.004	0.003	0.002	0.002	0.001				
27	0.007	0.005	0.003	0.002	0.002	0.001	0.001				
28	0.006	0.004	0.002	0.002	0.002	0.001	0.001				
29	0.005	0.003	0.002	0.002	0.001	0.001	0.001				
30	0.004	0.003	0.002	0.001	0.001	0.001					
40	0.001										

APPENDIX TABLE 7-B. Present Value of $1 Received Annually at the End of Each Year for N Years

Years (N)	1%	2%	4%	6%	8%	10%	12%	14%	15%	16%	18%
1	0.990	0.980	0.962	0.943	0.926	0.909	0.893	0.877	0.870	0.862	0.847
2	1.970	1.942	1.886	1.833	1.783	1.736	1.690	1.647	1.626	1.605	1.566
3	2.941	2.884	2.775	2.673	2.577	2.487	2.402	2.322	2.283	2.246	2.174
4	3.902	3.808	3.630	3.465	3.312	3.170	3.037	2.914	2.855	2.798	2.690
5	4.853	4.713	4.452	4.212	3.993	3.791	3.605	3.433	3.352	3.274	3.127
6	5.795	5.601	5.242	4.917	4.623	4.355	4.111	3.889	3.784	3.685	3.498
7	6.728	6.472	6.002	5.582	5.206	4.868	4.564	4.288	4.160	4.039	3.812
8	7.652	7.325	6.733	6.210	5.747	5.335	4.968	4.639	4.487	4.344	4.078
9	8.566	8.162	7.435	6.802	6.247	5.759	5.328	4.946	4.772	4.607	4.303
10	9.471	8.983	8.111	7.360	6.710	6.145	5.650	5.216	5.019	4.833	4.494
11	10.368	9.787	8.760	7.887	7.139	6.495	5.988	5.453	5.234	5.029	4.656
12	11.255	10.575	9.385	8.384	7.536	6.814	6.194	5.660	5.421	5.197	4.793
13	12.134	11.343	9.986	8.853	7.904	7.103	6.424	5.842	5.583	5.342	4.910
14	13.004	12.106	10.563	9.295	8.244	7.367	6.628	6.002	5.724	5.468	5.008
15	13.865	12.849	11.118	9.712	8.559	7.606	6.811	6.142	5.847	5.575	5.092
16	14.718	13.578	11.652	10.106	8.851	7.824	6.974	6.265	5.954	5.669	5.162
17	15.562	14.292	12.166	10.477	9.122	8.022	7.120	6.373	6.047	5.749	5.222
18	16.398	14.992	12.659	10.828	9.372	8.201	7.250	6.467	6.128	5.818	5.273
19	17.226	15.678	13.134	11.158	9.604	8.365	7.366	6.550	6.198	5.877	5.316
20	18.046	16.351	13.590	11.470	9.818	8.514	7.469	6.623	6.259	5.929	5.353
21	18.857	17.011	14.029	11.764	10.017	8.649	7.562	6.687	6.312	5.973	5.384
22	19.660	17.658	14.451	12.042	10.201	8.772	7.645	6.743	6.359	6.011	5.410
23	20.456	18.292	14.857	12.303	10.371	8.883	7.718	6.792	6.399	6.044	5.432
24	21.243	18.914	15.247	12.550	10.529	8.985	7.784	6.835	6.434	6.073	5.451
25	22.023	19.523	15.622	12.783	10.675	9.077	7.843	6.873	6.464	6.097	5.467
26	22.795	20.121	15.983	13.003	10.810	9.161	7.896	6.906	6.491	6.118	5.480
27	23.500	20.707	16.330	13.211	10.935	9.237	7.943	6.935	6.514	6.136	5.492
28	24.316	21.281	16.663	13.406	11.051	9.307	7.984	6.961	6.534	6.152	5.502
29	25.066	21.844	16.984	13.591	11.158	9.370	8.022	6.983	6.551	6.166	5.510
30	25.808	22.396	17.292	13.765	11.258	9.427	8.055	7.003	6.566	6.177	5.517
40	32.835	27.355	19.793	15.040	11.925	9.779	8.244	7.105	6.642	6.234	5.548
50	39.196	31.424	21.482	15.762	12.234	9.915	8.304	7.113	6.661	6.246	5.554

APPENDIX TABLE 7-B. *(continued)*

Years Hence	20%	22%	24%	25%	26%	28%	30%	35%	40%	45%	50%
1	0.833	0.820	0.806	0.800	0.794	0.781	0.769	0.741	0.714	0.690	0.667
2	1.528	1.492	1.457	1.440	1.424	1.392	1.361	1.289	1.224	1.165	1.111
3	2.106	2.042	1.981	1.952	1.923	1.868	1.816	1.696	1.589	1.493	1.407
4	2.589	2.494	2.404	2.362	2.320	2.241	2.166	1.997	1.849	1.720	1.605
5	2.991	2.864	2.745	2.689	2.635	2.532	2.436	2.220	2.035	1.876	1.737
6	3.326	3.167	3.020	2.951	2.885	2.759	2.643	2.385	2.168	1.983	1.824
7	3.605	3.416	3.242	3.161	3.083	2.937	2.802	2.508	2.263	2.057	1.883
8	3.837	3.619	3.421	3.329	3.241	3.076	2.925	2.598	2.331	2.108	1.922
9	4.031	3.786	3.566	3.463	3.366	3.184	3.019	2.665	2.379	2.144	1.948
10	4.192	3.923	3.682	3.571	3.465	3.269	3.092	2.715	2.414	2.168	1.965
11	4.327	4.035	3.776	3.656	3.544	3.335	3.147	2.752	2.438	2.185	1.977
12	4.439	4.127	3.851	3.725	3.606	3.387	3.190	2.779	2.456	2.196	1.985
13	4.533	4.203	3.912	3.780	3.656	3.427	3.223	2.799	2.468	2.204	1.990
14	4.611	4.265	3.962	3.824	3.695	3.459	3.249	2.814	2.477	2.210	1.993
15	4.675	4.315	4.001	3.859	3.726	3.483	3.268	2.825	2.484	2.218	1.995
16	4.730	4.357	4.033	3.887	3.751	3.503	3.283	2.834	2.489	2.216	1.997
17	4.775	4.391	4.059	3.910	3.771	3.518	3.295	2.840	2.492	2.218	1.998
18	4.812	4.419	4.080	3.928	3.786	3.529	3.304	2.844	2.494	2.219	1.999
19	4.844	4.442	4.097	3.942	3.799	3.539	3.311	2.848	2.496	2.220	1.999
20	4.870	4.460	4.110	3.954	3.808	3.546	3.316	2.850	2.497	2.221	1.999
21	4.891	4.476	4.121	3.963	3.816	3.551	3.320	2.852	2.498	2.221	2.000
22	4.909	4.488	4.130	3.970	3.822	3.556	3.323	2.853	2.498	2.222	2.000
23	4.925	4.499	4.137	3.976	3.827	3.559	3.325	2.854	2.499	2.222	2.000
24	4.937	4.507	4.143	3.981	3.831	3.562	3.327	2.855	2.499	2.222	2.000
25	4.948	4.514	4.147	3.985	3.834	3.564	3.329	2.856	2.499	2.222	2.000
26	4.956	4.520	4.151	3.988	3.837	3.566	3.330	2.856	2.500	2.222	2.000
27	4.964	4.524	4.154	3.990	3.839	3.567	3.331	2.856	2.500	2.222	2.000
28	4.970	4.528	4.157	3.992	3.840	3.568	3.331	2.857	2.500	2.222	2.000
29	4.975	4.531	4.159	3.994	3.841	3.569	3.332	2.857	2.500	2.222	2.000
30	4.979	4.534	4.160	3.995	3.842	3.569	3.332	2.857	2.500	2.222	2.000
40	4.997	4.544	4.166	3.999	3.846	3.571	3.333	2.857	2.500	2.222	2.000
50	4.999	4.545	4.167	4.000	3.846	3.571	3.333	2.857	2.500	2.222	2.000

8.

Uncertainty Analysis: The Theory of Chance Events

> We are merely reminding ourselves that human decisions affecting the future, whether personal or political or economic, cannot depend on strict mathematical expectation since the basis for making such calculations does not exist; and that it is our innate urge to activity which makes the wheels go round, our rational selves choosing between the alternatives as best we are able, calculating where we can, but falling back for our motive on whim or sentiment or chance.[1]

According to Webster's dictionary, diversification implies variety— to make things different. In the investment field diversification has sometimes been rather loosely explained: "Don't put all your eggs into one basket." While the conventional wisdom on which this cliché is based may be sound, it does not provide any useful insights from the point of view of portfolio selection.

Modern portfolio theory seeks to explain how diversification can be achieved, and how, once achieved, efficient diversification affects trade-offs between expectation and risk. Capital market theory, by contrast, seeks to explain the market implications were all investors to seek efficient diversification. These theories do not explain how to pick out the "best" individual stocks—this is the object of fundamental security analysis that is the subject of Section 2 of this book.

An analysis for investment decision must be comprehensive. The investor's specific investment goals must be considered, and these goals must be contrasted with the investor's willingness and ability to bear risk. Each investment alternative must be carefully evaluated, and a determination of how each part of an investment program relates to the whole must be made. Efficient diversification cannot be achieved by

---

[1] John Maynard Keynes, *The General Theory of Employment, Interest, and Money* (New York: Harcourt Brace & World, 1936).

merely purchasing "good" stocks or by investing in stock averages. Effective diversification is achieved by combining the assets in an investment portfolio in such a way as to provide a meaningful hedge against chance factors. The purchase of stocks, for example, whose rates of return are perfectly correlated would provide no hedge against market contingencies regardless of how many such stocks were purchased.

The theory of investment is concerned primarily with normative issues—that is, with the question of "how" an investment decision should be made. Recent developments, which have their origin in operations research, statistics, and the theory of games and decision, have significantly affected (and in many instances challenged) the traditional theory of investment. These new approaches are mathematically elegant, which is a source of advantage as well as disadvantage. The use of mathematical terminology and abstraction makes possible the precise formulation of an investment problem. The application of a mathematical model, unfortunately, may also require the exercise of various assumptions that are so unrealistic as to call into question the usefulness of the model or theory. As with any theory, therefore, the theory of investment must be approached with caution.

In order to present modern and traditional theories of investment analysis in a rigorous way, a vocabulary equal to the task is needed. The first step in the development of such a vocabulary is to establish the relevance of the theory of chance events to the topic of investment. Various sources of uncertainty that affect investment outcome are described in this chapter. The meaning of uncertainty is explained, and a concept of probability that is appropriate for application under conditions of uncertainty is introduced. The use of probability in forming expectations and in the evaluation of risk is illustrated. Various risk concepts that do not hinge on probability logic are also discussed.

CERTAINTY, UNCERTAINTY, AND RANDOM PROCESSES

When all the facts bearing on the outcome of an investment decision are known in advance, the environment of decision is called "certain." Barring mere miscalculation, investment decisions made under *conditions of certainty* are considered riskless in the sense that ex-post (after the fact) results should agree with ex-ante (before the fact) expectations. Decisions made under conditions of *uncertainty* would obviously not be riskless in this sense.

Deterministic Analyses

An investment problem is called *deterministic* when its solution can be determined or inferred from known facts. Assume, for example, that a $1,000 treasury bill that matures in 90 days can be purchased today for \$975.61. As a liability of the federal government, the future rate of return, r_f, can be calculated from these "known facts" as follows:

$$r_f = \left[\frac{(p_{t+1} - p_t)}{p_t} \right] \quad (4)$$

$$= \left[\frac{\$1,000.00 - \$975.61}{\$975.61} \right] \quad (4)$$

$$= 0.10.$$

The quarterly rate of return is multiplied by 4 in this calculation in order to obtain an annual figure.

Random Processes and Random Outcomes

The outcome of a random process defines a *random variable*. Conversely, any chance event, such as rate of return, represents an outcome of some random process. The one-period rate of return on stock (i) in period (t) is defined as follows:

$$\tilde{r}_{it} = \frac{(p_{t+1} - p_t) + D_t}{p_t},$$

where

p_t = the price of stock i in period t,
p_{t+1} = the price of stock i in period $t + 1$,
D_t = the dividend paid on stock i in period t,

and the tilde is used to emphasize the point that the rate of return on a risky asset is a random variable.

When at least some of the essential facts, such as the amount or timing of future cash flows, cannot be known for certain at the time of decision, then it is not possible to be sure that a particular investment will achieve ex-post what is "expected" of it ex-ante. When knowledge is imperfect, the environment of investment decision is called *uncertain*. Any asset purchased on the basis of imperfect information—which includes most assets—is a *risky asset;* and, conversely, every investment decision that involves the purchase of a risky asset is tantamount to a gamble whose outcome is determined, at least in part, by chance factors.

Suppose, for example, that the current price of some hypothetical stock is \$10. When investors purchase risky assets of this sort, they hope for the best. However, with the purchase of a particularly risky asset, one, in effect, purchases a turn at a *wheel of fortune*, or gaming device, such as that shown in Figure 8–1. Each rotation of the wheel of fortune determines the outcome of a random variable; the random vari-

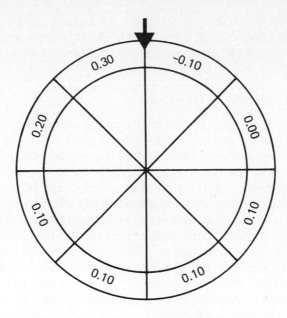

FIGURE 8-1. Wheel of Fortune, One-Stock Example

able of this illustration is rate of return. Suppose that the gaming device is activated over and over again and that the outcome of each trial is recorded. In a long run of trials, the relative frequency with which each possible *event* (one of the possible rates of return) will occur will approach a *limit* or number that represents the *objective probability* of the event. A *subjective probability*, on the other hand, would be the result of introspection. The *rule of randomness* that governs the possible outcomes of this illustration is shown in Table 8-1.

This state of affairs is not at all the same as owning a right to a *sure* stream of future dividend payments whose "intrinsic value" might be calculated by deterministic methods. Notice, moreover, that the pur-

TABLE 8-1. Rates of Return and Probabilities for a Single Hypothetical Stock

States of Nature	Probability	Rate of Return
θ_1	0.125	−0.10
θ_2	0.125	0.00
θ_3	0.500	0.10
θ_4	0.125	0.20
θ_5	0.125	0.30

chase of, say, two shares of the same $10 stock does not entitle the holder to two independent turns at the wheel of fortune, but rather to the proceeds of a $20 bet placed on the outcome of a single turn of the wheel.

Rules Governing Random Outcomes

Associated with each mutually distinct, possible rate of return that may result from an investment in a risky asset (i) is a number that is bounded by zero and one. This number is a probability; it measures the relative likelihood that the random variable $\tilde{r}_{it}$ will take on a particular value at a particular point in time. The set of all the relative likelihoods for any random variable is called a *probability distribution*. A probability distribution is a *rule of randomness;* it provides a mathematical description of the random process that governs the outcome of a random variable. A rule of randomness may be described in mathematical terms or by complete enumeration of every event and corresponding probability.[2] A spin of the "wheel of fortune"[3] shown in Figure 8-1, for example, sets in motion a random process in the same sense that the purchase of a share of common stock does.

Sources of Probability Information

Prior information about the next outcome of a random process may be obtained from various sources:

1. Deductive models that describe the distribution of events such as the outcome of a toss of a coin.
2. Subjectivity that is based on limited objective evidence or pertinent experience.
3. Historical information regarding the behavior of a random process over many trials, such as is provided by any economic time series.

The use of historical data as a basis for forming probability judgments does not necessarily imply that "history will repeat itself." This interpretation is wrong and untutored. Regardless of the source of information about a random process, to the extent that an individual is willing to base actions on probability distributions, *probability* measures the degree of belief that one is willing to attach to a particular outcome or event, which we call a *state of nature*. Such a probability is inherently subjective, even where the source of one's information may be objective.

---

[2] A random variable is "discrete" when it can assume only a finite number of possible values. A random variable is "continuous" when, in any interval, it can assume an infinite number of possible values. Complete enumeration of an infinity of possible outcomes, of course, is not possible.

[3] This example is a modification of one which has been used by Markowitz and many others. See Harry M. Markowitz, *Portfolio Selection* (New Haven: Yale University Press, 1959), p. 39.

A state of nature is a probability-determining event. Such an event describes a state of being such as the level of interest rates or the average price of a share of stock. The price of a particular stock, for example, may go up or down from its previous high, or not change. Thus, three mutually distinct and collectively exhaustive states of nature can be defined.[4] In assigning probabilities to states of nature, one assumes that the individual concerned is "reasonable." The possibility is not overlooked, of course, that "two reasonable individuals faced with the same evidence may have different degrees of confidence in the truth of the same propositions."[5]

Caveat

When the outcome of decision is determined by chance factors, as we have stated, the environment of decision is called "uncertain." A proper evaluation of any risky investment requires not only recognition of the fact that uncertainty exists but also understanding of the source and possible consequences of this uncertainty.

There are two types of uncertainty, and a proper distinction must be made between them. One type of uncertainty is a consequence of the pattern of variation that is described by some rule of randomness. A second type of uncertainty arises "when it is not known which laws of randomness apply."[6] It is one thing, for example, to suppose that the rate of return on a share of stock is governed by a rule of randomness; it is quite another thing to suppose that one can possibly know for sure *which* rule of randomness applies.

The purchase of a risky asset is similar to the purchase of an ordinary lottery in one sense only—the outcome of each is governed by some rule of randomness. When purchasing a lottery, the professional gambler knows the set of possible outcomes and can calculate the odds. The same is true of a life insurance actuary. On the other hand, an investor who purchases a risky asset can only have approximate knowledge about the set of possible outcomes; the investor can never know the "odds" in the same sense that a gambler might know them. The quantification of knowledge about a risky asset may result in probabili-

---

[4] We adopt a well-established convention of representing states of nature by subscripted Greek letters. The rationale that underlies this convention is twofold. First, the Greek letter should represent to the reader an event over which the decision maker has no control; such an outcome is, from the point of view of the decision maker, governed by chance. Second, there is the parallel practice in classical statistics of denoting probability-determining parameters by Greek letters. This is done to distinguish parameters from sample statistics.

[5] Leonard J. Savage, *The Foundations of Statistics* (New York: Wiley, 1954), p. 3.

[6] Herman Chernoff and Lincoln Moses, *Elementary Decision Theory* (New York: Wiley 1959), p. 1.

ties that are useful in the assessment of risk. However, the resulting probability distributions are always "fuzzy" in the sense that one can never firmly establish which rule of randomness applies on the basis of statistical estimation.[7]

The mere fact that one can or does calculate a descriptive statistic such as mean or variance does not, in itself, mean that (1) the statistic is free from error or (2) there is anything, in reality, to be "described." For example, where the underlying process is known to be unstable, this fact should not be ignored. Even where one is not willing to suppose that the underlying statistical process is a *stationary process*, the use of historical data may be justified, as where the data represent a significant part of knowledge. Good or bad, one does not throw away potentially useful information.

JOINTLY DISTRIBUTED RANDOM OUTCOMES

The investor who seeks to combine assets to form an investment portfolio is faced with a myriad of alternatives. To simplify matters, we will assume for the moment that there are just two risky assets available on the market—call them stock i and stock j.

The purchase of either risky asset—viewed in isolation—can be likened to the purchase of a turn at a wheel of fortune whose *gaming* properties are unique to it. Representative wheels of fortune, corresponding to the hypothetical risky assets of this example, are shown in Part (a) of Figure 8-2. If one's entire investment budget or fund is devoted to the purchase of a single asset, then, as previously explained, the investment outcome will be determined by a single random device. When the investment fund is to be divided—in any combination—between the two risky assets, however, then matters are not as simple and straightforward as before.

Joint Events

The wheels of fortune of this illustration cannot rotate independently, as their individual outcomes represent the rates of return on risky assets that trade in the same market. A more graphic illustration of this idea is presented in Part (b) of Figure 8-2. In Part (b) of the figure, a pulley is attached to each wheel of fortune and to a *market*

---

[7] Economists, following a tradition popularized by Frank H. Knight, have tended to dismiss problems in which probability distributions cannot be known precisely as being beyond the scope of "scientific method." The adherence to this view explains in part the tendency to treat problems where uncertainty may obviously apply as problems that are amenable to solution by deterministic techniques. This tendency has been reversed, if only gradually, by the reintroduction of a subjectivist view of probability that took place in statistics during the fifties. See Leonard J. Savage, *The Foundations of Statistics.*

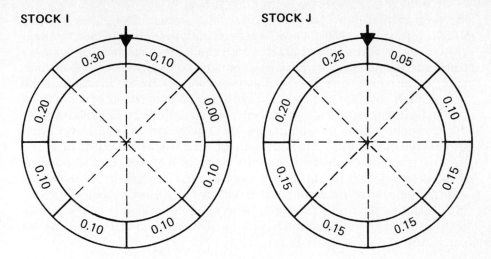

FIGURE 8-2a. Wheels of Fortune, Two-Stock Case

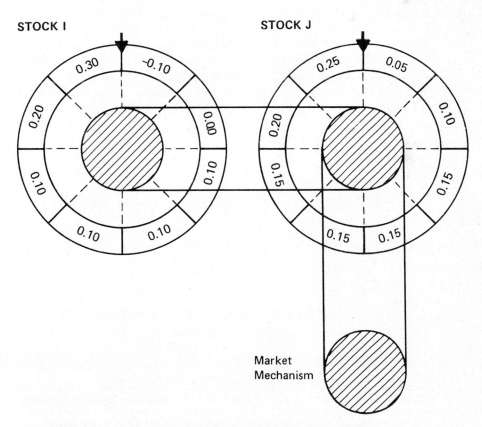

FIGURE 8-2b. Market Mechanism for Positively Correlated Returns

mechanism that provides the required momentum. The pulleys in this illustration are identical in every respect, and belts are attached to them so that every force that originates with the market mechanism—as if by the press of a button—is transmitted equally to each wheel.[8] Every rotation of one wheel, therefore, is matched precisely by the rotation of the other. Each rotation, moreover, results in the generation of a matched pair of outcomes. Such a matched pair of outcomes is called a *joint event.* Suppose that the gaming device is activated over and over again as before, and that the joint outcome of each trial is recorded. In a long run of trials, the relative frequency with which each of the possible joint events occurs will approach the *objective probability of that joint event.* The rule of randomness that governs the joint outcomes of this illustration is shown in Table 8-2. Five possible outcomes of the jointly distributed random variable $[\tilde{r}_i$ and $\tilde{r}_j]$ are shown in the table, one for each state of nature θ_t, $t = 1, 2, \ldots, 5$.

Expected Rate of Return. Rates of return on stocks i and j are related by means of a mutual dependence on the market mechanism. The question before us now has to do with the nature of this relationship and with how it might be measured statistically. Taking stocks i and j one at a time, the *expected rate of return* may be obtained by multiplying each possible value that the random variable $\tilde{r}$ may assume by the probability of the corresponding state, and summing. Thus, from Table 8-2 we obtain

$$E(\tilde{r}_i) = \sum_{t=1}^{5} P(\theta_t)\tilde{r}_{it}$$

$$= (0.125)(-0.10) + (0.125)(0.00) + \ldots + (0.125)(0.30)$$

$$= 0.10;$$

$$E(\tilde{r}_j) = \sum_{t=1}^{5} P(\theta_t)\tilde{r}_{jt}$$

$$= (0.125)(0.05) + (0.125)(0.10) + \ldots + (0.125)(0.25)$$

$$= 0.15,$$

---

[8] According to Webster's dictionary, a pulley is "a wheel that turns or is turned by a belt so as to transmit or apply power." Readers unfamiliar with the workings of mechanical devices that employ pulleys may find an examination of the engine compartment of the family automobile instructive. These readers are further advised to look and not touch!

TABLE 8-2. Joint Distribution of Rates of Return for Two Hypothetical Stocks

States of Nature	Probability	Joint Event Stock i	Joint Event Stock j
θ_1	0.125	-0.10	0.05
θ_2	0.125	0.00	0.10
θ_3	0.500	0.10	0.15
θ_4	0.125	0.20	0.20
θ_5	0.125	0.30	0.25

where

$\tilde{r}_{it}$ = the rate of return on stock i for the tth trial;
$\tilde{r}_{jt}$ = the rate of return on stock j for the tth trial.

In general,

$$E(\tilde{r}_{kt}) = \sum_{t=1}^{T} P(\theta_t)\tilde{r}_{kt},$$

(8.1)

where

$\tilde{r}_{kt}$ = the rate of return on stock k for the tth trial[9];
T = the number of trials for which there are observations.

The Variance and Standard Deviation. The *variance*, like the standard deviation, measures the degree of spread of a distribution relative to its mean—the moment of central tendency. Taking stocks i and j one at a time, as before, the variance of rate of return

$$\text{Var}(\tilde{r}_k) = \sum_{t=1}^{T} P(\theta_t)[\tilde{r}_{kt} - E(\tilde{r}_k)]^2$$

(8.2)

may be obtained by finding the squared difference of each possible value of the random variable $\tilde{r}_k$ and its expectation, $E(\tilde{r}_k)$; weighting each of the squared differences by the probability of the corresponding state; and then summing the products. The *standard deviation*

_____
[9] The subscript k is used as a general symbol, which may be represented by i or j or by any other letter that is used to represent a particular security.

$$\text{SD}(\tilde{r}_k) = \sqrt{\text{Var}(\tilde{r}_k)} \qquad (8.3)$$

is simply the square root of the variance. Notice that the variance of rate of return (8.2) and the standard deviation (8.3), like the expected rate of return (8.1), are defined by the *weighted average of a random variable*. In terms of the algebra, the only difference in the calculations is the random variable itself.

Covariance. A different weighted average, which will be less familiar to most readers, is also of interest. The *covariance* of two random variables measures the simultaneous variation of two random variables about their respective means. The covariance of rate of return for stocks i and j may be defined as follows:

$$\text{Cov}(\tilde{r}_i, \tilde{r}_j) = \sum_{t=1}^{T} P(\theta_t)[\tilde{r}_{it} - E(\tilde{r}_i)] [\tilde{r}_{jt} - E(\tilde{r}_j)]. \qquad (8.4)$$

The product that appears on the right-hand side of the expression, over which the weighted average is taken, is called a *cross-product*. Notice that each term in the cross-product is an unsquared difference that appears on the right-hand side of Equation (8.2). The calculation of the variance, standard deviation, and covariance of rate(s) of return is illustrated with the aid of Table 8–3.

The joint distribution of Table 8–2 is compacted into columns 1 through 4 of Table 8–3. Deviations of the random variable $\tilde{r}_i$ about its mean and $\tilde{r}_j$ about its mean are shown in columns 5 and 6, respectively. These deviates enter into the *partial calculations*, which are presented by the rows of the remaining columns of the table. The variance

$$\text{Var}(\tilde{r}_i) = 0.01250,$$

according to Equation (8.2), is a weighted average of squared deviations. The standard deviation,

$$\text{SD}(\tilde{r}_i) = 0.11180$$

by Equation (8.3), is simply its square root. These weighted averages are obtained by summing over the rows of column 7 in Table 8–3. The variance

$$\text{Var}(\tilde{r}_j) = 0.00313$$

and standard deviation

TABLE 8-3. Calculation of Variance and Covariance

(1) θ	(2) $P(\theta)$	(3) $\tilde{r}_i$	(4) $\tilde{r}_j$	(5) $[\tilde{r}_i - E(\tilde{r}_i)]$	(6) $[\tilde{r}_j - E(\tilde{r}_j)]$	(7) $P(\theta)[\tilde{r}_i - E(\tilde{r}_i)]^2$	(8) $P(\theta)[\tilde{r}_j - E(\tilde{r}_j)]^2$	(9) $P(\theta)[\tilde{r}_i - E(\tilde{r}_i)][\tilde{r}_j - E(\tilde{r}_j)]$
θ_1	0.125	-0.10	0.05	-0.20	-0.10	0.0050000	0.0012500	0.0025000
θ_2	0.125	0.00	0.10	-0.10	-0.05	0.0012500	0.0003125	0.0006250
θ_3	0.500	0.10	0.15	0.00	0.00	0.0000000	0.0000000	0.0000000
θ_4	0.125	0.20	0.20	0.10	0.05	0.0012500	0.0003125	0.0006250
θ_5	0.125	0.30	0.25	0.20	0.10	0.0050000	0.0012500	0.0025000
						0.0125000	0.0031250	0.0062500

$$SD(\tilde{r}_j) = 0.05595$$

are similarly obtained from column 8 of the table. These calculations are summarized in Figure 8-3.

Covariance, as the name implies, is a measure of statistical covariation. Invoking Equation (8.4) and summing over the rows of column 9 of Table 8-3, we obtain

$$Cov(\tilde{r}_i, \tilde{r}_j) = 0.00625$$

in this application. How shall we interpret this number?

When two random variables are positively related, they move together in the same direction and the covariance statistic is positive. When the random variables tend to move in opposite directions, the covariance is negative. There is nothing ambiguous about the meaning of the sign. However, from its definitional equation, Equation (8.4), we see that the *absolute magnitude* of a covariance statistic is a positive function of the

$$E(\tilde{r}_i) = \sum_{t=1}^{5} P(\theta_t)\tilde{r}_{it} \qquad\qquad Var(\tilde{r}_i) = \sum_{t=1}^{5} P(\theta_t)[\tilde{r}_{it} - E(\tilde{r}_i)]^2$$

$$= 0.10000 \qquad\qquad\qquad\qquad = 0.01250$$

$$E(\tilde{r}_j) = \sum_{t=1}^{5} P(\theta_t)\tilde{r}_{it} \qquad\qquad Var(\tilde{r}_j) = \sum_{t=1}^{5} P(\theta_t)[\tilde{r}_{jt} - E(\tilde{r}_j)]^2$$

$$= 0.15000 \qquad\qquad\qquad\qquad = 0.00313$$

$$Cov(\tilde{r}_i, \tilde{r}_j) = \sum_{t=1}^{5} P(\theta_t)[\tilde{r}_{it} - E(\tilde{r}_i)][\tilde{r}_{jt} - E(\tilde{r}_j)]$$

$$= 0.00625$$

$$Cor(\tilde{r}_i, \tilde{r}_j) = \frac{Cov(\tilde{r}_i, \tilde{r}_j)}{SD(\tilde{r}_i)SD(\tilde{r}_j)}$$

$$= \frac{0.00625}{\sqrt{0.012500}\,\sqrt{0.003125}}$$

$$= 1.00000$$

FIGURE 8-3. Summary Statistics

relative dispersion of two random variables about their respective means. We seek a standardized measure of statistical covariation—one that is not affected by dispersion.

Positive Correlation. The *coefficient of correlation* is a standardized measure of statistical covariation—co-movement of two random variables. The coefficient of correlation is obtained from the covariance by adjusting for dispersion:

$$\text{Cor}(\tilde{r}_i,\tilde{r}_j) = \frac{\text{Cov}(\tilde{r}_i,\tilde{r}_j)}{\text{SD}(\tilde{r}_i)\,\text{SD}(\tilde{r}_j)}. \tag{8.5}$$

Negative Correlation. To obtain a joint distribution of rates of return that exhibits perfect negative correlation, the gaming device that is featured in Table 8-2 is modified. The wheels of fortune shown in Figure 8-4 are precisely the same as before, as are the market mechanism and the pulleys. Contrasting the gaming devices of Figures 8-2 and 8-4,

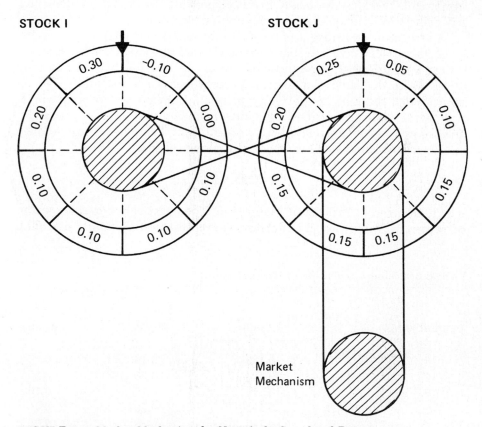

FIGURE 8-4. Market Mechanism for Negatively Correlated Returns

however, we see that one belt has been crisscrossed—the wheels of fortune now move in opposite directions. The jointly distributed rates of return shown in Table 8-2 exhibit perfect positive correlation. The jointly distributed random variables of Table 8-4, by contrast, exhibit perfect negative correlation. The random variables of Table 8-4 represent outcomes that correspond to wheels of fortune, which rotate in opposite directions and produce two series of numbers that are diametrically opposed. The expected rates of return are the same as before, as are the corresponding variance statistics, but $\text{Cor}(\tilde{r}_i, \tilde{r}_j) = -1.00$.

The Correlation Model

The rates of return on stocks that trade in the same market tend, on average, to vary *systematically* in response to market forces and, therefore, systematically in relation to one another. In practice, however, variation in rate of return also occurs in response to random factors that are independent of the market mechanism. This category of variation is called *residual variation*. Strictly speaking, a *residual* is something left over or left unexplained by an econometric model.

Correlation describes a pattern of mutual linear dependence—where it exists between two random variables. The jointly distributed rates of return of Table 8-2, for example, exhibit perfect positive correlation, while those of Table 8-4 exhibit perfect negative correlation. Where two random variables are perfectly correlated, the pattern of joint variation is completely described by some *linear function*—that is, a straight line. The positively correlated rates of return of Table 8-2, for example, may be represented by points that plot along the line

$$\tilde{r}_{it} = -0.20 + 2.0\tilde{r}_{jt},$$

which is shown in Part (a) of Figure 8-5. The negatively correlated rates of return of Table 8-4, by contrast, are represented by points that plot

TABLE 8-4. Joint Distribution of Rates of Return

States of Nature	Probability	Stock i	Stock j
		Joint Event	
θ_1	0.125	-0.10	0.25
θ_2	0.125	0.00	0.20
θ_3	0.500	0.10	0.15
θ_4	0.125	0.20	0.10
θ_5	0.125	0.30	0.05

along a different line

$$\tilde{r}_{it} = 0.40 - 2.0\tilde{r}_{jt},$$

which is shown in Part (b) of Figure 8-5.

Over a long run of actual investment experience, patterns of covariation emerge. In the real world, however, statistical patterns of this sort result *not* from the simultaneous movement of wheels, pulleys, and belts as in the previous illustration, but from the interplay of social, legal, and economic factors. Therefore, the resulting joint events, in general, do not take the form of discrete points that plot neatly on a straight line, but are part of a *continuum* of possible outcomes that may be distributed about a statistical trend.[10]

Suppose, for example, that a sample history of rates of return is obtained from a time series for two stocks. Such a history provides, in effect, a snapshot of a *continuous* process—one that produces jointly distributed rates of return. Where the rates of return in the population are perfectly correlated, as in Parts (a) and (b) of Figure 8-5, the jointly distributed random outcomes,

$$[\tilde{r}_{it} \text{ and } \tilde{r}_{jt}]$$

of the sample will plot as points on a straight line about which there is no variation or dispersion. Perfect correlation, positive or negative, hardly ever occurs in practice; but the rates of return on most stocks are positively correlated.

In Part (c) of Figure 8-5 a representative scatter diagram is presented illustrating high, but less than perfect, positive correlation. The coefficient of correlation in this case is about 0.90. A representative scatter diagram illustrating high negative correlation is presented in Part (d) of the figure; the coefficient of correlation in this case is about -0.90. Notice that the distribution of points in either case traces out a rather compact ellipse. Where the *degree of linear relationship* is lower (but still significantly greater than zero), the scatter of points will be elliptically shaped, but more spread out, as in Part (e) of the figure. The coefficient of correlation for a scatter of points such as that shown in Part (e) would be in the neighborhood of 0.50. Where the rates of return are independent, the coefficient of correlation is 0.00. Part (f) of the figure shows a representative scatter diagram for a situation in which there is no apparent linear relationship between two random variables.

------

[10] The analogy of the previous illustration has served its purpose and is now discarded. The major implication of the change that is about to take place is that random variables such as rate of return will be treated (more realistically) as continuous random variables. A *continuous random variable* is one that can take on any value in the interval between adjacent points.

(a) Perfect Positive Correlation

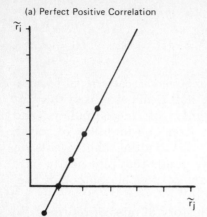

(b) Perfect Negative Correlation

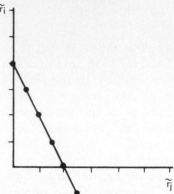

(c) High Positive Correlation

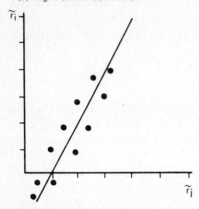

(d) High Negative Correlation

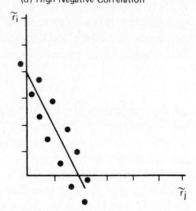

(e) Substantial Positive Correlation

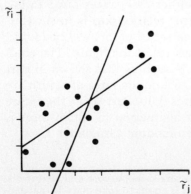

(f) No Correlation

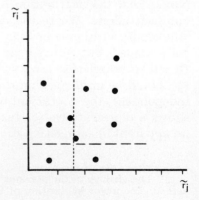

FIGURE 8–5. Correlated Rates of Return

A straight line can be fitted to any scatter diagram using ordinary regression techniques.[11] In the context of the correlation model, however, the trend line would be of little interest and is difficult to interpret in any event. Our concern here is not with a line of trend as such but with how compactly the points in a scatter diagram are distributed about a trend line. The coefficient of correlation provides a measure of the *degree of linear relationship*, and this value can be calculated directly from the data in a sample.

Equations (8.1) through (8.5) are appropriate for use with subjective data that may be discrete. By simple modification of these equations, one obtains a new set of equations for use with historical data that are never discrete. Let T represent the number of periods for which data are available, and let $\tilde{r}_{it}$ represent the rate of return in period t on stock i. The arithmetic mean of the rates of return in a sample is obtained by means of the familiar expression

$$\bar{r}_i = \frac{\left[\displaystyle\sum_{t=1}^{T} \tilde{r}_{it}\right]}{T}. \tag{8.6}$$

The variance of rate of return is simply the weighted average sum of squared deviations about the mean rate of return

$$\mathrm{Var}(\tilde{r}_i) = \frac{\left[\displaystyle\sum_{t=1}^{T} (\tilde{r}_{it} - \bar{r}_i)^2\right]}{T-1}, \tag{8.7}$$

where $T - 1 =$ the number of degrees of freedom for calculating a sample variance,[12] and the standard deviation of rate of return

$$\mathrm{SD}(\tilde{r}_i) = \sqrt{\mathrm{Var}(\tilde{r}_i)} \tag{8.8}$$

is the square root of the variance as before. The covariance of rates of return for any pair of stocks i and j is the weighted average sum of cross-products

---

[11] The regression and correlation models are different models and are based on different assumptions about the variables of the model. The regression model is introduced in Chapter 10.

[12] One degree of freedom is lost because the sum of squares is being taken about a sample mean and not the true parameter which, in practice, is always an unknown.

$$\text{Cov}(\tilde{r}_i,\tilde{r}_j) = \frac{\left[\sum\limits_{t=1}^{T} (\tilde{r}_{it} - \bar{r}_i)(\tilde{r}_{jt} - \bar{r}_j) \right]}{T - 1}, \qquad (8.9)$$

where $T - 1$ = the number of degrees of freedom for calculating a sample covariance.[13] The coefficient of correlation is obtained by adjusting the covariance for dispersion as before:

$$\text{Cor}(\tilde{r}_i,\tilde{r}_j) = \frac{\text{Cov}(\tilde{r}_i,\tilde{r}_j)}{\text{SD}(\tilde{r}_i)\text{SD}(\tilde{r}_j)}. \qquad (8.10)$$

As an illustration, real data on monthly rate of return were obtained for two stocks, covering a period of one year starting January, 1971.[14] The rates of return are shown in columns 1 and 2 of Table 8-5. The deviations of these rates of return about their respective means are shown in columns 3 and 4, and the cross-products of the deviations are shown in column 5. The deviations of columns 3 and 4 of Table 8.5 are squared and presented in columns 6 and 7, respectively. The mean rate of return for each stock is shown under "Summary Statistics" in the table. These statistics were obtained by Equation (8.6), using the column totals of columns 1 and 2, respectively, in the numerator and 12 degrees of freedom in the denominator. The variance statistics were similarly obtained by Equation (8.7), using the column totals of columns 6 and 7, respectively, in the numerator and 11 degrees of freedom in the denominator for each calculation. Calculating the covariance requires just one operation. The sum of cross-products which appears in the numerator of Equation (8.9) is obtained from the column total of column 5 of the table. One degree of freedom is lost. Thus, 11 degrees of freedom are used in the denominator of Equation (8.9) in this application. The resulting covariance is 23.35, which tells us very little about covariation. We standardize this measure by calculating the coefficient of correlation, using Equation (8.10). The resulting coefficient of correlation is 0.81 (after rounding), which indicates a very high degree of linear covariation.

The Variance-Covariance Matrix. A *variance-covariance matrix* and a *correlation matrix* are also presented under "Summary Statistics" in Table 8-5. Most standard computer programs report the results of these

---

[13] Two sample means are calculated, but only one degree of freedom is lost.

[14] The period, but not the stocks, was chosen at random. We will show later that these stocks are very unlikely to be chosen for the same investment portfolio. *Monthly rate of return* is defined as the change in price during the month plus a twelfth of the annual dividends, divided by the beginning price.

TABLE 8-5. Sample Calculation Using Monthly Data for One Year (in percent)

(1) $\tilde{r}_{1t}$	(2) $\tilde{r}_{2t}$	(3) $(\tilde{r}_{1t} - \bar{r}_1)$	(4) $(\tilde{r}_{2t} - \bar{r}_2)$	(5) $(\tilde{r}_{1t} - \bar{r}_1)(\tilde{r}_{2t} - \bar{r}_2)$	(6) $(\tilde{r}_{1t} - \bar{r}_1)^2$	(7) $(\tilde{r}_{2t} - \bar{r}_2)^2$
5.85000	19.19000	3.77750	17.02750	64.32138	14.26951	289.93576
-2.82000	- 7.03000	-4.89250	- 9.19250	44.97431	23.93656	84.50206
4.68000	4.45000	2.60750	2.28750	5.96466	6.79906	5.23266
2.82000	10.49000	.74750	8.32750	6.22481	.55876	69.34726
-4.12000	-11.04000	-6.19250	-13.20250	81.75648	38.34706	174.30601
2.02000	1.19000	- .05250	- .97250	.05106	.00276	.94576
1.16000	-10.08000	- .91250	-12.24250	11.17128	.83266	149.87881
3.24000	4.83000	1.16750	2.66750	3.11431	1.36306	7.11556
1.27000	5.58000	- .80250	3.41750	-2.74254	.64401	11.67931
2.18000	- 1.55000	.10750	- 3.71250	- .39909	.01156	13.78266
1.38000	- .18000	- .69250	- 2.34250	1.62218	.47956	5.48731
7.21000	10.10000	5.13750	7.93750	40.77891	26.39391	63.00391
24.87000	25.95000			256.83775	113.63847	875.21707

Summary Statistics

Variable	Mean	Variance	Variance-Covariance		Correlation	
1	2.07250	10.33077	10.33077	23.34888	1.00000	0.81440
2	2.16250	79.56518	23.34888	79.56518	0.81440	1.00000

calculations in precisely this way. In a two-stock application such as the present one, each matrix has two rows and two columns. By drawing a line connecting the upper left-hand corner of either matrix to the lower right-hand corner of that matrix, the reader will have traced out a *matrix diagonal*. We call this matrix diagonal the "main diagonal."

The elements along the main diagonal of any variance-covariance matrix are variance statistics.[15] The terms that lie above or below the main diagonal of a variance-covariance matrix are covariance statistics. In a two-stock case, of course, there is only one unique covariance. In this illustration the elements above and below the main diagonal are identical and, after rounding, equal to 23.35.[16]

Each element lying along the main diagonal of a correlation matrix is represented by unity—any random variable is perfectly correlated with itself. The elements above and below the main diagonal of a correlation matrix are statistics that represent the coefficients of correlation. In a two-stock example, of course, there is only one unique coefficient of correlation, which is equal to 0.81 in the preceding example.

Calculation and Interpretation

In practice there is no need for the financial analyst to perform any calculations by hand. Computer programs are widely available, easy to use, and specifically designed for this purpose. All that is required of the analyst is (1) to understand what *inputs* are required by the computer program and (2) to have some appreciation for the *output* that results. For use by most standard computer programs, for example, the input would include the basic data such as that presented in columns 1 and 2 of Table 8–5 and a few *control statements*. The computer program must be told (1) how many stocks there are, (2) what summary statistics are desired, and (3) which statistical model to apply—correlation, regression, or something else. There is no need, therefore, to burden the reader with more on the specifics of calculation or with the various computational forms that exist to facilitate hand calculation. We now turn to a purpose to which these concepts may be put.

RISK

Decisions made under conditions of certainty should turn out, after the fact, to be correct. When such conditions apply, there are no sources of variation or uncertainty to worry about, and there is no risk. Various

---

[15] The covariance of a random variable with itself is the variance of that random variable.

[16] The variance-covariance matrix and the correlation matrix are called "square symmetric." "Square" because the number of rows equals the number of random variables under study. "Symmetric" because that portion of the matrix above the main diagonal is the mirror image of the portion that lies below. Let n equal the number of stocks under study in an investment analysis. The number of unique covariance terms in any variance-covariance matrix is given by $(n^2 - n)/2$.

concepts of risk can be defined, as previously noted. In this section we expand on previous discussions and attempt to treat the topic in a unified way.

Downside Risk

The purchase of a risky asset, in effect, creates an uncertainty. When uncertainty applies, prior expectations are seldom realized after the fact. When the mathematical expectation, $E(\tilde{r}_k)$, coincides with the target rate of return, any outcome that is less desirable than the mathematical expectation is called an adverse event. The downside risk is measured in terms of a mathematical expectation: the weighted average of the consequences of all possible adverse events, with each such consequence weighted by the probability of occurrence.[17] For example, let r_f denote the rate of return on a riskless asset, and let $\tilde{r}_p$ be the rate of return on a portfolio of risky assets. The expectations of an investor who purchases a portfolio of risky assets may or may not be fully realized. Failure to realize one's ex-ante expectations ex-post may be called "tough luck," but it is not an adverse event in the present sense. If after the fact $\tilde{r}_p > r_f$, the investor would have lost nothing, relative to the riskless rate, by investing in a risky portfolio. Where $\tilde{r}_p < r_f$, however, the purchase of a portfolio of risky assets involves an opportunity cost relative to what might have been achieved with the riskless asset. An adverse event should be defined in terms of one's real investment alternatives, not in terms of a pipe dream.

The Variance as a Measure of Risk

The variance is a measure of spread of a distribution about its mean; it is not a measure of downside risk. However, if a distribution, say, of rate of return, is symmetric about its mean, then the variance or standard deviation will give precisely the same signals (that is, have the same implications) as would a measure of downside risk.[18]

Suppose, for example, that the expected rates of return on two stocks, i and j, are the same:

$$E(\tilde{r}_i) = E(\tilde{r}_j),$$

but that the variance of the first is greater than the variance of the second:

$$\mathrm{Var}(\tilde{r}_i) > \mathrm{Var}(\tilde{r}_j).$$

---

[17] Markowitz, *Portfolio Selection.*
[18] *Ibid.*

Assume, moreover, that the distribution of rate of return for any risky asset is symmetrically distributed about its mean. These assumptions are represented graphically by Figure 8-6.

Each distribution in the figure represents a rule of randomness that is governed by the same expectation. The fat-tail distribution, which we call "diffuse," is more spread out—it has the higher variance. Notice, moreover, that the riskless rate, r_f, is represented by a point in the left tail of either distribution. Points that lie to the left of r_f represent the adverse events of this example—the further to the left of r_f, the less desirable the event. It follows, therefore, that the area under a curve to the left of r_f corresponds to the probability of getting some adverse event.

Figure 8-6 shows that the probability of obtaining an adverse event is higher when the rule of randomness is represented by a diffuse distribution than when the distribution is highly concentrated about its mean. A distribution that is highly concentrated about its mean is called "peaked." Thus we arrive at the following generalization: for distributions that are at least roughly symmetric about their means, a measure of spread such as the variance or the standard deviation would have the same implications for investment decision as would a measure of downside risk.

The probabilities that one assigns to the possible outcomes of an investment decision may be objective or subjective in origin, and the resulting probability distribution may be symmetric or skewed. In any

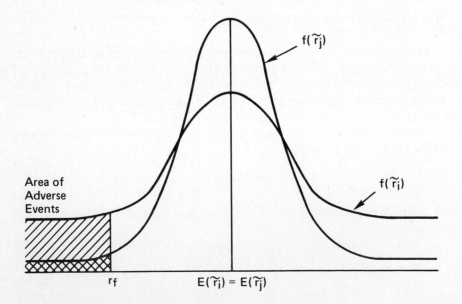

FIGURE 8-6. Prior Distributions on Rate of Return

case, the more diffuse one's *prior probability distribution* on the next outcome of a random variable, say, rate of return, the more uncertain one must be as to what the next outcome will be. A measure of dispersion may be interpreted, therefore, as a measure of one's degree of uncertainty about the next outcome or future outcomes of a random process. In this additional sense, the variance or the standard deviation may serve as a measure of risk. It will be shown in Chapter 9 that there are instances in which the variance measure is more convenient to use and other instances in which the standard deviation would have more appeal. Do understand, however, that their implications as measures of risk are perfectly equivalent.

Correlation and Covariance

Where the rates of return on all financial assets are perfectly correlated, risk reduction through diversification cannot be achieved. However, where rates of return are less than perfectly correlated, to the extent that these interrelationships can be known and appreciated by investors, they can be exploited to reduce or eliminate a component of investment risk. In the context of portfolio selection, correlation and covariance are indicators (as distinct from measurements) of the degree of risk reduction that can be achieved by including a particular security in an investment portfolio. Stock whose rates of return are highly correlated with the market, for example, possess a high degree of *nondiversifiable risk*. Such a stock, taken by itself, is not necessarily very risky. Taken in conjunction with other stocks, however, such a stock would contribute little toward risk reduction and is called "risky" in this very limited sense.

The Markowitz covariance portfolio selection approach is presented in Chapter 9. A computational alternative is presented in Chapter 10. According to this market's concept, total investment risk can be dichotomized into two components: a *systematic* component of risk that cannot be diversified away and a *nonsystematic* component of risk that can be reduced or eliminated by efficient diversification. Chapter 12 will show how the covariance and correlation concepts are useful for determining the risk associated with individual financial assets, while a measure of spread such as the standard deviation or variance would be more appropriate as a measure of risk for a diversified collection of risky financial assets.

SUMMARY

The object of financial diversification is risk reduction. Where the rates of return on securities in an investment portfolio are perfectly correlated, risk reduction through diversification cannot be achieved.

Whatever advantage is to be gained through financial diversification is due to the covariance effects. Where rates of return are less than perfectly correlated, therefore, effective risk reduction can be achieved by exploiting these interrelationships.

When all the facts that bear on an investment decision are known in advance, the environment of decision is called "certain." Decisions made under certainty should turn out, after the fact, to be correct. When purchasing a risk-free asset, there are no sources of variation to worry about, and there is no risk.

Where the outcome of an investment decision is determined by chance events, however, the environment of decision is uncertain. An asset that is purchased on the basis of imperfect knowledge about future events—and this includes virtually all financial assets—is called "risky." The purchase of risky financial assets is tantamount to the purchase of a financial lottery whose analogy might consist of a complex array of interdependent gaming devices—such as the wheels of fortune illustrations. A theory for rational asset selection under conditions of uncertainty must invoke both logic and techniques for dealing with random events.

The use of historical data in forming probability judgments does *not* necessarily imply that one believes that "history will repeat itself." In no sense of the word, moreover, can uncertainty about future events be resolved by mere estimation, regardless of how rich are one's sources of historical data. Regardless of one's sources of information—qualitative or quantitative, objective or subjective—to the extent that an individual bases his or her actions on the resulting probabilities, such probabilities represent one's "degrees of belief" or betting odds.

A probability distribution is a rule of randomness; it provides a mathematical description of a random process. There are two types of uncertainty. In investment decision one type of uncertainty is a consequence of the pattern of variation that is described by *some* rule of randomness. A second type of uncertainty is due to the fact that, for a risky asset, we can never know for sure which rule of randomness actually applies. In investment analysis, probability distributions are always "fuzzy," and any pretense to the contrary is misleading and pointless.

An analysis for investment decision must be comprehensive. The investor's specific investment goals must be considered, and these goals must be contrasted with willingness and ability to bear risk. But the environment of investment decision is complex. A rational approach for investment decision, therefore, will embrace information from whatever source it can be obtained. Such an approach calls for a blend of both art and science and for the integration of modern and traditional techniques and philosophies. These points will be demonstrated in the chapters that follow.

Questions

1. Distinguish between (a) certainty and uncertainty analysis; (b) a deterministic vs. a stochastic problem situation.

2. For each statement that follows, write a brief explanation.
   (a) The outcome of a random process defines a random variable.
   (b) The outcome of each random process is governed by some rule of randomness.
   (c) A probability distribution describes a rule of randomness.
   (d) The rate of return on a risky asset is a random variable.
   (e) The purchase of a risky asset is tantamount to participation in a financial lottery.
   (f) A summary statistic, such as expected return or variance, is a number; it is not a self-fulfilling prophecy.
   (g) There are two types of uncertainty: One type is due to and described by some rule of randomness; a second type results from uncertainty as to which rule of randomness applies.
   (h) The use of historical data in forming probability beliefs does not imply that "history will repeat itself," but only that historical data is a useful source of information (and often the only source) about an unknown probability distribution.
   (i) Regardless of one's source of information about a random process, to the extent that one is willing to base one's actions on the resulting probability distribution, probability measures degree of belief.

3. Risk may be defined as the expected consequence of an adverse event. From this point of view:
   (a) Contrast the variance and semivariance statistics as measures of risk.
   (b) Contrast these with other concepts and measures of risk discussed in the chapter.

4. Explain the meaning of each of the following:
   (a) a random process.
   (b) a random variable.
   (c) a probability distribution.
   (d) a rule of randomness.
   (e) a jointly distributed random variable.
   (f) a joint event.

5. What is the difference between a discrete random variable and a continuous random variable? What does one encounter more frequently in practice?

6. For each of the following mathematical concepts (a) explain the meaning of the concept in English, and (b) write out its definitional equation *both* for a discrete and for a continuous random process:
   (a) the mean of a distribution.

    (b) the expected value of a random variable.

    (c) the variance of a random variable.

    (d) the standard deviation.

    (e) a covariance statistic.

    (f) the coefficient of correlation.

7. Why is it necessary to standardize a covariance measurement and what is the result?

8. Explain each of the following terms:

    (a) a vector.

    (b) a matrix.

    (c) the main diagonal of a matrix.

    (d) a square-symmetric matrix.

    (e) a matrix partition.

9. A share of stock can be purchased today at a market price of p_t = $10. Tomorrow's price, and the dividend to be received during the holding period, is governed by chance events. The rule of randomness and the possible outcomes are as follows:

θ	$P(\theta)$	P_{t+1}	D_t
θ_1	0.05	$11	$0.00
θ_2	0.10	12	0.00
θ_3	0.70	13	1.00
θ_4	0.10	14	1.50
θ_5	0.05	15	2.00

    (a) Calculate the rate of return, $\tilde{r}_t$, corresponding to each state of nature.

    (b) Calculate the expected value of $\tilde{r}$.

    (c) Calculate the variance of $\tilde{r}$.

10. The data summary report shown in Table 8–A is based upon dividend adjusted rates of return calculated from monthly price and dividend information for a 14-year period. The means are expressed in percentage form. Explain each category of information presented and the use to which such information may be put in deciding upon the composition of an investment portfolio. (Note: this question will be asked again at the conclusion of the next chapter, at which point your answer should be somewhat more detailed.)

11. Multiply each of the numbers shown in columns 1 and 2 of Table 8–5 by 0.5. Having done so, one obtains two entirely new distributions of rates of return. For these new distributions perform the necessary calculations and make up a new data summary report to replace the one shown at the bottom of Table 8–5. Compare your summary statistics with the originals shown in the table and explain your observations.

APPENDIX TABLE 8-A.

Sec.	Company Name	Mean	Variance	SD
1	Bucyrus-Erie Co	34.97	28.31	5.32
2	Cities Service Co	11.85	8.14	2.85
3	Burroughs Corp	31.17	22.38	4.73
4	U.S. Steel Corp	5.31	2.38	1.54
5	Johnson & Johnson	26.42	11.76	3.43
6	CBS Inc	13.17	12.97	3.60
7	Bristol-Meyers Co	11.15	4.73	2.18
8	Procter & Gamble Co	11.19	4.07	2.02
9	Standard Oil Co (Ohio)	21.15	6.45	2.54
10	Delta Air Lines Inc	25.04	24.22	4.92

Variance-Covariance Matrix

Sec.	1	2	3	4	5	6	7	8	9	10
1	28.31	7.73	-.41	4.94	-2.74	-8.67	-1.74	-4.39	10.07	-2.04
2	7.73	8.14	-.23	1.65	-3.04	-1.53	-1.59	-1.97	1.83	1.83
3	-.41	-.23	22.38	-1.90	9.41	1.41	5.51	2.38	.63	9.94
4	4.94	1.65	-1.90	2.38	-.53	-.90	-.29	-.81	1.80	-1.27
5	-2.74	-3.04	9.41	-.53	11.76	3.80	3.29	4.44	1.23	5.97
6	-8.67	-1.53	1.41	-.90	3.80	12.97	3.78	1.98	-.92	10.07
7	-1.74	-1.59	5.51	-.29	3.29	3.78	4.73	.94	.23	5.81
8	-4.39	-1.97	2.38	-.81	4.44	1.98	.94	4.07	-1.08	-.10
9	10.07	1.83	.63	1.80	1.23	-.92	.23	-1.08	6.45	1.73
10	-2.04	1.83	9.94	-1.27	5.97	10.07	5.81	-.10	1.73	24.22

Correlation Matrix

Sec.	1	2	3	4	5	6	7	8	9	10
1	1.00	.51	-.02	.60	-.15	-.45	-.15	-.41	.75	-.08
2	.51	1.00	-.02	.37	-.31	-.15	-.26	-.34	.25	.13
3	-.02	-.02	1.00	-.26	.58	.08	.54	.25	.05	.43
4	.60	.37	-.26	1.00	-.10	-.16	-.09	-.26	.46	-.17
5	-.15	-.31	.58	-.10	1.00	.31	.44	.64	.14	.35
6	-.45	-.15	.08	-.16	.31	1.00	.48	.27	-.10	.57
7	-.15	-.26	.54	-.09	.44	.48	1.00	.21	.04	.54
8	-.41	-.34	.25	-.26	.64	.27	.21	1.00	-.21	-.01
9	.75	.25	.05	.46	.14	-.10	.04	-.21	1.00	.14
10	-.08	.13	.43	-.17	.35	.57	.54	-.01	.14	1.00

PART 3
The Portfolio Selection Framework

9.

The Markowitz Covariance Model

This chapter builds on the material in Chapter 8 and introduces the Markowitz covariance model for portfolio diversification. This model is easy to grasp and is more general than those that follow in the sense that a minimum of restrictive assumptions is called for. If one is willing to suppose, however, that the rates of return on various risky financial securities are related only in terms of common correlations with some underlying causative factor, such as the rate of return on the market for all risky assets, then a simplification of the full Markowitz variance-covariance computational technique is possible. A "simplified" market index model is introduced in Chapter 10. By virtue of this market-based index model, various theoretical insights are achieved. It will be shown that the risk associated with any financial security can be dichotomized into two components—a component of risk due to market fluctuations and a component of risk due to factors that are unique to that particular security. These ideas are extended in Chapter 11.

Further simplification is possible if one is willing to act in accord with an even more restrictive set of assumptions; i.e., that

> . . . capital markets are perfect in the sense that all assets are infinitely divisible, there are no transactions costs or taxes, information is costless and available to everybody, and borrowing and lending rates are equal to each other and the same for all investors.[1]

A capital market theory that assumes these conditions of general equilibrium apply is reserved for Part 4.

A portfolio selection model can be developed in an idealized setting but can never be applied in one. The problem of estimation, for example, is an integral part of the application of any analytic procedure for

---

[1] Eugene F. Fama, "Risk, Return, and Equilibrium: Some Clarifying Comments," *Journal of Finance*, Vol. 23, No. 1 (March, 1968), p. 30.

portfolio selection—clearly the required inputs cannot come out of thin air. In practice, data banks and statistical methods are used to estimate the means, variances, and covariances required by the model. Estimation, unfortunately, is a source of error, and such error is not accounted for by existing portfolio selection procedures. The differential effects of taxation, moreover, are virtually ignored by the current literature on portfolio selection and capital markets, but this is a very real problem in any real-world application. Such issues are not ignored here but are reserved for Chapters 11 and 13 and subsequent sections of the book.

MODERN PORTFOLIO THEORY

Modern portfolio theory is based on the pioneering work of Harry M. Markowitz.[2] Markowitz was the first to give rigorous content to the concept of portfolio diversification and to propose an analytic procedure by which it might be brought about. By *analytic procedure* we mean a procedure that begins with an unambiguous statement of objective, followed by analysis, and which culminates when one or more possible solutions to a problem—which satisfies a stated objective—are identified.

The Markowitz analytic procedure provides a method for identifying portfolios that are efficient in the sense that they satisfy certain efficiency criteria and various preconditions that may be imposed by a portfolio manager. A portfolio is called *efficient* if it (1) offers a higher expected rate of return than any other portfolio having the same level of risk and (2) offers a lower level of risk than any other portfolio having the same expected rate of return. These efficiency criteria are appropriate for use by investors who are[3]

1. Risk averse in the sense that they are made happy by anticipation of gain but are vexed by uncertainty about future rates of return.
2. Willing to base investment decisions about risky assets on estimated means, variances, and covariances of rate of return.

Application of quantitative portfolio selection techniques would not necessarily preempt any of the portfolio manager's accustomed discretionary options or the manager's responsibility for selecting portfolios that balance expected rate of return and risk in a way that satis-

---

[2] Harry M. Markowitz, *Portfolio Selection* (New Haven: Yale University Press, 1959).

[3] Formally, Tobin has established that the following are necessary and sufficient conditions for application of the mean-variance efficiency criteria: (1) that investor utility functions be quadratic or (2) that rate of return be a normal random variable. See James Tobin, "Liquidity Preference as Behavior Towards Risk," *Review of Economic Studies*, Vol. 26, No. 1 (February, 1958), pp. 65–86.

fies the client's investment objectives. Neither is it the purpose of normative portfolio theory to dictate to an investor what are proper investment objectives.[4] The Markowitz portfolio selection model provides the portfolio manager with a computationally efficient and logically consistent procedure for constructing portfolios that are ex-ante efficient. The means are also provided by which to determine what trade-offs between expected rate of return and risk might be achieved.

Whatever knowledge may exist at the time of decision about what may occur after the fact, of course, must be in the form of estimations. Modern portfolio theory does not relieve the security analyst of the responsibility for performing the necessary estimations, or of passing on the reasonableness of data that may be obtained from a subordinate or service. Neither is there any reason to suppose that bad estimation, naive application of highly abstract models, or both, can lead to good investment results. These new investment techniques must be used with discretion, and to do so requires an understanding of the theory on which they are based.

SECURITIES AND PORTFOLIOS

In portfolio selection the emphasis is on the collection and on how each part of a collection relates to the whole. The portfolio selection problem addressed here, therefore, is that of diversifying the investments in a portfolio in such a way that their future rates of return would not vary in unison.

Variable Representation

Many securities trade in the marketplace, but not all of these would be under active consideration by every investor at each point in time. In general, suppose that n securities are under active consideration for inclusion in an investment portfolio. A particular combination of n securities can be identified by means of a weights vector[5]

$$\underline{x} = [x_1, x_2, \ldots, x_n],$$

whose ith element represents the proportion of that combination that is represented by an investment in the ith security. Such a combination of n securities is called a portfolio. In a similar way, the expected rates of

---

[4] A normative theory seeks to explain *how* to accomplish a goal. Positive theory, by contrast, seeks to explain *what is* the situation or *what happens*, in general, when certain conditions are met.

[5] A single underscore attached to a letter identifies a vector. In general, an n component vector is an *ordered array* of n numbers. The vector x is an ordered array of n numbers, positive or zero, which sum to unity.

return on the n securities can be identified by means of the *expectations vector*[6]

$$E = [E_1, E_2, \ldots, E_n],$$

where the ith element

$$E_i = E(\tilde{r}_i)$$

represents the expected rate of return on the ith stock. The variance and covariance estimates may be set out in the form of a *variance-covariance matrix*[7]

$$C = \begin{bmatrix} C_{11} & C_{12} & \cdots & C_{1n} \\ C_{21} & C_{22} & \cdots & C_{2n} \\ \cdot & \cdot & \cdot & \cdot \\ \cdot & \cdot & \cdot & \cdot \\ \cdot & \cdot & \cdot & \cdot \\ C_{n1} & C_{n2} & \cdots & C_{nn} \end{bmatrix},$$

which is a *square-symmetric matrix*. The matrix is *square* because it has n rows and n columns, representing the n securities. The matrix is *symmetric* because each element

$$C_{ij} = \text{Cov}(\tilde{r}_i, \tilde{r}_j)$$

is equal to the corresponding element

$$C_{ji} = \text{Cov}(\tilde{r}_j, \tilde{r}_i).$$

The terms on the main diagonal

$$C_{ii} = \text{Cov}(\tilde{r}_i, \tilde{r}_i)$$
$$= \text{Var}(\tilde{r}_i)$$

are variance statistics.

An expectations vector and a variance-covariance matrix may be obtained for any collection of n securities by statistical methods, as explained in Chapter 8. What do such estimations represent in the context

---

[6] For ease of typography, a more compact notation is used to represent the elements of a vector or matrix. The terms are fully defined in the chapter.

[7] A double underscore attached to a letter identifies a matrix.

of portfolio selection? A mathematical expectation, $E(\tilde{r}_i)$, which is itself a random variable, estimates the mean of a random process that *may* determine tomorrow's rate of return on stock i.[8] A variance estimate, $\text{Var}(\tilde{r}_i)$, represents to the best of one's knowledge at the time of decision, the degree of spread of that random process relative to its *true mean*. A covariance statistic $\text{Cov}(\tilde{r}_i, \tilde{r}_j)$ estimates the degree of covariation of rates of return on stocks i and j relative to their respective means. Each covariance estimate can be standardized, in the sense explained in Chapter 8, by means of a very simple transformation on information that is contained in the variance-covariance matrix which follows from Equation (8.10):

$$R_{ij} = \frac{C_{ij}}{\sqrt{C_{ii}}\sqrt{C_{jj}}}$$

$$= \frac{\text{Cov}(\tilde{r}_i, \tilde{r}_j)}{\text{SD}(\tilde{r}_i)\,\text{SD}(\tilde{r}_j)}.$$

An estimate R_{ij} is an element of a different matrix

$$\underline{\underline{R}} = \begin{bmatrix} R_{11} & R_{12} & \cdots & R_{1n} \\ R_{21} & R_{22} & \cdots & R_{2n} \\ \cdot & \cdot & \cdot & \cdot \\ \cdot & \cdot & \cdot & \cdot \\ \cdot & \cdot & \cdot & \cdot \\ R_{n1} & R_{n2} & \cdots & R_{nn} \end{bmatrix},$$

whose elements along the main diagonal

$$R_{ii} = 1.00 \qquad \text{for all } i$$

are equal to unity and whose remaining elements

$$R_{ij} = \text{Cor}(\tilde{r}_i, \tilde{r}_j) \qquad \text{for all } i \text{ not equal to } j$$

are the coefficients of correlation. The symbol $\underline{\underline{R}}$ identifies the correlation matrix which, like C, is a square-symmetric matrix.

A Sample Application

Consider a simplified situation in which there exist just two securities. The mean and variance of annual rate of return and the covariance

---

[8] We say "may" because an estimate may be grossly in error or matters may change overnight. Clearly, an estimator is one thing, and a crystal ball is quite another.

TABLE 9-1. Securities Used in the Example

	Security Number	
	1	2
Mean returns:		
Percent	16.64	6.64
Standard deviations:		
Percent	4.58	4.08
Covariances:		
With security 1	21.02	-1.15
With security 2	-1.15	16.64
Correlations:		
With security 1	1.00	-0.06
With security 2	-0.06	1.00
Firm	Chrysler	N.Y. Ship

were calculated for two securities from annual data covering a representative period.[9] These values are shown in Table 9-1.

Any linear combination

$$\underline{x}_p = [x_1, x_2]$$

of these securities is a unique combination. Such a combination is called a *portfolio*. If one assumes that investments are *perfectly divisible* so that the smallest part of any security could be purchased, we would be left with an infinite number of possible combinations to consider. This, of course, would be perfectly ridiculous as securities are sold share for share at the market price, and, in general, are not divisible into parts of a share. To simplify matters, therefore, we will allow the investment weights x_i to vary from 0 to 1 in steps of 0.1, defining 11 different portfolios in the two-security case. These are shown in Table 9-2. An asterisk is used to identify the efficient portfolios.

The expected rate of return on any portfolio is a simple weighted average of the expected rates of return on the securities that are its component parts:

---

[9] Data from the examples in this section, and various illustrations, were adapted from two of the author's published papers. See George M. Frankfurter, Herbert E. Phillips, and John P. Seagle, "Portfolio Selection: The Effects of Uncertain Means, Variances, and Covariances," *Journal of Financial and Quantitative Analysis*, Vol. 6, No. 5 (December, 1971), pp. 1251-62; and, by the same authors, "Performance of the Sharpe Portfolio Selection Model: A Comparison," *Journal of Financial and Quantitative Analysis*, Vol. 11, No. 2 (June, 1976), pp. 195-204.

TABLE 9-2. Portfolio Summary Report, Two-Security Case

Portfolio Number	Portfolio Weights		Expected Return	Portfolio Variance	Portfolio SD
1*	10	0	16.64	21.02	4.58
2*	9	1	15.64	16.98	4.12
3*	8	2	14.64	13.75	3.71
4*	7	3	13.64	11.31	3.36
5*	6	4	12.64	9.68	3.11
6*	5	5	11.64	8.84	2.97
7*	4	6	10.64	8.80	2.96
8	3	7	9.64	9.56	3.09
9	2	8	8.64	11.12	3.33
10	1	9	7.64	13.48	3.67
11	0	10	6.64	16.64	4.08

$$E(\tilde{r}_p) = \sum_{i=1}^{n} x_i \, E(\tilde{r}_i). \qquad (9.1)$$

Each weight, x_i, represents the proportion of portfolio p that is invested in security i. In this illustration, and in most applications, an expectation, $E(\tilde{r}_i)$ in Equation (9.1), is obtained from the mean of historical rates of return as shown in Table 9-1. The expected rate of return for each one of the 11 portfolios identified in column 1 of Table 9-2 (and defined by the weights vectors of column 2) was calculated as follows. The expectations vector

$$\underline{E} = [16.64, \quad 6.64]$$

was formed from the means of historical rates of return, which are shown in Table 9-1. Equation (9.1) was applied to the elements of $\underline{E}$ and, for each portfolio, to the elements of $\underline{x}$—the elements of $\underline{x}$ vary from portfolio to portfolio as shown in column 2 of Table 9-2. The resulting expectations are shown in column 3 of the table. For example, for portfolio number 7

$$E(\tilde{r}_p) = (0.4)(16.64) + (0.6)(6.64)$$

$$= 10.64.$$

The other expected rates of return are calculated in the same way.

The corresponding portfolio variances are shown in column 4, Table 9-2. These calculations are not difficult to explain. The variance-covariance matrix

$$C = \begin{bmatrix} 21.02 & -1.15 \\ -1.15 & 16.64 \end{bmatrix}$$

is formed from information presented in Table 9-1. Notice that the terms along the main diagonal of the variance-covariance matrix

$$C_{11} = 21.02$$

and

$$C_{22} = 16.64$$

are variance statistics. Note also that the covariance term

$$C_{12} = \text{Cov}(\tilde{r}_1, \tilde{r}_2)$$

is the same as

$$C_{21} = \text{Cov}(\tilde{r}_2, \tilde{r}_1)$$

in the variance-covariance matrix. The variance of any portfolio p is a weighted average of all the elements of the variance-covariance matrix:[10]

$$\text{Var}(\tilde{r}_p) = \sum_{i=1}^{n} \left[\sum_{j=1}^{n} x_i x_j C_{ij} \right]$$

$$= \sum_{i=1}^{n} \left[\sum_{j=1}^{n} x_i x_j \text{Cov}(\tilde{r}_i, \tilde{r}_j) \right] . \tag{9.2}$$

Equation (9.2) is perfectly general in the sense that it holds for any number of securities. In the two-security case, however, algebraic expansion of Equation (9.2) is quite simple:

$$\text{Var}(\tilde{r}_p) = x_1 x_1 C_{11} + x_1 x_2 C_{12} + x_2 x_1 C_{21} + x_2 x_2 C_{22}.$$

Rearranging terms and simplifying, we get

$$\text{Var}(\tilde{r}_p) = x_1^2 C_{11} + x_2^2 C_{22} + 2[x_1 x_2 C_{12}] . \tag{9.3}$$

---

[10] Braces are provided in Equation (9.2) for the benefit of readers who may be unfamiliar with double summation operations. This practice will *not* be continued. The double summation operation of Equation (9.2) is illustrated by the algebraic expansion that leads to Equation (9.3).

According to Equation (9.2), portfolio variance is a weighted average of *all* the elements of the variance-covariance matrix. The standard deviation, of course, is simply the square root of this weighted average. In this weighted average, each element C_{ij} is weighted by the *product* of two weights x_i and x_j. For terms *along the main diagonal* (i.e., where $i = j$) that are variance terms:

$$x_i x_j = x_i^2.$$

For elements that are not on the main diagonal, the following is true:

$$x_i x_j C_{ij} = x_j x_i C_{ji}.$$

Two products in the algebraic expansion of Equation (9.2) are the same. The expansion can be simplified further, therefore, as in Equation (9.3). Where there are more than two securities, as in the more general cases that follow, the algebra does not reduce to a form as easy to follow as here. It will be instructive, therefore, to exploit the relative simplicity of the two-security case to show how diversification comes about before going on to more general cases.

Risk Reduction Through Diversification

By substitution of definitions for the elements of the variance-covariance matrix in Equation (9.3), one obtains the following definition of *portfolio variance* in the two-security case:

$$\text{Var}(\tilde{r}_p) = x_1^2 \text{Var}(\tilde{r}_1) + x_2^2 \text{Var}(\tilde{r}_2) + 2[x_1 x_2 \text{Cov}(\tilde{r}_1, \tilde{r}_2)]. \quad (9.4)$$

The variance of portfolio number 7, shown in column 4 of Table 9-2, for example, is

$$\text{Var}(\tilde{r}_p) = (0.4)^2(20.97) + (0.6)^2(16.64) - 2[(0.4)(0.6)(1.15)]$$

$$= 8.80.$$

This is a *minimum variance portfolio.*

Two interesting facts emerge from this calculation. First, portfolio Number 7, such as any portfolio shown in Table 9-2, is merely a linear combination of two securities. Nevertheless, the variance of this particular combination

$$\text{Var}(\tilde{r}_p) = 8.80$$

is *smaller* than the variance of either security taken by itself. This minimum variance portfolio, moreover, does *not* result from investment of equal amounts in each security, as in *naive diversification*. This example provides an illustration of *risk reduction* through diversification, which, really, is the one and only point of the Markowitz approach.

A second important fact that emerges from the calculation is that the covariance product

$$2x_1 x_2 \text{Cov}(\tilde{r}_1, \tilde{r}_2)$$

is subtracted from the weighted sum of the variances rather than added to it as in Equation (9.4). How so? Notice that the rates of return on these securities are negatively correlated, and that, therefore, the covariance term must have a negative sign. Clearly, subtraction of the covariance product in Equation (9.4) results in a smaller sum than addition of a covariance would.

Rates of return do not have to be negatively correlated, however, to achieve effective risk reduction through diversification. This point is made clearer by modification of Equation (9.4). It follows from Equation (8.10) that the covariance term in Equation (9.4) can be written

$$\text{Cov}(\tilde{r}_1, \tilde{r}_2) = \text{SD}(\tilde{r}_1)\, \text{SD}(\tilde{r}_2)\, \text{Cor}(\tilde{r}_1, \tilde{r}_2).$$

By substitution into Equation (9.4) one gets

$$\begin{aligned} \text{Var}(\tilde{r}_p) = {} & x_1^2 \text{Var}(\tilde{r}_1) + x_2^2 \text{Var}(\tilde{r}_2) \\ & + 2[x_1 x_2 \text{SD}(\tilde{r}_1)\, \text{SD}(\tilde{r}_2)\, \text{Cor}(\tilde{r}_1, \tilde{r}_2)], \end{aligned} \qquad (9.5)$$

which shows that risk reduction through diversification is impossible *only* when rates of return are perfectly correlated. As the coefficient of correlation in Equation (9.5) gets small, on the other hand, the product term on the right gets small also. For security rates of return that are uncorrelated, the product term that contains the correlation coefficient drops out of the expression altogether. Where rates of return are negatively correlated, as in the example, the situation is even more favorable to the achievement of risk reduction through diversification—the product term has a negative sign.

Risk Reduction and Correlation

Portfolio risk may be represented in either variance or standard deviation form. The critical results of a portfolio selection problem would not be affected by which measure is used. The variance measure is used in this text for computational convenience, but the standard deviation is useful here to dramatize a point.

The standard deviation of portfolio rate of return may be obtained from the square root of Equation (9.5):

$$\begin{aligned} \text{SD}(\tilde{r}_p) = {} & [x_1^2 \text{Var}(\tilde{r}_1) + x_2^2 \text{Var}(\tilde{r}_2) \\ & + 2\{x_1 x_2 \text{SD}(\tilde{r}_1)\, \text{SD}(\tilde{r}_2)\, \text{Cor}(\tilde{r}_1, \tilde{r}_2)\}]^{1/2}. \end{aligned} \qquad (9.6)$$

When the coefficient of correlation is *unity* (that is, where security rates of return are perfectly correlated), Equation (9.6) simplifies to

$$SD(\tilde{r}_p) = [x_1^2 Var(\tilde{r}_1) + x_2^2 Var(\tilde{r}_2) + 2\{x_1 x_2 SD(\tilde{r}_1) SD(\tilde{r}_2)\}]^{1/2},$$

which has a perfect square root

$$SD(\tilde{r}_p) = x_1 SD(\tilde{r}_1) + x_2 SD(\tilde{r}_2).$$

When the coefficient of correlation is unity, therefore, portfolio risk may be expressed by a simple linear function of the standard deviations. When the coefficient of correlation is not equal to unity, on the other hand, Equation (9.6) does not reduce to a form that has a perfect square root, and therefore is not a simple linear function of the standard deviations.

The portfolio standard deviation in a two-security problem, such as that described by Table 9-1, can be plotted as a function of the decision weights, as in Figure 9-1. Corner (a) of the figure represents a portfolio that consists entirely of investments in the more risky security; corner (b) represents a pure investment in the less risky security. As we

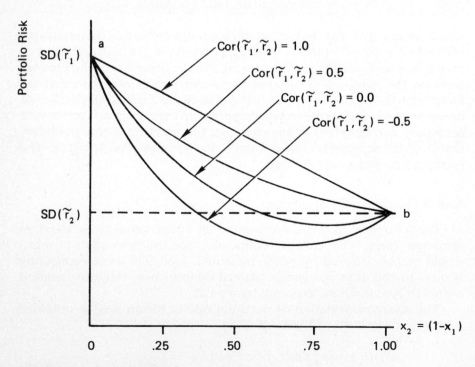

FIGURE 9-1. Portfolio Risk

move from corner (a) to corner (b) along any path, of course, portfolio risk will be reduced. Several alternative paths are shown in the figure, each corresponding to a different assumption about the coefficient of correlation.

Turning to expected rate of return, according to Equation (9.1), the expected rate of return on any portfolio is a weighted average of the rates of return on the component securities. In the two-security case this expectation is given by the linear function

$$E(\tilde{r}_p) = x_1 E(\tilde{r}_1) + x_2 E(\tilde{r}_2),$$

whose graph is given by a straight line, as shown in Figure 9-2.

Corner (a) of Figures 9-1 and 9-2, respectively, represents the same portfolio, and similarly for corner (b). Movement from corner (a) to corner (b) comes about by changing the portfolio weights—purchasing less of the more risky security. Such a shift will result in a reduction of risk at the expense of expected rate of return. The expected rate of return, of course, changes at a constant rate of change regardless of the coefficient of correlation; this follows from the fact that its graph is represented by a straight line. Portfolio risk, by contrast, changes at a

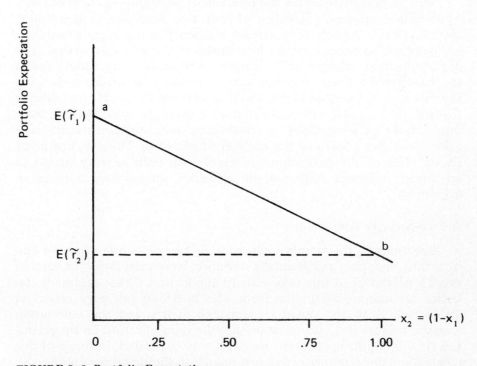

FIGURE 9-2. Portfolio Expectation

constant rate of change *only* when the rates of return on the component securities are perfectly correlated. When rates of return are less than perfectly correlated, on the other hand, portfolio risk will go down as one moves from corner (a) to corner (b), but at a faster rate of change than portfolio expected rate of return. Diversification, in a sense, comes about as a result of a favorable balance of trade between expectation and risk. The smaller the coefficient of correlation, the more favorable is the rate at which one can exchange expectation for risk.

Notice also that when the coefficient of correlation is *small enough*, the graph of Figure 9-1 will plot, in part, below the horizontal line drawn through $SD(\tilde{r}_2)$ in the figure. For points below this line, the risk associated with *some* combinations of securities is smaller than the risk associated with a pure investment in either security. These combinations are not arbitrary combinations, however—one does not achieve effective risk reduction by random selection even when the rates of return are less than perfectly correlated. Indeed, one does not achieve significant risk reduction at all unless the intercorrelations among rates of return are low enough.

PORTFOLIO EFFICIENCY ANALYSIS

This section begins with the problem of portfolio selection out of a hypothetical universe consisting of only two securities. In this simple setting, various aspects of portfolio efficiency analysis are illustrated, applying the covariance model introduced in the previous section. The environment of decision is then made more realistic by adding first a third and then a fourth security to the universe of securities under consideration. With each addition, the marginal benefit of efficient diversification is illustrated and contrasted with previous cases. Finally, these implications are generalized by considering cases involving security universes that may consist of any number of securities. The marginal benefit of efficient diversification decreases with each security added to an already efficient collection of securities, approaching zero as an asymptote.

A Two-Security Application

Returning to the sample application of Table 9-1, the expected rate of return, variance, and standard deviation were calculated for each of the 11 portfolios of this two-security application. These summary statistics are represented in the form of a *portfolio summary* report in Table 9-2. Both the variance-covariance matrix and the correlation matrix of Table 9-1 clearly show that the rates of return on the securities of this sample application are negatively correlated. In terms of this illustration, therefore, effective risk reduction should be possible.

A portfolio report, such as that shown in Table 9-2, takes all the *information* that is implicit in an expectations vector E and a variance-covariance matrix C (see Table 9-1) and compacts it, reducing the portfolio selection problem to a two-dimensional problem to be resolved on the basis of expectation and variance. A graphic representation of this problem is presented in Figure 9-3.

The portfolios of Table 9-2 plot as points in a two-dimensional grid, shown in Figure 9-3, where portfolio expectation is measured along the vertical axis and portfolio variance is measured along the horizontal axis. Such a two-dimensional grid is called an *EV space*, as its dimensions are defined in terms of portfolio expectation and variance. The portfolios of Table 9-2 are represented by discrete points in the figure, but a curve has been drawn through the points for ease of reference.

A portfolio is *efficient* if (1) it maximizes the expected rate of return for a given level of risk and (2) minimizes risk for a given level of expectation. Portfolios marked by an asterisk in Table 9-2 are efficient portfolios. These portfolios are represented by points that lie along the *efficient frontier* in Figure 9-3.

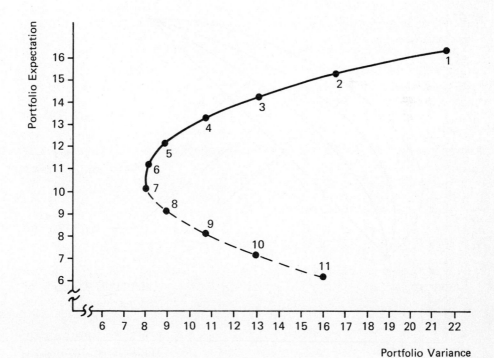

FIGURE 9-3. Portfolio-Efficient Frontier—Two-Security Case

In Figure 9–3 points that plot along that portion of the curve (which begins at point 7 and works its way upward and to the right) trace out the efficient frontier of the *feasible region* for these securities. For each portfolio that plots below and to the right of point 7, there is *at least* one point on the efficient frontier that offers (1) a lower level of risk for the same or a higher expectation and (2) a higher level of expectation for the same or a lower level or risk.

Correlation and the Shape of the Efficient Frontier. The efficient portfolios of Table 9–2 are shown plotted in EV space in Figure 9–3. Similar curves are presented in Figure 9–4 under various assumptions about the coefficient of correlation for two hypothetical securities. In Figure 9–4, however, portfolio risk is measured in terms of the standard deviation rather than the variance statistic.

We see from the figure that when the coefficient of correlation is high enough, no dominance relationship can be established—all possible combinations of two securities are efficient in the sense of the model. When the coefficient of correlation is small enough, by contrast, then some security combinations will be dominated by other combinations.

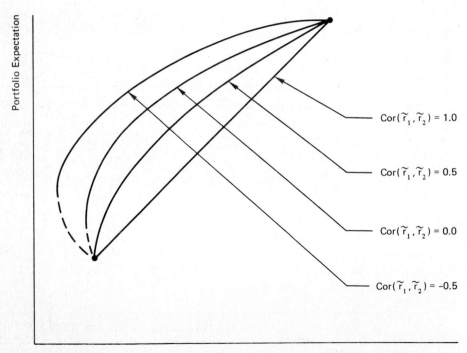

FIGURE 9–4. Correlation and Risk Reduction

The slope of the curve at any point represents the rate at which expectation can be substituted for risk at the margin. In all cases but one, this function increases at a decreasing rate. That is, where rates of return are less than perfectly correlated, risk reduction may be accompanied by a less than proportionate decrease in portfolio expected rate of return. Where security rates of return are perfectly correlated, on the other hand, portfolio expectation and risk will exchange at a constant rate. In this sense risk reduction cannot be achieved where rates of return are perfectly correlated.

Curvature: A Question of Space. From the point of view of the mathematics of portfolio analysis, the variance measure has several advantages over the standard deviation. From the point of view of actual results, on the other hand, which measure is used makes no difference. Table 9-2 shows that each portfolio that plots along the efficient frontier in EV space also plots along the efficient frontier when portfolio risk is measured in terms of the standard deviation and in the same order relative to other efficient portfolios.

The efficient frontier in EV space, however, has more curvature and no linear segments. Where mathematical programming techniques are applied, this nonlinearity is important. In models that follow the Markowitz tradition, moreover, an investor's investment objective can be described by a linear function in EV space; such an *objective function* is introduced below.

The portfolios of this two-security example plot as discrete points along the curve shown in Figure 9-3. If the restriction that the weights, x_i, be permitted to vary from 0 to 1 only if steps of 0.1 were relaxed, then the set of possible portfolios would grow from 11 to infinity. The boundary (both on and below the efficient frontier) would fill with points, but the space that is bounded by the curve would be empty. However, with the introduction of a third security, this space too would fill with points, as illustrated in the next section.

A Three-Security Application

A third security is added to the securities of Table 9-1. The mean, variance, and covariance of rate of return with each of the other securities were calculated, as before, from annual data. The resulting statistics are shown in Table 9-3. Notice that the variance-covariance matrix that appears in Table 9-1 is a partition of the variance-covariance matrix of Table 9-3.

The correlation matrix is not presented in Table 9-3 as it is not needed; the correlation statistics and the standard deviations may be obtained from the variance-covariance matrix.

TABLE 9-3. Expectations, Variances, and Covariances—
Three-Security Case

	Security Number		
	1	2	3
Mean returns:			
Percentage	16.64	6.64	21.35
Covariances:			
With security 1	21.02	-1.15	11.15
With security 2	-1.15	16.64	-0.37
With security 3	11.15	-0.37	22.23
Firm	Chrysler	N.Y. Ship	Bulova

By allowing an investment weight, x_i, to vary from 0 to 1 in steps of 0.1 as before, 66 unique combinations, where

$$\sum_{i=1}^{3} x_i = 1.00$$

and

$$x_i \geqslant 0.00 \quad \text{for all } i$$

are possible. A portfolio summary report for the portfolios of this three-security sample application is presented in Table 9-4. We see from the table that, of the 66 possible portfolios, 21 portfolios will lie on the efficient frontier in this application.

Every *feasible* combination of the means and variances of Table 9-4 plots as a point in the *feasible region* of EV space. Points that plot outside the feasible region are, according to the sample data, not obtainable. Where there are three or more mutually distinct securities, moreover, and no constraints are placed on the investment weights other than

$$\sum_{i=1}^{n} x_i = 1.00$$

and

$$x_i \geqslant 0.00 \quad \text{for all } i,$$

TABLE 9-4. Portfolio Summary Report

Portfolio Number	Portfolio Weights			Mean Return	Portfolio Variance	Portfolio Number	Portfolio Weights			Mean Return	Portfolio Variance
1*	0	0	10	21.35	22.23	34	7	2	1	15.11	12.41
2*	1	0	9	20.88	20.22	35*	4	3	3	15.05	09.19
3*	2	0	8	20.41	18.63	36	1	4	5	15.00	09.30
4*	3	0	7	19.94	17.46	37	8	2	0	14.64	13.75
5	0	1	9	19.88	18.10	38	5	3	2	14.58	09.48
6*	4	0	6	19.46	16.72	39*	2	4	4	14.52	08.54
7*	1	1	8	19.41	16.30	40	6	3	1	14.11	10.19
8	5	0	5	18.99	16.38	41*	3	4	3	14.05	08.20
9*	2	1	7	18.94	14.92	42	0	5	5	14.00	09.53
10	6	0	4	18.52	16.47	43	7	3	0	13.64	11.31
11*	3	1	6	18.47	13.96	44	4	4	2	13.58	08.27
12	0	2	8	18.41	14.77	45	1	5	4	13.53	08.56
13	7	0	3	18.05	16.98	46	5	4	1	13.11	08.76
14*	4	1	5	17.99	13.42	47*	2	5	3	13.05	08.00
15*	1	2	7	17.94	13.18	48	6	4	0	12.64	09.68
16	8	0	2	17.58	17.91	49*	3	5	2	12.58	07.86
17	5	1	4	17.52	13.29	50	0	6	4	12.53	09.37
18*	2	2	6	17.47	12.00	51	4	5	1	12.11	08.14
19	9	0	1	17.11	19.25	52	1	6	3	12.06	08.60
20	6	1	3	17.05	13.59	53	5	5	0	11.64	08.84
21*	3	2	5	17.00	11.25	54	2	6	2	11.58	08.25
22	0	3	7	16.94	12.23	55	3	6	1	11.11	08.31
23	10	0	0	16.64	21.02	56	0	7	3	11.06	10.00
24	7	1	2	16.58	14.30	57	4	6	0	10.64	08.80
25*	4	2	4	16.52	10.91	58	1	7	2	10.58	09.44
26*	1	3	6	16.47	10.84	59	2	7	1	10.11	09.29
27	8	1	1	16.11	15.43	60	3	7	0	09.64	09.56
28	5	2	3	16.05	10.99	61	0	8	2	09.58	11.42
29*	2	3	5	16.00	09.88	62	1	8	1	09.11	11.06
30	9	1	0	15.64	16.98	63	2	8	0	08.64	11.12
31	6	2	2	15.58	11.49	64	0	9	1	08.12	13.64
32*	3	3	4	15.52	09.32	65	1	9	0	07.64	13.48
33	0	4	6	15.47	10.49	66	0	10	0	06.64	16.64

Note: Mean returns are given in percentages, variances in (percent)$^2 \times 10^{-2}$. Weights are fractions multiplied by 10. Efficient portfolios are indicated by an asterisk.

Source: George M. Frankfurter, Herbert E. Phillips, and John P. Seagle, "Portfolio Selection: The Effects of Uncertain Means, Variances, and Covariances," *Journal of Financial and Quantitative Analysis*, Vol. 6, No. 5 (December, 1971).

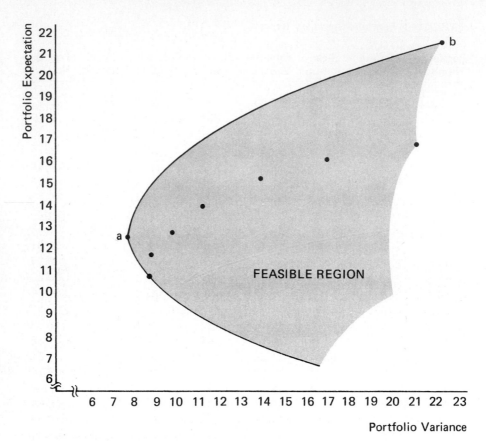

FIGURE 9-5. EV Space—Three-Security Case

then the feasible region is a bounded region that is filled with points, both within and along its frontier. The feasible region for the securities of this application is shown in Figure 9-5.

When calculating the means and variances that make up a portfolio summary report, such as that presented by Table 9-4, the analyst in effect *estimates* the betting probabilities for alternative financial lotteries. To what extent, if any, the resulting probabilities properly reflect real-world random processes is a matter of real concern; this question is taken up in Chapter 11. Nevertheless, to the extent that one's probabilistic judgments can be established on the basis of *sample* mean, variance, and covariance statistics, a portfolio efficiency analysis reduces to a contrast between alternative probability distributions on rate of return.

Each portfolio that lies on the efficient frontier dominates some interior portfolio that lies below and to its right. Each portfolio that does not lie on the efficient frontier, by contrast, is dominated by some portfolio that does. It suffices, therefore, to consider only those portfolios that lie on the efficient frontier.

No portfolio that lies on the efficient frontier is dominated by any other portfolio. Which efficient portfolio, in application, would best suit a particular investor depends on how *risk averse* that investor happens to be.[11] Different investors may prefer different EV combinations along the efficient frontier.[12] In this context the shape of the efficient frontier is both of theoretical and practical importance.

Referring to Figure 9–5, we see that a frontier of efficiency that is drawn in EV space will start at some minimum point (a) and rise at a decreasing rate (as measured by the slope of the curve, evaluated at any point) until some finite limit (b) is reached. An investor who is absolutely risk averse, but for some reason is intent on purchasing risky assets, would purchase the minimum risk portfolio (a). As one moves beyond point (a) along the efficient frontier, higher expectation is obtained in exchange for a higher level of risk. Curvature is important. As one moves up the curve and to the right, the curve gets flatter. With each increase in expectation, therefore, one is required to accept *more than a proportionate* increase in risk. This is a market phenomenon and is perfectly consistent with established theory in the area of value and capital.[13]

Risk Reduction with Go-Go Stocks? In this section a third security was added to those of the previous illustration. Contrasting Table 9–1 and 9–3, we see that the smaller variance-covariance matrix of Table 9–1 is a partition of the larger one and that the additional stock is less than perfectly correlated with the securities of the previous illustration. Contrasting the portfolio summary reports of Tables 9–2 and 9–4, we see that the 11 feasible portfolios of the two-security case form a subset (i.e., are a part) of the feasible region of the three-security case.

The new security offers the highest level of expected rate of return but also sports the highest level of risk. Does one have to be a risk lover to justify the inclusion of a relatively risky asset in an otherwise conser-

---

[11] An investor's degree of risk aversion can be described in terms of the rate at which the investor would be just willing to exchange expectation for risk at the margin. Fortunately, "descriptions" of this sort are unnecessary. In applications of the model, a client can be presented with a list of efficient options. Investors, quite typically, get born, pay taxes, and die with little, if any, thought devoted to the fact that a different course of action might be more fun. Investors, left to their own devices—uncluttered by formalistic utility axioms—will make decisions.

[12] The introduction of a riskless asset would, given certain assumptions, lead us to a different conclusion. This logic will be developed in Part 4, below.

[13] J. R. Hicks, *Value and Capital* (Oxford: The Clarendon Press, 1962), pp. 125-126.

vative investment portfolio?[14] Hardly! Figure 9–5 shows that the efficient portfolios of the two-security case (see Table 9–2) plot as points in the *interior region* of the feasible region of the three-security case. We see from the portfolio summary report of Table 9–4, moreover, that each efficient portfolio contains positive amounts of security 3, which,

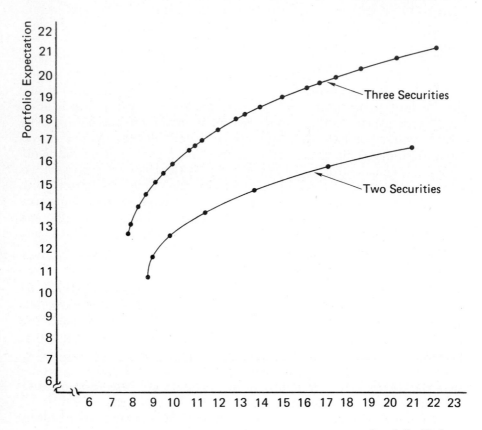

FIGURE 9–6. Portfolio-Efficient Frontiers—Contrast of Two- and Three-Security Applications

[14] This question is of more than mere academic interest. Investment managers have been sued by clients for investing in "unseasoned, speculative and volatile securities . . . involving a high level of investment risk." See *The Trustees of Hanover College* v. *Donaldson, Lufkin & Jenrette*, U.S. District Court, Southern District of Indiana, Indianapolis Division, Docket N. 71–C–686, December 7, 1971. Existing legal regulations which govern the conduct of investment trusts, and the investment lists that exist in some states, predate modern portfolio theory and are grossly incompatible with it. See Peter Barack, "The Regulation of Risky Investments," *Harvard Law Review*, Vol. 83 (January, 1970), pp. 603–625.

while far from being a go-go stock, is a riskier financial asset than the other securities of this application.

Portfolio Efficiency. The efficient frontiers of the two- and three-security cases are plotted in Figure 9-6. We see from the figure that the addition of a stock that is less than perfectly correlated with the other two results in (1) a shift upward of the efficient frontier, (2) an upward tilt of the efficient frontier, and (3) more curvature along the efficient frontier. Any level of expected rate of return, therefore, that was feasible before can now be achieved at a substantially lower level of risk. The minimum risk portfolio corresponds to a lower level of risk than before and a higher level of expected rate of return. At any level of risk, moreover, the net change in expected rate of return that results from the addition of the next unit of risk is greater in the three-security case. Figure 9-6 illustrates how risk reduction through diversification is achieved by the addition of more securities to an investment portfolio. As argued below, this process cannot continue forever; however, first a fourth security is introduced to this sample application and its impact examined.

A Four-Security Application

A third security was added to the securities of the two-security case in Table 9-3. In this section, a fourth security is added to the securities of the previous two- and three-security applications. As before, expectations, variances, and covariances are obtained from sample estimations. The basic data for this four-security application are presented in Table 9-5.

TABLE 9-5. Expectations, Variances, and Covariances—Four-Security Case

	Security Number			
	1	2	3	4
Mean returns:				
Percentage	16.64	6.64	21.35	19.91
Covariances:				
With security 1	21.02	-1.15	11.15	0.44
With security 2	-1.15	16.64	-0.37	-2.68
With security 3	11.15	-0.37	22.23	8.15
With security 4	0.44	-2.68	8.15	17.97
Firm	Chrysler	N.Y. Ship	Bulova	Avis Corp.

TABLE 9-6. Portfolio Summary Report of Efficient Portfolios—Four-Security Case

Portfolio Number	Portfolio Weights				Expected Return	Portfolio Variance	Portfolio Number	Portfolio Weights				Expected Return	Portfolio Variance
1	0	0	10	0	21.35	22.23	21	2	1	2	5	18.22	8.67
2	0	0	9	1	21.21	19.65	22	3	1	2	4	17.89	8.27
3	0	0	8	2	21.06	17.55	23	3	1	1	5	17.75	8.04
4	0	0	7	3	20.92	15.93	24	4	1	1	4	17.42	8.00
5	0	0	6	4	20.77	14.79	25	1	2	3	4	17.36	7.89
6	0	0	5	5	20.63	14.13	26	4	1	0	5	17.28	7.84
7	0	0	4	6	20.49	13.94	27	1	2	2	5	17.22	7.77
8	1	0	5	4	20.30	13.05	28	2	2	3	3	17.03	7.52
9	1	0	4	5	20.16	12.46	29	2	2	2	4	16.89	6.99
10	1	0	3	6	20.02	12.34	30	2	2	1	5	16.75	6.93
11	2	0	4	4	19.85	11.74	31	3	2	1	4	16.42	6.50
12	2	0	3	5	19.69	11.21	32	4	2	0	4	15.95	6.43
13	2	0	2	6	19.54	11.15	33	2	3	2	3	15.56	6.10
14	3	0	3	4	19.36	10.84	34	2	3	1	4	15.42	5.80
15	3	0	2	5	19.22	10.37	35	3	3	1	3	15.09	5.75
16	4	0	2	4	18.89	10.36	36	3	3	0	4	14.95	5.52
17	1	1	4	4	18.83	10.08	37	2	4	1	3	14.09	5.47
18	4	0	1	5	18.75	9.96	38	2	4	0	4	13.95	5.41
19	1	1	3	5	18.69	9.71	39	3	4	0	3	13.62	5.33
20	2	1	3	4	18.36	8.96							

By allowing the investment weights to vary from 0 to 1 in steps of 0.1, 11 possible combinations resulted in the two-security case; 66 resulted in the three-security case; and 286 possible combinations resulted in this four-security application. A portfolio summary report, presented in Table 9-6 describes only the efficient set of portfolios, which has grown to 39. Efficient frontiers for the two-, three-, and four-security applications are presented in a single graph in Figure 9-7.

A common misconception is to suppose that high risk results merely from investment in risky securities. Of course, this notion is not entirely incorrect, but it is quite beside the point. We see from Table 9-4 that the riskiest security, stock 3, is represented by a positive investment weight in the minimum risk efficient portfolio; the riskiest efficient portfolio, on the other hand, represents a pure investment in this single

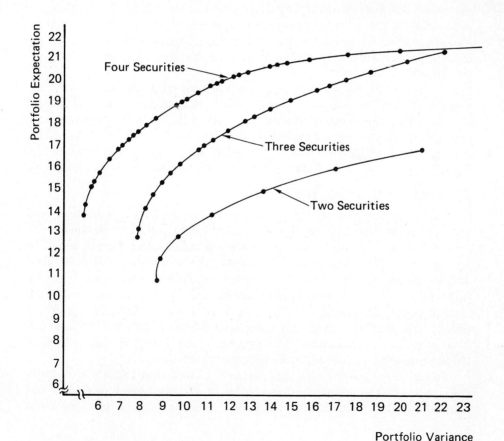

FIGURE 9-7. Portfolio-Efficient Frontiers—Two-, Three-, and Four-Security Applications

security. A more complete portfolio summary report would show, moreover, that many of those portfolios that lie farthest from the efficient frontier place little or no weight on security 3.

Table 9-6 illustrates the point that for efficient portfolios high risk is generally the result of concentration on just a few securities. Under these conditions, of course, there is little diversification, and, thus, little risk reduction. One can suffer roughly the same effect, unwittingly, by investing in a barrelful of securities whose rates of return are highly correlated. Portfolios that are concentrated in blue chip stocks, for example, are not efficiently diversified portfolios. Such a portfolio subjects the holder to a disproportionately high level of risk when measured against expected rate of return. There is some question, moreover, whether the new index funds now in vogue are diversified in a Markowitz sense. But this is a topic for Chapter 13.

Figure 9-7 shows that the reward for bearing very high levels of investment risk can be quite small. As one moves out to the right along any efficient frontier, one gains less with each step in terms of higher, ex-ante, expected rate of return. Therefore, in the long run, prudently managed portfolios are likely to outperform those governed by daredevil instinct.

We see from Figure 9-7 that the addition of a fourth security has resulted in a higher degree of risk reduction than was available before. Nevertheless, the efficient frontier is getting flatter and converges on a point that was previously obtainable with only three securities. This illustration is suggestive of the fact that there may be a limit to the degree of risk reduction that can be achieved by efficient diversification.

The Limits of Diversification

The only purpose of financial diversification is risk reduction, and any risk reduction that results from diversification is due to the covariance effect of rates of return. As more and more securities are added to an existing *efficient portfolio*, however, the difficulty will be to find any securities whose rates of return are *not* highly correlated with the rates of return on securities that are already included. Beyond some critical point, therefore, the efficient frontier of the feasible region will rise by less and less with each additional security, and the surface will lose most of its curvature. The process of meaningful risk reduction through diversification will not continue indefinitely.

In an early paper Evans and Archer showed that there is a relationship between the number of securities in an investment portfolio and portfolio risk.[15] According to Evans and Archer, as is clear from

---

[15] John L. Evans and Stephen H. Archer, "Diversification and the Reduction of Dispersion: An Empirical Analysis," *Journal of Finance*, Vol. 23, No. 5 (December, 1968), pp. 761-767.

Figure 9–7, this relationship takes the form of a rapidly decreasing asymptotic function. Evans and Archer plotted the marginal benefit of diversification as a function of portfolio size by adding securities one by one, as we have done in this chapter, and then applying equal weights. The resulting portfolios were called *naively diversified*. On the basis of these naively diversified portfolios, they concluded that there is some doubt "concerning the economic justification of increasing portfolio sizes beyond 10 or so securities."[16]

In fact, naive diversification is one thing and efficient diversification is quite another. We see from Figure 9–7 that the rate of convergence of the efficient frontier on a state of zero curvature is very rapid along that region where high, almost daredevil, risk would be taken but is not so rapid in the region that corresponds to more conservative investment strategies. Therefore, real-world efficient portfolios will, in the main, be somewhat larger than Evans and Archer assumed. Nevertheless, the major point of this research is clearly correct: the marginal benefit of diversification will get small as more and more securities are added to an investment portfolio. Therefore, as will be argued below, strategies that call for "buying the market" are not compatible with Markowitz logic.

Investment in Large Numbers of Securities

In order to hold the number of portfolios down to a manageable level for purpose of illustration, a somewhat artificial restriction was imposed on each investment weight. With only two securities in the sample application, there were 11 possible portfolios. This number grew to 66 in the three-security case and to 286 with the addition of a fourth security. If the process of addition were permitted to continue, the "brute force" computational scheme featured above would quickly be dwarfed by the enormity of the problem. The addition of a fifth security, for example, would bring the number of possible portfolios to 1,001, and with ten securities this number would grow to 92,378.[17] In real-world applications one's alternatives would number in the millions.

Fortunately, the portfolio selection problem can be posed as a quadratic programming problem. A compact representation of this procedure is presented in Chapter 11. Computer programs that are easy to use and require no advanced mathematical training on the part of the user are widely available. Most programs accept as input either time series data on rate of return or an expectations vector and variance-covariance matrix, and return a complete description of the efficient

---

[16] *Ibid.*, p. 767.
[17] Rowland Hill, "An Algorithm for Counting the Number of Possible Portfolios Given Linear Restrictions on the Weights," *Journal of Financial and Quantitative Analysis* (September, 1977).

frontier. Indeed, mathematical solution of a portfolio selection problem is so easy from the point of view of a user, even when dealing with hundreds of different securities, that there is danger in becoming enamored with computer output and reports, and missing the forest for the trees. We will return to this issue in Chapter 13.

LENDING AND BORROWING PORTFOLIOS

The introduction to the portfolio selection model of lending or borrowing funds—at appropriate market interest rates—will have a bearing on one's portfolio efficiency analysis and on choice. In this section the alternatives of lending and borrowing are introduced and a number of common misconceptions are highlighted. More detailed discussions appear in Part 4.

The Riskless Lending Rate

At any point in time, there is some interest rate, r_f, at which loanable funds can be lent with virtual assurance that both principal and interest will be returned. A 90-day treasury bill, for example, is a riskless asset in this sense, and its rate of return is a very convenient, if not an altogether appropriate, proxy for the riskless rate, r_f.

Once the opportunity to purchase a risk-free asset is introduced to a portfolio analysis, the situation is changed. A Markowitz feasible region is shown in Figure 9–8. An investor with only risk alternatives would select some portfolio along the efficient frontier of this region. With the introduction of a risk-free asset, however, one's options are expanded. From the point of view of portfolio analysis, one can

1. Invest everything in the risk-free asset, with a lower certain return.
2. Invest everything in risky assets.
3. Purchase some mix consisting of both risky assets and the riskless one.

These options are represented by portfolios that plot as points along the ray from point r_f to point f in the figure. Such portfolios, which consist of linear combinations of portfolio f and the riskless asset, are called *lending portfolios*. Portfolio f takes on a very special meaning in Part 4 (but not here), where conditions of general equilibrium are assumed.

Suppose, for example, that an investor who is confronted with only risky investment alternatives would purchase portfolio d, which is the minimum risk efficient portfolio consisting entirely of risky assets. With the introduction of a risk-free asset as an investment option, clearly this investor might choose to invest everything in the riskless asset. Suppose, on the other hand, that a rate of return that is in excess of the rate of return on the riskless asset is desired. What then? Rates of return that are in excess of the risk-free rate of return on loanable funds come

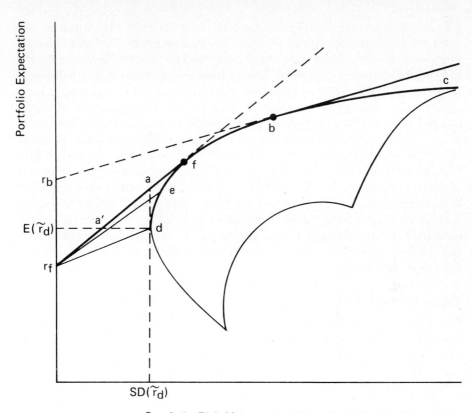

Portfolio Risk Measured in Units of the Standard Deviation

_____

*In order that expectation and risk be measured in units of rate of return, so that the functions will be linear, we substitute standard deviation for variance in the figure.

FIGURE 9–8. Lending and Borrowing Portfolios

about as a reward for bearing risk. Presumably investors who seek such a rate of return would invest at least a part of their wealth in an efficient portfolio made up of risky assets. Might the investor, therefore, who was previously at point d on the Markowitz frontier continue to invest in portfolio d?

Even an investor who, for some reason, has a particular attachment for portfolio d would be at least tempted by the fact that portfolio a offers a higher expectation for the same level of risk. Portfolio a is obtained by investing a portion, x_a, of one's wealth in the risk-free asset, and the remainder, $1 - x_a$, in a different, and *more risky*, efficient collection of risky assets. Clearly portfolio a dominates portfolio d; but portfolio a' dominates portfolio d also. Portfolio a' offers the same expectation as d but at a lower level of risk. In fact, we arrive at the delightful conclusion that every combination of portfolio f and the riskless asset, which is described by a point in the line segment a' a on the ray from r_f to point f on the efficient frontier, dominates portfolio d.

Perhaps we have found the best game in town. Why not search for a ray that lies above the one from r_f to point f? The answer is obvious: point f is the *point of tangency* with the Markowitz efficient frontier of a line passing through r_f on the vertical axis. This is the highest point that one can reach on the frontier of the feasible region. Investors who would previously have invested in efficient portfolios that plot as points along the efficient frontier below f in the figure would now invest in some combination of portfolio f and the riskless asset. Other investors, who would previously have invested in portfolios that plot as points along the efficient frontier at or above point f, would not be enticed by the riskless asset. Such investors, however, might find bliss in a different prospect—leveraging.

The Borrowing Rate

At any point in time there exists some interest rate, r_b, at which loanable funds can be borrowed by the investor in order to purchase even greater amounts of a portfolio than personal funds will allow. The borrowing rate, r_b,

1. Is higher than the riskless lending rate r_f for any borrower other than the Treasury.
2. Will vary from one borrower to the next, and from one day to the next, depending on the purpose of the loan.

In Figure 9-8 a hypothetical borrowing rate is shown by a point, r_b, on the vertical axis. A line has been drawn through r_b, tangent to the Markowitz efficient frontier at point b. An investor who would previously have purchased a portfolio that is represented by a point along this frontier beyond point b could, according to this logic, improve the situation by *portfolio leveraging*. Portfolios that plot as points along the ray from point b to point c are called *borrowing portfolios*. A borrowing portfolio is obtained by investing all of one's own funds and borrowed funds as well in portfolio b. By so doing, of course, one substitutes the *differential risk* associated with a point that lies beyond point b on the efficient frontier for a *fixed commitment risk*—the commitment to make a fixed interest payment in each period.

Some Questions About Lending and Borrowing

According to theory, investors who would otherwise purchase efficient portfolios that plot as points below point f along the efficient frontier of Figure 9-8 would, if given an opportunity to do so, purchase lending portfolios. An investor whose *bliss point* plots beyond point *b* on the efficient frontier, on the other hand, would purchase a borrowing portfolio by leveraging his or her investments. All one must do, according to theory, is identify the Markowitz efficient frontier and plot two tangent lines. Having done this, a portfolio manager would be free to pick a client's poison! In practice, however, a number of questions might be raised.

If, as is commonly done, the 90-day treasury bill rate is used as a proxy for the riskless lending rate, then a good idea might be to note that the 90-day bill rate is a *known constant* for a 90-day period only. Each 90 days the investor would either be required to roll over the loan, almost certainly at a different rate, or to rebalance the entire portfolio. More obvious still is the question of taxation. Stock dividends and interest coupon payments are taxed at the ordinary income tax rate, but capital gains are treated more favorably. Turning to the question of portfolio leveraging, note that any borrowing rate, r_b, is an extremely short-term rate. If, as matters unfold, one's ex-ante expectations are not realized, then the nasty problem of having to cover a position will inevitably arise. Portfolio leveraging is accomplished by acquiring a *fixed commitment risk*. To lump this form of risk together with random portfolio risk may be to mix apples and oranges. Portfolio rate of return variation may not be a proper representation of risk for a leveraged portfolio. We will take up questions of this sort in Part 4.

Summary

When the means and variances of a portfolio summary report are calculated, one, in effect, estimates the betting odds on alternative financial lotteries. Whether the odds are actually calculated or not makes no difference. The purchase of an investment portfolio that is concentrated in risky assets is tantamount to a gamble, and it does no harm to recognize this fact.

The Markowitz portfolio selection model is useful as a theoretical construct and also as a practical tool for financial management. The model gives rigorous content to the concept of diversification and shows how risk reduction through efficient diversification can be brought about on an ex-ante basis. In this regard the traditional theory of investment presents the financial analyst with a total void; there was no comprehensive theory of diversification before Markowitz. As with any quantitative approach, however, the resulting charts, figures, and graphs must be interpreted with care and used with discretion.

Portfolios that plot along an efficient frontier in EV space are only nominally efficient; that is, the efficiency of such portfolios is established on the basis of sample information and not on the basis of known facts. Modern portfolio theory provides a framework in which to account for statistical covariation among rates of return on financial assets. To use this theory effectively, however, one must understand its limitations and shortcomings and how to adjust for them. Such limitations and shortcomings are discussed in Chapters 11 and 13.

Questions

1. (a) In what sense is an analytic approach different from a mathematical model?
   (b) What are the objectives of the Markowitz portfolio selection model?
   (c) In what sense are these objectives different from those employed by traditional portfolio managers? In what sense are they the same?
2. (a) What are the Markowitz efficiency criteria?
   (b) What conditions were placed on the application of such criteria by Tobin?
   (c) For whom are these criteria appropriate?
   (d) For whom might the mean-variance efficiency criteria be inappropriate?
3. Does the Markowitz portfolio selection model represent a scheme for portfolio selection by which relatively expensive security analysts could be eliminated?
4. (a) What is the objective of efficient diversification?
   (b) How does the concept of efficient diversification differ from the traditional security valuation concept of diversification?
   (c) Can efficient diversification be achieved with securities whose rates of return are perfectly correlated?
   (d) Can risk reduction through efficient diversification be achieved with securities whose rates of return are perfectly correlated?
5. (a) Does a portfolio consisting entirely of blue chip stocks represent the sort of "well-balanced package" that, according to traditional logic, might be prescribed for a very risk averse investor?
   (b) In what sense is the holder of such a collection exposed to risk levels that are disproportionate? Disproportionate in terms of what?
   (c) Does one have to be a risk lover to add a share or two of Fly By Night or Wildcat Oil to such a collection?
6. (a) What are the limits of risk reduction through efficient diversification?
   (b) What asymptotic relationship was identified by Evans and Archer?

(c) How might this relationship be used to explain the lackluster performance of mutual funds in recent years?

7. (a) Describe the characteristics of an efficient frontier drawn in EV space.
   (b) Why is curvature important?
   (c) Why is convexity important?
   (d) Lay out the equations of the Markowitz model.
   (e) Explain the properties of the efficient frontier in terms of these equations.

8. Only efficient portfolios are described in the portfolio summary report of Table 9-6.
   (a) Using the equations of the Markowitz model, calculate the expected rate of return and variance of rate of return for several of the efficient portfolios shown there; check your answers against the reported figures.
   (b) Would portfolio No. 16 in the table appeal to an entirely different sort of an investor than portfolio No. 17?

9. The introduction of lending at the risk-free rate or of portfolio leveraging will have important implications in portfolio selection.
   (a) What are the implications regarding the composition of the set of feasible investment opportunities?
   (b) What happens to the frontier of efficiency?
   (c) Might it be reasonable to assume that individual investors could borrow to leverage their investment portfolios at the same rate that the Treasury can borrow? What if they could?

10. The data summary report presented in Table 8-A, page 195, is the subject of Question 10 of the previous chapter. Review your answer to this question, and modify your answer where appropriate.

11. Referring to Table A of Chapter 8, suppose that the relevant stock universe consists of the ten stocks listed there.
    (a) Calculate the expected rate of return and variance for a portfolio that consists of an equal proportionate investment in each stock (i.e., under naive diversification).
    (b) Calculate the expected rate of return and variance for the portfolio whose weights vector is as follows:

$$x = (0.1, 0.0, 0.1, 0.0, 0.5, 0.3, 0.0, 0.0, 0.0, 0.0).$$

    (c) How might risk reduction through efficient diversification be brought about by portfolio analysis applied to these ten stocks?
    (d) Equal weighting is called "naive diversification." Contrast the implications of naive and efficient diversification.

10.

Sharpe's Single Index Model: A Computational Alternative

In portfolio selection the emphasis is on the collection and on how each part of a collection relates to the whole. Recall from Chapter 9 that when the rates of return on the risky assets in an investment portfolio are perfectly correlated, risk reduction through diversification cannot be achieved. The portfolio selection problem addressed here, therefore, is that of diversifying the investments in a portfolio in such a way that their future rates of return would not vary in unison.

Markowitz was the first to give rigorous content to a concept of risk reduction through diversification that depends entirely on co-variance. For all of its genius, the simple covariance model of Chapter 9 is modest in its objectives, limited in its scope, and not too unreasonable in its assumptions.[1] The model does not attempt to explain how "beliefs about the future" should be formed, for example, and is quite general in this respect.[2] There is no need to exercise the fiction, moreover, that all investors are the same one-period, expected utility maximizers with the same opportunities and expectations. Such assumptions, which are obviously both extreme and incorrect, are invoked by the *capital asset pricing model* as conditions for general equilibrium. This development appears in the next chapter. It is important to note that no such extreme assumptions have yet been exercised, nor shall they be in this chapter.

Markowitz realized that any realistic application of the full variance-covariance model would be laborious.[3] To facilitate practical applica-

---

[1] Carried to an extreme, the quadratic utility assumption can lead to some ridiculous implications. See John W. Pratt, "Risk Aversion in the Small and in the Large," *Econometrica*, Vol. 32, No. 1 (January–April, 1964), pp. 122–136. Within the bounds of realistic application, however, the Markowitz utility or preference ordering assumptions are not too difficult to justify.

[2] Harry M. Markowitz, "Portfolio Selection," *Journal of Finance*, Vol. 7, No. 1 (March, 1952), p. 77.

[3] Harry M. Markowitz, *Portfolio Selection* (New Haven: Yale University Press, 1959), pp. 96–97.

tion of his portfolio selection approach Markowitz first suggested,[4] and Sharpe later developed, the implications of an alternative computational scheme. According to this modification of the full covariance model, "the returns on various securities are related only through common relationships with some basic underlying factor,"[5] which is the rate of return on a broad market index. This market index model,[6] which is clearly distinguished from the capital asset pricing model in this text, is introduced in this chapter.

A MARKET INDEX MODEL

In portfolio selection, risk reduction through diversification is achieved by exploiting whatever knowledge may exist at the time of decision about a pattern of variation among rates of return. A "simplified" portfolio selection model that is based on a regression structure is introduced in this section.

The Regression Model

The regression and correlation models are different, although highly related, models that are based on different assumptions about the variables of the model. The correlation model which was introduced in Chapter 8 applies when the variables are to be treated as *mutually dependent* random variables. The regression model applies when the variation in one random variable, called the "dependent variable," is *dependent* on the outcome of another variable that varies *independently*. In regression, one has *strict dependence* and not mutual dependence as in correlation.

The mean-variance portfolio selection approach is modified by assuming that the rates of return on various securities are related *only* in terms of their common correlations with the rate of return on a broad stock market index (as distinct from a market portfolio). Each rate of return, therefore, may be represented by the simple linear relationship

$$\tilde{r}_{it} = \alpha_i + \beta_i r_{mt} + \tilde{\epsilon}_{it}, \tag{10.1}$$

which is plotted in Figure 10–1, where

$\tilde{r}_{it}$ = a random variable which is the rate of return on stock i in period t,

---

[4] *Ibid.*, pp. 97–101.
[5] William F. Sharpe, "A Simplified Model of Portfolio Analysis," *Management Science*, Vol. 9, No. 2 (January, 1963), p. 280.
[6] *Ibid.*, pp. 277–293.

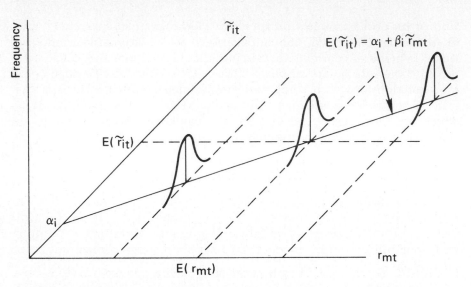

FIGURE 10-1. The Market Index Model—Characteristic Line and Residual Distributions

r_{mt} = the rate of return in period t on a broad stock market index,

α_i = an intercept term representing the expected rate of return on stock i when $r_{mt} = 0$,

β_i = the slope of a line showing the extent to which security i rates of return are affected by r_{mt},

$\tilde{\epsilon}_{it}$ = a random error term, or residual, with zero mean and variance σ_ϵ^2 which is *not* zero.

The figure, which is drawn in three dimensions, shows a straight line about which a number of representative normal probability distributions are drawn. The straight line is a regression line. Each point on this particular regression line represents the expected rate of return on stock i that corresponds to a particular level of rate of return on a broad market index—the independent variable r_{mt}. The *line of causation* in this model, therefore, flows from the independent variable to the dependent variable.

Equation (10.1) is the equation of a simple regression structure. From the point of view of portfolio selection, however, the equation represents a proposition about the facts. This proposition may be true or false; we will take this matter up later.

Residual Variation

In any regression model the random error term is extremely important; the market model is no exception to this rule. A residual $\tilde{\epsilon}_{it}$ represents that portion of the rate of return on stock i that is not explained by (i.e., is independent of) the rate of return on the market for all risky assets, and, therefore, is a factor unique to stock i. According to the proposition of Equation (10.1), the rates of return on any stock i are normally distributed about the line of central tendency

$$E(\tilde{r}_{it}) = \alpha_i + \beta_i E(r_{mt}),\qquad (10.2)$$

which is shown in Figure 10-1. Each random error, $\tilde{\epsilon}_{it}$, must therefore be the result of a random draw from a normal distribution whose mean is zero and whose variance we denote as $\sigma_{\tilde{\epsilon}}^2$.

Each point on the line of central tendency represents the mean of a normal distribution of rates of return whose location in the graph is determined by the rate of return on a broad stock market index. The proposition of Equation (10.1), therefore, further implies that for each different possible value of r_{mt} there is a different normal distribution of rates of return, $\tilde{r}_{it}$, about the line of central tendency, and that each of these different distributions of $\tilde{r}_{it}$ has the *same degree of spread*, which is also measured by $\sigma_{\tilde{\epsilon}}^2$. It follows, therefore, that the residual variance, $\sigma_{\tilde{\epsilon}}^2$, is not affected by r_{mt}. If the residuals are truly indepen-dent, however, then these random errors must be uncorrelated from one observation to the next.[7]

In the context of portfolio selection, residual variation in rate of return on stock i is not a systematic effect of market forces but is a factor unique to stock i. Therefore, at any point in time the residuals must be uncorrelated from one security to the next. This point merely serves to underscore the idea that a part of the variation in rate of re-turn on stock i must be due to factors that are unique to stock i, and thus is independent of general market movements. This is the portion of risk that we call *the nonsystematic* component of risk, and it may be reduced or eliminated by diversification. The systematic component is nondiversifiable.

The Problem of Unknown Parameters

The market index model of Equation (10.1) is merely a theoretical construct. In application one might begin with this proposition, but one would have no way of knowing the true parameters. In application of the model, therefore, the unknown parameter values are estimated using standard statistical methods. This idea is made explicit by rewrit-ing Equation (10.1) in terms of the estimators:

$$\tilde{r}_{it} = \hat{\alpha}_i + \hat{\beta}_i r_{mt} + \tilde{e}_{it},\qquad (10.3)$$

[7] J. Johnston, *Econometric Methods*, 2d ed. (New York: McGraw-Hill, 1972), p. 122.

where

$\tilde{e}_{it}$ = a random error term in the regression of $\tilde{r}_{it}$ on r_{mt}, whose mean is zero, and whose variance is denoted $\text{Var}(\tilde{e}_i)$

and the *random variables* $\hat{\alpha}_i$ and $\hat{\beta}_i$ are least-squares estimators that are defined by the *normal equations*

$$\hat{\beta}_i = \frac{\displaystyle\sum_{t=1}^{T} (\tilde{r}_{it} - \bar{r}_i)(r_{mt} - \bar{r}_m)}{\displaystyle\sum_{t=1}^{T} (r_{mt} - \bar{r}_m)^2} \tag{10.4}$$

and

$$\hat{\alpha}_i = \tilde{r}_i - \hat{\beta}_i\bar{r}_m, \tag{10.5}$$

where

$$\bar{r}_i = \sum_{t=1}^{T} \tilde{r}_{it}/T$$

$$\bar{r}_m = \sum_{t=1}^{T} r_{mt}/T.$$

The least-squares regression estimator

$$\text{Var}(\tilde{e}_{it}) = \sum_{t=1}^{T} \tilde{e}_{it}^2/T\text{-}2 \tag{10.6}$$

is a measure of spread of residuals

$$\tilde{e}_{it} = \tilde{r}_{it} - [\hat{\alpha}_i + \hat{\beta}_i r_{mt}]$$

about a least-squares regression line.

An example of the use of these normal equations is presented in Table 10-1. Dividend-adjusted monthly rates of return were obtained for a broad market index covering a period of one year starting with

TABLE 10-1. Sample Calculation Using Monthly Data for One Year (In percent)

(1) r_{mt}	(2) $\tilde{r}_{1t}$	(3) $\tilde{r}_{2t}$	(4) $(r_{mt} - \bar{r}_m)$	(5) $(\tilde{r}_{1t} - \bar{r}_1)$	(6) $(\tilde{r}_{2t} - \bar{r}_2)$	(7) $(r_{mt} - \bar{r}_m) \times (\tilde{r}_{1t} - \bar{r}_1)$	(8) $(r_{mt} - \bar{r}_m) \times (\tilde{r}_{2t} - \bar{r}_2)$	(9) $(r_{mt} - \bar{r}_m)^2$
7.70	5.85	19.19	5.73333	3.77750	17.02750	21.65765	97.62428	32.87107
4.10	-2.82	-7.03	2.13333	-4.89250	-9.19250	-10.43732	-19.61064	4.55110
4.60	4.68	4.45	2.63333	2.60750	2.28750	6.86641	6.02374	6.93443
4.60	2.82	10.49	2.63333	.74750	8.32750	1.96841	21.92906	6.93443
-2.40	-4.12	-11.04	-4.36667	-6.19250	-13.20250	27.04060	57.65096	19.06781
.30	2.02	1.19	-1.66667	-.05250	-.97250	.08750	1.62084	2.77779
-2.20	1.16	-10.08	-4.16667	-.91250	-12.24250	3.80209	51.01046	17.36113
4.00	3.24	4.83	2.03333	1.16750	2.66750	2.37391	5.42391	4.13443
-1.50	1.27	5.58	-3.46667	-.80250	3.41750	2.78200	-11.84735	12.01780
-4.30	2.18	-1.55	-6.26667	.10750	-3.71250	-.67367	23.26501	39.27115
.60	1.38	-.18	-1.36667	-.69250	-2.34250	.94642	3.20142	1.86779
8.10	7.21	10.10	6.13333	5.13750	7.93750	31.50998	48.68331	37.61774
23.60	24.87	25.95				87.92398	284.97500	185.40667

Summary Statistics

Variable	Mean	Variance	Alpha	Beta	Variance-Covariance			Correlation		
m	1.96667	16.85515			16.85515	7.99309	25.90682	1.00000	0.60574	0.70744
1	2.07250	10.33077	1.13987	0.47422	7.99309	10.33077	23.34884	0.60574	1.00000	0.81440
2	2.16250	79.56519	-0.86033	1.53703	25.90682	23.34884	79.56519	0.70744	0.81440	1.00000

January 1971.[8] Rates of return on the market index are shown in column 1 of the table. Rates of return for two stocks, numbered 1 and 2, are shown in columns 2 and 3. The deviations of the rates of return about their respective means are shown in columns 4, 5, and 6. The cross-product of the deviations of rates of return on the market about the average market rate of return and the rates of return on stock 1 about the mean rate of return on stock 1 are shown in column 7. The cross-product of deviations of rates of return on the market and stock 2 are shown in column 8. The deviations of rates of return on the market index about its mean (which are shown in column 4) were squared, and the results are shown in column 9. A typical bivariate regression summary report is shown under "Summary Statistics" in the table.

Estimation and Prediction

The equation of the market index model is given by Equation (10.1) and the trend line by Equation (10.2). Equation (10.3), by contrast, is a statistical representation. The "true" parameters of Equations (10.1) and (10.2) can never be known, but the variables of Equation (10.3) can always be obtained by statistical methods—that is, by regressing historical rates of return for each individual stock on the index, r_{mt}. Once the parameters of the market model have been estimated, the trend relationship is modified to predict the future:[9]

$$E(\tilde{r}_{it}) = \hat{\alpha}_i + \hat{\beta}_i E(\tilde{r}_{mt}). \qquad (10.7)$$

In Equation (10.7), $E(\tilde{r}_{mt})$ represents the expected rate of return on a broad market index in the next period. This expected value, of course, is itself a prediction about a future event and differs from $E(\tilde{r}_{mt})$, which

---

[8] Commonly used indices are the Dow Jones or Standard and Poor's indices. In this illustration we use the geometric mean rate of return on a universe of 760 common stocks from which the stocks of this illustration were taken. The geometric mean of a large number of stocks is also a common index which is superior in many respects to either the Dow Jones or Standard and Poor's indices as the latter were originally designed for an entirely different purpose. This point will be pursued in Chapter 13.

[9] Formally, the expectations operator is applied to both sides in Equation (10.1) as follows:

$$E(\tilde{r}_{it}) = E(\alpha_i + \beta_i r_{mt} + \tilde{\varepsilon}_{it})$$
$$= E(\alpha_i) + E(\beta_i r_{mt}) + E(\tilde{\varepsilon}_{it})$$
$$= \alpha_i + \beta_i E(r_{mt}) + 0$$
$$= \alpha_i + \beta_i E(r_{mt}).$$

We then obtain Equation (10.7) by replacing each unknown constant by an estimated value.

appears in Equation (10.2) and which represents an average of past events that are known after the fact.

The expected rate of return on a broad market index may be obtained by objectivist statistical methods, or subjectively by use of a Bayesian normal prior.[10] In either case the model treats the next period's rate of return on the market index, $\tilde{r}_{mt}$, as a random draw from a normal distribution whose mean is denoted $E(\tilde{r}_{mt})$, and whose variance we denote $\text{Var}(\tilde{r}_{mt})$.[11] It is clear from Equation (10.5) that a regression line must pass through that point in the grid that corresponds to the intersect of two means; this is illustrated in Figure 10–1. Sharpe exploited this property of regression in order to represent both the market model characteristic line and the normal estimator distribution of $\tilde{r}_{mt}$ on a single graph. The model is set out graphically in Figure 10–2 by modifying Sharpe's original drawing only with respect to our system of notation.[12]

Sharpe's Analogue

According to an analogue by William F. Sharpe, "the return of a portfolio can be considered to be the result of (1) a series of investments in n basic securities and (2) an investment in the index."[13] This analogue can be exploited to define the *weighted average response* of rate of return on the securities in portfolio p to the rate of return on the market index:

$$\beta_p = \left\{ \sum_{i=1}^{n} x_i \beta_i \right\}. \tag{10.8}$$

This weighted average response, or *portfolio beta score*, is the slope of the characteristic line for portfolio p.

---

[10] When objectivist statistical methods are to be used, the rate of return on the market can be forecasted using a moving average time series approach. See Charles R. Nelson, *Applied Time Series Analysis* (San Francisco: Holden-Day, Inc., 1973), Chapter 2. An alternative approach that from the point of view of this author would be easier to justify logically is the subjectivist approach. A normal probability curve called the prior can be obtained by Bayesian methods. See Ward Edwards, Harold Lindman, and Leonard J. Savage, "Bayesian Statistical Inference for Psychological Research," *Psychological Review*, Vol. 70, No. 3 (May, 1963), pp. 209–212. Regardless of how the rate of return on the market is to be estimated, everything in this model, and those that follow, hinges on the analyst's ability to estimate this value—and here we have a problem. For purpose of prediction, the most common practice has been to use a simple weighted average of historical rates of return on the market. This procedure clearly leaves much to be desired.

[11] Sharpe recognizes that the future level of the index "is determined in part by random factors," but he maintains the fiction throughout that the slope and intercept of the characteristic line for each security "are parameters." Sharpe (1963), "A Simplified Model of Portfolio Analysis," p. 281.

[12] *Ibid.*, p. 283.

[13] *Ibid.*, p. 282.

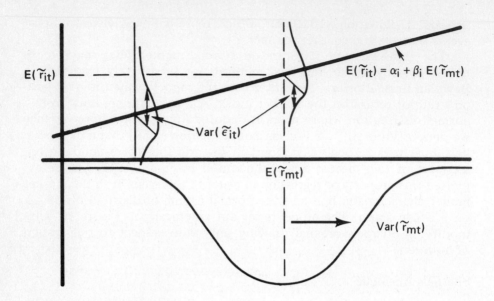

FIGURE 10-2. The Model

The analogue is further exploited to obtain an expression for the *expected rate of return* on portfolio p[14]

$$E(\tilde{r}_{pt}) = \sum_{i=1}^{n} x_i \hat{\alpha}_i + \left[\left\{ \sum_{i=1}^{n} x_i \hat{\beta}_i \right\} E(\tilde{r}_{mt}) \right] \qquad (10.9)$$

---

[14] To derive the expected rate of return, Equation (10.9), one begins with the definition

$$\tilde{r}_{pt} = \sum_{i=1}^{n} x_i \tilde{r}_{it}.$$

Substitution from Equation (10.1) yields

$$\tilde{r}_{pt} = \sum_{i=1}^{n} x_i (\alpha_i + \beta_i r_{mt} + \tilde{\epsilon}_{it})$$

$$= \sum_{i=1}^{n} x_i \alpha_i + \left\{ \sum_{i=1}^{n} x_i \beta_i \right\} r_{mt} + \sum_{i=1}^{n} x_i \tilde{\epsilon}_{it}.$$

Applying the expectations operator to this last expression, and substituting estimated values for the unknown constants, yields Equation (10.9).

and the *variance of rate of return*

$$\text{Var}(\tilde{r}_{pt}) = \sum_{i=1}^{n} x_i^2 \, \text{Var}(\tilde{e}_{it}) + \left[\left\{ \sum_{i=1}^{n} x_i \hat{\beta}_i \right\}^2 \text{Var}(\tilde{r}_{mt}) \right] \quad (10.10)$$

= *unsystematic risk + systematic risk.*

According to one of the basic postulates in statistics, the variance of a sum is equal to the sum of the variances. The risk associated with an investment in any risky security, according to the Sharpe analogue, is equal to the sum of two parts. One part results from factors that are unique to that risky security, and the other part results from factors that are common to all risky securities that trade in the same market for risky securities. Thus, *portfolio risk*, according to Equation (10.10), is defined as the sum of two weighted average risk measures. The *unsystematic* component of portfolio risk refers to that portion of risk that results from factors that are unique to the various securities of an investment portfolio. The unsystematic component of risk in Equation (10.10) is therefore a weighted average of the residual variances. In this model the unsystematic component of risk is important.

The variance of a forecast, $\text{Var}(\tilde{r}_{mt})$, by contrast, is viewed as a measure of uncertainty about a prediction $E(\tilde{r}_{mt})$. The *systematic* component of risk for any portfolio p must therefore be related to one's uncertainty about the rate of return on the market index or underlying factor. According to Equation (10.10), the *systematic risk* for portfolio p is the scalar product of (1) the weighted average response of the rates of return on the risky securities contained in portfolio p to the rate of return on the market index, and (2) a measure of one's uncertainty about next period's rate of return on the index.

Historical Justification for the Market Index Model

A portfolio's expected rate of return and variance can be calculated on the basis of estimated parameters using either the more general variance-covariance model of Chapter 9 or the market index model. Computer programs are available to work out all of the details as explained in the next section of this chapter, but the security analyst must provide the necessary inputs. At first glance the market index model would seem to result in a simplification of this task relative to the more complete model. Contrary to a popular misconception, however, this is not necessarily so.

Number of Required Inputs. In order to apply the full variance-covariance model, one needs

1. A vector of n expected rates of return;
2. A vector of n variance terms, which is the main diagonal of an (n by n) variance-covariance matrix;
3. A quantity, $(n^2 - n)/2$ unique covariance terms, which is the number of terms above the main diagonal of an (n by n) variance-covariance matrix (or below).

In total, $2n + [(n^2 - n)/2]$ inputs must be provided for application of the variance-covariance portfolio selection model. When there are 100 securities, for example, 5,150 estimations must be performed.

In application of the market index model, by contrast, less information would seem to be required. One needs

1. A vector of n alpha scores, which are the intercept terms;
2. A vector of n beta scores, which are the slope coefficients;
3. A vector of n residual variance terms, which measure the dispersion of unsystematic variation about the characteristic lines;
4. A forecast of next period's rate of return on the market for all risky assets;
5. A variance term that measures the degree of one's uncertainty about the rate of return on the market for all risky assets.

A total of $3n + 2$ inputs are required for application of the market model. In the 100-security case, for example, only 302 inputs are required for application of the market model, which, taken at face value, contrasts rather favorably with the 5,150 inputs required for application of the variance-covariance model.

A Fallacy About Numbers. Unfortunately Markowitz made a small error in logic on this point, arguing that

> . . . it is reasonable to ask security analysts to summarize their researches in 100 carefully considered variances of return. It is not reasonable, however, to ask for 5,000 carefully and individually considered covariances.[15]

Sharpe repeats this argument as part of his own justification.[16] This line of argument leads to a rather interesting contradiction. Actually, the "simplified" index model of Markowitz and Sharpe is no more economical, from the point of view of estimation, than it is "simple." According to Equations (8.9) and (8.10) of Chapter 8, the coefficient of correlation is the ratio of a (degree of freedom adjusted) cross-product term to the product of two standard deviations. A beta term, according to Equation (10.4) of this chapter, is the ratio of a similar cross-product term to a sum of squared deviations. If readers would review the illustrative example of Table 10-1, they would find that all

---

[15] Markowitz (1959), *Portfolio Selection*, pp. 96–97.
[16] Sharpe (1963), "A Simplified Model of Portfolio Analysis," p. 282.

of the calculations (i.e., sums of squares) required for application of the full variance-covariance portfolio selection model must be performed before a single beta score can be found. To make matters worse for the market index model, the data matrix for the more complete variance-covariance model consists of n rows and n columns. For the market model, on the other hand, the data matrix consists of $n + 1$ rows and $n + 1$ columns. The addition of a row and a column, and thus of $2n - 1$ calculations, results from the addition of an index. This index, moreover, is difficult to define in practice and even more difficult to measure and predict.[17] The real world, therefore, presents us with an entirely different picture in terms of estimation economy than did the highly idealized and rhetorical settings assumed by Markowitz and Sharpe.

Other Economies

The market index model was originally proposed as an alternate computational procedure to facilitate practical application of the Markowitz portfolio selection model. Once the parameters of the market index model have been estimated, the inputs to the original Markowitz model can be approximated by means of the following identities:

$$E(\tilde{r}_{it}) = \hat{\alpha}_i + \hat{\beta}_i E(\tilde{r}_{mt}), \tag{10.11}$$

$$\text{Var}(\tilde{r}_{it}) = \hat{\beta}_i^2 \text{Var}(\tilde{r}_{mt}) + \text{Var}(\tilde{e}_{it}), \tag{10.12}$$

$$\text{Cov}(\tilde{r}_{it}, \tilde{r}_{jt}) = \hat{\beta}_i \hat{\beta}_j \text{Var}(\tilde{r}_{mt}). \tag{10.13}$$

These definitions follow from well-known postulates, but *assume* that the linearity assumption underlying the market model formulation is correct. On this point, there is conflicting evidence.[18]

In terms of estimation efficiency the market index model is a mixed blessing. The amount of computer time required for solution of a portfolio selection problem expressed in terms of the market index model is lower than where the full covariance model is invoked.[19] These techniques are discussed in the next chapter. This economy may come at a very high cost, however, as the efficient frontiers obtained by use of the

---

[17] George M. Frankfurter and Herbert E. Phillips, "Alpha-Beta Theory: A Word of Caution," *Journal of Portfolio Management*, Vol. 3, No. 4 (Summer, 1977), pp. 35–40.

[18] William E. Blume, "On the Assessment of Risk," *Journal of Finance*, Vol. 26, No. 1 (March, 1971), p. 2. See especially footnote 3.

[19] Sharpe (1963), "A Simplified Model of Portfolio Analysis," pp. 91–96.

market index model are not necessarily the same efficient frontiers that would be obtained by use of the more general and complete covariance approach of Chapter 9.[20] We will have more to say on this topic in Chapter 11.

Summary

In portfolio selection the emphasis is on the collection and on how each part of a collection relates to the whole. Markowitz was the first to give rigorous content to the concept of portfolio diversification and to provide a methodology whereby risk reduction through diversification could be achieved. This methodology, which was introduced in Chapter 9, exploits the covariance relationships that exist among rates of return.

The market index model, which is the subject of this chapter, was originally intended as a means for simplifying the analyst's task of providing needed inputs. This argument, though widely reported, is in fact incorrect; it supposes that the required inputs could be obtained by fundamental security analysis. Unfortunately, the inputs required by portfolio selection models that follow the Markowitz tradition deal in abstractions such as covariance or beta. Fundamental security analysis, which is the subject of Section 4 of this text, is not equipped to deal very effectively with mathematical abstractions of this sort. The required inputs for effective utilization of these portfolio selection models are obtained by statistical methods. Various problems that result from the use of such methods are discussed in Chapter 11. We also suggest there an approach for integrating this methodology with other methodologies, and the need to do so.

The market index model has one distinct advantage: it provides an ideal setting for an analogue which is truly worthwhile in terms of the insights that it provides. According to this analogue, the rate of return on a portfolio may be viewed, in part, as the result of (1) factors that are unique to the securities of that portfolio and (2) factors that are common to all risky securities that trade in the same market for risky securities. Portfolio risk, therefore, can very conveniently (perhaps too conveniently) be dichotomized into two component parts—a systematic component and a nonsystematic component.

Computer programs are widely available to solve the portfolio selection problem in either format, by invoking the full covariance model or the market model. The market index model is more efficient in that the

---

[20] George M. Frankfurter, Herbert E. Phillips, and John P. Seagle, "Performance of the Sharpe Portfolio Selection Model: A Comparison," *Journal of Financial and Quantitative Analysis*, Vol. 11, No. 2 (June, 1976), pp. 202-204.

amount of computer time required to identify the portfolios of the efficient frontier, and thus the risk return trade-offs that are available for risky securities, is substantially reduced relative to the full covariance approach.

Questions

1. (a) Set out the equations of the Markowitz covariance model and briefly explain each.
   (b) Set out the equations of the market index model and briefly explain each.
2. (a) What are the objectives of the Markowitz portfolio selection model and what are the underlying assumptions about investor behavior?
   (b) In what sense is the market index model an extension of the full variance-covariance model?
   (c) In what sense are the assumptions underlying the market index model more restrictive than those underlying the full variance-covariance model? Might this added restriction limit the usefulness of the model?
3. Markowitz realized that any realistic application of the full variance-covariance model would be laborious. To facilitate practical application of his portfolio selection approach, Markowitz first suggested, and Sharpe later developed, an alternative computational scheme according to which it would be assumed that "the returns on various securities are related only through common relationships with some basic underlying factor."
   (a) In what way does this assumption lead to analytic simplification?
   (b) This assumption represents a proposition about the facts that might be true or false. Explain.
   (c) Would rejection of the market model as an alternative computational scheme lead inevitably to rejection of the full variance-covariance model? Explain.
4. It is widely supposed that the number of inputs required for application of the market index model is less than that required for application of the full variance-covariance model.
   (a) Identify the inputs required for application of each model.
   (b) Assuming that these inputs are to be obtained by "objective" (or traditional) statistical methods, show the equations necessary to obtain the inputs for the models from raw data.
   (c) Describe the raw data.
   (d) The market index model does require fewer inputs than the full variance-covariance model, as is commonly supposed, but the calculation of these inputs requires more raw data. Explain in terms of your answers to parts (a), (b), and (c) above.

5. One of the primary attributes of the market index model is that it provides the setting for an analogue which is truly worthwhile in terms of the insights that it provides.
   (a) Describe the equations of Sharpe's analogue.
   (b) Explain the dichotomization of risk that results.
   (c) What are the implications of this dichotomy regarding the degree of risk reduction that may result from efficient diversification? (This point will be expanded upon in Chapter 11.)
6. Two stocks are described in Table 10–1. Recall in Chapter 9 that by allowing the investment weights x_i to vary from 0 to 1 in steps of 0.1, 11 different portfolios are defined in the two-security cases (see Table 9–2). Based on the information in Table 10–1:
   (a) Calculate the expected rate of return and variance for each of the 11 possible portfolios by application of (1) the full variance-covariance model and (2) the market model. (Note: You will have to calculate the variance of the residuals for each security on your own from information contained in the table as this has not been done for you.)
   (b) For each case separately, use your results to identify the portfolios of the efficient set.
   (c) In what sense if any are the efficient sets (1) the same, (2) different?

11.

Portfolio Selection and Security Identification: Shortcomings of Models and an Integrative Solution

Oh, Dr. Freud. Oh, Dr. Freud. How we wish that you had been differently employed. But this set of circumstances sure enhances the finances of the followers of Dr. Sigmund Freud. (From pop song popular in the fifties; author unknown)

The theory of finance has long been captivated by a valuation logic and a notion of intrinsic value that is an outgrowth of deterministic and not stochastic logic.[1] Such logic, of course, is not easily modified to account for uncertainty, and in any event results in implications that are not entirely satisfactory. For example, the

... hypothesis (or maxim) that the investor does (or should) maximize discounted return must be rejected. If we ignore market imperfections the foregoing rule never implies that there is a diversified portfolio which is preferable to all non-diversified portfolios. Diversification is both observed and sensible; a rule of behavior which does not imply the superiority of diversification must be rejected both as a hypothesis and as a maxim.[2]

This position, which is due to Markowitz, might easily be construed as a direct attack on traditional valuation theory, and perhaps it was so intended.

One must realize, however, that modern portfolio theory and traditional valuation theory address truly different aspects of the security investment problem; they are not really competing or conflicting approaches. As we shall see in Section 4, traditional valuation theory is concerned with the classification of individual financial assets according

---

[1] J. B. Williams, *The Theory of Investment Value* (1938: reprint ed., Amsterdam, The Netherlands: North Holland Publishing Co., 1964).
[2] Harry M. Markowitz, "Portfolio Selection," *Journal of Finance*, Vol. 3, No. 1 (March, 1952), p. 77.

to various investment criteria or "quality." Modern portfolio theory, by contrast, is concerned with the selection of investment assets and the combination of investment assets in such a way as to reduce risk.

The formation of an investment portfolio is a matter of decision strategy that depends on inputs; it is not a matter of classification as such. The disagreements that do arise between modern portfolio selection theorists and traditional security analysts or advisers typically result from a difference in emphasis and vocabulary. This lack of effective communication is particularly unfortunate, as existing security evaluation and portfolio selection approaches are imperfect at best. Various shortcomings of existing methodologies and models can be substantially overcome, however, by working toward the following goals:

1. A better understanding of the real issues and what deficiencies are to be overcome.
2. Better communication between modern portfolio theorists and fundamental security analysts.
3. An integration of methodologies.

Various problems that arise in application of existing portfolio selection models are discussed in this chapter. A detailed discussion of traditional valuation theory is put off to Section 4, but a means for integrating such knowledge in a Markowitz-type portfolio selection model is discussed here.

COMPACT REPRESENTATION OF PORTFOLIO SELECTION PROBLEM AND OVERVIEW

Suppose that n securities are being considered for inclusion in an investment portfolio. An infinite number of different portfolios can be formed from any collection of n securities, provided, of course, that n is greater than 1. Any unique portfolio may be identified by means of a vector

$$\underline{x} = [x_1, x_2, \ldots, x_n], \tag{11.1}$$

whose i^{th} element $(i = 1, 2, \ldots, n)$ represents the proportion of that particular combination of investment assets that are invested in security i.

A portfolio selection problem may be stated compactly, and thus set up for computer solution, as follows: First we define a relationship

$$\phi = \text{Var}(\tilde{r}_p) - \lambda E(\tilde{r}_p), \tag{11.2}$$

which we call the *objective function*. For any level of expected rate of return, an efficient portfolio is one that minimizes the level of risk required to achieve that level of expected rate of return. Thus we seek to minimize the function ϕ. One way to minimize risk, in the sense of $\text{Var}(\tilde{r}_p)$, however, is to do absolutely nothing. A second way, which is a bit more extreme, is to sell off all of the securities we already own. We must place constraints, therefore, on the possible solutions of a portfolio selection problem.

We add at least two constraints. The first is a *lower limit* constraint, which in general is

$$x_i \geqslant 0 \text{ for all } i \quad i = 1, 2, \ldots, n. \tag{11.3}$$

The second constraint, which tells us to exhaust an investment budget by purchasing securities, is typically written as follows:

$$\sum_{i=1}^{n} x_i = 1.00. \tag{11.4}$$

Other constraints may, of course, be added to reflect special requirements. An upper limit, for example, must often be imposed on x_i as well as a lower limit. Where no upper limit is imposed, 100 percent of the investment budget might conceivably be invested in a single stock. This is unlikely to occur, however, unless λ in equation (11.2) is very large.

Notice that the objective function defined by equation (11.2) is a linear function and plots as a straight line in EV space. Four lines are shown in Figure 11-1, each corresponding to a different level of objective ϕ. Only five lines are drawn, but an infinite number of lines are possible—each with the same slope λ. In the model λ is called the *coefficient of risk aversion*. It represents the rate at which a particular investor is just *willing* to exchange expected rate of return for risk.

Clearly, an investor whose choices are represented by Figure 11-1 would desire the highest level of expected rate of return possible commensurate with the risk required to achieve it. All other things equal, therefore, the investor would prefer to be on the highest of the lines shown in Figure 11-1. This is impossible, however, as every point on this line represents an EV combination that cannot be achieved. The highest level of investment return that can be achieved by an efficient solution to the portfolio selection problem set out by equation (11.2) is represented by the point of tangency of the fourth line in Figure 11-1 to the feasible region. This point represents a solution to the problem in the sense that the rate at which the investor in question is just *willing* to exchange expectation for risk is precisely equal to the rate at which his or her opportunities will allow. The resulting solution, moreover, identifies a portfolio that lies on the efficient frontier. That is, the tangency condition identifies an efficient portfolio.

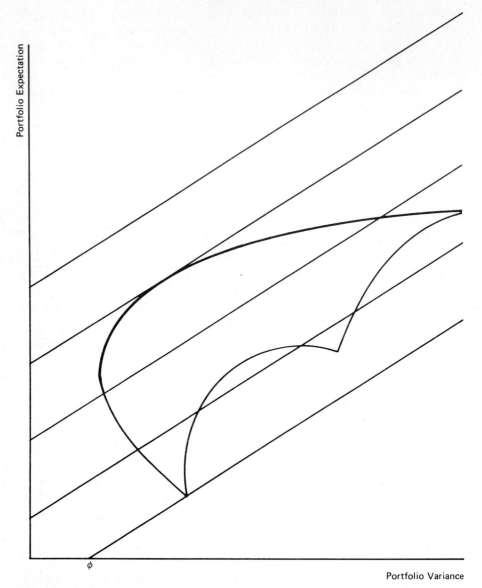

FIGURE 11-1. Representative Lines and Feasible Region

Quadratic Programming Solution

If one knows the coefficient of risk aversion, λ, for a particular investor, then mathematical methods exist to solve the portfolio selection problem in the sense just illustrated. The method is called *quadratic programming*. We need not concern ourselves with the details of quadratic programming here. What is important is to realize that computer programs exist to find a point of tangency, such as that shown in Figure 11-1, and thus to solve the portfolio selection problem by means of quadratic programming.

The coefficient of risk aversion, unfortunately, is an abstraction at best. Only a clairvoyant could claim such knowledge. All is not lost, however. If a methodology exists for finding one solution, then the same methodology can be used to find many solutions. Starting with $\lambda = \infty$ in Figure 11-2, we can vary the coefficient of risk aversion from ∞ to 0 in a number of discrete steps and at each step identify the efficient portfolio that is optimal for that level of λ. In the end we will thus have identified the entire efficient frontier. This process is precisely the one that is represented in Figure 11-2, which provides an intuitive outline of how some standard computer programs work.

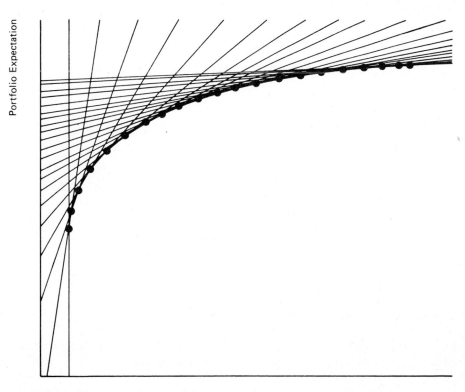

FIGURE 11-2. Representative Programming—Solution of the Portfolio Selection Problem

We may not know λ for a particular investor, but we do know that the appropriate value is bounded by 0 and ∞. Once the efficient frontier has been identified by a computer-based portfolio selection model, the investor must "reveal" his or her preference (i.e., coefficient of risk aversion) by selecting one of the efficient solutions provided. Unfortunately, the computer program requires certain inputs that must be provided by the investor or portfolio selection analyst.

The Data Inputs Required for Solution

Solution of the portfolio selection problem described compactly by equation (11.2) is based on the portfolio mean and variance estimators discussed in Chapters 9 and 10. Specifically, one must first decide whether to solve in terms of the full variance-covariance model of Chapter 9 or the computational alternative provided by the market index model discussed in Chapter 10. Depending on the outcome of this decision, the portfolio mean and variance estimators are then appropriately defined as follows:

Variance-covariance model

$$E(\tilde{r}_p) = \sum_{i=1}^{n} x_i E(\tilde{r}_i)$$

$$\text{Var}(\tilde{r}_p) = \sum_{i=1}^{n} \sum_{j=1}^{n} x_i x_j \text{Cov}(\tilde{r}_i \tilde{r}_j)$$

(11.5)

Market index model

$$E(\tilde{r}_{pt}) = \sum_{i=1}^{n} x_i \hat{\alpha}_i + \left[\left\{\sum_{i=1}^{n} x_i \hat{\beta}_i\right\} E(\tilde{r}_{mt})\right]$$

$$\text{Var}(\tilde{r}_{pt}) = \sum_{i=1}^{n} x_i^2 \text{Var}(\tilde{e}_{it}) + \left[\left\{\sum_{i=1}^{n} x_i \hat{\beta}_i\right\}^2 \text{Var}(\tilde{r}_{mt})\right]$$

(11.6)

To solve the portfolio selection problem by means of the full variance-covariance model, therefore, requires n means, n variances, and $(n^2-n)/2$ covariance terms. To solve by means of the market index model requires n intercept terms, n beta estimates, n residual variance terms, an estimate of the market index in the next period, and a variance term that represents the precision of the estimated market index.

If in either application the inputs were "known" in the sense that they could be represented by actual parameter values in application of the models, our discussion would end here with the suggestion that the process of security investment be reduced to a simplistic application of the computer-based model described above. Unfortunately, the inputs can never be "known" in this sense. In any application of either model, the inputs are necessarily represented by statistical estimates of the desired parameters—not by "known" parameter values.

UNCERTAIN MEANS, VARIANCES, AND COVARIANCES

The process of selecting a portfolio may be divided into two stages. "The first stage starts with observation and experience and ends with beliefs about the future performance of available securities. The second stage starts with the relevant beliefs about future performance and ends with the choice of portfolio."[3] The portfolio selection models outlined in Chapters 9 and 10 deal with the second stage only. As we shall see in this chapter, the inputs are important.

The Markowitz portfolio selection model is useful as a theoretical construct and also as a practical tool for use by financial management. The model gives rigorous content to the concept of diversification and shows how risk reduction through efficient diversification can be brought about on an ex-ante basis. In this regard the traditional theory of investment presents the financial analyst with a total void; there was no comprehensive theory of diversification before Markowitz. Portfolios that plot along an efficient frontier in EV space are only nominally efficient; that is, the efficiency of such portfolios is established on the basis of sample information and not on the basis of known facts. Modern portfolio theory provides a framework in which to account for statistical covariation among rates of return on financial assets. To use this theory effectively, however, one must understand its limitations and shortcomings and how to adjust for them.

In a very real sense Markowitz portfolio theory is preoccupied with finding optimal solutions to a nonexistent problem, one in which estimation is not an integral part. In practice, estimates, which are themselves random variables, serve in place of known parameter values. There has been a tendency, moreover, to view attempts to deal with the problem of uncertain estimation as being somehow beyond the scope of science.[4] Model builders, unable to deal very precisely with the problem of uncertain parameter values, often assume the problem away.

---

[3] *Ibid.*

[4] Frank H. Knight, *Risk, Uncertainty and Profit* (Boston: Houghton-Mifflin, 1921), Chapter 2.

Sharpe, for example, states that "portfolio theory cannot directly help those for whom probability distributions are fuzzy."[5] Such a position, we feel, is tantamount to a refusal to play the only real game in town.

The simple truth is that probability distributions are always "fuzzy." Implicit in every application of normative theory is a source of variation that cannot be accounted for within a formal mathematical optimization model. This source of variation is due to error in estimation. Estimation error can take various forms, and each different aspect of this phenomenon has an important bearing on the efficacy of normative theory.

Accuracy of Financial Measurements

Failure to recognize the random nature of expectations, variances, and covariances that are available for use in application of normative models can lead to a rather simplistic and dangerous interpretation of quantitative information. The efficient portfolios whose means and variances are presented in the portfolio summary reports of Chapter 9 plot as points along the efficient frontiers of Figure 9–7. The sample statistics of this illustration are reported in percentage form; four-place accuracy (to one-hundredth of one percent) is thus implied by the data. As if this were not sufficiently presumptuous, the model attempts to distinguish between efficient portfolios (see portfolios 16 and 17 of Table 9–6) on the basis of sample differences that are as small as 0.01 percent in weighted average rate of return. Who would be foolish enough to suppose that sample data could be rich enough, or a mere model responsive enough to the facts, to support such minute distinctions?

If, on average, a portfolio selection model can successfully distinguish between portfolios that lie on or near the efficient frontier and those that do not, the model will have served a very useful purpose. If, in addition, the model can provide the portfolio manager with even a rough ranking of portfolios according to average ex-post rate of return and risk, then the model will have accomplished all that can reasonably be expected of quantitative methods. As we shall see, the absolute magnitudes, and even the signs, attached to the reported statistics are of dubious value and should not be taken too seriously.

The Deleterious Effects of Estimation Error

It is commonly recognized that estimation error cannot be avoided in practical application of normative portfolio selection models. Also widely accepted as fact is that sampling error will average out to zero for the securities of an investment portfolio. This fallacy results from

---

[5] William F. Sharpe, *Portfolio Theory and Capital Markets* (New York: McGraw-Hill, 1972), p. 26.

the mistaken belief that the law of large numbers applies. According to the law of large numbers, the average error of the mean will approach zero as a random sample gets larger and larger. The trick, of course, is to realize that efficient portfolios are not random collections, and therefore that the law of large numbers does not apply.

Selection Bias and Disappointed Clients. A recent study has shown that mere random error in estimation of security means, variances, and covariances is sufficient to cause a systematic bias when estimating the future rates of return and risk for efficient investment portfolios.[6] As a result of such bias, investors will find that portfolios selected even by the most cautious application of the normative portfolio selection models of Chapters 9 and 10 will, on average, result in lower levels of rate of return and in greater dispersion than would have been anticipated before the fact.[7] This form of bias, which is called *selection bias*, was first identified by Black, Jensen, and Scholes[8] and was subsequently observed in empirical work by Blume.[9]

Selection bias is easy to explain. When estimating the means, variances, and covariances of rates of return for securities that are being considered for inclusion in an investment portfolio (or the alpha and beta scores and residual risk statistics where the market index model of Chapter 10 is applied), random error in estimation will almost certainly be a factor. Sometimes, for example, one will understate the future rate of return on a stock and simultaneously overstate the variance and average covariance with other stocks (or the market). A computer-based portfolio selection code, such as that described above, is programmed to discriminate against such a stock (which is a shortcoming). One can also, however, no matter how rich the data, simultaneously (1) overstate the future rate of return on a particular security, (2) understate its variance, and (3) understate its average covariance with the other securities in the market. Such a fortuitous combination of estimation errors (which in practice will occur in excess of 25 percent of the time) can make *Fly By Night, Inc.*, look to the computer code like the best thing to come along since ice cream, and its combination with *Sinai Enterprises, Ltd.*, to be mistaken for risk avoidance. Regardless of the ef-

---

[6] George M. Frankfurter, Herbert E. Phillips, and John P. Seagle, "Bias in Estimating Portfolio Alpha and Beta Scores," *Review of Economics and Statistics*, Vol. 56, No. 3 (August, 1974), pp. 412-414.

[7] George M. Frankfurter and Herbert E. Phillips, "Alpha-Beta Theory: A Word of Caution," *Journal of Portfolio Management*, Vol. 3, No. 4 (Summer, 1977), pp. 35-40.

[8] Fischer Black, Michael C. Jensen, and Myron Scholes, "The Capital Asset Pricing Model: Some Empirical Tests," in *Studies in the Theory of Capital Markets*, edited by Michael Jensen (New York: Praeger, 1972).

[9] Marshall E. Blume, "On the Assessment of Risk," *Journal of Finance*, Vol. 26, No. 1 (March, 1971), pp. 1-10.

fectiveness of one's estimation process, or how rich the data, the application of any standard computer code for identifying portfolios that are Markowitz efficient is tantamount to the conduct of an efficient search for precisely this combination of random errors.[10]

Garbage In, Garbage Out. In order to function properly, or even sensibly, the statistical data used in application of normative models must be carefully selected. For every estimated mean, variance, and covariance, for example, one should know the source of the raw data used in calculation, how many periods are covered, which periods are covered, what definitions were used to compile the data, and the standard error associated with each mean and variance.

One common practice, for example, is to merge time series data from various sources to obtain statistical coverage. In most applications this practice is totally invalid. Unless the periodicity of the data in two time series is precisely the same, and the definitions and system of aggregation used to compile the data are identical, time series data cannot justifiably be merged. Moreover, means, variances, and covariances that are estimated on the basis of data obtained from one source cannot, in general, be put side by side with statistics that have been obtained from another. For example, one should not attempt to estimate covariances (or beta statistics) objectively and then resort to subjectivist approaches to determine the means and variances. To do so is to mix apples and oranges.

Even the most astute financial analysts sometimes fail to recognize the various shortcomings ever present in economic data and in statistical estimations based on economic data. There is a tendency, moreover, even among those who are ordinarily very cautious about using historical data, to take at face value published reports such as beta surveys. Such reports are mere compilations of descriptive statistics that are obtained by elementary statistical methods such as those reported in Chapters 8 and 10. In addition, the technical staffs employed by agencies that issue financial reports such as beta reports are not necessarily accomplished statisticians; under such conditions conceptual blunders are commonplace.

Error Due to Nonrandom Factors

In practical application of any portfolio selection model, various inputs, such as covariance statistics or beta scores, must be provided by

---

[10] George M. Frankfurter, Herbert E. Phillips, and John P. Seagle, "Portfolio Selection: The Effects of Uncertain Means, Variances, and Covariances," *Journal of Financial and Quantitative Analysis,* Vol. 6, No. 5 (December, 1971), pp. 1251–1262; "Performance of the Sharpe Portfolio Selection Model: A Comparison," *Journal of Financial and Quantitative Analysis,* Vol. 6, No. 2 (June, 1976), pp. 195–204.

the financial analyst. Unfortunately, there is nothing in the analyst's practical experience that corresponds even approximately to the set of complex mathematical relationships envisaged by theory. Existing portfolio selection algorithms fail to account for the fact that estimates must serve in place of known parameters. Thus, while preserving the fiction that all inputs obtained from the financial analyst are deterministic or subjective in nature, in fact the inputs that enter into normative applications must be obtained by statistical methods. Some effects of random estimation error were considered in the last section. In this section we consider some statistical problems that result from nonrandom factors.

Model Misspecification. According to the market index model introduced in Chapter 10, the rates of return on various securities are related only in terms of common correlations with an underlying market factor, which is represented in the model by the rate of return on a broad market index. In order to produce useful results, a normative model must provide a good approximation of reality. How good an approximation of reality is provided by the market index model is open to question. The general assumption is that "the linearity assumptions of the model are adequate."[11] Of course, this is not quite the same thing as saying that the linearity assumption is precisely correct. To the extent that the linearity assumption is not precisely correct, the model is a misspecification of reality—or *misspecified* for short. The market index model has been shown to perform worse when long data histories are available upon which to perform the required estimations than when only short data histories are available.[12] This topsy-turvy relationship is a direct result of *model misspecification*. The longer the period covered by a data history—all other things being equal—the more precise are the resulting estimations. Very precise estimation in combination with the wrong model will lead to convergence on the wrong relationship. This type of error, moreover, will not necessarily show up in *t* scores such as those used in statistical inference.

Misspecification Caused by the Use of a Proxy. Most published statistical series are subject to both measurement error and sampling error. Moreover, a published statistical series does not always report final figures. From the point of view of the financial analyst, therefore, a published statistical series may represent only a rough measure of what the analyst would actually like the data to measure. The statistical series used to represent the index in the market model, for example, is typically thought to represent rates of return on the market portfolio.

---

[11] Blume, "On the Assessment of Risk," p. 2.
[12] Frankfurter, *et al.*, "Performance of the Sharpe Portfolio Selection Model."

Where general equilibrium assumptions are not imposed, however, as in the market model, even to provide an adequate definition of a market portfolio is impossible, much less to measure its rate of return over time. When using a proxy for such a series, moreover, the analyst must be content with a data collection that consists of something less than a complete universe.

The use of a proxy introduces a different kind of misspecification than that considered in the previous section. An example of this form of misspecification is the following: Let the variable y be linear in the variable x, with the "true" model given by

$$y = a + bx.$$

Suppose, however, that observations on x are not available, but observations on a different variable z are. By definition, the variables x and z are not one and the same, for then we would know x. Thus, the use of z as a proxy for x results in yet a different form of model misspecification. Estimates obtained on the basis of a model that is subject to this sort of misspecification are, in general, biased estimates. This point was made in a different context by Morgenstern: "Faulty definitions, in the sense that a figure is taken to measure something which in fact it does not try to measure, or faulty application of a definition when the method for collecting the data is constructed, may each lead to bias."[13]

The statistical series used to represent the index in applications of the market index model performs a dual role. Future values of the index, which according to the model are determined by random factors, are used to predict ex-ante rates of return. Historical values of the index, on the other hand, are used to estimate alpha and beta scores and residual variance terms. Thus, the use of a proxy affects not one, but each of the variables that enter into application of the model. When we turn to estimation in the context of capital market theory, the situation becomes even more complex.

The Time Horizon Problem. Relationships that describe short-term market movements can be different relationships from those that describe longer-term market movements. In the shortest of short runs, for example, the rates of return on most stocks would be highly correlated. As the period between observations gets longer, however, a new relationship would emerge in which the rates of return on most financial assets would be less highly correlated.

---

[13] Oskar Morgenstern, *On the Accuracy of Economic Observations* (Princeton: Princeton University Press, 1963), p. 56.

A recent study has shown that correlations among the rates of return on various securities are not necessarily the same when the length of the time between observations is changed, as where time series of different duration are used.[14] The study shows that high positive correlation among rates of return calculated on the basis of short-term data can be perfectly consistent with negative correlation among the same returns when the interval between successive observations on rate of return is longer. These results are consistent with the casual observation that short-term price movements tend to occur in unison and, in general, are in the same direction. The fact that short-term price changes are positively correlated, therefore, can mask both the magnitude and direction of longer-term divergences.

The use of annual, quarterly, monthly, or even daily data as a basis for estimation raises an important question: How current should the data be and how many observations are necessary in order to produce useful results? By obtaining observations on rates of return more frequently than annually, the number of observations in a time series can be made quite large; from a statistics point of view, this should lead to more precise estimates. If the additional observations obtained by the use of short-term data are to be considered an unmixed blessing, however, they must provide more precise estimates of the very same economic relationships estimated with longer-term data. This does not seem to be the case. A consideration of the investment objectives of a particular portfolio is needed to determine a proper investment horizon, which in turn is needed to establish the appropriate period of aggregation. Unfortunately, there does not exist a firm theoretical basis for this determination; the time horizon problem would have to be considered on a case-by-case basis by the financial analyst. These results, incidentally, cast considerable doubt on the usefulness of so-called beta scores, which are calculated from daily data.

AN INTEGRATIVE PORTFOLIO SELECTION APPROACH

In practice, reliable inputs are difficult to define, let alone obtain. In standard applications of existing algorithms, securities are distinguished from one another on the basis of statistical scores, which, in many instances, could not exhibit significant differences. Under these conditions, a rationale for optimization (in the mathematical programming sense) is difficult to pin down. The need, therefore, is for a change in emphasis away from formalistic optimization models that do not cope with real-world data problems toward an approach that recognizes the shortcomings ever present in empirical work.

---

[14] Herbert E. Phillips and John P. Seagle, "Data: A Mixed Blessing in Portfolio Selection?" *Financial Management*, Vol. 4, No. 3 (Autumn, 1975), pp. 50–53.

Once the portfolio selection problem is recognized as the sum of the parts—estimation, analysis, and choice—normative theory can be redirected toward the only relevant aspect—decision. In a recent paper by Frankfurter and Phillips,[15] the portfolio selection problem is posed as a global problem that involves each of these parts, and a multistage portfolio selection method is proposed. The market index model is incorporated as part of this procedure because of its relative simplicity and economy of application, and because its linear structure provides virtually an ideal framework for this multistage approach. The approach is integrative in the sense that final choice is based on fundamental security analysis as well as the precepts of modern portfolio theory.

Portfolio Selection: A Two-Stage Procedure

Stage One: Security Grouping. The object of analysis in the context of modern portfolio theory is to identify those portfolios that maximize expected rate of return for a given level of risk and simultaneously minimize the level of risk exposure required to achieve a given level of expected rate of return. According to the modification of the procedure suggested here, securities are collected into groups by means of quantitative measurements that are meaningful from the point of view of modern portfolio theory. A framework for analysis and grouping is provided by the model.[16]

According to the market index model, the rate of return, $\tilde{r}_{it}$, in period t on security i is expressed as follows:

$$\tilde{r}_{it} = \alpha_i + \beta_i r_{mt} + \tilde{\epsilon}_{it} \qquad i = 1, \dots, N, \qquad (11.7)$$
$$t = 1, \dots, T,$$

where the tilde denotes a random variable, and

$\tilde{r}_{it}$ = the periodic rate of return on security i in period t,
r_{mt} = the rate of return on a market index in period t,
α_i = the point at which a regression line intercepts the vertical axis,
β_i = the slope of a regression line showing the extent to which security returns are affected by r_{mt},
$\tilde{\epsilon}_{it}$ = a random residual error term, with zero mean and variance $\text{Var}(\tilde{\epsilon}_{it})$.

From the point of view of the market index model, the characteristics of a security's rate of return are completely described by the values

---

[15] George M. Frankfurter and Herbert E. Phillips, "Portfolio Selection: An Analytic Approach for Selection of Securities from a Large Universe," *Journal of Financial and Quantitative Analysis*, Vol. 15 (June, 1980), pp. 357–378.

[16] For a more detailed and rigorous discussion, see Frankfurter and Phillips, *ibid.*

of α_i, β_i, and $\text{Var}(\tilde{\epsilon}_{it})$, which are the parameters of equation (11.7). Unfortunately, such parameters are necessarily unknown quantities and, thus, the subject of statistical estimation procedures, which, in application, are imperfect at best. The most commonly used method of estimation is the method of least squares.

For each of the N securities of a universe of securities, suppose that estimates $\hat{\alpha}_i$, $\hat{\beta}_i$, and $\text{Var}(\tilde{e}_{it})$, where $\tilde{e}_{it}$ is the residual of a regression estimate and $\hat{\alpha}_i$ and $\hat{\beta}_i$, estimate α_i and β_i, respectively, are based on T pieces of historical data that are available to the portfolio manager or analyst. In application of such an estimation procedure, the resulting estimates will vary considerably and reflect both real differences and purely random estimation error. Thus, the observed differences in the security profiles, be they large or small, do not necessarily reflect any real differences. Such observations must, in any event, be regarded as but one source of information about securities and about the future rates of return on portfolios that may be fashioned on them. A procedure is needed, therefore, that is capable of recognizing (explicitly) that estimation error and other data problems are present in any estimation.

Securities may be arranged into groups of securities by means of factor analysis and statistical cluster analysis. The resulting groupings represent "homogeneous" collections of securities in the sense that the data suggest they are homogeneous. No pretense is made that such groupings can serve to uncover any parametric relationships, but only that group characteristics can provide better estimates of the unknown parameters than would simple least-squares values obtained for each security separately. From the point of view of decision making, moreover, the groupings have added meaning: given the sample information, they reflect the portfolio manager's ability, or lack of ability, to distinguish members of a universe of securities. Such groupings are called *quasi-securities* because they are treated as such. Primary diversification is achieved in the Frankfurter and Phillips model on the basis of quasi-securities.[17]

According to the market index model, the rate of return on any security is the result of two factors: a systematic component that is market related and factors that are unique to a given security. In equation (11.7) the parameters are given by α_i and β_i. In any application, however, we should be concerned not only with the alpha and beta but also with the level of our uncertainty about the estimates. The grouping procedure separates securities into groups such that each security is most similar in terms of its statistical characteristics to those that belong to the group. We seek a collection of groupings that are distinguishable from one another on both subjective and statistical grounds.

---

[17] *Ibid.*

Securities are categorized based on their systematic response to general market conditions and according to nonsystematic factors. The securities within each group identified in this way are more homogeneous as regards the investment characteristics that are important in the sense of the portfolio selection model than would be securities grouped according to traditional industry classifications or according to naive beta statistics. No pretense is made, however, that the security groupings derived in this way serve to uncover important long-term fundamental characteristics of the securities of interest. This is the purpose of the fundamental security analysis, which is a part of the second stage of analysis.

The first stage of analysis is completed by application of the market index model in conjunction with quasi-securities (i.e., clusters) rather than on the basis of the real (individual) securities. The Markowitz frontier of efficiency is determined on this basis. That is, the optimal combination of quasi-securities is determined for every feasible level of rate of return and risk. These efficient combinations of quasi-securities provide the framework in which the second stage of analysis takes place.

Stage Two: Portfolio Selection. The model tells the security analyst what proportions to invest in each grouping so as to achieve efficient diversification among clusters of securities, but the analyst must also decide (1) which securities to purchase within each group and (2) in what relative proportions. The analyst may be in possession of information that is not properly reflected in historical data. On this basis the analyst may wish to suggest certain modifications, such as the inclusion of a security that might otherwise be excluded, the holding of a higher proportion of cash or cash equivalents, or perhaps a change in the proportion of risk-free assets and stocks.

Security selections are justified on the basis of what they contribute toward effective diversification of risk and also on the basis of their fundamental investment characteristics. In deciding which securities to select from among those identified by the portfolio selection model (used in conjunction with the grouping technique), the analyst must consider various qualitative and quantitative factors in addition to the purely quantitative information provided by the model. Such qualitative factors, for example, include a professional assessment of the quality of a firm's management, the appropriateness of its research and development efforts, the status of demand for its product, and relatedly, its prospects for future earnings and growth. The quantitative factors include the rate of return data and market forecasts and various other financial reports and data.

The analyst who enters in the second stage of the portfolio selection process is provided with a list of optimal portfolio weights. These weights are attached to groups of securities that are homogeneous from the point of view of the model as regards their investment characteristics. The analyst does not modify these weights in any way but must decide which of the securities within each group to select and in what combination.

Thus optimality in the sense of the portfolio selection model is not in any way destroyed by the security analyst's inputs. On the contrary, the analyst enjoys the advantage of a comprehensive framework that is established on the basis of the optimal portfolio weights. The analyst is then at liberty to concentrate his or her efforts on the systematic evaluation of a security universe that has been reduced to manageable proportions by the grouping approach. The in-depth analysis required for effective decision and comprehensive justification would be impossible to achieve were the analyst required to consider every stock publically traded.

Thus a system of checks and balances may be incorporated into the portfolio selection process. Such a system involves an interaction between specialists in the area of modern portfolio selection and quantitative analysis and fundamental security analysis. The final decision as to which of the competing portfolios to select is left to human judgment.

By interacting directly with the security analyst, the diversification model described above provides the basis for an effective integrative approach. Such an integration of methodologies, moreover, is accomplished without violating the essential precepts of traditional or modern theory. Other integrative approaches, which are perhaps better known, fail in this regard. Most importantly, the quantitative model provides both a basis for efficient diversification and an algorithm for assigning optimal portfolio weights to meaningful collections of securities, rather than to industry averages or to groups that can be justified only on the basis of naive beta statistics. Thus a fundamental analyst is able to exploit the portfolio selection framework provided by the model rather than—as is more common—merely to pay lip service to it.

LENDING AND BORROWING PORTFOLIOS

The introduction to the portfolio selection model of lending and borrowing funds—at appropriate market interest rates—will have a bearing on one's portfolio efficiency analysis and on choice. In this section the alternatives of lending at a riskless rate of interest and/or borrowing at an appropriate borrowing rate are introduced.

The Riskless Lending Rate

At any point in time, there is some interest rate, r_f, at which loanable funds can be lent with virtual assurance that both principal and interest will be returned. A 90-day treasury bill, for example, is a riskless asset in this sense, and its rate of return is a very convenient, if not an altogether appropriate, proxy for the riskless rate, r_f.

Once the opportunity to purchase a risk-free asset is introduced to a portfolio analysis, the situation is changed. A Markowitz feasible region is shown in Figure 11-3.[18] An investor with only risk alternatives would select some portfolio along the efficient frontier of this region. With the introduction of a risk-free asset, however, one's options are expanded. From the point of view of portfolio analysis, one can

1. Invest everything in the risk-free asset, with a lower certain return.
2. Invest everything in risky assets.
3. Purchase some mix consisting of both risky assets and the riskless one.

These options are represented by portfolios that plot as points along the ray from point r_f to point f in the figure. Such portfolios, which

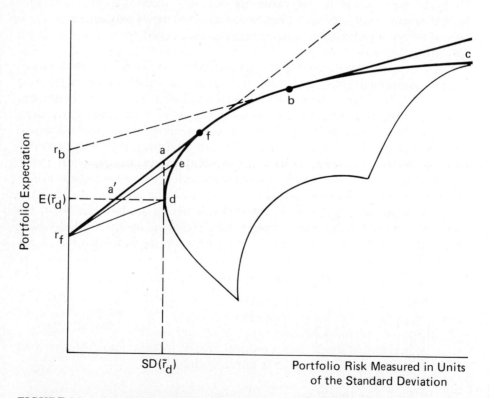

FIGURE 11-3. Lending and Borrowing Portfolios in EV Space

---

[18] Notice that the horizontal axis in Figure 11-3 is measured in terms of the standard deviation rather than variance. This is done so that the relationships involving lending and borrowing will be linear relationships.

consist of linear combinations of portfolio f and the riskless asset, are called *lending portfolios*. Portfolio f takes on a very special meaning in Chapter 12 (but not here), where conditions of general equilibrium are assumed.

Suppose, for example, that an investor who is confronted with only risky investment alternatives would purchase portfolio d, which is the minimum risk-efficient portfolio consisting entirely or risky assets. With the introduction of a risk-free asset as an investment option, clearly this investor might choose to invest everything in the riskless asset. Suppose, on the other hand, that a rate of return in excess of the rate of return on the riskless asset is desired. What then? Rates of return in excess of the risk-free rate of return on loanable funds come about as a reward for bearing risk. Presumably investors who seek such a rate of return would invest at least a part of their wealth in an efficient portfolio made up of risky assets. Might the investor, therefore, who was previously at point d on the Markowitz frontier continue to invest in portfolio d?

Even an investor who, for some reason, has a particular attachment for portfolio d would be at least tempted by the fact that portfolio a offers a higher expectation for the same level of risk. Portfolio a is obtained by investing a portion, x_a, of one's wealth in the risk-free asset, and the remainder, $1 - x_a$, in a different, and *more risky*, efficient collection of risky assets. Clearly, portfolio a dominates portfolio d; but portfolio a' dominates portfolio d also. Portfolio a' offers the same expectation as d but at a lower level of risk. In fact, we arrive at the delightful conclusion that every combination of portfolio f and the riskless asset, which is described by a point in the line segment $a'\,a$ on the ray from r_f to point f on the efficient frontier, dominates portfolio d.

It seems as though we have found the best game in town. Why not search for a ray that lies above the one from r_f to point f? The answer is obvious: point f is the *point of tangency* with the Markowitz efficient frontier of a line passing through r_f on the vertical axis. This is the highest point that one can reach on the frontier of the feasible region. Investors who would previously have invested in efficient portfolios that plot as points along the efficient frontier below f in the figure would now invest in some combination of portfolio f and the riskless asset. Other investors, who would previously have invested in portfolios that plot as points along the efficient frontier at or above point f, would not be enticed by the riskless asset. Such an investor, however, might find bliss in a different prospect—leveraging.

The Borrowing Rate

At any point in time there exists some interest rate, r_b, at which loanable funds can be borrowed by the investor to purchase even greater amounts of a portfolio than personal funds will allow. The borrowing rate, r_b, is higher than the riskless lending rate, r_f, for any borrower other than the Treasury and will vary from one borrower to the next and from one day to the next.

In Figure 11-3, a hypothetical borrowing rate is shown by point r_b on the vertical axis. A line has been drawn through r_b, tangent to the Markowitz efficient frontier at point b. An investor who would previously have purchased a portfolio that is represented by a point along this frontier *beyond* point b could, according to this logic, improve the situation by portfolio leveraging. A borrowing portfolio is obtained by investing all of one's own funds and borrowed funds as well in portfolio b. Unfortunately, this strategy may look better on paper than it is in fact.

Portfolio leveraging, in the sense of the figure, involves the substitution of a fixed commitment risk for a differential in portfolio risk—the two are really quite different. If, for example, as matters unfold, one's ex-ante expectations are not realized, then the nasty problem of having to cover a position (i.e., transfer additional funds to the lender) will inevitably arise. To lump this form of risk together with random portfolio risk is clearly to mix apples and oranges. Portfolio variance does not provide a very good representation for the risk that is involved in leveraging operations. Such an operation should be undertaken, therefore, only on the basis of logic that goes beyond the representation shown in Figure 11-3. The portfolio selection model, of course, is subject to other limitations.

BOND SELECTION STRATEGIES

A strategy is a rule for action. A rational investment strategy, therefore, is one that seeks to maximize expected rate of return (or yield) for the degree of risk exposure accepted. To this point in the development of normative theory, portfolio selection strategies have been proposed for applications which assume—by implication—that a risky asset is necessarily a common stock. A bond is also a risky asset, however, and should be thought of as such.

A high-grade bond offers the holder a relatively stable and highly predictable pattern of cash flow over the holding period that is contracted for, assuming that the bond is held to maturity. Each element of cash flow associated with bond investment—both coupon and the return of principal—are fixed in regard to both timing and amount by the contract. This does not guarantee payment, of course, but legal remedies exist in the event of nonpayment. There are no similar remedies—expressed or implied—available to stock investors.

A bond purchaser agrees in principle to accept a fixed return on an investment, and by so doing must forego any claim to a share in the future growth in earnings of the issuer. A common stockholder, by contrast, is entitled to a proportionate share of future net earnings—as may be affected by either success or economic adversity. The holders of variable income securities, therefore, by virtue of their holdings, enjoy some protection against diminution of capital caused by inflation, but they accept in exchange risk that is inherent in an auction market for variable income securities. A high-grade, long-term bond offers its holder no hedge against inflation, but for the investor who plans to hold the security until maturity, some protection is provided against unanticipated variation in either periodic cash flow or the nominal yield.

Any attempt to compare the determinants of yield on stocks and investment quality bonds is bound to be frustrated by the fact that these are fundamentally different investment mechanisms, with vastly different characteristics and holding periods. Bond demand is highly segmented, representing the varied objectives of individuals and financial institutions that make up the market. Each such group is subject to legal and institutional constraints, tax programs, and investment priorities that are unique to it in various respects. It would be utter nonsense, therefore, to suppose that bond investors are, in general, unconstrained, one-period, mean-variance utility maximizers who trade in perfectly liquid markets where there are no barriers to entrance or exit. Nevertheless, an appropriate strategy for investment decision is one that considers the interrelationships between financial variables and deals rigorously and explicitly with the risk-return trade-offs that are a characteristic of financial markets.

Various Concepts of Risk

Except for the shortest of short-term debt issues of the federal government, a limited-income security—regardless of quality rating—is a risky financial asset and should be regarded as such. Both from a theoretical and a pragmatic point of view, bond risk is a very complex phenomenon that defies simple categorization according to its various components.[19]

Default Risk. Standard bond ratings allude, somewhat imprecisely, to the unconditional probability of default on or before maturity.[20] The consequence of default, however, is not a direct function of the

---

[19] Steven Katz, "The Price Adjustment Process of Bonds to Rating Reclassifications: A Test of Bond Market Efficiency," *Journal of Finance*, Vol. 29 (May, 1974), pp. 551-559. Also see Ronald W. Melicher and David F. Rush, "Systematic Risk, Financial Data and Bond Rating Relationships in a Regulated Industry Environment," *Journal of Finance*, Vol. 29 (May, 1974), pp. 537-544.

[20] George E. Pinches and J. Clay Singleton, "The Adjustment of Stock Prices to Bond Rating Changes," *Journal of Finance*, Vol. 33 (March, 1978), pp. 29-44.

unconditional probability of default at some point in the life cycle of a bond. What matters is the *conditional probability* of default at each point in time and the remaining consequence of default measured in terms of (1) interest payments and/or the return of principal foregone and (2) the expected proceeds under liquidation or reorganization.

   Systematic Risk. The existence of a term structure of interest rates implies that bond prices vary in a systematic fashion over time in tune with market interest rate changes. The resultant investment risk, however, is not a stable function of just one market interest rate, or even of a particular schedule of interest rates, as the characteristics of the term structure vary over time in line with varying business conditions and changes in Federal Reserve policy. The probability of default and the value of a firm under liquidation are affected by business cycle fluctuations that are lead indicators of the market interest rate cycle. As one approaches a peak in the business cycle, for example, default is not common, even among lower-quality issues. As one passes the peak and heads for the trough, however, the situation is entirely changed— the probability of default goes up, and the value of assets used to secure a firm's debt (where there are such provisions) goes down. Clearly, aggregate data compiled on an ex-post basis (such as that compiled by Hickman and discussed below) would be of little value in assessing systematic risk on an ex-ante basis. Systematic factors of risk are in any event confounded with factors that are unique to individual firms and the contracts that they enter into.

   Nonsystematic Risk. The systematic and nonsystematic components of bond investment risk are not easily and neatly dichotomized as they are in a one-period hold stock market model. Nevertheless, certain factors are unique to individual issues just as certain factors are affected by the market. Where it is appropriate to consider only longer holding periods (i.e., longer than one year), unfortunately, systematic and nonsystematic factors of risk interact rendering it impossible to separate the two. As a long-term bond is a commitment on the part of both lender and borrower for a period longer than a year—typically much longer—the application of a one-period hold logic, such as in the calculation of covariance or beta statistics, would be utter nonsense. A second casualty of the multiperiod nature of bond investment, from the point of view of modern portfolio theory, has to do with the nature and efficacy of diversification.

Limited Relevance of Modern Portfolio Theory

   The characteristic logic and equations of models that follow the Markowitz ilk do not directly apply to the analysis of portfolios that consist wholly or in part of long-term debt securities. We cannot, for example, describe the precise makeup of the Markowitz efficient frontier in this case. Neither would it be reasonable to assume that for efficient portfolios all but the systematic component of risk will have been diversified away—even in the context of general equilibrium the systematic and nonsystematic components of risk interact. Given the diverse nature and objectives of bond investors, moreover, the assumption that bond investors are, in general, one period mean-variance utility maximizers would be so much at variance with reality as to lead to no useful implications or conclusions. Nevertheless, if one were willing to accept the more modest proposition that bond investors generally seek the highest after-tax yield given any degree of risk exposure deemed to be appropriate and in light of whatever institutional constraints may apply, then some of the relationships of modern portfolio theory are approximately correct and provide useful insights for bond investors. A more detailed discussion is presented in Chapter 23.

Summary

The object of portfolio diversification is risk reduction. Efficient diversification in the sense of the Markowitz portfolio selection model refers to the combination of financial assets into an investment portfolio in such a way as to reduce risk. To this point in the discussion, however, consistent with the literature on the subject, we have concentrated primarily on stock investment. A number of points have come to light in the present chapter.

We noted that even when restricted to stock investment, existing portfolio selection methods and algorithms are seriously deficient in a number of respects. Indeed, in any application of the standard model there is a component of random variation that is not at all accounted for by the model—this source of variation is due to random estimation error. A model that is credited to Frankfurter and Phillips was outlined. The purpose of this model is more efficient estimation through grouping and more effective selection through integration. We would anticipate the development of new and improved integrative approaches in the years ahead.

Also noted in this chapter, as if it were necessary to point out, was that an optimally diversified investment portfolio is not typically restricted to stock investment. Unfortunately, extending the Markowitz methodology, as such, much beyond the realm of stock investment is difficult. The logic, however, is perfectly general. Argued here, and further demonstrated later in the book, is the point that while solutions to real-world portfolio selection problems may, in fact, be somewhat less precise (in the sense of mathematical optimization) than the portfolio selection literature would lead us to believe, the underlying logic is helpful and relevant.

Questions

1. Effective, as distinct from efficient, diversification is achieved by combining assets in an investment portfolio in such a way as to provide a meaningful hedge against chance factors.
   (a) What sort of factors are included among the chance factors?
   (b) To what extent might the following statement be justified: "Modern portfolio theory is concerned with optimal solution of a nonexistent problem—one for which estimation is not an integral part."

2. One can always calculate a statistic, such as covariance or beta, on the basis of financial information that is readily available. It does not follow, however, that the resulting estimation will be free from error or that there is anything in reality to be estimated. You may support or take issue with this proposition, which lies at the heart of an existing controversy; it is to be presumed, however, that you will take a position. Do so in as rigorous a fashion as you are able.

3. (a) What is the difference between true efficiency and nominal efficiency?
   (b) In what sense are objective probabilities "fuzzy"?
   (c) Why should anyone wish to use a fuzzy probability? Does one have any choice?
   (d) The notion that by using historical information one implies that "history will repeat itself" is clearly simplistic. Would it be any less simplistic to suppose that a statistical estimate can fully substitute for an unknown parameter value in application of an optimization model? Explain.

4. If the required level of accuracy in estimation cannot be achieved with annual data because there are too few observations, and monthly data proves to be better from this point of view, might not daily data be better still? Explain.

5. Left to its own devices, a computer-based application of a portfolio selection model might, very systematically, search out the very worst securities and/or portfolios. Why might this happen and in what sense are the resulting selections bad?

6. According to Markowitz, "a rule of behavior which does not imply the superiority of diversification must be rejected both as a hypothesis and as a maxim." His diversification model, however, does not account for perhaps the most important stage in the process of portfolio selection. Discuss.

7. As pointed out in the chapter, an upper limit must often be imposed on the proportion of an investment portfolio that may be invested in a particular security.
   (a) Set the portfolio selection problem up as a quadratic programming problem, assuming an upper limit of 5 percent.

    (b) What would be the affect of this additional constraint on (1) the number of securities likely to be included in an investment portfolio and (2) the shape of the resulting efficient frontier?

8. Explain the workings of a computer-based portfolio selection model, in terms of inefficient portfolios as well as efficient portfolios.

9. An integrative portfolio selection approach is described in this chapter.
    (a) In what sense is this approach "integrative"?
    (b) What are some of the shortcomings of more standard approaches, as described in Chapters 9 and 10, which this approach seeks to overcome?
    (c) How do the security groupings used by the model differ from standard industry groupings?
    (d) Investment weights are obtained in the first stage; the security analyst does not have any role until the second stage. Why is it necessary that this sequence not be reversed?

10. What are the essential disadvantages accruing to the purchaser of fixed-income securities? The major advantages?

11. Would a highly risk-adverse investor be wise to confine bond purchases to issues in the most stable industries in our economy? Discuss.

12. (a) What should be the objectives of a bond investment strategy?
    (b) Explain the relevance and applicability of the Markowitz portfolio selection approach.

PART 4
Capital Market Theory

12.

The Capital Asset Pricing Model

Modern portfolio theory, which is the subject of Part 3 of the book, seeks to explain (1) how risk reduction through efficient diversification can be achieved and (2) how, once achieved, efficient diversification would affect the rate at which one could efficiently trade expectation for risk when making portfolio selections. Efficient portfolios comprised entirely of risky assets may be represented by points that plot along an efficient frontier, as illustrated by Figure 9-1. Figure 11-3 shows that the introduction of lending and borrowing as alternatives when forming an investment portfolio would have an important bearing on portfolio selection and on the shape and composition of the efficient frontier.[1]

No very extreme assumptions have been necessary to this point as our concern has been limited to normative theory. As our sights turn from normative approaches to positive theory, we are at once confronted by a change in objectives and a need to impose restrictions that may be both unrealistic and extreme. Capital market theory, for example, assumes that all investors can both borrow and lend at the same riskless rate of interest r_f,[2] which is clearly not so. Such assumptions are *restrictive assumptions*.

POSITIVE VS. NORMATIVE THEORY

The portfolio selection models of Part 3 are normative in scope. The objective of *normative theory* in the context of portfolio selection is to serve as a guide to action. This theory seeks to explain how indi-

---

[1] This relationship was first introduced by Professor William F. Sharpe of Stanford University, and Figure 11-3 should be credited to him. See William F. Sharpe, "A Simplified Model of Portfolio Analysis," *Management Science*, Vol. 9, No. 2 (January, 1963), p. 286.

[2] William F. Sharpe, "Capital Asset Prices: A Theory of Market Equilibrium Under Conditions of Risk," *Journal of Finance*, Vol. 14, No. 3 (September, 1964), p. 431.

vidual investment portfolio decisions should be made. Normative portfolio theory does not seek to explain how, in the aggregate, individual investment decisions will affect the behavior of securities markets or what actual effects may be.

The purpose of *positive theory*, by contrast, is to help us understand a complex situation. The environment of investment decision, for example, is extremely complex. One cannot possibly know all of the factors that affect the pricing of capital assets; and to suppose that the totality of such factors will remain constant over time would indeed be heroic. Nevertheless, capital market theory seeks to explain the positive implications of modern portfolio theory—that is, what would be the *general equilibrium* implications for capital asset prices and other market relationships were all investors to behave in the manner prescribed by modern portfolio theory.

Positive theory is intended as a guide for drawing inferences that are quite general. As a first step in the development of a positive theory, a logical framework must be established wherein matters may be simplified. This is accomplished by imposing restrictions or limiting assumptions. An artificial environment is set up in which purely theoretical relationships and interrelationships may be studied. The object is to construct a model so that conclusions can be reached which, from the point of view of theory, are mutually consistent with the assumptions. Once this is accomplished the model builder may try to relax the restrictive assumptions one by one to see if useful implications can be obtained in a more realistic theoretical setting. Such attempts, as in the case of capital market theory, often fail to produce a very precise replicate of reality. Ultimately the model builder will test the empirical validity of the model; that is, the ability of the model—notwithstanding the restrictive assumptions on which it is based—to permit conclusions to be reached that generally apply in the real world.

A model that is itself an abstraction may serve a useful purpose, but such an abstraction must never be confused with the real thing. Matters must be kept in perspective. No serious scholar, for example, would be willing to suppose that a totality of market relationships and interrelationships could, in any meaningful sense, be reduced to a few abstract symbols or equations. The authors of this text make no strong claims for capital market theory other than to suggest that, used with discretion, some useful insights regarding the behavior of securities markets may be obtained.[3]

_____

[3] Stronger claims are made elsewhere (as, for example, in a number of competing textbooks), but such strong claims are quite deservedly coming under stronger and stronger attack. See Richard Roll, "A Critique of the Asset Pricing Theory's Tests" [Part I: On Past and Potential Testability of the Theory], *Journal of Financial Economics,* Vol. 4 (March, 1977), pp. 129–176; Herbert E. Phillips, "Capital Asset Pricing Model and Traditional Risk for Capital Budgeting: A Comment," *Financial Review* (Fall, 1977), pp. 91–96.

THE MEANING OF GENERAL EQUILIBRIUM

Equilibrium is a concept borrowed from the physical sciences that is widely applied in the area of macroeconomic analysis. *Equilibrium* refers to a state of balance between opposing forces—a position from which there is no tendency to move. The *conditions of equilibrium*, by contrast, are conditions which, if satisfied, will result in such a balance.

In theory, an equilibrium system begins with an abstraction—the model and its assumptions. Such a system may be static or dynamic, partial or general. A *static equilibrium* system is "timeless in the sense that there are no links with the past or with the future; we are not interested in how we got there or in what will happen later."[4] An equilibrium system is dynamic, on the other hand, when it deals with dated variables that "relate to different moments or periods of time and have links with the past and future."[5] A *partial equilibrium* state is one in which certain variables are held constant. Such restrictions may apply to variables that are internal to the model or to externalities. An equilibrium system is called *general*, however, when nothing is held constant. The only thing "general" about general equilibrium is the name, as the conditions (i.e., assumptions) of such an equilibrium system are necessarily restrictive.

Herein lies a very important difference between modern portfolio theory and capital market theory. In the portfolio selection framework of Part 3, no equilibrium conditions are expressed or implied. These models are *not* equilibrium restricted. Capital market theory, by contrast, *is* equilibrium restricted. Equilibrium in this context, moreover, is both general and dynamic.

THE NEED FOR REALISTIC ASSUMPTIONS

Capital market theory is, in a sense, "an exercise in positive economics."[6] Given certain assumptions that may be both unrealistic and extreme, *capital market theory* seeks to explain what would be the market implications in general equilibrium were all investors to seek to hold investment portfolios that are Markowitz efficient. Simply to raise the question, of course (i.e., to ask what if), does not in itself suggest that general equilibrium can or does exist in securities markets or that, in the main, market participants do behave in the manner that is prescribed by modern portfolio theory. Interesting questions can be raised in this regard, but such questions are not directly relevant to the present discussion.

---

[4] R. G. D. Allen, *Macro-Economic Theory: A Mathematical Treatment* (New York: St. Martin's Press, 1968), p. 76.

[5] *Ibid.*

[6] William F. Sharpe, *Portfolio Theory and Capital Markets* (New York: McGraw-Hill, 1972), p. 77.

From the point of view of positive theory, "the relevant question to ask about the assumptions of theory is not whether they are descriptively realistic, for they never are, but whether they are sufficiently good approximations for the purpose at hand."[7] From the point of view of normative theory, on the other hand, the underlying assumptions had better be "descriptively realistic," as normative theory must apply to a reality where specific actions are to be taken. In recent years various normative approaches, such as so-called beta theory and the formation of index funds, that rely on the positive implications of capital market theory for justification have been introduced. A discussion of these approaches, and the backward induction that is required to justify their application, is presented in Chapter 13.

WHAT THE MODELS ASSUME

The portfolio selection and general equilibrium frameworks are different frameworks, appropriate to different purposes, and based on vastly different assumptions. There is a very common tendency to downplay or to entirely disregard the distinction that one should draw, for example, between portfolio theory and capital market theory; the result is widespread confusion. Any attempt at understanding, and at meaningful contrast, must begin with a consideration of the assumptions on which theory is based.

The Portfolio Selection Framework

The portfolio selection framework of the Markowitz model is not equilibrium restricted. In this framework one assumes that choices are made in accord with a preference ordering system that supposes the investor to be made happy by anticipation of financial gain but vexed by uncertainty about future benefits and losses.[8] In application of the model the investor has only to form expectations about future one-period rates of return (subjectively or objectively), and be willing to express these expectations in probabilistic form as required by the model—in terms of the means, variances, and covariances of the relevant probability distributions.[9]

An analytic procedure for portfolio selection is made up of two stages. In the first stage one forms beliefs about the future. There are no preconditions as to how this is to be accomplished; one may use fundamental analysis, follow the data, or employ the services of a clair-

---

[7] Milton M. Friedman, "The Methodology of Positive Economics," *Essays in Positive Economics* (Chicago: The University of Chicago Press, 1953), p. 15.

[8] Harry Markowitz, *Portfolio Selection* (New Haven: Yale University Press, 1959), Chapter 1.

[9] James Tobin, "Liquidity Preference as Behavior Towards Risk," *Review of Economic Studies*, Vol. 26, No. 1 (February, 1958).

voyant. The second stage of analysis begins only after one's beliefs about the future have been formed; this stage ends with action—an investment portfolio is actually chosen. Markowitz was very careful to point out that his model begins with the second stage.[10]

The reader must note that up to this point in the development of theory absolutely no restrictions have been placed on the way that investors, individually and collectively, form their expectations. There has been no assumption that all investors form the same expectations or that they purchase the same portfolio of risky assets.

The General Equilibrium Framework

To the rather modest assumptions that apply to the portfolio selection framework, capital market theory adds the following:

1. All investors have the same decision horizon.
2. Capital markets are perfect in the sense that all assets are infinitely divisible, there are no transactions costs or taxes, information is costless and available to everybody, and borrowing and lending rates are equal to each other and the same for all investors.
3. Expectations and portfolio opportunities are "homogeneous" throughout the market. That is, all investors have the same set of portfolio opportunities and view the expected returns and standard deviations of return provided by the various portfolios in the same way.[11]

The market analogy assumed by the general equilibrium framework of the capital asset pricing model, therefore, is a rather "extreme" version of the *perfect markets proposition* in which "prices at any time *fully reflect* available information."[12] These propositions carry the further implication that all ex-ante investor expectations are realized ex-post.[13]

THE CAPITAL ASSET PRICING MODEL

By virtue of the limiting assumptions, a logical framework has been established in which to examine the positive implications of modern portfolio theory. Were all investors to behave in the manner prescribed by modern portfolio theory, they would each form expectations about future rates of return and express these expectations in terms of means,

---

[10] Harry M. Markowitz, "Portfolio Selection," *Journal of Finance*, Vol. 7, No. 1 (March, 1952), p. 91.

[11] Eugene F. Fama, "Risk, Return, and Equilibrium: Some Clarifying Comments," *Journal of Finance*, Vol. 23, No. 1 (March, 1968), p. 30.

[12] Eugene F. Fama, "Components of Investment Performance," *Journal of Finance*, Vol. 27, No. 3 (June, 1972), p. 554. Emphasis is ours.

[13] Stewart C. Myers, "On the Use of β in Regulatory Proceedings: A Comment," *Bell Journal of Economics and Management Science*, Vol. 3, No. 2 (Autumn, 1972), pp. 622-627.

variances, and covariances of rates of return.[14] In order to establish the conditions of general equilibrium in the capital markets, however, these expectations would have to be compatible with equilibrium (i.e., a position from which there is no tendency to move). In the general equilibrium framework of the capital asset pricing model, this question of compatibility is resolved by assuming that all investors form the same expectations about the future. A further assumption is that there are no transactions costs or taxes. Thus, from the point of view of theory, investors must view their individual opportunities for diversification when purchasing risky assets in terms of the same opportunity set. The efficient frontier of this opportunity set is shown in Figure 12-1.

The Capital Market Line

According to the idealized assumptions of the model, each investor is faced with the same investment opportunities and with the same op-

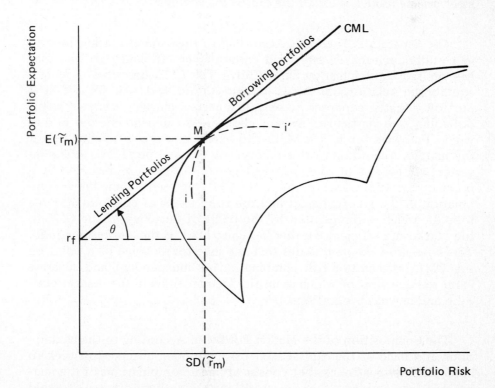

FIGURE 12-1. The Capital Market Line

---

[14] An investor may form the entire variance-covariance matrix as in Chapter 9, or the diagonalized version of it as explained in Chapter 10.

portunities to borrow and lend.[15] The choices open to each investor, then, are the following:

1. To invest everything in the risk-free asset whose certain rate of return is r_f.
2. To purchase some mix consisting of both risky assets and the riskless one.
3. To purchase an unleveraged investment portfolio that consists entirely of risky assets.
4. To purchase a leveraged portfolio that consists entirely of risky assets.

According to the assumptions of the model, the lending and borrowing rates are the same and are equal to the riskless rate r_f for all investors. This restrictive assumption yields the following important implication: In equilibrium each investor will be able to achieve any expectation-risk combination that lies on a single straight line that is drawn through point r_f on the expectations axis in Figure 12–1 and tangent to the efficient frontier at point M. This straight line, which describes one of the central equilibrium relationships of the capital asset pricing model, is called the *capital market line*.

The Separation Theorem. According to this capital market theory, in equilibrium each investor will choose some efficient portfolio that lies on the capital market line (CML). The CML describes a general equilibrium relationship between expectation and risk for efficient portfolios that is supposed to exist in a perfect market. Which efficient portfolio, p, a particular investor chooses will depend on the rate at which that investor is just willing to exchange expectation for risk at the margin. According to this theory, the optimal portfolio for any investor will consist of some efficient portfolio that is represented by a point on the CML. Each point on the CML represents some linear combination of the risk-free asset and the risky assets of portfolio M. Portfolio M, which is represented by the point of tangency of the CML to the Markowitz efficient frontier in Figure 12–1, is the *market portfolio*. The *separation theorem* states that the investor's choice of a point on the CML (expectation-risk combination) is independent and separate from the question of which securities are contained in the market portfolio and in what proportions.

The Composition of the Market Portfolio. According to the assumptions and logic of the capital asset pricing model, all investors seek to hold efficient portfolios that consist of linear combinations of the market portfolio and the riskless asset. All investors, therefore, seek to hold

---

[15] The implications of borrowing and lending alternatives on the criteria for portfolio efficiency are discussed in Chapter 11 and outlined by Figure 11–3. Readers who have not mastered this material should do so before proceeding.

the securities of portfolio M, which is unique.[16] As all investors seek to purchase the same securities in a market that is characterized by atmospheric competition, and where the conditions outlined under assumption (2) above apply,[17] the relative prices of financial securities will adjust perfectly in tune with changes in supply and demand. In equilibrium, therefore, the market portfolio must—consistent with these assumptions—be composed of a proportionate share of all risky securities that are available on the market. The fraction of portfolio M that is represented by any security i, $i = 1, 2, \ldots, m$, therefore, must be proportional to the equilibrium value of a single share of security i and the value of the market as a whole. Thus, in equilibrium, the mean and variance of the market portfolio are unique, and are defined as follows:

$$E(\tilde{r}_m) = \sum_{i=1}^{m} x_i E(\tilde{r}_i) \qquad (12.1)$$

$$\text{Var}(\tilde{r}_m) = \sum_{i=1}^{m} \sum_{j=1}^{m} x_i x_j \text{Cov}(\tilde{r}_i, \tilde{r}_j) \qquad (12.2)$$

The Reward to Variability Ratio: Efficient Portfolios. In Figure 12-1 the riskless rate, r_f, represents the pure price of time, which is, among other things, the maximum return that one can realize by an investment in a financial asset without bearing risk. All points to the right of point r_f on the CML correspond to higher expectations, but also to positive levels of risk. According to this model, therefore, any expectation of financial reward that is in excess of the risk-free rate of return on loanable funds must be a reward for bearing risk.[18] In equilibrium, for example, the excess return on some portfolio p, $[E(\tilde{r}_p) - r_f]$, is the financial reward for bearing risk by investing a proportion, x_p, of one's

---

[16] If the assumption of homogeneous expectations were relaxed, the CML would degenerate into a relationship between a single, risk-free interest rate and an infinite number of market portfolios. If the assumption of a single lending and borrowing rate were relaxed, the situation would degenerate even more.

[17] In order for the price system to work perfectly in bringing about the required adjustments, all assets must be perfectly divisible. Even so, the differential effects of unequal transactions costs and taxes would, at least in theory, prevent the required adjustments from taking place. For this reason these effects are assumed away according to the restrictions set out under assumption (2) above.

[18] This result has both intuitive and aesthetic appeal. Indeed, this rationale scratches at the heart of the capitalist ethic that we all know and love. The capital asset pricing model, however, deals in specifics as well as in pleasing generalities. These generalities, moreover, might be arrived at by an alternative path, or even by assertion; the capital asset pricing model, therefore, must be understood for its specifics and accepted or rejected on that basis.

wealth in the risky assets of portfolio M, and the remainder in the riskless asset. The expected reward for bearing risk by investing all of one's wealth in the risky assets of portfolio M, by contrast, is the excess return on the market portfolio, $[E(\tilde{r}_m) - r_f]$, relative to the rate of return on the riskless asset. This idea is set out graphically in Figure 12-1.

The intercept term in the figure, r_f, represents the pure rate of interest—the maximum rate of return on loanable funds that can be obtained without bearing risk. The slope

$$\beta_{CML} = \text{Tan } \theta$$

$$= \frac{[E(\tilde{r}_m) - r_f]}{SD(\tilde{r}_m)} \tag{12.3}$$

is the *reward to variability ratio* for efficient portfolios under conditions of market equilibrium. This ratio represents the rate at which financial rewards that are in excess of the riskless rate can be substituted for higher risk in an optimal fashion. And conversely, the slope term β_{CML} may be viewed as the *equilibrium price of risk reduction for efficient portfolios*.

In equilibrium a very simple relationship exists between expected rate of return and risk for efficient portfolios. This relationship, which is described by the CML, may be stated formally as follows:

$$E(\tilde{r}_p) = r_f + \beta_{CML} SD(\tilde{r}_p). \tag{12.4}$$

According to this characteristic expression for the CML, the expected rate of return on any efficient portfolio is the rate of return on a risk-free asset plus the reward to variability ratio multiplied by a measure of dispersion.

The appropriate measure of dispersion, or risk, for efficient portfolios according to this model is standard deviation. Substituting the reward to variability ratio of Equation (12.3) into the characteristic expression for the CML of Equation (12.4), we obtain an alternate form of this characteristic expression:

$$E(\tilde{r}_p) = r_f + [E(\tilde{r}_m) - r_f] \frac{SD(\tilde{r}_p)}{SD(\tilde{r}_m)}. \tag{12.5}$$

The ratio $SD(\tilde{r}_p)/SD(\tilde{r}_m)$ has a useful interpretation: Values greater than unity apply to leveraged portfolios, while values less than unity apply to portfolios that contain positive amounts of the risk-free asset. For a pure investment in portfolio M, of course, the ratio is unity; in this case Equation (12.5) reduces to a tautology:

$$E(\tilde{r}_m) = E(\tilde{r}_m).$$

The Security Market Line

In the previous section a very simple relationship was found to exist in equilibrium between expected rate of return and risk for efficient portfolios. But the basic building blocks of portfolios are securities, and a single security does *not*, in general, constitute an efficient portfolio. A different equilibrium relationship is needed, therefore, to describe trade-offs between expectation and risk that result from holding individual securities. This relationship is provided by the *security market line*.

Analytic Derivation of SML.[19] Any risky asset, i, may be combined with a different risky asset, i', to form a portfolio of two risky assets. Likewise, any risky asset, i, can be combined with an existing portfolio of risky assets to form a new portfolio—this is true whether or not asset i is a part of the original portfolio. In this way the composition of the market portfolio can be varied by adding or subtracting positive amounts of security i. The curve iMi' in Figure 12-1 shows how the expected rate of return and standard deviation of the resulting portfolio are altered by varying its composition regarding a particular security i.

The slope of the capital market line, shown in Figure 12-1 and described by Equation (12.3), is a constant. The slope of the curve iMi' shown in Figure 12-1, on the other hand, is not a constant, but varies from one point to the next along the curve. The curve iMi' is tangent to the CML at point M, however, and thus at point M the two relationships must have the same slope.[20] At point M, therefore, the rate at which one can exchange expectation for risk by moving along the CML is precisely the same as the rate at which one can exchange expectation for risk by varying the composition of the market portfolio by adding or subtracting small amounts of security i.

The slope of the curve iMi' may be obtained by calculus and can be shown to be equal to

$$\frac{[E(\tilde{r}_i) - E(\tilde{r}_m)]\,\mathrm{SD}(\tilde{r}_m)}{\mathrm{Cov}(\tilde{r}_i,\tilde{r}_m) - \mathrm{Var}(\tilde{r}_m)} \tag{12.6}$$

at any point along the curve, including point M.[21] At point M, however,

---

[19] The material presented in this section is fairly abstract. Readers who are not especially interested in mathematical derivation may skip this section—that is, to Equation (12.8)—without serious loss of continuity.

[20] The slope of a curve evaluated at a point is equal to the slope of a straight line which is tangent to the curve at that point.

[21] This expression is obtained by mathematical methods which are beyond the scope of this text and is therefore presented here without proof. For the derivation, see Fama (1968), "Risk, Return, and Equilibrium," p. 35. We do not give a formal symbol to this identity as its only purpose in this development is served in forming the following equality.

the curve iMi' is tangent to the CML. Thus, at point M the slope of the curve iMi' is equal to the slope of the CML. By Equations (12.3) and (12.6), therefore, we have at point M:

$$\frac{[E(\tilde{r}_m) - r_f]}{\mathrm{SD}(\tilde{r}_m)} = \frac{[E(\tilde{r}_i) - E(\tilde{r}_m)]\,\mathrm{SD}(\tilde{r}_m)}{\mathrm{Cov}(\tilde{r}_i,\tilde{r}_m) - \mathrm{Var}(\tilde{r}_m)}. \tag{12.7}$$

By transposing terms in Equation (12.7) and simplifying the results, we get

$$[E(\tilde{r}_i) - r_f] = \frac{[E(\tilde{r}_m) - r_f]}{\mathrm{Var}(\tilde{r}_m)}\,\mathrm{Cov}(\tilde{r}_i,\tilde{r}_m), \tag{12.8}$$

which is the relationship we are seeking.

The Security Market Line: Covariance Form. Equation (12.8) of the previous section describes an equilibrium relationship that applies to all risky financial assets in the market. The term on the left of the expression, $[E(\tilde{r}_i) - r_f]$, represents the *expected reward for bearing risk* by holding security i. On the right, the ratio

$$\frac{[E(\tilde{r}_m) - r_f]}{\mathrm{Var}(\tilde{r}_m)} \tag{12.9}$$

is the *reward to variability ratio* for individual securities. Inspection of Equation (12.3) shows that this is not the same reward to variability ratio that applies for efficient portfolios. Notice that

$$\beta_{\mathrm{CML}} = \frac{[E(\tilde{r}_m) - r_f]}{\mathrm{Var}(\tilde{r}_m)}\,\mathrm{SD}(\tilde{r}_m). \tag{12.10}$$

Thus, in equilibrium the reward to variability ratio would be higher for efficiently diversified portfolios than for undiversified securities, and therefore the cost of risk reduction would be lower.

In equilibrium, expectation and risk combinations for efficient portfolios plot as points along the capital market line as shown in Figure 12-2. Expectation and risk combinations for undiversified securities do not, in general, plot as points along the CML, but are described by a different economic relationship called the *security market line*. The security market line is shown drawn in *covariance form* in Figure 12-3(a). The equation of this line may be obtained by rearranging terms in Equation (12.8), written as follows:

$$E(\tilde{r}_i) = r_f + \frac{[E(\tilde{r}_m) - r_f]}{\text{Var}(\tilde{r}_m)} \text{Cov}(\tilde{r}_i, \tilde{r}_m). \qquad (12.11)$$

This analysis yields the following important economic implication: For efficient portfolios, the appropriate measure of risk is the standard deviation $\text{SD}(\tilde{r}_p)$, or the variance $\text{Var}(\tilde{r}_p)$, which is perfectly equivalent

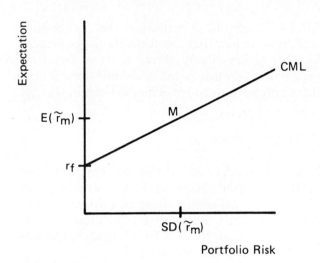

FIGURE 12-2. The Capital Market Line

(a) In Covariance Form   **(b) In Beta Form**

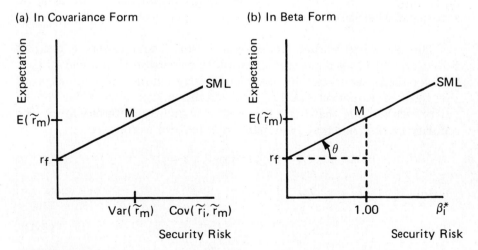

FIGURE 12-3. The Security Market Line

as a measure of dispersion. The appropriate measure of risk for undiversified securities, on the other hand, is covariance. According to Equation (12.11), the expected rate of return on any security i would be equal to the risk-free rate of return, plus the reward to variability ratio that applies to undiversified securities, times the appropriate measure of risk. Notice from Equation (12.11) that the reward to variability ratio for undiversified securities is the same for all securities on the market, but that the risk measure—which is covariance—varies from one security to the next.

Points along the SML in Figure 12–3 represent the equilibrium trade-offs between expectation and risk that are available for individual securities on the market. The figure clearly shows as does Equation (12.11), that the SML must pass through point r_f on the vertical axis and through a point M that corresponds to the expected return, $E(\tilde{r}_m)$, and variance

$$\text{Var}(\tilde{r}_m) = \text{Cov}(\tilde{r}_m, \tilde{r}_m)$$

on the market. Securities whose expectation and risk combinations plot below point M on the SML are called defensive securities; those that plot above point M on the SML are called aggressive securities. By definition, a *defensive security* is a security whose risk, as measured by covariance with the market, is lower than the market risk. An *aggressive security* is one whose risk is higher than the market risk.

The reader has to understand that the security market line is an *equilibrium restricted relationship.* That is, the derivation of the SML outlined in the previous section and the interpretations offered in this section assume that the model's conditions for general equilibrium actually apply. In the absence of general equilibrium, there could be no security market line.

The Security Market Line: Beta Form. The covariance term in Equation (12.11) is a measure of absolute dispersion for individual (i.e., undiversified) securities. By means of a very simple transformation of the term of Equation (12.11), one obtains an expression for the security market line that is represented in a slightly different form. The security market line may be written in *beta form* as follows:

$$E(\tilde{r}_i) = r_f + \beta_i^*[E(\tilde{r}_m) - r_f], \tag{12.12}$$

where

$$\beta_i^* = \frac{\text{Cov}(\tilde{r}_i, \tilde{r}_m)}{\text{Var}(\tilde{r}_m)}. \tag{12.13}$$

The term β_i^* in Equations (12.12) and (12.13) is a measure of *rela-*

tive variation. This is not the same beta term that shows up in the characteristic expression of the market index model, which is given by Equation (10.1). We use an asterisk here to distinguish between these two beta terms. We emphasize that, although they are often confused, the models set out by Equations (10.1) and (12.12) are based on different assumptions and are thus different models.[22] We will return to this point in Chapter 13.

In equilibrium every security plots along the security market line. Points along the SML (written in either form) represent the trade-offs between expectation and risk that would be possible were capital markets perfect markets where conditions of general equilibrium apply.[23] Under these restrictive assumptions the risk associated with an undiversified stock may be represented in *absolute form* as in Equation (12.11), or in a form, as in Equation (12.12), which is *relative to the risk associated with the market portfolio.* In either of the expressions for the security market line, as shown in Figure 12–3(b), the graph of the SML must pass through point r_f on the expectations axis and through a point such as *M* in the figure. Inspection of Figure 12–3 clearly shows that regardless of which form is used the graph of the SML is the same but for the scale of measurements used to represent risk.

When the security market line is shown in beta form, as it is in Figure 12–3(b), point *M* corresponds to the expectation $E(\tilde{r}_m)$ on the vertical axis, and a degree of dispersion that is represented by

$$\frac{\text{Cov}(\tilde{r}_m, \tilde{r}_m)}{\text{Var}(\tilde{r}_m)} = 1.00$$

on the risk axis. Consistent with previous logic, therefore, a security whose beta is less than unity is called a *defensive security*, and a security whose beta is greater than unity is called an *aggressive security*.

Summary

The portfolio selection models introduced in Part 3 are normative models. The capital market theory introduced in this chapter is posi-

---

[22] The security market line represents an equilibrium restricted relationship characteristic of a perfect market where borrowing and lending is permitted *in any amount* at the same risk-free interest rate, r_f. The market model of Chapter 10, by contrast, is not equilibrium restricted. No general equilibrium assumptions are expressed or implied; markets may be perfect or imperfect; and any borrowing or lending that takes place will take place under conditions that the model does not seek to explain.

[23] Once these restrictive assumptions are relaxed, it is not at all clear that the SML yields any useful implications or insights beyond those already stated. It should be emphasized, in this regard, that this is a controversial issue about which there are other points of view.

tive. Normative theory should be strictly distinguished from positive theory regarding both purpose and technique. A normative model serves as a guide for action. Positive theory, by contrast, is not intended or designed to serve as a guide for action. The purpose of positive theory is to simplify and explain—to serve as a guide for drawing meaningful inferences about the economic environment in which action takes place.

Equilibrium is a term borrowed from the physical sciences. It refers to a state of balance between opposing forces from which there would be no tendency for change. In mechanics, a common practice is to discuss the outcome of events that take place in a vacuum; useful inferences are drawn on this basis about events that do not necessarily take place in a vacuum. In a social science, such as economics or capital market theory, equilibrium exists only in the abstract. An abstract environment must first be established in which equilibrium may exist; one then attempts to derive useful implications that hold in general. A proper test of positive theory, therefore, is not the reasonableness of the assumptions that must be imposed but the usefulness and generality of the implications that result.

Capital market theory seeks to explain what would be the positive implications of normative portfolio theory were all investors to behave in the manner prescribed by theory. The important positive implications that may be derived from the capital asset pricing model are the following:

1. The appropriate measure of risk for efficient portfolios is the standard deviation of portfolio rates of return.
2. The appropriate measure of risk for an individual (i.e., undiversified) security is the covariance of the rates of return on such a security with the rate of return on the market portfolio.
3. Were equilibrium possible in the capital markets, and were these markets perfect in the sense of the capital asset pricing model, then in equilibrium the market portfolio would consist of a weighted average of all risky assets that are available.
4. In such an equilibrium state individual investors would seek to hold some portion of their wealth (possibly zero) in a riskless asset and some portion in the market portfolio.

These are indeed interesting implications, but they apply directly only to an abstraction and do not necessarily hold in reality. The capital asset pricing model is an equilibrium restricted model. The question is, are these interesting and thought-provoking implications truly useful? This question is taken up in the next chapter.

Questions

1. (a) What is the difference between positive and normative theory? Contrast in terms of (1) the objectives of each, (2) the need for

realistic assumptions, (3) equilibrium conditions if any, and (4) appropriate application. (Note: A modification of this question will be asked again at the conclusion of Chapter 11, at which point your answer should be somewhat more detailed.)

(b) What would constitute a "proper test" of positive theory?

(c) What would constitute a proper test of normative theory?

2. (a) What do we mean by equilibrium? What is the difference between general and partial equilibrium? Between static and dynamic equilibrium?

(b) What is the purpose of imposing restrictive equilibrium conditions on a model when one knows perfectly well that such conditions cannot even be approximated, much less precisely realized, in the real world? Regarding the potential usefulness of such assumptions, does it make a difference whether one's objectives are positive or normative?

3. (a) What happens to the Markowitz frontier of the region of feasibility when one introduces the option of investing in a risk-free asset?

(b) What further effects on the boundary of the feasible region come about when portfolio leveraging is introduced?

(c) How does portfolio leveraging come about in the real world?

(d) To support a margin account, can an individual borrow at the same short-term rate of interest as the U.S. Treasury? What are the implications of your remarks?

(e) What would happen to the efficient boundary of the feasible set of expectation and risk trade-offs if one were actually able to borrow and lend in any amount at the same risk-free interest rate?

4. How might federal, state, and local tax programs enter into the picture and affect one's choice between lending and borrowing portfolios, or the purchase of an unleveraged portfolio consisting entirely of risky assets? Would the fact that investors are, in general, taxed at different rates and subject to different exclusions have yet further implications?

5. (a) Set out the assumptions that underlie the general equilibrium framework of the capital asset pricing model and contrast these assumptions with those that underlie the portfolio selection framework which is common to (1) the full variance-covariance model (Chapter 9), and (2) the market model (Chapter 10).

(b) Which of these frameworks seem most appropriate for the purpose of analyses that are to result in actual portfolio decisions by individual investors, as distinct from analyses whose only purpose is to explain—in very general terms—the workings of a macroeconomic system? Justify your answer.

(c) Allow the assumptions that underlie the capital asset pricing model to be relaxed one by one; at each step explain what happens to the model. (A modification of this question is presented at the conclusion of Chapter 13, at which point your answer should be somewhat more detailed.)

6. Several very different models are presented in this and in previous chapters. *Without resort to mathematical detail*, write a brief description of each of the following frameworks, models, or approaches.
   (a) A portfolio selection framework for analysis.
   (b) A general equilibrium framework for analysis.
   (c) The Markowitz variance-covariance model (Chapter 9).
   (d) The market model (Chapter 10).
   (e) The capital asset pricing model (Chapter 12).
   (f) Markowitz efficiency analysis.
   (g) Beta theory.
   (h) Portfolio indexing.
   (A modification of this question is presented at the conclusion of Chapter 13, at which point your answer should be somewhat more detailed.)

7. (a) Set out the equation of the capital market line. Explain how it is derived, in what context, and what useful implications result,
   (b) Set out the equation of the security market line. Explain how it is derived, in what context, and what useful implications result.

8. (a) Explain the meaning and implications of the separation theorem.
   (b) Describe the composition of the market portfolio, and explain what assumptions are necessary in order to suppose that there exists a market portfolio.
   (c) What would any proxy for the market portfolio, such as an S&P or Dow stock index, have in common with the market portfolio? Explain as fully as you can. We will take this question up more formally in Chapter 13.

9. (a) Describe the reward to variability ratio for efficient portfolios in mathematical terms and explain its implications.
   (b) Describe the reward to variability ratio for individual securities in mathematical terms and explain its implications.

10. What are some objectives of positive economics, such as the Keynesian theory of the consumption function? Do these objectives come closer to the objectives of the Markowitz variance-covariance model featured in Chapter 9 or to those of the capital asset pricing model featured in the present chapter.

11. The security market line may be presented in covariance or in beta form. Does it make a great deal of difference which form one chooses? Explain, supporting your answer with both equations and graphs.

12. Various portfolio and security performance indexes have been proposed.
    (a) Describe each of the performance indexes introduced in this chapter.
    (b) Are these relationships "equilibrium restricted"? Explain.
    (c) Are these relationships difficult to estimate?
    (d) When using a performance index to, say, evaluate the ex-post performance of a particular mutual fund or fund manager.
        (1) Is one involved in positive analysis or normative analysis?
        (2) Are the economic relationships which are being invoked the product of normative theory or positive theory? Explain.
13. What are the useful implications that result from the capital asset pricing model?

13.

The Various Facets of Beta: Issues and Controversies

THE CAPITAL ASSET PRICING MODEL (CAPM)

Given various assumptions, which as we have seen may be both un-realistic and extreme, capital market theory seeks to explain what would be the market implications in equilibrium were all investors to seek to hold investment portfolios that are Markowitz efficient. The purpose of imposing restrictive assumptions of this sort is discussed in Chapter 12. Questions having to do with the relaxation of the assump-tions that underlie capital market theory are considered elsewhere.[1] It is only fair to point out that the same facts, seen through different eyes, sometimes lead to vastly different conclusions. Jensen, for ex-ample, points out that "the currently available empirical evidence seems to indicate that the simple version of the asset pricing model . . . does not provide an adequate description of the structure of security returns." Moreover, he recognizes that "virtually all of its assumptions have been criticized as inappropriate, and questioned as a source of . . . empirical inadequacy." Jensen nevertheless maintains that "most of the assump-tions of the model are capable of relaxation without destroying the essential nature of the results."[2] In this section we examine much the same information that Jensen did, but we arrive at a different conclusion.

Relaxation of the Assumptions

As we have seen, capital market theory is in a sense "an exercise in positive economics,"[3] wherein all investors are assumed to be one-period, mean-variance expected utility maximizers. A rather "extreme

---

[1] Michael C. Jensen, "The Foundations and Current State of Capital Market Theory," in *Studies in the Theory of Capital Markets,* edited by Michael C. Jensen (New York: Praeger, 1972), pp. 14-38.

[2] *Ibid.,* pp. 37-38.

[3] Sharpe (1972), *Portfolio Theory and Capital Markets,* p. 77.

version of the efficient markets" hypothesis is invoked, according to which "prices at any time fully reflect available information."[4] A further assumption is that capital markets are perfect in the sense that "there are no transactions costs or taxes, information is costless and available to everybody, and borrowing and lending rates are equal to each other and the same for all investors."[5]

According to theory, therefore, all investors have the same expectations about the future, enjoy the same opportunities, and seek to hold the same market portfolio, M, which lies on the CML and consists of a weighted average of every risky asset on the market. While accepting these assumptions is impossible, the implications of the model can be accepted. Two questions are in order, however: (1) Why were such extreme assumptions necessary in the first place? (2) On what basis are we to accept or reject the model or its implications? The first question is discussed at length in Chapter 12; the second is taken up here.

Investors Are Markowitz Efficient. In the portfolio selection context, a particular investor needs only to be Markowitz efficient over *some* decision horizon, which the investor is free to decide. Those for whom the model has no appeal are free to do what they have always done—something else.

In the context of this capital market theory, on the other hand, each investor who participates in the market must be *the same*, one-period, mean-variance expected utility maximizer. Relaxation of this assumption, which is obviously not even approximated by the facts, would result in a total disintegration of the capital asset pricing model; for then, some investors might not seek to be on a Markowitz frontier, much less on a particular Markowitz frontier to which a CML might be drawn tangent. Under these conditions, there would be no market portfolio and no incentive for all investors to hold the same market portfolio.

The Efficient Markets Hypothesis. Risk reduction through diversification comes about in portfolio selection by exploiting one's knowledge about the interrelationships among rates of return on risky financial assets. No assumption, or even a concept, of market efficiency is required. In the context of this capital market theory, on the other hand, prices must somehow adjust. In equilibrium the market portfolio M must be composed of a proportionate share of all risky assets, and the proportion of each risky asset in M must equal its proportionate value to the market as a whole. If security prices do not, in fact, fully

---

[4] Eugene F. Fama, "Components of Investment Performance," *Journal of Finance*, Vol. 27, No. 3 (June, 1972), p. 554.

[5] Eugene F. Fama, "Risk, Return, and Equilibrium: Some Clarifying Comments," *Journal of Finance*, Vol. 23, No. 1 (March, 1968), p. 30.

reflect all available information at any point in time, unfortunately we could not be sure that equilibrium, in the sense of the model, would ever be established.

We are not aware of a single empirical work that actually supports the efficient markets hypothesis in any of the various forms in which it may be put. Failure to reject an extreme null hypothesis, of course, may be regarded as corroboration of sorts, but it is not "support" in the sense of statistical inference.[6] Indeed, "the definitional statement that in an efficient market prices fully reflect available information is so general that it has no empirically testable implications."[7] Add to this the fact that "to a large extent the empirical work in this area preceded the development of theory,"[8] which is a breach of scientific method,[9] and one is forced to conclude that the validity of the perfect markets proposition has, as yet, not been firmly established. The cynic, therefore, or even some unpretentious person who is intent on finding an undervalued security or two, must be guilty of something less than heresy.

Homogeneous Expectations. When the means and variances of a portfolio summary report are calculated, one, in effect, estimates the betting odds on alternative financial lotteries. The simple truth is that such estimations are always subject to uncertainty. Speaking in terms appropriate to the subject of this chapter, Stewart C. Myers makes the point very nicely as follows:

> Will anyone really be foolhardy enough to find an estimated β, using six months' data, and to assume that this estimate reveals anything about the risk of the company in question? Any such person will be demolished by a simple question: "What is the standard error of your estimated β?"[10]

This problem of generalized uncertainty is not adequately treated in

---

[6] A null hypothesis is said to "stand," unless the evidence to the contrary is sufficiently strong to knock it down. Failure to reject the null hypothesis, of course, when a level of significance which is specifically intended to limit the probability of false rejection is used, is grounds on which to "withhold judgment," but is not grounds on which to arrive at strong conclusions. Nevertheless, advocates of the efficient markets hypothesis persist at stating the hypothesis that is of primary concern to them in the form of the null hypothesis, thus stacking the deck in favor of a preconceived notion.

[7] Eugene F. Fama, "Efficient Capital Markets: A Review of Theory and Empirical Work," *Journal of Finance*, Vol. 25, No. 2 (May, 1970), p. 384.

[8] *Ibid.*

[9] Tjalling C. Koopmans, "Measurement Without Theory," *Review of Economic Statistics*, Vol. 29 (August, 1947). Reprinted in Robert A. Gordon and Lawrence R. Klein (eds.), *Readings in Business Cycles*. American Economic Association (Homewood, Ill.: Richard D. Irwin, 1965), pp. 186-203.

[10] Stewart C. Myers, "On the Use of β in Regulatory Proceedings: A Comment," *Bell Journal of Economics and Management Science*, Vol. 3, No. 2 (Autumn, 1972), p. 626.

the current literature of portfolio selection. In the context of this capital market theory, moreover, it is absolutely essential that the problem of generalized uncertainty be assumed away. There is no problem in doing so, moreover, as the efficient markets hypothesis does precisely that. Under generalized uncertainty, during which individual investors might arrive at their own betting odds on the same financial lotteries, there would be a myriad of efficient frontiers; under these conditions there could be no CML, no equilibrium, and thus, no SML.

Equal Borrowing and Lending Rates. Chapter 11 already established the simple fact that different lending and borrowing rates result in two tangent lines rather than in a single one. When one considers that both lending and borrowing rates will change from one period to the next, and, regarding the latter, from one investor to the next, the theory is placed in yet further jeopardy. Empirical evidence by Friend and Blume has shown that the assumption of an equal borrowing and lending rate results in bias and in conflicting conclusions:

> These findings suggest that an optimal portfolio consisting of positive investments in both a risky portfolio and a riskless asset does not contain the market portfolio as its risky component, contrary to the usual assumption.[11]

Transactions Costs and Taxes. A portfolio selection model is easily corrected to account for "known" transactions costs; the impact of taxation, moreover, on expected rates of return and risk can be approximated. In terms of the capital asset pricing model, on the other hand, it is not possible to properly account for the differential impact of transaction costs that may vary from investor to investor, and the differential impact of taxation which certainly varies from investor to investor. There is no possibility, therefore, of being able to adjust the "useful" implications of this capital market theory to account for the reality of practice.

Equilibrium Restricted Relationships

According to theory, in equilibrium each investor will choose some efficient portfolio that lies on the capital market line. The CML is a mathematical abstraction that is absolutely dependent on each of the assumptions outlined previously; it represents a proposition about an equilibrium relationship that is supposed to exist between expectation and risk for efficient portfolios.

---

[11] Irwin Friend and Marshall Blume, "Measurement of Portfolio Performance Under Uncertainty," *American Economic Review*, Vol. 60, No. 4 (September, 1970), p. 569. See especially footnote 17 on the same page.

According to the model, expectation and risk combinations for efficient portfolios plot as points along the capital market line. Expectation and risk combinations for individual (i.e., undiversified) securities, by contrast, are described by a different equilibrium relationship—the security market line. According to this relationship, the expected rate of return on any share of common stock is equal to the risk-free rate of return plus a premium for bearing risk. According to the model, the risk premium for holding a particular stock is equal to a reward to variability ratio, which is the same for all stocks, times the appropriate measure of dispersion—the covariance of rate of return on that security with the rate of return on the market portfolio.

The capital asset pricing model is essentially positive, but the current emphasis in the literature of finance is on deriving the normative implications of the model.[12] Most normative applications invoke the following logic:

> The risk premium for an individual security is proportional to the risk premium for the market. The constant of proportionality β_i can therefore be interpreted as a measure of risk for individual securities.[13]

Although assertions of this sort are widely accepted and employed, the justification for normative application of models that build on this particular proposition may be questioned on grounds such as those outlined below.

The Stability of General Equilibrium. Any adjustment to disequilibrium conditions that may apply in the capital markets (or in the product markets) may, as this capital market theory supposes, result in a change in the relative prices of financial securities. To the extent that capital markets are perfect markets, this would be the primary mechanism of adjustment. According to the model, however, any variation in the relative prices of financial securities must result in a change in the composition of the market portfolio and, thus, in a simultaneous pivoting of the capital market line and the security market line. Any adjustment to disequilibrium, therefore, results in the creation of a new set of general equilibrium conditions and not in a return to the old ones. This carries the added implication that beta, in the context of this equilibrium restricted model, is inherently unstable.

Estimation. The security market line is, as we have seen, an equilibrium restricted relationship. In any application of the model, the security market line would have to be an estimable function that could

---

[12] Stewart C. Myers (ed.), *Modern Developments in Financial Management* (New York: Praeger, 1976).
[13] Marshall E. Blume, "On the Assessment of Risk," *Journal of Finance*, Vol. 26, No. 1 (March, 1971), p. 3.

be obtained on the basis of data that might be available at the time when inference or decision is attempted—that is, by application of statistical methods. Even if these relationships were, in general, stable relationships "we should forget about equilibrium restricted regressions."[14] The application of regression techniques in estimating the parameters of the security market line, for example, assumes not only equilibrium ex-ante but also that expectations are realized ex-post.[15]

From the point of view of positive theory, the capital asset pricing model does not require that equilibrium be stable over time.[16] From the point of view of normative applications, however, to be "operationally useful" the underlying relationships would have to be "reasonably stable."[17] No valid empirical test exists on the stability of general equilibrium (i.e., of beta) in the context of this capital market theory, however, because (1) the model is clearly misspecified mathematically[18] and (2) no viable technique has yet been devised by which to distinguish between random error in a diffuse estimator and periodic nonstability.

Assumptions regarding investor decision horizons create an additional problem for theory which, in a statistical sense, translates into one concerned with the periodicity of data in a time series. It is demonstrated elsewhere and previously reported that "the fact that short-term price changes are positively correlated . . . can mask both the magnitude and direction of longer term divergences."[19] Thus, economic relationships that describe short-term market movements are not necessarily the same relationships that describe longer-term market movements. The application of any standard estimator, therefore, would carry the added implication that not only are expectations homogeneous (i.e., the same for all investors), but also investment decision horizons. This implication may be disqualified on the basis of the casual observation that the real capital markets are dichotomized into different term structures with both overlapping and nonoverlapping participation in each.

Use of a Market Proxy: Equilibrium Restricted Models. One of the major characteristics of the market index model of Chapter 10 is the

---

[14] Stewart C. Myers, "On the Use of β in Regulatory Proceedings: A Comment," *Bell Journal of Economics and Management Science*, Vol. 3, No. 2 (Autumn, 1972), p. 623.

[15] *Ibid.*

[16] *Ibid.*, p. 625.

[17] *Ibid.*

[18] See Friend and Blume, "Measurement of Portfolio Performance Under Uncertainty"; and Fischer Black, Michael C. Jensen, and Myron Scholes, "The Capital Asset Pricing Model: Some Empirical Tests," in *Studies in the Theory of Capital Markets,* edited by Michael Jensen (New York: Praeger, 1972).

[19] Herbert E. Phillips and John P. Seagle, "Data: A Mixed Blessing in Portfolio Selection?" *Financial Management*, Vol. 4, No. 3 (Autumn, 1975), p. 53.

assumption that the rates of return on various securities are related only in terms of common correlations with some basic underlying factor.[20] No equilibrium assumptions are expressed or implied in the portfolio selection framework. In the general equilibrium framework of the capital asset pricing model, by contrast, the index (i.e., the independent variable) becomes a true market portfolio whose composition this capital market theory purports to explain.

One of the strong implications of the capital asset pricing model is that in equilibrium each investor would seek to hold one of the ex-ante efficient portfolios that lie along the capital market line. Turning matters about, we see from Chapter 12 that the existence of a unique market portfolio depends on the existence of a capital market line that is tangent to the Markowitz efficient frontier at a single point "M." Clearly, this point "M" should be a member of the Markowitz efficient set.

Professor Richard Roll has created quite a storm in the literature of finance by showing that "the only viable (i.e., rejectable) hypothesis" to grow out of positive applications of the capital asset pricing model is the proposition that "the market portfolio is mean-variance efficient."[21] The deck has been so stacked in favor of this proposition, unfortunately, that rejecting it on statistical grounds alone, even if it were known to be quite false, would be difficult. The rate of return on any highly (as distinct from efficiently) diversified portfolio is likely to lie close enough to the efficient frontier to frustrate any statistically based attempt to demonstrate that such a portfolio, serving as a proxy for the market portfolio, is not a member of a Markowitz efficient set.[22]

Various market indices are used to represent the market portfolio in both positive and normative applications of the capital asset pricing model. Indices published by Dow Jones, Standard and Poor's, and other such agencies, were in existence long before the introduction of the capital asset pricing model. Clearly, therefore, not one of these indices was specifically designed to represent the market portfolio (i.e., in the sense of the capital asset pricing model), and chances are that not one comes very close to doing so.

The failure of theory to identify uniquely the market portfolio would obviously place severe limitations on the ability of researchers to test various propositions adequately, such as that beta is an adequate

_____

[20] William F. Sharpe, "A Simplified Model of Portfolio Analysis," *Management Science*, Vol. 9, No. 2 (January, 1963), p. 280.

[21] Richard Roll, "A Critique of the Asset Pricing Theory's Tests" [Part I: On Past and Potential Testability of the Theory], *Journal of Financial Economics*, Vol. 4 (March, 1977), p. 138.

[22] A privileged null hypothesis may be rejected only when the statistical evidence to the contrary is statistically significant.

measure of systematic risk. As Roll points out, "No two investigators who disagree on the market's measured composition can be made to agree on the theory's test results."[23] The validity of the capital asset pricing model, therefore, and most of its important implications, are as yet open to question. Other problems involved in testing the model have been identified by Miller and Scholes, and by Black, Jensen, and Scholes.[24]

USEFULNESS OF THE MODEL—AND MISUSE

The general equilibrium framework of the capital asset pricing model is not the same portfolio selection framework that we discussed in Part 3 of the book. To what extent the two frameworks are consistent or mutually inconsistent depends on the use—or misuse—to which CAPM is put.

The capital asset pricing model seeks to explain what would be the equilibrium implications of risk-return trade-offs in an efficient capital market were all investors to attempt to maximize the same one-period objective function. This objective function, moreover, is assumed to differ from one investor to the next only in terms of one's degree of risk aversion λ. In equilibrium, according to theory, every security will plot as a point on the security market line, whose equation is the characteristic equation of the capital asset pricing model.

In order to derive the SML, there must first exist a capital market line. The CML describes the equilibrium risk-return trade-offs for efficient portfolios. The CML, moreover, is tangent to the Markowitz efficient frontier in equilibrium. Thus, in equilibrium all investors seek to hold the same portfolio of risky assets, and this portfolio is the market portfolio M.

Useful Aspects of the Model

In the sense of positive theory, the capital asset pricing model does provide many useful insights into the workings of real capital markets as well as ones that exist only in theory. The usefulness of such insights and implications, moreover, does not hinge on the question of validity of the underlying assumptions or the sensitivity of the model to relaxation of these assumptions. Indeed, the usefulness of the implications does not even hinge on the question of whether or not the theory—in some abstract sense—is really true, or on an empirical basis if one can

---

[23] Roll, "A Critique of the Asset Pricing Theory's Tests," p. 131.

[24] M. H. Miller and M. Scholes, "Rates of Return in Relation to Risk: A Re-Examination of Some Recent Findings"; F. Black, M. C. Jensen, and M. Scholes, "The Capital Asset Pricing Model: Some Empirical Tests." Both papers in Jensen, ed., *Studies in the Theory of Capital Markets* (New York: Praeger, 1972).

argue that it is true. There is no question, however, that in the absence of valid empirical evidence, or even a logical basis for obtaining it, proponents of a theory should be a bit more humble in its application than proponents of CAPM have been.

Fortunately, in the context of positive theory as explained in Chapter 12, "usefulness" is not necessarily an empirical question. In a more intuitive sense than that, the capital asset pricing model does succeed at identifying a number of key variables and relationships that are important in understanding the workings of a capital market—efficient or otherwise. This is not to say that it provides a very accurate picture of this complex environment, but rather that it provides a useful framework for reference and study.

The model does have some real problems. Most issues and controversies that arise, however, are not due to inherent shortcomings in the model, but rather to the sheer heroics of some of the model's most outspoken proponents—and an army of Shumpetian imitators. Merely to recognize that there are issues, and perhaps a number of unanswered questions, is not at all the same thing as saying that the model is of no value.

Some Misapplications

The capital asset pricing model is a positive model. Yet in recent years its primary area of application—and therefore misapplication— has been in the area of normative application. In this section we present a number of examples, which, while not exhaustive, are surely provocative.

Portfolio Indexing. The first extension of the Markowitz covariance approach was achieved with the introduction of the market index model discussed in Chapter 10, according to which the rates of return on various securities were assumed to be related only through common correlations with some underlying factor. In most applications of Sharpe's single index model,[25] which is not to be confused with the capital asset pricing model,[26] the rate of return on a broad stock market index is typically used to represent that underlying common factor. The point has already been made, moreover, that such an index is not to be confused with an efficient portfolio, and certainly not with

---

[25] William F. Sharpe, "A Simplified Model of Portfolio Analysis," *Management Science*, Vol. 9, No. 2 (January, 1963), pp. 277-293.

[26] William F. Sharpe, "Capital Asset Prices: A Theory of Market Equilibrium Under Conditions of Risk," *Journal of Finance*, Vol. 19, No. 3 (September, 1964), pp. 425-442.

a market portfolio. Nevertheless, the practice of portfolio indexing amounts to nothing more than the purchase of an index, which, by implication, serves as a proxy for the market portfolio M.

Model Mixing. If one wishes to justify a normative procedure on the basis of the capital asset pricing model, then one must also be prepared to operate entirely within its framework. For example, seeking justification in terms of the general equilibrium framework of the capital asset pricing model but returning to the portfolio selection framework (i.e., the simple linear regression structure) of the market index model in search of an unbiased estimator function is entirely inconsistent. Various authors have confused the issue entirely,[27] while others have emphasized technical aspects of the issue.[28] The essential point, however, is that the portfolio selection and general equilibrium frameworks are different frameworks; the variables of each (no matter how much they may look alike) are not interchangeable. Thus the mixing of justifications and/or empirical models is tantamount to mixing apples and oranges.

Performance Measurements. When measuring investment performance, one must do more than merely consider what results were achieved or not achieved by investment; one must also consider the risk exposure necessary to achieve these results. From this point of view, the capital asset pricing model provides a very appealing, if not an altogether convincing, framework of reference. As we have seen in Chapter 12, for example, the slope of the capital market line

$$\beta_{CML} = \frac{[E(\tilde{r}_m) - r_f]}{SD(\tilde{r}_m)}$$

represents the ex-ante reward to variability ratio for efficient portfolios. Similarly, the slope of the security market line

$$\beta_{SML} = \frac{[E(\tilde{r}_m) - r_f]}{Var(\tilde{r}_m)}$$

represents the ex-ante reward to variability ratio for undiversified capital assets. Notice that these are not only ex-ante measurements but equilibrium restricted ones. Various performance measurements, which

---

[27] See Bar Rosenberg and James Guy, "Beta and Investment Fundamentals," *Financial Analysis Journal*, Vol. 32, No. 4 (July–August, 1976), p. 70.
[28] See footnote 24.

in fact are simply variations on a single theme, have been proposed.[29] What is involved in each case is the calculation of an ex-post reward to variability ratio and a contrast with β_{CML} or β_{SML}, depending on what one is trying to prove. Such attempts, unfortunately, involve not only model mixing (in the sense explained above) but also the mixing of ex-ante and ex-post concepts. To make matters worse, the term in the denominator of either reward to variability ratio shown above is based on a measurement (i.e., the sum of squares) that is more sensitive to small changes in the data than is the difference in the numerator. In other words, in addition to being logically invalid, these evaluation approaches can also be manipulated by "playing with the data."

Portfolio Analysis and Corporation Finance. In 1969 Hamada published a rather theoretical paper demonstrating, among other things, that under the general equilibrium assumptions of the capital asset pricing model, the effect of corporate financial leverage on investment risk would be captured in beta and would translate into a shift to the right along the SML.[30] Hamada's derivation is a delightful example of good academic work, which the present authors themselves exploit in the appendix to Chapter 16. This development, probably more than any other, has also had an impact on the journal and textbook literature of corporation finance, which the present authors regard as unfortunate at best. One has only to refer to a recently published textbook in the area of corporation finance or financial management to learn that at least some classes of capital budgeting problems reduce to calculation of beta scores and contrast with *stock market* beta scores that plot along the SML—in the context of the general equilibrium framework of the capital asset pricing model. Many objections can be raised to this development, but we will end this section and chapter by calling the reader's attention to only one. Capital budgeting problems are, in the main, normative problems, but the so-called mean-variance synthesis of corporation finance is based on a body of positive theory that simply does not apply.

Questions

1. The assumptions that underlie the capital asset pricing model, and the general equilibrium framework on which it is based, are out-

---

[29] William F. Sharpe, "Mutual Fund Performance," *Journal of Business*, Vol. 39, No. 1 (January, 1966), pp. 119-138. Also see Jack L. Treynor, "How to Rate Management of Investment Funds," *Harvard Business Review*, Vol. 43, No. 1 (January-February, 1965), pp. 63-75; and Michael C. Jensen, "Risk, the Pricing of Capital Assets, and the Evaluation of Investment Portfolios," *Journal of Business*, Vol. 42, No. 2 (April, 1969), pp. 167-247.

[30] Robert S. Hamada, "Portfolio Analysis, Market Equilibrium and Corporation Finance," *Journal of Finance*, Vol. 24 (March, 1969), pp. 13-31.

lined in Chapter 12. Set out these assumptions one by one, and, for each assumption, attempt to relax it. Discuss the implications of each such attempt.

2. Review your answer to question 1 of Chapter 12, which deals with a contrast of positive and normative theory. Modify your answer in light of the issues and controversies discussed in this chapter.

3. Professor Richard Roll has created quite a storm both in the literature of finance and the professional community by showing that "the only viable (i.e., rejectable) hypothesis" to grow out of positive applications of the capital asset pricing model is the proposition that "the market portfolio is mean variance efficient."
   (a) Outline some major issues raised by Professor Roll.
   (b) Many empirical studies have dealt with various aspects of the capital asset pricing model. Some of these papers are by outstanding scholars and are published in the leading academic and professional journals. Virtually all of these oft-cited publications purport to do precisely what Professor Roll claims cannot be done. What is to be made of this?

4. Set out the equations (1) of the market index model (Chapter 10) and (2) of the security market line (Chapter 12).
   (a) These are equations of different lines that are based on different assumptions and therefore represent vastly different propositions about the facts. You are to support or take issue with this proposition—as you see fit—and are to do so in a rigorous fashion.
   (b) In each of these models there appears a symbol called "beta." Outline the statistical process for estimating beta (1) in the portfolio selection context of the market model (Chapter 12), and (2) in the general equilibrium context of the capital asset pricing model.
   (c) Can the resulting beta statistics be treated interchangeably? Explain.
   (d) Professor Stewart C. Myers raises a number of interesting issues regarding attempts at "equilibrium restricted regression." What single pivotal assumption is needed to justify such attempts? Explain.

5. (a) What implications (if any) of the Markowitz portfolio selection model would lead one to the conclusion that in equilibrium all but the systematic component of risk would have been diversified away by efficient diversification?
   (b) What implications (if any) of the market model would lead to this conclusion?
   (c) What implications (if any) of the capital asset pricing model would lead to this conclusion?
   (d) What implications, and of what model or models, would lead to the conclusion that one should "buy the market"?

6. (a) What is portfolio indexing, and on what basis is it sometimes justified?
   (b) Is a portfolio selected according to this scheme Markowitz efficient?

7. You are being interviewed for a job by a well-known "beta theorist" whose firm is one of the leading beta services. You need and want the job, of course. Explain to your interviewer why beta is or is not a valid measure of risk for individual securities. Also for the interviewer's benefit—regardless of what view you take—outline some of the major issues and controversies regarding beta that have been reported in this chapter or elsewhere.

8. Discuss some misapplications of the capital asset pricing model and contrast these with some useful applications of the model.

9. What is an indexed portfolio? How might portfolio indexing be justified according to the logic of the capital asset pricing model. Can such a portfolio selection approach be justified from the point of view of Markowitz efficiency analysis?

10. To what extent, if any, are the findings of Professor Roll applicable also to the issue of portfolio indexing?

11. Discuss some issues raised under the heading of "Model Mixing" in this chapter. Which models are being referred to and what underlying assumptions are being brought into question?

12. Refer to any recently published textbook in the area of corporation finance or financial management (preferably the textbook that you yourself used in the basic course). Contrast the developments in that book which deal with beta analysis in the context of corporation finance with the points raised under the heading "Portfolio Analysis and Corporation Finance" in this chapter. Your comments should be of a critical nature. That is, either the present authors or the author or authors of the reference text should be criticized. You should take one, the other, or both, to task.

PART 5
Historical Patterns, Changing Investment Environment, and Regulation

Chapter 14
Historical Behavior of Security Markets

Chapter 15
Security Markets and Regulation

Chapter 16
The Growth of Pension Funds and the Inflation Issue

14.

Historical Behavior of Security Markets

In equilibrium (which is explained in Chapter 12) savings in an economy equals investment. This is *not* to say that savings causes investment or that the two are always in balance at desired levels of economic activity, but that they are always related. Investors should understand how savings flow through the capital markets. This chapter describes the savings process and explains how interest rates and the prices of securities fluctuate in relation to the supply and demand for loanable funds.

SAVINGS IN THE UNITED STATES

Savings may be described in gross or net terms. *Gross savings* refer to the total private domestic investment for a period, prior to any allowance for depreciation (capital used up in producing the income of that period), plus net foreign investment. The principal categories of gross savings as identified in the national income accounts are (1) personal savings, (2) corporate savings (undistributed corporate profits), and (3) corporate and noncorporate capital consumption allowances. Capital consumption allowances represent a source of funds in the sense that such allowances have been charged against earnings as an expense but do not represent an actual cash outlay or using up of current production output in that period. A budget surplus by government would add to gross savings, but such additions are uncommon. *Net savings* differ from gross savings in that an allowance is made for capital consumed in the production of product for that period.

Business Savings

An indication of how savings flow through the financial markets is provided by flow of funds statistics that appear monthly in the *Federal Reserve Bulletin*. Sources and uses of funds analyses are also published each year by Banker's Trust Company of New York and Salomon

Brothers and form the basis for their interest rate forecasts and stock market expectations for the next year.

Summaries of sources and uses of funds for business corporations are provided in Tables 14-1 and 14-2. The relative importance of internal sources of funds fell sharply from 71.1 percent of total sources in 1965 to 56.8 percent in 1974. This occurred mainly because of a marked increase in corporate needs for funds while growth in profits was at a much slower rate. Undistributed corporate profits actually fell through 1972 and did not rise above the 1965 level until 1973. The relative importance of internally generated funds rose sharply to 77.4 percent of total funds raised in 1975 as the economy recovered. Internal sources of funds then represented 66 to 68 percent of total funds raised, about the average from 1900 to 1966, during the years 1976 to 1979. The relative importance appears to have risen a bit further in 1980 and 1981 to about 70 percent, but the 1981 figures are only projections.

Capital consumption allowances represent the larger portion of internally generated funds. Changes brought about by the Economic Recovery Tax Act of 1981 are likely to accelerate further the growth in capital consumption allowances. The act permits faster recovery of fixed capital investments and encourages additional capital investments by relaxing the rules pertaining to the amount and timing of the investment tax credit.

Corporate borrowing has remained high in the 1970s, while new stock issues were relatively unimportant as a source of funds, especially during the years 1977 to 1979. Sharp increases in net new stock issues, as occurred in 1980 and 1981, may limit the ability of the stock market to rise because of the increased supply of common stocks. The high debt position of many corporations could suggest that they will bring new issues to market to create better balance in the capital structure whenever stock prices rise significantly.

Total corporate debt rose approximately 200 percent during the decade beginning in 1966 and has continued to grow since 1975. "Short-term borrowings amounted to more than 46 percent of total corporate debt at the end of the second quarter of 1981 . . . , up from less than 40 percent in 1977 and 33 percent in 1962."[1] The earnings available to cover each dollar of interest paid, moreover, have shrunk sharply since 1965, on average, as revealed in Figure 14-1. Henry Kaufman, chief economist at Salomon Brothers, has estimated that interest expense amounted to about 45 percent of corporate net profits before taxes in 1980, while being only about 14 percent in the 1960s.[2] Many

_____
[1] "Companies Facing Severe Problems Because of Rising Short-Term Debt," *Wall Street Journal,* October 26, 1981, page 29.
[2] *Ibid.*

TABLE 14-1. Sources of Funds—Business Corporations (in billions of dollars)

	1976	1977	1978	1979	1980	1981 (est.)	1982 (proj.)
Cash flow							
Undistributed profits*	58.1	67.8	80.3	101.3	92.8	83.0	80.0
Capital consumption allowances**	90.7	104.1	116.0	131.9	149.7	174.2	209.0
Total	148.8	171.9	196.3	233.2	242.5	257.2	289.0
Long-term funds							
Net new bond issues	22.8	21.0	20.1	21.2	30.4	20.5	24.4
Net new stock issues	9.8	2.7	-.1	-3.9	12.9	2.6	4.0
Total net new issues	32.6	23.7	20.0	17.3	43.3	23.1	28.4
Mortgages	12.1	19.7	22.1	22.6	20.7	17.5	20.0
Industrial revenue bonds	3.0	4.3	4.1	4.2	4.4	6.3	4.0
Term bank loans	-1.2	5.2	15.7	17.7	12.5	13.0	12.0
Total	46.5	52.9	61.9	61.8	80.9	59.9	64.4
Short-term funds							
Open market paper	2.8	2.2	4.1	9.4	4.4	14.7	10.5
Short-term bank loans	6.2	15.6	14.6	26.2	17.5	20.0	15.0
Finance company loans	8.6	13.5	11.5	10.1	3.4	9.0	7.0
Total	17.6	31.3	30.2	45.7	25.3	43.7	32.5
Other short-term sources							
Unpaid taxes	7.5	-1.3	3.4	- -	-6.7	-8.5	- -
Direct foreign investment in U.S.	4.3	3.7	7.9	11.9	10.9	14.0	15.0
U.S. Government loans	.2	- -	1.7	1.2	1.5	1.5	1.5
Total	12.0	2.4	13.0	13.1	5.7	7.0	16.5
Total sources	224.9	258.5	301.4	353.8	354.4	367.8	402.4

MEMORANDA

Bank loans

Term	-1.2	5.2	15.7	17.7	12.5	13.0	12.0
Short-term	6.2	15.6	14.6	26.2	17.5	20.0	15.0
Total	5.0	20.8	30.3	43.9	30.0	33.0	27.0

Corporate profits

Profits before taxes	166.3	192.6	223.3	255.4	245.5	234.0	238.0
Tax liability	63.8	72.6	83.0	87.6	82.3	78.7	79.2
Profits after taxes	102.5	120.0	140.3	167.8	163.2	155.3	158.8
Cash dividends	37.4	39.9	44.6	50.2	56.0	63.3	68.3

Undistributed profits

	65.1	80.1	95.7	117.6	107.2	92.0	90.5
Nonfinancial corporations	58.1	67.8	80.3	101.3	92.8	83.0	80.0
Financial corporations	7.0	12.3	15.4	16.3	14.4	9.0	10.5

a Includes foreign branch profits.
b Before capital consumption adjustment.

Source: Bankers Trust Company, *Credit and Capital Markets 1982*, p. 367.

TABLE 14-2. Uses of Funds—Business Corporations (in billions of dollars)

	1976	1977	1978	1979	1980	1981 (est.)	1982 (proj.)
Short-term funds							
Open market paper	5.0	4.0	3.0	3.9	3.9	5.6	4.5
Consumer credit	2.6	3.3	4.1	3.7	2.8	5.4	5.4
Net trade credit	5.7	10.0	14.1	10.6	4.2	8.2	7.5
Total	13.3	17.3	21.2	18.2	10.9	19.2	17.4
U.S. Government and agency securities							
U.S. Government securities[a]	2.1	−3.7	−4.5	.9	−2.5	5.0	5.5
Federal agency securities	- - -	−.4	.7	−1.3	.5	.2	.5
Total	2.1	−4.1	−3.7	−.4	−2.1	5.2	6.0
State and local securities	−1.1	- - -	.2	- - -	−.2	- - -	- - -
Total funds	14.3	13.2	17.7	17.8	8.6	24.4	23.4
Physical assets							
Plant and equipment	129.0	149.4	175.0	202.0	212.6	239.7	262.0
Residential structures	2.5	3.7	2.4	.6	.1	−1.3	1.5
Inventories—book value	27.5	34.3	44.2	56.2	43.3	44.5	40.0
Total	159.0	187.4	221.6	258.8	256.0	282.9	303.5

Cash assets	6.2	7.7	6.0	11.5	4.9	8.5	9.5
Other assets							
Investment abroad[b]	11.6	11.5	15.7	23.7	18.2	11.5	17.5
Miscellaneous assets[c]	12.8	10.0	13.4	12.6	21.9	16.0	16.2
Total	24.4	21.5	29.1	36.3	40.1	27.5	33.7
Total Uses	203.9	229.8	274.4	324.4	309.6	343.3	370.1
Discrepancy—sources less uses	21.0	28.7	27.0	29.4	44.8	24.5	32.3
MEMORANDUM							
Growth of liquid assets	14.5	4.7	10.9	17.7	13.1	19.0	22.2

[a] Does not include securities held under repurchase agreements.
[b] Net of bond issues abroad.
[c] Includes securities purchased on resale agreements.
Source: Bankers Trust Company, *Credit and Capital Markets 1982*, p. 368.

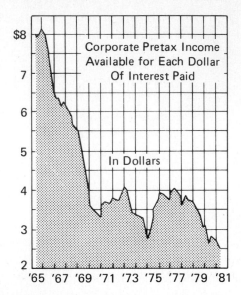

FIGURE 14-1. Corporate Pretax Income Available for Each Dollar of Interest Paid

bankers and financial analysts have expressed a growing concern that serious financial problems, perhaps even widespread bankruptcies, could occur. They believe that U.S. businesses, having built too much debt into their capital structures, are more vulnerable to recession than at any time since the 1930s.

Capital structures, especially the debt situation, deserve particular attention in any company analysis today. High interest rates have sharply increased the cost to refund maturing debt and coupled with inflation have led to rising costs that many companies have been unable to offset. A heavy debt position raises the cost of both debt and equity financing since risk is increased. A heavy debt position also raises questions about the ability of the firm to finance future growth. Purchase of a common stock would be hard to justify if growth is not expected to offset the lower dividend yield relative to fixed income instruments and the added risk.

Both pretax and after-tax corporate profits have fallen sharply as a percentage of gross national product since 1948 (see Table 14-3). Government deficits, moreover, have been large and increasing through 1981; they are forecasted to rise to new highs in 1982, 1983, and 1984. Such deficits represent claims against future savings, and other sectors of the economy find that generating the capital needed for growth becomes more difficult. Recent government policy, on the other hand, has encouraged savings and business investment. Still, interest rates re-

TABLE 14-3. Corporate Profits and Gross National Product, 1948–1980

Year	GNP	Corporate Profits Before Taxes		All U.S. Corporations After Taxes	
		$	% of GNP	$	% of GNP
1948	489.8	43.0	8.8	23.0	4.7
1949	492.2	37.7	7.7	22.5	4.6
1950	534.8	48.4	9.1	20.6	3.9
1951	579.4	51.9	9.0	18.8	3.2
1952	600.8	45.7	7.6	18.7	3.1
1953	623.6	45.0	7.2	17.5	2.8
1954	616.1	42.3	6.9	19.3	3.1
1955	657.5	55.9	8.5	26.1	4.0
1956	671.6	50.3	7.5	22.2	3.3
1957	683.8	47.2	6.9	21.4	3.1
1958	680.9	40.3	5.9	18.7	2.7
1959	721.7	52.6	7.3	25.4	3.5
1960	737.2	48.2	6.5	23.6	3.2
1961	756.6	49.2	6.5	24.1	3.2
1962	800.3	58.5	7.3	31.8	4.0
1963	832.5	65.8	7.9	36.7	4.4
1964	876.4	73.5	8.4	42.8	4.9
1965	929.3	85.3	9.2	51.1	5.5
1966	984.8	88.8	9.0	52.2	5.3
1967	1,011.4	82.5	8.2	49.4	4.9
1968	1,058.1	85.1	8.0	46.2	4.4
1969	1,087.6	75.1	6.9	38.2	3.5
1970	1,085.6	56.1	5.2	27.4	2.5
1971	1,122.4	63.8	5.7	33.5	3.0
1972	1,185.9	72.5	6.1	39.3	3.3
1973	1,255.0	75.4	6.0	37.4	3.0
1974	1,248.0	55.1	4.4	18.4	1.5
1975	1,233.9	67.1	5.4	35.2	2.9
1976	1,300.4	79.9	6.1	40.5	3.1
1977	1,371.7	89.3	6.5	47.5	3.5
1978	1,436.9	91.6	6.4	46.6	3.2
1979	1,483.0	84.5	5.7	41.4	2.8
1980	1,480.7	69.5	4.7	34.7	2.3

Source: Economic Report of the President, January 1981, pp. 234, 247.

main relatively high, large deficits loom, and unemployment continues to increase in 1982. Economic conditions, coupled with the rising corporate debt-equity ratios discussed above, increase investment risk and raise questions as to the ability of corporations to generate revenues adequate to (1) service this debt, (2) meet needs for replacement and growth capital, and (3) generate profits sufficient to offer equity investors adequate incentive to buy and/or hold stock.[3] Inflation aggravates the problem. Depreciation charges (based on historical cost), for example, tend to fall behind the cost of replacement capital. Reported profits, therefore, are overstated to the degree that capital consumption charges and inventory costs are understated, leading to the incurrence of tax liabilities in excess of those that would be incurred if true economic income were reported. Estimates are, for example, that after-tax profits by corporations, adjusted for inflation, were close to reported profits in 1965, but by 1973 were less than half of reported profits. In security or portfolio analysis, one should be aware of possible distortions in the data caused by inflation.

In summary, investors should pay close attention to the impact of inflation on a given company's operations, the need for growth capital, the debt position of the corporation, and the potential sources of funds available to the company. The drop in pretax tax corporate earnings from 8.8 percent of GNP in 1948 to 4.7 percent of GNP in 1980, inflation, and the rising supply of new stock issues brought to the market in the mid 1970s and early 1980s certainly help explain the inability of the major stock averages to surpass the highs reached in the 1966–1968 period and again in the 1972–1973 period.

Personal Savings

Most of the gross increase in financial asset holdings by individuals has been achieved by flows into the capital markets through financial institutions. Individuals, moreover, have been net sellers of equity securities in practically every year since 1960 (see Table 14–4). Although many individuals became owners of equity securities for the first time during the 1970s and many others added to their stock holdings, individuals have, on balance, been net sellers of stocks for many years. Financial institutions, by contrast, have increased their holdings.

Equity Investments of Institutional Investors

The extent to which financial institutions invest in equities is indicated in Table 14–5. At the end of World War II, the equity securities owned by financial institutions represented a value equal to about 10

---

[3] This point is more rigorously developed in the appendix to Chapter 16.

TABLE 14-4. Saving by Individuals, 1946-1980[1] (billions of dollars; quarterly data at seasonally adjusted annual rates)

Year or quarter	Total	Increase in financial assets									Net investment in			Less: Net increase in debt		
		Total	Currency and demand deposits	Savings accounts	Money market fund shares	Securities			Insurance and pension reserves[5]	Miscellaneous financial assets[6]	Nonfarm homes	Consumer durables	Noncorporate business assets[7]	Mortgage debt on nonfarm homes	Consumer credit	Other debt[7,8]
						Government securities[2]	Corporate equities[3]	Other securities[4]								
1946	24.4	18.8	5.6	6.3		-1.5	1.1	-0.9	5.3	2.8	3.6	6.1	2.1	3.6	3.1	-0.5
1947	20.2	13.2	.1	3.4		1.6	1.1	-.8	5.4	2.4	6.7	8.8	2.0	4.7	3.7	2.2
1948	24.5	9.1	-2.9	2.2		1.3	1.0	.0	5.3	2.2	9.1	9.8	7.1	4.6	3.2	2.8
1949	21.3	9.9	-2.0	2.6		1.8	.7	-.4	5.6	1.6	8.4	10.9	2.0	4.4	3.2	2.2
1950	30.9	13.7	2.6	2.4		-.1	.7	-.7	6.9	1.9	11.8	14.9	7.0	6.7	4.8	5.0
1951	34.7	19.1	4.6	4.7		-.6	1.8	.3	6.3	1.9	11.7	11.3	4.4	6.6	1.6	3.6
1952	30.7	23.2	1.6	7.8		2.5	1.6	.0	7.7	2.0	11.3	8.4	2.0	6.2	5.3	2.8
1953	31.6	22.8	1.0	8.1		2.5	1.0	.3	7.9	2.1	12.3	9.4	.8	7.6	4.2	1.9
1954	27.7	22.2	2.2	9.1		1.0	.8	-.9	7.8	2.1	12.7	6.9	1.5	8.7	1.5	5.5
1955	33.4	28.0	1.2	8.6		5.8	1.0	.8	8.5	2.1	16.7	11.9	2.4	12.2	7.2	6.4
1956	36.7	30.2	1.8	9.4		3.9	2.0	1.2	9.5	2.5	15.6	8.7	.5	11.2	3.9	3.2
1957	35.8	28.6	-.4	11.9		2.3	1.5	1.0	9.5	2.8	13.2	7.6	2.1	8.9	2.9	3.8
1958	33.4	31.6	3.8	13.9		-2.5	1.5	1.1	10.4	3.5	12.1	3.4	2.3	9.5	.5	6.0
1959	35.6	37.4	.8	11.1		10.1	.6	-.4	11.9	3.3	15.9	6.9	3.4	12.8	8.0	7.2
1960	35.6	32.5	1.0	12.1		2.4	-.5	2.4	11.5	3.6	14.3	6.7	3.1	11.7	4.4	4.8
1961	34.1	35.9	-.9	18.3		1.8	.3	.1	12.1	4.3	12.0	4.1	3.3	12.2	2.5	6.5
1962	40.3	40.6	-1.2	26.1		1.8	-2.0	.1	12.7	3.2	12.8	8.2	6.3	14.1	6.3	7.2
1963	45.2	47.3	4.2	26.3		1.2	-2.6	1.4	13.9	2.9	13.4	11.8	8.5	16.2	8.9	10.6
1964	55.7	56.1	5.2	26.1		5.1	-.1	.4	16.1	3.2	13.9	15.1	7.7	17.5	9.8	9.8
1965	63.8	59.0	7.5	27.8		3.9	-2.1	1.3	16.9	3.7	13.4	20.2	11.2	17.0	10.6	12.6
1966	72.1	58.4	2.4	19.0		11.7	-.6	2.4	19.2	4.4	12.6	22.8	9.4	13.8	6.5	10.8
1967	77.6	70.4	9.9	35.3		-.7	-4.2	4.8	18.6	6.7	10.9	20.9	8.5	12.5	5.7	15.0
1968	82.2	76.2	11.1	31.1		5.7	-6.4	6.8	19.8	8.1	14.3	26.3	9.4	17.1	11.5	15.3
1969	73.7	64.5	-2.5	9.1		25.3	-3.6	10.7	21.5	4.0	14.2	26.2	11.4	18.5	10.8	13.3
1970	86.1	78.8	8.9	43.6		-7.2	-1.5	5.7	23.9	5.4	11.7	20.2	9.8	14.1	5.4	14.8
1971	98.7	103.0	12.2	67.8		-10.1	-5.1	5.0	27.4	5.8	18.8	26.2	13.5	26.4	14.7	21.7
1972	116.3	128.8	13.9	74.5		1.9	-5.6	3.3	29.4	11.4	26.0	35.1	17.7	41.5	19.8	29.9
1973	138.4	148.5	14.1	63.8		24.1	-6.7	11.2	33.0	9.1	28.2	41.1	20.3	47.1	26.0	26.5
1974	128.9	142.4	7.1	55.9	2.4	27.7	-2.2	6.8	36.2	8.5	23.1	28.6	2.8	35.4	9.9	22.7
1975	150.0	167.2	4.0	84.0	1.3	23.0	-3.5	3.9	43.5	11.0	20.8	26.6	-.2	38.1	9.7	16.7
1976	164.6	208.1	14.9	109.3	-.0	12.1	-3.2	2.7	52.6	19.7	33.1	40.6	-1.0	61.3	25.6	29.2
1977	172.8	241.7	22.7	109.2	.2	18.3	-6.1	6.3	65.3	25.8	48.1	50.9	5.9	93.2	40.6	40.0
1978	198.2	275.3	18.3	105.2	6.9	30.3	-6.2	13.2	77.9	29.7	59.2	57.5	6.9	103.8	50.6	46.2
1979	198.8	291.6	14.2	81.0	34.4	50.3	-11.9	16.0	74.7	32.9	55.6	52.6	10.5	110.2	44.2	57.2
1978:																
I	176.6	243.4	26.7	91.2	6.9	35.3	-8.8	2.8	71.0	25.4	56.6	48.1	5.3	95.3	43.4	38.1
II	196.7	286.4	17.2	113.7	5.4	32.5	-.7	13.8	73.2	31.3	58.3	59.5	5.2	102.8	56.9	53.0
III	205.4	288.6	14.7	117.1	5.8	26.5	-5.1	6.6	90.7	32.4	59.8	58.8	6.7	104.1	48.8	55.7
IV	214.2	282.9	14.7	98.8	9.6	27.1	-10.2	36.8	76.4	29.8	62.0	63.4	10.4	113.2	53.3	38.0
1979:																
I	184.4	273.6	-8.3	85.9	28.8	66.5	-7.5	16.0	63.1	29.1	59.3	60.1	8.5	112.3	51.4	53.3
II	213.3	305.3	23.7	67.8	31.6	60.7	-10.6	16.7	81.1	34.3	56.9	50.8	9.7	110.8	45.2	53.4
III	204.2	313.3	31.3	103.5	33.1	22.5	-14.3	26.0	76.7	34.4	54.3	50.8	10.3	108.5	46.9	69.0
IV	193.2	271.1	9.8	66.7	44.1	51.3	-15.0	4.7	77.8	31.6	52.0	48.5	13.7	109.3	31.1	51.8
1980:																
I	221.6	311.9	-4.5	82.7	61.3	84.3	-17.4	-6.1	76.8	34.7	45.7	47.8	7.5	104.4	25.9	61.0
II	220.1	232.8	-3.9	106.1	62.5	-39.6	7.8	-17.5	91.7	25.8	35.2	18.6	-5.3	56.5	-44.2	48.9
III	215.1	314.8	27.7	122.8	5.1	38.1	-9.2	6.0	89.9	34.5	22.9	27.3	-2.6	77.2	6.1	64.1

[1] Saving by households, personal trust funds, nonprofit institutions, farms, and other noncorporate business.
[2] Consists of U.S. savings bonds, other U.S. Treasury securities, U.S. Government agency securities and sponsored agency securities, and State and local obligations.
[3] Includes investment company shares.
[4] Corporate and foreign bonds and open market paper.
[5] Private life insurance reserves, private insured and noninsured pension reserves, and government insurance and pension reserves.
[6] Noncorporate business proprietors' equity, etc.
[7] Includes data for corporate farms.
[8] Other debt consists of security credit, policy loans, noncorporate business mortgage debt, and other debt.

Source: Economic Report of the President, 1981 (Washington, D.C.: U.S. Government Printing Office, 1981), p. 261.

TABLE 14-5. Estimated Holdings of NYSE Listed Stocks by Selected Institutional Investors (billions of dollars)

Type of Institution	1949	1965	1973	1974^r	1975^p
Insurance companies:					
Life	$ 1.1	$ 6.3	$ 20.0	$ 16.3	$ 21.9
Nonlife	1.7	10.1	16.4	10.4	11.3
Investment companies:					
Open-end	1.4	29.1	38.5	27.1	35.2
Closed-end	1.6	5.6	5.9	4.0	5.4
Noninsured pension funds:					
Corporate & other private	0.5	35.9	82.1	58.2	82.2
State & local government	*	1.4	19.6	15.9	22.8
Nonprofit institutions:					
Foundations	2.5	16.4	21.5	16.9	22.1
Educational endowments	1.1	5.9	7.7	5.5	7.2
Other	1.0	7.7	9.5	6.6	8.7
Common trust funds	*	3.2	5.8	4.7	6.1
Mutual savings banks	0.2	0.5	2.1	1.7	2.3
Total	$11.1	$122.1	$229.1	$167.3	$225.2
Market value of all NYSE listed stock	$76.3	$537.5	$721.0	$511.1	$685.1
Estimated % held by institutional investors	14.5%	22.7%	31.8%	32.7%	32.9%

*Less than $50 million.
^{r}Revised estimates.
^{p}Preliminary estimates.
Source: New York Stock Exchange, Fact Book, 1977, p. 53.

percent of the total value of all stocks listed on the New York Stock Exchange. By the end of 1972 their holdings had risen to about $269.7 billion and then dropped to $167.3 billion in the sharp market decline of 1973 and 1974. Actually, the proportion of NYSE listed stocks held by institutional investors increased to about 33 percent by 1974, even though the market value of the stocks they held fell sharply.

The influence of institutional investments on the New York Stock Exchange market is even greater than would be implied by their ownership of 33 percent of the value of all listed stocks as of 1975. A New York Stock Exchange "Public Transactions Study" covering the total number of shares traded during 1974 disclosed that institutions accounted for about 45 percent of the shares traded and 51 percent of the dollar value of transactions.

Money Market Funds

A sharp increase in shorter-term investments in the 1970s was brought about by (1) rising short-term interest rates, exceeding the yields offered on long-term debt instruments at many times during the period 1975 to 1981 and (2) apprehension over the prospects for longer-term debt instruments and equity securities in rising interest rate markets. Money market funds that dealt exclusively in short-term instruments such as treasury bills, commercial paper, and bankers' acceptances experienced rapid growth. Individual investors often are unable to participate effectively in the market for such short-term instruments because of the relatively large minimum purchases that are required. Such funds not only offered yields that typically exceeded those available on savings accounts and savings certificates offered by banks, but also offered immediate access to funds without the penalty associated with competitive bank certificates generally tied to the treasury bill rate. Money market funds do not offer the government guarantee that backs bank savings insured by the FDIC or FSLIC, but they do offer the other advantages noted above. Money market funds, therefore, provide an alternative to savings accounts that is of considerable interest to individual investors.

INTEREST RATES

An interest rate is a price paid for loanable funds. Such rates, of course, are determined by supply and demand for loanable funds and vary with risk and maturity.

Interest Rates and Stock Dividend Yields

The periodic rate of return on common stock is a function of both capital gain and dividend yield. Our concern in this section is with the behavior of ex-post bond coupon yields and stock dividend yields in the post–World War II period. We see from Table 14–6 that bond yields have steadily increased over the period, exceeding 15 percent for Baa bonds in 1980, and from Table 14–7 that stock dividend yields steadily decreased until 1972. The picture, of course, is incomplete as debt and equity represent different forms of investment that cannot adequately be compared on the basis of yield statistics alone. Nevertheless, a number of conclusions can be reached.

From the point of view of both individual and institutional investors, debt and equity securities are competing forms of investment.

TABLE 14-6. Bond Yields and Interest Rates, 1929-1980 (percent per annum)

Year or month	U.S. Treasury securities				Corporate bonds (Moody's)		High-grade munici-pal bonds (Stand-ard & Poor's)	New-home mortgage yields (FHLBB) [3]	Prime com-mercial paper, 4-6 months	Prime rate charged by banks [4]	Discount rate, Federal Reserve Bank of New York [4]	Federal funds rate [5]
	Bills (new issues) [1]		Constant maturities [2]		Aaa	Baa						
	3-month	6-month	3 years	10 years								
1929					4.73	5.90	4.27		5.85	5½-6	5.16	
1933	0.515				4.49	7.76	4.71		1.73	1½-4	2.56	
1939	.023				3.01	4.96	2.76		.59	1.50	1.00	
1940	.014				2.84	4.75	2.50		.56	1.50	1.00	
1941	.103				2.77	4.33	2.10		.53	1.50	1.00	
1942	.326				2.83	4.28	2.36		.66	1.50	[6] 1.00	
1943	.373				2.73	3.91	2.06		.69	1.50	[6] 1.00	
1944	.375				2.72	3.61	1.86		.73	1.50	[6] 1.00	
1945	.375				2.62	3.29	1.67		.75	1.50	[6] 1.00	
1946	.375				2.53	3.05	1.64		.81	1.50	[6] 1.00	
1947	.594				2.61	3.24	2.01		1.03	1½-1¾	1.00	
1948	1.040				2.82	3.47	2.40		1.44	1¾-2	1.34	
1949	1.102				2.66	3.42	2.21		1.49	2.00	1.50	
1950	1 218				2.62	3.24	1.98		1.45	2.07	1.59	
1951	1.552				2.86	3.41	2.00		2.16	2.56	1.75	
1952	1.766				2.96	3.52	2.19		2.33	3.00	1.75	
1953	1.931		2.47	2.85	3.20	3.74	2.72		2.52	3.17	1.99	
1954	.953		1.63	2.40	2.90	3.51	2.37		1.58	3.05	1.60	
1955	1.753		2.47	2.82	3.06	3.53	2.53		2.18	3.16	1.89	1.78
1956	2.658		3.19	3.18	3.36	3.88	2.93		3.31	3.77	2.77	2.73
1957	3.267		3.98	3.65	3.89	4.71	3.60		3.81	4.20	3.12	3.11
1958	1.839		2.84	3.32	3.79	4.73	3.56		2.46	3.83	2.15	1.57
1959	3.405	3.832	4.46	4.33	4.38	5.05	3.95		3.97	4.48	3.36	3.30
1960	2.928	3.247	3.98	4.12	4.41	5.19	3.73		3.85	4.82	3.53	3.22
1961	2.378	2.605	3.54	3.88	4.35	5.08	3.46		2.97	4.50	3.00	1.96
1962	2.778	2.908	3.47	3.95	4.33	5.02	3.18		3.26	4.50	3.00	2.68
1963	3.157	3.253	3.67	4.00	4.26	4.86	3.23	5.89	3.55	4.50	3.23	3.18
1964	3.549	3.686	4.03	4.19	4.40	4.83	3.22	5.82	3.97	4.50	3.55	3.50
1965	3.954	4.055	4.22	4.28	4.49	4.87	3.27	5.81	4.38	4.54	4.04	4.07
1966	4.881	5.082	5.23	4.92	5.13	5.67	3.82	6.25	5.55	5.63	4.50	5.11
1967	4.321	4.630	5.03	5.07	5.51	6.23	3.98	6.46	5.10	5.61	4.19	4.22
1968	5.339	5.470	5.68	5.65	6.18	6.94	4.51	6.97	5.90	6.30	5.16	5.66
1969	6.677	6.853	7.02	6.67	7.03	7.81	5.81	7.80	7.83	7.96	5.87	8.20
1970	6.458	6.562	7.29	7.35	8.04	9.11	6.51	8.45	7.72	7.91	5.95	7.18
1971	4.348	4.511	5.65	6.16	7.39	8.56	5.70	7.74	5.11	5.72	4.88	4.66
1972	4.071	4.466	5.72	6.21	7.21	8.16	5.27	7.60	4.69	5.25	4.50	4.43
1973	7.041	7.178	6.95	6.84	7.44	8.24	5.18	7.95	8.15	8.03	6.44	8.73
1974	7.886	7.926	7.82	7.56	8.57	9.50	6.09	8.92	9.87	10.81	7.83	10.50
1975	5.838	6.122	7.49	7.99	8.83	10.61	6.89	9.01	6.33	7.86	6.25	5.82
1976	4.989	5.266	6.77	7.61	8.43	9.75	6.49	8.99	5.35	6.84	5.50	5.05
1977	5.265	5.510	6.69	7.42	8.02	8.97	5.56	9.01	5.60	6.83	5.46	5.54
1978	7.221	7.572	8.29	8.41	8.73	9.49	5.90	9.54	7.99	9.06	7.46	7.93
1979	10.041	10.017	9.71	9.44	9.63	10.69	6.39	10.77	[7] 10.91	12.67	10.28	11.19
1980	11.506	11.374	11.55	11.46	11.94	13.67	8.51	12.65	12.29	15.27	11.77	13.35

See next page for continuation of table.

TABLE 14-6. Bond Yields and Interest Rates, 1929-1980 (percent per annum) (continued)

Year or month	U.S. Treasury securities				Corporate bonds (Moody's)		High-grade munici-pal bonds (Stand-ard & Poor's)	New-home mortgage yields (FHLBB)³	Prime com-mercial paper, 4-6 months	Prime rate charged by banks⁴	Discount rate, Federal Reserve Bank of New York⁴	Federal funds rate⁵
	Bills (new issues)¹		Constant maturities²		Aaa	Baa						
	3-month	6-month	3 years	10 years								
1978:												
Jan	6.448	6.685	7.61	7.96	8.41	9.17	5.60	9.15	6.79	7¾ -8	6 -6½	6.70
Feb	6.457	6.740	7.67	8.03	8.47	9.20	5.51	9.18	6.80	8 -8	6½ -6½	6.78
Mar	6.319	6.644	7.70	8.04	8.47	9.22	5.49	9.26	6.80	8 -8	6½ -6½	6.79
Apr	6.306	6.700	7.85	8.15	8.56	9.32	5.71	9.30	6.86	8 -8	6½ -6½	6.89
May	6.430	7.019	8.07	8.35	8.69	9.49	5.97	9.37	7.11	8 -8½	6½ -7	7.36
June	6.707	7.200	8.30	8.46	8.76	9.60	6.13	9.46	7.63	8½ -9	7 -7	7.60
July	7.074	7.471	8.54	8.64	8.88	9.60	6.18	9.57	7.91	9 -9	7 -7¼	7.81
Aug	7.036	7.363	8.33	8.41	8.69	9.48	5.98	9.70	7.90	9 -9¼	7¼ -7¾	8.04
Sept	7.836	7.948	8.41	8.42	8.69	9.42	5.93	9.73	8.44	9¼ -9¾	7¾ -8	8.45
Oct	8.132	8.493	8.62	8.64	8.89	9.59	5.95	9.83	9.03	9¾-10¼	8 -8½	8.96
Nov	8.787	9.204	9.04	8.81	9.03	9.83	6.03	9.87	10.23	10½-11½	9½ -9½	9.76
Dec	9.122	9.397	9.33	9.01	9.16	9.94	6.33	10.02	10.43	11½-11¾	9½ -9½	10.03
1979:												
Jan	9.351	9.501	9.50	9.10	9.25	10.13	6.25	10.18	10.32	11¾-11¾	9½ -9½	10.07
Feb	9.265	9.349	9.29	9.10	9.26	10.08	6.19	10.20	10.01	11¾-11¾	9½ -9½	10.06
Mar	9.457	9.458	9.38	9.12	9.37	10.26	6.16	10.30	9.96	11¾-11¾	9½ -9½	10.09
Apr	9.493	9.498	9.43	9.18	9.38	10.33	6.14	10.36	9.87	11¾-11¾	9½ -9½	10.01
May	9.579	9.531	9.42	9.25	9.50	10.47	6.10	10.47	9.98	11¾-11¾	9½ -9½	10.24
June	9.045	9.062	8.95	8.91	9.29	10.38	5.99	10.66	9.71	11¾-11½	9½ -9½	10.29
July	9.262	9.190	8.94	8.95	9.20	10.29	6.05	10.78	9.82	11½-11¾	9½-10	10.47
Aug	9.450	9.450	9.14	9.03	9.23	10.35	6.10	11.01	10.39	11¾-12¼	10 -10½	10.94
Sept	10.182	10.125	9.69	9.33	9.44	10.54	6.40	11.02	11.60	12¼-13½	10½-11	11.43
Oct	11.472	11.339	10.95	10.30	10.13	11.40	6.98	11.21	13.23	13½-15	11 -12	13.77
Nov	11.868	11.856	11.18	10.65	10.76	11.99	7.19	11.37	⁷13.26	15¼-15½	12 -12	13.18
Dec	12.071	11.847	10.71	10.39	10.74	12.06	7.09	11.64	12.80	15½-15¼	12 -12	13.78
1980:												
Jan	12.036	11.851	10.88	10.80	11.09	12.42	7.21	11.87	12.66	15¼-15¼	12 -12	13.82
Feb	12.814	12.721	12.84	12.41	12.38	13.57	8.04	11.93	13.60	15¼-16¾	12 -13	14.13
Mar	15.526	15.100	14.05	12.75	12.96	14.45	9.09	12.62	16.50	16¾-19½	13 -13	17.19
Apr	14.003	13.618	12.02	11.47	12.04	14.19	8.40	13.03	14.93	19½-19½	13 -13	17.61
May	9.150	9.149	9.44	10.18	10.99	13.17	7.37	13.68	9.29	⁸18½-14	13 -12	10.98
June	6.995	7.218	8.91	9.78	10.58	12.71	7.60	12.66	8.03	14 -12	12 -11	9.47
July	8.126	8.101	9.27	10.25	11.07	12.65	8.08	12.48	8.29	12 -11	11 -10	9.03
Aug	9.259	9.443	10.63	11.10	11.64	13.15	8.62	12.25	9.61	11 -11½	10 -10	9.61
Sept	10.321	10.546	11.57	11.51	12.02	13.70	8.95	12.35	11.04	11½-13	10 -11	10.87
Oct	11.580	11.566	12.01	11.75	12.31	14.23	9.11	12.61	12.32	13½-14½	11 -11	12.81
Nov	13.888	13.612	13.31	12.68	12.97	14.64	9.55	13.04	14.73	14½-17¾	11 -12	15.85
Dec	15.661	14.770	13.65	12.84	13.21	15.14	10.09	13.27	16.49	17¾-21½	12 -13	18.90

¹ Rate on new issues within period; bank-discount basis.
² Yields on the more actively traded issues adjusted to constant maturities by the Treasury Department.
³ Effective rate (in the primary market) on conventional mortgages, reflecting fees and charges as well as contract rate and assuming on the average, repayment at end of 10 years. Rates beginning January 1973 not strictly comparable with prior rates.
⁴ Average effective rate for the year, except for prime rate for 1929-33 and 1947-48, which are ranges of the rate in effect during the period; opening and closing rate for the month.
⁵ Since July 19, 1975, the daily effective rate is an average of the rates on a given day weighted by the volume of transactions at these rates. Prior to that date, the daily effective rate was the rate considered most representative of the day's transactions, usually the one at which most transactions occurred.
⁶ From October 30, 1942, to April 24, 1946, a preferential rate of 0.50 percent was in effect for advances secured by Government securities maturing in 1 year or less.
⁷ Beginning November 1979, data are for 6-months paper.
⁸ On May 1, range of 18½-19 was in effect.

Source: Economic Report of the President, 1981 (Washington, D.C.: U.S. Government Printing Office, 1981), pp. 308-309.

TABLE 14-7. Common Stock Prices and Yields, 1949-1980

| Year or Month | Common Stock Prices[1] | | | | | | Common Stock Yields (percent)[5] | |
| | New York Stock Exchange Indexes (Dec. 31, 1965=50)[2] | | | | Dow-Jones industrial average[3] | Standard & Poor's composite index (1941-43=10)[4] | Dividend-price ratio[6] | Earnings-price ratio[7] |
	Composite	Industrial	Transpor-tation	Utility	Finance				
1949	9.02					179.48	15.23	6.59	15.48
1950	10.87					216.31	18.40	6.57	13.99
1951	13.08					257.64	22.34	6.13	11.82
1952	13.81					270.76	24.50	5.80	9.47
1953	13.67					275.97	24.73	5.80	10.26
1954	16.19					333.94	29.69	4.95	8.57
1955	21.54					442.72	40.49	4.08	7.95
1956	24.40					493.01	46.62	4.09	7.55
1957	23.67					475.71	44.38	4.35	7.89
1958	24.56					491.66	46.24	3.97	6.23
1959	30.73					632.12	57.38	3.23	5.78
1960	30.01					618.04	55.85	3.47	5.90
1961	35.37					691.55	66.27	2.98	4.62
1962	33.49					639.76	62.38	3.37	5.82
1963	37.51					714.81	69.87	3.17	5.50
1964	43.76					834.05	81.37	3.01	5.32

1965	47.39	46.18	50.26			910.88	88.17	3.00	5.59
1966	46.15	51.97	53.51	45.41	44.45	873.60	85.26	3.40	6.63
1967	50.77	58.00	50.58	45.43	49.82	879.12	91.93	3.20	5.73
1968	55.37	57.44	46.96	44.19	65.85	906.00	98.70	3.07	5.67
1969	54.67			42.80	70.49	876.72	97.84	3.24	6.08
1970	45.72	48.03	32.14	37.24	60.00	753.19	83.22	3.83	6.45
1971	54.22	57.92	44.35	39.53	70.38	884.76	98.29	3.14	5.41
1972	60.29	65.73	50.17	38.48	78.35	950.71	109.20	2.84	5.50
1973	57.42	63.08	37.74	37.69	70.12	923.88	107.43	3.06	7.12
1974	43.84	48.08	31.89	29.79	49.67	759.37	82.85	4.47	11.59
1975	45.73	50.52	31.10	31.50	47.14	802.49	86.16	4.31	9.15
1976	54.46	60.44	39.57	36.97	52.94	974.92	102.01	3.77	8.90
1977	53.69	57.86	41.09	40.92	55.25	894.63	98.20	4.62	10.79
1978	53.70	58.23	43.50	39.22	56.65	820.23	96.02	5.28	12.03
1979	58.32	64.76	47.34	38.21	61.42	844.40	103.01	5.47	13.46
1980	68.10	78.70	60.61	37.35	64.25	891.41	118.78	5.26	
1979:									
Jan	55.77	61.31	43.69	38.83	57.59	837.39	99.71	5.33	
Feb	55.08	60.37	42.27	39.21	56.09	825.18	98.23	5.48	
Mar	56.19	61.89	43.22	38.94	57.65	847.84	100.11	5.41	13.09
Apr	57.50	63.63	45.92	38.63	59.50	864.96	102.07	5.35	
May	56.21	62.21	45.60	37.48	58.80	837.41	99.73	5.58	
June	57.61	63.57	47.54	38.44	61.87	838.65	101.73	5.53	13.58
July	58.38	64.24	48.85	38.88	64.43	836.95	102.71	5.50	
Aug	61.19	67.71	52.48	39.26	68.40	873.55	107.36	5.30	
Sept	61.89	69.17	52.21	38.39	67.21	878.50	108.60	5.31	13.38

TABLE 14-7. Common Stock Prices and Yields, 1949-1980 *(continued)*

Year or Month	Common Stock Prices[1] New York Stock Exchange Index (Dec. 31, 1965=50)[2]					Dow-Jones industrial average[3]	Standard & Poor's composite index (1941-43=10)[4]	Common Stock Yields (percent)[5]	
	Composite	Industrial	Transportation	Utility	Finance			Dividend-price ratio[6]	Earnings-price ratio[7]
Oct	59.27	66.68	48.09	36.58	61.64	840.39	104.47	5.56	
Nov	59.02	66.45	47.61	36.55	60.64	815.78	103.66	5.71	
Dec	61.75	69.82	50.59	37.29	63.21	836.14	107.78	5.53	13.77
1980:									
Jan	63.74	72.67	52.61	37.08	64.22	860.74	110.87	5.41	
Feb	66.06	76.42	57.92	36.22	61.84	878.22	115.34	5.24	
Mar	59.52	68.71	51.77	33.38	54.71	803.56	104.69	5.87	14.98
Apr	58.47	66.31	48.62	35.29	57.32	786.33	102.97	6.05	
May	61.38	69.39	51.07	37.31	61.47	828.19	107.69	5.77	
June	65.43	74.47	54.04	38.53	65.16	869.86	114.55	5.39	13.08
July	68.56	78.67	59.14	38.77	66.76	909.79	119.83	5.20	
Aug	70.87	82.15	62.48	38.18	67.22	947.33	123.50	5.06	
Sept	73.12	84.92	65.89	38.77	69.33	946.67	126.51	4.90	
Oct	75.17	88.00	70.76	38.44	68.29	949.17	130.22	4.80	
Nov	78.15	92.32	77.23	38.35	67.21	971.08	135.65	4.63	
Dec	76.69	90.37	75.74	37.84	67.46	945.96	133.48	4.74	

[1] Averages of daily closing prices, except New York Stock Exchange data through May 1964 are averages of weekly closing prices.
[2] Includes all the stocks (more than 1,500) listed on the New York Stock Exchange.
[3] Includes 30 stocks.
[4] Includes 500 stocks.
[5] Standard & Poor's series, based on 500 stocks in the composite index.
[6] Aggregate cash dividends (based on latest known annual rate) divided by aggregate market value based on Wednesday closing prices. Monthly data are averages of weekly figures; annual data are averages of monthly figures.
[7] Ratio of quarterly earnings after taxes (seasonally adjusted annual rate) to price index for last day of quarter. Annual ratios are averages of quarterly ratios.

Note—All data relate to stocks listed on the New York Stock Exchange.

Source: Economic Report of the President, 1981 (Washington, D.C.: U.S. Government Printing Office, 1981), pp. 308–309.

Some advantages and disadvantages of each have been previously explained in Chapters 2 and 3. All other things being equal, however, the higher bond yields are relative to stock dividend yields, the more attractive the bond investment will be—and similarly for preferred stocks. The exodus of individual investors from the stock market during this period, and the simultaneous increase in institutional holdings, is explained in part by the tendency of individual investors to place a higher premium on current period yield than do institutional investors. This follows, of course, from an understandable difference that exists between individuals and institutions regarding both investment horizon and time preference.

The Structure of Interest Rates

There is not just one interest rate, but a complex structure of interest rates which describes the pattern of interrelationships of various maturities and risks. The phrase "structure of interest rates" refers to the varying yields offered at a given time by securities identical in all respects except for maturity.[4] Typical yield patterns are shown in Figures 14-2 and 14-3. Generally, but not always, all interest rates move in the same direction, regardless of maturity, with short-term rates moving over a wider range. The longer the maturity, usually, the higher the rate. Interest rate risk is, of course, a function of maturity. There are exceptions, however. Short-term rates have at times exceeded intermediate-term rates and even long-term rates. Also, within each maturity category quality ratings differ. Within each category, the higher the quality grade, the lower the rate. Moreover, yields are calculated on a before-tax basis; therefore, tax-exempt securities appear to offer much lower yields than other securities. Investors should be careful to adjust reported yields to reflect their tax circumstances when comparing potential returns offered by alternative investments.

In periods of economic growth, rates on lower-quality debt issues tend to move closer to the yields on high-grade issues; in periods of economic contraction, they tend to move apart. This narrowing and widening of the yield spread between Aaa and Baa bonds is shown in Figure 14-3. The change in yield patterns has generally been explained in terms of changes in investor psychology that take place over the cycle. The optimism generated on the upswing is thought to cause investors to become less concerned about financial risk, while the pessimism generated on the downside is thought to have the opposite effect.

Interest rate patterns reflect demand and supply factors at work in the markets. The higher the demand, given a fixed supply, the higher the rate, and vice versa. The demand curve for loanable funds is subject to greater volatility than is the supply curve and is, in this respect, more

_____
[4] The phrase "structure of interest rates" is further discussed in Chapter 23.

CHART I—Short-Term Interest Rates—1970-77

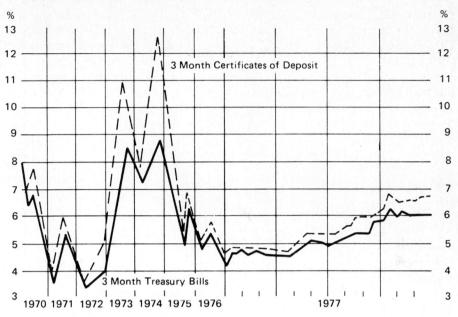

CHART II—Long-Term Interest Rates—1970-77

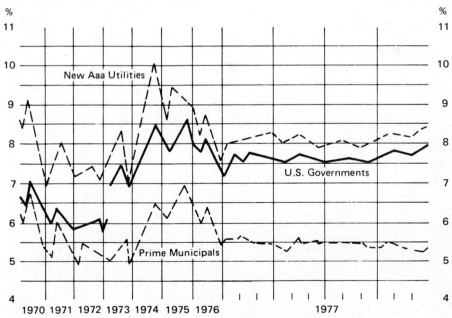

Source: Salomon Brothers, *1976 Annual Review of the Bond Market*, p. 3.

FIGURE 14-2. Yield Fluctuations in Different Maturity Categories

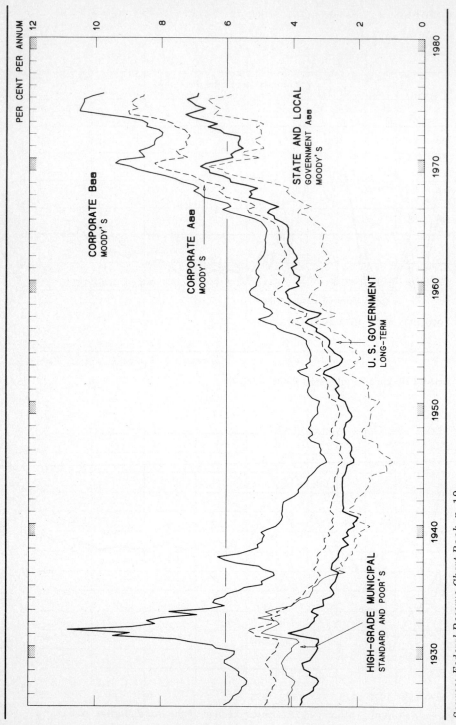

Source: Federal Reserve Chart Book, p. 19.

FIGURE 14-3. Long-Term Bond Yields

important in establishing rates. In addition to the normal economic demand and supply factors, entry of the Federal Reserve into the market on either the demand or the supply side also affects interest rates, especially in the short-term markets. In periods of economic expansion, a point is approached whereby the demand for loanable funds will exceed the supply leading to rising interest rates. Conversely, in periods of economic contraction supply expands relative to demand and therefore interest rates decline, as in late 1975 and early 1976.

A major reason why interest rates for different maturity categories do not always move in the same direction and why short-term rates sometimes exceed long-term rates is that there are different demand and supply forces at work in each category. A large segment of capital market funds does not move freely from one maturity category to another.

The Federal Reserve, moreover, operating mainly in the short-term end of the market, may intensify the trend upward or downward and on occasion may counteract the normal trend set by economic forces.

Expectations of future rates are important. When long-term rates are expected to decline, investors bid up prices (lower yields) on long-term securities in anticipation of realizing capital gains. Borrowers, on the other hand, tend to crowd demand in the short-term market, raising short-term yields, with the intention of refinancing when long-term rates fall. Such expectations will tend to lower long-term rates relative to short-term rates, leading to a relatively flat yield curve or even a downward sloping curve at times.

Historical Record of Interest Rates and Prices of Debt Instruments[5]

Figure 14-3 demonstrates the long-term secular trend in interest rates from 1925 to 1977. Since 1900 there have been three major secular trends:

1. From 1900–1920, a secular rise in interest rates and decline in bond prices.
2. From 1920–1946, a secular decline in interest rates and rise in bond prices.
3. From 1946–1981, a secular rise in interest rates and decline in bond prices.

Prior to the 1930s, an absolute low for bond yields in the United States was reached in 1899 when the average yield of municipal bonds (New England) and prime corporate bonds fell to between 3.07 percent and 3.20 percent. From 1899 to 1920 bond yields rose substantially, from the 3.20 percent level in 1899 to 5.56 percent in May 1920.

The period from 1920 to 1946 was a period of secular decline in

[5] A detailed history of interest rates is provided by Sidney Homer, *A History of Interest Rates—2000 B.C. to the Present* (New Brunswick, N.J.: Rutgers University Press, 1963) and also B. G. Malkiel, *The Term Structure of Interest Rates—Expectations and Behavior Patterns* (Princeton, N.J.: Princeton University Press, 1963).

interest rates and thus a secular rise in bond prices. During this long period of secular decline, the yields on prime corporate bonds declined from 5.50 percent in May 1930 to 2.3 percent in April 1946. However, the yields on U.S. government securities were maintained by pegging operations conducted by the Federal Reserve during World War II; we can learn little from this pattern, therefore.[6]

The period from 1946 to 1981 was a period of secular rise in interest rates, interrupted only temporarily during various recessions that occurred during the period. Interest rates surpassed the highs of the 1920s and rose so that in 1967–1970 the yields on prime corporate bonds, treasury bills, and municipals had surpassed even those of the post–Civil War period. Yields on the longest term U.S. government bonds rose from an absolute low of 2.08 percent in April 1946 to a high of 7.29 percent in September–October 1975. Yields on U.S. government issues with three- to five-year maturities reached 8.22 percent in September 1975. The yield on long-term high-quality municipals rose from a low of 0.90 percent in 1946 to a high of 7.41 percent in November 1975.

In most cases, higher yields can be found in the secondary markets, in which previously issued bonds are traded when bond prices are generally rising (falling yields), and in the new issues market when bond prices are declining (yields rising). This occurs because price adjustments are usually reflected first in new issues. Inventories of bonds tend to grow in dealers' hands during declining markets, and new issue prices are quickly adjusted downward to assure sale and avoid burdensome inventory levels. At the same time, most dealers are hesitant to mark down inventoried bonds unless the market shows real evidence of further deterioration. In rising markets, sales are brisk and dealers have no hesitancy to raise prices on new issues.

Nominal and Real Interest Rates

Figure 14–4 expresses interest rates in "real" terms by subtracting the rate of change in consumer prices during the period from rates on three-month treasury bills. The chart shows an unusually large swing in real rates from a minus 4.5 percent in 1979 to a plus 5.5 percent in 1981. Alfred Malabre, in an article containing the chart, stated:

> There was nothing like the recent 10-point swing earlier in the 16-year period covered by the chart. Nor can such a huge turnabout be found in still earlier years since World War II.[7]

---

[6] Interestingly, treasury bill yields fell to a negative yield for a very short period during the bank holiday in the 1930s. This occurred because investors were seeking a safe place to keep money during the bank failures. Yields stayed very low after this, reflecting a search for security and huge idle reserves of banks.

[7] Alfred L. Malabre, Jr., "Interest Rates, Adjusted for Rising Prices, Show Unprecedented Minus-to-Plus Swing," *The Wall Street Journal*, October 2, 1981, p. 56.

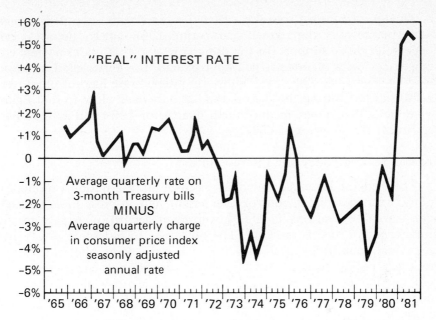

Source: Alfred L. Malabre, Jr., "Interest Rates, Adjusted for Rising Prices, Show Unprecedented Minus to Plus Swing," *The Wall Street Journal*, October 2, 1981, p. 56. Reprinted by permission of *The Wall Street Journal*, © Dow Jones & Company, Inc., 1981. All Rights Reserved.

FIGURE 14-4. The Real Interest Rate, 1965-1981

The recent sharp swing in real rates probably, at least in part, reflects the swift steep decline in the inflation rate in the 1980–81 period. A relatively restrictive monetary policy followed by the FED and large federal budgets that are expected to continue through 1984 also are part of the explanation. The money supply actually fell from the end of 1977 to October 1981. Financing budget deficits, moreover, under tight monetary conditions does tend to drive interest rates higher.

One can observe that the last time "real" rates were driven from plus to minus was in 1976, a period of accelerating inflation. The plus to minus swings to 1972 and 1956 also occurred during a period of rising inflationary pressures.

The recent sharp rise in real interest rates has made borrowing costs painful and has contributed to the recessionary environment present in late 1981. James O'Leary, economic consultant of U.S. Trust Co., notes that long-term lenders have been burnt during the past 16 years as the rate of inflation ratcheted upward and interest rates also rose. He suggests that lenders will need convincing proof that the decline in the inflation rate by year-end 1981 is the beginning of a trend, not merely a temporary cyclical decline, before long-term interest rates are likely to fall much.

Finally, of interest to note is that the "real" interest rate has been quite volatile over the sixteen-year period 1965–1981. Historical evidence offers little support for the popular notion that under normal circumstances rates of interest will approximate the anticipated inflation rate plus 3 percent. The "real" quarterly interest rate has not once averaged 3 percent during the period and has only been close to that figure twice—at 2.95 percent in the fourth quarter of 1966 and at 2.83 percent in the first quarter of 1967.

Federal Reserve Policy and Interest Rates

The Federal Reserve, which is executor of the nation's monetary policy, exercises direct control over credit and interest rates through open-market operations in U.S. government securities, largely in the short-term end of this market.[8] The objectives of monetary policy are, in general, countercyclical in nature. During economic downturns, monetary policy seeks to foster recovery by strengthening credit and reducing the cost of money. During economic upswings, it seeks to maintain momentum while damping inflationary forces that may tend to rise.

Generally, throughout the post–World War II years, Fed policy was to tighten credit as expansion became strong and to ease credit during recessions. But during the 1961–1969 business expansion (the longest on record), while stating its desire to prevent inflation and asking for fiscal restraints in late 1965 and 1966–1968, the Fed continued to expand credit most of the time at an unusually rapid rate, thus contributing to inflation in an environment of rising federal deficits. For a short time in 1966 (June–October) the Federal Reserve did let credit tighten. The result, in light of monetary demands for funds for all segments of the economy and from rising federal deficits, was a serious "credit crunch" or liquidity crisis. The federal government deficits during this period were related to the Viet Nam War and suggest that the Fed is not immune from political pressures and patriotic zeal.

The Fed had typically increased the money supply during the 1970s at a substantially greater rate than the productivity of the economy had increased, thereby contributing to economic instability and inflationary pressures. An economic downturn in 1971, coupled

---

[8] When the Fed purchases securities on the open market, it pays with a check drawn on the Federal Reserve Bank of New York, which eventually is credited to the reserve account of some commercial bank member of the Federal Reserve System, thus increasing this bank's ability to expand loans and investments. When the Fed sells securities in the open market, the eventual result is the reduction of the reserves of member banks as their reserve accounts with the Fed are charged with the check received by the Fed. In this case the reserves of commercial banks are reduced and likewise their ability to increase loans and investments.

with high and rising inflationary pressures, led to the imposition of wage and price controls. Interest rates dropped sharply in late 1971 when the Fed eased monetary policy but began to rise again by March 1972. Wage and price controls had become unpopular by this time and were abandoned.

Economists generally agree that government deficits do not have to be inflationary since the gap between expenditures and receipts can be bridged by borrowing. The inflation problem arises when the Fed monetizes the deficit by printing money and buying treasury obligations, thereby pumping reserves into the banking system. Table 14–8 shows that the monetizing of the deficit proceeded at a fairly high level during most of the 1970s. The percentage of the deficit monetized shrank sharply in 1980 and 1981, and the rate of inflation did fall sharply. Balance-of-payments problems, large projected U.S. government deficits and related funding needs, and financial market fears that high unemployment in the early 1980s will lead to resumption of government policies (including Federal Reserve policy) that will sharply increase inflationary pressures all suggest that interest rates will remain at relatively high levels during the decade of the 1980s.

STOCK YIELDS

The yield on a stock refers to the current dividend yield offered by that stock, calculated by dividing the latest annual dollar dividend paid by the current price of the stock. Historical yields on both preferred

TABLE 14-8. The Monetization of the Federal Deficit, 1973-1981
(billions of dollars)

Year	Federal Deficit	Purchases of Debt by Fed	Percentage of Deficit Monetized
1973	$ 7.9	$9.2	116
1974	10.9	6.1	56
1975	75.1	8.5	11
1976	56.6	9.8	17
1977	50.9	7.1	14
1978	43.8	6.9	16
1979	28.1	7.7	27
1980	67.8	4.5	7
1981[a]	24.3	1.6	6

[a]9 months

Source: Paul Blustein, "The Deficit Follies: What, Me Worry?" *The Wall Street Journal*, December 29, 1981, p. 1. Reprinted by permission of *The Wall Street Journal*, © Dow Jones & Company, Inc., 1981. All Rights Reserved.

and common stocks are reviewed below. Historical prices of common stocks are also reviewed, since total returns to a stockholder would include any realized capital gain or loss through the sale of a security as well as dividend income.

Preferred Stock

A preferred stock is similar to a bond in that it is a limited income security. The dividend on a preferred stock, however, is not guaranteed. The market yield on preferred stocks, therefore, is highly correlated with the yield on similar quality bonds because of the limited income feature.

Since 1965 the average yield on preferred stocks has been consistently below the average yield offered by high-grade corporate bonds. However, it would be incorrect to suggest that this implies that preferred stocks are of higher quality than bonds. Although the yield spread between preferred stocks and bonds is affected by the perceived risk for each type of security, tax considerations are a major factor explaining why preferred stock yields have typically fallen below equivalent quality bond yields in recent years. For corporate investors, interest received on debt is fully taxable at ordinary corporate income tax rates, but the tax on dividends received, either from common or preferred shares, is applied to only 15 percent of the dividends received. Therefore, since the corporate tax rate is currently 48 percent, the effective corporate tax rate on total dividends received is only 7.2 percent, as opposed to the full 48 percent applied to interest received. Thus a corporate investor would have had a strong incentive to purchase preferred stocks yielding approximately 12 percent on average during 1981 rather than corporate bonds yielding nearer 15 percent on average. The corporate investor would realize an after-tax yield of 11.13 percent by investing in the preferred stock yielding 12 percent, while only about 8.5 percent would be realized after tax by investing in a 15 percent bond.

Individual investors, on the other hand, pay their full ordinary income tax bracket rate on preferred dividends received; they therefore do not have the same incentive to choose nonconvertible preferred stocks over bonds.

Common Stocks

An understanding of the historical behavior of stock prices helps to identify some of the major forces affecting stock prices and provides useful background for estimating possible future behavior.

Stock Price Indexes. Stock price indexes are often used to suggest general movement of stock prices, although admittedly a stock price index is not the market. Prior to 1966 the major stock price indexes (Dow Jones Industrial Stock Average, Standard & Poor's 425 Stock Price Index, and the New York Stock Exchange Price Index[9]) were highly correlated. Since 1966 the indexes, including a much larger number of stocks than the Dow Jones averages, have portrayed a more bullish picture.

Interestingly, in early 1973 all three indexes climbed to new highs, yet many individual investors were not showing good results from investment in stocks. This indicates that the averages are not necessarily representative of portfolios held by many individual investors.

Common Stock Price Trends. Stock prices, as represented by the major stock averages, were in an upward trend from 1946 through 1966, growing at an unusually high rate (see Table 14–9 and Figure 14–5). Earnings and dividends also grew at an exceptionally high rate during this period. Since 1966, however, stock price movement has been virtually horizontal. Dividend and earnings growth have also fallen to lower rates than during the 1946–1966 period.

Stock prices, based on the S&P 500 Composite Index, rose 329.2 percent during the period 1949–1961, while earnings per share for the index rose only 37.5 percent. The much greater rise in the price index is explained by a sharp increase in the mean price-earnings ratio for the index from 6.5 in 1949 to a peak of 20.4 in 1961. The mean price-earnings ratio then fell back to 15.1 by 1966, but the price index continued to rise because of a sharp increase in corporate earnings.

TABLE 14-9. Compound Annual Growth Rates for the Standard & Poor's 500 Composite Stock Price Index Data-Mean Price, 1900-1975

Years	Stock Prices S&P 500	Earnings S&P 500	Dividends S&P 500
1900–1975	3.6%	3.9%	3.5%
1900–1966	4.1	3.8	3.6
1900–1929	6.3	4.6	4.4
1929–1966	3.0	3.4	3.0
1946–1966	8.3	8.7	7.2
1960–1966	7.3	9.2	6.7
1966–1975	0.0	4.1	2.8
1966–1979	1.5	7.8	5.4
1970–1979	2.4	12.5	6.8

---

[9]The Standard & Poor's 425 Index was changed to an index of 400 stocks as of July 1, 1976.

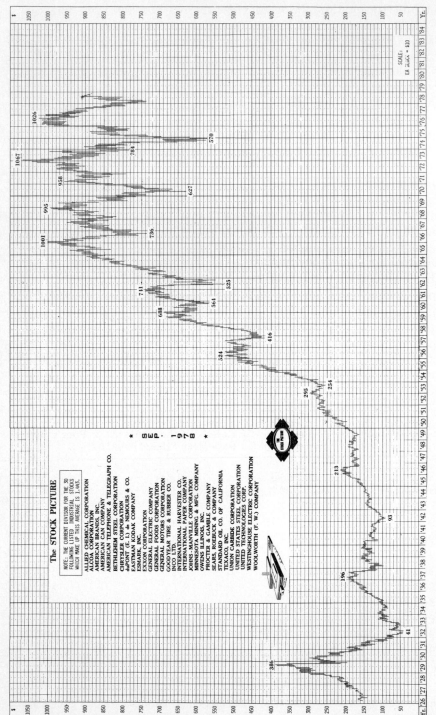

Source: The Stock Picture (September, 1978), p. 2. Published by M. C. Horsey & Co., Salisbury, Maryland.

FIGURE 14–5. The Dow Jones Industrial Average, 1926–1978

After-tax corporate earnings with inventory valuation and capital consumption adjustments (see Table 14–10) rose from $25.8 billion in 1961 to $51.4 billion in 1966 for a 99.2 percent increase.

TABLE 14–10. Corporate Profits with Inventory Valuation and Capital Consumption Adjustments, 1946–1980 (billions of dollars, quarterly data at seasonally adjusted annual rates)

Year or Quarter	Corporate Profits with Inventory Valuation and Capital Consumption Adjustments	Corporate Profits Tax Liability	Profits After Tax with Inventory Valuation and Capital Consumption Adjustments		Undistributed profits with inventory valuation and capital consumption adjustments
			Total	Dividends	
1946	16.6	9.1	7.5	5.6	1.9
1947	22.3	11.3	11.0	6.3	4.7
1948	29.4	12.4	17.0	7.0	10.0
1949	27.1	10.2	16.9	7.2	9.7
1950	33.9	17.9	16.0	8.8	7.2
1951	38.7	22.6	16.1	8.5	7.6
1952	36.1	19.4	16.7	8.5	8.2
1953	36.3	20.3	16.0	8.8	7.2
1954	35.2	17.6	17.5	9.1	8.4
1955	45.5	22.0	23.4	10.3	13.1
1956	43.7	22.0	21.8	11.1	10.7
1957	43.3	21.4	21.8	11.5	10.3
1958	38.5	19.0	19.5	11.3	8.2
1959	49.6	23.6	26.0	12.2	13.8
1960	47.6	22.7	24.9	12.9	12.1
1961	48.6	22.8	25.8	13.3	12.5
1962	56.6	24.0	32.6	14.4	18.2
1963	62.1	26.2	35.9	15.5	20.4
1964	69.2	28.0	41.2	17.3	23.9
1965	80.0	30.9	49.1	19.1	30.0
1966	85.1	33.7	51.4	19.4	32.0
1967	82.4	32.5	49.9	20.2	29.7
1968	89.1	39.2	50.0	22.0	27.9
1969	85.1	39.5	45.6	22.5	23.1

TABLE 14-10. (*Continued*).

Year or Quarter	Corporate Profits with Inventory Valuation and Capital Consumption Adjustments	Corporate Profits Tax Liability	Profits After Tax with Inventory Valuation and Capital Consumption Adjustments		Undistributed profits with inventory valuation and capital consumption adjustments
			Total	Dividends	
1970	71.4	34.2	37.2	22.5	14.8
1971	83.2	37.5	45.7	22.9	22.8
1972	96.6	41.6	55.0	24.4	30.5
1973	108.3	49.0	59.3	27.0	32.3
1974	94.9	51.6	43.3	29.9	13.4
1975	110.5	50.6	59.9	30.8	29.1
1976	138.1	63.8	74.3	37.4	36.9
1977	164.7	72.6	92.2	39.9	52.3
1978	185.5	83.0	102.5	44.6	57.9
1979	196.8	87.6	109.2	50.2	59.1
1980^p	181.7	80.1	101.6	56.0	45.6
1978:					
I	163.6	71.2	92.4	42.3	50.1
II	185.2	83.3	101.9	43.5	58.4
III	190.5	85.0	105.4	45.4	60.0
IV	202.7	92.3	110.4	47.3	63.1
1979:					
I	201.9	88.5	113.3	49.0	64.3
II	196.6	86.4	110.2	49.8	60.5
III	199.5	88.4	111.1	50.2	60.9
IV	189.4	87.2	102.2	51.6	50.6
1980:					
I	200.2	94.2	106.0	53.9	52.1
II	169.3	71.5	97.8	55.7	42.1
III	177.9	78.5	99.5	56.7	42.8

p = preliminary

Source: Economic Report of the President, 1981 (Washington, D.C.: U.S. Government Printing Office, 1981), p. 325.

Corporate profits reached a peak in 1966 that was not exceeded until 1972. The inventory valuation and capital consumption adjustments made to the reported profit data do offer some adjustment for the impact of inflation but certainly not a complete adjustment. For example, after-tax profits for all manufacturing corporations, as reported in various Federal Reserve bulletins and adjusted by dividing each year by the consumer price index for all items, suggest that the 1966 profits were not exceeded until 1976. The corporate profit record in real terms has been rather discouraging during the decade beginning in 1966. Corporate profits in real terms did grow markedly in 1978–79, but little growth in stock prices took place. The DJIA has not yet exceeded the highs reached in 1966, but the S&P 500 Index does show substantial growth from 85.26 in 1966 to 118.78 in 1980, or 39.3 percent. The growth in stock prices suggested by the S&P indexes, however, is substantially less than the growth in profits (97.7 percent) and the growth in the consumer price index during the period of 153.8 percent.

Investors became very dividend yield conscious in the 1970s and tended to be unwilling to push up the price of stocks in the absence of dividend increases. Concern with historically high inflation rates, the uncertain world political and economic situation, and fear of recession and large potential government deficits for the next few years all combined to depress the stock market in late 1981.

Common Stock Prices and the Economic Cycle. Thirteen business cycle peaks and troughs have been identified from 1920 through 1980. Table 14–11 shows that business cycles and stock market cycles are highly related, although stock market indexes typically peak and hit their troughs before business cycle indicators do. This seems to suggest that investors could have profited by selling stocks prior to the peak of the business cycle and then purchasing stocks again prior to the start of each economic recovery. But no one is able to forecast economic cycles perfectly, and earnings of individual companies have not correlated well with the movement of aggregate corporate earnings. Brealey estimated that only 21 percent of the movement in the earnings of individual companies was on the average correlated with the movement of aggregate corporate earnings.[10] Furthermore, the relative prices of stocks in an efficiently diversified portfolio are—by definition—not perfectly correlated with a stock index and thus would not be perfectly correlated with any business cycle indicators. Investors would not necessarily benefit even if they were able to forecast business cycles accurately.

_____

[10] Richard A. Brealey, *An Introduction to Risk and Return from Common Stocks* (Cambridge, Mass.: The MIT Press, 1969), pp. 104–105.

TABLE 14-11. Major Stock Market Cycles and Business Cycles

Stock Market Peaks	Business Cycle Peaks	Stock Market Lows	Business Cycle Troughs
January 3, 1920	January, 1920	August 24, 1920	July, 1921
March 20, 1923	May, 1923	October 27, 1923	July, 1924
August 14, 1926	October, 1926	January 25, 1927	November, 1927
October 9, 1929	August, 1929	July 4, 1932	March, 1933
March 10, 1937	May, 1937	March 31, 1938	June, 1938
*	February, 1945		October, 1945
June 15, 1948	November, 1948	June 13, 1949	October, 1949
January 5, 1953	July, 1953	September 14, 1953	August, 1954
July 12, 1957	July, 1957	October 22, 1957	April, 1958
January 5, 1960	May, 1960	October 25, 1960	February, 1961
December 2, 1969†	November, 1969	May 26, 1970	November, 1970
January 11, 1973	July, 1973	December, 1974	February, 1975
September 21, 1976	November, 1978	March, 1978	May, 1980

*No peak until May 29, 1946, in stock market.
†1961 economic expansion carried into 1969.

MARKET TIMING

The questions of *which* investment assets should be considered and *what* dollar amount should be allocated to each investment have received careful attention. The question of *when* to buy or sell given investment assets can be raised as a separate issue. Of course, all investors want to "buy low and sell high," but this does not offer a very precise answer as to when to buy or sell.

The long-term trend of stock prices is interrupted by intervening bull and bear market trends. Major bull and bear markets are generally associated with the rise and fall of corporate profits, which in time are associated with business cycles, as we have just discussed. This relationship is not surprising since the potential earning power of corporations is the basis for dividend payments and stock value. As noted, efforts to forecast economic cycles so as to profit from the relationships described above have not usually been successful, for good reason.

However, while taking advantage of cyclical patterns has always proved difficult, it has been almost necessary to reflect market movements in one's buying and selling patterns to achieve worthwhile investment returns from common stock investment since 1966. The market has moved pretty much in a channel bonded at the top by DJIA 1000 since 1966 with a flat trend. A single buy and hold approach, unless a majority of purchases were made near the lows, would not have produced much in the way of capital gains for a highly diversified portfolio.

Forecasting Bull and Bear Markets by Technical Methods

There is a continuing debate between those who believe in a relatively efficient market wherein stock prices adjust rapidly to new information making current prices an unbiased estimate of the intrinsic value, and those who believe in technical analysis in which it is assumed that stock prices move in identifiable trends that persist and that can be detected by studying the pattern of past price movements. Although a wide review of empirical evidence leads the authors to believe that technical methods for forecasting have not proved rewarding, those who use technical analysis obviously subscribe to a different view.

Evidence of Random Price Behavior. The random walk theory suggests that in a perfect market stock prices change in a random fashion rendering prior predictions impossible.[11] This theory, for which there is considerable analytic support, contradicts the assumptions of chartists and technical analysts that there are systematic patterns to be found in stock price series. Many empirical tests have been conducted that show that stock prices change in a random fashion. This work has concentrated on testing the hypothesis that successive price changes are independent. The results support the assumption of independence of price movements and/or lack of a systematic pattern of movement.[12]

A number of studies have been undertaken, but none that we are aware of lend much support to the proposition of efficacy of mechanical trading rules.[13]

The Dow Theory. The Dow theory, the oldest of the technical theories, was first developed in an editorial in the *Wall Street Journal* by Charles H. Dow and W. P. Hamilton around the turn of the century. The theory assumes that investors can profit by taking advantage of primary market trends. No attempt is made to forecast the beginning of primary trends once they are established. The identification of trends is purposely put on an ex-post basis to avoid mistaking short-term trends for primary trends.

One can assume in a primary uptrend (bull market) that each suc-

---

[11] See Paul H. Cootner (ed.), *The Random Character of Stock Market Prices* (Cambridge, Mass.: The MIT Press, 1964).

[12] Examples are: (a) Paul H. Cootner, "Stock Prices: Random vs. Systematic Changes," *Industrial Management Review*, Vol. 3 (Spring, 1962), pp. 24–45, or Eugene F. Fama, "The Behavior of Stock Market Prices," *Journal of Business*, Vol. 38 (January, 1965), pp. 34–105. (b) M. G. Kendall, "The Analysis of Economic Time Series—Part 1: Prices," *Journal of the Royal Statistical Society*, 96 (Part 1, 1953), pp. 11–25. (c) A. B. Moore, "A Statistical Analysis of Common Stock Prices" (Doctoral dissertation, Graduate School of Business, University of Chicago, 1962).

[13] For a survey of such work, see George Pinches, "The Random Walk Hypothesis and Technical Analysis," *Financial Analysts Journal* (March, 1970).

ceeding cycle will produce a peak higher than the last preceding one and also a trough in declines higher than the preceding one. Conversely, in a primary downtrend (bear market), each secondary peak will be lower than the last preceding peak and each secondary trough lower than the last preceding one. If this is true, then once a new peak exceeds the last peak and the succeeding low is above the last trough, then a bull market signal has been given. Conversely, when a peak is below the last preceding peak, and the subsequent trough is below the last preceding trough, a bear market signal has been presented.

Many Dow theorists still believe that the action of the Dow Jones Transportation Average must confirm the action of the Dow Jones Industrial Average before a true bull or bear market signal has been posted. Others believe that the use of the transportation average in this respect has lost much of its validity.

Some critics of the theory point to a period such as 1946-1949 or January 1956 to mid-1957, when the trend was horizontal, to prove that those following the Dow theory, being purposely late, entered the market just before it was to take a major downtrend and exited just before there was a major uptrend. Another valid criticism is that many Dow theorists frequently disagree in identifying the secondary peaks and troughs to be used as signals. They even disagree as to whether the Dow Jones figures can be rounded in determining a signal or whether the figure must be carried to the second decimal point.

Although many analysts have written advising the use of the Dow theory, few if any have published evidence of successful results to be achieved by following the theory. Others argue that the Dow theory has many followers who by their actions make the theory work, but we are not aware of any evidence to support this view.

Other Technical Theories. The more publicized of the other technical theories are commented on only briefly in the following paragraphs, largely because of lack of evidence and justification. Their proponents may well state that these theories are not fully interpreted in these brief comments.

Resistance Points. Some investors argue that for stocks, taken individually or in combination, resistance points can be calculated in the same manner as for the Dow averages, a previous low or high point. Market prices going through these resistance points are an indication of a downward or an upward trend. Volume figures are also considered important. A rising volume in a rising market is a bullish indication; but volume drying up in a rising market is an indication that the trend is slowing down or may be reversed. These much-heralded resistance points fell like kingpins in the 1966 and 1969 bear markets. Still, such points as previous bull market highs or lows appear to offer some value as resistance points or reference points in later markets, but by no means are they infallible reference-resistance points. In the case of individual stocks, previous bear market lows and bull market highs have quite frequently acted as resistance points.

Odd-Lot Index. Another technique used by technical market analysts rests on the study of daily odd-lot statistics. The interpretation of these statistics rests on the "theory of contrary opinion." Odd-lot trading is considered to reflect the investment decisions of small investors. The collective decisions of small investors are usually wrong according to this theory, and investment success may be achieved by consistently acting contrary to the odd-lot figures. Some investors simply argue that the odd-lot figures are useful indicators of popular opinion and that when such opinion becomes "too uniform" one should take an opposite position in the market.

The absolute levels of odd-lot buying and selling are of less significance than the ratio of odd-lot sales to purchases—the odd-lot index. The odd-lot index is calculated daily and is plotted against a stock price index such as the DJIA. The analyst looks for differences in the directions of the odd-lot index and the stock price index.

Investors do tend to shift from waves of optimism to waves of pessimism and they generally overdo it at both extremes, but the difficulty is in pinpointing the turning point. An examination of the period from 1960 through 1969 suggests that utilization of the odd-lot technique would have led to poor timing results. The odd-lot index and other such approaches are too simple to be really effective. Also, an investor buys particular stocks, not a market index. Mechanistic approaches will never replace good judgment on the part of the investor in any aspect of investing.

Volume. Many traders consider a market rising on rising volume a strong plus sign, and they apply the same reasoning to individual stocks. Conversely, they argue that declining volume on the downside is a signal that the market, while temporarily declining, is basically sound and that a new uptrend can be expected.

Although there is certainly some merit in this thinking, the fact is that the greatest optimism will bring out the greatest volume at or near market peaks; conversely, the greatest pessimism will generate the greatest volume at or near market lows—a selling climax. This is the great weakness of the theory. The theory is applied both to individual stocks and to the market.

Year-End Tax Selling. There is always some tax selling to establish tax losses for the calendar year. However, relatively large amounts of tax selling occur in years when the market is relatively low in the last quarter.

In years when the market is depressed during the last quarter of the year, it frequently has a significant recovery in the first quarter of the following year. Therefore, in years when the market makes its low for the year in the last four months of the year, there has frequently been an opportunity to obtain capital gains by buying in that quarter compared to the first quarter of the following year.

Short Selling. While short selling has been severely restricted under the Securities Exchange Act of 1934, it can still attain material importance. Some traders assume that if the short interest is especially high, the shorts are usually wrong. They also assume that the short interest provides a cushion for a market decline at some point as the shorts cover. In the case of individual stocks, some traders calculate the ratio of stock that is short to one day's normal volume for that stock. If the short interest is equal to two or more days's normal volume, they consider that the downside risk is significantly reduced—that the shorts will cover any weakness in the stock.

Breadth of the Market. It is certainly true that the more stocks there are participating in a market trend, the more indication there is of a unanimity of opinion. More stocks participating is indicative of an upsurge. Conversely, if the number of stocks participating in a rally, especially the number making new highs, decreases, the rally is considered to be weakening. If fewer and fewer stocks make new lows, the decline may be coming to an end.

Horizontal Channels for Specific Stocks. If a stock moves horizontally for some time, it is said to form a channel and, sooner or later there should be a breakout from this channel. While it appears, from empirical evidence, that the odds favor such an action on the upside, it is more a question of interesting odds than certainty in predicting whether a stock has actually broken out of its channel from an established base.

Confidence Index. The Confidence Index, published by Barron's, is an attempt to measure the psychology of bond traders regarding their outlook for the market and the economy. It is the ratio of the yield of Barron's High Grade Corporate Bonds to that of the Dow Jones 40 Bond Index, which includes both high- and low-quality bonds. When traders are dubious about the outlook, they move away from lower-quality, higher-yielding bonds toward higher-quality, lower-yielding ones, causing the ratio to decline. Followers suggest that this movement takes place well in advance of the start of a bear market. The record indicates that as a lead indicator at tops the Confidence Index has been effective, though the lead time could be criticized as too long. For example, the 1956 sell signal came about 14 months prior to the break in the market, and it was 7 months prior to the January 1973 high of the DJIA. The record at bottoms (buy signals) has been quite erratic and does not suggest usefulness, possibly because bond buyers are more concerned with capital preservation at tops than consistency in shifting tactics at bottoms.

Inflation and Common Stocks

Persistent increases in the cost of living since World War II have seriously reduced the purchasing power of funds committed to fixed-income securities, savings accounts, or idle cash balances. Common stocks are often suggested as an inflation hedge, based on assumed continued growth in corporate earnings and dividends and, therefore, the value of common stocks. In an effort to review the effectiveness of common stocks as an inflation hedge, Table 14–12 contrasts the change in price, earnings per share, and dividends per share for the Standard & Poor's 500 Stock Index against that of the Consumer Price Index (CPI) over the period 1945–1980.

Table 14-12 shows that stock prices rose substantially more than did the CPI over the entire period studied, and dividends paid also rose substantially. Common stocks, on average, did offer an effective inflation hedge over the entire time period, in fact offering substantial growth in real wealth.

However, the rise in stock prices since 1965 has not compensated for the loss in purchasing power suggested by the CPI, and would just about do so if growth in dividends is allowed for. We must point out, however, that an analysis such as this is deficient on two accounts. First, a stock average is not a very realistic proxy for an efficient portfolio. Second, the CPI may not represent the effect of inflation on a particular individual.

The early stages of an inflationary period are commonly marked by large increases in the supply of money and credit, and thus by relatively low interest rates. Prices tend to rise faster than the money supply, reflecting inflationary anticipations, and the real supply of money then begins to decline. Interest rates then rise sharply. The resulting tight liquidity situation and high interest rates are reflected in lower values for many financial assets, especially those offering fixed payouts to the holders. However, once the inflation rate begins to level off or starts to decline, even though prices continue to rise, stocks should begin to show more favorable price rises in line with expected growth in earnings and dividends. Thus, stocks perform poorly during an accelerating phase of inflation but in the long run may more than offset the effects of inflation, provided that corporate profits and dividends grow at a rate exceeding the average rate of inflation.

TABLE 14–12. Growth in Stock Prices, Earnings per Share, and Dividends, Standard & Poor's 500 Stocks (selected periods)

Years	S&P 500 Stocks			Consumer Price Index
	Year-end price	Earnings per share	Dividends per share	
1945	17.36	0.96	0.66	53.9
1950	20.41	2.84	1.47	72.1
1955	45.48	3.62	1.64	80.2
1960	58.11	3.27	1.95	88.7
1965	92.43	5.19	2.72	94.5
1970	92.15	5.13	3.14	116.3
1976	102.01	9.91	4.05	175.3
1977	98.20	10.89	4.67	181.5
1980	135.75	14.77	6.16	245.8
(Percentage Change)				
1945–1950	17.57%	195.83%	122.73%	33.8%
1950–1955	122.08	27.05	11.06	11.2
1955–1960	27.08	-9.07	18.09	10.6
1960–1965	59.01	58.07	39.05	6.5
1965–1970	-.01	0.01	15.04	23.1
1970–1977	6.56	112.28	48.73	50.7
1945–1977	466.67	1,034.37	607.58	225.2
1950–1977	381.14	283.45	217.69	143.1
1965–1977	6.24	109.83	71.69	92.6
1945–1980	682.03	1,438.54	833.33	356.0
1950–1980	565.16	420.07	319.05	240.1
1965–1980	46.88	185.59	126.47	160.1
1970–1980	47.32	187.91	96.18	111.4

Source: Standard & Poor's *Statistical Service,* and *Security Price Index Record* (and *Current Statistics*), various, through April, 1981.

Alchian and Kessel[14] stress the importance of whether the firm is a net monetary debtor or creditor in evaluating its prospects for serving as an effective inflation hedge. A *monetary asset* is defined as an asset whose market value is independent of changes in the price level, such as money, accounts and notes receivable, and fixed-income securities that were purchased. A *monetary liability* is defined as a liability whose

---

[14] Armen A. Alchian and Reuben A. Kessel, "Redistribution of Wealth Through Inflation," *Science*, Vol. 130, No. 3375 (September 4, 1959), pp. 535–539.

amount is independent of changes in the price level—that is, denominated in dollars and payable in terms of the contractual amount no matter what happens to the price level during the time the debt is owed. Therefore, while banks are large debtors and would tend to gain during an inflationary period by repaying these debts with depreciated dollars, they are even larger creditors and lose when repaid with depreciated dollars. Therefore, on average, bank stocks have not proven to be good inflation hedges. Also, banks are characterized by large amounts of labor per dollar of invested capital, and wage costs for banks have tended to rise faster during inflationary periods than have the prices charged for bank services.

Summary

In summary, an acclerating period of inflation is not good for stock prices. Restrictive monetary and fiscal policies typically used to restrain inflationary pressures lead to relatively high interest rates, reduced real demand, and therefore lower volumes of output. While unemployment often results, organized labor is able to increase dollar wage costs, and unit production costs tend to increase. Competition and political pressure make it difficult to raise prices sufficiently to maintain nominal, let alone real, profit margins, and corporate profits tend to decline in real terms. History does suggest that when inflation rates slow down appreciably, stock prices move up substantially from lows recorded during the height of the inflation. When and if inflation rates recede, future returns on stocks are likely to be largely a function of corporate earnings and dividend growth, which in turn depends on the ability of corporations to earn an adequate return on invested capital.

Questions

1. Distinguish between gross and net savings. What are the basic sources of gross savings?
2. (a) Are depreciation allowances as charged by accountants a source of funds to businesses? Discuss.
   (b) Are corporate debt issues or stock issues of greater importance as external sources of funds to business in recent years? Why?
3. Concern has been expressed about a possible capital shortage for American business during the decade beginning in 1975. What factors lead to this concern? Of what significance is this issue to investors?
4. Why might investors be interested in the amount of new stock issues corporations are likely to bring forth in coming years?
5. Are individuals or financial institutions becoming relatively larger

holders of equity securities in recent years? What is the significance of this?

6. How do you explain the exodus of individual investors from the stock market since 1966?

7. (a) What is meant by the term structure of interest rates?
   (b) Do short-term and long-term interest rates always move in the same direction? If not, explain the conditions under which opposite movements might occur.

8. (a) Of what significance are the actions of the Federal Reserve System to the investing public?
   (b) How does the Fed operate to influence the economy?

9. During the tight money period of 1968–69, high-grade bonds fell in price while low-grade issues often maintained their prices, or even rose in price. How do you explain this?

10. Should individual investors have been purchasing high-grade, non-convertible preferred stocks in recent years? Discuss.

11. In recent years high-grade bond yields have often been one and a half to two times as great as the dividend yield for the Standard & Poor's 400 Stock Index. How can this be justified on the basis of the relative risks involved?

12. In early 1973 the major stock indexes all climbed to new highs, yet the performance of many individual investors' portfolios was not favorable. How would you explain this?

13. (a) Was the sharp rise in stock prices during the period 1949–1961 basically a reaction to growth in corporate earnings? Discuss.
    (b) Was the corporate profit record particularly favorable during the years 1966–1976?

14. Are common stocks an effective hedge against inflation? Discuss.

Work-Study Problems

1. Using the *Wall Street Journal* and/or other sources compare the Dow Jones Industrial Index with the Standard and Poor's 400 Stock Index (425 Stock Index prior to 1976) and the New York Stock Exchange Index.
   (a) Would it matter which index was used in portraying average behavior of stock prices in the market?
   (b) How do you explain differences in the picture suggested by the different indexes?

2. Assume an investor purchased 100 shares of each of the following stocks at the closing price on December 31, 1966:
   I.B.M.
   E. I. du Pont
   Chase Manhatten Bank

General Motors
Texaco
Florida Power & Light
General Electric
General Foods

(a) What would the investor have realized if the stocks were sold on December 31, 1977, at the closing price? Determine for each individual stock and in total.

(b) Determine the dividends that would have been received during the 11-year period, by individual stock and in total.

(c) Would this particular grouping of stocks serve as an effective inflation hedge during the 11-year period?

(d) Would the inflation protection have been different if the listed groups of stocks had been purchased at the closing prices on May 31, 1970?

(e) Rank the stocks from high to low in terms of overall return on funds committed over the period 12/31/66 to 12/31/77. Do they rank about as you would have expected in terms of inflation protection? Discuss.

15.

Security Markets and Regulation

A securities market is a place where securities transactions take place. Securities may be traded on a formally organized exchange developed for the purpose of trading existing issues or in the relatively informal and loosely organized over-the-counter market, which deals primarily in issues not listed on the organized exchanges.

The primary purpose of a securities market is to provide for the orderly transfer of both product and information between buyer and seller. Efficient securities markets facilitate continuous modifications and transfer of portfolio holdings, so as to meet the changing needs of investors.

TYPES OF SECURITIES MARKETS

Securities markets are classified according to geographical location, nature of claims traded, and time to maturity of claims traded.

The Capital Market

The *capital market* is the composite of all markets where long-term securities are originated and traded. The *new issues market*, a part of the capital market, acts to transfer savings to those with productive ideas by means of the sale of new issues to the investing public. The investment banker is the backbone of the new issues market, although other specialized financial institutions (such as pension and retirement funds and insurance companies) also supply funds.

The Money Market

Short-term securities, with maturities ranging from one day up to a year, are traded in the *money market*. Investors with temporarily surplus funds may commit them to this market until needed or until longer-term decisions are made.

Primary and Secondary Markets

A *primary market* is a market where new issues originate, while existing issues are traded in the *secondary market*. Trading may take place on an organized exchange (such as the New York Stock Exchange), or in a relatively informal and loosely organized market such as that characterized by the *over-the-counter market*.

The functions of the various markets are overlapping. An investor may, for example, apportion part of a portfolio between short- and long-term markets, between debt and equity securities, and between new and existing issues. The holdings in a particular portfolio, moreover, may be liquidated at any time to revert to an alternative form of savings or cash. Efficient securities markets facilitate such continuous modifications and transfers.

THE ROLE OF INVESTMENT BANKING

Investment banking is a form of financial intermediation. The primary function of an investment banker is to bring together the suppliers and demanders of long-term investment funds—both debt and equity capital—through a variety of arrangements, such as the following:

1. Purchasing (*underwriting*) an entire new security issue at an agreed price and reoffering it to investors at its own risk.
2. Agreeing to use "best efforts" to sell an issue without making a commitment to an underwriting agreement.
3. Guaranteeing to subscribe to and resell any portion of a new issue not already subscribed to by the existing securityholders of that issue (*standby underwriting*).
4. Acting as *finder* for a fee in the case of issues sold directly by issuers to investors (*private placements*).

In addition to its role as a financial intermediary, the investment banker also performs other related functions. An investment banker may act as a wholesaler or retailer of securities. The wholesaler's function consists of selling an issue, purchased by the banker acting as the underwriter, to other investment firms that deal directly with the public. Investment bankers usually also manage a purchase group, which buys an issue and retails that issue to the public.

Through their knowledge of the objectives of various classes of investors, investment bankers serve in an advisory capacity by providing issuers with information and advice regarding such matters as what type of securities to bring to market, the timing of the issue, and provisions to be included in the contract. The investment banker also assumes an investigative function that provides the information needed to make a decision as to whether to underwrite an issue. This investigation provides most, if not all, of the material needed for the registration statement and the prospectus that must be filed with the Securities and Exchange Commission under provisions of the Securities Act of 1933.

The Underwriting Function

The issues that investment bankers purchase and resell to investors are obtained either by private negotiation with the issuer or by successful bidding against other investment bankers in competitive bidding. The typical arrangement calls for an investment banker to underwrite an entire issue at a specified price to the issuer and to assume all risks associated with its sale. The issuer will commonly assume responsibility for the expenses associated with preparing the issue for sale, including the costs of preparing and printing the necessary copies of the registration statement and prospectus.

The Underwriting Contract. Most underwriting contracts are firm underwriting contracts. With a *firm underwriting*, a group of investment bankers agrees to purchase an entire issue, contracting to pay the full purchase price on a specified date. The investment bankers expect to resell the entire issue within a very brief period. Commonly, the risk is spread among a large number of investment bankers. The underwriting contract may include an escape clause that permits cancellation of the contract by the underwriter prior to sale. However, most bond underwriting contracts allow very few "outs" for either party.

At times underwriters may accept very speculative issues as best-efforts deals, meaning that they will be committed to use their *best efforts* to sell the issue rather than make a firm commitment to buy the entire issue. In cases where a corporation has issued rights to a new issue, the corporation may also sign a *standby-underwriting agreement* with the investment bankers, which is a firm underwriting contract for a fee to purchase all securities not purchased by those exercising the rights to the new issue.

Purchase and Selling Groups. An investment banker will usually form groups to pool the rather considerable risk that may be associated with the sale of an entire issue. A *purchase group* may be formed to spread the risk associated with underwriting an issue. Under such an arrangement, the originating investment banker may be given the designation of syndicate manager to act on behalf of the other members of the group. A *syndicate manager* is responsible for overseeing all written agreements with the issuer, allocating shares among the members, and determining which sales, if any, are to be allowed specified concessions below the offering price. The syndicate manager may also engage in various transactions aimed at stabilizing the market for the new issue, as provided in the federal Securities Acts.

In addition to a purchase group, a selling group may also be formed. A *selling group* is concerned directly with marketing the issue. Determination of whether to form a selling group is made by members of the purchase group, who must decide whether they need the greater potential market added by the new members of the selling group or whether they can handle the selling of the issue alone. Members of the purchase group will ordinarily also be members of the selling group.

Underwriting Spreads. The *spread* is the difference between the price paid the issuer for the securities and the price at which they are sold to the public. It varies considerably among different issues. It may be less than $1\frac{1}{4}$ percent of the par value of high-grade bonds and as much as 10 to 25 percent of the cost of smaller, unseasoned (recently issued), speculative common stock issues.

Members of the purchase group are entitled to the full spread on securities they buy and retail. A discount from the public offering price is allowed on that part of the issue that is wholesaled to the selling group, thus reducing the spread on such portions as are wholesaled. This discount is the selling group's compensation. The remainder of the spread on securities retailed by the selling group accrues to the purchase group.

The underwriting spread actually consists of payment for three elements: (1) the expenses of origination and distribution of the issue, (2) the risk involved in underwriting the issue, and (3) the equivalent of a commission for selling the issue.

Making a Public Offering. The public offering begins when the selling group manager—who may or may not be the purchase group manager—officially "opens the books" by entering approved subscriptions from members of the selling group and from other dealers who may participate in the distribution. When dealers *oversubscribe*, the books are opened and immediately closed; such an issue is said to have "gone out the window." An issue that does not sell well, by contrast, is called "sticky." For such an issue the books may remain open for a considerable time.

Advertising the Issue. While the Securities Act of 1933 prohibits any public offering except by means of the final prospectus, the SEC not only has officially encouraged the use of the preliminary *red herring prospectus,*[1] but also has recognized the necessity for the public

---

[1] This is a preliminary prospectus circulated during the registration period and bearing a red-ink legend that it is to be used for information only and is not deemed an offer to sell or a solicitation of an offer to buy.

advertising of issues in journals and newspapers. It has approved two types of advertising. The *tombstone prospectus*, often published in newspapers on the public offering date or immediately thereafter, is an extremely brief advertisement giving a few specific facts about the issue and listing the syndicate members. It specifically states that it is "not an offer to sell or solicitation of an offer to buy." The *newspaper prospectus* presents the more important facts about the issue in abbreviated form, and the SEC approves the omission from this advertisement of many of the details that must be included in the red herring prospectus and in the final prospectus.

Competitive Bidding. Most underwriting agreements are struck by direct negotiation between an underwriter and the issuer, but for certain regulated industries competitive bidding is required. Under this arrangement the issuer invites competitive (i.e., sealed) bids from members of the investment banking community, and the contract is awarded to the highest bidder. The Securities and Exchange Commission, consistent with the Public Utility Holding Company Act of 1935, requires competitive bidding on all issues offered by registered public utility holding companies and their subsidiaries. The Federal Power Comission requires competitive bidding on issues by utilities that are subject to regulation under the Federal Power Act. Various state commissions have similar requirements, although exceptions can be made where competitive bidding would not serve the public interest. The Interstate Commerce Commission, which regulates railroad financing, requires competitive bidding on almost all railroad securities, although private placement of some equipment issues has been permitted in recent years. Finally, competitive bidding is used in connection with most federal, state, and municipal bonds. The tax-exemption feature and standardization of these securities obviate the necessity for banking connections. Moreover, public issuers are understandably sensitive to charges of political favoritism, and in some instances formal statutes require competitive bidding.

Private Placement of Securities

Investment bankers may be bypassed in several ways by corporations seeking new funds. The two most common ways are for the corporate issuer (1) to sell the issue directly to present stockholders or (2) to obtain by negotiation private placement with one or a few institutional investors. Private placement avoids many of the delays, legal complications, and costs coincident with making a public offering. Private placements are not subject to the registration provisions of the Securities Act of 1933, while most public offerings must be registered. Since private placements are accomplished by negotiation, the contractual provisions are flexible and may be tailor-made to fit the needs of both issuer and purchaser in a way that is not possible with a public offering. Moreover, renegotiation between issuer and purchaser, as situations arise, is feasible under private placement. A degree of confidentiality and an economy of spread that cannot be achieved with a public offering are possible with a private placement. Finally, a direct placement may be consummated with a speed that is not possible with publicly issued securities.

The major disadvantage of a private placement lies in its narrow distribution and resulting potential lack of liquidity and its check on price. Furthermore, the lack of a large number of shareholders can act as a deterrent to selling additional securities at some future date.

Investment bankers may serve as finders for private placements and receive a finder's fee for this service. They may also aid the issuers in preparing the papers necessary to submit the proposal to potential institutional investors.

THE OVER-THE-COUNTER MARKET

Both new and existing issues trade on the over-the-counter market (OTC). This market offers a wider variety of selections with regard to number and quality of shares than do the organized exchanges. Most bond issues trade on the OTC, as do all open-end mutual fund shares, most insurance company stock issues, virtually all bank stocks, and some common stocks. Indeed, the volume of transactions that takes place on the OTC exceeds, by a substantial margin, that which takes place on all organized exchanges combined.[2]

The OTC lacks a central marketplace but is nevertheless well organized in its operations. Current bid-and-ask prices are provided by a computerized communications network called NASDAQ (National Association of Security Dealers Automated Quotations), which also provides OTC stock price indexes and volume reports. The operations of thousands of brokerage houses nationwide are tied together by this system.

Investment bankers, brokers, and dealers participate in the over-the-counter market, but dealers constitute the backbone of the market. There are thousands of dealers, but the bulk of all business on the OTC is done by a relatively few who buy or sell for their own accounts or sell directly to customers. Some dealers take positions in particular issues for trading purposes, while others attempt to keep the volume of buying and selling of each issue roughly in balance. A dealer who takes

---

[2] Frank Reilly, "First Look at OTC Volume," *Financial Analysts Journal*, Vol. 25, No. 1 (January–February, 1969), pp. 124-128.

a position in a particular issue does so in order to create or maintain a market for that issue.

Unlike the organized exchanges, the over-the-counter market is a negotiated market. Dealers create and maintain markets for given issues. Prices are bid-and-asked offers, and these prices or quotes form the basis of negotiation—not the actual price at which the issue has been bought or sold. The differential, or spread, is the dealer's gross profit margin.

The over-the-counter market is regulated by the Securities and Exchange Commission, along with various state-enforced requirements and the self-regulation provided by the National Association of Securities Dealers (NASD). In 1964 Congress amended the Securities Exchange Act of 1934 to subject firms with $1,000,000 in assets and 500 or more stockholders to the same disclosure, proxy, and other regulations as are required for companies whose securities are listed on the organized exchanges. This was a tremendous help to those seeking to analyze and evaluate over-the-counter securities.

ORGANIZED SECURITY EXCHANGES

An organized security exchange is a place where securities are bought or sold according to formal and rigidly enforced rules. There are twelve organized exchanges in the country. Of these, all but the Honolulu Stock Exchange are subject to the registration requirements of the SEC; Honolulu is exempted because of the small number of transactions that take place in this location. The following is a list of the twelve organized exchanges:

1. American Stock Exchange
2. Boston Stock Exchange
3. Chicago Board of Trade
4. Chicago Board Options Exchange
5. Cincinnati Stock Exchange
6. Honolulu Stock Exchange
7. Intermountain Stock Exchange
8. Midwest Stock Exchange
9. New York Stock Exchange
10. Pacific Coast Stock Exchange
11. Philadelphia-Baltimore-Washington Stock Exchange
12. Spokane Stock Exchange

The New York Stock Exchange (NYSE) is the largest and best known of the organized exchanges, and the American Stock Exchange (ASE) is second largest. The larger regional exchanges include the Midwest Stock Exchange, the Pacific Coast Stock Exchange, and the Philadelphia-Baltimore-Washington Stock Exchange. All the regional exchanges combined account for but a small portion of either total dollar volume or number of shares traded on organized exchanges. The primary function of these regional exchanges is to maintain an organized market for regional issues that do not qualify for listing on the national exchanges. Interestingly, many NYSE-listed issues trade on the Pacific Coast Stock Exchange, which is a regional exchange.

New issues trade in the over-the-counter market and not on the organized exchanges. Nevertheless, as previously explained, by maintaining an efficient and convenient mechanism for the orderly transfer of existing issues for other issues or for cash, the organized stock exchanges constitute a vital link in the nation's saving-investment process and in the capital flow to the new issues markets. Moreover, by providing a market for rights to new issues, the exchanges aid in the sale and distribution of new issues.

Trade on the OTC is by negotiation. An organized exchange, by contrast, is an auction market. The prices of securities traded on the OTC are maintained by specialists who maintain positions in particular issues. The market prices of securities that trade on the organized exchanges, on the other hand, are determined by the forces of supply and demand. In each transaction, a broker representing a buyer and one representing a seller bid competitively against other brokers on the floor of an organized exchange.

The regular trading unit on an organized exchange is 100 shares, which is called a *round lot*. Units of less than 100 shares are called *odd lots*. In some instances the unit of trading has been established at 10 shares.

The securities traded on the organized exchanges are primarily *listed* securities. These are the securities of firms that have (1) applied for listing and (2) satisfied all requirements of the exchange for listing. The American Stock Exchange does a small portion of its business in unlisted securities; this exchange, moreover, offers some unseasoned issues, while the activity of regional exchanges is devoted almost entirely to newer and local issues. Only seasoned and listed securities, by contrast, are permitted to trade on the New York Stock Exchange.

MEMBERSHIP IN THE NEW YORK STOCK EXCHANGE

A member is currently defined by the New York Stock Exchange as a person who has agreed to be regulated by a national securities exchange or a registered securities association, and to comply with the rules of the exchange. The number of members was fixed at 1,366 in 1933, and therefore membership can now only be attained by purchasing a "seat" from an existing member. A member, with the approval of the board of directors of the exchange, may combine with others to form a partnership or corporation.[3] An exchange must accept whomever buys a seat unless that person cannot meet specified standards of conduct, financial responsibility, or competency. Trading on the floor of the exchange is carried on exclusively by members.

Formal application for admittance as a member must be made to the Department on Members of the exchange, and as noted above is acquired through purchasing the "seat" of an existing member. The price of a seat is arrived at by private negotiation or auction, and is determined primarily by expected profitability of membership.[4] Exchange policy and regulations governing the conduct of members are established by a Board of Governors consisting of ten exchange members, ten public members, and a paid chairperson.

Types of Memberships

Members of the NYSE are classified as commission brokers, specialists, odd-lot dealers, or registered traders. Their functions are briefly described in the following paragraphs.

Commission Brokers. *Commission brokers* act as agents, executing buy and sell orders received from customers. A security firm may have more than one commission broker to handle business that has to be conducted simultaneously at different posts on the exchange floor.

Specialists. *Specialists* may act both as brokers and as dealers. As brokers, specialists execute orders for other brokers and receive commissions for doing so. As dealers, they buy and sell the stock they specialize in for their own accounts, accepting the risk of future price declines and realizing gains if the prices rise. Specialists may not act for themselves as a principal and for a customer as an agent in the same transaction. They must always give precedence to orders other than their own. Specialists almost always specialize in more than one stock. However, except in the case of a very few large-volume stocks, there is only one specialist for each stock.

Floor brokers generally allow specialists to execute on their behalf any customers' market orders and orders to sell or buy above or below market (limit or stop orders). Floor brokers would find it prohibitively expensive, and in fact physically impossible, to follow their customers' limit or stop orders and to execute them efficiently. Specialists record

---

[3] There were 486 Exchange member organizations (220 partnerships and 266 corporations) at year-end 1976. See *New York Stock Exchange Fact Book*, 1977 ed., p. 57.
[4] The highest price ever paid was $625,000 in 1929, and the lowest was $17,000 in 1942.

on their books all such orders and automatically execute them if the target price is realized.

Specialists are expected to maintain a fair and orderly market in stocks assigned to them. When sell orders exceed buy orders, the specialists acquire stock for their inventories; when buy orders exceed sell orders, they sell from their inventories to meet the demand. In this fashion the specialists help maintain an orderly change in prices (tending to hold price changes to small incremental amounts) and a continuous market.

The specialist records all limit and stop orders in a book, which gives the specialist a select, although incomplete, picture of the market for the stock or stocks specialized in. For this reason, the specialist is very strictly regulated and supervised. The specialist may not disclose any information concerning orders on the books except to authorized members of the SEC or to executives of the NYSE in the course of their official duties.

The specialist system has been severely criticized in recent years, and some experts have suggested eliminating the system. Charges are that the specialist system excludes competition, that many specialists are inadequately capitalized, that their earnings are too high, and that many of the functions of the specialist could be better handled through a computerized system. The role of the specialist in the centralized market system currently being developed is unclear. To fairly evaluate these arguments based on available public information is difficult, if not impossible. Still, the possibility for abuse by the specialist is clearly recognized.

Odd-Lot Dealers. *Odd-lot dealers* and *brokers* deal principally in odd-lot orders—that is, transactions involving less than 100 shares. There is only one major odd-lot firm with whom most member firms of the NYSE deal. Odd lot orders are discussed later in this chapter.

Floor Traders. Members who act exclusively for their own accounts as speculators seeking quick profits are known as *floor traders.* They do not act either for the public or for other members. Because they are purely speculators, they have been subject to considerable criticism since the passage of the Securities Exchange Act of 1934. As a result of restrictions on their activities, the number of members primarily engaged in floor trading has dwindled until there are now less than 20.

Bond Traders. Certain members of the NYSE trade only in bonds, either as brokers or as dealers. The bond market is also an auction market. The total number of bond issues listed on the exchange at year end 1976 was 2,708 with a par value of $400 billion. Even in the case of listed bonds, most of the trading in bonds is in the over-the-counter markets. In recent years, the volume of bond trading on the NYSE has not been very significant, approximating $5.3 billion in 1976.

Listing of Securities

Initiative for listing securities comes from the issuing corporation, often with the support and encouragement of a member of the NYSE. The corporation's listing application places at the disposal of the exchange information necessary to determine the suitability of the security for trading on the exchange and provides the public with information useful in appraising the investment merits of the security. In determining eligibility for listing, the exchange is particularly concerned with the degree of national interest in the company, its relative position and stability in its industry, and whether it is engaged in an expanding industry with prospects of maintaining its position. While each case is decided on its own merits, the minimum standards are as follows:

Number of stockholders holding 100 shares or more (The number of beneficial holders of stock held in the name of NYSE member organizations will be considered in addition to holders of record. NYSE will make any necessary check of such holdings.)	2,000
Number of shares publicly held	1,000,000
Market value of publicly held shares (While greater emphasis is placed on market value, an additional measure of size is $16 million minimum net tangible assets.)	$16,000,000
Demonstrated earning power before federal income taxes under competitive conditions	
Latest fiscal year	$ 2,500,000
Each of preceding two years	$ 2,000,000

Listing information filed by an applicant to conform with New York Stock Exchange and Securities and Exchange Commission requirements must be kept up to date. Corporations meet this requirement by filing annually with the exchange copies of their published certified financial statements and other supplemental information required by the NYSE and the SEC. The issuer is required to maintain a transfer agent and a registrar in New York City. The company pays the exchange's initial listing fee and, in addition, pays an annual fee for the continued listing privilege.

The exchange has the right to de-list a security or suspend dealings in it at any time it judges such action advisable, but with the prior approval of the SEC. A security may be de-listed if it becomes inactive and is likely to remain so, or if the issuing corporation contracts in size to the point where it no longer meets initial listing standards.

Trading on the Exchange

Orders received by a brokerage firm are transmitted to a representative of that firm on the exchange floor. The representative then enters the bidding at the "post" at which the stock ordered is traded or gives the order to the specialist in that stock. Once the transaction has been completed, the participating brokers notify their firms, and the customer receives confirmation of the execution of the order. The transaction is reported on the ticker tape by the New York Quotations, a subsidiary corporation of the Exchange.[5]

Cash Purchase. A purchase on the NYSE may be made on a 100 percent cash basis. The buyer may take possession of the stock certificate, leave it with the broker for safekeeping, or have the broker retain it in the firm's name as a "street certificate" to facilitate its transfer at some later date without the necessity of endorsing the certificate.

Margin Buying. Buying on margin permits the buyer to purchase securities without paying the full price with personal funds. In effect, the buyer obtains the difference between the required margin and the cash price as a loan from the broker, who retains the securities purchased as collateral for the loan. Although the certificate is in a "street name" (broker's name), the customer, as beneficial owner of the stock, is entitled to receive any dividends and to vote on corporation policy through the broker. Margin requirements are initially determined by the Federal Reserve Board under authority provided by the Securities Exchange Act of 1934. In 1974 the margin requirement was set at 50 percent for stocks, 50 percent for convertible bonds, and 50 percent for short sales (see pages 357–358 for a discussion of short selling).

If a customer's equity falls below 25 percent of the market value of the securities after purchase, the broker must request additional margin or sell the securities for protection against loss. Most brokers require that the equity be at least 33 percent. A broker may also rehypothecate the certificate with a bank, and most brokers do so to obtain the loanable funds.

Delivery and Settlement. Transactions in stocks and bonds are normally made in one of three ways:

1. Regular way, requiring settlement on the fifth business day following the day of the contract. (The bulk of transactions follow this pattern.)
2. Cash, requiring delivery of the securities and payment for them on the day of the contract.

_____

[5] Most member firms now use one of several types of reporting machines based on computer operations that provide not only current price quotations, but also dividend yields and price-earnings ratios.

3. Seller's option, requiring delivery on the day of the expiration of the option, or at the option of the seller on any prior business day upon one day's written notice, provided such notice is not given before 4 p.m. nor before the day when delivery would be due in the regular way.

In 1968 the number of failures to deliver the securities as required reached a peak and became a very serious problem for many firms. The total was over $3 billion. But since then, such failures have declined substantially and were not a problem when record volumes occurred in 1975–1976.

Market and Limit Orders. Generally, *market orders* (to be executed "at the market") are more satisfactory for securities with good marketability, whereas *limit orders* (to be executed only at specified prices) are more advantageous in securities of limited marketability with a wide spread between bid and asked prices. Orders to buy and sell "at the market" are to be executed as soon as possible at the best price obtainable by the broker on the trading floor. The "best price" is the lowest price for a buy order and the highest price for a sell order. The obvious advantage of a market order is its rapid execution, which can be a particularly important factor when the market is rising or declining sharply. The basic disadvantage of a market order is that the "best price available" may be quite unsatisfactory. Caution is advised with respect to market orders in inactive stocks or in issues performing erratically and fluctuating over a wide range. If considerable time has elapsed since the last quotation, ask for a "bid and ask" quotation before placing an order.

Unlike a market order, which may be executed without limitations regarding price, a limit order instructs the broker to execute the order within a certain price limit set by the customer; this limit can be no higher than the limit price in a buy order and no lower than the limit price in a sell order. Under existing exchange rules, once a stock is ex-dividend (i.e., a dividend has been declared but has not been paid), all limit orders in the stock are adjusted for the amount of the dividend. The primary disadvantage of the limit order is that the order may never be executed and the investor may have "missed the market" only by a small margin.

Stop-Loss Order. A *stop-loss order* is a special type of limit order. Once the stock on the exchange has sold at or beyond the stop-loss price, the stop order becomes a market order. The difficulty with stop-loss orders, in fact with all limit orders, is that the customer may forget that they have been placed, with the result that they may be executed at a time when the customer may no longer want them executed.

Selecting the points at which stop-loss orders will be placed is a difficult problem. A small price decline often can launch a wave of stop-loss selling that may appreciably accelerate the price drop in the stock. Stop-loss orders are used defensively to minimize or prevent losses automatically if the market suddenly changes direction. In numerous cases, when a specialist notifies a member of the Board of Governors that the current price of a stock is close to the stop price on a large volume of orders, the exchange will bar all stop orders on the stock until congestion is cleared away.[6]

Day Orders and Open Orders. A *day order* is one that automatically expires at the close of the day it is placed if not executed by that time. Orders are usually considered as day orders unless otherwise specified. *Open orders*, however, may be entered for some limited period, such as a week or month, or may remain effective until executed or canceled, known as "good-'til-canceled" or GTC orders. Under New York Stock Exchange rules, all GTC orders outstanding must be confirmed or renewed with the floor specialist at six-month intervals, on the last days of April and October. Brokerage firms also typically check their orders with their customers at least once a month.

Odd-Lot Orders. An order for the purchase or the sale of less than the unit of trading is an odd-lot order. Typically the round-lot unit of trading is 100 shares, although in a few issues 10 shares is considered a round lot. An odd-lot differential of $\frac{1}{8}$ point per share is added to the price of the stock for most purchases and sales on the NYSE. The odd-lot differential is the odd-lot dealer's compensation and is in addition to the broker's commission. The differential increases the cost of the purchase of stock and decreases the proceeds from the sale of stock. If, for example, the next round-lot sale is at 41, the price to the seller of an odd lot is $40\frac{7}{8}$, and the price to the buyer of an odd lot is $41\frac{1}{8}$. The firm of Carlisle DeCoppatt & Co. handles all odd-lot transactions and maintains the $\frac{1}{8}$ point difference, although the NYSE permitted the differential to be determined competitively in the fall of 1975. Merrill-Lynch has since announced a plan to trade odd-lots without the differential. This plan is supported by the Securities and Exchange Commission and opposed by the NYSE.

Short Selling. A *short sale* is the sale of stock by a seller who borrows the stock to make delivery and later returns the stock to the lender. There are several reasons why individuals may wish to sell short. The primary purpose is to speculate on the anticipation of a price de-

_____
[6] The New York Stock Exchange in recent years has ordered cancellation of all stop orders on certain stocks when the volume of such orders has created a potential situation detrimental to an orderly market. The American Stock Exchange also has followed the same policy.

cline in the stock. The short seller hopes to acquire the stock to "cover" the sale at a lower price in the future, realizing a profit measured by the difference between the selling price and the later purchase price after commissions and other expenses. There is no limit to the short seller's loss if the market rises and the short seller does not "buy in." To prevent "bear raiding" and demoralization of the markets by short sellers deliberately depressing the market, the Securities and Exchange Commission has ruled that a short sale must be so designated when the order is placed and may not be executed at a price below the last preceding regular sale. A short sale must be made on an "uptick" or may be made at the price of the last regular trade only if the previous price change was upward.

When selling short, the customer's broker makes a loan of the stock or borrows the stock from another customer or broker. To provide security for the loan of stock, the borrowing broker deposits with the lending broker the market price of the borrowed shares obtained from the short sale transaction. Dividends declared to stockholders of record during the time a short sale is in effect seemingly belong to two parties: the registered owner of the shares and the lender of those shares. In actuality the corporation pays the dividend to the registered owner, and the short seller pays the dividend to the lender.[7]

Commissions. For many years, commissions prepared by the exchanges with the approval of the SEC were calculated on the basis of a fixed schedule of minimum charges, based on a round lot of 100 shares. Under this arrangement, the commissions for handling an order of 1,000 shares were exactly ten times that of an order for 100 shares. This did not allow for the economies of scale involved in handling larger orders. In addition, financial institutions had to resort to devices such as the "third" market, which will be discussed later, to avoid the fixed commission system used on the NYSE. Finally, in December 1968 the NYSE was forced to allow discounts on transactions in excess of 1,000 shares.

Continued pressure on the part of the SEC and market participants led to negotiated rates, first on orders exceeding $500,000 and later on those in excess of $300,000. In September 1973 the SEC announced that it would require termination of fixed commission rates after April 30, 1975. Many industry people feared that the advent of negotiated rates would cause members to leave the exchange to avoid the cost and regulatory responsibilities required by the exchanges. Fears were that

---

[7] A stock sold when a dividend has been declared but not paid is *ex-dividend*, and its market price is usually lower to reflect this fact. Thus, a short seller who must pay a dividend to the lender of the stock usually does not suffer a loss because the lower market price generally reflects the value of the dividend.

this would bring about the demise of auction markets for securities and a lessened role for the specialist, and thus would not be in the public interest.[8] Markets could become dominated by big institutions, and the extraordinary liquidity of U.S. markets would be threatened. The small investor, not in a position to negotiate effectively, would face sharply higher costs. On the other hand, supporters of negotiated rates believe they will lead to sound competition, elimination of inefficient brokerage firms, and through this process, a reduction in brokerage costs.[9]

With the advent of negotiated rates, new brokerage firms appeared offering execution of orders at minimal commissions. Services such as research reports are not provided at these rates. This allows investors to pay only for those services they need, which seems eminently fair. However, there is an argument that this will cause the cost of such services to rise and will encourage unsound judgments on securities. Still, it seems the investor should have the opportunity to pay only for those services that are needed and are fairly priced.

Trading costs have risen somewhat for the small investor, but commissions charged have not changed drastically since the days of fixed-rate schedules. Commissions typically approximate 2 percent of the total dollar value of a stock transaction for the average small investor. Bonds are cheaper. Typically a $5 charge per $1,000 bond is made.

THE THIRD MARKET

The *third market* refers to over-the-counter trading in securities listed on an exchange by nonmembers of that exchange. This market developed in the 1960s in response to the dissatisfaction of institutional investors who were not being given volume discounts for large block trading on the organized exchanges. The volume of business of institutional investors (mainly mutual funds, insurance companies, and pension funds) has increased markedly in recent years, and thus the third market business has also increased. The ratio of third market volume to NYSE volume on a share basis increased from 2.7 percent to 7.3 percent in 1972, and then fell off to about 4.7 percent in 1975. The ratio in terms of dollar volume of transactions rose from 3.4 percent in 1965 to 8.5 percent in 1972, and then dropped to about 6 percent in 1975.[10]

Certain large brokerage firms (such as Weeden & Co.) operate in this market in much the same fashion as wholesalers in the OTC market; they maintain inventories of listed stocks and stand ready to buy or sell

---

[8] New York Stock Exchange, *Maintaining Exchange Auction Markets in an Era of Competitive Commission Rates*, December 5, 1974.

[9] For example, see David L. Ratner, "The NYSE's Day of Judgment," *The Wall Street Journal*, November 19, 1974, p. 26.

[10] *The New York Stock Exchange Fact Book*, 1976, p. 17.

at a quoted price.[11] Typically, the profit lies in the spread between a bid and offered price, and commissions are not charged. Such firms (and some that never take a dealer's position) act to bring together buyers and sellers with large blocks to trade. A price quoted by a third market dealer is often better than the combination of an exchange price and the commission to acquire the same stock. Furthermore, market interest and trading does not receive unwanted publicity. Broker-dealers (nonmembers of the NYSE) thus enjoy an opportunity to deal in listed stocks, at least in terms of block transactions.

Some speak of a "fourth market" representing institution to institution dealing through the facilities of Instinet (owned by Institutional Networks Corporation). Instinet is a system enabling direct trades via computer terminals at costs that are generally less than stock exchange commissions. Subscribers may enter indications of interest in trades, and other subscribers may either communicate with the former by teletype, negotiate, or accept firm bids or offers thereby executing transactions. No broker-dealer is used as an intermediary, as in the third market.

THE EXPANDING ROLE OF FINANCIAL INSTITUTIONS

Financial institutions have enjoyed dramatic growth since 1960 and have increased markedly the proportion of equity securities held in their portfolios. At the end of World War II, financial institutions owned stocks having a value equal to about 10 percent of the total value of all stocks listed on the New York Stock Exchange. Table 15–1 shows that these holdings had risen to about 33 percent of the market value of all NYSE-listed stock by the end of 1975, and the institutions accounted for over half the exchange's dollar volume during the year. Of course, financial institutions also hold large amounts of other equities as well.

The expanding role of financial institutions has led to serious concerns within industry and governmental circles. For example, concern has been expressed that buying power is concentrated in too few hands. Some argue that the institutions, with their huge buying power, tend to bid their favorite stocks to a higher level than justified by the underlying facts, while other companies do not attract the interest commensurate with their real potential contribution to the economy. Also, some fear that the growing concentration of investment activity in financial institutions will adversely affect the strong marketability of U.S. stocks, which was always a feature of past investor markets domi-

---

[11] Donald Weeden, Chairman of the Board of Weeden & Co., has described this market as, ". . . the over-the-counter marketplace dealing in exchange-listed stocks."

TABLE 15-1. Estimated Holdings of NYSE Listed Stocks by Financial Institutions (billions of dollars)

Type of Institution	1949	1960	1965	1966	1967	1968	1969	1970	1971	1972	1973	1974	1975
Insurance companies:													
Life	1.1	3.2	6.4	6.2	7.4	9.3	9.7	10.9	16.1	21.5	21.0	16.3	21.9
Nonlife	1.7	6.0	10.1	9.2	11.4	12.8	11.7	12.2	15.6	19.8	16.5	10.4	11.3
Investment companies:													
Open-end	1.4	12.4	26.5	25.4	33.0	43.9	39.8	39.4	46.8	51.4	38.5	27.1	35.2
Closed-end	1.6	4.2	5.6	4.0	4.6	5.5	4.1	4.4	5.6	6.5	5.9	4.0	5.4
Noninsured pension funds:													
Corporate	0.5	13.5	32.5	31.4	43.0	49.2	46.9	51.7	75.2	104.5	83.1	58.2	82.2
Other private	*	0.8	1.9	2.0	2.7	3.0	2.8	3.0	4.5				
State and local government	*	0.5	2.0	2.2	3.2	3.2	4.6	5.0	12.4	13.6	17.1	15.9	22.8
Nonprofit institutions:													
College and university endowments	1.1	2.9	5.4	4.9	6.0	7.6	6.8	7.1	7.8	8.8	7.7	5.5	7.2
Foundations	1.1	5.3	11.0	9.7	11.9	13.5	13.9	14.1	14.3	23.9	20.5	16.9	22.1
Other	1.0	4.4	7.7	6.9	8.7	9.8	8.9	9.0	10.1	11.8	9.5	6.6	8.7
Common trust funds	*	1.4	3.2	2.9	3.8	4.3	4.1	4.2	5.3	6.4	5.5	4.7	6.1
Mutual savings banks	0.2	0.2	0.5	0.5	0.6	0.7	0.8	0.9	1.5	1.5	1.4	1.7	2.3
TOTAL	9.7	54.8	112.8	105.3	136.3	162.8	154.1	161.9	215.2	269.7	226.7	167.3	225.2
Market value of *all* NYSE-listed stock	76.3	307.0	537.5	482.5	605.8	692.3	629.5	636.4	741.8	871.5	721.0	511.1	685.1
Estimated percent held by above institutions	12.7	17.9	21.0	21.8	22.5	23.5	24.5	25.4	29.0	30.9	31.4	32.7	32.9

*Less than $50 million.

Source: *New York Stock Exchange Fact Book* (various issues).

nated by individuals. The specialist's role is not clear in a centralized market dominated by financial institutions. At present, when someone wants to sell a stock and there are no buyers, the specialist's duty is to "make a market" by buying the stock. Financial institutions customarily deal in such large volumes that it is reasonable to question whether any single specialist can guarantee a stable market. C. Bradford Cook, in his last days as chairman of the SEC, said, "I feel constrained to warn: the individual investor has acquired the status of an endangered species."[12]

There have also been positive effects from growing institutional dominance. The institutions were instrumental in bringing about the demise of the fixed minimum commission rate structure of the NYSE, which in effect rewarded inefficiency by requiring all brokers to charge the same commission on a trade. Also, the institutions have sought membership on the exchanges and have forced them to reexamine their basic operating practices. Hopefully, this will bring about a more efficient automated marketplace in the future.

THE MARKET SYSTEM OF THE FUTURE

A new central stock market appears to be in the making, but the experts disagree on the shape that this market will take. The SEC has stated:

> Our objective is to see a strong central market system created to which all investors have access, in which all qualified broker-dealers and existing market institutions may participate . . . , and which is controlled not only by appropriate regulation but also by the forces of competition.[13]

The SEC has since further developed its ideas in a series of policy statements.[14] Furthermore, the Securities Acts Amendments of 1975 serve as a congressional mandate to the SEC to work for a central national market system.

William McChesney Martin, Jr., former chairman of the Board of Governors of the Federal Reserve System and the first paid president of the NYSE, also prepared a report recommending a central market system. But he described it as "a single national auction market for each security qualified for listing."[15] Under the Martin proposal, each of the existing markets being joined into the central system would retain

---

[12] *Business Week*, June 2, 1973, p. 58.
[13] Letter of Transmittal, Securities and Exchange Commission, *Institutional Investor Study Report*, March 10, 1971, pt. 1, p. xxv.
[14] Securities and Exchange Commission, *Policy Statement on the Future Structure of the Security Markets*, February, 1972, and *Policy Statement*, March, 1973.
[15] Report by William M. Martin, Jr., to the New York Stock Exchange, August 5, 1971.

many of its individual standards, and financial institutions would be barred from membership. Furthermore, Martin defended the concept of a fixed minimum commission, which the SEC opposes. The NYSE continues to advocate the Martin proposal.

The SEC, in a report to Congress on September 2, 1975, proposed the elimination of Rule 394 that prohibited member firms of the NYSE from taking orders off the floor, even when a better price could be obtained in the OTC. This further stimulated discussion of plans for reorganization of the security markets. By early September 1976, Weeden & Company, a leading third market firm, was displaying a new computerized stock market system built around 65 utility stocks. This minimarket was kept on exhibit for two months to aid industry executives in judging how a large electronic system might perform. Merrill-Lynch has proposed a largely electronic stock market with competing market makers as the central securities market of the future.[16] The current specialist system would be abolished under this plan, and stock exchange trading floors and exchanges themselves would be eliminated. The NYSE opposes this approach, suggesting instead a single central marketplace with competition excluded and the NYSE operating an exclusive market for securities of major corporations.

There will no doubt be a major overhaul of security markets in the future. However, the exact direction this overhaul will take is not now clear. Many problems of implementation of any centralized market system remain to be solved. We would expect the actual realization of a central securities market to evolve slowly.

PROTECTION FOR THE INVESTOR

A comprehensive national legal framework to regulate all aspects of securities transactions did not exist prior to the enactment of the various federal acts that will be described in this section. However, both prior to the enactment of federal legislation and subsequent to it, there has been state regulation of securities transactions that has proved by itself quite inadequate because of the national scope of the securities markets. State legislation takes the form of registration of securities and security dealers; in some states, such as New York, Connecticut, Delaware, and Maryland, it takes the form of antifraud legislation.

Securities Act of 1933

Congress passed the Securities Act of 1933 "to provide full and fair disclosure of the character of securities sold in interstate and foreign commerce and through the mails and to prevent fraud in the sale there-

---

[16] *The Wall Street Journal,* October 17, 1975, p. 4.

of, and for other purposes." The act required that, with certain specific exceptions as to type and size of issue, before new corporate securities may be sold or offered for sale, a registration statement and prospectus must be filed with the SEC. We have discussed these in connection with sources of company information.

Under the Securities Act of 1933, a large number of persons can be liable for false and misleading statements in the registration statement or prospectuses and may be sued for damages under civil law. Persons who *willfully* violate any of the provisions of the act or rules and regulations, or who *willfully* make a false statement or omit a material fact in a registration statement, may be held *criminally* liable and subject to fine, imprisonment, or both. If any part of an effective registration statement makes a false statement of a material fact or has omissions of essential data, the issuer, underwriters, and responsible parties may be sued by any purchaser of the security offered.[17]

Securities Act of 1934

The passage of this act brought national security exchanges under federal control "to insure the maintenance of a fair and honest market in such transactions." Voluntary regulations by the exchanges, nevertheless, continue to govern much of stock exchange procedure, and self-regulation by the National Association of Security Dealers governs much of the operation of the over-the-counter securities markets in accordance with the significance attached to the concept of industry self-regulation.

The principal objectives of the Securities Act of 1934 may be summarized as follows:

1. To provide the public with reliable information about securities listed on national security exchanges.
2. To eliminate manipulation, fraud, and dissemination of false information in the securities markets.
3. To insure just and equitable trading in the security markets.
4. To regulate the use of credit for the purpose of security trading.
5. To regulate trading by insiders in the security markets.
6. To regulate the use of proxies by corporate officials.

---

[17] In addition to all persons who sign the registration statement, these individuals are liable: (1) every person who was a director or a partner in the issuing firm at the time of filing of the part of the registration statement under question; (2) every person who, with consent, is named in the registration statement as a director or a partner; (3) all accountants, engineers, appraisers, or other persons whose professions give authority to their statements and who with their consent have been named as having prepared or certified any part of the registration, but liability attaches only to those portions actually prepared or certified by the individuals; (4) every underwriter of the security. Liability was becoming more of a problem for accountants in the 1970s and also for lawyers.

Furthermore, the act makes provision for both civil and criminal liabilities for those who violate its requirements.

Provisions Controlling and Regulating Security Trading. The 1934 act provides comprehensive regulation of security trading and the prevention of manipulation in any form. To establish a fair and equitable market, certain practices are prohibited and others are controlled. The following are among the more important practices specifically prohibited:

1. Creating a misleading appearance of active trading through wash sales (an order to buy and an order to sell given at the same time), matched orders, or pool operation.
2. Creating trading activity to raise or depress the price of a registered security for the purpose of inducing buying or selling by others.
3. Disseminating information for the purpose of creating a change in price.
4. Making false and misleading statements regarding a security to create market activity or to induce buying or selling by others.
5. Pegging (fixing or stabilizing prices) except by investment bankers during underwriting.

Regulation of Corporate "Insiders." Officers, directors, and beneficial owners of 10 percent or more of a company's voting securities are generally known as *insiders.* To discourage insiders from capitalizing on confidential information, the SEC requires such owners of 10 percent or more of a company's equity securities (common and preferred stocks, convertible bonds, and bonds with stock warrants) to file a monthly statement of their transactions in the securities. To prevent unfair use of information by insiders, the law requires that any profits realized from security transactions within a 6-month period must be forfeited to the corporation. A suit to recover short-term profits may be instituted by the corporation or any stockholder. The SEC was very active in this area in the 1968–1976 period.[18] The Appeals Court in the Texas Gulf Sulphur case stated that, "anyone in possession of material inside information is an insider and must refrain from telling anyone or refrain from trading in or recommending the securities concerned while such information remains undisclosed." The Newmark-RKO case extended the theory of insiders to include "corporate insiders" as well as individuals.

The Securities and Exchange Commission, by publishing the *Official Summary of Security Transactions and Holdings*[19] on a monthly

---

[18] Two SEC landmark "insider" cases are: *Securities and Exchange Commission* v. *Texas Gulf Sulphur Co.,* 258 F. Supp. 262 (1966), 401 F2d 833 (1968); and *Newmark* v. *RKO General, Inc.,* 425 F2d 348 (1970).

[19] The *Official Summary of Security Transactions and Holdings,* a monthly, annual subscription may be ordered from the Superintendent of Documents, GPO, Washington, DC 20402.

basis, makes available to the general public reports of insider transactions. As we have mentioned earlier in this chapter, the *Insiders' Chronicle*, a weekly commercial publication, publishes a selected listing of purchases and sales of insiders' stock holdings. Its publishers claim, "If a transaction is filed by Thursday, we give it to you the following week. That's five weeks ahead of SEC publications!" The governmental source is a more complete record, however.

Letter Stock. The SEC carefully regulates the sale of letter stock, also discussed on page 399, under their rules 144 and 237.[20] Unregistered stock (letter stock) of newly public companies poses a risk to investors since an unknown number of shares could be liquidated suddenly, lowering the price.[21] For registered stock the SEC requires the disclosure in the prospectus of a company's float of unregistered shares.

Tender Offers. Related to insider trading is tender offer solicitation. By this is meant an offer or request to acquire stock with intent to gain control of a company. Usually one company offers, for a specific period of time, to buy another's shares at a price higher than the prevailing market price. In August 1976, the SEC proposed to set this time period requiring the tender offer to be open for 15 business days, and 10 days after any increase in price.[22]

A 1970 amendment to the Exchange Act required the reporting of any attempt to acquire 5 percent of a company's equity securities whether by buying them on a regular exchange or in any market such as the fourth market. In recent years foreign ownership of U.S. companies has been on the increase. By the end of 1975 foreign holdings amounted to about 5 percent of the value of publicly traded stocks.[23] Because of this a congressional committee supported required reporting of information on the residence and nationality of all investors holding a 5 percent or more interest in U.S. companies.

Section 12(m) of the Exchange Act, together with the 1975 amendments, called for a study of the practice of having securities recorded in a name other than that of the beneficial owner. This was known as the "Street Name Study."[24] During the fall of 1975 the staff con-

---

[20] See the *37th SEC Annual Report* for a discussion of these rules.

[21] Richard D. Moran, "Risk Exposure Up On New Offerings?" *Insiders' Chronicle*, November 4, 1976, pp. 1, 16.

[22] Robert D. Hershey, Jr., "S.E.C. Proposes New Tender Rules: Bidder Would Be Guaranteed Access to Target's Stockholder List," *New York Times*, August 3, 1976, p. C37.

[23] Edwin L. Dale, Jr., "U.S. Stock Abroad Totals $37.2 Billion," *New York Times*, May 4, 1976, p. 55.

[24] From the *SEC Annual Report*, 1976, p. 20.

ducted extensive research into both the historical background of street name registration and the scope of its recent use. Study of the effect of this practice on appropriate disclosure of the beneficial ownership of corporate securities and on issuer-shareholder communications was undertaken in 1976 and continued into 1979.

Regulation of Proxies. Regulation X-14 issued by the SEC requires a proxy solicitation to contain (1) a statement of the stockholder's rights concerning revocation and the right of dissension; (2) the identity of those who will pay the cost of solicitation; (3) a statement concerning on whose behalf the solicitation is being made and the interests of the party in the corporation; and (4) complete information with respect to voting rights, classes of stock outstanding, directors and officers and their remuneration, candidates for election, and the specific types of action to be undertaken for the corporation.[25]

Regulation of the Over-the-Counter Markets. The over-the-counter markets are subject to federal regulation under Section 15 of the Securities Exchange Act of 1934 and under the Maloney Act of 1938 that amended the legislation by the addition of Section 15(a) to the act. The Maloney Act provides for the self-regulation of the over-the-counter dealers and permits the NASD (National Association of Security Dealers) to allow discounts in trading between its own members. It was the 1964 amendment to the Securities Exchange Act that for the first time extended the registration, periodic reporting, proxy solicitation, and insider reporting and trading provisions to issuers of securities traded over-the-counter having total assets of $1 million and a class of equity security held of record initially by 500 or more persons, if the issuer is engaged in interstate commerce or its securities are traded by means of the instruments of interstate commerce. The required registration statement that must be filed under new Section 12(g) of the act is similar to that required on an exchange.

Public Utility Holding Company Act of 1935

In administering the Public Utility Holding Company Act, the SEC regulates interstate public utility holding company systems and their operating company subsidiaries engaged in the electric utility business and/or in the retail distribution of gas. A holding company is defined by the act as one that directly or indirectly owns, controls, or holds

---

[25] *Rule 10b-5. Employment of Manipulative and Deceptive Devices.* Numerous lawsuits have been instituted by the SEC and by stockholders (especially in regard to proxies, prospectuses, and registration statements) under this rule. In 1969 the SEC ruled that this section and tender offers of the 1934 act also covered proxies issued in mergers and tender offers.

with power to vote 10 percent or more of the outstanding voting stock. All such holding companies are required by law to register and file annual reports with the SEC.

Trust Indenture Act of 1939

The contract (indenture) between the issuer of corporate securities and the bondholders sets forth the relationship of the trustee to the issuer and the bondholders. The act applies to securities required to be registered under the Securities Act of 1933 and securities issued in exchange for other securities of the same corporation or under a reorganization plan approved by a court, which may not be required to be registered.

The major purpose of the act is to continue the theory of full disclosure first developed in the Securities Act of 1933. The information required by the act protects the bond or debenture holder from a trustee who might have conflicting interests and from an issuer who might not have sufficient capital. The issuer is required by the act to send periodic reports through the trustee to the bondholders, and the corporate trustee is required to maintain bondholder lists to provide a method of communication between the bondholders and the issuers in accordance with the provisions of the indentures.

Investment Company Act of 1940

This legislation had two main purposes: (1) full disclosure and (2) the prevention of the speculative abuses and management manipulation characteristic of the late 1920s. The act was broadly amended in 1970.[26]

> The Investment Company Act of 1940 provides for the registration and regulation of companies primarily engaged in the business of investing, reinvesting, owning, holding, or trading in securities. The Act, among other things, requires disclosure of the financial condition and investment policies of such companies; prohibits changing the nature of their business or their investment policies without shareholders' approval; regulates the

---

[26] Major 1970 amendments provided the following: "(a) Investment advisers . . . have a fiduciary duty with respect to the receipt of compensation for services or payments of a material nature paid . . . to the adviser or an affiliate of the adviser; (b) the NASD may by rule prohibit . . . offering such shares at a price which includes an excessive sales load; and (c) front-end-load sales charges on contractual plans may be imposed under either of two alternative methods: (1) "spread load" alternative—the sales load is restricted to not more than 20 percent of any payment and not more than an average of 16 percent over the first four years of the plan, or (2) periodic payment plan certificates may still be sold with a 50 percent front-end-load, but plan sponsors must refund to any investor surrendering his certificate within the first 18 months . . . that portion of the sales charges which exceeds 15 percent of the gross payments made as well as pay him the value of his account."

means of custody of the companies' assets; requires management contracts to be submitted to security holders for approval; prohibits underwriters, investment bankers and brokers from constituting more than a minority of the directors of such companies; and prohibits transactions between such companies and their officers, directors, and affiliates except with approval of the Commission. The Act also regulates the issuance of senior securities. . . . The Companies must issue prospectuses when offering new stock which must be periodically updated to conform to SEC requirements.[27]

Investment Advisers Act of 1940

The Act requires persons engaged for compensation in the business of advising others with respect to securities to register with the Commission and to conform to statutory standards designed to protect the public interest. The Act prohibits fraudulent, deceptive or manipulative acts or practices. . . . Advisers are also required to make, keep or preserve books and records in accordance with the Commission's rules and the Commission is empowered to conduct inspection of such books and records.[28]

The Investment Company Amendments Act of 1970

The Securities and Exchange Commission initiated the changes in the 1940 Investment Company Act, which culminated in the Investment Company Amendments Act of 1970. This was the first major revision in 30 years. Important provisions are the imposition of a "fiduciary duty" upon the investment adviser, the injunction that there should be no "excessive sales load," and provision for certain refund rights for buyers of mutual funds.

Nearly a year later an amendment to the 1970 amendments "restricted the refund rights for mutual funds to participants in contract investment plans under which sales charges exceeding 9 percent of any payment were deducted."[29]

Securities Investor Protection Act of 1970

The Securities Investor Protection Act set up a nonprofit corporate agency, the Securities Investor Protection Corporation, to administer an insurance fund that would pay for any losses investors might incur if their brokers should become insolvent. Each account was to be insured up to $50,000; and $20,000 of that could be a cash deposit. This insurance fund would be financed by assessing the broker-dealer members one-half of one percent of their commissions until $150 million was accumulated. After that the assessment was to be reduced. If the entire

---

[27] From the *32d Annual Report*, 1966, SEC, p. 98.
[28] From the *32d SEC Annual Report*, 1966, p. 109.
[29] *Congressional Quarterly Almanac*, Vol. 27 (1971), p. 864.

reserve fund should ever be depleted, the SIPC (the Securities Investor Protection Corporation) could borrow up to $1 billion from the U.S. Treasury. All this came about because investors suffered heavy losses when a large number of brokerage houses failed in the late sixties. Bankruptcies were attributed chiefly to poor management and speculative activity. High volume during those years made for a great deal of paperwork, and management often was not prepared to handle the unexpected increase.

Until the Security Act Amendments of 1975, there existed very little uniformity in capital requirements among the national securities exchanges. Section 15(c)(3) directed the SEC to establish, no later than September 1, 1975, minimum requirements for all brokers and dealers. The commission satisfied this directive on June 26, 1975, with Rule 15(c)(3)—1, which retained the traditional "aggregate indebtedness" standard of capital sufficiency but introduced something new— the "alternative net capital requirement." The first concept, that of aggregate indebtedness, measures a broker's financial well-being by means of the ratio of liabilities to liquid (or convertible) assets. "The alternative net capital requirement, which is available at the election of qualified brokers and dealers, prescribes net capital requirements graduating in direct proportion to the magnitude of a firm's customer-related obligations."[30]

Securities Act Amendments of 1975

On May 22, 1975, Congress passed an omnibus measure revising federal securities regulations and increasing SEC supervisory powers. It culminated a four-year effort toward reform of the securities industry.

Major important provisions include the following:

1. It directed the Commission to facilitate the establishment of a national market system for securities and a national system for the prompt and accurate clearance and settlement of securities transactions.
2. It established a 15-member National Advisory Board to supervise development of the national market system.
3. It prohibited stock exchanges from fixing commission rates. Fixed rates may be restored by the SEC only after formal proceedings.
4. It retained the so-called "New York Rule" that permits the New York Stock Exchange to require its members to trade their listed stocks within the exchange.
5. It prohibited stock exchanges from denying membership to any broker-dealers who meet the SEC qualifications and barred exchanges from reducing their membership ranks below those existing on May 1, 1975.
6. It empowered the SEC to oversee bank performance in clearing securities transactions and required banks to keep records on security transactions.

_____

[30] 42d *SEC Annual Report,* 1976, p. 14.

7. It directed the SEC to establish minimum capital requirements for brokers. (We have discussed this in conjunction with the Securities Investor Protection Act of 1970.)
8. It provided that eventually a stock exchange member would be prohibited from buying securities for a personal account or for any other business with which the member is affiliated.
9. It provided for a Municipal Securities Board to make the rules for trading in state and local government bonds.
10. It required institutional investment managers to make annual disclosures of their transactions in equity securities.
11. It protected investment managers against charges of violating their fiduciary duties when paying brokerage commissions higher than the lowest available fees.

Congress has always passed securities industry legislation with the intention of (1) furthering an efficient capital market, (2) working for the public interest, and (3) protecting the investor. What makes the Security Act Amendments of 1975 different is the drive for the emphasis on competition within the industry. The findings of many special congressional studies that preceded the act had pointed out the need for these reforms.

SEC Accounting Regulations

By virtue of authority granted by the Securities Act of 1933, the SEC has defined accounting terms and prescribed the form in which required financial statements must be presented, stipulating the method to be used in the determination of depreciation and depletion, the valuation of assets and liabilities, the treatment of recurring and nonrecurring charges or profits, the manner in which operating income is to be segregated from income obtained from other sources, and other matters. The SEC has adhered quite closely to sound accounting principles as generally understood by the accounting profession and the AICPA. SEC rulings are published in the form of Accounting Series Releases.

The commission generally has not attempted to impose its ideas on the accounting profession but instead has chosen to cooperate closely with it, first submitting any proposed regulation to the Financial Accounting Standards Board which, in 1973, supplanted the APB (the Accounting Principles Board) as the rule-making body for the profession. The SEC generally has assigned full responsibility for adequate disclosure in financial reports filed with it to management, not to the accountants certifying the statements. In recent years, however, the number of suits against accounting firms has risen. On March 30, 1976, in the case of an investor's suit against a large accounting firm, *Hochfelder* v. *Ernst and Ernst*, the Supreme Court ruled that victims of securities frauds cannot sue the auditing firm for not recognizing fraud.[31] The intent to deceive must be present to result in liability.

Summary

The primary purpose of a securities market is to provide for the orderly transfer of both securities and information concerning those securities between buyer and seller. Efficient securities markets facilitate continuous modifications and transfers of portfolio holdings so that investors can adjust to changing circumstances.

Security markets may be classified in two basic ways. First, one may distinguish between the capital market where long-term securities originate and are traded and the money market where short-term securities are traded. Second, one may speak of the primary market where new issues originate and are sold, and the secondary market where existing securities are traded. Trading of existing securities may take place in the relatively informal and loosely organized over-the-counter market or on a formally organized exchange. The mechanics of trading in these markets and other aspects of security market operations that affect investors have been discussed.

Several proposals for a new central stock market that would be quite different than current markets are briefly reviewed. Quite clearly a major overhaul of security markets is coming, but the exact direction this overhaul will take is not now certain.

Federal and state securities regulation is aimed at providing fair and equitable trading markets for investors and furnishing investors with sufficient and reliable information on securities to enable them to make intelligent decisions. Investors should, therefore, familiarize themselves with security legislation so as to be aware of the protection afforded.

Questions

1. (a) Distinguish between primary and secondary markets.
   (b) What is the economic function of these markets? How does each contribute to the basic economic function?
2. (a) State the primary function of an investment banker.
   (b) Name three other functions performed by investment bankers.
3. Discuss briefly the purpose of the investigation of an issuing company by an investment banker.
4. (a) Describe the type of agreement entered into in a "best-efforts" underwriting. Under what circumstances will an investment banker usually insist on this form of agreement?

---

[31] See *Facts on File*, Vol. 36, No. 1849 (April 17, 1976), p. 262.

     (b) Define a firm underwriting. Is a standby underwriting a firm underwriting? Discuss.

5. Describe the basic function of the purchase group in an underwriting.

6. (a) Define the term "underwriters' spread."

     (b) Why may there be wide differences among spreads for various types of securities?

7. Compare competitive bidding and "origination by negotiation."

8. Discuss briefly the significance of private placements as a means of selling new issues.

9. Differentiate between a broker and a dealer and indicate how compensation is derived for each.

10. (a) Name the categories into which active members of the NYSE are placed. Differentiate as to the role played by each category.

     (b) Discuss briefly the functions of a specialist on the NYSE.

11. (a) Who can trade on the floor of the exchanges?

     (b) Of what significance to the investor is the fact that a company whose securities are being considered for investment is listed on the New York Stock Exchange?

     (c) What information of value to a prospective investor could be found in a New York Stock Exchange listing statement?

12. (a) Distinguish between a limit order and a stop-loss order. When would each be used?

     (b) What are the advantages and disadvantages of placing a market order?

     (c) What are the advantages and the major risks of buying stock on margin?

13. Define a short sale. What are the regulations governing short sales?

14. What is the "third market"?

15. Why should the securities market be reorganized and what kind of system is currently being proposed?

16. (a) What type of information might one find in a Form 10-K report filed with the Securities and Exchange Commission?

     (b) How does a Form 10-K report differ from a Form 8-K report?

17. (a) Explain briefly the reasons for the passage of federal statutes regulating the securities business.

     (b) Did the passage of federal statutes eliminate the need for state blue-sky laws?

18. (a) What is the purpose of the Securities Act of 1933?

     (b) To what branch of the securities business does the Securities Act of 1933 apply?

     (c) Name at least four classes of securities that are exempted from the provisions of the Securities Act of 1933. Why were they exempted?

19. (a) Distinguish between a registration statement and a prospectus.

(b) What is the purpose of a prospectus?

(c) What is a red herring? Why is it issued?

20. (a) What is the SIPC? Why was it established?

(b) What is fiduciary duty?

21. Discuss briefly the liabilities arising from false registration under the Securities Act of 1933. Compare these to liabilities under the Securities Act of 1934.

22. (a) What are the basic objectives of the Securities Exchange Act of 1934?

(b) What is a wash sale and why is it prohibited under the Act of 1934?

(c) Under what circumstances is pegging or price stabilizing permitted?

23. (a) Discuss the regulation of corporate officers and "insiders" under the Securities Exchange Act of 1934.

(b) What is tender offer solicitation?

(c) What are restricted securities?

24. (a) What is the main purpose of the Securities Act Amendments of 1975?

(b) What class of investors was helped most by the abolition of fixed commission rates May 1, 1975?

25. What was the significance of the *Hochfelder* v. *Ernst & Ernst* decision of the Supreme Court in 1976?

Work-Study Problems

1. Describe the activities of a large investment banking firm, covering in particular the following:

(a) The types of security issues normally originated by competitive bidding and the types of security issues normally originated by negotiated deal.

(b) The four categories normally covered in a thorough investigation of an issuing company by an investment banking firm.

(c) The spread.

(d) The agreement among the underwriters.

(e) The underwriting agreement.

(f) The advantages and the disadvantages of private placement and the role of the investment banking houses in private placement.

2. Write a short paper giving the reasons why an industrial concern:

(a) Would seek to have its securities listed on the New York Stock Exchange.

(b) Would prefer to have its securities traded over the counter.

3. Explain whether the following actions or lack of action would be considered violations subject to possible penalty by the Securities and Exchange Commission. Explain the rules involved in each case.

(a) After the Securities and Exchange Commission has allowed the registration statement for a security to become effective and it is being sold, the salesperson may verbally, but not in writing, tell a prospective customer that the Securities and Exchange Commission has approved the issue.

(b) The bonds of a company with investment rating of A or better can be sold a few days after registration without waiting for the 20-day waiting period.

(c) The issuer may withdraw on written notice, without penalty, the registration of a security filed with the SEC:
    (1) After the effective date of registration.
    (2) Before the effective date of registration.

(d) A company does not have to disclose that it is being sued for a large amount of money for a patent infringement if the company has legal advice that the claim is probably groundless.

(e) A company that fails to mention that goodwill is carried at $1 might be subject to a severe penalty.

(f) Failure to register a new issue with New York State officials in Albany, New York, would subject the issuer to penalties for securities sold in New York State.

(g) Registration is not necessary for the sale of securities of (1) the Bank for Reconstruction and Development, (2) the Port of New York Authority, (3) The First National City Bank of New York, (4) the Consolidated Edison Company of New York, Inc., (5) (5) Mack Trucks, Inc., and (6) the Chesapeake and Ohio Railway Co.

(h) An individual owning 9 percent of the common stock of a company listed on the New York Stock Exchange would be liable to penalties if any or all of this stock was sold without reporting the transaction to the Securities and Exchange Commission.

(i) Disclosure by the Securities and Exchange Commission of information filed by an issuer is a cause of action against the Securities and Exchange Commission.

(j) A company did not include a copy of its Form 10-K report in the annual report sent to shareholders.

4. In the *Federal Register*, under the Securities and Exchange Commission, find a proposal and trace it to see if it ever became a rule or regulation.

16.
The Growth of Pension Funds and the Inflation Issue

Employee pension plans come in different sizes, shapes, and formats. We should first distinguish between defined contribution and defined benefit pension plans. A *defined contribution* pension plan is one in which the firm's contribution rate is fixed—usually in terms of covered wages or salaries. When an employer's contribution rate is fixed, the pension benefit that an employee may eventually receive must be regarded as variable. A *defined benefit* pension plan, by contrast, "is one in which the benefits are established in advance by formula and the employer contributions are treated as the variable."[1]

Defined benefit pension plans fall into the following three major categories:

1. *Fixed Dollar per Month Benefit Pay Plan.* According to the provisions of such a plan, "benefits are determined by crediting a specific dollar amount (generally based on current pay levels) for each year of service."[2]
2. *Career Average Benefit Pay Plan.* A career average benefit formula may be viewed as similar to a fixed dollar per month formula "except that the pay to which the benefit formula is applied is average pay over the employee's entire career with the employer."[3]
3. *Final Pay Period Benefit Plan.* In the case of a final pay scheme, benefits are typically determined on the basis of an average taken over the final few years of employee service.

Our concern in this chapter is with the implications of employee pension plan programs, looked at from the following points of view:

1. The legal and legislative framework;
2. The nature of the liabilities that are undertaken by firms and the implications of these liabilities on firm financial risk;

---

[1] Dan M. McGill, *Fundamentals of Private Pensions*, 3d ed. (Homewood, Ill.: Richard D. Irwin, 1975), p. 98.
[2] *Business Roundtable*, "Study of Retirement Benefit Levels, Costs and Issues," Towers, Perrin, Forster & Crosby, Washington, D.C. (August, 1978), p. 6.
[3] *Ibid.*

3. The impact of inflation on the efficacy of an employee pension benefit program and on the financial interests of both the providers and eventual recipients of pension plan benefits;
4. The special problems that arise in the management of employee pension plan asset portfolios.

THE EMPLOYEE RETIREMENT INCOME SECURITY ACT OF 1974

In response to various abuses and ambiguities that existed among employee pension plans, the Employee Retirement Income Security Act (ERISA) was enacted by Congress in 1974. Title IV of the act established a program to ensure, subject to certain limitations, the vested rights of participants in certain qualified defined benefit employee pension plans. According to the act, such covered benefits are guaranteed by the Pension Benefit Guaranty Corporation (PBGC). Housed within the Labor Department, the PBGC was organized for the purpose of administering the act. In order to accomplish this goal, of course, the act also (and for the first time)

1. Set standards for the proper funding of vested benefits of plans that fall under its purview;
2. Established procedures for the termination of existing plans or freezing (i.e., halting the accumulation) of benefits;
3. Amortized unfunded vested benefits for terminated as well as ongoing plans.

According to the act, the sponsor of a plan who terminates the plan at a time when its assets are not sufficient to fund that portion of the vested benefits that are guaranteed by PBGC is liable to PBGC up to a limit of 30 percent of net worth.[4] Thus the act, in effect, "converted employer pension obligations from gratuities to corporate liabilities enforceable at law."[5] Few would argue that the enactment of ERISA has altered the capital structure of every firm having an unfunded pension liability. What is perhaps less obvious, but equally germane to the issue, is that the act also altered the financial risk profile of every firm that at some future date might find itself in such a position.

Legal Versus Financial Realities

Conditions that apply in the private sector of the economy are often affected by legislation in ways that were not anticipated before the fact or well understood after the fact. The primary issues that arose

---

[4] Modification of the act to increase this limit to 100 percent is now under consideration.

[5] Jack L. Treynor, Patrick J. Regan, and William W. Priest, Jr., *The Financial Reality of Pension Funding Under ERISA* (Homewood, Ill.: Dow Jones-Irwin, 1976), p. vii.

in implementation of a defined benefit pension guaranty program under ERISA were based on law, actuarial science, and accounting, but the variables that the resulting act most directly affect are financial variables. In a particularly insightful passage, Treynor, Regan, and Priest make the following point:

> The 200 pages of rules and exceptions to rules is the legal reality of ERISA. The standard mortality tables, turnover ratios, and historical rate of return studies constitute the actuarial reality. True to form, the accountants are still debating the accounting reality. But the marketplace dictates the financial reality.[6]

Financial Reality and Investment Implications

One point that Congress seems to have overlooked is that the ultimate source of the pension benefits that ERISA seeks to protect is not some mystical creature called a firm or the sponsor but very real creatures called investors. In a private enterprise economy, moreover, the earnings needed to fund a pension plan program properly are fueled not by government regulation but by sales and by credit and capital that only savers and investors can provide.

Financial Leverage Effects. The introduction of a defined benefit pension plan under ERISA by a firm is tantamount to the introduction of a fixed commitment obligation. This points to a very important distinction that should be made between a defined contribution and a defined benefit pension program. Under a defined contribution program, the only "fixed commitment" is to fund the firm's contribution agreement properly. This commitment can be undone, however, by termination of the program or by a properly negotiated freeze.

Under a defined benefit scheme, by contrast, the employer's fixed commitment is to provide an eventual benefit, not merely to fund it properly. Such benefits, moreover, may be viewed in terms of both stocks and flows. The *stock* of vested benefits, which already exists at any point in time as a fixed commitment, survives termination of a plan. There is also a *flow* component to this fixed commitment. Period by period, benefits accumulate according to the benefit formula. As we shall see in the next section, in addition to new vested benefits accumulating period by period for an ongoing plan, under either a career average or final pay scheme, the stock of existing benefits is constantly being redefined in accord with a monotonically increasing function of the price level and wage rates.

The introduction of a new fixed commitment obligation into the capital structure of a firm simultaneously introduces a source of possible

---

[6] *Ibid.*, p. 2.

insolvency and a constraint on the distribution of the firm's future earnings. The redefinition of existing vested benefits in tune with inflationary and other increases in wages, moreover, is tantamount to increasing a stockholder's degree of uncertainty as to the survival characteristics of the firm and his or her share in the flow of future earnings.

Firm financial leverage will result in an increase in the rate of return on owners' equity if, and only if, the source of leverage (say the proceeds from issuing a debt security) can be invested in such a way as to result in net proceeds that exceed the cost. According to this logic, to the extent that it applies, there is justification for the position that a firm's defined benefit programs produce nothing of value to the firm's stockholders. Some disadvantages, on the other hand, are clearer.

Clearly, the ability of an unleveraged firm to pay a dividend and/or to accumulate wealth to the advantage of the common stockholders goes down in hard times and up in good. A leveraged firm travels much the same path but with a vengeance and fewer departures from trend. In periods of economic decline, for example, fixed charges must still be met. What is truly unusual about the stock and flow of vested benefits that have to be funded under a defined benefit pension plan is that the changing level of resulting fixed commitment obligations is difficult to control or to correlate with the level of business activity.

The introduction of financial leverage through a firm's defined benefit pension plan program, as we have seen, is tantamount to introducing a constraint on the distribution of future earnings by the firm. We show in the appendix to this chapter that such a constraint produces a covariance effect. That is, as is shown in the appendix, the rate of return on a firm's equity shares becomes more highly correlated with the rate of return on the market as the level of fixed commitments increases relative to the firm's capital structure, and thus the degree of investment risk to be associated with the firm's shares is also affected.

Enter ERISA. ERISA established standards under which firms are required to determine actuarially and amortize pension fund benefits and unfunded past service costs as they accumulate. In this way, as we have seen, ERISA strengthened the claim that plan beneficiaries have on the distribution of future earnings. In this sense, and otherwise, the act has a bearing on firm financial risk profiles and on market risk premiums. The resulting market risk profiles, moreover, will be higher

1. The more closely related future benefit levels are to inflation-related variables;
2. The narrower a firm's equity cushion;
3. The narrower the spread between marginal revenue and cost;
4. The more variable, unconditionally, the firm's total revenue function;
5. The higher the degree of statistical relationship between a firm's total revenue function and the status of business conditions in general.

IMPACT OF INFLATION

A defined benefit pension plan seeks, as the name suggests, to define a flow of benefits that plan participants will eventually receive. Benefit formulas, on the other hand, vary according to their basic elements and quantitative specifics that include the means (if any) for integration of private pension benefits with Social Security benefits. Regardless of form or specifics, however, the purpose of an overall pension program is not merely to provide so many (unadjusted) dollars of income at retirement, but rather an amount that is sufficient to fund some target standard of living for the retiree. In a world of uncertain future inflation rates and changing social patterns, such a benefit package is difficult to define very precisely before the fact and may prove impossible to achieve after the fact.

Recent Developments in the Public and Private Sectors

Pension planners, employee representatives, legislators, and the various administrative agencies concerned are aware of the fact that inflation has a particularly onerous effect on fixed (i.e., unadjusted) dollar income recipients. Political action by interest groups has resulted in pressure for change in both the public and private sectors of the economy to alleviate the problem of inflation and more equitably distribute its burden.

The Social Security Act, for example, has recently been amended to link benefits to a price inflator. There is widespread concern, however, as to the adequacy of these changes as well as to the impact of the resulting cash drain on the current generation of producers and wage earners and on future generations. Some interesting dimensions of the Social Security program have been outlined as follows:[7]

1. The Social Security tax rate in 1978 was 6.05 percent on covered annual wages of $17,700, and this rate is paid equally by employers and by employees for a total of 12.1 percent. (Self-employed individuals pay $1\frac{1}{2}$ times the 6.05 percent rate.) By 1987, the tax rate will increase to 7.15 percent on an estimated $42,600 in annual wages. The Social Security Administration estimates that by 1987, 92 percent of wages and salaries will be covered by Social Security as opposed to 85 percent today.
2. Based on the above relationships, an employer's Social Security tax rate will increase from an average of 5.14 percent of payroll that applied in 1978 to 6.58 percent in 1987, a 28 percent increase.
3. By the end of 1977, there were 100 million workers with covered earnings taxed by Social Security; 17.1 million retired workers received benefits totaling $46.9 billion in fiscal 1977. This does not include payments to other beneficiaries under Social Security.

---

[7] *Business Roundtable*, "Study of Retirement Benefit Levels, Costs and Issues," Towers, Perrin, Forster & Crosby, Washington, D.C. (August, 1977), p. 2.

4. The gross national product for 1977 was $1,890.4 billion. Social Security benefits under all programs in 1977 totaled $103.2 billion (5.46 percent of the GNP).

Each generation thus is blessed with the task of funding the promises and/or miscalculations of the previous generation. Such a continuity of responsibility, though not explicit, is an integral part of the Social Security system and is highlighted by recent amendments to it. The same may be said of the private pension system to the extent that future benefits are linked to inflation, as in a final pay scheme.

In order for one generation of producers and wage earners to subsidize a previous one, however, in the form of benefit improvements and/or by bearing all or a part of the burden imposed by inflation, output (measured in real terms) must be growing at a rate that is sufficient to fund the resulting benefits. If output does not grow at the required rate, just two alternative possibilities remain: (1) the pension system must renege or (2) there must be a continuous relocation of wealth flowing from producers to nonproducers and denigration in the claim that producers have on the fruits of their own labor or capital. Such forces, moreover, once set in motion in a private enterprise economy, are self-propelling. In the face of the declining worker productivity figures that we have witnessed in recent years, declining birth rates, and increased life expectancies, therefore, there seems ample justification for concern about the financial implications of pension programs that have been undertaken in both the public and private sectors.

Over the past several decades, private pension plans have become an important source of retirement income for a growing number of workers. According to recent figures of the U.S. Chamber of Commerce, "private pension coverage extends to roughly half of the nongovernment working population."[8] Furthermore, most large corporations "have for the last quarter-century extended pension plan coverage to substantially their entire work force."[9] Most significantly, the period from 1970 to 1975, according to a 1975 Bankers Trust Company study, witnessed a trend toward liberalization of vesting provisions, both prior to the passage of ERISA in 1974 and at an accelerated rate in the period immediately thereafter.[10] Early retirement provisions were likewise liberalized, and pension benefits were generally improved—especially at the lower end of the income scale.

This trend toward liberalization and improvement was highlighted by a movement away from career average and fixed dollar benefit formulas and in the direction of benefit schemes based on final pay. Of

---

[8] *Ibid.*, p. 3.
[9] *Bankers Trust Company, 1975 Study of Corporate Pension Plans.* Bankers Trust Company, New York, N.Y., p. 6.
[10] *Ibid.*

course, the numbers and specific algebra that enter into a defined benefit pension plan formula vary from plan to plan and from firm to firm, but there is one implication that all plans of the "exclusively final pay" type hold in common. To the extent that the final period pay figures to which these plans relate are correlated with the inflation rate (i.e., with a price inflator such as the CPI), the cost of the pension programs must also be correlated with inflation. That is, "the annual cost of a pension plan to an employer will vary from plan to plan based on the composition of the participating group, the level of benefits to be paid, current levels of plan funding and the investment experience of the pension funds."[11]

Each of these variables, with the exception of composition, however, may be impacted by inflation. This relationship, moreover, which is mitigated only by the nature and extent of integration of future plan benefits with Social Security benefits, introduces the rather ominous prospect that future pension fund costs may increase in accord with an exponential function of time (in accord with inflation rates) that is increasing at a fairly high rate.

Income Distribution Effects

Inflation imposes financial hardship on pensioners whose incomes are either fixed at the date of retirement or will fail to keep up. A pensioner whose income is continuously adjusted by a price inflator, by constrast, might actually benefit by inflation. The most commonly used price inflator, after all, is based on the change in price of the market basket consumed by a hypothetical blue-collar urban worker supporting a mate and two offspring. The use of such an index as a continuous adjustment factor applied to pensioner benefits would clearly result in a redistribution of wealth in favor of the recipients of such a flow of benefits. That is,

> Inflation is generally measured by changes in the consumer price index (CPI). However, there is some question as to whether the CPI accurately reflects inflation because some of the factors reflected in price changes of goods and services (e.g., quality improvements) should probably be discounted. There is even more concern over the adequacy of the CPI as a measure of how inflation affects retired persons.[12]

The impact of relatively high inflation rates such as we have experienced in recent years can, perhaps, be better appreciated by noting that an inflation rate of *only* 8 percent would cause prices approximately to double every nine years and to increase more than tenfold in thirty

---

[11] *Business Roundtable*, 1977, p. 7.
[12] *Ibid.*, p. 8.

years. An individual at age 35, for example, who plans to retire at age 65, must contemplate the prospect that a pension plan benefit of $10,062 a month would be required to support the same standard of living that a $1,000-a-month benefit would support today, disregarding taxes. Assuming an inflation rate of 10 percent, this figure jumps to $17,449.40 a month, and using a 15 percent rate we break the bank with a $66,211.77-a-month requirement. This result, in light of recent inflation rates, has important implications regarding both the funding of pension plan obligations and the management of pension plan asset portfolios.

FUNDING THE PENSION PLAN

As previously stated, ERISA "converted employer pension obligations from gratuities to corporate liabilities enforceable at law."[13] Prior to the passage of ERISA, pension fund obligations were commonly used as a surreptitious source of "cheap" capital. As a result, employee pension plans were often seriously and intentionally underfunded. Under these conditions, moreover, the incentive might occasionally arise (as in the business downturn that followed the so-called October war of 1973) to terminate expensive employees before they can become fully vested. The 1974 act, however, established standards for funding and vesting.

Actuarial funding formulas are, in general, driven by two primary variables:

1. The interest rate assumption, r, which represents the annual rate of return that the actuary "expects" the pension fund assets to earn.
2. The wage assumption, w, which represents the annual rate at which covered wages are expected to grow.

The interest rate assumption is a key actuarial assumption. "The higher the expected investment return, the smaller the unfunded pension liability and the lower the required company contribution."[14] Indeed, all other things being equal, "a 1 percent increase in the interest rate assumption allows for an increase in pension benefits or a decrease in pension contributions of 16 percent to 30 percent."[15] In reality, however, the setting of an interest rate assumption is, in general, more art than science. Beauty, of course, is in the eyes of the beholder.

One must realize that the IRS has a vital interest in the way a pension plan is set up and funded. In order for the employer contributions

---

[13] Treynor *et al.*, *The Financial Reality of Pension Funding Under ERISA*, p. vii.
[14] *Ibid.*, p. 18.
[15] *Ibid.*

to a pension plan to "qualify" for tax-exempt status, the plan must be "general." A plan, for example, which is *obviously* set up to serve the interests of the boss or a chosen few does not qualify in this sense.[16] One factor that explicitly or implicitly affects the parameters of a rate-setting formula, therefore, is the tax-exempt status of the firm's contributions—which is of obvious interest to the IRS.

The current yield to maturity being offered on long-term corporate bonds has always served not so much as a basis for setting but as a means for justifying the present interest rate assumption of a proposed change. This is so for at least two reasons. First, according to ERISA, bonds held to maturity can be carried at book value regardless of what changes take place in actual market value in response to changing market interest rates. Actuaries are generally not financial specialists and, in the interests of being "prudent," need some sort of benchmark.

There are a number of fallacies, however, which—from the point of view of finance as distinct from actuarial science—we may wish to consider. First, the interest rate assumption cannot be changed often enough to reflect actual market movements. As recently as 1976, for example, the norm was 5 or 6 percent. Partly in response to the bond market movements in 1980 and 1981, and partly in response to the fact that external capital became very expensive during that period, the rates used by a number of major plans edged upward during the period to the 9 to 11 percent range. For some reason that is difficult to understand, however, the wage assumption tends to be somewhat less volatile than the interest rate assumption.

A second problem with this procedure stems from the fact that pension plan asset portfolios usually are not pure bond portfolios. Indeed, there is no restriction under ERISA on the portion of a pension plan asset portfolio that may be invested in equity securities, provided only that all investments be in accord with a prudence rule that we take up in the next section. Add to this the fact that actuaries, who generally set the interest rate assumption, do not typically participate in the management of the asset portfolio. Indeed, one of the major shortcomings in the private pension field is a general lack of coordination, or even effective communication, among actuaries, money managers, and the firm's financial managers (who, more often than not, are not directly involved in questions having to do with employee pension plans).

The situation is clearly distressing. What is even more distressing is the fact that although the 1974 act did succeed in correcting a number

---

[16] This is not to say, of course, that plans in general, and defined benefit pension plans in particular, have not been sold to employers on precisely this basis. Our point here is that the IRS takes a very dim view of the use of this particular tax exemption for any purpose other than the one originally intended—to encourage the development of private pension plans in the interests of employees in general.

of situations that needed correcting, it succeeded also at exacerbating a number of other problems. With its emphasis on the legal, actuarial, and accounting realities of pension plans (in that order), it fails to come to grips with the financial realities.

MANAGING THE PENSION PLAN ASSETS

The concept of risk reduction through diversification has much intuitive appeal. So much so, in fact, that the *catch words* of modern portfolio theory were virtually written into the act. According to the Prudent Man Rule, as worded in the original act and interpreted more recently in a Labor Department pronouncement under the heading "Investment of Plan Assets by Fiduciaries Under ERISA the Prudence Rule,"

1. The relative riskiness of a specific investment or investment course of action does not render such investment or investment course of action either per se prudent or per se imprudent.
2. The prudence of an investment decision should not be judged without regard to the role that the proposed investment or investment course of action plays within the overall plan portfolio.
3. The regulation is not intended to suggest either that any relevant or material attributes of a contemplated investment may properly be ignored or disregarded, or that a particular plan investment should be deemed to be prudent solely by reason of the propriety of the aggregate risk/return characteristics of the plan's portfolio.[17]

Strictly interpreted, therefore, this Labor Department interpretation would seem to mandate that pension plan asset portfolios be managed according to the principles of portfolio efficiency and portfolio diversification, as outlined in Part 3 of this book and in accord with an integrative philosophy such as that outlined in Chapter 11. In fact, by contrast, the Markowitz portfolio selection technique has had little or no effect on the community of professional money managers and no impact at all on the legal profession or the field of actuarial science.

Although the Prudent Man Rule does require professional money managers to "consider" various measurements, it says nothing about what in the world to do with them. Certainly, one would infer from the rule that diversification is a good thing; however, one cannot possibly infer from this wording what precisely is meant by diversification or whether or not it is also mandated. Clearly it would be imprudent for a money manager to accept an unnecessary risk.

---

[17]*BNA Pension Reporter*, No. 245, June 25, 1979, the Bureau of National Affairs, Inc., Washington, D.C., 20037, pages unnumbered. See in particular section headed, "Labor Department Issues: Final Regulation of Prudent Investment of Plan Assets."

There is nothing in the act, however, that explains at what rate it is "prudent" to exchange increased expected return for higher risk, and at what point (or within what range) such an exchange would be deemed imprudent. Presumably, the act anticipates (with or without justification) that the ex-ante interest rate assumption used in calculating a funding rate should correspond, at least approximately, to ex-post rates of return. But the act does not tell the money manager how to weigh the market risk associated with higher rates of return against the risk that a pension plan asset portfolio may not earn enough over time to fund the benefits that have been promised. Nor does the act warn that the plan sponsor may not be financially able to make up the difference.

The Role of Acadamic Finance

Even though the pension fund area has received a considerable amount of attention in recent years, for some reason the problem has received little or no comment in the literature of academic finance. This is most unfortunate, as the variables of real interest now are financial variables. There is, as we have pointed out elsewhere in the text, a pressing need for an integration of methodologies in finance. There is also a pressing need for better integration than now exists with other specialties—especially actuarial science. As a useful first step, we suggest that pension funding approaches proceed according to the following rationale.

Principle of Efficient Diversification. The object of portfolio diversification is risk reduction. Efficient diversification in the sense of a firm's pension fund investment policy refers to the combination of financial assets in a pension plan portfolio in such a way as to minimize the degree of risk required to achieve a particular target rate of return. Such a target rate of return should be decided on the basis of

1. The firm's benefit formula;
2. The actuarially defined interest rate assumption;
3. Present security market conditions;
4. The reward to variability ratio that is commensurate with present market conditions under efficient diversification.

Fundamental Security Analysis. Diversification in the sense of risk reduction is achieved on the basis of quantitative measurements that can be misleading, as was shown in Chapter 11. The Labor Department's pronouncement cited above emphasizes the importance of such measurements, but it also stresses the need to consider other sources of information. We believe that the integrative approach suggested in Chapter

11 provides a useful basis for considering both quantitative and qualitative information in the context of optimization analysis.

Periodic Review of Portfolio Composition. Security market conditions change frequently. The efficiency of a pension plan asset portfolio should be reestablished whenever the critical balance is broken by changing market conditions. A pension plan asset portfolio should be reviewed at least on a quarterly basis and otherwise as conditions may warrant.

Periodic Trading. The need for periodic review does not imply a need for periodic trading. Trading should be kept to an absolute minimum, and securities should be traded only when there is a clear and compelling reason to do so. In this regard, firms that execute trades for a fee should not also be employed as pension fund money managers.

Periodic Review of Pension Fund Portfolio Managers. The principle of portfolio efficiency outlined in Part 3 of the book provides a clear and systematic objective to be realized in managing a pension plan asset portfolio. It also provides a criteria for judging the adequacy of a portfolio manager's ex-post performance. The investment performance of a pension plan asset portfolio should be periodically reviewed according to these criteria and also on the basis of how well the risk-rate of return characteristics of the asset portfolio conforms to the ex-ante policy that should have been jointly agreed to by (1) the firm's financial managers, (2) the pension actuary, and (3) the investment manager—whether he or she be internal or external. Investment strategies, such as various technical approaches or ad-hoc purchasing schemes, that cannot be justified *both* on the basis of diversification and fundamental security analysis should be regarded as being imprudent, regardless of the level of ex-post return.

Asset Portfolio Investment Policy. The plan sponsor is ultimately responsible in the case of a defined benefit pension plan to deliver (i.e., fund) the benefits promised by the plan. The plan sponsor, therefore, or a consulting service acting on behalf of the plan sponsor, should participate directly in establishing an investment policy for the asset portfolio. Matters of policy should not be left to the money manager. Most firms, incidentally, do not at present have such a policy—at least not in written form. When one considers the nature of the commitment undertaken by an employer with a defined benefit pension plan, and the importance of the "guaranteed" benefits to his or her employees, one can only suppose that such indifference results, at least in part, from a general failure to grasp a single essential point—the pension plan obligations under ERISA are real corporate liabilities enforceable at law.

Appendix

Firm Pension Plans, ERISA, and Investor Attitudes Toward Risk

The introduction of financial leverage is tantamount to introducing a constraint on the distribution of future earnings by the firm. Hamada has shown that such a constraint produces a covariance effect—that is, rates of return on the firm's equity shares become more highly correlated with the rate of return on the market and thus become subject to a greater degree of systematic risk.[18] We argue in the chapter that the introduction of a defined benefit pension plan into the capital structure of a firm is a form of leverage that produces a covariance effect similar to the one demonstrated by Hamada. The purpose of this appendix is to demonstrate this result in a rigorous fashion.

According to the general equilibrium framework of the capital asset pricing model introduced in Chapter 12, the expected rate of return on security i in period t may be written as follows:

$$E(\tilde{r}_{it}) = r_f + \delta \operatorname{Cov}(\tilde{r}_i, \tilde{r}_m), \tag{16.1}$$

where

r_f = the risk free rate of interest;
$\{\tilde{r}_i\}$ = the rates of return on security i;
$\{\tilde{r}_m\}$ = the rates of return on the market portfolio, whose variance is denoted $\operatorname{Var}(\tilde{r}_m)$;

and the reward to variability ratio

$$\delta = \frac{[E(\tilde{r}_m) - r_f]}{\operatorname{Var}(\tilde{r}_m)}$$

is the same for all individual capital assets that trade in the same market.

Assume that financial markets are perfect markets and in equilibrium. Assume, moreover, that a particular firm's dividend policy has no effect on the market's valuation of its equity shares. Now let

$\tilde{V}_{it}$ = the equilibrium market value of firm i in period t,
$E(\tilde{V}_{i, t+1})$ = the expected market value of the same firm one period later,
$E(\tilde{C}_{it})$ = the expected dividend to be paid by firm i in period t,
$E(\tilde{Y}_{it})$ = the expected earnings of firm i in period t net of depreciation but prior to the deduction of interest and tax payments.

---

[18] Robert S. Hamada, "Portfolio Analysis, Market Equilibrium and Corporation Finance," *Journal of Finance*, Vol. 24 (March 1969), pp. 13-31.

According to these definitions,

$$E(\tilde{r}_{it}) = \frac{[E(\tilde{V}_{i,t+1}) - \tilde{V}_{it}] + E(\tilde{C}_{it})}{\tilde{V}_{it}} \tag{16.2}$$

$$= \frac{E(\tilde{Y}_{it})}{\tilde{V}_{it}},$$

where

$$E(\tilde{Y}_{it}) = [E(\tilde{V}_{i,t+1}) - \tilde{V}_{it}] + E(\tilde{C}_{it}).$$

Now suppose that firm i alters its capital structure by issuing debt whose market value is D and on which it pays the riskless rate r_f. Assume further that there are no transactions costs and that firm i uses the net proceeds from the sale of bonds to buy back its own equity from the market and at the market price $\tilde{p}_{it}$. Let us further assume that firm i alters none of its policy variables, so that it is the same real firm before and after such a transaction in its own securities. An asterisk is used to identify firm i's equity after the transaction. Thus from Equation (16.2) we get

$$E(\tilde{r}_{it}^*) = \frac{E(\tilde{Y}_{it}) - r_f D}{\tilde{V}_{it}^*}. \tag{16.3}$$

By substitution from Equation (16.1) we get

$$\frac{E(\tilde{Y}_{it})}{\tilde{V}_{it}} = r_f + \delta \operatorname{Cov}(\tilde{r}_i, \tilde{r}_m) \tag{16.2a}$$

$$\frac{E(\tilde{Y}_{it}) - r_f D}{\tilde{V}_{it}^*} = r_f + \delta \operatorname{Cov}(\tilde{r}_i^* \tilde{r}_m). \tag{16.3a}$$

By isolating $E(\tilde{Y}_{it})$ in Equations (16.2a) and (16.3a), respectively, and equating terms, we get[19]

$$\tilde{V}_{it}[r_f + \delta \operatorname{Cov}(\tilde{r}_i, \tilde{r}_m)] = \tilde{V}_{it}^*[\delta \operatorname{Cov}(\tilde{r}_i^* \tilde{r}_m) + r_f(1 + D/\tilde{V}_{it}^*)]. \tag{16.4}$$

Exploiting the definitions of Equation (16.2), we get the following covariance form:

---

[19] The reader who reaches a dead end in his or her attempt to transform (16.3a) into the term shown on the right-hand side of (16.4) should multiply both sides of the expression by $1/\tilde{V}_{it}$ at that point.

$$\text{Cov}(\tilde{r}_i,\tilde{r}_m) = E\{[E(\tilde{Y}_{it})/\tilde{V}_{it} - E(\tilde{Y}_{it}/\tilde{V}_{it})][\tilde{r}_m - E(\tilde{r}_m)]\} \quad (16.5)$$
$$= \text{Cov}[E(\tilde{Y}_{it}),\tilde{r}_m]/\tilde{V}_{it}.$$

By substitution from Equation (16.3), by similar logic but noting that the variability of earnings before fixed charges is not affected by the fixed changes, we obtain

$$\text{Cov}(\tilde{r}_i^*,\tilde{r}_m) = \text{Cov}[E(\tilde{Y}_{it}),\tilde{r}_m]/\tilde{V}_{it}^*. \quad (16.6)$$

By substitution (16.5) and (16.6) into (16.4), one obtains

$$\tilde{V}_{it}\left\{\frac{\delta}{\tilde{V}_{it}}\text{Cov}[E(\tilde{Y}_{it}),r_m] + r_f\right\} + \tilde{V}_{it}^*\left\{\frac{\delta}{\tilde{V}_{it}^*}\text{Cov}[E(\tilde{Y}_{it}),r_m] + r_f\left(1 + \frac{D}{\tilde{V}_{it}^*}\right)\right\}$$

which reduces to

$$\tilde{V}_{it} = \tilde{V}_{it}^* + D, \quad (16.7)$$

which is the result we seek. We note from (16.7) that

$$\tilde{V}_{it}^* < \tilde{V}_{it}.$$

By logical substitution into (16.5) and (16.6), it follows immediately that

$$\text{Cov}(\tilde{r}_i^*,\tilde{r}_m) > \text{Cov}(\tilde{r}_i,\tilde{r}_m), \quad (16.8)$$

which is no longer an intuitive result but a proven one.

One may relax the assumption, implicit in Equation (16.3), that the market charges a risky firm (on its fixed commitments) a periodic rate r_f appropriate to a riskless asset. If a leveraged firm i^* is riskier than the unleveraged (but otherwise identical) firm i, then the leveraged firm i^* is even more risky the more onerous is the nature of its fixed commitments. The relationship between Equations (16.2) and (16.3) is not destroyed by relaxing this assumption, therefore, but is made stronger. The neat mathematical solution survives also but is reduced to the status of a boundary condition.

One assumption, however, we do not wish to relax because it provides a near-perfect analogy of the defined benefit pension plan setting. The purpose of assuming that firm i^* uses the proceeds of a sale of fixed commitment financial obligations to retire an appropriate portion of firm i's equity shares is merely to change the capital structure of the same real firm without at the same time affecting its stock of real capital. This is tantamount to introducing a *constraint* on the distribution of future earnings to be derived from that stock of real capital. This constraint is what leads to the covariance effect described by Equation (16.8). The more onerous is the resulting constraint, moreover, the greater will be the disparity between the two sides of the inequality in (16.8).

Precisely in accord with this logic, the 1974 ERISA Act converted the defined benefit pension plan obligations of firms from gratuities to corporate liabilities. That is, the act mandated that firms "actuarially determine and amortize" Unfunded Past Service Costs (UPSC), and thus "strengthened the claim that plan beneficiaries have on corporate earnings."[20] Thus the act imposed new constraints on the distribution of future earnings and an onerous redefiniton of an existing one. The 1974 act, therefore, does have a direct bearing on firm risk profiles in the sense of Equation (16.8) and on market expectation and risk trade-offs.

Questions

1. Distinguish between a defined contribution and a defined contribution employee pension plan in terms of the nature of the commitment and risk undertaken by management.
2. In the case of defined benefit pension plan agreements, there are a variety of benefit formulas in use. Three different types of defined benefit pension plan benefit schemes are discussed in the chapter. Discuss and contrast these three agreements in terms of the different commitments undertaken by management and the implied risk.
3. Much has been said about the Employee Retirement Income Security Act of 1974. In what sense did this act change the "financial reality" of employee pension plans in general, and of defined benefit pension plans in particular.
4. Under ERISA, can an employer terminate a plan at any time that he or she feels that the firm can no longer afford the trouble or expense of sponsoring one?
5. It has been stated that ERISA altered the capital structure of every firm having an unfunded pension liability.
   (a) What is the difference between an unfunded and a funded pension plan liability?
   (b) Does "proper funding" at present rates ensure that tomorrow's liability, ex-post, may not turn out to be at least partly underfunded?
   (c) In what sense does an unfunded pension liability "alter the capital structure of the firm"?
   (d) In what sense, moreover, might pension plan obligations not

_____
[20] *Moody's Bond Survey*, Vol. 70, No. 8 (February 20, 1978).

yet accrued by the sponsor be viewed, ex-ante, as unfunded liabilities?

(e) What is the impact of such liabilities on the degree of risk that a stockholder assumes by the purchase of the firm's equity shares, and how does this risk (i.e., which is specific to the pension fund variables) manifest itself?

6. ERISA places constraints on the management of firms that sponsor pension plans in general, and defined benefit pension plans in particular. The act also places constraints on other parties, however. Identify these other parties and explain the nature of the constraints that are imposed upon them.

7. In what sense is the introduction of a defined benefit pension plan a form of financial leverage, and in what sense is it not a form of financial leverage? That is, in what sense is the analogy appropriate and in what sense is it not?

8. In the case of a benefit freeze, what sort of benefits are "frozen" and what sort are not?

9. Explain some impacts of inflation on employee benefits and the value of employee benefits under each of the pension benefit arrangements discussed in the chapter.

10. Explain the impact that inflation is likely to have on the degree of risk assumed by the pension fund sponsor under each of the pension benefit plan arrangements discussed in the chapter.

11. In what sense may an employer "liberalize" his or her pension plan arrangement?

12. What is a social security offset?

13. In what sense, under inflation, might the pension fund result in a redistribution of income and wealth effect?

14. What is an interest rate and a wage assumption? How are they used? By whom are they used? How and why are they derived?

15. Why should the IRS have any interest in how an employee pension benefit plan is funded and for whose benefit it was established?

16. It was pointed out in the chapter that bonds held to maturity may be carried on the books at "book," regardless of what happens to the market interest rate (not so of stock, of course). Under these conditions, should a firm invest a relatively high or low percentage of the pension fund benefits in bonds? Might your answer be influenced, at least in part, by differential rates of return on various investment assets that are available on the market and by the firm's interest rate and wage assumptions? Discuss.

17. There is clear evidence that the management of sponsoring firms has not, in the past, paid as much attention to the management of pension plan assets as would be appropriate. The evidence in this regard, of course, goes considerably deeper and further than what

is presented in this brief introductory chapter. Nevertheless, a strong case is made in the chapter. Discuss.

18. Some shortcomings of the capital asset pricing model, its tests of validity and assumptions, are discussed in Chapter 13. Obviously, the present authors are not especially sympathetic to the cases made by various proponents of the model. Nevertheless, the capital asset pricing model is used and applied in the appendix to this chapter to make our own case. Are we justified in using the model in this way, in light of the case we have made against it and our criticism of others? Discuss.

PART 6
Stock Analysis

17.

Sources of Information

We will devote the greater part of Chapter 17 to an overview of frequently used investment information sources currently available and, in addition, suggest methods for locating titles of sources not discussed.

The subjects of sources of information and security market regulation are interrelated since the federal securities legislation has as its purpose not only to provide fair and equitable trading markets for investors but also to furnish investors with sufficient, reliable, and accurate information on securities that will enable them to make decisions. Reports filed with the Securities Exchange Commission are an important source of data and will, therefore, be briefly discussed in this chapter.

Information on economic and security market trends and knowledge about industry and company developments are necessary ingredients for intelligent investment decisions. Sources of such information include financial news periodicals, statistical services, government publications, trade journals, industry publications, company annual and interim reports, offering prospectuses, and significant literature furnished by the research-oriented brokerage houses.

GENERAL REFERENCE SOURCES

Overall guides and business encyclopedias are available to aid in locating a variety of source material dealing with a specific subject. Their titles can be found at the end of this chapter in Appendix B, General Investment Reference Sources.

If one must choose among all the "tools," Lorna Daniells's "Business Information Sources" could well be the most useful. For example, under mutual funds are found listings such as the *United Mutual Fund Selector*, United Business Service Company's semimonthly newsletter, which gives performance comparisons; Wiesenberger Services' *Invest-*

ment Companies (annual and supplements); *Barron's* "Quarterly Mutual Fund Record"; *Financial World*, which reports on mutual funds on a quarterly basis; and *Forbes'* August 15 "Annual Mutual Fund Survey." Paul Wasserman's *Encyclopedia of Business Information Sources* serves a purpose similar to Daniells's guide. Arranged alphabetically by subject, its table of contents lists all subjects convered with cross-references to additional and related topics.

Major Indexes—General Business News

The major indexes for general business news are the *New York Times Index*, *Facts on File*, *The Wall Street Journal Index*, the *Funk and Scott Index of Corporations and Industries*, the *Funk and Scott Index International*, and *Business Periodicals Index*.

Brief descriptions of these publications follow:

1. *The New York Times Index*. Biweekly index that cumulates annually. Published approximately two months after the period covered. News items are arranged by subject in chronological order. An adequate indication of the substance of each article is indicated.
2. *Facts on File*. Published by Facts on File, Inc. A weekly publication with index cumulated semiannually and annually. Usually received one week after the news date. Valuable because of its prompt availability. Has concise summaries of important events and is quite comprehensive.
3. *The Wall Street Journal Index*. A monthly index cumulated annually. Arrangement is in two sections: Corporate News and General News. Includes list of book reviews.
4. *Funk & Scott Index of Corporations and Industries*. A weekly publication cumulated monthly, quarterly, and annually. Indexes "over 750 financial publications, business-oriented newspapers, trade magazines, and special reports." Covers general economic information as well as companies, products, and industry information.
5. *Funk & Scott Index International: Industries, Countries, Companies*. A monthly, cumulated annually. Covers similar information about the rest of the world gleaned from the world's leading newspapers, business publications, trade journals, and bank reviews. Over 6,000 abstracts each month.
6. *Business Periodicals Index*. Published monthly except August by the H. W. Wilson Company. A subject index to approximately 275 periodicals covering many fields of business. Arrangement is alphabetical by subject. Book reviews are listed following the main body of the index.

Other Reference Sources

In addition to indexes there are reference sources with which anyone concerned with business research should be familiar. A few of these are the *Congressional Quarterly*, the *Federal Register*, *Directory Information Service*, and Ulrich's serial directories.

A brief description of their coverage follows:

1. *Congressional Quarterly Weekly Report.* News on Congress, government, and politics. Good coverage of court decisions involving securities.
2. *Federal Register.* In 1935 the Federal Register Act established the *Federal Register* as a daily publication to record all executive orders and administrative regulations of the various agencies of the government. All regulations must be published in it to be legally binding. Each issue is indexed. Monthly indexes cumulate quarterly and annually. Each issue contains three sections: Notices, Proposed Rules, and Rules and Regulations (those which have taken effect).
3. *Directory Information Service.* A reference periodical that covers business and industrial directories, professional and scientific rosters, and other lists and guides of all kinds. Published by Information Enterprises. Broad coverage and currency make this service valuable.
4. *Ulrich's International Periodicals Directory, Ulrich's Irregular Serials and Annuals,* and *Ulrich's Quarterly.* The *Quarterly,* which began in March 1977, presents information on new serial titles, title changes, and cessations.

GENERAL ECONOMIC AND BACKGROUND INFORMATION

Investors are interested in the behavior of fundamental economic factors underlying corporate earnings and performance. They also should have knowledge of changing market conditions. Current general economic and market information is available from many sources.

Financial News Sources

Many investors obtain most of their *daily* financial information by reading the financial pages of newspapers. Company earnings reports and items on new products and manufacturing processes, mergers, acquisitions, proxy contests, and current business and industry trends are featured. Financial sections of newspapers include statistics and indexes of general business activity; complete transactions and prices for securities listed on major exchanges, and bid and asked prices for securities traded over-the-counter; the well-known and much quoted Dow Jones and Standard & Poor's market averages; and conditions in the money market. Among the most useful daily publications are the *New York Times, The Wall Street Journal,* and the *Journal of Commerce.* Useful weekly publications include *Barron's National Business & Financial Weekly,* the *Insiders' Chronicle,* the *M/G Financial Weekly Market Digest,* and the *Wall Street Transcript.* The weekly publications differ greatly. *Barron's* regular features include corporate reports, weekly highs and lows, sales, P/E ratios and yields for the New York Stock Exchange composite transactions, large block transactions, the American Stock Exchange composite transactions, options trading on all exchanges where traded, over-the-counter market transactions including highs and lows for the week, highs and lows for selected securities on other exchanges, listed bond quotations, Ginnie Mae pass-through issues, mutual funds data, and futures trading statistics.

Barron's "Pulse of Industry and Trade" statistics range from auto output to gasoline inventories to building contracts; and *Barron's* "Economic and Financial Indicators" are good sources for recent figures. For example, finding published elsewhere as recent a figure for the gross federal debt is difficult.

The *Insiders' Chronicle*, the name given to the editorial section of the *Commercial and Financial Chronicle*, publishes selected listings (approximately 400 companies) of purchases and sales of insiders' stock holdings.

Another feature of the *Insiders' Chronicle* is the listing of the 144 letter stocks outstanding. Letter stocks, or "restricted securities" as they are often called, are issues not involving any public offering, sold to investors who supposedly do not require knowledge of the information in a registration statement. These investors sign a "letter" stating that they are purchasing the stock for investment only. To prove this they must hold the stock for a period of time, usually two years.

The *Insiders' Chronicle* has a statistical section that retains the *Commercial and Financial Chronicle* name. In contrast with *Barron's* weekly figures, the *Chronicle* provides the highs and lows for each day of the week for consolidated trading for all New York Stock Exchange issues, the stock record from the Pacific Stock Exchange, the consolidated trading for all American Stock Exchange issues, the stock record from the Midwest Stock Exchange, and the stock record from the Toronto Stock Exchange.

The *Media General Financial Weekly Market Digest*, the youngest of the four publications, serves a very special purpose in providing so many—over 90 pages—statistics aimed at helping the investor measure the profitability of an investment. Figure 17-1 illustrates the type of comparative information given for each stock. The other three weekly publications do not give similar detailed indicators of price movements and trends. Figure 17-2 illustrates Media General's section on stocks by industry, which was added with the August 15, 1977, issue. It facilitates comparison within an industry.

The *Wall Street Transcript* covers speeches given by company representatives before security analysts' meetings. Each issue has one or more "Roundtables" in which several industry experts report on the outlook for their industry. The *Transcript's* "Technical Corner," "Options Corner," "Connoisseur's Corner" (collectibles as an investment), "Executive's Corner" (the speeches by company executives), "Tax Notes," "Wall to Wall Street" (general financial news such as mergers, new processes, etc.), and "Executive Alert" (advice for the busy executive concerning labor, insurance, accounting rules, health, etc.) are popular attractions for today's business person and investor.

New York Stock Exchange

Abb-All — Price and Volume

Name	Ind Grp	Symbol	Weekly High	Weekly Low	Weekly Close	Change Amt	Change Pct	200-Day Mov Avg: Avg	200-Day Mov Avg: % of Avg Today	52-Week High	52-Week Low	Volume Weekly Total	Pct of Shares Outstndg	20-Day Moving Avg: Avg	20-Day Moving Avg: % of Avg This Week	$ Volume Weekly
-	-	-	$	$	$	$	%	$	%	$	$	00	%	00	%	$000
Abbott Labs	151	ABT	50¼	49⅛	49¾	+ ¼	+ .5	45.63	109	54¼	38⅞	1,373	.46	308	89	6,826
ACF Industries	284	ACF	33⅜	31⅝	33⅜	+ ⅞	+ 2.7	35.32	94	39⅜	31⅜	538	.62	66	163	1,739
Acme-Clevelnd	291	AMT	11¼	11	11¼	0	.0	12.11	93	13⅜	8½	59	.13	17	69	65
Adams Drug	501	ADG	3	2¾	2⅞	- ⅛	- 4.2	2.94	98	3½	2⅝	18	.04	24	15	5
Adams Express	272	ADX	12⅜	12⅛	12⅛	- ¼	- 2.0	12.15	100	13¼	11	262	.18	35	150	321
Adams-Millis	562	ALL	4⅞	4⅝	4⅝	- ⅛	- 2.6	4.19	110	5⅛	3¾	100	.44	16	125	47
Addresso-Mult	081	AIN	13⅛	12½	12⅞	- ⅛	- 1.0	12.72	101	15⅜	9¾	472	.57	123	77	605
Aetna Life Cas	261	AET	33⅞	32½	33⅞	+ ⅜	+ 1.1	33.75	100	38⅜	28⅜	3,450	.65	752	92	11,499
Aguirre Co	442	AGG	14⅜	14	14¼	- ¼	- 1.7	13.88	103	16	9	41	.27	6	137	58
Ahmanson H F	541	AHM	18⅞	18½	18⅞	+ ⅛	+ .7	18.06	105	21½	13⅞	136	.06	94	29	254
Aileen Inc	562	AEE	3	2⅝	3	+ ⅛	+ 4.3	3.06	98	3⅞	2⅝	142	.28	23	123	40
Air Pd & Chem	101	APD	25¼	24⅛	24⅞	+ ⅜	+ 1.5	25.83	96	35⅛	21	587	.21	211	56	1,445
Airborne Frgt	223	ABF	14	13⅝	13⅞	+ ¼	+ 1.8	13.30	104	16¾	11½	314	.76	41	153	435
Airco Inc	101	AN	33¼	30⅝	30¾	0	.0	30.49	101	34⅛	24¾	2,995	2.54	303	198	9,496
Akzona Inc	101	AXO	15	14½	14½	- ⅛	- .9	16.67	87	19⅛	13⅜	51	.04	17	60	76
Alabama Gas	602	AGA	17⅛	16¾	17	+ ⅛	+ .7	16.22	105	18⅜	14⅛	25	.13	5	100	42
Alaska Intste	341	AKI	14¾	12¾	14¾	0	.0	17.62	84	22	12¾	706	2.19	76	186	955
Albany Intl	294	ABY	15⅝	15½	15⅝	- ⅛	- .8	17.54	89	20⅛	15¼	6	.01	5	24	9
Alberto-Culver	121	ACV	7½	7⅛	7¼	0	.0	6.90	105	8⅛	5¾	202	.47	25	162	149
Albertsons Inc	511	ABS	26⅜	25½	26¼	- ⅛	- .5	23.14	113	27¼	19	230	.31	48	96	595

Trend to Market, Earnings Per Share, Relative Price

Name	200-Day Price Index Vs Market	200-Day Price Index Vs Industry	Price Trend (% Per Day) Last 30 Days	Price Trend (% Per Day) Last 5 Days	Volume Trend (% Per Day) Last 30 Days	Volume Trend (% Per Day) Last 5 Days	Last Fiscal Year	Latest Change Amt	Latest Change Pct	5-Year Annual Growth Rate	Profit Margin	P/E Ratio Today	Mkt Value To Revenue	Percent of Market Norm	Percent of Industry Norm	5-Yr Price High	5-Yr Price Low
	-	-	%	%	%	%	$	$	%	%	%	-	%	%	%	$	$
Abbott Labs	119	120	+ .10	- .42	+1.68	- .86	3.26	+ .48n	+ 21	+23	8.5↑	13.3	136	184	124	55.25	15.25
ACF Industries	106	105	- .11	+ .57	- .64	+ 5.38	3.92	- .01s	0	+12	5.3↓	8.5	45	130	118	40.87	19.18
Acme-Clevelnd	104	105	- .18	+ .35	-2.65	-54.26	.65	+ .04n	+ 8	-10	1.5↓	16.3	26	76	96	18.50	7.00
Adams Drug	101	109	+ .09	- .82	+2.68	+10.71	.59	+ .03s	+ 17	- 1	1.8↑	4.6	9	53	80	26.75	1.37
Adams Express	100	102	+ .24	- .84	+1.47	-27.44	NA	NA	NA	NA	NA	NA	NA	NA	NA	14.75	7.00
Adams-Millis	113	111	+ .71	- .51	+2.32	-39.63	.52	+ .04s	+ 24	- 3	1.9↑	8.3	17	59	77	13.37	1.75
Addresso-Mult	106	103	- .09	+ .00	-5.45	-11.39	- 1.70	- 2.52f	NE	-30	- 2.4↓	NE	18	153	135	49.50	3.00
Aetna Life Cas	113	107	+ .02	+ .05	+ .58	+ 6.36	3.91	+ 1.88s	+115	+ 7	2.9↑	5.9	25	123	105	41.00	15.12
Aguirre Co	137	119	+ .08	- .59	-5.14	+21.88	.10	- .04n	NE	-37	1.4↓	237.5	150	268	230	17.00	4.37
Ahmanson H F	129	107	- .29	- .14	- .69	- .97	3.00	+ .85s	+ 69	+13	10.0↑	4.9	63	76	113	33.12	5.62
Aileen Inc	105	104	+ .23	+ .86	+1.14	+16.10	- .13	- .02n	NE	-25	- .9↓	NE	22	126	129	22.87	1.37
Air Pd & Chem	85	93	+ .20	+ .16	-2.03	- 2.72	2.40	+ .18f▲	+ 8	+32	7.1↓	10.4	74	170	152	40.62	11.87
Airborne Frgt	106	94	+ .20	- .50	+ .41	+ 9.92	1.22	- .03s	- 6	+31	3.9↓	11.7	43	139	138	16.75	2.87
Airco Inc	117	128	+ .26	- 1.43	-2.81	-64.42	4.37	+ .12n▲	+ 3	+31	6.4→	6.8	43	107	94	34.37	10.00
Akzona Inc	95	104	+ .03	- .65	- .40	+11.54	.45	+ .27n	+ 40	-30	.8↑	20.1	25	80	69	35.50	8.75
Alabama Gas	114	106	+ .14	- .32	+3.15	+10.00	2.03	+ .34n	+ 13	+ 7	3.8↓	7.2	30	82	90	18.37	7.25
Alaska Intste	87	87	- .41	+ 2.72	+1.65	-14.10	2.23	- .46s	- 35	+29	4.5↓	8.3	27	94	90	54.12	5.62
Albany Intl	93	94	+ .15	- .06	-2.86	-80.00	2.74	+ .21s	+ 16	+ 2	6.0→	5.3	34	80	88	39.50	12.87
Alberto-Culver	104	102	+ .23	- .29	+2.94	- 8.22	.53	+ .08f▲	+ 18	-17	1.5↑	13.7	20	55	99	29.25	4.00
Albertsons Inc	129	129	+ .08	- .19	- .28	+26.06	2.41	+ .36s	+ 32	+20	1.2↑	9.5	13	222	162	27.25	10.00

Dividends, Shareholdings, Financial Position

Name	Indicated Dvd Rate Amt	Indicated Dvd Rate Yield	Payout Fiscal Year	Payout Last 5 Years	Last X-Dvd Date	Shares Outstanding Total	Held by Banks-Funds	Insider Mo Net Change	Short Interest Ratio	Revenue (In $Millions)	Earnings (In $Millions)	Current Ratio	Per Share Long Term Debt	Per Share Stock Equity	Last Bal Sheet Date
	$	%	%	%	-	000	000	000	Days	$	$	-	$	$	-
Abbott Labs	1.20	2.4	26	31	10/07/77	29,751	9,388	- 1	1.7	1,084.9	92.5	2.2	6.72	19.50	12/76
ACF Industries	2.00	6.0	45	52	08/26/77	8,687	2,874	+ 1	.0	639.9	34.0	2.5	27.18	31.52	12/76
Acme-Clevelnd	.60	5.3	77	60	08/30/77	4,410	361	0	.0	194.1	2.9	3.8	8.80	18.37	09/76
Adams Drug	.04	1.4	7	6	09/09/77	4,063	824	0	.0	136.3	2.4	2.7	4.01	5.19	12/76
Adams Express	.52	4.3	NA	NA	09/13/77	14,548	110	0	.0	NA	NA	NA	NA	NA	NA
Adams-Millis	.15	3.2	0	22	08/11/77	2,282	111	+ 0	.0	62.1	1.2	2.3	1.62	9.21	12/76
Addresso-Mult	.10	.8	NE	56	09/27/77	8,348	176	0	23	596.3	- 14.4	1.8	9.02	23.77	07/77
Aetna Life Cas	1.60	4.7	28	32	09/01/77	53,428	14,968	+ 0	.7	7,179.4	210.0	NA	3.82	32.67	12/76
Aguirre Co	.00	.0	0	0	NA	1,498	40	0	.0	14.2	.2	3.2	1.41	12.63	07/76
Ahmanson H F	.80	4.2	7	8	08/15/77	22,761	6,818	0	.0	683.9	68.3	NA	20.46	24.62	12/76
Aileen Inc	.00	.0	0	0	NA	5,061	40	0	.0	68.2	- .6	4.5	2.43	10.12	10/76
Air Pd & Chem	.40b	1.6	8	6	09/27/77	28,209	8,911	- 2	3.1	947.2	67.7†	1.4	7.84	13.01	09/76
Airborne Frgt	.70	5.0	41	32	08/02/77	4,148	1,055	+ 1	.0	132.9	5.2	1.7	.00	4.77	12/76
Airco Inc	1.35	4.4	25	33	08/15/77	11,794	1,398	+ 2	.2	837.4	54.0	2.7	15.52	31.76	12/76
Akzona Inc	1.20	8.3	G	69	09/13/77	12,460	860	0	.7	728.6	5.6	2.7	14.79	24.60	12/76
Alabama Gas	1.40	8.2	63	65	11/07/77	1,974	0	0	.0	111.9	4.2	1.0	19.25	18.14	09/76
Alaska Intste	.66	4.5	27	9	09/02/77	3,222	109	+ 1	8.2	175.2	7.9	1.8	24.09	22.08	12/76
Albany Intl	.80	5.1	23	25	12/02/77	5,261	270	0	.0	238.8	14.4	2.7	8.25	23.84	12/76
Alberto-Culver	.36	5.0	68	65	10/31/77	4,273	86	0	.1	152.1	2.3†	2.4	.66	11.42	09/76
Albertsons Inc	.80	3.0	30	28	10/31/77	7,310	1,193	+ 3	.9	1,490.8	18.2	1.5	4.68	14.28	01/77

z – Sales in full.
x – Ex-dividend.
y – Ex-dividend and sales in full.
vj – In bankruptcy or receivership or being reorganized under the Bankruptcy Act, or securities assumed by such companies.

a – Stock dividend.
b – Cash + stock dividend.
* – Actual amount for interim period, other than a quarterly multiple, resulting from a fiscal year change.

Latest change in earnings and latest change in profit margin based on:
q – First quarter.
s – First six months.
n – First nine months.
f – Fiscal year.
▲ – New earnings this week.

↑ – Trend up.
↓ – Trend down.
→ – No change in trend.
† – Revenues and earnings from preliminary report for year later than date shown.
c – Currency in country of origin.

G – Value calculated greater than allowed range.
L – Value calculated less than allowed range.
NA – Item not applicable to this type of stock.

NC – Data required for calculation currently incomplete in our files.
NE – Negative earnings invalidate calculation.
NT – No trades; prices and calculations shown are based on latest recorded trading.

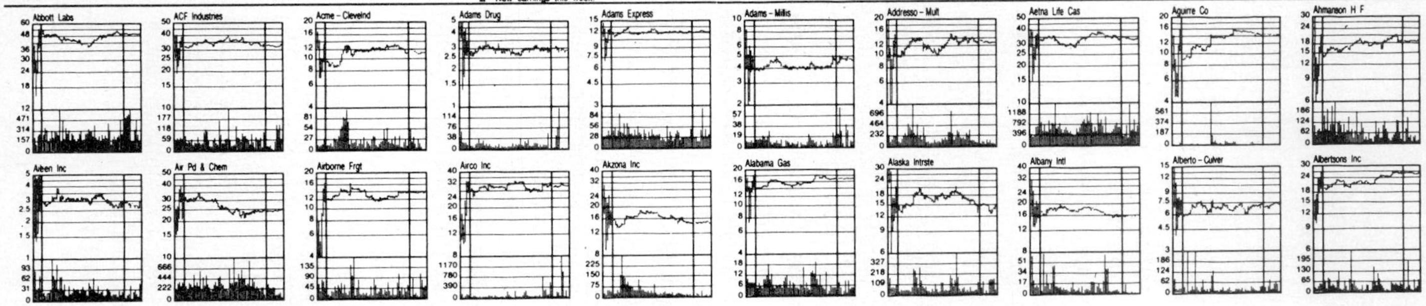

Source: M/G Financial Weekly, October 31, 1977, p. 7.

FIGURE 17-1. Section from *M/G Financial Weekly* Showing Type of Information Given for Each Stock

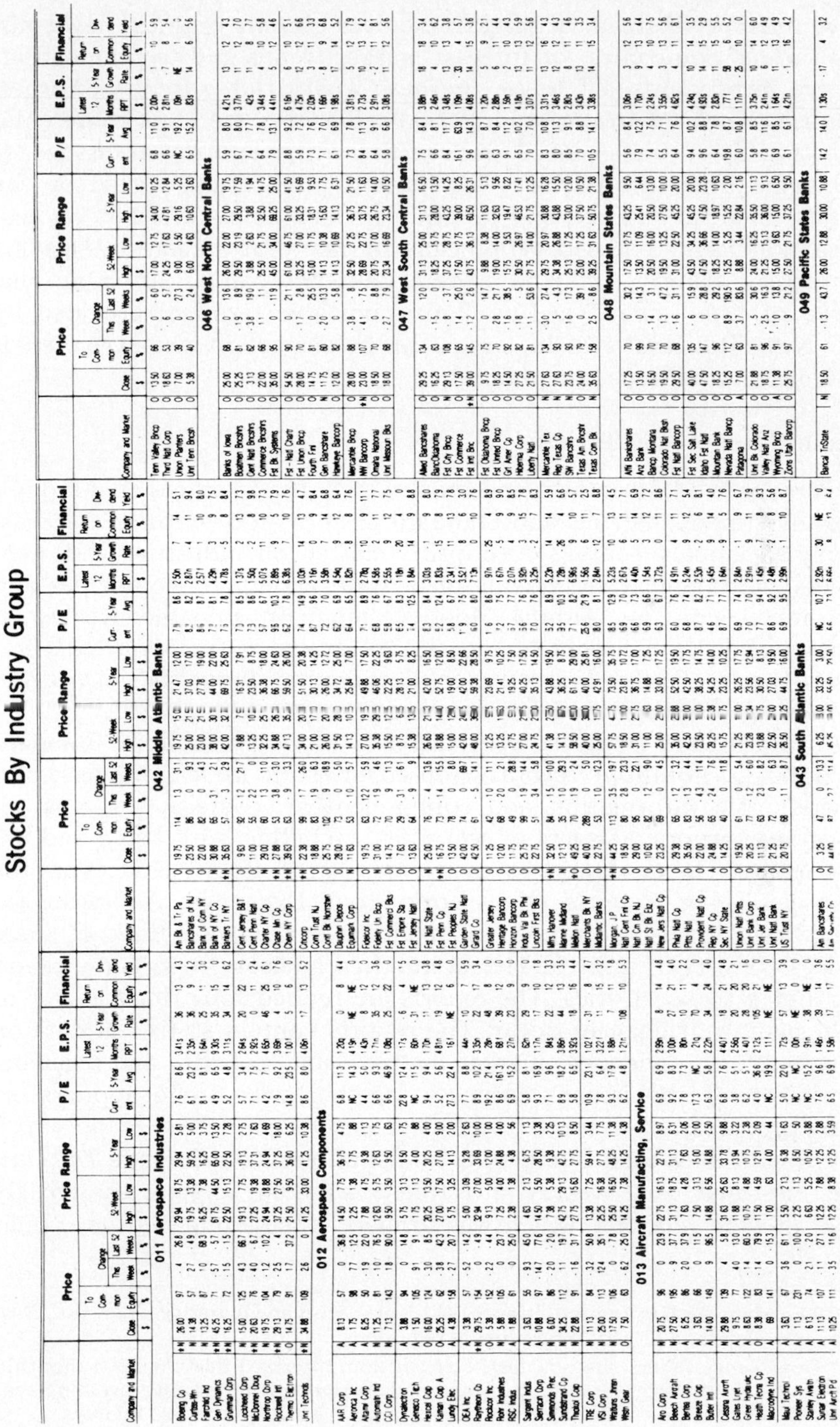

Stocks By Industry Group

Source: M/G Financial Weekly, October 31, 1977.

FIGURE 17-2. Section from *M/G Financial Weekly* Showing Information Given on Their "Stocks by Industry Group"

A number of financial magazines cover current business news, discuss various companies, or forecast market trends and recommend attractive investments. Of these, *Business Week, Dun's Review, Forbes, Financial World, Fortune*, and *Nation's Business* are most representative. In addition, many investors read the letters and reports issued by brokerage firms, the advisory letters and publications issued by the various financial services, and monthly reviews or bank letters on economic conditions released periodically by many of the nation's leading commercial banks[1] and the Federal Reserve banks. An additional source of "spot news" is Dow Jones' portable terminal provided by their News/Retrieval system, which can be plugged in wherever there is an electric outlet and a telephone.[2]

Financial Reporting Services

Perhaps the best-known and most widely used services are Moody's large investment manuals and Standard & Poor's *Corporation Records*. Moody's manuals contain descriptive matter on industries and companies and financial statements on a wide variety of companies and government entities. Annual Moody's manuals, updated weekly or twice weekly by a loose-leaf service, are available for *Municipals and Governments, Banks and Finance Companies, Industrials, Over-the-Counter Industrials, Public Utilities*, and *Transportation*.

Although not nearly so specialized as Moody's volumes, Standard & Poor's *Corporation Records*, housed in six loose-leaf binders, also provide basic information and comprehensive coverage of almost all important corporate issuers of securities, including both listed and unlisted issues. The next most extensive Standard & Poor's services are the loose-leaf *Stock Reports* (New York Stock Exchange, American Exchange, and over-the-counter and regional exchanges). Each of these services consists of a set of several hundred advisory reports on important and active securities. The reports are revised four times a year or when significant changes occur. The reports contain statistical data on sales, earnings, dividends, market history, and so forth, and a general description of the issuer's business together with some appraisal of future prospects.

Other widely used Standard & Poor's publications include *The Outlook*, designed as a weekly investment advisory service; the weekly *Fixed Income Investor*, which was formerly their *Bond Outlook;* their

---

[1] The Monthly Economic Letters of Citibank; Morgan Guaranty Trust Co., New York; and Cleveland Trust Co. are highly regarded.

[2] Dow Jones offers their *News/Retrieval* computerized system for a monthly fee plus a time charge for use. You can dial for current news plus anything that appeared in either *The Wall Street Journal* or *Barron's* within the last 90 days.

two monthly periodicals, the *Stock Guide* and *Bond Guide*, together with their weekly *Option Guide*, all three of which are similar in size and format; the *Analysts Handbook*, an annual statistical service supplemented by monthly issues, providing composite corporate per share data for a ten-year span on earnings, dividends, and yields on a corporate and industry basis; the *Dividend Record*, containing annual and current data on dividend payments and declaration dates; and the three-volume *Register of Corporations, Directors and Executives*, an annual publication listing the company's home office address, its officers, sales volume, number of employees, products, and appropriate Standard Industrial Classification (SIC) numbers.[3]

Moody's also issues many publications comparable to Standard & Poor's services; for example, *Moody's Dividend Record, Bond Record*, and *Bond Survey*.

Two popular advisory publications should be mentioned along with Standard & Poor's *The Outlook*. They are Arnold Bernhard and Company's *Value Line Investment Survey* and United Business Service's *United Business and Investment Report*. Of the two, the United Business Service publication is more like *The Outlook* in format and content. All three are published weekly.

The *Value Line Investment Survey* is published in three parts: Part 1, Summary of Advice & Index; Part 2, Ratings and Reports; and Part 3, Selection and Opinion. Part 1 is replaced each week. It updates the rankings, earnings, and prices of the 1,650 stocks monitored and provides tabular information useful for option writers and other investors. The Selection and Opinion (Part 3) "reviews the economy and stock market, contains special highlighted recommendations, and presents up-to-date studies of new accounting methods and business developments." Part 2 has full-page reports and evaluations of each of the 1,650 stocks. These are updated on a weekly schedule to provide quarterly revisions. Figure 17–3 illustrates the type of full-page report in Part 2.

Each week *Value Line*, in their Part 1 Summary and Index, lists up-to-date ratings for each stock relative to all the others, as follows:

1. Rank for probable price performance in the next 12 months—ranging from one (highest) down to five (lowest).
2. Rank for investment safety (from one down to five).

---

[3] SIC numbers are used in so many business directories that it is wise to familiarize yourself with the purpose and pattern of the numbers by examining the most recent (1972) *Standard Industrial Classification Manual*. A classification number is assigned to each product or type of service. Since companies diversify so much now, one company may easily need several SIC numbers. A 15-page supplement to the 1972 *SIC Manual* was issued in 1978. A broader review of the Standard Industrial Classification system is scheduled for completion by 1982.

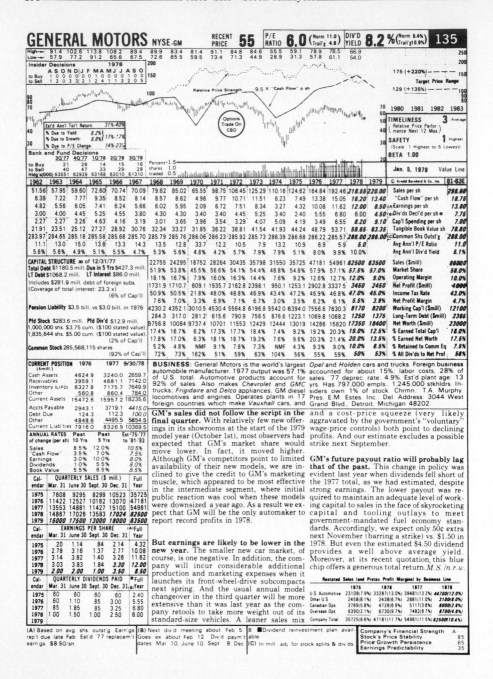

Source: Ratings and Reports, *Value Line Investment Survey* (New York: Arnold Bernhard & Co., 1978).

FIGURE 17-3. *Value Line* Investment Survey of General Motors

3. Estimated yield in the next 12 months.
4. Estimated appreciation potential in the next three to five years—showing the future "target" price range and percentage change from current price.
5. P/E ratio and current price, plus estimated annual earnings and dividends in current 12 months. Also latest quarterly results against a year ago.

In addition to the *Value Line Investment Survey*, Arnold Bernhard and Company publishes the *Value Line OTC Special Situations Service*, a service that follows some 70 relatively volatile stocks, most of which are traded over-the-counter, and *Value Line Options and Convertibles*, which rates and evaluates over 1,000 convertibles and their underlying common stocks and recommends a special few.

The *United Business and Investment Report* summarizes the favorable and unfavorable factors in the current situation, forecasts the nation's economic growth, recommends stocks and bonds, and has many special features including "Buying Advice of Other Services," "Selling Advice of Other Services," and "Views of Other Authorities."

Industry Surveys and Publications

Analysis and judgment of the nature and prospects of the industry or industries (if a conglomerate) in which the company operates underlie analysis of a specific company. There are many sources of industry information. A frequently used source is Standard & Poor's *Industry Surveys*, which covers 69 major domestic industries. There is a *Basic Analysis* issued approximately once a year, which is supplemented two or three times during the year by a briefer survey entitled *Current Analysis*. These surveys contain lengthy discussions of the forces affecting developments within an industry as well as statistical data pertinent to an in-depth analysis of an industry's prospects, stability, profits, and growth. Also, Standard & Poor's *Trade and Securities Statistics* supplies historical statistics on securities markets and important industries and is updated by a monthly supplement. There are also many industry or "trade" publications.[4]

---

[4] Excellent sources of listings of trade publications are: Charlotte M. Devers, Doris B. Katz, and Mary M. Regan, *Guide to Special Issues and Indexes of Periodicals* (2d ed.; New York: Special Libraries Association, 1976); Craig Colgate, Jr., and Mattie Ellen Gustafson (eds.), the annual *National Trade and Professional Associations of the United States and Canada and Labor Unions* (Washington: Columbia Books, 1977); and the "Guide to Industry Publications," compiled by the New York Society of Security Analysts, comprising a chapter within Sumner Levine's *Financial Analyst's Handbook, Volume II Analysis by Industry* (Homewood, Ill.: Dow Jones-Irwin, 1976).

U.S. Government Publications

The federal government and its agencies, as well as the Board of Governors of the Federal Reserve System, regularly prepare and release numerous bulletins, publications, and studies on the nation's business as well as statistical studies and information on particular industries. The general source for listings of government publications is the *Monthly Catalog of United States Government Publications*, issued by the Superintendent of Documents. Entries in the *Monthly Catalog* are indexed for access by author, title, subject, and series/report. With the July 1976 issue, the *Monthly Catalog* changed over to the MARC format (the machine readable cataloging format). There are semiannual and annual indexes. There is also a special annual issue known as the "Serials Supplement," which describes all periodicals and subscription publications issued by the federal government's various departments and agencies.

The annual *Statistical Abstract of the United States* provides economic and statistical information on many industries and indicates the issuing agency and title of the source from which the statistics are taken. An excellent, and probably unnoticed, guide to the sources used can be found in the back of the volume. At times the sources are publications of private entities and they are so indicated in this descriptive section in the back of the volume.

The U.S. Department of Commerce Publications are widely used and are the bases for much of the material included and interpreted by private business services and publications. The major publications of the U.S. Department of Commerce are as follows:

1. *Survey of Current Business.* A monthly publication supplemented by a biennial known as *Business Statistics.* The biennial is a historical compilation of statistics. The monthly is the most important source of the government's economic series statistics and of articles on business activity that the Bureau of Economic Analysis writes after studying incoming reports to government agencies. These comprise information on both U.S. domestic and foreign commerce. An additional publication, *Weekly Business Statistics*, was formerly a weekly statistical supplement to the monthly *Survey.* It still serves as such.

2. *Business Conditions Digest.* A monthly report that "brings together many of the economic time series found most useful by analysts and forecasters."[5] International series are included. Appendixes provide series descriptions. Revised in 1977 to put emphasis on cyclical indicators. A computer tape containing data for most of the series is available for purchase.

3. *U.S. Industrial Outlook.* Annual that assesses trends in over 200 industries with a five-year projection for each.

----

[5] Quoted from the description of *Business Conditions Digest* in *Business Service Checklist.*

The Bureau of Labor Statistics of the U.S. Department of Labor publishes periodicals that contain information useful in estimating the economic growth of the nation, the states, regional groupings of states, and occasionally foreign industrial countries. The following are two major publications of the Bureau of Labor Statistics:

1. *Monthly Labor Review.* A monthly containing articles on employment, labor force, wages, prices, productivity, unit labor costs, labor developments here and abroad, and forecasts of labor developments. Like the *Survey of Current Business*, it has a special statistical section. MLR's section includes figures on employment data, hours and earnings data, unemployment insurance data, price data, productivity data, and labor-management data (wage settlements, work stoppages, etc.). The *Handbook of Labor Statistics* furnishes more detailed data and historical coverage for most of the statistical series presented in the *Monthly Labor Review.* Press releases provide the latest statistical information.
2. *Chartbook on Prices, Wages, and Productivity.* A monthly prepared in the Office of Economic Growth in collaboration with the Office of Publications. Trends in key economic indicators are shown in both tabular and graphic form.

Important monetary statistics are found in the *Federal Reserve Bulletin*, a monthly publication of the Board of Governors of the Federal Reserve system. It contains articles having to do with the Federal Reserve System and monetary conditions, and a lengthy statistical section containing both U.S. and international monetary statistics. These include tables on the Federal Reserve's index of industrial productivity, U.S. government securities, bank debits, bank reserves, commercial banks by deposits, open-market paper, etc. The *Federal Reserve Chart Book*, an annual publication, furnishes a graphic presentation of many of the banking statistics found in the *Bulletin*. These monthly issues are cumulated annually (in September) into the *Historical Chart Book* available from the Federal Reserve, Washington, DC 20551. Many other Federal Reserve publications, including some staff studies, are available free of charge. Those available are listed in each monthly issue of the *Federal Reserve Bulletin*.

Three other sources of essential business statistics are as follows:

1. *Economic Indicators.* A monthly prepared by the U.S. Council of Economic Advisers for the Joint Economic Committee. Basic U.S. economic indicators are offered in tabular and chart form. Includes federal finance and international statistics. Figures are often given for most recent ten years.
2. *The Annual Report of the Council of Economic Advisers*, which is always published together with the *Economic Report of the President.* Includes statistical tables relating to income, employment, and production. Statistics, for the most part, go back to 1946. They include tables on corporate profits and finance, money stock, credit, and many more.

3. *The Quarterly Financial Report for Manufacturing, Mining, and Trade Corporations*, issued by the Division of Financial Statistics of the Federal Trade Commission. The main purpose of the QFR is to provide timely, accurate data for use by government and private sector organizations and individuals. The Commerce Department regularly employs *Quarterly Financial Report* data as an important component in determining corporate profits for GNP and National Income estimates. The data consist of estimated aggregate income statements and balance sheets and related financial and operating ratios for manufacturing, mining, and wholesaling corporations. More than 3,000 aggregates or ratios are estimated each quarter. The QFR publishes information on the most recently closed quarter for manufacturing, mining, and wholesaling, and the preceding quarter's data for retailing except in the fourth quarter, when the 95-day publication lag permits synchronized presentation.

National Technical Information Service

The government has always been an inexpensive source of help in providing factual information concerning both domestic and international business. Since 1970 the National Technical Information Service of the U.S. Department of Commerce[6] has served as a clearinghouse for disseminating to the public the multitude of Department of Commerce publications as well as those of other government bureaus and agencies. Many university and private research organization publications funded by the government are included.

This wealth of information, going back to 1964, is available for online computer searching. A special search by subject for a possible answer to a current problem would cost around $100 for up to 100 microfiche copies of research summaries.[7] A search usually requires a ten-day wait. The magnetic tape containing the abstracts is available for lease annually for a basic fee of $2,000 plus a negotiated use fee; a subscriber receives current tapes biweekly.

For those interested in a particular subject area, NTIS puts out 26 *Weekly Government Abstract* newsletters. One is on *Business & Economics;* others are on more specific subjects such as *Transportation and Natural Resources.* Each costs $40 for an annual subscription.

---

[6] NTIS publishes a *General Catalog* describing its information services. It can be obtained free of charge by writing to National Technical Information Service, Department of Commerce, 5285 Port Royal Road, Springfield, VA 22161.

[7] Microfiche, sometimes shortened to "fiche," are 4- × 6-inch sheets. The printed page is reduced to $\frac{1}{24}$ th its original size; there is a space for approximately 98 pages on a single microfiche.

COMPANY INFORMATION

The basic information for company analysis comes from the company, either directly in the form of annual, semiannual, and quarterly reports and intermittent news releases or indirectly through a regulatory body (in the latter case, to a large extent, material filed with the SEC). However, for quick reference the Standard & Poor's *Stock Reports and Industry Surveys*, together with Moody's reports, receives the most use.

Company Reports to Stockholders

As a result of pressure from the securities exchanges, professional analysts, the American Institute of Certified Public Accountants, and institutional investors and other investors, company annual reports have shown a marked improvement over the years, and the trend is fortunately continuing. From the standpoint of disclosure, great progress has been made, but there is still a long way to go to improve the uniformity of corporate financial reporting. Investors should read the text of annual reports completely to determine company policy and goals, research, new products, labor relations, and so forth. By studying a series of reports covering a period of years, investors may determine the extent to which policies were advocated and goals realized. The financial information must be studied, ratios calculated, and results analyzed. Company semiannual and quarterly reports bring some of the most important financial information up to date. Finally, intermittent news releases inform the investor of major current happenings affecting the company.

Reports Filed with the SEC

Today most companies that the analyst will wish to study must file reports with the SEC. In 1964 the Securities Exchange Act of 1934 was amended, providing under a new section (12g) for the registration of securities traded over-the-counter whose issuers have total assets in excess of $1 million and a class of equity securities held of record by at least 500 persons. Information filed with the SEC and available to the general public is filed under the forms discussed in the following paragraphs.

Registration Statement—Form S-1 (1933 Act). A registration statement is submitted and signed by the principal executive and the financial officers of the issuing company and by a majority of its board of directors. It becomes effective 20 days after it is filed, or 20 days after the filing of an amendment. Since most registration statements have an amendment, the time period is usually much longer than the statutory 20 days.

The following is indicative of the type of information required in the registration statement and summarized in the prospectus: (1) purpose of the issue, (2) the price at which the issue is to be publicly offered, (3) disclosure of any purchase options agreements, (4) underwriters' commissions or discounts, (5) net proceeds of the issue to the company, (6) description of the business and its development during the past five years, and (7) detailed financial statements.

Realizing that a registration statement is too time-consuming for most to read, Congress provided for the filing of a prospectus that summarizes the information in the registration statement. It must be offered to every person solicited and to all who purchase or indicate an interest in the securities at or before the actual offering. Its purpose is to provide the investor with the data required to analyze the issue. Originally the required prospectus was voluminous, but the SEC later approved smaller pocket-sized prospectuses, now in use for many years. Since the time span between actual public announcement of an offering and the selling of new securities is often only a matter of hours, the SEC has permitted a relaxation of the regulations to give prospective buyers information on the issue *during* the registration period but prior to the sale by allowing the distribution of a preliminary prospectus referred to as a "red herring." It is so named because it must have on its cover in red ink a statement to the effect that it is not yet effective.

Acceptance by the SEC implies only that the disclosure requirements have been met—not that the offering has any merit. Any implication on the part of any dealer that acceptance by the SEC implies a recommendation is against the law.

Annual Report—Form 10-K (1934 Act). This is the annual report to update registration statements. Most companies must file this annual Form 10-K report, which includes financial statistics and supplementary statements. Briefly, the annual report must contain the following items:

Part I

Item 1. Business. If more than one line of business, total sales for last five years for any line which accounted for 10 percent or more of sales during the last two years.

Item 2. Summary of operations.

Item 3. Properties. Location, type at each location, and if owned or leased.

Item 4. Parents and subsidiaries.

Item 5. Legal proceedings.

Item 6. Increases and decreases in outstanding securities.

Item 7. Approximate number of equity security holders.

Item 8. Executive officers of the registrant.

Item 9. Indemnification of directors and officers.
Item 10. Financial statements and exhibits filed.

Part II

Item 11. Principal security holders and security holdings of management.
Item 12. Directors of the registrant.
Item 13. Remuneration of directors and officers.
Item 14. Options granted to management to purchase securities.
Item 15. Interest of management and others in certain transactions.

Part I must be filed within 90 days of the end of a company's fiscal year. Part II must be filed within 120 days unless a proxy, in accordance with Regulation 14A, or information statement, in accordance with Regulation 14C, is filed within that period. If either is, Part II may be omitted.

There are additional financial statements or "schedules" that must be filed as required by Regulation S-X, Article 5-04. The regulation spells out who must file.

In September 1975, the commission ruled that companies must append to the 10-K selected quarterly information for the two most recent fiscal years. For the most part this includes net sales, gross profits, income, and per share data. Only companies that have had a net income of $250,000 for each of the last three years, or $200 million in assets at the end of the last fiscal year, need to do this. Large companies having nonfinancial assets exceeding $100 million were required to append to their 10-K annual reports for 1976 and 1977 cost estimates for replacing their physical plant and equipment.

Interim Reports—Form 8-K (1934 Act). This so-called current report must be filed only when certain significant events occur. It must be filed 15 days after the event when there are changes in control of the registrant, acquisition, or disposition of assets, the inception of lawsuits involving bankruptcy or receivership proceedings, and changes in certifying accountants. Material developments such as questionable payments must be reported ten days after the first of the following month.

Quarterly Reports—Form 10-Q (1934 Act). A quarterly financial report must be filed by most companies within 45 days after the end of each of the first three fiscal quarters. Balance sheets for the corresponding quarter of the preceding fiscal year must be shown along with that for the current quarter. There must be a statement of source of funds as well as data showing application of funds. Management must include a written analysis of operations during the quarter. Information on legal proceedings, changes in registered securities, changes in collateral for registered securities, material defaults on senior securities, and information as to matters submitted to vote of security holders must be reported on the 10-Q.

Investors' Access to SEC Filings. The statistical services extract and summarize important information from the SEC filings, but useful information is often included in the filings that is not reported in company annual reports or by the statistical services. An analyst making an in-depth study of a company can inspect the SEC filings directly at the offices in Washington, New York, Chicago, or Los Angeles. Large public libraries may have available microfiche of the 10-K reports of the largest companies. Exchanges also have these reports.

A commercial company, Disclosure, Inc., a division of the Reliance Group, Inc., has a contract with the SEC to copy all material in the commission's public files. It supplies it in either photocopy or microfiche at reasonable cost. It has devised an elaborate index so that it can search its on-line system for the answer to any question concerning company information within the reports. When companies are its customers, it offers a service called Corporate Competitive Surveillance.[8] It will alert a customer to a single type of action on the part of rival companies or furnish all recorded activities of a given list of competitors.

Reports Filed with Regulatory Commissions Other Than the SEC.

When an industry is regulated, prescribed accounting methods and a fair degree of standardization in reporting is the rule. Reports filed with regulatory bodies provide a wealth of material for financial analysis, although not all information on file with regulatory agencies is available to the public. The major regulatory authorities other than the SEC with which reports must be filed are as follows:

1. Interstate Commerce Commission (ICC).
2. Civil Aeronautics Board (CAB).
3. Energy Information Administration.
4. State public utility commissions.
5. State insurance commissions.
6. Federal Reserve Board.
7. Federal Deposit Insurance Corporation (FDIC).
8. Comptroller of the Currency.
9. State banking commissions.

Information Obtained Directly from the Company

Analysts frequently seek to obtain additional information not published by the company by direct interviews with officers of the company. The professional analysts—members of the Financial Analysts Federation—have over the years placed considerable pressure on man-

---

[8] See "Washington's New Sleuths," *Dun's Review* (October, 1976), pp. 70–73.

agement to disclose pertinent information that is often not obtainable in published reports; but if such information is disclosed to one or more analysts, it must immediately be publicly and broadly disclosed. The type of questions that a professional analyst usually asks when visiting companies on a "field trip" are outlined in Appendix A at the end of this chapter.[9]

COMPUTERIZED FINANCIAL DATA

The computer has proved to be extremely useful to the financial community, not simply because it can do computations more easily and accurately than people, but because of its ability to store, retrieve, and manipulate information as directed.

Data Bases

Data bases are proliferating. One company after another is forming in order to collect a data base aimed at supplying a particular type of needed information. Some of the better-known data bases are briefly reviewed below.

Media General Financial Services offers access to their broad data base of some 3,700 common stock issues through their customized services *Stock Reference Report, Executive Stock Report, Media General Screen & Rank, the M/G StockVue,* and *DataBank.* Each service allows the subscriber to choose the stocks and/or criteria wanted for analysis.

Value Line, mentioned earlier, has a data base that is available via computer tape and computer time-sharing for a yearly subscription fee of $5,000. Its annual data go back as far as 1954; its quarterly figures, to 1963. Its data base contains the following information:[10]

1. Complete income statements.
2. Complete balance sheets.
3. Sources and uses of funds statement.
4. Sales and income as reported.
5. Sales and income restated for mergers.
6. Restated sales and earnings by product line.
7. Precalculated ratios, return rates, per share data.
8. Measures of earnings predictability.
9. Stock price characteristics including beta, r-square.

---

[9] Also see *How to Interview Corporate Executives* (New York: The New York Society of Security Analysts, August 7, 1972).

[10] From the description of data services in *Investing in Common Stocks with the Aid of the Value Line Rankings and Other Criteria of Stock Value* by Arnold Bernhard, the *Value Line Investment Survey*, 1975.

10. Identification of key accounting methods for inventories, depreciation, tax credits, and leases.
11. Footnote information including the accrued pension liability and the debt due in five years.
12. Year ahead dividend estimates.
13. Calendarized earnings forecasts.
14. Three- to five-year stock price ranges.
15. The recent stock price.
16. Average annual, average quarterly, and quarter-ending stock prices.
17. Monthly high and low stock prices.
18. Monthly trading volume statistics.
19. Composite records for individual industries.
20. A composite file combining the historic annual and quarterly results of U.S. industry.

Investors Management Services, a subsidiary of Standard & Poor's Corporation, maintains one of the better machine-readable collections of corporate financial data currently available. On-line service is offered as well as the *Compustat* tapes for those who wish to purchase them. Based on reports filed with the Securities and Exchange Commission, balance sheet and income statement data for all listed firms and selected over-the-counter issues are available on an annual, quarterly, and monthly basis, reported on separate industrial, over-the-counter, and bank tapes. The price, dividend, earnings tape, also available, is a special-purpose tape containing price, dividend, and earnings data for more than 3,000 firms, arranged on a monthly basis for a maximum of 14 years. Similar information is presented for a number of important stock averages.

One of the largest nationwide computer time-sharing networks that specializes in financial and investment data is *Interactive Data Corporation*. The corporation provides historical data bases in depth, including all available data from the government's economic time series, census statistics, and Federal Reserve statistics, plus data from over 100 foreign countries. It offers, with these, intricate systems for analysis.

Literature Search Services

Commercial bibliographic search services have a growing repertoire of data bases that have been reprogrammed for use on computer terminals in libraries. Academic and research libraries subscribe to these on-line search services, and the academic libraries may offer these to their nonstudent clientele at a price above their cost.[11] Two well-

---

[11] Ryan E. Hoover, "Patron Appraisal of Computer-Aided On-Line Bibliographic Retrieval Services," *Journal of Library Automation* (December, 1976), pp. 335–350.

known literature search services are the Lockheed Information Systems' DIALOG and System Development Corporation's ORBIT.

Summary

The investor must select securities as a result of thorough financial analysis. This analysis depends on information that is available from such sources as company annual and periodic reports, the statistical services and their computer banks, governmental bureaus or agencies such as the SEC, other federal and state agencies and commissions and reports issued under their regulations, the U.S. Department of Commerce, and industry publications. Only after passage of federal securities acts in the 1930s and subsequent amendments did reliable information become available to investors.

As further aids to investors, the professional societies such as the Financial Analysts Federation and the American Institution of Certified Public Accountants (AICPA) have published a considerable quantity of high-quality material that enables investors to interpret available sources of information properly.

Investors should also familiarize themselves with the financial data provided under federal and state securities legislation, especially reports required by the SEC. The best advice to investors is to investigate thoroughly before they invest and seek to obtain the best relative values available at any point in time. The judgment of the investor or analyst in assessing the probable effect of available information on future earnings is paramount.

Appendix A
Types of Questions Analysts Ask When Visiting Companies[12]

Sales

1. Percentage gain or loss, year to date vs. year before.
2. Estimates for full year:
   (a) Units and dollars.
   (b) Identical store sales (retailing).
3. Explanation of sales changes, either way.
4. Sales breakdowns (year to date):
   (a) By divisions.
   (b) By major product groups.
   (c) By major consuming markets.

---

[12] Joseph M. Galanis, "A Primer for Field Contact Work," *Financial Analysts Journal* (August, 1956).

5. Explanation of sales trends above or below the industry average.
6. Demand prospects: near, intermediate, and longer term.
7. Inventory status of company, its distributors, ultimate users.
8. Price levels vs. year ago—impact on unit and dollar sales.
9. Outlook for selling price: firm, up or down. Why?
10. Company's percent of industry sales (i.e., "trade position").
11. Foreign sales aspects:
    (a) Percent of export sales.
    (b) Percent contributed by foreign branches.
    (c) Outlook abroad by countries.
12. Percent of sales derived from government business—type of work.

Selling and Distribution

1. Methods used: direct to users, via wholesalers, retailers, branch warehouses, or combination of these.
2. Percent of selling costs to total sales.
3. Methods of compensation to selling forces: number of salesmen employed.
4. Advertising and promotional efforts, use of TV and other publicity media, with actual costs of this type of expense.
5. Extent of geographic coverage of the nation; plans, if any, to extend marketing areas, add new distributors, etc.
6. Economic radius of distribution from individual points; importance of freight rates.

Competition

1. What concerns are viewed as chief competitors?
2. Few or many competitors?
3. Is competition cutthroat or live-and-let-live type?
4. Are competitors strongly or weakly financed units?
5. In what way do company's products and services have an advantage, if any, over competition?
6. Is new competition entering field?
7. Where does company rank in its field or fields?
8. Importance of brand names, trademarks, patents, or servicing methods.

Patent Aspects

1. Importance re sales and prices.
2. Expiration dates of basic or supplementary patents; expected impact on sales, price structure, profit margins, etc., upon expirations.

Production

1. Rate of operations to date vs. year ago; prospective rates of operation over foreseeable future.
2. Basis of operations: 1-2-3 shift, 7-8 hour day, or continuous operations?
3. Overtime premium pay?

4. Number of plants and character of their construction; multistory or single-story (modern)?
5. Status of equipment: new, modernized, or obsolete?
6. Does company rate as a low-cost, high-cost, or average-cost producer?
7. Steps, if any, being taken to improve production methods and to increase productive efficiency.

Raw Materials

1. Major raw materials used; sources, domestic and foreign. Ample supplies or storage?
2. Price history of raw materials used. Volatility?
3. Extent of integration.
4. Is LIFO method of inventory valuation used?

Financial

1. Most recent capitalization and changes.
2. Any current bank loans outstanding? Explanation.
3. Adequacy of working capital in relation to current and anticipated sales, compared with earlier years.
4. Near term maturities? Refundings? Retirements? Comment on ability to meet these obligations.
5. Any new financing in offing? Kind.
6. Insured, replacement, or appraisal value of fixed assets (especially natural resources) vs. book value.

Dividend Policies and Prospects

1. Payout policy, percent of earnings, percent of cash flow.
2. Prospect for extras.
3. Prospect for stock dividends.
4. Chances for increase (or decrease) in regular annual rate.

Earnings

1. Trend of labor and materials costs, percent of each to sales.
2. Ability to adjust selling prices to higher costs.
3. Cost savings programs, and comments.
4. Profit margins vs. year ago.
5. Trend of earnings to date vs. year ago.
6. Per share earnings for full year.
7. Nonrecurring items. Explanation.
8. Nonoperating sources of income vs. year ago.

Miscellaneous Topics

During the average interview, the analyst will think of spur-of-the-moment questions induced by information or comments of the contact.

In addition, it may prove advisable to request comment on such individual topics as

1. Status of current litigation.
2. Impact of Government Consent Decree.
3. Status of particular long-term sales contracts.
4. Problems arising as result of a current strike or aftermath of one settled.
5. Extent of insurance coverage in connection with floods or other disasters.

Expansion

1. Details of program: plant locations, additions, product lines to be added.
2. Capital outlays involved; methods of financing, if any, contemplated.
3. Percent to be added to plant capacity on a square foot basis, or in physical units, or in dollar sales volume.
4. Any certificates of necessity or fast amortization of new facilities involved?
5. Any new acquisitions in mind?
6. Costs of new construction and equipment per unit of added production vs. one to five years ago.
7. Expected sales per $1 of new plant account investment vs. other years.

Research

1. Amounts, or percent, of sales spent annually on research.
2. Number employed and number possessing advanced degrees.
3. Record of recent patents granted as result of research.
4. New products on the fire and their prospects.
5. Percent of current sales from new products traceable to research over the past five to fifteen years. (This is the most important factor in evaluating research.)

Management

1. Does management show continuity or frequent changes?
2. Average age of top management officials.
3. Is the company a one-man outfit?
4. Methods of recruiting and training executives.
5. Is management centralized or decentralized?

Employee Relations

1. Long-term strike record.
2. Percent of employees unionized—which plants?
3. Management policies on labor relations.
4. Chief employee benefits.
5. Labor turnover rates.

Appendix B
General Investment Reference Sources

Current Periodical Publications in Baker Library. Boston: Baker Library, Graduate School of Business Administration, Harvard University. Issued annually. One volume in three parts: Title, Subject, Geographic Region. The Baker Library also puts out exceedingly helpful subject mini-lists which they revise as needed. Mini-List No. 3 is "Investment Sources"; No. 15 is "Sources of Information for Industry Analysis."

Daniells, Lorna M. *Business Information Sources*. Berkeley: University of California Press, 1976. An excellent successor to Edwin T. Conan's *Sources of Business Information*.

Devers, Charlotte M., Doris B. Katz, and Mary Margaret Regan (eds.). *Guide to Special Issues and Indexes of Periodicals*, 2d ed. New York: Special Libraries Association, 1976.

Grant, Mary McNierney, and Norma Cote. *Directory of Business and Financial Services*, 7th ed. New York: Special Libraries Association, 1976.

Levine, Summer N. (ed.). *The 1977 Dow Jones-Irwin Business Almanac*. Homewood, Ill.: Dow Jones-Irwin, 1977.

Mechanic, Sylvia. *Course Syllabus for Information Sources for Business and Economics*. Brooklyn, N.Y.: Pratt Institute, Graduate School of Library and Information Science, 1977.

Wasserman, Paul (ed.). *Encyclopedia of Business Information Sources*, 3d ed. Detroit: Gale Research Company, 1976.

Woy, James B. *Investment Methods:* A Bibliographic Guide. New York: R. R. Bowker, 1973.

Wyckoff, Peter. *The Language of Wall Street*. New York: Hopkinson and Blake, 1973.

Questions

Due to the nature of the material in this chapter no questions or work-study problems are provided.

18.

Economic and Industry Analysis and Forecasting

Growth has always been considered the most important factor in equity investments. Growth in revenues, earnings, and cash flow is expected to provide growth in dividends and stock prices for common stocks and adequate protection for payment of interest and principal repayments for bonds. Therefore, it is highly important that the analyst form some judgment as to the future long-term secular growth of the economy (GNP and its major components), of industrial production and its major components, and also an opinion concerning the cyclical outlook for the economy. Finally, the analyst should make an estimate of the long-term trend of price-earnings ratios and stock prices as a background for company analysis and stock selection.

Although the future is never a mirror of the past, reviewing the past as a base from which to make projections can be useful. We will, therefore, first review briefly the long-term past record and then the post–World War II record. By doing this we can remove many illusions held by investors whose judgment is often the result of their own relatively short experience.

THE LONG-TERM RECORD OF ECONOMIC GROWTH

Since World War II, real GNP has grown at a 3.4 percent rate and industrial production at a 4.3 percent rate, with marked variations in the short run (see Table 18–1). Table 18–1 also shows that the growth rate for industrial production has, over any extended period, consistently been higher than the growth rate for real GNP, and that the cyclical fluctuations have been much wider for industrial production than for real GNP. Moreover, the cycles in industrial production have been much closer in amplitude to cycles in corporate profits than have the cycles of GNP. Therefore, the cycles of industrial production may

TABLE 18-1. Real Growth Rates for GNP and Industrial Production, Selected Periods

Years	Real GNP	Indus. Prod.	Years	Real GNP	Indus. Prod.
1890-1970	3.3%	4.1%	1920-1923	4.3%	4.3% = Prosperity most years
1900-1970	3.2	4.2	1919-1939	0.3	0.0 = Depression 1930-33 & 1938
1910-1970	3.0	3.3	1939-1945	9.2	11.2 = World War II, 1939- mid-1945
1920-1970	3.3	4.1	1946-1956	2.9	5.6
1930-1970	3.5	4.5	1946-1966	3.8	5.3
1940-1970	3.9	4.1	1946-1976	3.3	4.4
1950-1970	3.6	4.5	1946-1980	3.4	4.3
1960-1970	4.0	4.9	1956-1966	4.0	4.9
1965-1970	3.1	3.7	1966-1976	2.6	2.7
			1966-1980	3.2	2.9

The 1970s

Years	Real GNP	Indus. Prod.	Years	Real GNP	Indus. Prod.
1970	-0.2%	-0.3%	1975	-1.1%	8.9%
1971	3.4	1.7	1976	5.4	10.2
1972	5.7	9.2	1977	5.5	6.0
1973	5.8	8.4	1978	4.8	5.7
1974	-0.6%	-0.4	1979	3.2	3.9
			1980 est.	-0.2	-3.9

Source: U.S. Department of Commerce, Bureau of Economic Analysis, *Long-Term Economic Growth 1860-1970* (Washington, D.C.: U.S. Government Printing Office, 1973), pp. 105-110. Also issues of *Monthly Labor Review*.

have greater significance to the investor than the cycles of GNP. Table 18-2 contrasts the industrial production and GNP cycles. The average durations of cycles of industrial production are summarized in Table 18-3.

BUSINESS CYCLES AND THE INVESTOR

For the investor cyclical trends are at least as important as longer secular trends. In fact, the business profits and stock market cycles since 1961-1968 have clearly been major factors in causing many investors to question the desirability of investment in common stocks—to such a degree that the total number of individual investors, which had

TABLE 18-2. Business Cycles and Cycles of Industrial Production

Business Cycles			Industrial Production		
Trough	Peak	Duration (Months) Peak to Peak	Trough	Peak	Duration (Months) Peak to Peak
	Jan. 1893			Mar. 1892	
1. June 1894	Dec. 1895	35	1. Oct. 1893	Nov. 1895	44
2. June 1897	June 1899	42	2. Sept. 1896	June 1900	55
3. Dec. 1900	Sept. 1902	39	3. Oct. 1900	July 1903	37
4. Aug. 1904	May 1907	56	4. Dec. 1903	May 1907	46
5. June 1908	Jan. 1910	32	5. May 1908	Mar. 1910	34
6. Jan. 1912	Jan. 1913	36	6. Jan. 1911	Jan. 1913	34
7. Dec. 1914	Aug. 1918	67	7. Nov. 1914	May 1917	52
8. Mar. 1919	Jan. 1920	17	8. Mar. 1919	June 1920	32
				Feb. 1920	
9. July 1921	May 1923	40	9. Apr. 1921	May 1923	39
10. July 1924	Oct. 1926	41	10. July 1924	Mar. 1927	46
11. Nov. 1927	Aug. 1929	34	11. Nov. 1927	July 1929	28
12. Mar. 1933	May 1937	93	12. July 1932	May 1937	34
13. June 1938	Feb. 1945	93	13. May 1938	Nov. 1943	78
			No Trough		
14. Oct. 1945	Nov. 1948	45	Determined	July 1948	
15. Oct. 1949	July 1953	56	14. Oct. 1969	July 1953	60
16. May 1954	Aug. 1957	49	15. Apr. 1954	Feb. 1957	43
17. Apr. 1958	Apr. 1960	32	16. Apr. 1958	Jan. 1960	35
18. Feb. 1961	Dec. 1969	116	17. Feb. 1961	Sept. 1969	116
19. Nov. 1970	Nov. 1973	47	18. Nov. 1970	Nov. 1973	50
20. Mar. 1975	Jan. 1980	74	19. Mar. 1975	Mar. 1979	64

Source of data: Business Conditions Digest (December, 1980).

risen steadily to about 33 million in the long 1950–1966–1968 bull market, has now declined by about 6 to 7 million. By December 1981 substantial capital losses had been experienced by many investors. For example, an investment in a portfolio of common stocks in 1968 that behaved as did the S&P stock indexes would have shown a loss in January 1979, and would only have been higher in 1972–1973. The S&P 500 stock index dropped 9.6 percent in 1981 when the economy experienced a recession.

TABLE 18-3. Business Cycle Expansions and Contractions in the United States, 1854-1980

Business Cycle Reference Dates		Duration in Months		Cycle	
		Contraction (Trough from Previous Peak)	Expansion (Trough to Peak)	Trough from Previous Trough	Peak from Previous Peak
Trough	Peak				
December 1854	June 1857	(X)	30	(X)	(X)
December 1858	October 1860	18	22	48	40
June 1861	April 1865	8	46	30	54
December 1867	June 1869	32	18	78	50
December 1870	October 1873	18	34	36	52
March 1879	March 1882	65	36	99	101
May 1885	March 1887	38	22	74	60
April 1888	July 1890	13	27	35	40
May 1891	January 1893	10	20	37	30
June 1894	December 1895	17	18	37	35
June 1897	June 1899	18	24	36	42
December 1900	September 1902	18	21	42	39
August 1904	May 1907	23	33	44	56
June 1908	January 1910	13	19	46	32
January 1912	January 1913	24	12	43	36
December 1914	August 1918	23	44	35	67
March 1919	January 1920	7	10	51	17
July 1921	May 1923	18	22	28	40
July 1924	October 1926	14	27	36	41
November 1927	August 1929	13	21	40	34
March 1933	May 1937	43	50	64	93
June 1938	February 1945	13	80	63	93
October 1945	November 1948	8	37	88	45
October 1949	July 1953	11	45	48	56
May 1954	August 1957	10	39	55	49
April 1958	April 1960	8	24	47	32
February 1961	December 1969	10	106	34	116
November 1970	November 1973	11	36	117	47
March 1975	January 1980	16	58	52	74

TABLE 18-3. Business Cycle Expansions and Contractions in the United States, 1854-1980 *(continued)*

Business Cycle Reference Dates		Duration in Months			
				Cycle	
		Contraction (Trough from Previous Peak)	Expansion (Trough to Peak)	Trough from Previous Trough	Peak from Previous Peak
Trough	Peak				
Average, all cycles:					
28 cycles, 1854–1975		19	33	52	52[a]
16 cycles, 1854–1919		22	27	48	49[b]
6 cycles, 1919–1945		18	35	53	53
6 cycles, 1945–1980		11	49[c]	59	60[c]
Average, peacetime cycles:					
23 cycles, 1854–1980		20	28[d]	46	47[d]
14 cycles, 1854–1919		22	24	46	47[e]
5 cycles, 1919–1945		20	26	46	45[f]
4 cycles, 1945–1980		11	39[f]	45	49[f]

Note: Underscored figures are the wartime expansions (Civil War, World Wars I and II, Korean War, and Vietnam War), the postwar contractions, and the full cycles that include the wartime expansions.
[a] 29 cycles. [c] 7 cycles. [e] 13 cycles. [f] 5 cycles.
[b] 15 cycles. [d] 24 cycles.

Source: Business Conditions Digest (October, 1980), p. 105.

The record of business cycles during the period 1854–1980, as reported by the U.S. Department of Commerce in *Business Conditions Digest* (BCD), is shown in Tables 18-2 and 18-3. While each cycle reflects particular characteristics that determined its length, we believe there is reason to examine the length of past cycles as a guide to the length of any current cycle. Many economists might have had a better forecasting record had they considered the average length of past cycles—three-year minimum, five-year maximum—rather than estimating each one separately.

The mean length of the 28 cycles, 1854–1975, either from trough to trough or peak to peak, was 52 months (4 years and 4 months). There were 12 cycles, 1919–1980, with a mean length of 56 months trough to trough and 59 months peak to peak.

In the nine-year period 1888 to 1980 there have been only two cycles significantly over five years in length. These were the 88-month cycle, trough June 1938 to trough October 1945, and the 117-month cycle from February 1961 to November 1970, trough to trough. These were exceptional in length. The first, 1938–1945, was certainly prolonged well beyond the "average" cycle because the economy reflected the outbreak of war in Europe in 1939 and our subsequent entry into the war in December 1941. The first-quarter 1961 to fourth-quarter 1969 cycle was peculiar in that the stated expansion to 1969 included a mini-recession in 1967 that ended the 1961–1966 profits expansion of 83 percent even though the economic expansion continued to December 1969. Corporate profits after taxes did not exceed the 1966 level until 1972, a major factor in the poor stock market performance of 1966–1971.[1]

Therefore, as far as investors were concerned, the economic profits recovery and expansion that began the first quarter of 1961 ended in 1966 (five years), not in 1969 (nine years); and the stock market, as so often is the case, discounted and signaled in advance this major change when it declined 27 percent in 1966 and 37 percent later from December 1968 to May 1970, discounting the 1970 decline in profits.

In summary, all cycles beginning in 1888 (except the World War II cycle and the 1961–1969 cycle) have been approximately five years or less in length. Only one, in the early 1920s, was significantly less than five years (28 months). Therefore, the probabilities are strong that a full cycle will last at least three years but probably not much over five years. We have noted that the stock market discounts in advance, sometimes substantially in advance, expansions and contractions. What it really discounts is expected changes in the trend and level of corporate profits. A continued economic expansion may not mean a continued profit expansion. The stock market correctly discounted the fact that corporate profits, after rising 83 percent (1961–1966), would decline somewhat in 1967 and not recover to the 1966 level for some years—in fact, not until 1972. This was a major change in the trend of profits. The fact that the stock market has made major bear market *lows* every four *calendar* years (not every 48 months) in 1949, 1953, 1957–58, 1962, 1966, 1970, 1974, and 1978 reflects in part the constant repetition of the business cycle recurring on the average of every three to five years. This pointed to a bear market low that would be reached in 1978 or 1979, but the anticipated behavior of corporate profits is the important variable.

---

[1] Corporate profits after taxes (in billions of dollars) for all U.S. corporations for these years were

$	$	$	$
1966—47.1	1969—43.8	1972—54.6	1975— 70.6
1967—44.9	1970—37.0	1973—67.1	1976— 91.7
1968—46.2	1971—44.3	1974—74.5	1977—102.1

CORPORATE PROFITS GROWTH

Statistics on corporate after-tax profits for all U.S. corporations only go back as far as 1929. For earlier data we must use figures that link Cowles Commission earnings-per-share data (dating back to 1871) to DJIA or S&P indexes. The record of growth of corporate profits is given in Table 18-4. These are long-term secular growth rates that obscure interruptions in the growth of profits.

Over the very long term, 1871-1980, corporate profits have grown at a slower pace than real GNP (3.0 percent versus 3.6 percent) and, of course, more slowly than industrial production. However, in the 1929-1977 period, profits grew at a somewhat faster rate than real GNP (4.6 percent for all U.S. corporations versus 3.1 percent for GNP) but at a slower rate than current dollar GNP (4.6 percent versus 6.2 percent). Current dollar corporate profits have rather consistently declined as a percentage of current dollar GNP during the post–World War II years 1946-1980. Furthermore, the record of corporate profits has been far more erratic than the growth of current dollar GNP, real GNP, and industrial production. For example, the Cowles Commission demonstrated that earnings per share (for the Cowles Stock Index) reached a peak in 1873-1882 and did not again reach this level for twenty years. This type of record has been typical, not exceptional.

There have been only three five-year periods of truly strong corporate earnings growth during the years 1910-1980. Except for the two war years of 1916 and 1917, corporate earnings per share did not recover and exceed the 1915 level until 1923. Earnings then rose 83 percent between 1925 and 1929. Corporate profits fell during the Great

TABLE 18-4. Compound Annual Growth Rates

Years	Current Dollar GNP	Real GNP Constant Dollars	Current Dollar Profits All U.S. Corp.	Cowles Commission EPS 1871 to 1929 Linked to DJIA 1929 to 1980	Current Dollars		
					DJIA	S&P 500	S&P 400
1871-1929	6.10%	4.0%	N.A.	2.4%	N.A.	N.A.	N.A.
1929-1977	6.20	3.1	4.6%	3.7	3.9%	3.9%	4.5%
1971-1978	10.60	3.7	14.8	N.A.	9.7	11.3	11.2
1929-1980	6.55	3.1	5.5	3.5	10.9	3.0	3.6
1933-1980	8.54	4.1	—[a]	8.8	11.4	5.5	6.2
1871-1980	6.31	3.6	N.A.	3.0	N.A.	N.A.	N.A.

[a]Profits were negative in 1933. Therefore, no meaningful calculation is possible.

Depression of the 1930s and did not recover to the 1929 level until 1947. Corporate profits grew very slowly during the period 1947–1948 through 1960–1961, rising only from $20.2 billion in 1947 to $25.8 billion in 1961, or 13.6 percent (less than 1 percent per year). Profits then rose 83 percent to $47.1 billion dollars during the five-year period ending in 1966. Corporate profits did not again exceed the 1966 level until 1972 and then rose nearly 100 percent for the category "All U.S. Corporations" during the years 1972–1978.

THE LONG-TERM RECORD OF STOCK PRICES

In the period 1881–1898 the price record of common stocks was quite unsatisfactory as price trends were down for most of that eighteen-year period, reflecting no net increase in corporate earnings (see Figure 18–1). Then, in the period 1899–1906, stocks surpassed their 1881 level for the first time, reflecting the first significant rise in earnings since 1881.[2] The stock price index was $6.25 in 1881 and $6.29 in 1899. It then rose to $9.64 in 1906 and $9.71 in 1909. This price index did not rise above its 1906–1909 level until the 1925–1929 bull market sixteen years later, suggesting the higher wartime earnings, 1915–1920, were considered abnormal and temporary. It was twenty-five years before the price index reached or surpassed its 1929 level (in 1954). In the sixteen years, from 1950 to 1966, stock prices rose spectacularly: DJIA, 160 to 1000, and the S&P 400 (425) Industrials, 16 to 100. The rise until 1954 was merely a recovery to the 1929 level and reflected a substantial rise in price-earnings ratios as stock prices rose three times as fast as earnings. History soon proved that the rapid growth in stock prices during the 1949–1966 period would not be sustained. During the period 1968–1981 stock prices rather generally moved horizontally. Prices did not surpass their 1966–1968 highs, except temporarily in the period mid-1972 to mid-1973, and again briefly in 1976 and April 1981.

Price-earnings (P/E) ratios are calculated by dividing current market price per share by the latest twelve months earnings per share. They indicate the amount investors are willing to pay for each currently reported dollar of earnings. Beginning with 1973, P/E ratios declined from an average for U.S. corporations of 17 to 19, where they had stabilized for about fifteen years, to a level of 6 to 12, which had existed during the 1946–1951 period. Therefore, while earnings per share for the corporations included in the DJIA rose approximately 87 percent

---

[2] Cowles Commission earnings per share reached peaks in

1880	1882	1899	1901	1902	1906	1909	1915
3.28	3.22	3.60	3.91	4.96	6.11	6.19	7.07

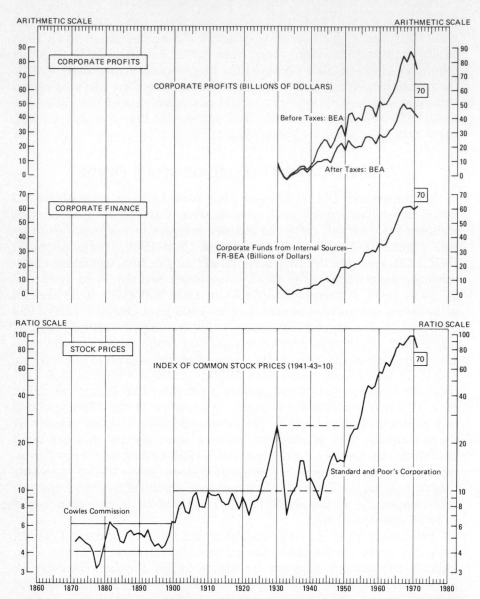

Source: U.S. Department of Commerce, Bureau of Economic Analysis, *Long-Term Economic Growth, 1860–1970* (Washington, D.C.: Government Printing Office, 1973), pp. 54–55.

FIGURE 18-1. Corporate Profits and Stock Prices

from the 1966 average level, the DJIA never rose more than 5 percent above its February 1966 level of 1000 and was substantially below that level in December 1981 (about 870). Investors understand that earnings growth does not guarantee a rise in stock prices, let alone a rise paralleling the growth in earnings. The capitalization factor applied by the market in valuing those earnings must be assessed as well as growth in earnings. Behavior of P/E ratios for the most commonly utilized stock price indexes for the period 1947 to 1980 are contained in Table 18–5. Undoubtedly, they will stabilize in the 6 to 12 range in the 1980s.

TABLE 18–5. Mean P/E Ratios, 1947–1979

		Mean P/E Ratios		
		DJIA	S&P 400 (425)	S&P 500
1947	Period I	9.3	9.2	9.5
1948		7.8	6.5	6.4
1949		7.7	6.1	7.2
1950		7.0	6.3	7.2
1951		9.7	8.9	9.7
Average 1947–1951		8.3	7.4	8.0
1952	Period II	11.1	10.2	11.1
1953		10.1	9.6	9.9
1954		12.1	10.7	13.0
1955		12.1	11.3	12.6
1956		14.7	14.0	13.7
1957		13.0	13.6	11.9
Average 1952–1957		12.2	11.6	12.0
1958	Period III	18.3	17.3	19.1
1959		18.3	17.3	17.7
1960		19.4	17.9	17.8
1961	Peak-Mean	21.1	20.4	22.4
1962		17.2	16.8	17.2
1963		17.2	17.1	18.7
1964		17.9	17.7	18.6
1965		16.9	16.8	17.8
1966		15.1	15.2	14.5
1967		16.1	16.9	18.1
1968		15.3	17.3	18.0
1969		15.3	17.3	15.9
1970		14.4	16.4	18.0
1971		15.9	17.9	17.9
1972		14.3	18.0	18.4
Average 1958–1972		16.9	17.4	18.0
1973	Period IV	10.7	13.4	12.0
1974	A return to	7.4	7.3	7.7
1975	Period I Level	9.7	11.1	11.6

TABLE 18-5. Mean P/E Ratios, 1947-1979 *(continued)*

	DJIA	Mean P/E Ratios	
		S&P 400 (425)	S&P 500
1976	9.7	12.6	12.1
1977	9.4	10.1	9.9
1978	7.1	8.2	7.8
1979	6.7	7.3	7.3

Note: P/E ratios for the Dow Jones Industrial Average can be found in issues of *Barron's,* a Dow Jones publication. P/E ratios for Standard and Poor's 400 Industrials and the 500 Composite can be found in issues of their publication, *The Outlook,* as well as their *Trade and Securities Statistics.*

GROWTH AND THE OVERALL RATE OF RETURN FOR COMMON STOCK

Common stocks represent residual claims subordinate to those of creditors. Therefore, as a class they embody more risks than bonds, and it seems logical that the rate of return on common stocks should exceed the rate of return on bonds by a sufficient margin to compensate for the higher risks.

Based on that assumption, dividend yields on common stocks (the stock indexes) consistently exceeded yields in bonds through 1957–1958. There was one exception. In the highly speculative bull stock markets of 1928 and 1929, stock yields temporarily fell below bond yields (see Table 18-6). However, in 1957–1958, as the yield on bonds equaled and then rose above the yield on common stocks, the case for the purchase of common stocks had to rest on the argument that the overall rate of return on common stocks (dividend yields plus capital appreciation) would exceed the yields on bonds by a sufficient margin to justify the purchase of common stocks.

The experience of investors from 1966 to 1980 was unsatisfactory, based on the averages, whether investing was in long-term bonds or common stocks. For common stock investors this fourteen-year period was far different from the 1949–1966–1968 period.[3] Investors in long-term bonds saw high-grade bond yields rise from 5.44 in September 1966 (4.74 in January 1966) to 9.25 in 1978 and a corresponding decline in the bond price index from 82.58 to 55.62. We have already noted that stock prices moved horizontally during this period.

---

[3] The consumer price index rose from 48.8 in 1942 to 100 by 1967, but the DJIA had risen from 100 to 1000 and the S&P 425 from 10 to 100. The DJIA Index rose from 42 in 1932 after declining from 381 in 1929.

TABLE 18-6. Bond Prices—Bond Yields and Stock Yields, 1926-1979

	S&P High-Grade Bonds		S&P Municipal Bond Yields	DJIA	S&P 400 (425)	S&P 500
	Prices	Yields				
1926	90.11	4.77	4.08	NA	4.86	4.90
1927	91.63	4.65	3.98	NA	4.73	4.76
1928	91.82	4.63	4.05	NA	3.93	3.98
1929	89.09	4.86	4.27	4.4	3.61	3.47
1930	90.85	4.71	4.07	4.9	4.84	4.51
1931	92.82	4.55	4.01	6.3	6.40	6.15
1932	84.36	5.28	4.65	7.1	7.74	7.43
1933	91.10	4.69	4.71	4.3	4.06	4.21
1934	89.10	4.14	4.03	3.7	3.37	3.72
1935	105.5	3.61	3.40	3.7	3.52	3.82
1936	109.6	3.34	3.07	4.3	3.39	3.44
1937	110.2	3.30	3.10	5.7	4.83	4.86
1938	111.7	3.20	2.91	3.9	4.9	5.18
1939	114.7	3.02	2.76	4.4	3.87	4.05
1940	116.3	2.92	2.50	5.3	5.51	5.59
1941	117.7	2.84	2.10	6.3	6.62	6.82
1942	117.4	2.85	2.36	6.0	7.04	7.24
1943	118.3	2.80	2.06	4.8	4.76	4.93
1944	118.7	2.78	1.86	4.6	4.64	4.86
1945	121.6	2.61	1.67	3.9	4.13	4.17
1946	123.4	2.51	1.64	4.0	3.81	3.85
1947	122.1	2.58	2.01	5.3	4.90	4.93
1948	118.2	2.80	2.40	5.8	5.47	5.54
1949	121.0	2.65	2.21	6.5	6.63	6.59
1950	121.9	2.59	1.98	7.2	6.69	6.57
1951	117.7	2.84	2.00	5.9	6.17	6.13
1952	115.8	2.95	2.19	5.6	5.88	5.80
1953	112.1	3.18	2.72	5.6	5.86	5.80
1954	117.2	2.87	2.37	5.0	4.92	4.95
1955	114.4	3.04	2.53	4.3	3.97	4.08
1956	109.1	3.38	2.93	4.1	3.95	4.09
1957	101.3	3.91	3.60	4.3	4.18	4.35
1958	102.9	3.80	3.56	3.7	3.87	3.97
1959	94.59	4.38	3.95	3.1	3.11	3.23
1960	94.64	4.41	3.73	3.3	3.36	3.47
1961	95.22	4.36	3.46	3.2	2.90	2.98
1962	96.16	4.29	3.18	3.5	3.32	3.37
1963	96.76	4.24	3.23	3.3	3.12	3.17

TABLE 18-6. Bond Prices—Bond Yields and Stock Yields, 1926–1979 *(continued)*

| | S&P High-Grade Bonds | | S&P Municipal Bond | | S&P 400 | S&P |
	Prices	Yields	Yields	DJIA	(425)	500
1964	95.14	4.37	3.22	3.1	2.96	3.01
1965	93.88	4.47	3.27	3.1	2.94	3.00
1966	86.88	5.13	3.82	3.5	3.32	3.40
1967	81.75	5.53	3.98	3.4	3.07	3.20
1968	76.41	6.05	4.51	3.5	2.91	3.07
1969	68.63	6.93	5.81	3.7	3.07	3.24
1970	61.55	7.84	6.51	4.3	3.62	3.83
1971	65.01	7.38	5.70	3.5	2.94	3.14
1972	65.86	7.26	5.27	3.4	2.61	2.84
1973	63.65	7.56	5.18	3.8	2.79	3.06
1974	58.80	8.25	6.09	5.1	4.13	4.47
1975	56.23	8.63	6.89	4.9	3.96	4.31
1976	58.03	8.36	6.49	4.1	3.48	3.77
1977	59.59	8.12	5.56	5.5	4.43	4.62
1978	55.58	8.74	5.90	5.3	5.06	5.28
1979	51.09	9.53	6.39	5.4	5.20	5.47

Source: Standard and Poor's *Trade and Securities Statistics 1977*, pp. 215–235.

The annual returns generated on investment in various types of securities are presented in Table 18-7, as calculated by Ibbotson and Sinquefield for the period 1926-1978. Remember, however, that although the returns on stocks (on average) have been excellent in some years (1976, for example), an investor who purchased a portfolio of stocks represented by the Standard & Poor 500 Index and held it through 1981 has not offset the adverse effects of inflation.

Table 18-7 indicates that the annual returns on stocks are much more variable than those on debt instruments; therefore, stocks are a riskier investment. However, the average return over the years 1926-1978 has been substantially higher on stocks, demonstrating that the market does reward for risk taking.

Industry Performance

While a broad holding of many stocks (such as those included in the Standard & Poor's 400 Index) would have recorded little or no capital gains since 1965, a portfolio invested in selected industry groupings could have shown excellent performance. Of the 46 Moody's Industry

TABLE 18-7. Annual Returns: Stocks, Bonds, and Treasury Bills and Change in the Consumer Price Index

| Year | Stocks | Total Returns | | T. Bills | Change in the Consumer Price Index |
		Long-term Govt. Bonds	Long-term Corp. Bonds		
1926	11.62	7.77	7.37	3.27	-1.49
1927	37.49	8.93	7.44	3.12	-2.08
1928	43.61	.10	2.84	3.24	-.97
1929	-8.42	3.42	3.27	4.75	.19
1930	-24.90	4.66	7.98	2.41	-6.03
1931	-43.34	-5.31	-1.85	1.07	-9.52
1932	-8.19	16.84	10.82	.96	-10.30
1933	53.99	-.08	10.38	.30	.51
1934	-1.44	10.02	13.84	.16	-2.03
1935	47.67	4.98	9.61	.17	2.99
1936	33.92	7.51	6.74	.18	1.21
1937	-35.03	.23	2.75	.31	3.10
1938	31.12	5.53	6.13	-.02	-2.78
1939	-.41	5.94	3.97	.02	-.48
1940	-9.78	6.09	3.39	.00	.96
1941	-11.59	.93	2.73	.06	9.72
1942	20.34	3.22	2.60	.27	9.29
1943	25.90	2.08	2.83	.35	3.16
1944	19.75	2.81	4.73	.33	2.11
1945	36.44	10.73	4.08	.33	2.25
1946	-8.07	-.10	1.72	.35	18.17
1947	5.71	-2.63	-2.34	.50	9.01
1948	5.50	3.40	4.14	.81	2.71
1949	18.79	6.45	3.31	1.10	-1.80
1950	31.71	.06	2.12	1.20	5.79
1951	24.02	-3.94	-2.69	1.49	5.87
1952	18.37	1.16	3.52	1.66	.88
1953	-.99	3.63	3.41	1.82	.62
1954	52.62	7.19	5.39	.86	-.50
1955	31.56	-1.30	.48	1.57	.37
1956	6.56	-5.59	-6.81	2.46	2.86
1957	-10.78	7.45	8.71	3.14	3.02
1958	43.36	-6.10	-2.22	1.54	1.76
1959	11.95	-2.26	-.97	2.95	1.50
1960	.47	13.78	9.07	2.66	1.48
1961	26.89	.97	4.82	2.13	.67
1962	-8.73	6.89	7.95	2.73	1.22
1963	22.80	1.21	2.19	3.12	1.65

TABLE 18-7. Annual Returns: Stocks, Bonds, and Treasury Bills and Change in the Consumer Price Index *(continued)*

		Total Returns			Change in the Consumer Price Index
Year	Stocks	Long-term Govt. Bonds	Long-term Corp. Bonds	T. Bills	
1964	16.48	3.51	4.77	3.54	1.19
1965	12.45	.71	-.46	3.93	1.92
1966	-10.06	3.65	.20	4.76	3.35
1967	23.98	-9.19	-4.95	4.21	3.04
1968	11.06	-.26	2.57	5.21	4.72
1969	-8.50	-5.08	-8.09	6.58	6.11
1970	4.01	12.10	18.37	6.53	5.49
1971	14.31	13.23	11.01	4.39	3.36
1972	18.98	5.68	7.26	3.84	3.41
1973	-14.66	-1.11	1.14	6.93	8.80
1974	-26.48	4.35	-3.06	8.00	12.20
1975	37.20	9.19	14.64	5.80	7.01
1976	23.84	16.75	18.65	5.08	4.81
1977	-7.18	-.67	1.71	5.12	6.77
1978	6.56	-1.16	-.07	7.18	9.03
Average	11.18	3.37	4.10	2.54	2.65
Std. dev.	22.16	5.71	5.55	2.22	4.78

Source: Roger G. Ibbotson and Rex A. Sinquefield, *Stocks, Bonds, Bills, and Inflation, 1926–1978* (Charlottesville, Va.: Financial Analysts Research Foundation, 1979).

Groups shown in Table 18-8, about half did as well as or better than the published market averages over the period 1957–1959 to February 1981. A portfolio that consisted proportionately of representative stocks of the best six performing groups (oil service through drugs in Table 18-8) would have risen more than $6\frac{1}{2}$ times, while the DJIA only about doubled during this period. However, while one can easily select the best-performing industries ex-post, the evidence suggests that investors in the aggregate have had great difficulty doing so at the time investment funds are committed (witness the inability of many mutual funds and bank trust portfolios to outperform the stock averages over time).

A firm's profits would usually be affected by economywide factors (for example, interest rate and price level fluctuations), by factors specific to the product line areas (industry) in which the firm operates (for example, changes in demand or supply for the products sold by the

TABLE 18-8. Moody's Index of Market Price Trends of Industry Groups, 1957–1959 to February 1981 (1957–1959 = 100)

Industry	Approximate Increase to 1980	Moody's Feb. 1981
1. Oil service	39X	3,924.9
2. Electronics	$8\frac{1}{4}$-$8\frac{3}{4}$X	883.4
3. TV radio broadcasting		827.3
4. Cosmetics	$7\frac{1}{4}$-$7\frac{3}{4}$X	769.0
5. Soft drinks		723.4
6. Drugs	$6\frac{1}{2}$X	645.8
7. Cigarettes		549.1
8. Printing & publishing		522.7
9. Machinery & equipment	5-$5\frac{1}{2}$X	513.4
10. Machine tools		502.5
11. Business equipment		500.3
12. Liquor		411.9
13. Railroad equipment		396.9
14. Aerospace		394.8
15. Oil	$3\frac{3}{4}$-4X	390.3
16. Apparel		381.7
17. Soap		371.9
18. Railroads		335.3
19. Airlines		330.6
20. Insurance—property & casualty		313.0
21. Farm equipment		303.8
22. Foods	$2\frac{3}{4}$-$3\frac{1}{2}$X	295.4
23. Natural gas		280.0
24. Automotive equipment		278.5
25. Insurance—life		251.4
26. Appliances		249.5
27. Nonferrous metals		247.4
28. Building materials	2-$2\frac{1}{2}$X	246.6
29. Banks		237.4
30. Retail stores		231.0
31. Electrical equipment		218.5
32. Textiles		196.7
33. Finance companies		170.2
34. Containers		162.1
35. Paper & products		156.6
36. Chemicals		145.6
37. Grocery chains	1-$1\frac{3}{4}$X	140.2
38. Service companies		127.1

TABLE 18-8. Moody's Index of Market Price Trends of Industry Groups, 1957–1959 to February 1981 (1957–1959 = 100) *(continued)*

Industry	Approximate Increase to 1980	Moody's Feb. 1981
39. Aluminum		124.4
40. Cement		109.5
41. Copper		104.0
42. Automobiles	Decreases	96.6
43. Electric power	"	89.7
44. Savings & loan	"	85.1
45. Tires & rubber	"	76.6
46. Steel	"	71.9

Source: Moody's Handbook of Common Stocks, Moody's Investors Service, Inc., February, 1981, column taken from Spring 1981 edition, p. 13a.

firm), and by factors specific to the firm (for example, quality of management, firm size, and locational factors). Therefore, a part of the earnings dividends and market performance of a corporation is determined by forces common to a grouping of companies that sell similar product lines. When income was defined as tax-adjusted return on capital employed, Ball and Brown estimated that 35 to 40 percent of the variability in an average firm's earnings per share could be associated with effects common to all firms.[4] Brealey found that 21 percent of the changes in annual earnings for the typical company of a sample of 217 companies in 20 industries during the 1948–1966 period were correlated with changes in the aggregate earnings of the companies in its industry.[5] However, the industry influence varied considerably among companies (and we would suspect would also vary markedly if different time periods were studied). For stock prices the industry effect was not large relative to the overall market effect.[6]

Limitations of Industry Analysis. Recognizing the limitations of an industry approach as a basis for organizing an investment analysis is of great importance. As noted above, the industry influence varies consid-

---

[4] Ray Ball and Phillip Brown, "Some Preliminary Findings on the Association Between the Earnings of a Firm, Its Industry, and the Economy," *Empirical Research in Accounting: Selected Studies, 1967, Supplement to Volume 5 of the Journal of Accounting Research,* pp. 55–77.

[5] Richard A. Brealey, *An Introduction to Risk and Return from Common Stocks* (Cambridge, Mass.: The MIT Press, 1969), pp. 104–111.

[6] B. F. King, "Market and Industry Factors in Stock Price Behavior," *Journal of Business,* Vol. 39 (January, 1966), pp. 134–190.

erably among companies. Elton and Gruber[7] have shown that industry groupings often include companies whose operations and performance are so dissimilar from one another that so-called industry factors may be more misleading than helpful in attempting to assess future potential returns from an investment in these companies. For example, while International Business Machines and Sperry-Rand are both important producers in the computer area, their investment performance has been quite different over time. In fact, classifying a company such as Sperry-Rand in terms of an industry classification is difficult since they also operate in the farm equipment area (Holland Division), the electric shaver area (Remington Division), and other product line areas. When the variations between various segments of a highly diversified product line company are substantial in terms of profitability, risk, and opportunities for growth, concentration on aggregate data is meaningless.

Moreover, an attractive company may at times be found in what otherwise would be considered an industry with unattractive prospects over the next few years. For example, the merchandizing industry grew only modestly during the 1960s, but S. S. Kresge Company proved to be a highly profitable investment opportunity during this period.

Product Line Analysis. Product line growth underlies company growth, and analysis of broad market factors is necessary to assess sales and profit potential. Cost and revenue considerations such as labor relations, competitive conditions, and the impact of technological change can often be best initially assessed in a broader context, such as industry groupings, than in the framework of a given company. Governmental attitudes and legislation may also be better analyzed initially on a product line or industry basis as a background for specific company analysis. The aim of such analysis is to develop probabilistic expectations for company and stock price performance by applying economic and product line expectations to company data. For these reasons, a study of industry data and factors, especially in a product line sense, is useful when evaluating company performance and potential. Industry and product line analysis can provide useful inputs for making financial projections but must be used with great care and awareness of the limitations of such data.

Growth in earnings for the period of 1970–1980 for the industry groupings shown in Table 18-9 suggests one reason for the unfavorable stock price performance experienced by so many investors. Earnings per share grew at about 11 percent per year for the average corporation during the period. Since the rate of inflation averaged about 10 percent per year during this period, earnings growth for the average corporation

---

[7] Edwin J. Elton and Martin J. Gruber, "Improved Forecasting Through the Design of Homogeneous Groups," *Journal of Business*, Vol. 44, No. 4 (October, 1971), pp. 432–450.

merely kept pace with inflation. Note that the industry groups that did
show relatively high appreciation in the market price of their stock in
Table 18-8 would typically be included among the high earnings groups
in Table 18-9.

TABLE 18-9. Industry Earnings per Share Growth, 1970-1980:
Ranked from Highest to Lowest Growth Rate

Industry	Compound Growth Rate, 1970–1980
1. Oil service & supply	28%
2. Food & lodging	22
3. Aerospace	19
4. Trucking	19
5. Nonbank financial	16
6. Savings & loan	16
7. Special machinery	16
8. Conglomerates	15
9. Paper	15
10. Publishing, radio & TV	15
11. Service industries	15
12. Building materials	14
13. General machinery	14
14. Instruments	14
15. Office equipment, computers	14
16. Chemicals	13
17. Drugs	13
18. Electrical, electronics	13
19. Railroads	13
20. Natural resources (fuel)	12
21. Tobacco	12
22. Food processing	11
23. Leisure time	11
24. Real estate & housing	11
25. Personal care products	10
26. Banks & bank holding co's.	9
27. Beverages	9
28. Metals & mining	9
29. Retailing (nonfood)	9
30. Textiles, apparel	9
31. Containers	8
32. Retailing food	8
33. Tires & rubber	6

34. Utilities	5
35. Steel	1
36. Appliances	-2
37. Airlines	NM
38. Automotive	NM
All industry composite	11

NM (not measurable)

Source of data: "Corporate Scoreboard," *Business Week,* May 18, 1981, pp. 75–104.

Industry Growth and the "Life Cycle"

Some writers, notably the late Julius Grodinsky,[8] have drawn a rough parallel between industry growth and the human life cycle. They point out correctly that when new industries are born, there is often a rush by many companies to enter the field in the period of initial and usually rapid growth. This is generally followed by a shakeout period with only a relatively few survivors and by a continuing period of strong growth, although the rate of growth is slower than in the initial period. Grodinsky described these first two periods as (1) the pioneering stage and (2) the expansion stage. Finally, industries are expected to stop growing, either living a relatively stable existence for an extended period or dying.

Grodinsky pointed out the great risk in selecting stocks of companies in the pioneering stage prior to the first shakeout and survival of the few. Those with luck or skill, or a combination of both, who have selected the few survivors may have done well, but the difficulties of such selection in the pioneering stage are great. Security analysis, valuation, and selection require adequate information. If there is little or no past record, there is little to guide future projections. Some suggest participating in the pioneering phase by buying the stocks of several companies in the new industry and thereby spreading the risks. This admits inability to predict the successful survivors and assumes the profits on the survivors will result in a return high enough to be satisfactory for the high level of risk accepted, even after allowing for losses on those companies that do not survive.

The life-cycle theory at least implies, even where not explicitly stated by proponents, that investors should purchase only securities of companies whose earnings have grown and are expected to grow at a significantly faster rate than earnings of corporations overall. Thus, it in fact becomes the "growth" theory of investment that so many investors have adopted. But, by definition, only an extremely small proportion

---

[8] Julius Grodinsky, *Investments* (New York: The Ronald Press, 1953), Part II.

of all stocks can meet the test. If an important proportion of investment funds attempts to crowd into this small select group, the prices of such stocks can and very frequently do get pushed to extremely high prices (high price-earnings ratios) and extremely low or nonexistent dividend yields. Conversely, other stocks may be relatively neglected by institutions and they become undervalued in the market place.

Those strongly favoring investing only in growth stocks dismiss lightly the suggestion that many, if not most, such stocks sell at relatively high P/E ratios that may more than discount their "growth" potential. Growth advocates state that high P/E ratios are merely an illusion because expected fast growth in earnings will bring the P/E ratio in line with other companies over time. The experience with "growth" favorites in the mid-sixties has proven the importance of considering relative prices and values when selecting securities.

Most companies must, by definition, be in industries in the maturity stage, still growing but only at about the same rate as the economy (or a slightly higher or slightly lower rate). Other companies must be in industries growing at a significantly slower rate, while a relatively few industries and companies may be experiencing a definite secular downturn. Under the life-cycle or growth stock thesis, all of these companies should be avoided regardless of the prices at which their securities sell on the market. This would preclude a portfolio that was a cross-section of the American economy, which would grow only with the economy and would, of course, preclude the "index fund" policy.

The life-cycle approach could also eliminate investment in industries and companies that were experiencing temporary periods of decline in earnings even though projections are that they will experience an earnings recovery. Industries do not necessarily decline at some given point in their life. New products are developed—for example, double knits in the wool industry or new uses for cement—after a period of decline. Furthermore, many modern companies operate in more than one industry and frequently change their product lines. The difficulty lies in classifying companies within given industries according to assumed life-cycle stages.

Forecasting End-Use Demand Through Input-Output Tables

Above-average growth for a company is usually predicated on expected rapid growth of the industry in which the company operates. However, a company may accomplish above-average growth by gaining an increasing share of total industry demand. Forecasting end-use demand is therefore important to the analyst, although quite difficult to accomplish.

Historically, analysts would first obtain from industry and company sources the major end uses of the products produced. Next they would forecast the demand for each of these end uses, and then they would include these forecasts in final total industry demand projections. This process started with the past end-use demand statistics and the historical patterns found. The analyst then tried to forecast future trends and shifts in demand leading to estimates of new potential end-use demand. The problem of substitutes and competing products, of course, had to be considered in such forecasts. In many industries this involved an analysis of foreign as well as domestic demand and supply.

Input-output tables indicate how much each industry requires of the production of each other industry to produce each dollar of its own output. The various industrial subdivisions are listed both vertically and horizontally and resemble an intercity milage chart on a road map. The individual inputs into a given industry are read vertically, while the industry's dollar sales to other specific industries are read horizontally. This is called an input-output flow table, as it shows the flow of dollar sales from each industry to other industries. Another table that is based on the flow table is prepared, but that divides each column in the flow table by the output of the using industry. This table effectively presents the requirements of an industry for each dollar of its output and therefore is called an input-output coefficient table. None of this has yet been reduced to a company base, and up-to-date tables are not available.[9]

ANALYZING GROWTH

After making projections for GNP and its components and for specific industries, the analyst will proceed to analyze past growth of a company and current factors that could cause changes in past growth rates. This forms the basis for projections for that company.

Charting as an Aid in Analyzing Growth

In analyzing growth the analyst will find it helpful to chart certain data from available statistics in areas such as sales, net income, cash flow, and earnings per share. Comparisons over time can then be made, with a given company's data compared to past records and projections for competing companies and industry and economic aggregates.

In such charting use of semilogarithmic chart paper is helpful. Arithmetically spaced paper can give misleading results as equal space on the chart reflects equal absolute quantities, not rates of growth. On the other hand, with semilogarithmic chart paper equal space changes

---

[9] For further details on pursuing an input-output industry analysis, see M. F. Elliott-Jones, *Input-Output Analysis: A Nontechnical Description* (New York: The Conference Board, 1972). Also Clopper Almon, Jr., *Matrix Methods in Economics* (Reading, Mass.: Addison-Wesley, 1967) offers a discussion of how to utilize "matrix inversion" to determine from the basic input-output tables the amount of a given product sales, say copper, accounted for by given expenditure categories, such as personal consumption expenditures.

represent equal percentage changes, and thus changes in rates of growth are highlighted. The slope of a line and the changing character of the slope on semilogarithmic paper indicate the stability or the accelerating or decelerating nature of the rate of growth.

The first stage would be simply to extrapolate the average growth of at least the past five years. Then the important factor is the judgment of the analyst—whether factors for the industry or company lead the analyst to believe that the future growth rate will be about the same or is likely to be higher or lower than the past and how much higher or lower. At this point the analyst, being interested in earnings growth and its implications for investor returns, must consider cost factors as well as sales. Business cycle anticipations must also be considered in assessing earnings growth and market reaction. Statistical techniques such as correlation and trend analysis are often utilized to aid in generating projections. However, mathematical models will not replace the need for sound judgment on the part of the analyst, and no method will eliminate the possibility of incorrect forecasts.

Growth in Sales or Gross Revenues

Growth in earnings, and especially in earnings per share, is what the investor is most concerned with because this growth provides the basis for increased dividends and higher stock prices. It will be exceptional for earnings to increase for any extended period of time if this increase is not the result of a growth in sales supported by growth in invested capital. Therefore, the analyst first concentrates on the record of sales growth and a projection for sales. The compound rate of growth of sales and earnings should be calculated for a period of years (at least five and preferably ten years), and the regularity or irregularity of growth determined. The resistance or lack of resistance of company sales to general economic recession is also of interest, as well as the trend in sales. The sales record and rate of growth should be compared with those of competing industries to the extent that such comparisons are meaningful; for example, aluminum vs. copper, glass containers vs. tin, aluminum vs. paper containers, and synthetic fibers vs. natural fibers. Finally the sales record should be compared with the record of GNP and major components of GNP that provide meaningful comparison. For example, sales of department stores, autos, or drug companies might best be correlated with disposable personal income since their products are consumer goods. A true "growth" situation will show a more rapid growth than the economy as a whole and the major components of GNP to which it is related. Furthermore, an economic recession is expected to only slow, not stop, the growth.

An analysis of total sales dollars of a company may give a misleading impression of growth. During an inflationary period a company may well report rising dollar sales that do not represent growth in real demand for the company's output but merely rising prices with a constant or declining number of units being sold. Unit sales should be analyzed as well as dollar sales. In most cases, unfortunately, the analyst can obtain only units produced rather than sold. Production may be going into inventory, as in the case of steel in the first six months of 1977, rather than representing sales. Later sales may draw not only on production but also on inventory. However, over any extended period in a well-managed company, unit production should correlate closely with unit sales.

The analyst can secure unit production data from numerous sources. The U.S. government's yearly *Statistical Abstract of the United States* furnishes a great amount of data on this subject. Current data can be obtained from the *Survey of Current Business*, trade periodicals, and industry associations. In addition, the *Federal Reserve Bulletin* furnishes the Index of Industrial Production monthly in total, and subdivided into many industry groupings. In the latter case, indexes are shown rather than actual production units; but for the purpose of analyzing growth, they serve the same purpose as actual unit production figures and could even be converted to units for approximations.

Sales should be analyzed in terms of product lines for purposes of forecasting future growth. The SEC has proposed criteria for the breakdown of sales and earnings data of diversified companies. While this data is useful to the analyst, the problem of allocation of common costs may seriously distort the reported profit data. Such allocations are to a large extent arbitrary, and it would be preferable if profitability data were provided on the basis of the contribution margin of each segment reported (i.e., revenues less direct costs that are specifically traceable to that product line).

Industry price data should also be analyzed. There is a strong tendency in industries in the pioneering stage for prices to be relatively high compared to costs. This is usually followed by a declining price trend as the advantages of large-scale production are evidenced and the industry reaches out for larger markets. As increasing competition is encountered in the expansion stage, the desire to utilize unused capacity often spurs price reductions, which have a different implication than the declining price trend associated with economies of scale. There is also a problem if inflationary forces are strong in the nation as in 1941–1957 and 1966–1981. Under such conditions the costs of labor and materials rise, and industries attempt to raise prices to maintain profit margins. For various reasons some industries do not have a demand situation that will support raising prices sufficiently to offset rising costs, and government action may attempt to restrict price increases. The price record is one good indication of the strength and the growth of demand. Grodinsky felt that a relatively greater rise in prices compared with a competitive industry or the general price level was one danger signal suggesting maturity and/or decline.[10]

In the final analysis the analyst must ascertain the determinants of the sales record being studied. The analyst is attempting to forecast future sales trends and must decide whether the sales pattern that existed in the past will persist in the future. If changes seem likely, the estimated extent and nature of the changes must be determined. Mere extrapolation is not a sound forecasting technique.

Growth in Earnings

The investment value of a stock and its market price over any period of time are determined by its expected earnings and dividends. While gross revenues (mainly sales) are the basic source of funds to a corporation, there may be sales or revenue growth over the years without a correlated growth in earnings. This situation has occurred in many industries since 1966. Costs have often risen faster than sales prices could be increased. Also, exceptionally high profits may attract entry of other firms and, therefore, competition that will slow future growth.

In the final analysis investors are interested not in growth in total corporate net earnings as such, but in growth in earnings per share. There can be growth in total dollar earnings, but a slower or even negative growth in earnings per share because of an increase in the number of shares outstanding (earnings dilution). Growth in earnings per share can be the result of either growth in the rate of return on the stockholders' equity or growth in the total equity per share, or both, as shown below, where EAC equals earnings available to common stockholders.

$$\frac{EAC}{Common\ Equity} \times \frac{Common\ Equity}{Number\ of\ Shares} = \frac{EAC}{Number\ of\ Shares}.$$

Over any extended period of time there usually must be an increase in total invested capital and in stockholders' equity to provide increases in earnings per share. Simply to have an increased rate of return on a more or less stable capital base would be unusual. A growth in stockholders' equity and in equity per share is the result of either earnings retention or the sale of additional stock at prices in excess of book value. The most important source of the growth of assets of industrial corporations has been retained earnings, and for many corporations this has been the sole source of growth.

For other corporations the source of growth of assets has been a combination of retained earnings, the sale of debt instruments (increasingly common in recent years) or other increases in liabilities (such as

---

[10] Grodinsky, *Investments*, pp. 81–85.

increases in liability "reserves" of insurance companies or deposits in banks), and the sale of common and preferred stock. An increase in assets resulting from an increase in liabilities does not increase the stockholders' equity at the time of the increase in liabilities, but does so only if earnings on the additional assets exceed the cost of the increased liabilities (favorable financial leverage).

As a result of retaining earnings, the rate of growth of earnings per share is the product of the rate of return earned on equity times the proportion of earnings retained, assuming past rates earned on owners' capital can at least be maintained. A more meaningful way to calculate the annual rate of return on equity is to use as the equity base an average of the equity at the beginning and the end of the fiscal period, thus allowing for the flow of retained earnings into investment and into equity during the year.

If corporations overall or in terms of the DJIA or the Standard & Poor's indexes retain 45 percent of earnings and if they earn pretax 10 to 13 percent (average $11\frac{1}{2}$ percent) on their total equity, then the annual compound rate of growth of earnings per share can be calculated as $11\frac{1}{2}$ percent $\times$ 45 percent, or 5.18 percent per year.

RATE OF RETURN ON SALES AND ON EQUITY

The analyst is interested not only in the historical rate of return on equity but also in the reasons for this rate. The net rate of return on sales is one source of the rate of return on equity, and the turnover of invested capital is the other.[11] Given a stated rate of return on sales, the higher the turnover rate of stockholders' equity, the higher the rate of return on this equity.

Rate of Return on Assets

The analyst will find it useful to analyze return on owners' capital in terms of the leverage factor and the return on corporate assets. This allows more critical and meaningful analysis. The relationships can be shown as follows, where EAC refers to earnings available to common stockholders:

$$\frac{EAC}{Total\ Assets} \times \frac{Total\ Assets}{Owners'\ Equity} = \frac{EAC}{Owners'\ Equity};$$

$$\frac{EAC}{Net\ Sales} \times \frac{Net\ Sales}{Total\ Assets} = \frac{EAC}{Total\ Assets}.$$

_____

[11] $\dfrac{EAC}{Net\ Sales} \times \dfrac{Net\ Sales}{Owners'\ Equity} = \dfrac{EAC}{Owners'\ Equity}$, where EAC refers to earnings available to common stockholders.

Table 18-10 shows the historical record of return on stockholders' equity and the margin earned on sales for durable and nondurable goods industries. Table 18-11 gives detailed industry breakdowns for 1979-1980.

TABLE 18-10. Relation of Profits after Taxes to Stockholders' Equity and to Sales, All Manufacturing Corporations, 1947-1980

Year or Quarter	Ratio of Profits After Income Taxes (Annual Rate) to Stockholders' Equity—Percent[a]			Profits After Income Taxes Per Dollar of Sales—Cents		
	All Manufacturing Corporations	Durable Goods Industries	Nondurable Goods Industries	All Manufacturing Corporations	Durable Goods Industries	Nondurable Goods Industries
1947	15.6	14.4	16.6	6.7	6.7	6.7
1948	16.0	15.7	16.2	7.0	7.1	6.8
1949	11.6	12.1	11.2	5.8	6.4	5.4
1950	15.4	16.9	14.1	7.1	7.7	6.5
1951	12.1	13.0	11.2	4.8	5.3	4.5
1952	10.3	11.1	9.7	4.3	4.5	4.1
1953	10.5	11.1	9.9	4.3	4.2	4.3
1954	9.9	10.3	9.6	4.5	4.6	4.4
1955	12.6	13.8	11.4	5.4	5.7	5.1
1956	12.3	12.8	11.8	5.3	5.2	5.3
1957	10.9	11.3	10.6	4.8	4.8	4.9
1958	8.6	8.0	9.2	4.2	3.9	4.4
1959	10.4	10.4	10.4	4.8	4.8	4.9
1960	9.2	8.5	9.8	4.4	4.0	4.8
1961	8.9	8.1	9.6	4.3	3.9	4.7
1962	9.8	9.6	9.9	4.5	4.4	4.7
1963	10.3	10.1	10.4	4.7	4.5	4.9
1964	11.6	11.7	11.5	5.2	5.1	5.4
1965	13.0	13.8	12.2	5.6	5.7	5.5
1966	13.4	14.2	12.7	5.6	5.6	5.6
1967	11.7	11.7	11.8	5.0	4.8	5.3
1968	12.1	12.2	11.9	5.1	4.9	5.2
1969	11.5	11.4	11.5	4.8	4.6	5.0
1970	9.3	8.3	10.3	4.0	3.5	4.5
1971	9.7	9.0	10.3	4.1	3.8	4.5
1972	10.6	10.8	10.5	4.3	4.2	4.4
1973	12.8	13.1	12.6	4.7	4.7	4.8
1973: IV	13.4	12.9	14.0	4.7	4.5	5.0

TABLE 18-10. Relation of Profits after Taxes to Stockholders' Equity and to Sales, All Manufacturing Corporations, 1947-1980 (continued)

	Ratio of Profits After Income Taxes (Annual Rate) To Stockholders' Equity—Percent[a]			Profits After Income Taxes Per Dollar of Sales—Cents		
Year or Quarter	All Manu- facturing Corpora- tions	Durable Goods Industries	Non- durable Goods Industries	All Manu- facturing Corpora- tions	Durable Goods Industries	Non- durable Goods Industries
New series:						
1973: IV	14.3	13.3	15.3	5.6	5.0	6.1
1974	14.9	12.6	17.1	5.5	4.7	6.4
1975	11.6	10.3	12.9	4.6	4.1	5.1
1976	13.9	13.7	14.2	5.4	5.2	5.5
1977	14.2	14.5	13.8	5.3	5.3	5.3
1978	15.0	16.0	14.2	5.4	5.5	5.3
1979	16.4	15.4	17.4	5.7	5.2	6.1
1977:						
I	13.0	13.0	13.0	5.0	5.0	5.0
II	16.0	17.1	15.0	5.8	6.0	5.6
III	13.3	12.9	13.7	5.0	4.8	5.3
IV	14.4	15.1	13.7	5.3	5.4	5.2
1978:						
I	12.4	12.7	12.1	4.7	4.7	4.8
II	16.7	18.7	14.8	5.9	6.2	5.6
III	14.9	15.5	14.4	5.4	5.4	5.4
IV	16.1	17.0	15.3	5.6	5.6	5.6
1979:						
I	15.7	16.2	15.3	5.6	5.5	5.6
II	18.1	18.4	17.8	6.1	6.0	6.3
III	16.3	14.0	18.4	5.7	4.8	6.4
IV	15.7	13.4	17.9	5.3	4.6	6.0
1980:						
I	15.4	12.6	18.1	5.3	4.4	6.1
II	13.7	10.6	16.5	4.8	3.8	5.7
III	12.6	9.2	15.7	4.5	3.4	5.5

[a]Annual ratios based on average equity for the year (using four end-of-quarter figures). Quarterly ratios based on equity at end of quarter only.

Note: Based on data in millions of dollars.

Source: Economic Report of the President, January, 1981, p. 329.

TABLE 18-11. Relation of Profits after Taxes to Stockholders' Equity and to Sales, All Manufacturing Corporations, by Industry Group, 1979–1980

Industry	Ratio of Profits After Income Taxes (Annual Rate) to Stockholders' Equity—Percent[a]					Profits After Income Taxes Per Dollar of Sales—Cents				
	1979		1980			1979		1980		
	III	IV	I	II	III	III	IV	I	II	III
All manufacturing corporations	16.3	15.7	15.4	13.7	12.6	5.7	5.3	5.3	4.8	4.5
Durable goods industries	14.0	13.4	12.6	10.6	9.2	4.8	4.6	4.4	3.8	3.4
Stone, clay, and glass products	19.4	13.9	5.9	11.5	14.4	6.8	5.2	2.5	4.6	5.4
Primary metals industries	13.3	5.7	16.8	11.8	5.6	4.4	1.9	5.4	4.2	2.1
Iron and steel	11.7	-2.3	12.8	8.2	3.4	3.7	-.7	3.9	2.7	1.2
Nonferrous metals	15.8	18.2	22.9	17.1	8.7	6.0	6.7	7.9	6.7	3.6
Fabricated metal products	15.8	15.4	16.6	13.3	12.3	4.5	4.4	5.0	4.0	3.8
Machinery, except electrical	16.0	17.2	14.1	15.6	13.9	6.8	7.2	6.0	6.6	6.3
Electrical and electronic equipment	16.4	17.6	16.0	14.8	14.2	5.3	5.5	5.1	4.8	4.8
Transportation equipment[b]	5.2	7.9	3.8	-3.6	-6.2	1.7	2.5	1.2	-1.2	-2.1
Motor vehicles and equipment	-.5	3.5	-2.2	-14.1	-18.1	-.2	1.2	-.8	-5.2	-6.9
Aircraft, guided missiles, and parts	17.9	18.3	16.5	16.5	15.4	5.1	5.0	4.5	4.3	4.3
Instruments and related products	16.2	17.0	16.2	17.3	17.6	8.4	8.7	8.5	8.9	9.1
Other durable manufacturing products	19.7	15.7	12.5	9.0	12.2	5.2	4.1	3.6	2.7	3.6

TABLE 18-11. Relation of Profits after Taxes to Stockholders' Equity and to Sales, All Manufacturing Corporations, by Industry Group, 1979-1980 (continued)

| Industry | Ratio of Profits After Income Taxes (Annual Rate) to Stockholders' Equity—Percent[a] | | | | | Profits After Income Taxes Per Dollar of Sales—Cents | | | | |
| | 1979 | | 1980 | | | 1979 | | 1980 | | |
	III	IV	I	II	III	III	IV	I	II	III
Nondurable goods industries	18.4	17.9	18.1	16.5	15.7	6.4	6.0	6.1	5.7	5.5
Food and kindred products	17.2	13.8	12.8	13.4	15.1	3.9	3.1	3.0	3.1	3.4
Tobacco manufactures	21.6	18.4	21.2	20.2	22.3	13.1	10.8	13.1	12.1	13.0
Textile mill products	13.4	12.5	10.9	7.9	6.7	3.7	3.2	2.8	2.0	1.8
Paper and allied products	20.5	13.4	13.3	13.1	10.8	8.2	5.4	5.4	5.5	4.6
Printing and publishing	20.1	16.8	15.0	16.5	17.3	6.8	5.5	5.2	5.6	5.8
Chemicals and allied products[b]	15.9	15.3	18.0	15.3	15.0	7.2	7.0	8.0	7.1	7.1
Industrial chemicals and synthetics	13.3	13.6	16.1	12.3	9.6	5.9	6.1	6.8	5.7	4.7
Drugs	18.4	17.9	21.6	18.3	22.6	12.4	11.9	14.0	12.4	15.1
Petroleum and coal products	21.1	24.6	24.3	21.5	18.2	9.0	9.5	9.0	8.4	7.2
Rubber and miscellaneous plastics products	8.8	5.6	7.7	5.6	6.2	2.7	1.7	2.4	1.8	2.0
Other nondurable manufacturing products	19.0	14.3	10.5	10.3	16.0	3.7	2.8	2.2	2.2	3.1

[a] Ratios based on equity at end of quarter.
[b] Includes other industries not shown separately.
Source: Economic Report of the President, January, 1981, p. 330.

Operating and nonoperating factors that enter into determining the return on total assets can be studied separately by utilizing net operating earnings and nonoperating earnings separately as the numerators for the margin component in the previous equations (EAC/Net Sales). The efficiency of corporate operating assets is best judged in terms of net operating earnings, since leverage resulting from debt financing and tax factors are separate variables. When analyzing operating efficiency, the analyst should be careful to separate recurring and nonrecurring factors. Projections should only reflect recurring factors.

As with all other ratios, the trends in the ratios and the factors underlying these trends are what is important. Ratios raise questions; they do not answer questions. If the ratio of sales to operating assets is increasing for a given firm, it may indicate increasing efficiency in the use of assets, but it may also indicate a need for more investment in assets. Conversely, if the ratio is declining, it may indicate declining ability to effectively utilize assets with serious profit implications, or it may reflect a recent rapid plant expansion which has not yet been completed or for which there has not yet been time to utilize the assets to reach future potential markets. The analyst must assess the underlying causes for the changing patterns found, and their implications for future profitability, not merely mechanically calculate and read ratios.

The Leverage Factor

Corporations are in business to make a profit, and the major tests of corporate management are the rates of return earned on sales, on total assets, on total capital, and on stockholders' equity. The difference between the latter two ratios indicates the effect of financial leverage. Table 18-12 shows the effect of financial leverage over a five-year period for selected companies. The leverage factor is discussed in greater detail in Chapter 20.

MANAGEMENT AND EARNINGS GROWTH

Management has the responsibility of generating sales (or gross revenues) and the responsibility of controlling costs to maximize profits. Financial success is the result of high-quality management, and failure is the result of poor management. Rate of return *and* its volatility are important.

Measuring the quality of management other than as indicated above is very difficult, but professional analysts are constantly attempting to make qualitative judgments. They attempt to learn as much as possible concerning management policies and the direction of these policies. However, they will have more faith in stated management policies and the direction in which management says it is headed if past statements

TABLE 18-12. Effect of Capitalization (Financial) Leverage, Five-Year Period, 1976-1980

	Return on Total Capital	Return on Equity
Continental Telephone Corp.	5.3%	12.8%
Panhandle Eastern Pipe Line Co.	7.1	15.6
General Telephone & Electronics Corp.	5.8	12.7
Texas Utilities Co.	6.1	11.9
RCA Corporation	7.8	12.4
Trans World Airlines, Inc.	2.7	7.1
Beneficial Corp.	2.6	10.7
General Dynamics Corp.	9.9	10.6
American Airlines, Inc.	2.4	4.5
Eastern Air Lines, Inc.	2.3	7.0
Crown Cork & Seal Company, Inc.	13.0	13.5
Georgia-Pacific Corp.	9.6	14.0
Celanese Corp.	6.0	8.8
Owens-Illinois, Inc.	5.8	8.4
Pittston Co.	9.4	10.7
Tenneco Inc.	8.6	16.5
Kaiser Aluminum & Chemical Corp.	8.2	12.9
Uniroyal, Inc.	-5.0	-8.7
Reynolds Metals Co.	5.9	8.7

of management policies, including those in past annual reports, have actually resulted in the realization of the stated goals.

The financial analyst visiting with management will attempt to assess the intensity of management's desire for the company to grow rather than the desire to rest on its laurels. In this respect, the age of management is often quite important. As management ages, there can be a tendency to slow down. This tendency can be offset by the regular influx of younger blood into top management as shown by a policy of mandatory retirements and the training and development of junior management for positions of responsibility. The analyst must be aware of one negative factor disclosed by numerous studies: a close correlation in many cases between the size of a business and management compensation. Therefore, the analyst must determine if the company places emphasis on growth in profits and not merely growth in total assets and sales.

In analyzing management the investor must realize that our economy is in a constant state of change—in some areas gradual change and in others revolutionary change. An example of the latter is the recent shift from low-cost to high-cost energy. Sales growth will usually result from product and marketing research and sound capital expenditures. Management must therefore follow policies that will anticipate and contribute to appropriate change in its product mix. Markets may be broadened not only by innovations but also by means taken to reduce costs and therefore reach larger markets by lowering sales prices.

RESEARCH AND DEVELOPMENT AND
GROWTH OF SALES AND EARNINGS

Because management realizes the importance placed on research and development, there is a tendency for some managements to inflate reported expenditures on research and development. The analyst can avoid this trap by concentrating on an analysis of the results of research and development in terms of products, sales, and profits. The analyst can get some help in determining the amounts spent by checking the companies' registration statements under both the SEC Act of 1933 and the SEC Act of 1934.

In analyzing company research and development, some companies provide assistance to the analyst by dividing research and development expenses into three headings: (1) basic research, (2) product-oriented research, and (3) specialized research, the latter usually under contract with the government. Although contract research for the government does not directly and immediately help the company's civilian business knowledge and experience, gains are often transferable to civilian products. The Burroughs Corporation illustrates this factor.

Most companies do not spend an important part of research and development expenditures on basic research, although the hope of such research is that it will produce some practical results in the long run. Usually, only the very large and profitable companies believe they can justify significant expenditures for basic research. Companies tend to stress product research.

On the other side of the research and development problem is the record of many new companies started by engineers and scientists to capitalize on their research ideas. In many cases the results have been unsatisfactory since innovators have often lacked practical business know-how. But there have been a number of spectacular successes that have caused this type of "investment" to be attractive to many investors.

Innovation involves risk, and success is usually the result of a balance between fostering innovation without accepting exceptionally large risks requiring large amounts of capital. On the other hand, management that overemphasizes the risk aspect will be deterred from obtaining exceptional growth. Exceptional profit growth will usually be the result of accepting above-normal risk.

The size of a company also affects ability to accept risk. Large companies (such as RCA Corporation and International Business Machines) can accept substantial dollar amounts of risk that cannot be assumed or even financed by smaller companies. In respect to size, the marketing aspect of converting innovations into sales and profits is as important as innovation itself and most of the time exceeds substantially the research and development expenses. Size tends to provide both the funds and the opportunity to promote new products successfully.

GROWTH THROUGH MERGERS

The post–World War II years have witnessed the largest and by far the greatest merger movements in our history. In fact, stock market speculation during 1981 focused strongly on merger and acquisition activity.[12] Some expect that merger and acquisition activity will accelerate in 1982 because of the favorable effects on cash flow of businesses of the cuts in corporate tax rates that will take effect. Mergers provide the fastest method of corporate growth.

One of the major problems involved in mergers of successful companies is the problem of management of the numerous companies involved. Top management of the constituent companies being absorbed may find that it is no longer the top management but is subservient to new top management. This can interfere with the successful operations of the companies in the merged enterprise. Historically, the major justification for mergers has been the argument that the merged companies can operate more efficiently and with lower overhead. The advantages of economy of size include lower operating costs and smaller financial costs. In recent years numerous mergers have apparently placed undue emphasis on the financial aspect of the merger rather than on opportunities for higher profits for the constituent companies as compared with their results when they were separate entities.

Numerous managements in the 1960s took advantage of the relative popularity of conglomerates and the resulting high P/E ratios for such stocks. A merger could result in increased earnings per share without any real growth in combined earnings after taxes when shares were exchanged at the market P/E ratios for the companies being merged. This is illustrated in Table 18–13. When the parent builds a capital structure using convertible securities, leverage may also result in reported

_____
[12] Merger and acquisition activity was estimated to involve about $80 billion in 1981 in an article in the *Wall Street Journal,* January 4, 1982, p. 11.

TABLE 18-13. Earnings per Share Effects of an Assumed Merger Between Companies A and B

	Earnings After Taxes	Number of Shares	Earnings Per Share	P/E Ratio
		Before Merger		
Company A	$10,000	10,000	$1.00	20
Company B	5,000	5,000	1.00	10
		After Merger		
Company A	$15,000	12,500*	$1.20	

*Assumes shares are exchanged on the basis of the P/E ratios, or each stockholder of Company B receives one share of Company A for each two shares of B.

earnings-per-share growth that is superior to actual earnings growth of the constituents.

The poor market performance of the stocks of major corporations since 1966 has no doubt stimulated merger and acquisition activity. As previously noted, the stock prices were relatively flat during the period, while the price level (as measured by the consumer price index) has roughly tripled. On an inflation-adjusted basis stocks are valued at only about one-third of their 1966 value; many companies, therefore, would find expansion through acquisition less expensive than expansion by means of new capital investment.

As a company grows, the problems of top management in handling the larger company also increase. In the case of conglomerates, the problems may multiply sharply, especially during general economic recessions. Managements that were successful in managing companies of a given size and in only one industry may prove to be less successful in meeting the problems of rapidly expanding companies. The analyst must constantly measure the performance of management as a company grows, particularly if the growth is spectacular as a result of mergers and strong diversification.

Historically, management has usually been faced with a period of digestion as it has acquired companies of any significant size. This has been a period of adjustment before the expected economies are effected. One seeming phenomenon of the merger movement of the 1960s was the apparent ability of management to escape the difficulties of such an adjustment period. But the record of 1970–1978 brought out the major weaknesses in many of the former popular conglomerates. Drastic declines in stock prices resulted, and considerable divestiture was required.

Summary

Investors should understand that the growth of the economy and of industries and companies is an essential environment for successful investing. The condition and levels of the financial markets in the 1930s, a period of stagnation with a very low level of growth for the decade, give a clear indication of the essential nature of growth required for successful investing. The stagflation of the 1970s also indicates the problems of investing in an environment of relatively high inflation while experiencing difficulties in real growth. It is very difficult for industries and companies to grow satisfactorily if the overall economy is not demonstrating satisfactory growth.

Therefore, the first factor in financial analysis is a determination of the expected rate of growth for the economy and major segments of the economy such as industrial production. Publications of the U.S. Department of Commerce and the National Planning Association are particularly helpful in this respect. After judgments are made as to the expected growth of the economy and its subdivisions, the investor must make projections for specific industries and relate them to projections for the economy. Finally, the investor must make projections for individual companies related to projections for the economy and for industries. Growth for companies may be internally generated or the result of mergers or acquisitions. In any case, it is important that growth results in growth in earnings and earnings per share—that is, that dilution does not significantly reduce or eliminate for stockholders the advantages of growth of revenues.

The investor must realize that all projections are based on subjective judgments depending on the ability of the analyst and that the results obtained are in any case only probabilities. The further projections are made into the future, the greater the uncertainties and the less their reliability for the future.

To prepare reasonable projections for the economy and its subdivisions, the investor should understand the past history, composition, and causes and effects of business cycles and subcycles, such as cycles of industrial production and of industries. While each cycle differs in certain aspects from past cycles, there are certain significant repetitive aspects of expansions and contractions with the seeds of the following phase of a cycle generated in the preceding phase of the cycle.

The investor must understand that cycles of profits are generally more volatile than business cycles and that the volatility of profits differs quite widely among industries and companies. Furthermore, corporate dividends demonstrate much more stability during business cycles than do earnings.

Questions

1. It has been said that "growth" is the normal characteristic of the American economy. Review the past as a base for projecting possible future growth.
2. Discuss business cycles and the investor.
3. Discuss reasonable industry selection versus wide diversification.
4. (a) What are input-output tables? In your answer distinguish between the input-output flow table and the input-output coefficient table.
   (b) Of what use might such tables be to investment analysts?
5. Analyze the past record of interest rates and bond prices.
6. Discuss the usefulness and the limitations of the "industrial life cycle" concept from the standpoint of investment analysis.
7. Discuss the charts you would draw to aid in analyzing sales growth of a company and what you would specifically look for in the analysis of those charts. Note specifically the data you would include in the charts, the time period you would study, and the scale you would use in constructing the charts.
8. (a) Why should the analyst carefully study unit sales data as well as dollar sales data?
   (b) Of what significance is the product price record of a company?
9. (a) What are the two basic factors underlying growth in earnings per share? Why is volatility as important as growth?
   (b) How would you assess the likely effect of earnings retention on future earnings per share?
   (c) Carefully explain the relationship between profit margins and rate of return on equity capital and on total capital for a given company.
10. (a) How would a security analyst attempt to determine whether or not management had a sufficiently broad conception of its market?
    (b) What factors would you study in evaluating the management of a company? Do analysts often rely on their intuition in this respect?

Work-Study Problems

1. Select three industries you believe will outperform the economy over the next five years and justify your choices.
2. (a) Select two companies in the same industry, with quite different price-earnings ratios, and prepare charts that you feel would be helpful in studying their growth trends in sales and earnings and their volatility.

(b) Prepare sales and earnings projections for these companies for the next five years, carefully noting the assumptions underlying your projections.

(c) What factors underline differences in growth rates and volatility of earnings of the two companies as observed by you?

19.

Security Analysis: Approach and Basic Issues

The objective of security analysis is to screen and classify financial assets in terms of investment quality (basically financial risk) and intrinsic value.[1] The security analyst utilizes expectations for the economy in the aggregate and for industry groupings (product line analysis) for the purpose of forecasting dividends and stock prices of particular companies as a basis for estimating expected returns from an investment.[2] Expected returns are then related to investment quality gradings of the companies (a surrogate for risk) as a basis for appraising relative attractiveness of the various securities under consideration. The remaining chapters of this part will develop the fundamental analysis approach; applications to special classes of securities will be presented in Part 8 of the book.

THE PROBLEMS OF QUALITY GRADING

Quality grading for bonds is discussed at some length in Chapter 23. The major emphasis when grading bonds is on ability to meet all obligations in years of poor as well as good economic conditions. The highest quality ratings for bonds suggest coverage for obligations by earnings and cash flow to such an extent that the probability that the company will not be able to meet its obligations is practically nonexistent. Such quality ratings are based on analysis of one type of risk—the financial risk—and ignore other aspects of risk.

---

[1] Intrinsic value was defined in Chapter 7 as the present value of all future income expected from an asset. For common stocks, it is often estimated by multiplying normalized earnings per share by an appropriate price-earnings multiplier.
[2] Forecasts of earnings, dividends, and stock prices would best be prepared in the form of probability distributions, recognizing the uncertainty underlying such forecasts.

460

Quality grading of common stocks also emphasizes the risk that a series of expected cash receipts for a given security will not be realized. The less the uncertainty foreseen in realizing expected dividends and earnings growth, and the stronger the underlying financial condition of the company, the higher the grade of the securities being evaluated in terms of financial risk. Standard and Poor's, for example, explains that their common stock ratings are designed to indicate by the use of symbols the relative stability and growth of earnings and dividends of the most recent ten years while also making adjustments for corporate size and "special considerations such as natural disasters, massive strikes and nonrecurring accounting adjustments."[3] Standard and Poor's is careful to point out that "a ranking is not a forecast of future market performance but is basically an appraisal of past performance of earnings and dividends. . . ."[4]

Investors in bonds and stocks face purchasing power risk, interest rate risk, and market risk, as well as financial risk. Quality ratings are therefore not an effective indicator of the total risk exposure of an investor. Modern portfolio theory provides the only consistent and integrated approach to handling risk and return but has not really been developed to handle bonds. Still, all aspects of risk must be considered when making investment decisions. Published quality ratings for common stocks are much less widely used than those for bonds, possibly because bonds have often been bought as a defensive investment emphasizing the yield to maturity and relative certainty of receiving that yield rather than growth.

VALUATION: A CORNERSTONE
OF FUNDAMENTAL ANALYSIS

Valuation of common stocks rests on the ability of the analyst to anticipate the future performance of a company. As discussed in Chapter 7, valuation would be relatively easy in a world of certainty, but once uncertainty about future earnings, dividends, and stock prices is recognized, fundamental analysis can suggest only a range of values based on assumed conditions with varying degrees of probability of occurrence.

Such an analysis does, however, provide a basis for varying assumptions concerning the factors underlying valuation, so that the security analyst can ask "what if" questions. The tools of uncertainty analysis, as developed in Chapter 8, provide a framework for moving from the

---

[3] *Stock Guide* (New York: Standard & Poor's Corporation, November, 1981), p. 7.
[4] *Ibid.*

rather sterile certainty approach to valuation to the more meaningful realization that the usefulness of valuation analysis lies in the original framework it provides for exploring the interaction of the many factors that affect the returns from an investment. Financial analysis must terminate in a projection of future returns and a classification of securities in terms of relative risk if it is to be useful.

Portfolio Selection and Fundamental Analysis

Portfolio selection literature suggests a different approach to security selection than that advocated by fundamental analysis. Stock selection is based largely on expected means, variances, and covariances of rates of return, where such information may be based on subjective or objective sources, with the emphasis on realizing efficiently diversified portfolios as described in Section II, Part 3.

The fundamental approach suggests selecting that stock whose intrinsic value is highest relative to current market price. Risk is taken into account on a subjective and ad-hoc basis by varying the discount rate or capitalization factors used in calculating intrinsic value. This procedure does not imply a one-stock portfolio.[5] If all investors calculated the same intrinsic value (certainty assumption), the demand for that security would quickly push up its price until the margin of intrinsic value over current market price would be greater for other securities. A given security would only be most attractive at a given moment in time; since investors commit funds over time and change their expectations over time, one would expect them to acquire more than one security. Of course, acquiring more than one security would in no way assure that meaningful diversification had been accomplished.

Valuation analysis incorporates a different concept of risk than that utilized in portfolio selection models. By concentrating on individual securities it fails to recognize the importance of covariation of returns and the logically related idea that risk for an individual security and risk for that security as part of a portfolio of securities are two different things. Risk reduction through diversification can only be meaningfully attained when the covariance relationships are taken into account. Portfolio theory has added a new and important dimension to the problem of security selection that is not considered in the fundamental analysis approach alone to selecting securities. An integration of the two approaches is needed.

Optimal portfolio decisions require dependable estimates of risk and return characteristics for individual securities. Basic changes do occur in a firm's characteristics over time, such as changes in product

---

[5] See Harry Markowitz, "Portfolio Selection," *Journal of Finance,* Vol. 7, No. 1 (March, 1952), pp. 77–78, where such an interpretation might be suggested.

mix, technological change, the introduction of new products, variations in capital structure, and merger. A concentration on empirical past return and variance data could lead to improper selection if some attempt is not made to recognize these changes. According to Markowitz,

> these procedures should combine statistical techniques and the judgment of practical men. Our feeling is that statistical computations should be used to arrive at μ_{ii} and σ_{ij}. Judgment should then be used in increasing or decreasing some of these μ_{ii} and σ_{ij} on the basis of factors or nuances not taken into account by the formal computations.[6]

An approach to integration following this logic has been developed in Chapter 11.

Capital Market Theory and Fundamental Analysis

In a perfectly efficient capital market[7] stock prices always fully reflect all publicly and privately available information concerning the securities traded. Security prices would adjust instantaneously and in an unbiased manner to new information as it enters the market. Furthermore, price changes in such efficient markets would perform a random walk—that is, behave in a patternless manner reflecting the random introduction of new information.

It is true that in a perfectly efficient market no technique or analytical tool can be expected to yield systematically above-average returns. However, security analysis is essential to market efficiency since only if investors make conscientious and competent efforts to learn about and apply relevant information promptly and perceptively can efficient markets exist. In the real world users of available information do not necessarily agree on the implications that information has for future corporate performance and stock prices. Furthermore, information is not costless to market participants. Finally, transactions costs do exist. Existing capital markets are probably reasonably efficient, but disequilibrium situations are likely to exist, at least in the short run. Such disequilibrium situations are most likely to come about because of varying and changing interpretations by the various participants in the market, and they are likely to be short lived.

The analyst must recognize that acceptance of the idea that capital markets are relatively efficient and that stock prices perform a random walk does not imply that security analysis is useless. As noted above, security analysis is essential if capital markets are to be efficient. Fundamental analysis, unlike technical approaches and charting, is not

---

[6]*Ibid.*, p. 91. The Greek symbols represent the expected rates of return and covariances, respectively.
[7]For a discussion of the underlying assumptions to such a market, see Chapter 12.

based on historical price data. The analyst is attempting to uncover information that is not generally known. It is consistent with the concept of relatively efficient capital markets to recognize that proper use of such information could result in above-average gains.

The major contribution of security analysis in relatively efficient markets will be the understanding it brings about of effects of firm and economywide events on security prices and alertness in directing attention to new developments. Opportunities for gains that may result from effective analysis may well be short lived in our capital markets, and originality in analysis and alertness in applying the results are necessary conditions for successful security analysis.

THE INGREDIENTS OF SECURITY ANALYSIS

In making an analysis of securities, both qualitative and quantitative factors are considered. *Qualitative* factors refer to subjective information (such as the quality of management or research and development effort) and to projections of quantitative data such as earnings and dividends. *Quantitative* factors are historical numerical data as reported in financial statements or concerning the economy and financial markets. Quantitative data appear to be quite objective, but the determination of the figures reported often depends on numerous subjective judgments, as we will see. Expressing qualitative factors in quantitative terms does not change the fact that such data are subjective in nature.

The data that analysts utilize in their decision-making process are often best thought of in terms of probability distributions rather than point estimates as typically presented. The job of the analyst is to develop the probability distributions. The fact that projections and other data are qualitative and subjective in nature does not mean that such data are not useful or even essential; the data merely emphasize the uncertainties and the need for an analysis capable of dealing with uncertain situations.

Ratio Analysis: A Basic Tool of Security Analysis

Investors have long used ratio analysis as a major tool for evaluating and interpreting the financial statements of companies. The object of ratio analysis is to reduce the large number of items contained in the statements to a relatively small number of meaningful relationships. Mere examination of the absolute figures included in financial statements cannot be expected to lead to definite conclusions in regard to the financial status of a business. Assume, for example, that Company A reports earnings after taxes of $100,000 while Company B reports earnings after taxes of $1,000,000. To assume that Company B is ten times as profitable as Company A would be incorrect. Suppose the balance sheet of A showed total invested capital of $200,000 while that of Company B showed total invested capital of $10,000,000. Company A is earning 50 percent on invested capital while Company B is earning only 10 percent. The overall objective of a business is to earn a satisfactory return on the funds invested in it, consistent with maintaining a sound financial position, and a return on invested capital ratio is a logical test of the success experienced in achieving this objective.

Interpretation requires comparison of meaningful components. Appropriate relationships (ratios) will depend on the purpose of the analysis but should fulfill the following criteria: (1) the ratios selected should relate components in which a logical decision-making relationship exists between the two variables, as for profits and invested capital; (2) the numerator and denominator chosen should be based on commonly calculated values. For example, cost of sales (not net sales) should be used as the numerator in an inventory turnover ratio since the denominator (inventory) is valued at cost and the purpose is to assess the adequacy of the physical turnover of that inventory.

Ratios are like the thermometer to the medical doctor. A ratio, like a temperature, can suggest favorable or unfavorable health. Ratios do not provide a definitive answer; their real value lies in the questions they raise. Specific ratios and their interpretations will be presented in Chapters 20, 21, and 22, in association with the specific areas of analysis they are felt useful for. We now turn our attention to considering the limitations inherent in ratio analysis and the issues raised by using the ratio approach.

Guidelines for Interpreting Ratios

The literature on ratio analysis offers little in the way of a theoretical framework or explicitly stated standards for interpreting ratios.[8] The most frequently suggested standards are (1) experience of the analyst, (2) budgetary goals that suggest what performance is expected to be under the prevailing circumstances, (3) historical standards in terms of comparing current performance with past figures, and (4) industry standards, such as the average ratios published by Dun and Bradstreet, Inc.[9] Each of these suggested bases for interpreting ratios has its faults.

If the analyst is not experienced or not particularly competent, experience offers little as a basis for judging the ratios calculated. How-

---

[8] See G. E. Penches, K. A. Mingo, and J. K. Caruthers, "The Stability of Financial Patterns in Industrial Organizations," *Journal of Finance* (May, 1973), pp. 389–396.

[9] For example, see R. Brealey and S. Myers, *Principles of Corporate Finance* (New York: McGraw-Hill, 1981), p. 590; or J. F. Weston, *Financial Management* (Homewood, Ill.: Richard Irwin, 1982), pp. 24-25.

ever, standards based on the experience of the analyst, while highly subjective, are preferable to mechanical comparisons. Rules of thumb, such as that the current ratio should be at least two to one, ignore operating differences between companies. A two for one current ratio might well suggest excessive liquidity and missed profit opportunities for a company that has a very rapid turnover of inventory, such as a bakery. On the other hand, a two for one current ratio could suggest serious liquidity problems for a liquor company where inventory must be aged four or more years before it is ready for sale.

When actual performance corresponds with budgetary performance, there is a reasonable inference that performance is good. However, the budgeted figures may not have been well set in the first place. Moreover, budgetary goals reflect assumptions concerning economic and operating conditions that were expected to prevail during the period, but if the assumptions were incorrect, the budgeting figures are likely to be improper as measures of desirable results. If because of a recession that was not forecasted, or an unexpected event such as a strike or new unfavorable government legislation, profits turn out to be lower than budgeted, one cannot necessarily say that failure to reach the budgeted goal reflects "poor" managerial performance. Of course, the failure to reach budgeted goals does suggest situations that should be carefully investigated by investors in terms of their long-run implications. Unfortunately budget information is not readily available to investors and therefore does not help in providing a basis for judging the ratios calculated.

Historical standards show only that the ratio is higher or lower than in the past, but the past may not provide a sound basis for judgment. The fact that returns on invested capital increased from 2 percent to 3 percent suggests movement in the right direction but still poor performance. The analyst is interested in trends and patterns over time since they provide a useful basis for attaining an understanding of company operations that can serve as a basis for forecasting future returns from owning that stock. This, however, is quite different than suggesting that there is anything ideal about past performance.

Operating circumstances, environmental conditions, and accounting differences all raise serious questions when "industry averages" are used as a basis of comparison for company ratios. However, they do provide an external check on performance relative to competing companies that can prove useful, assuming allowance can be made for the limitations inherent in such data.

In short, of real interest to the analyst are the underlying factors causing changes in ratios, not the ratios in and of themselves. Ratios are merely a convenient way of spotting problem areas, such as inadequate liquidity or inefficient operating performance, that analysts have found useful through experience. Ratios act as symptoms that help guide the analyst in an investigation.

Analyzing Financial Ratios

Both time series analysis and cross-sectional analysis are used when analyzing ratios. *Time series analysis* is used to search for systematic patterns that offer a basis for performance predictions. This approach to predictions depends on the process continuing to behave in the future as it has in the past. At a minimum the analyst hopes to gain a better understanding of the basic mechanism governing the process to be predicted through such historical analysis.

Cross-sectional analysis implies comparison with industrywide measures as a check on selective performance. Chudson[10] found significant differences for liquidity and turnover ratios among industry groupings. Horrigan also found significant differences for turnover ratios and the net income to sales ratios among industries.[11] In addition, Horrigan found that firm size affected ratios. None of these studies attempted to separate the size effect, the industry effect, or other possible effects, and much work remains to be done in appropriately stratifying cross-sections.

Finally, any individual ratio means little by itself. Financial analysis aims at a comprehensive evaluation of a firm's economic situation, and interdependencies among the various ratios must be recognized. A simultaneous consideration of several ratios is necessary to avoid being misled by a single ratio. For example, a current ratio might appear adequate, but inventory (a current asset) might be excessive and therefore liquidity problems may occur. Multivariate analysis, in which several ratios are combined into a model or an index providing a unique signal, has been suggested to overcome this problem.[12] Serious difficulties exist in choosing the right ratios and the appropriate weights for each ratio, and the aggregation process may disguise the interrelationships the analyst is looking for.[13]

---

[10] W. A. Chudson, *The Patterns of Corporate Financial Structure: A Cross-Section of Manufacturing, Mining, Trade and Construction, 1937* (New York: National Bureau of Economic Research, 1940), pp. 68, 118-128. 141-142.

[11] J. O. Horrigan, *An Evaluation of Financial Ratio Analysis* (Ph.D. dissertation, University of Chicago, 1967), p. 112.

[12] For example, see A. Wall and R. W. Dunning, *Ratio Analysis of Financial Statements* (New York: Harper Brothers, 1928), pp. 152-165; or M. Tamari, "Financial Ratios as a Means of Forecasting Bankruptcy," *Management International Review* (Fall, 1966), pp. 15-21.

[13] For an interesting presentation and evaluation of multivariate models, see Baruch Lev, *Financial Statement Analysis: A New Approach* (Englewood Cliffs, N.J.: Prentice-Hall, 1974), Parts I and II.

THE FINANCIAL REPORTING PROBLEM

The dissatisfaction of investors and other financial analysts with corporate financial reports is evident from the following selected remarks:

> If accountants want to continue to enjoy a role in the investment management process, they should prepare to focus their energies on supplying whatever data a workable theory of security valuation requires, rather than defending the present ritual.[14]

> Congress has become increasingly alert to the lack of uniformity in accounting rules and to the deleterious effects this situation can have on the legislature's attempts to write laws.[15]

> It is going to be difficult to detect from 1973 financial reports whether a company's fundamentals are deteriorating since there are many accounting, operating and financial gimmicks that management can use in the short-run to hide the effect on profits of a deterioration in fundamentals.[16]

The federal securities acts discussed in Chapter 15 have gone a long way toward eliminating fraudulent or purposely misleading financial statements. However, the Equity Funding case proves that fraudulent financial reports have not been entirely eliminated, and it must be remembered that some small and intrastate firms are exempt from federal reporting requirements. Investors do have to depend on the certification of corporate reports by outside accountants as protection from inadequate reporting and fraudulent practice.

Inadequate Disclosure vs. Lack of Uniformity

For some years a battle has raged over whether the information problem is largely one of "inadequate disclosure" or one of "lack of uniformity" in corporate reporting. Disclosure problems certainly exist, but the SEC is exerting considerable effort to assure full, accurate, and adequate disclosure of material corporate financial information. Sufficient information should be given, either in the body of the report or in footnotes, to facilitate comparisons among firms using alternative accounting techniques. Admittedly, the cost of gathering and reporting this additional information would have to be weighed against its usefulness in performing a sound analysis. Where adjustments are relatively

---

[14] J. L. Treynor, "The Trouble with Earnings," *Financial Analysts Journal*, No. 28 (September–October, 1972), p. 43.

[15] "Who Will Set CPA Rules?" *Dun's Review* (September, 1976), p. 62. Reprinted with the special permission of *Dun's Review*, September 1976. Copyright 1976, Dun & Bradstreet Publications Corporation.

[16] David F. Hawkins, "Accounting Dodos and Red Flags—A Guide to Reading 1973 Annual Reports," *Financial Executive* (May, 1974), p. 84.

easy and necessary for useful comparison—for example, the investment tax credit—sufficient information should be given for adjustment from the method used to other acceptable methods. Footnotes, explanations, and qualifications to the annual reports taken by the accountants for preceding years should be repeated in current annual reports and in comparative statements to the extent that they continue to be of significance. Differences between net income reported to stockholders and that reported to the Internal Revenue Service should be explained. The analyst should not be required to spend time and effort searching SEC filings and old reports to gather the information necessary to interpret the data currently reported.

Accountants should prepare statements that are useful to the user. Users desire statements that are reliable and informative for the purpose of appraising the financial strength and profitability of the firm and for making interfirm comparisons. Users are not so much interested in a past accounting of stewardship as in developing a base useful for projecting earnings, dividends, and financial strength. What is needed is disclosure of *material* information necessary for proper evaluation of a corporation's securities, not greater disclosure per se. Under SEC regulations, S-X-Rule 1–02 states, "The term 'material' when used to qualify a requirement for the furnishing of information as to any subject, limits the information required to those matters on which an average prudent investor ought reasonably be informed." Rule 3–06 goes beyond this to say, "The information required with respect to any statement shall be furnished as a minimum requirement to which shall be added such further material information as is necessary to make the required statements, in the light of the circumstances under which they are made, not misleading."[17] A mere proliferation of details may only make sifting out the really significant information more difficult. As G. K. Chesterton pointed out, "The best place to hide a leaf is in a forest."

Absolute uniformity in accounting data should not be expected or sought. The complex and varied nature of business operations and a rapidly changing economy suggest a need for flexibility in reporting. Firms should be allowed to continue choosing among generally accepted accounting principles, but they should also be required to disclose in dollar amounts the impact on net income and balance sheet values of the accounting alternative chosen.

The analyst has the responsibility to interpret the information and recognize economic reality, assuming the facts are fully and accurately disclosed. Accountants and management should seek to present the in-

_____
[17] William Holmes, "Materiality—Through the Looking Glass," *Journal of Accountancy* (February, 1972), p. 45.

formation in the form most useful to users. Reports should not be so prepared that only a very experienced professional analyst can dig out, rearrange, and adjust published figures by interpretation of notes to financial statements and other supplementary information to make them useful.

Published Forecasts in Annual Reports

The financial literature has long stressed the fact that the value of a security or a business must rest on the future, not the past. This has led to suggestions for the disclosure of budgets and earnings forecasts in the financial reports.[18]

View of the AICPA. Chang and Liao, when discussing the AICPA view of including forecasts in published accounting reports, said, "Without endorsing the publication of financial forecasts, the AICPA issued specific guidelines for the preparation, presentation and disclosure of financial forecasts." The two authors summarized specific recommendations as follows:

1. A financial forecast should be expressed in specific monetary amounts representing the single most probable result with an appropriate warning to draw attention to the tentative nature of the forecast.
2. The ranges of, or probabilistic statements supplementing, the single most probable result should be developed and disclosed in order to emphasize even further the tentative nature of the forecast.
3. The assumptions management considers significant to the forecast or key factors on which the financial results of the enterprise depend should be disclosed to provide the most benefit to forecast users.
4. An expression of the relative impact of a variation in the assumption, when it would significantly affect the forecasted result, should be disclosed.[19]

View of the SEC. Late in 1975 the SEC proposed a requirement that all companies that make profit forecasts in published reports meet certain standards. The companies should report assumptions under which projections were made and should update them in subsequent reports, comparing actual results with forecasts. Intense opposition made the SEC in the spring of 1976 officially drop its proposal. They

---

[18] For example, see W. W. Cooper, N. Dopuch, and T. F. Keller, "Budgetary Disclosure and Other Suggestions for Improving Accounting Reports," *The Accounting Review,* No. 43 (October, 1968), pp. 640–648; or B. J. Belda, "Reporting on Forecasts of Future Development," *Journal of Accountancy,* No. 130 (December, 1970), pp. 54–58.

[19] Davis L. S. Chang and Shu S. Liao, "Measuring and Disclosing Forecast Reliability," *Journal of Accountancy* (May, 1977), p. 77.

did, however, continue to encourage voluntary filing of forecasts and proposed guidelines for companies to follow.

The Objections. The highly subjective and uncertain nature of such forecasts has been pointed out; the argument is that the forecasts might mislead readers of the reports. Furthermore, reporting future plans such as expansion of existing lines or introduction of a new product line might provide competitors with an advantage that is not in the stockholders' interest. Also, such estimates would be difficult, if not impossible, to audit and might increase the legal liability of management and auditors.

There is merit in the above objections, but investors must use estimates in their investment decisions. The publication of forecasts could be highly useful to investors, especially if adequate information about underlying assumptions was provided.

Product Line Reporting

Many corporations are multiline in product scope and multinational in operations. Effective analysis of sales and sales forecasts, therefore, requires product line data and geographic breakdowns to recognize different growth and stability characteristics. During 1969 an SEC release proposed the following criteria for the breakdown of sales and earnings of diversified companies:

> State for each of the registrant's last five fiscal years, or for each fiscal year ending after December 31, 1966, or for each fiscal year the registrant has been engaged in business, whichever period is less, the approximate amount or percentage of (i) total sales and revenues and (ii) income (or loss) before income taxes and extraordinary items, attributable to each line of business which during either of the last two fiscal years accounted for:
> (a) 10 percent or more of the total sales and revenues,
> (b) 10 percent or more of income before income taxes and extraordinary items computed without deduction of loss resulting from operations of any line of business, or
> (c) a loss which equaled or exceeded 10 percent of the amount of income specified in (b) above.[20]

Although these amendments require disclosure in SEC reports, they are not binding as reporting standards for annual reports to shareholders and are not followed in annual reports of all corporations.

The main problem in preparing profit breakdowns by product line is that of allocating common costs, such as administrative expense, to the various segments. Such allocations are to a large extent arbitrary.

---

[20] "Adoption of Amendments of Forms S-1, S-7 and S-10," Releases No. 4988 and No. 8650 (Washington: Securities and Exchange Commission, July 14, 1969).

From the analyst's standpoint it would seem preferable to report revenues less traceable costs (contribution margins) for each segment, rather than profits that involve allocations of joint costs. Such information could be quite valuable to an analyst.

Accounting for Inflation

Businesspeople, financial analysts, and accountants have long realized that traditional financial statements prepared on the historical cost basis for measuring income produce misleading results when prices are changing. The inflation rate in the United States prior to the 1970s, however, was relatively low, and many felt that the year-to-year changes in accounting data brought on by such inflation were relatively insignificant and would best be estimated by the analyst.

Recent years have been marked by unprecedented inflation rates that have led to strong pressure by accountants for change that would result in reporting inflation-adjusted data. The SEC (Accounting Series Release 190) in 1976, for the first time, required the nation's largest nonfinancial corporations to report in their 10-K filings estimates of the extent to which undervaluation of inventory and plant and equipment resulted in understatement of expenses and overstatement of profit in the income statement. Although not a comprehensive restatement of financial data to reflect the impact of inflation, the data generated were believed to offer a more useful suggestion of true earning power by many analysts.

Financial Accounting Standards Bulletin Number 33 (adopted September 1979) required the disclosure in annual reports of two different types of inflation-adjusted financial data by publicly held corporations with total assets of more than $1 billion or inventories and property and equipment valued at $125 million. Each of the two types of required inflation-adjusted data is discussed further in Chapter 21.

Summary

In this section of the text, we are dealing mainly with fundamental security analysis. In this respect the function of security analysis is to determine the best relative values and portfolio composition at any point of time. This requires the investor to screen and classify financial assets, first on the basis of quality (financial risk) and then in terms of intrinsic values that were described in Chapter 7. The necessary screening process has become significantly more practical since the introduction of computers and computer banks of corporate financial information.

In the two previous chapters we have discussed the type and reliability of information available to investors as well as the necessity for projections of the economy, its subdivisions, and of industries and specific companies. In addition, we have also discussed the problems inherent in such projections and recognized that the future is always uncertain and that projections determined are only probabilities.

The investor must understand the differing concepts of risk underlying fundamental analysis as compared with the portfolio selection models and that modern portfolio theory has added a new and important dimension to the problem of security selection. Historically this was not considered in the strictly fundamental analysis approach to security selection. Therefore, the material in this chapter recommends an integration of the two approaches.

The investor should be familiar with the development of capital market theory but also understand that in the real world users of available information do not necessarily agree on the implications that such information has for future corporate performance and stock prices and also that information is by no means costless to market participants.

Security analysis deals with both qualitative and quantitative data. Qualitative factors are by definition subjective—as, for example, the ability of management or the quality of research. All projections are qualitative, for they are strictly subjective although generally expressed in quantitative terms.

In analyzing quantitative accounting data, investors will use ratio analysis, which facilitates comparisons of meaningful components of financial statements. Once ratios are calculated, they must be interpreted in absolute terms and in terms of trends, which involves certain subjective judgments. Therefore, in our discussion of the most useful ratios, interpretations of the ratios are explained. In any case, the underlying factors that have resulted in the ratios and their trends are most important as a basis for future projections.

In spite of the great improvement in financial reporting, there still exist problems of inadequate disclosure and lack of uniformity in reporting financial data. The SEC, the Financial Analysts Federation, and the American Institute of Certified Public Accountants, as well as committees of the stock exchanges and the National Association of Security Dealers, are working cooperatively for continuing improvement in the area of financial reporting.

Questions

1. What is the basic purpose of security analysis?
2. Suggest standards that you would use for purposes of screening the myriad of securities available to select those securities worthy of in-depth study. In answering this question consider not only the material in this chapter, but the preceding chapters of this book.

3. Distinguish between grading and valuation of stocks.
4. Are Standard & Poor's common stock ratings guides to stock selection? Discuss.
5. (a) Can an intrinsic value be calculated for a common stock?
   (b) Discuss the usefulness of attempts to value common stocks by analysts.
6. (a) Are portfolio selection approaches and valuation approaches internally consistent? Discuss.
   (b) How does the concept of risk that is utilized in valuation theory relate to the concept of risk that enters into portfolio theory?
7. Does the concept of efficient capital markets suggest that fundamental analysis is useless? Discuss.
8. "Quantitative factors in security analysis are objective while qualitative factors are subjective." Do you agree with this statement? Discuss.
9. (a) What is the basic objective of ratio analysis?
   (b) What standards would you suggest for interpreting ratios?
   (c) Do ratios answer questions? Discuss.
10. What is meant by "materiality of disclosure"?
11. Accountants offer both constant dollar and current cost data to indicate the effects of inflation on reported historical statements. (See discussion in Chapter 21 when answering this question.)
    (a) How do constant dollar and current cost data differ?
    (b) Outline the pros and cons of (1) constant dollar data and (2) current cost data.

Work-Study Problems

1. Can a bond issue of a given corporation be graded high in terms of quality while the common stock of that same corporation is not given an investment quality rating? Discuss.
2. Review company annual reports or 10-K filings in order to find at least one example of a disclosure problem. Describe and discuss.
3. The Moss Amendment to the Energy Policy and Conservation Act of 1975 mandated the FASB, working with the SEC, to issue guidelines by the end of 1977 for uniform accounting for the oil and gas industry. What problems developed?
4. What did the President of the AICPA, Wallace E. Olson, state about the problems and conceptual framework of financial reporting in the July 1977 *Journal of Accountancy?*
5. (a) What rules cover reporting breakdowns of sales, income, and balance sheet data by corporations in terms of major product line activities in annual reports?
   (b) Are these requirements adequate for the purpose of effective security analysis? Discuss.

20.

Analysis of the Income Statement

For many years major emphasis has been placed on the income statement—not only in the case of common stock analysis but also in the case of bonds, private placements, and preferred stock analysis. The margin of safety for fixed-income security holders is provided by a corporation's earnings *and* cash flow. The value of a business reflects the amount that can be earned on the invested capital. Therefore, the analyst must determine, especially for the common stock investor, a true earnings base of recurring earnings from which growth and volatility of earnings and dividends may be projected. All a common stockholder can receive from an investment are dividends and/or capital appreciation, and both are dependent on future earnings—and expectations by investors of future earnings and dividends.

PREPARATION OF INCOME STATEMENTS

The most fundamental accounting principle applied to the income statement is that which requires the matching of revenues and expenses. Usually annual reports and reports filed with the SEC include statements from previous years; if these are to be in fact comparable, there must be consistency in the accounting principles followed.

Reporting Accounting Changes

The Accounting Principles Board issued APB *Opinion No. 20*, "Accounting Changes" in July 1971, which stated among other things:

1. A change in accounting . . . may significantly affect the presentation of both financial position and results of operations for an accounting period and the trends shown in comparative financial statements and historical summaries. The change should therefore be reported in a manner which will facilitate analysis and understanding of the financial statements.

15. . . . there is a presumption that an accounting principle once adopted should not be changed. . . . Consistent use of accounting principles from one accounting period to another enhances the utility of financial statements to users by facilitating analysis and understanding of comparative accounting data.
16. The presumption . . . may be overcome only if the enterprise justifies the use of an alternative acceptable accounting principle on the basis that it is preferable. . . .
17. The nature of and justification for a change in accounting principle and its effect on income should be disclosed in the financial statements of the period in which the change is made. The justification for the change should explain clearly why the newly adopted accounting principle is preferable.[1]

Forms to Use

There are two major forms of income statement. The first is the *current operating performance statement* or clean income statement (ordinary, recurring annual items); the second is the *all-inclusive income statement*, an example of which is shown in Table 20–1. The principal

TABLE 20–1. All-Inclusive Income Statement

Major Divisions	Comments
Gross sales or revenue	Sometimes not given.
Sales returns and allowances and cash discount	Sometimes not given.
Net sales or revenue	Often the first item in the income statement. SEC requires a breakdown of sales by line of business and a breakdown of profits for each industry segment for which sales comprise 10 percent of the total. Also a breakdown of sales and earnings by broad geographic areas outside the U.S.
Other income	Listed here in the AICPA recommended form; but if it is material, analysts prefer that it be listed below where indicated.
Cost of goods sold	Rarely broken down into its components.
Gross profit	Net sales less cost of goods sold.

[1] APB *Opinion No. 20*, "Accounting Changes," *Journal of Accountancy* (October, 1971), pp. 63–72. "This Opinion defines various types of accounting changes and establishes guides for determining the manner of reporting each type. It also covers reporting a correction of an error in previously issued financial statements. . . ."

TABLE 20–1. All-Inclusive Income Statement *(continued)*

Major Divisions	Comments
Gross profit margin	Percentage of gross profit to sales calculated by analyst.
Selling expenses	Promotion, selling, and distribution expenses.
General administrative expenses	Salaries, wages, office supplies, insurance, taxes other than income taxes, etc.
Profit from operations	
Profit from operations—margin	Percentage of sales; operating profit margin calculated by analyst.
Other income	Nonoperating income such as dividends and interest income. When it is regular and recurring in nature, the AICPA recommends showing it separately under net sales; but if the item is substantial, analysts prefer that it be located here in the statement.
Other expenses	Nonoperating expenses such as bond interest, note interest, amortization, and bond discount.
Income before income taxes	
Income taxes	Federal and foreign income taxes.
Income before extraordinary items	
Extraordinary income and extraordinary expenses	Usually nonrecurring items of material amount, net of applicable income tax. Major items should be explained.
Net income	
Net income—profit margin	Net profit on sales.
Retained earnings at beginning of year	
Cash dividends on common stock	Also preferred dividends if any.
Cash dividends as percentage of net income	Payout ratio.
Retained earnings at end of year	

Per share of common stock
  Income before extraordinary
    items
  Extraordinary items net of taxes
  Final net income
  Dividends	

advantages of the all-inclusive income statement are (1) inclusion of all operating items related to the current period, with segregation and disclosure of extraordinary items; (2) a reporting of current income from operations free from distortions resulting from material items directly related to prior periods; and (3) proper retroactive reflection in comparative financial statements of material adjustments relating directly to prior periods.[2]

APB *Opinion No. 15*, Paragraph 13 (May 1969), states that earnings per share should be shown on the face of the income statement, presenting amounts for (1) income before extraordinary items and (2) net income. If there are any extraordinary items, earnings per share amounts should be presented for these items separately.

The analyst should prepare a spread sheet of the company's income statement for the number of years considered necessary.[3] Extraordinary and nonrecurring items should be separated from those items determining recurring operating income so as to provide a useful base for projecting earnings into the future. To determine true recurring earnings, the analyst should also add back to income any deductions for arbitrary and contingency reserves. If there is a significant variation between reported earnings and earnings for tax purposes, the analyst should determine why since adjustments may be required to derive an income figure that is meaningful for comparative and projection purposes. Comparative analysis requires the recognition of the lack of uniformity in reporting (as, for example, different methods used for reporting depreciation and inventory) and adjustments where necessary.

Accounting for Consolidated Statements

Practically all large corporations are holding companies with subsidiaries and frequently with affiliates. A *subsidiary* is a corporation controlled by a parent company, the latter owning at least 50 percent of the voting stock of the subsidiary. In practice, an important proportion of subsidiaries are 100 percent owned. To file a consolidated tax return, the parent must own at least 80 percent of the voting and nonvoting stock of the subsidiary, but not including preferred stock. The definition of an *affiliate* is not so precise. An affiliate includes corporations that are effectively controlled even though there is less than a 50 percent ownership.

Noting the Extent of Consolidation. The annual report indicates whether statements are consolidated and the extent of their consolida-

---

[2] APB *Opinion No. 13* states that the *Opinion No. 9* requirement for all-inclusive income statements also applies to reporting by commercial banks.

[3] Standard & Poor's Compustat tapes contain income statement data and useful ratios covering many years for a large selection of companies. This data could facilitate preparation of spread sheets.

tion. It may state that "all subsidiaries are consolidated," or "all sub-sidiaries are consolidated except 'X' financial subsidiary," or "all domestic subsidiaries are consolidated but not foreign subsidiaries." The reason why a company's financial subsidiary is not consolidated is that such corporations have a very large debt-to-equity ratio, which would, if consolidated, significantly raise the debt-to-equity ratio on the consolidated balance sheet. A finance company, because of the liquid nature of its assets, is assumed to be able to safely carry a higher debt-to-equity ratio; but if consolidated, its relatively large debt could make debt appear excessive on an operating parent's consolidated statement.

Consolidated statements combine all the companies involved into one corporation. Intercompany transactions are eliminated to prevent double counting. All assets and liabilities are consolidated, and all earnings and losses are consolidated in one final net income or net loss figure. If a corporation consolidates when it did not do so previously, adjustments should be made in reports for previous years to make them comparable.

Equity Method vs. Cost Method of Accounting. When a corporation consolidates its 50 percent or more owned subsidiary, it consolidates the assets and liabilities of the subsidiary into the assets and liabilities of the consolidated balance sheet (eliminating intercompany transactions) and consolidates the income or losses of the subsidiary into the consolidated statement of income. In the past, when less than 50 percent of the stock of another corporation is owned, the practice has frequently been not to use the equity method of accounting but to merely report in the balance sheet the initial "cost" of the investment with no reflection of subsequent equity in retained earnings of the investee. Past practice has also been to report only actual dividends, if any, received in the consolidated income account and not to reflect in the income statement any equity in the earnings of the less than 50 percent owned company, except when dividends are paid from those earnings.

However, in March 1971 the AICPA issued *Opinion No. 18*. "The Equity Method of Accounting for Investments in Common Stock,"[4] which requires that the *equity method*, rather than the *cost method*, be applied both in consolidated financial statements and in parent company statements prepared for issuance to stockholders as the financial statement of the primary reporting entry to account for investment in voting stock of

---

[4] APB *Opinion No. 18*, "The Equity Method of Accounting for Investments in Common Stock," *Journal of Accountancy* (June, 1971), pp. 63–69; and "Applying APB Opinion No. 18: The Equity Method," *Journal of Accountancy* (September, 1971), pp. 54–62.

1. Unconsolidated subsidiaries (where at least 20 percent of the voting stock is owned).
2. Incorporated joint ventures.
3. Other companies, 50 percent or less owned, over whose operating and financial policies the investor (parent company) is able to exercise "significant influence."

Under the equity method, the investment is initially recorded at cost. The carrying amount is adjusted to recognize the investor's share of the earnings or losses of the investee subsequent to the date of investment, with the amount of the adjustment included in the determination of the investor's net income. Dividends received reduce the carrying amount of the investment. Opinion No. 18 requires that in applying the equity method, any difference between the cost of an investment and the investor's equity in the net assets of the investee at the date of investment be accounted for as if the investee were a consolidated subsidiary. Accordingly, the cost of the investment would first be allocated to the investor's share of the investee's net identified assets and liabilities on the basis of the fair value. Only excess of the cost of the investment over the sum of the amounts so allocated should be considered to be goodwill. Such goodwill should be amortized over a period not to exceed forty years as a reduction of the amount recognized each period by the investor as its equity in the earnings or losses of the investee.

ANALYSIS OF ITEMS ON THE INCOME STATEMENT

The remainder of this chapter is devoted to an analysis of the major divisions that appear on an all-inclusive income statement, including the items that may be listed under each division.

Net Sales or Revenue

The major purpose of a business corporation is to produce sales, or revenues, and to earn a profit on these revenues. Therefore, the analyst has a major concern with the size, trend, and composition of these revenues. The level of sales over the past five to ten years should be reviewed and, by using 100 percent statement analysis, the percentage that each major income statement item bears to sales determined. Until 1970 the major difficulty found in analyzing the revenues of nonregulated enterprises was, in most cases, the inability to obtain a breakdown of sales by line of business and by product line. The more diversified the business, the more serious the problem. The SEC adopted new rules in December 1977 requiring companies to report according to industry segments in stock registrations and annual reports. The segment reporting rules require companies to disclose revenues, profit, and asset information relating to their industry segments and geographic areas for a five-year period. Geographic and export sales data are required only for fiscal years beginning after December 15, 1976.[5]

Registered corporations are required by federal securities legislation to make interim reports. In reviewing quarterly, semiannual, and nine-month published income figures, investors must recognize the seasonal nature, if any, of certain corporate incomes. For example, the investor can be greatly misled by multiplying quarterly figures by four- or six-month figures by two. Instead, when there is an important seasonal element, the investor should review the quarterly and semiannual results of previous years, calculate the seasonal factor, and interpret current interim reports in the light of the past year's figures. Furthermore, the investor must realize that corporations customarily make final-year adjustments in the final quarter of the year—adjustments that have not been reflected in quarterly, semiannual, or nine-month reports. Reference to adjustments in the final quarter of previous years may aid the investor in estimating earnings for the current fiscal year, although this method cannot be assumed to be a complete answer since major differences may appear in different years.

The aim of sales analysis is to project revenues for possibly the next three to five years as a basis for generating cost and profit expectations. As developed in Chapter 18, appraisal of future sales potential would include analysis of (1) potential growth in terms of product line areas, (2) stability and resistance of company sales to negative economic and industry factors, and (3) potential risks arising from competitive or political factors. Sales per share of common stock (adjusted for splits and stock dividends) should be calculated and studied because the pattern of per share results determines the potential returns on the common stock.

Computers may be used to apply regression and/or trend analysis to historical data as an aid in forecasting; the analytical techniques used should be structured to offer maximum useful insights with minimum cost and expenditure of time. Care should be exercised to avoid excessive computations and detailed data gathering that contribute little in the way of significant insights.

Cost of Goods Sold

At the same moment that income is increased by revenues derived from the sale of a product sold, it is also decreased by the cost of that product in modern accounting. In actual practice accountants usually determine the cost of goods sold by adding the value of inventory on hand at the beginning of a period to that acquired during the period,

---

[5] *The Wall Street Journal*, December 28, 1977, p. 5.

thereby determining the cost of goods available for sale. The value of the goods on hand at the end of the period is subtracted from the total cost of goods available for sale to determine the cost-of-goods-sold figure used in the income statement. This figure should never be combined with selling and administrative expenses, as the details are needed to facilitate effective analysis. Unfortunately, however, many companies do not report these items separately.

Determining the appropriate cost to apply to the goods remaining in the ending inventory when price levels are changing requires choosing a costing method that assumes the order in which units of production will be sold. Most important in this respect are the *first-in, first-out* (Fifo) method and the *last-in, first-out* (Lifo) method of costing inventories.

Fifo and Lifo Inventory Accounting. Traditionally, inventories were carried on the Fifo basis, which assumed that the cost flow was first-in, first-out. This is consistent with the actual physical practice of using the goods received first. However, during the period since 1941, inflation has been a "way of life." Many companies have shifted to the Lifo method—last-in, first-out. This assumes, for accounting purposes, that the goods last acquired are the first sold. In a period of rising prices, the use of Fifo results in inventory profits that inflate total profits; and if reporting for tax purposes is on this basis, the use of Fifo results in higher taxes. The items included in "cost of goods sold" are the "first-in" or lowest cost items, and yet sales are on a current price basis. On the other hand, the use of Lifo results in the last or higher cost items being used in "cost of goods sold"; therefore, a lower profit is reported than if Fifo is used. In a period of rising prices, Lifo will result in lower profits in the income statement and therefore lower income taxes. Lifo will also result in a lower inventory figure in the balance sheet and a lower net worth figure because the higher cost figures have been removed from inventory. Finally, because Fifo accounting incorporates inventory gains and losses, profits usually appear to be more volatile during the course of the business cycle than under Lifo.

Rules Governing the Use of Lifo. The tax laws permit the use of Lifo by *all* companies who choose to do so, but they must comply with certain requirements. The inventories must be reported on a cost basis. Furthermore, the taxpayer who uses the Lifo method for tax purposes must also use the Lifo method in all published financial statements. However, if sound accounting practice dictates that inventories be marked down to market, which is below cost, this procedure may be followed in the company's annual published financial statement, but the amount of the reduction is not available as a tax deduction.

A corporation may change to Lifo simply by notifying the Treasury Department, giving the details of the type of inventories carried and the exact method to be used in valuing additions to inventories. The Treasury Department will then affirm or disapprove the specific details of the Lifo method that the company intends to use. Once the Lifo method is approved and is used, the corporation *must* continue to use the method until the Internal Revenue Service approves a request for change.[6] The company may not shift back and forth to benefit taxwise.

The analyst can use the following ratios in analyzing inventories: (1) inventories to net working capital, (2) current debt to inventories, (3) cost of goods sold to inventories[7] (inventory turnover), and (4) inventory to sales. Trends for "unfilled orders" are also analyzed. These ratios are discussed in Chapter 22.

Gross Profit and Gross Profit Margin

Net sales minus cost of goods sold yields gross profit on sales, which, taken as a percentage of sales, produces the gross profit margin. This tool is a useful one for comparison of different years for the same company and for comparison between companies assuming that the figures used are comparable—that is, that inventory accounting policies are similar and that the components of "cost of goods sold" are similar. As

---

[6] Sometimes Lifo is assumed, erroneously, to be a method of adjusting for overall or general changes in the price level. In "Reporting the Financial Effects of Price-Level Changes," *Accounting Research Study No. 6* (New York: American Institute of Certified Public Accountants, 1963), on page 40 the following statement is made: ". . . If the most recent purchase prices are used in calculating the Lifo cost of materials used or Lifo cost of goods sold, they will in most cases correspond closely to the replacement costs in the market at the end of the current period. Except by coincidence, these specific replacement costs (for specific products), whether taken directly from market data or approximated by the use of indexes of specific goods, *will not* coincide with the movement of prices in general as measured by an index of the general price level. Thus, the general price level could be stable, while the Lifo index moved up or down; the Lifo index could be stable, while prices in general were falling or rising."

"Furthermore, Lifo makes no adjustment at all for inventories on the balance sheet. The more the general price level moves, up or down, the further removed is a Lifo inventory from even approximating an inventory adjusted for changes in the general price level. Lifo is a method for excluding changes in the replacement costs of specific commodities from 'realized profits': it is not intended to and cannot cope with the measurement problem created by a change in the general purchasing power of money as measured by an 'all-commodity' index."

[7] If net sales is used as the numerator rather than cost of goods sold, variations in the inventory turnover could result either from changes in the turnover of inventory or from changes in the gross margin. It would not be possible to determine the origin of change without further investigation. Cost of goods sold, on the other hand, is calculated on the same basis as inventory, and changes will represent changes in the turnover of inventory, which is what the analysts are trying to isolate. Dun and Bradstreet do relate net sales to inventory in their publications, although cost of goods sold is superior from a logical standpoint.

noted above, if inventory methods have been changed, adjustments must be made if possible to make the past years' figures comparable. For a particular company a comparison of gross profit margins for a period of years may disclose that (1) sales prices are rising or falling in relation to the cost of goods sold or (2) there has been a change in the product mix.

Selling Expenses and General Administrative Expenses

These two items are sometimes combined and sometimes shown separately. In most cases companies report selling and administrative expenses "exclusive of items listed below." Examples of items that may be listed "separately below" are depreciation and rapid amortization, depletion, maintenance, and repair, research and development expenses, rental expenses, exploratory expenses, and employee compensation and benefit payments (mainly pension costs). The analyst should calculate each of these items as a percentage of sales and should note the trends in this regard over the period of years under review.

Depreciation, Rapid Amortization, and Depletion. This item, which is a noncash and nonfund item, is of major importance—so important that the next chapter is largely devoted to it. There is considerable lack of uniformity in corporate reporting of depreciation and the related investment credit.

Research and Development. Rapid growth of sales and earnings can be attributed largely to *quality* research and development (or mergers). Total expenditures in this area would best be analyzed by comparison with previous years and other companies, and by using this figure as a percentage of sales. However, the real test is the percentage of sales and profits that results from the company's previous research and development expenditures—that is, what research has produced.

Rental Expenses. Today we find a large number of corporations leasing instead of owning assets. Thus, lease rentals become very important expenses, as they always have been for many railroads. This important item should be, and often is, shown as a separate item in the income statement. As noted earlier, information on the details regarding lease agreements should be furnished, but such information is often presented in a sketchy and unsatisfactory manner. To an important extent, these are at least equivalent to fixed charges on debt for which the lease is a substitute, and the fixed charge element of the lease rental can force a company into financial difficulties just as readily as can fixed charges on funded or other debt. This topic will be discussed in detail in Chapter 22.

Exploratory Expenses, Including Intangible Drilling and Development Costs. In the case of oil, gas, and mining companies, this classification is a major expense item. Therefore, it must be considered in comparative analysis between companies and for the same company in past years. The problem has been that many companies use the "full cost" method to account for exploration costs incurred in searching for reserves, while others use the "successful efforts" method. The "successful efforts" method requires that the costs associated with unsuccessful attempts to find gas or oil be immediately charged against earnings; the costs associated with successful drillings are capitalized in an asset account and written off over time. In contrast, under full-cost accountin, all exploration costs incurred in searching for reserves are capitalized and amortized as expenses as the numerical resources are actually produced. A growing company doing a large amount of exploration will report lower earnings under the "successful efforts" method, and the company's reported earnings will probably be more volatile under this method.[8] On December 5, 1977, the Financial Accounting Standards Board in Statement No. 19 required that the "successful efforts" method be used to account for costs of exploration and development in the oil industry. This should help produce more uniform reports from oil companies.

Employee Compensation. This item is usually not shown separately in the income statement but is included within other expense items as applicable. However, the labor cost factor is highly important, and frequently the information will be presented separately from the income statement elsewhere in annual reports. Analysts often obtain this vital information from company sources, as do the statistical services.

Pension Costs and Other Employee Benefits. This item is, of course, an additional wage and salary cost and has been of rapidly increasing importance in the total labor cost picture. It has taken on so much importance since ERISA (The Employee Retirement Income Security Act of 1974) that the analyst needs a breakdown of assets included in the pension fund as well as knowledge of the actuarial cost method used. ERISA gave the government the power to take up to 30 percent of a company's assets if pension liabilities had to be paid off and the pension fund was insolvent.[9]

---

[8] For example, when Texaco switched to the "successful efforts" method in 1975, estimates were that full cost accounting had increased Texaco's reported profits by $500 million over the preceding ten years.

[9] See "Unfunded Pension Liabilities: A Growing Worry for Companies," *Business Week*, July 18, 1977, p. 86. Also see Chapter 16 of this book.

Profit from Operations and Operating Ratio

The profit from operations is the result of deducting all operating expenses, including the cost of goods sold, from net sales. It indicates the operating efficiency of the management. The operating ratio (total operating costs as a percentage of sales) is especially useful in comparative analysis of the efficiency of competing companies and of the same company over a period of years. One should be careful that the turnover of operating assets (net sales divided by total operating assets) is similar when comparing the operating ratios of different companies. To be meaningful, the composition of operating expenses must be presented in a consistent accounting manner.

Other Income

In the past, other income, if shown separately, was usually entered in the income statement following profit from operations. At present, if the item is substantial, it usually follows operating income and expenses but prior to extraordinary income and expenses, as shown in the form presented in Table 20-1 earlier in this chapter.

Other Expenses

In the past other expense items directly related to other income items were deducted with general expenses, and therefore other income as reported was gross of associated expenses; but other income now is generally reported net of expenses directly associated with such other income reported. Therefore, other expenses as now reported in the income statement generally consist only of recurring expenses that are not associated with other income; for example, such items as bond interest, note interest, and amortization of bond discount.

Income Before Income Taxes

This item represents income calculated by deducting all reported expenses from all reported income. The ratio of income *before* income taxes to sales is an important ratio in analyzing and determining the corporation's earning power and in comparative statement analysis. One should recognize, however, that it is only one of the two components determining return on asset investment and should be considered in relation to the asset turnover in comparative analysis.

Income Taxes

Current accounting practice requires that the income tax expense reported in the income statement be computed on book income, not taxable income. When there are differences between book and taxable income, an allocation of tax expense between reporting periods may be necessary; there may be either charges or credits to the expense account accompanied by entries to deferred accounts on the balance sheet—that is, deferred tax accounting. Current practice also requires that, where appropriate, income taxes be separately computed on (and reported with) income from ordinary operations and on income from extraordinary items.

The analyst should calculate the percentage of taxes applicable to income before taxes. If this figure is about 46 percent, the analyst can assume that the corporation's book income from ordinary sources is about the same as that reported for tax purposes. However, if the percentage is significantly different, the analyst should attempt to determine reasons for the disparity. Some of the reasons why a company may show differences between book and taxable income are discussed below.

Depreciation and Investment Credit. Accounting for depreciation and for the investment credit for tax purposes is often different from the reporting in published reports, as discussed in Chapter 21.

Depletion. Depletion accounting for natural resource companies is different from cost depreciation accounting because most companies use "percentage depletion" accounting for tax purposes rather than "cost depreciation," which almost always results in a much lower tax rate than the effective rate for companies not in industries with wasting assets. Although this depletion figure may be used for comparative purposes and in calculating cash flow, the analyst has no opportunity to check on its validity as to the particular company under analysis because of the sheer complexity and confidentiality of the data involved.

Tax-Exempt Income. The company that has invested in tax-exempt securities will include income from such securities but will pay no tax on this income. If such investments are substantial, they will account for a significantly lower effective tax rate on income than the current corporate tax rate. This is also true to the extent that any income received from subsidiaries or affiliates is considered a return of capital for tax purposes.

Dividends Received from Domestic Corporations. The dividends received from domestic corporations on both preferred and common stock are subject to the corporate income tax only to the extent of 15 percent of such dividends received; 85 percent of such dividends are not included in income for tax purposes. Therefore, assuming a corporate tax rate of 48 percent, the effective rate on dividends received is only 46 percent $\times$ 15 percent, or 6.9 percent. If a corporation has a large dividend income, such as is the case with fire and casualty companies or some holding companies, this could account for a much lower effective tax rate than a 46 percent rate.

Long-Term Capital Gains on Sale of Capital Assets. If capital assets are held more than one year, they are subject to a maximum capital gains tax of only 35 percent. Capital assets consist in the main of real property or securities. Except for corporations whose main business is dealing (purchases and sales) in capital assets, capital gains or losses should be entered in the extraordinary income and expense section of the income statement following income taxes.

Capitalized Items and Deferred Expense Items. There are numerous items that a corporation may expense in its tax return but capitalize in its published balance sheet. Many companies have followed a similar procedure in regard to advertising and promotional expenses. Analysts are cynical about capitalization and deferral of expense items.[10]

Other items that are sometimes capitalized in annual reports, although expensed in tax returns, are intangible drilling costs of oil and natural gas producers and exploration and development expenses of mining companies. These all raise a problem for the analyst attempting to place different companies on a comparable base.

Another item that must be mentioned is interest charged to construction credit, which is capitalized by public utility companies in their published statements but is expensed in their income tax reports. This item will be examined in detail in Chapter 26.

One further item should be mentioned because it is often capitalized in published balance sheets while being expensed in tax reports to the Internal Revenue Service. This is the item of cost applicable to "start-up" and related expenses for new plants. The analyst may decide that if the company is regularly expanding, capitalizing such expenses as is done in the company's published reports is justifiable. This item will almost always be expensed in the tax report. The reverse item is cost of plant closing, which should be reported separately before extraordinary items.

---

[10] When companies defer items that more properly should be currently expensed, the result is higher reported profit. For 1968 United Air Lines cushioned its decline in profits by deferring to later years the costs of training pilots, mechanics, and ground crews to handle new equipment. Estimates were that such deferrals of expenses amounted to $9 to $10 million. The analyst must make adjustments, increasing reported expenses and decreasing reported profits for these and similar expense items that should be expensed in the current year rather than deferred to later years.

Installment Sales. Many companies report the full effect of install-ment sales when the sales are made, thus reporting the full profit in that fiscal year. However, for tax purposes they report only actual income as payment is received. Therefore, reported taxes in published income statements will be at a rate lower than the regular corporate rate be-cause higher profits are being reported to stockholders than to the In-ternal Revenue Service. Because the taxes are deferred, the published report should include an estimate of deferred taxes applied to the sales reported in the published statement and should also provide sufficiently for estimated bad debts.

Goodwill. The item of goodwill, once so important in corporate bal-ance sheets, became relatively unimportant until the great acquisitions movement of the post–World War II years. In recent years costs of acquisitions have often been well in excess of the book value of the assets acquired, and a balancing item of goodwill has had to be added in the balance sheet where the "purchase of assets accounting procedure is used, unless this excess is charged off immediately and in total to the capital account."[11] The AICPA requires that the item of goodwill be amortized annually as a charge against income over a period of not more than forty years.

Net Operating Loss. Such losses sustained in any fiscal year may be applied to reduce previously reported profits for tax purposes, first in the three preceding years and then, if there is still an amount remaining, in the seven succeeding years. As applied to the three preceding years, this requires a recalculation of reported income previously filed with the Internal Revenue Service. Under this procedure, when the reported profits are reduced by the loss, the lower recalculated profits will result in a lower tax than was required when the original report was filed, and therefore a tax refund or tax credit will be secured. The result of the tax refund or tax credit is to reduce the effect of the tax loss by approx-imately one-half. As noted above, the remaining portion of the loss not absorbed in the three preceding years may be carried forward for seven years, reducing the tax that would otherwise be required against realized profits. While the tax saving is certainly real, it results from operating losses in previous years and has nothing to do with current and future operations in a recurring sense. Unfortunately, many companies simply

---

[11] In August, 1970, the Accounting Principles Board issued *Opinion No. 16*, "Business Combinations," resulting in the acceptance in practice of two methods of accounting for business combinations: "purchase," and "pooling of interests." The opinion makes it quite difficult to use the "pooling of assets" method that had been so popular because it did not require the addition of "goodwill" to the assets on the balance sheet. The two methods are discussed and contrasted in Chapter 21.

reduce taxes in the income statement and report net income and earnings per share only after such lower taxes without disclosing the actual tax adjustments.

Just as in the case of capital gains and losses, a tax credit item for previous losses carried forward should appear as a separate item in the extraordinary items section of the income statement following income taxes. As recommended by the AICPA, the earnings per share of common stock should be shown at the bottom of the income statement for (1) income per share before extraordinary items, (2) extraordinary items per share net of taxes, (3) final net income per share, and (4) dividends per share.

Acquisition of Companies Having Net Loss Carry-Forward Items. If such a company is acquired, the acquiring company can use this carry-forward loss to reduce future taxes even though the acquiring company had no loss itself in previous years. To avoid having corporations acquire such loss companies for the main or sole reason of the tax benefit, such acquisitions must be for business reasons—that is, continuation of the company's business or combining the company's business with that of the acquiring company. If the acquiring company cannot justify the acquisition on this "business purpose" basis, it loses the advantage of the tax carry-forward. In any case, if the tax carry-forward is used, it should appear in the extraordinary items section of the income statement.

Other Tax Privileges. Federal legislation provides tax privileges for the following categories:

1. Shipping lines, which receive subsidies from the federal government and are governed by legislation that both requires in some instances and permits in others the transfer of earnings, tax free, to reserve funds that may or may not later be subject to tax.
2. Life insurance companies, which receive favorable tax treatment leading to a lower tax base than that of other corporations.
3. Savings and loan associations, which are required by law to build up substantial reserves by the annual transfer of earnings, tax free, to their reserve accounts. Legislation requires that reserves be built up to 12 percent of the total of insured savings accounts and then be maintained at this level as the total of insured accounts increases. Annually 10 percent of net earnings *before* interest on savings accounts must be transferred to reserves until the requirement is met. Congress has placed an overall limitation for tax purposes on the accumulation of reserves, such accumulations being generally limited to 12 percent of withdrawable accounts. Most associations paid no federal income taxes before the changes in the Revenue Act of 1962. This was followed by the Tax Reform Act of 1969 under which associations still operate. The 1969 act established a new method for calculating taxes for associations. The new method provided for the basing of deductible additions to reserves (before taxes) on a percentage of mortgage loans outstanding. In tax years 1970–1975 the percentage was 1.8 percent. Thereafter,

deductible additions are reduced by 0.6 percent for each subsequent six-year period until they disappear completely in 1987. Associations in 1978 claimed that their effective tax rate is now higher than for commercial banks.

Extraordinary Items

These are items of an extraordinary and *nonrecurring* nature. The analyst attempts to determine the recurring annual earning power of the corporation to establish a base from which to project future earnings and dividends. Items that are not of a recurring nature should be isolated at the bottom of the income statement and eliminated in analysis of any particular year to calculate the normal recurring earning power of the business. The analyst should calculate income per share before extraordinary nonrecurring items and net income per share including such items, making necessary adjustments when items have been improperly reported.

Classification of Nonrecurring Items. Nonrecurring items fall into two categories: (1) they reflect events that occurred in previous years or (2) they represent items that did occur within the fiscal year under review but that do not represent normal recurrent operations and are, instead, items of an exceptional nature. The first category includes such items as tax adjustments covering previous years' operations (additional tax payments, refunds, or credits relating to past years), the settlement of claims such as lawsuits or government renegotiation claims that have been carried forward from previous years, and adjustments of depreciation charges made in past years. The second category includes such items as adjustments in the book value of investments, profits or losses resulting from the sale of investments (except of financial companies), the sale of other assets above or below their book value, the receipt of exceptional dividends from subsidiaries, and profits from bond retirements. If extraordinary items of a nonrecurring nature appear in the income statement, they should be identified as nonrecurrent, be segregated, and entered in the bottom section of the income statement.

Adjustments for Material Amounts. In line with the general principles regarding adjustments, the analyst in determining recurring earnings as a base for projecting earnings does not have to make any adjustments if the amount involved would not materially affect the final result.

INCOME STATEMENT RATIO ANALYSIS

As explained in earlier chapters, the value of an enterprise (and its divisional units of equity—shares of common stock) is essentially based on its projected earning power and dividends. Furthermore, the key tests of corporate management are the ratio of these earnings to total capital invested in the business and also the rate earned on equity capital and on assets.

Methods of Analyzing Income Statements

It is assumed that the analyst has made all the adjustments deemed necessary so that the income statement reflects true earning power, excluding extraordinary items.

The 100 Percent Income Statement. One method of analyzing income statements for a period of years is to take net sales as 100 percent and then to calculate the percentage that the major items in the income statement bear to net sales. Such items as cost of goods sold, operating expenses, depreciation, maintenance, labor costs, net operating income, other income, other expenses, and finally net income are then placed on a comparable percentage basis. An inspection of these 100 percent income statements on spread sheets for a period of years shows clearly the trends of the ratios of important items to net sales.

Base Period Analysis. Another method of income statement analysis for a period of years is to establish a base year (or a base period of several years) and to use this base year (or the average of the years in the base period) as equal to 100 percent. The analyst can then calculate the relationship of the major items in the income statements for each year to the base year.[12] This comparison will indicate the growth (or the decline) of these items year by year and for the entire period under review. Having calculated the percentage increase from the base year or base period, the analyst can then (through the use of compound interest tables) calculate the compound rates of annual growth for the period. The more regular the growth, the more significant the compound annual growth rate.

The analyst can thus compare the trends of related items to judge whether favorable or unfavorable tendencies are reflected by the data. Certainly one would expect operating costs to rise with increases in sales, but costs that increase at a faster rate than sales are a negative factor. The percentage increase in sales over a given time span can be contrasted against the percentage increase in GNP components such as disposable personal income, personal consumption expenditures, or expenditures for durable goods to determine if the company is growing as fast as the economy or a major component of the economy. The percentage

---

[12] In selecting a base year or years, the analyst will find it advantageous to use a base year or a base period that also serves as a base for U.S. Department of Commerce figures, which may be used for comparative purposes.

increase in sales can also be compared with industry sales to determine if the company is maintaining its share of the market. The rate of growth of sales can also be contrasted with the rate of growth of operating assets.

Most Significant Income Statement Ratios

The most significant ratios used in analyzing the income statement are discussed in the following paragraphs.

Gross Profit Ratio. This is the ratio of gross profit to net sales. It can be analyzed in terms of the trend over a period of years for the same company, along with its relationship to other companies in the same industry. As noted earlier, the method of inventory valuation used (for example, Lifo versus Fifo) is quite important, and the analyst must be sure that the figures used for comparison between companies and also for the same company are in fact comparable.

Operating Expense Ratio. This is the ratio of total operating expenses, including cost of goods sold, to net sales and indicates the operating efficiency of the management.

The analyst should also calculate (if data are available) the ratio of major components of operating expenses to net sales: depreciation, maintenance or repairs (especially for railroads), total labor costs, pension costs, and research and development and other expenses that, because of the nature of the industry and the company, are significant. Trends in these ratios, especially in relation to revenue trends, are particularly important.

Net Operating Margin. This is the ratio of net operating income to net sales. It is the complement of the operating expense ratio, since the two when added always equal 100 percent.

The net operating margin indicates the percentage of sales available to meet financial charges, pay taxes, and provide for dividends and retained earnings. In determining the quality of debt obligations, many analysts consider this percentage of equal importance with the number of times fixed charges are earned. In considering the amount of income remaining after operating expenses (the amount available to meet fixed financial charges), see the discussion of fixed charge coverage in Chapter 24.

Other Income and Other Expense as Percentages of Sales. If these items are material, their source and their regularity over the years should be analyzed. The ratio to net sales and also to final net income should be calculated.

Net Income Before Taxes as a Percentage of Sales. Net income before taxes as a percentage of sales is an intermediate determinant of the final rate of return on invested capital (ROI).[13] Industry statistics for profits per dollar of sales, before and after taxes, are given in Tables 20-2 and 20-3.

The ratio of net income before taxes to sales is the percentage of sales brought down to pretax net profit for the common stockholder. This percentage may be very low; but if inventory turnover and capital investment turnover are high, the rate of return on investment may still be high. Conversely, if the net income before taxes as a percentage of sales is high but inventory and capital investment turnover are low, the rate of return on investment may be low.

Extraordinary Item Percentages. If the total of all extraordinary items is material, it should be calculated as a percentage of net income *after* extraordinary items. Variations in the relative importance of extraordinary items should be analyzed.

Earnings per Share

A most commonly discussed figure in the financial community is earnings per share, along with its correlated ratio of market price to earnings per share (the P/E ratio). APB *Opinion Number 15* (May 1969) requires the presentation of two earnings per share figures on the income statement of companies with potentially dilutive securities (such as convertible securities or warrents): (1) primary earnings per share and (2) fully diluted earnings per share. The difference between these two can be illustrated in the following way. Assume a company has outstanding 20 million shares of common stock (on average) and that common equity totals $400 million in the balance sheet. Further assume that there is $400 million of 5 percent preferred stock outstanding, of which $200 million is convertible into 40 million common shares. Also assume there is $400 million of 10 percent long-term debenture bonds outstanding of which $200 million is convertible into 30 million common shares. Finally, assume this company has a profit before interest and taxes of $200 million and is subject to an effective income tax rate of 50 percent.

When a corporation has a complex capital structure—that is, it includes potentially dilutive convertible securities, options, or warrents—both primary earnings per share and fully diluted earnings per share must be presented in the income statement. The primary earnings per share is calculated on the basis of the number of common shares outstanding plus the shares referred to as common stock equivalents (shares

---

[13] Return on asset investment equals the operating margin times the turnover of asset investment.

TABLE 20-2. Profits per Dollar of Sales, by Industry (cents)

Industry	Before Income Taxes[b]					After Taxes				
	2Q 1980[c]	3Q 1980[c]	4Q 1980[c]	1Q 1981	2Q 1981	2Q 1980[c]	3Q 1980[c]	4Q 1980[c]	1Q 1981	2Q 1981
All manufacturing corporations	7.7	7.2	7.4	7.5	8.5	4.8	4.5	4.8	4.7	5.5
Nondurable manufacturing corporations	9.1	8.5	7.7	7.9	9.0	5.7	5.5	5.2	5.0	5.9
Food and kindred products	5.2	5.5	6.1	4.9	5.4	3.1	3.5	4.0	3.0	3.4
Tobacco manufactures	18.8	20.5	14.2	18.5	16.5	12.0	13.0	8.8	12.5	10.4
Textile mill products	4.1	3.6	3.8	4.0	5.7	2.1	1.8	2.2	2.3	3.3
Paper and allied products	8.4	6.6	6.4	7.8	8.3	5.5	4.5	4.9	5.3	5.6
Printing and publishing	9.9	10.0	9.5	8.5	9.3	5.6	5.8	5.5	4.8	5.2
Chemicals and allied products	10.5	10.0	9.0	10.9	10.5	7.1	7.1	6.3	7.3	6.8
Industrial chemicals and synthetics[a]	8.2	5.7	6.4	9.5	8.7	5.7	4.7	4.5	6.5	5.6
Drugs[a]	17.5	20.7	15.6	15.0	16.0	12.4	15.1	11.3	10.4	10.9
Petroleum and coal products	13.1	11.1	9.1	9.0	11.7	8.3	7.2	6.3	5.7	8.2
Rubber and miscellaneous plastics products	2.2	2.7	4.4	5.9	7.0	1.5	1.6	2.7	3.6	4.2
Other nondurable manufacturing corporations	4.4	5.6	5.3	4.9	5.2	2.5	3.3	3.2	2.7	3.2
Durable manufacturing corporations	6.2	5.6	6.9	7.0	8.1	3.8	3.4	4.5	4.3	5.0
Stone, clay and glass products	7.0	8.1	6.7	4.1	7.6	4.6	5.4	4.4	2.3	4.8
Primary metal industries	6.1	2.9	6.1	6.5	7.1	4.2	2.2	4.4	4.4	4.8
Iron and steel[a]	4.0	1.1	5.2	5.9	6.9	2.7	1.2	3.8	3.9	4.5
Nonferrous metals[a]	9.3	5.7	7.6	7.4	7.4	6.6	3.6	5.6	5.4	5.3
Fabricated metal products	6.4	6.3	6.6	7.1	8.1	4.0	3.8	4.1	4.2	5.0
Machinery, except electrical	10.1	9.6	10.5	9.8	11.0	6.5	6.2	7.3	6.1	6.6
Electrical and electronic equipment	8.1	7.9	8.4	9.2	8.8	4.8	4.8	5.2	5.7	5.4

TABLE 20-2. Profits per Dollar of Sales, by Industry (cents) (continued)

Industry	Before Income Taxes[b]					After Taxes				
	2Q 1980c	3Q 1980c	4Q 1980c	1Q 1981	2Q 1981	2Q 1980c	3Q 1980c	4Q 1980c	1Q 1981	2Q 1981
Transportation equipment	-1.1	-2.2	2.2	2.9	5.5	-1.2	-2.1	1.0	1.3	3.4
Motor vehicles and equipment[a]	-6.9	-8.9	-0.1	-0.5	4.5	-5.2	-6.9	-0.9	-1.4	2.7
Aircraft, guided missiles and parts[a]	7.0	6.8	5.8	8.7	7.0	4.3	4.3	4.0	5.7	4.5
Instruments and related products	15.2	15.3	14.1	15.3	14.5	9.4	9.5	9.4	10.0	9.2
Other durable manufacturing corporations	5.1	5.9	5.4	4.4	5.4	2.7	3.6	3.2	2.3	2.8
All mining corporations	15.4	19.1	18.2	18.5	16.7	10.3	13.4	13.1	12.0	10.0
All retail trade corporations	2.4	2.5	3.7	1.9	NA	1.6	1.6	2.4	1.1	NA
All wholesale trade corporations	2.8	3.0	2.6	2.5	2.9	1.8	1.9	1.6	1.5	1.8

[a] Included in major industry above.
[b] Based on profit figure which includes net income (loss) of foreign branches and equity in earnings (losses) of nonconsolidated subsidiaries, net of foreign taxes.
c Some of the rates in this column have been revised since their first appearance.

Source: Federal Trade Commission, Quarterly Financial Report for Manufacturing, Mining and Trade Corporations, Second Quarter, 1981, p. 12.

TABLE 20–3. Profits per Dollar of Sales, Manufacturing Corporations by Asset Size and Industry Group (cents)

Asset Size	Before Income Taxes[a]					After Taxes				
	2Q 1980	3Q 1980	4Q 1980	1Q 1981	2Q 1981	2Q 1980	3Q 1980	4Q 1980	1Q 1981	2Q 1981
All manufacturing corporations	7.7	7.2	7.4	7.5	8.5	4.8	4.5	4.8	4.7	5.5
Under $5 million[b]	4.8	4.9	3.8	4.7	5.7	2.7	2.8	2.1	2.7	3.6
$ 5 million to $ 10 million	5.6	4.9	5.0	5.6	6.7	2.7	2.4	2.6	3.0	3.7
$ 10 million to $ 25 million	5.0	4.9	5.8	4.8	6.3	2.4	2.6	3.1	2.3	3.3
$ 25 million to $ 50 million	5.7	5.9	5.2	5.2	6.1	3.1	3.2	2.8	2.7	3.2
$ 50 million to $ 100 million	6.4	6.4	7.3	6.4	6.9	3.6	3.5	4.4	3.6	3.7
$ 100 million to $ 250 million	6.7	6.8	5.8	6.1	6.9	3.9	3.8	3.4	3.4	4.0
$ 250 million to $1,000 million	7.7	7.6	6.9	6.9	7.5	4.6	4.6	4.2	4.1	4.3
$1,000 million and over	9.1	8.1	8.8	8.9	10.1	6.0	5.4	6.2	5.8	6.8
Durable goods	6.2	5.6	6.9	7.0	8.1	3.8	3.4	4.5	4.3	5.0
Under $5 million	5.8	5.5	4.4	5.4	6.7	3.3	3.1	2.3	3.1	4.2
$ 5 million to $ 10 million	6.7	5.8	6.3	6.9	8.0	3.2	2.8	3.4	3.8	4.7
$ 10 million to $ 25 million	6.0	5.6	7.1	5.5	7.4	2.9	2.9	3.7	2.7	3.9
$ 25 million to $ 50 million	6.7	6.1	5.3	6.4	7.1	3.6	3.1	2.7	3.2	3.6
$ 50 million to $ 100 million	7.0	6.8	8.2	7.9	8.6	3.8	3.6	4.8	4.4	4.7
$ 100 million to $ 250 million	7.1	6.6	6.7	7.2	8.3	4.1	3.8	3.9	4.1	4.8
$ 250 million to $1,000 million	7.6	7.5	7.7	7.7	8.2	4.6	4.7	5.0	4.7	4.6
$1,000 million and over	5.7	4.9	7.5	7.4	8.5	3.7	3.2	5.2	4.8	5.5
Nondurable goods	9.1	8.5	7.7	7.9	9.0	5.7	5.5	5.2	5.0	5.9
Under $5 million	3.6	4.2	3.3	3.9	4.5	2.0	2.4	1.8	2.3	2.9

TABLE 20-3. Profits per Dollar of Sales, Manufacturing Corporations by Asset Size and Industry Group (cents) (continued)

Asset Size	Before Income Taxes[a]					After Taxes				
	2Q 1980	3Q 1980	4Q 1980	1Q 1981	2Q 1981	2Q 1980	3Q 1980	4Q 1980	1Q 1981	2Q 1981
$ 5 million to $ 10 million	4.5	4.0	3.7	4.3	5.4	2.2	1.9	1.8	2.2	2.8
$ 10 million to $ 25 million	4.1	4.2	4.7	4.1	5.1	1.8	2.2	2.6	1.9	2.6
$ 25 million to $ 50 million	4.8	5.6	5.2	4.0	5.0	2.6	3.4	2.8	2.2	2.6
$ 50 million to $ 100 million	5.8	5.8	6.5	5.1	5.2	3.3	3.4	3.9	2.9	2.7
$ 100 million to $ 250 million	6.2	7.0	5.1	4.9	5.5	3.6	3.8	2.9	2.9	3.1
$ 250 million to $1,000 million	7.9	7.6	6.2	6.2	6.9	4.5	4.5	3.6	3.7	4.1
$1,000 million and over	11.8	10.6	9.8	10.0	11.5	7.7	7.1	6.9	6.6	7.8

[a] Based on profit figure which includes net income (loss) of foreign branches and equity in earnings (losses) of nonconsolidated subsidiaries, net of foreign taxes.
[b] Collapse of asset size data resulting from change in estimating techniques.

Source: Federal Trade Commission, Quarterly Financial Report for Manufacturing, Mining and Trade Corporations, Second Quarter, 1981, p. 13.

that could be acquired through conversion or exercise of convertibles, options, or warrents when the cash yield on such convertibles is less than $66\frac{2}{3}$ percent of their current bank prime rate of interest). The fully diluted earnings per share is calculated by assuming that all contingent issues that can be converted into common stock have been so converted.

An undiluted earnings per share figure and a diluted earnings per share figure are calculated in Table 20-4 to illustrate these concepts. The table shows primary earnings per share and fully diluted earnings per share are the same since all securities that could result in additional shares becoming outstanding were considered common stock equivalents. The fully diluted earnings per share was calculated by assuming (1) the conversion of all convertible securities and (2) the elimination of the related interest charges net of tax, and preferred dividends, related to the convertible securities. Note that the diluted earnings per share calculation does exclude the benefit of leveraging that the company would realize while the convertible securities remain unconverted. On the other hand, the calculation draws attention to the possibility that this leverage is only temporary since the securities will be converted if that becomes desirable for the holders of such securities. Moreover, a company can force conversion by calling the convertible security (assuming the security is callable) when the value of the common stock received through conversion would exceed the call price.

An evaluation of both undiluted and fully diluted earnings per share and the components that created that record provide a base for projection of future earnings and dividends.

There are two reasons why earnings per share figures should never be reviewed in isolation from a complete income statement review and analysis. First, accounting problems already discussed may make earnings per share figures noncomparable over time for a company or in the

TABLE 20-4. Calculation of Undiluted Earnings per Share (millions of dollars)

	Undiluted		Diluted
Earnings before interest and taxes	$200	$\left(\begin{array}{c}\$200 \text{ million} \\ \times \text{ }.10\end{array}\right)$	$200
Interest expense ($400 million $\times$ .10)	40		20
	160		180
Taxes at 50 percent	80		90
Earnings after taxes	80	$\left(\begin{array}{c}\$200 \text{ million} \\ \times \text{ }.05\end{array}\right)$	90
Preferred dividend ($400 million $\times$ .05)	20		10
Earnings available to common	60		80
Number of shares	20		90
Earnings per share	$3.00		$0.89

case of comparing different companies. Second, one should not concentrate attention on a single figure that may offer little basis for projection of future earnings results.

Dividends per Share

The stability and the growth of dividends from a base year or a base period should be calculated. Explanations should be sought for significant changes in policy. For most corporations dividend yield is important to investors. Only in the case of very rapid growth companies is it ignored by investors.

Having adjusted (or accepted) the reported earnings per share, the analyst can calculate the ratio of dividends per share to earnings per share. Assuming that the directors follow a fairly well-defined policy, this policy is indicated by a review of the payout ratio for a period of years and may be projected. Cash flow provides protection for dividends, and directors do not like to cut dividends. As previously noted, for the entire period of the 1930s, dividends exceeded earnings for all U.S. corporations but did not exceed cash flow. In no year did dividends exceed 75 percent of cash flow.

COMBINED STATEMENT RATIO ANALYSIS

The first test of profitability—net profit as a percentage of sales—has already been discussed. However, that is only an intermediate test of profitability and not a final test. The final tests are rates of return on assets, on total capital, and on common equity, as well as the past and expected growth rate of earnings.

Net Income Before Extraordinary Items
as a Percentage of Equity Capital

Stockholders supply the equity and are the residual claimants to the profits generated. Preferred dividends are deducted from net income after taxes, and the remainder is calculated as a percentage of the common equity.

If capitalization is leveraged, the difference between the rate of return on total capital and the rate of return on the common equity indicates the effect of trading on the equity.

The relationship between the rate of return on common equity and the rate earned on total invested capital is

$$\frac{\text{Net Profit}}{\text{Assets}} \times \frac{\text{Assets}}{\text{Owners' Equity}} = \frac{\text{Net Profit}}{\text{Owners' Equity}}.$$

Industry statistics on rates of profit on stockholders' equity, before and after federal income taxes, are presented in Tables 20-5, 20-6 and 20-7.

GROWTH AND STABILITY RATIOS AND MEASUREMENTS

As previously noted, the yield on high-quality bonds is substantially above the dividend yield offered by common stocks. An investor would not be interested in purchasing common stocks, therefore, unless growth supporting price appreciation was anticipated.

Price-Earnings Ratio

The P/E ratio may be the current price divided by (1) the latest available twelve months' earnings, (2) earnings projected for the next twelve months, (3) the average or midpoint of projected earnings for the next five or six years, or (4) the earnings expectation in a target year three to six years hence. On Wall Street the price-earnings ratio is the most commonly used method of determining relative values of various stocks. The earnings used are current earnings, but the actual capitalization rate applied to the earnings for specific stocks reflects investors' estimates of future earnings. The higher the expected growth rate and the less the volatility of earnings, the higher the P/E that will be awarded.

The latest two months' earnings are commonly used in calculating the P/E ratios reported in financial publications. Recommendations published by brokers typically calculate the P/E ratio based on earnings estimated for the current fiscal year or if near the end of that year, on an estimate for the next fiscal year. Such earnings are not the most appropriate representation of normal earning power. *Normal earning power* is best defined as earnings at the mid-point of the business cycle, where nonrecurring factors have been eliminated. However, when considerable stability in earnings or growth of earnings is present, current earnings may be a good proxy for normal earning power. Comparisons of relative value should be made on the basis of normalized P/E ratios. Such ratios assume that earnings have been adjusted to eliminate inconsistencies that can arise from utilizing different accounting techniques by the companies being compared.[14]

Growth Yields

Growth yield tables can be utilized to suggest the relative attraction of different stocks. As noted in Chapter 7, Samuel Elliot Guild provided

---

[14] For a good discussion of normalized P/E ratios, see Volkert S. Whitbeck and Manown Kisor, Jr., "A New Tool in Investment Decision Making," *Financial Analysts Journal*, Vol. 19, No. 3 (May–June, 1963), pp. 56–62.

TABLE 20–5. Annual Rates of Profit on Stockholders' Equity, by Industry (percent)

Industry	Before Income Taxes[b]					After Taxes				
	2Q 1980[c]	3Q 1980[c]	4Q 1980[c]	1Q 1981	2Q 1981	2Q 1980[c]	3Q 1980[c]	4Q 1980[c]	1Q 1981	2Q 1981
All manufacturing corporations	21.8	19.8	21.4	21.5	25.2	13.6	12.5	14.1	13.4	16.1
Nondurable manufacturing corporations	26.0	24.1	23.0	23.5	26.5	16.4	15.6	15.4	14.9	17.4
Food and kindred products	22.3	24.2	26.1	20.4	22.7	13.5	15.2	17.4	12.6	14.1
Tobacco manufactures	32.0	35.2	24.7	31.3	30.4	20.3	22.3	15.3	21.2	19.2
Textile mill products	16.0	13.3	15.3	15.6	23.4	7.9	6.6	8.6	8.8	13.8
Paper and allied products	19.5	15.3	15.1	18.7	20.4	13.0	10.6	11.6	12.5	13.7
Printing and publishing	29.3	29.8	29.1	24.0	27.3	16.5	17.2	16.7	13.6	15.2
Chemicals and allied products	22.5	21.1	19.1	24.4	23.5	15.3	15.0	13.3	16.3	15.3
Industrial chemicals and synthetics[a]	17.7	11.8	14.0	21.8	20.0	12.3	9.6	9.7	14.9	12.9
Drugs[a]	25.7	31.0	23.3	23.7	23.7	18.3	22.6	16.9	16.4	16.1
Petroleum and coal products	32.9	27.6	25.5	25.9	31.3	21.1	17.8	17.5	16.5	21.9
Rubber and miscellaneous plastics products	7.4	8.8	14.9	19.4	24.5	4.9	5.4	9.2	12.0	14.8
Other nondurable manufacturing corporations	20.3	27.7	24.6	21.0	22.5	11.4	16.3	14.6	11.5	13.8
Durable manufacturing corporations	17.3	15.0	19.6	19.3	23.7	10.6	9.1	12.7	11.8	14.6
Stone, clay and glass products	17.4	21.4	17.3	9.6	19.7	11.5	14.4	11.5	5.3	12.6
Primary metal industries	17.0	7.5	17.1	18.7	21.4	11.8	5.6	12.5	12.8	14.5
Iron and steel[a]	12.0	3.0	16.2	18.8	22.8	8.2	3.4	11.7	12.2	14.9
Nonferrous metals[a]	24.2	13.8	18.5	18.5	19.3	17.1	8.8	13.6	13.6	13.9
Fabricated metal products	21.3	20.1	21.8	23.0	27.7	13.3	12.3	13.5	13.6	17.0
Machinery, except electrical	23.9	21.2	24.0	22.0	25.3	15.4	13.7	16.6	13.8	15.2
Electrical and electronic equipment	25.0	23.3	25.2	26.1	25.8	14.8	14.1	15.6	16.2	15.8

TABLE 20–5. Annual Rates of Profit on Stockholders' Equity, by Industry (percent) (continued)

Industry	Before Income Taxes[b]					After Taxes					
	2Q 1980c	3Q 1980c	4Q 1980c	1Q 1981	2Q 1981	2Q 1980c	3Q 1980c	4Q 1980c	1Q 1981	2Q 1981	
Transportation equipment	-3.4	-6.4	7.5	9.7	20.6	-3.6	-6.2	3.4	4.3	12.6	
Motor vehicles and equipment[a]	-18.7	-23.0	-0.4	-1.8	16.8	-14.0	-18.0	-3.0	-4.3	10.0	
Aircraft, guided missiles and parts[a]	26.8	24.2	22.9	31.4	26.9	16.6	15.4	15.5	20.4	17.0	
Instruments and related products	28.8	28.5	27.0	27.4	27.4	17.8	17.8	17.9	17.9	17.5	
Other durable manufacturing corporations	16.9	19.7	18.8	14.1	18.8	8.8	12.0	11.2	7.4	9.9	
All mining corporations	27.0	30.8	31.7	31.1	27.7	18.0	21.7	22.9	20.3	16.6	
All retail trade corporations	18.4	19.9	31.7	15.7	NA	11.7	12.6	20.2	9.3	NA	
All wholesale trade corporations	27.3	29.5	26.7	24.6	28.3	17.6	18.8	16.5	15.1	17.9	

[a]Included in major industry above.
[b]Based on profit figure, which includes net income (loss) of foreign branches and equity in earnings (losses) of nonconsolidated subsidiaries, net of foreign taxes.
[c]Some of the rates in this column have been revised since their first appearance.

Source: Federal Trade Commission, Quarterly Financial Report for Manufacturing, Mining and Trade Corporations, Second Quarter, 1981, p. 14.

TABLE 20-6. Rates of Return, All Manufacturing Corporations, 1970–1981

Year and Quarter	Annual Rate of Profit on Stockholders' Equity (percent)		Profit Per Dollar of Sales (cents)	
	Before Taxes	After Taxes	Before Taxes	After Taxes
1970 Q1	16.0	9.2	7.1	4.0
2	17.9	10.4	7.5	4.4
3	15.1	9.0	6.6	3.9
4	13.8 T	8.7 T	5.9 T	3.7 T
1971 Q1	15.4	8.9	6.8	3.9
2	18.2	10.7	7.6	4.5
3	15.9	9.3	6.9	4.1
4	16.5	9.8	6.9	4.1
1972 Q1	16.8	9.5	7.1	4.0
2	19.7	11.3	7.8	4.5
3	17.4	10.1	7.2	4.2
4	19.8	11.5	7.7	4.4
1973 Q1	20.3	11.6	7.9	4.5
2	23.9	14.0	8.7	5.1
3	20.7	12.3	7.7	4.6
4	22.1	13.4	7.8	4.7
a 4	22.4	14.3	8.7	5.6

Year and Quarter	Annual Rate of Profit on Stockholders' Equity (percent)		Profit Per Dollar of Sales (cents)	
	Before Taxes	After Taxes	Before Taxes	After Taxes
1976 Q1	21.9	13.3	8.6	5.2
2	25.5	15.7	9.5	5.9
3	22.3	13.7	8.6	5.3
4	21.0	13.1	8.0	5.0
1977 Q1	21.3	13.0	8.2	5.0
2	26.3	16.0	9.6	5.8
3	21.7	13.3	8.2	5.0
4	23.4	14.4	8.6	5.3
1978 Q1	20.7	12.4	7.9	4.7
2	27.0	16.6	9.5	5.9
3	24.4	14.9	8.9	5.4
4	25.8	16.1	9.1	5.6
1979 Q1	25.4	15.7	9.0	5.6
2	28.8 P	18.1 P	9.7 P	6.1 P
3	25.1	16.3	8.7	5.7
4	23.7	15.7	8.0	5.3

TABLE 20-6. Rates of Return, All Manufacturing Corporations, 1970–1981 (continued)

Year and Quarter	Annual Rate of Profit on Stockholders' Equity (percent)		Profit Per Dollar of Sales (cents)	
	Before Taxes	After Taxes	Before Taxes	After Taxes
1974 Q1	22.4	14.3	8.8	5.6
2	26.5	16.7	9.6	6.0
3	24.8	15.4	9.2	5.7
4	19.7	13.2	7.2	4.8
1975 Q1	15.0	9.0	6.2	3.7
2	19.2	11.8	7.6	4.7
3	20.4	12.4	8.0	4.9
4	20.8	13.1	8.0	5.1

Year and Quarter	Annual Rate of Profit on Stockholders' Equity (percent)		Profit Per Dollar of Sales (cents)	
	Before Taxes	After Taxes	Before Taxes	After Taxes
1980 Q1	24.5	15.4	8.5	5.3
2	21.8	13.6	7.7	4.8
3	19.8	12.5	7.2	4.5
4	21.4	14.1	7.4	4.8
1981 Q1	21.5	13.4	7.5	4.7
2	25.2	16.1	8.5	5.5

P—Peak
T—Trough
[a]This line of data and all subsequent data reflect the new rules of consolidation. See page 85 of explanatory notes.
Source: Federal Trade Commission, Quarterly Financial Report for Manufacturing, Mining and Trade Corporations, Second Quarter, 1981, p. 16.

TABLE 20-7. Annual Rates of Profit on Stockholders' Equity, Manufacturing Corporations by Asset Size and Industry Group (percent)

Asset Size	Before Income Taxes[a]					After Taxes				
	2Q 1980	3Q 1980	4Q 1980	1Q 1981	2Q 1981	2Q 1980	3Q 1980	4Q 1980	1Q 1981	2Q 1981
All manufacturing corporations	21.8	19.8	21.4	21.5	25.2	13.6	12.5	14.1	13.4	16.1
Under $5 million[b]	25.8	25.7	20.2	24.6	31.2	14.8	14.8	11.1	14.2	19.6
$ 5 million to $ 10 million	23.6	21.1	21.9	23.4	30.3	11.2	10.2	11.2	12.5	16.9
$ 10 million to $ 25 million	20.1	19.7	24.5	19.2	25.4	9.5	10.3	13.1	9.2	13.3
$ 25 million to $ 50 million	20.6	21.1	19.4	18.5	22.5	11.0	11.6	10.2	9.5	11.5
$ 50 million to $ 100 million	21.2	20.5	23.5	20.6	23.8	11.8	11.2	14.0	11.6	12.8
$ 100 million to $ 250 million	22.0	21.1	19.4	20.2	23.4	12.8	11.9	11.3	11.5	13.5
$ 250 million to $1,000 million	22.3	21.9	20.5	19.6	22.1	13.2	13.3	12.6	11.8	12.8
$1,000 million and over	21.4	18.5	21.7	21.9	25.3	14.1	12.4	15.3	14.3	17.0
Durable goods	17.3	15.0	19.6	19.3	23.7	10.6	9.1	12.7	11.8	14.6
Under $5 million	27.4	25.2	19.6	24.3	32.0	16.0	14.4	10.6	14.0	20.0
$ 5 million to $ 10 million	23.5	19.0	22.1	23.7	29.6	11.0	9.3	11.8	12.9	17.2
$ 10 million to $ 25 million	20.4	18.8	25.4	18.5	25.7	10.0	9.9	13.3	9.0	13.6
$ 25 million to $ 50 million	20.4	18.2	15.7	18.7	22.3	10.9	9.1	8.2	9.4	11.2
$ 50 million to $ 100 million	20.0	18.9	22.3	21.0	24.6	10.9	9.8	13.1	11.6	13.4
$ 100 million to $ 250 million	20.5	17.7	19.0	20.0	24.7	11.9	10.2	11.1	11.3	14.2
$ 250 million to $1,000 million	20.3	19.1	19.8	19.2	21.7	12.4	11.9	12.9	11.7	12.2
$1,000 million and over	13.7	11.2	19.2	18.3	22.6	9.1	7.4	13.4	11.8	14.7

TABLE 20-7. Annual Rates of Profit on Stockholders' Equity, Manufacturing Corporations by Asset Size and Industry Group (percent) (continued)

Asset Size	Before Income Taxes[a]					After Taxes				
	2Q 1980	3Q 1980	4Q 1980	1Q 1981	2Q 1981	2Q 1980	3Q 1980	4Q 1980	1Q 1981	2Q 1981
Nondurable goods	26.0	24.1	23.0	23.5	26.5	16.4	15.6	15.4	14.9	17.4
Under $5 million	23.4	26.6	21.0	25.0	29.9	13.1	15.5	12.0	14.6	18.9
$ 5 million to $ 10 million	23.8	24.7	21.6	23.0	31.2	11.5	11.8	10.3	11.8	16.4
$ 10 million to $ 25 million	19.7	20.9	23.1	20.2	25.0	8.8	10.8	12.9	9.5	12.9
$ 25 million to $ 50 million	20.8	25.0	24.6	18.2	22.8	11.2	14.9	13.1	9.8	12.0
$ 50 million to $ 100 million	22.6	22.8	25.1	20.1	22.6	13.1	13.1	15.4	11.6	12.0
$ 100 million to $ 250 million	24.0	25.8	20.0	20.5	21.7	14.0	14.1	11.6	11.9	12.5
$ 250 million to $1,000 million	24.7	25.1	21.4	20.1	22.6	14.2	14.9	12.2	12.0	13.5
$1,000 million and over	27.0	23.8	23.5	24.5	27.3	17.8	16.1	16.6	16.1	18.7

[a]Based on profit figure which includes net income (loss) of foreign branches and equity in earnings (losses) of nonconsolidated subsidiaries, net of foreign taxes.

[b]Collapse of asset size data resulting from change in estimating technique.

Source: Federal Trade Commission, Quarterly Financial Report for Manufacturing, Mining and Trade Corporations, Second Quarter, 1981, p. 15.

a set of tables that enable an investor to calculate the rate of return that would be received on a given stock based on the following assumptions:

1. Expected duration of the growth period;
2. The estimated growth rate for earnings during this period;
3. The dividend payout ratio;
4. The assumed P/E ratio at which the stock would sell at the end of the growth period.

Soldofsky and Murphy created tables based on the Guild tables that are broader in scope.[15] These tables are based on dividends, not earnings growth rates. The tables consist of one-step and two-step growth yield tables. The one-step table assumes a continuous growth period with a constant growth rate. The two-step tables assume two growth periods with a different but constant growth rate for each. The figures in the body of the tables are price-dividend ratios.

The use of the two-step tables can be illustrated by assuming that the $11.52 dividend paid by IBM during 1977 will grow at a compound annual rate of 15 percent over the next ten years, and will then decline to 10 percent for the succeeding ten years and stay at that level. If the appropriate discount rate is assumed to be 7 percent, Table 20–8 suggests that the reasonable current price for IBM is approximately $896 (77.77 × $11.52). The market price of IBM was about $240 in April 1978, suggesting that if the estimated growth rate for dividends did in fact materialize over the next twenty years, the return to the investor would be substantially above the 7 percent discount rate used. One could make similar calculations for a stock index and/or other stocks to assess return expectations.

TABLE 20–8. Dividend Growth Yield

First Growth Period	Second Growth Period	Total Years	Dividend Growth Rates 15%, 10% Discount Rate		
			$6\frac{1}{2}\%$	$6\frac{3}{4}\%$	7%
5	5	10	40.89	39.13	37.51
10	10	20	87.00	82.20	77.77
15	10	25	133.90	125.42	117.67
20	15	35	254.56	234.54	216.49

Source: R. M. Soldofsky and James T. Murphy, *Growth Yields on Common Stock: Theory and Tables,* rev. ed. (Iowa City: Bureau of Business and Economic Research, State University of Iowa, 1964), p. 118.

---

[15] R. M. Soldofsky and James T. Murphy, *Growth Yields on Common Stock: Theory and Tables,* rev. ed. (Iowa City: Bureau of Business and Economic Research, State University of Iowa, 1964).

Growth Yield Limitations

The Soldofsky and Murphy tables assume an investor is interested only in the average rate of return received over a very long period; in other words, that investors are indifferent to the timing of anticipated income. This ignores the different objectives and constraints of investors. For example, a retired person may be highly interested in current income and even willing to trade higher potential income in the future for more current income. Furthermore, the longer the time period under which estimates are made, other things being equal, the greater the uncertainties involved in the estimates made to utilize the tables. The tables, however, do provide a tool for assessing the impact of changing expectations in which some factors are held constant.

Dividend Yield

The dividend yield is calculated by dividing the current annual dividend by the current market price. It is most meaningful in industries and companies that have demonstrated stability of earnings and dividends and consistent growth. Since 1938 a portfolio of common stocks representative of the major stock averages would have demonstrated excellent dividend stability and, in addition, substantial dividend growth. Therefore, overall dividend yield is a much more significant figure than it was prior to 1938 for stock portfolios. In the 1970s, especially beginning in 1972, dividend yields and their relationship to bond yields appeared to have a growing role in investor thinking.

Price Range of Stock

The price range of the stock—high, low, and mean—should be tabulated for the past five to ten years or longer. The prices should be adjusted for stock splits and stock dividends. Price charts and price-earnings ratios should be examined.

Net Working Capital or Net Current Asset Book Value per Share

This ratio is not actually based on net working capital or net current asset book value per share because it is calculated (1) by deducting *all liabilities* (short term and long term) from current assets, not just *current liabilities* and (2) then dividing the result by the number of outstanding shares (less treasury stock). Many stocks sell well below book value and quite a number at any point of time below net current asset book value, almost always because of poor earnings or actual losses. Even in the latter case an undervalued situation is not indicated unless a turnaround is expected or new, capable management is to take over or the company is expected to be taken over by another company. If the market price is below net current asset book value (less all liabilities), the stock may be a particularly good value in case of expected changes discussed above.

Physical Data Ratios

In addition to the statement ratios discussed in this chapter, analysts frequently use certain physical data ratios and often reduce them to a per share basis. This adds depth to the straight dollar figure analysis and is particularly significant in comparing competing companies in the same industry.

Physical Reserves. Reserves are of utmost importance to companies dependent on wasting assets for their operations. Reported reserves of major companies normally provide a conservative representation of such assets. The analyst should note carefully the quality or grade of reserves as well as the quantity, with special attention to changes in grade from year to year since these are largely indicative of current mining policy and possible "high-grading" (mining primarily the highest grade ores in the deposit) in any given year.

Reserves of oil and gas, normally stated in terms of millions of barrels and billions of cubic feet respectively, are frequently reported on a per share basis. The estimated value of reserves can be computed by multiplying the number of units in reserve by the going market price per unit.

Capacity. Producers and processors of various materials normally have specific productive or fabricating capacity that may be expressed in terms of physical units. Data of physical capacity are particularly valuable in determining the relative position of individual companies within an industry. These data can be reduced to a per share or a per employee basis for comparison between companies. Trends for a period of years may be significant. Capacity can also be related to order backlogs for units and dollars.

Production. Production data in units are of considerable interest to the analyst. Related to capacity figures, they provide an indication of the level of operations within a company, which in turn can be compared to industry figures. In companies concentrating primarily on one type of product (for example, crude oil, ingot steel, or copper), production data in units can be used to calculate selling prices, production costs, and profits per unit. Such data also enable the analyst to determine the effects of changes in costs and selling prices on the profit margins of the company.

Freight Volume. Detailed information relative to volume, product composition, and geographical distribution of freight carried is especially valuable to the analyst in appraising the outlook for a transportation company such as a railroad, airline, trucking service, or barge line.

Stock Dividends, Stock Splits, and the Sale of New Stock

The analyst must adjust all per share data for stock splits and stock dividends to ensure comparability over time, as discussed in Chapter 2. Although the sale of new stock also changes the number of shares outstanding, no adjustment similar to that for splits or dividends is necessary. The analyst should expect common stock financing to be justified by adequate earnings (rate of return) on the new funds in the future. As suggested by AICPA, "the computation of earnings per share should be based on the weighted average number of shares outstanding during the period," which will properly allow for the effect of a sale of new shares.[16] The financial services make such adjustments.

Mergers

Most corporations restate prior years' data to show on a pro forma basis the effects of a merger on both balance sheet and income account items. This represents proper procedure.

Summary

Careful analysis of the income statement is highly important since that statement presents the income earned by the business on its assets, total invested capital, and stockholders' net worth. The value of a business, its assets, and net worth depend on its earning capacity and the quality of its earnings. In combination with balance sheet data, the rate of return on assets, total invested capital, and stockholders' net worth can be calculated. As with all financial statements, the investor must review a period of past years and current conditions and then make projections for a period into the future.

To complete a satisfactory analysis, the investor must be familiar with basic accounting principles, the character of accounts appearing in the statements, the basis for construction of statements including consolidated statements, the type of judgments including subjective judgments, and the knowledge to interpret the accountant's notes to the statements properly. In addition to basic accounting knowledge, the investor should be familiar with the pronouncements of such groups as the American Institute of Certified Public Accountants (AICPA), the

—————————
[16] APB Opinion No. 9 and reaffirmed in Opinion No. 15.

Securities and Exchange Commission (SEC), other federal and state regulatory commissions and agencies, and the security exchanges. Also, the analyst must have the training and ability to make adjustments in reported figures to arrive at "true" earnings, which can form a basis for projecting the recurring earnings power of the business.

In reviewing a series of past "comparative" financial statements covering a period of years, the analyst must recognize that to be meaningful the statements must in fact be comparable. If there have been accounting changes (methods of reporting), then statements for a period of years should have been adjusted in accordance with pronouncements of the AICPA. In the Accounting Principles Board (APB) *Opinion No. 13*, the AICPA requires the use of the "all-inclusive statement" rather than the less-inclusive "operating performance" statement. The "all-inclusive" type of income statement includes operating income and related expenses, other income and related expenses, and extraordinary income and related expenses. The most fundamental of all accounting principles applied to the income statement is that which requires the matching of revenues and expenses.

Many, perhaps most, corporate financial statements being analyzed will be consolidated statements combining the performance of all 50 percent or more owned subsidiaries and eliminating all intercompany transactions. In 1971 the AICPA in APB *Opinion No. 18* required that the "equity method" rather than the "cost method" be applied in both consolidated statements and parent company statements. In applying the equity method, any difference between the cost of an investment and the investor's equity in the net assets of the investee at the date of investment must be accounted for as if the investee were a consolidated subsidiary. Any goodwill so generated must be amortized over a period not to exceed forty years as a reduction of the amount recognized each period by the investor as its equity in the earnings or losses of the investee.

The investor will review the trends of all major items on the income statement in respect to the company being analyzed and the trends of its industry or industries. The analysis essentially takes the form of ratio statement analysis as well as analysis of the specific record of absolute earnings and dividends per share. The analyst must also calculate certain combined statement ratios using both the income statement and balance sheet data to determine the rate of return earned on assets, total invested capital, and equity capital.

We have earlier explained the importance of growth and stability of earnings and dividends. In addition to analyzing such growth factors, the investor must examine the trends over a period of years of market data such as the price of the stock, price-earnings ratio, and dividend yields in relation to the trends of the general stock market and industry averages.

Certain physical data ratios are additional tools that are especially helpful in certain industries such as physical reserves (now required to be estimated in annual reports) and output capacity per share, and capacity and production ratios. Finally, the investor must determine the effects of stock dividends, stock splits, mergers, acquisitions, and actual and potential conversion of convertible securities.

Questions

1. Explain briefly the significance of consolidated financial statements from the standpoint of the security analyst.
2. (a) Distinguish between the equity method and the cost method in preparing consolidated statements. When is the equity method required?
   (b) When would "goodwill" be properly recorded in relation to an acquisition if the equity method were used? How should the goodwill account be handled over time?
3. (a) Distinguish between a subsidiary and an affiliate.
   (b) In what ways does the growing importance of foreign operations for many U.S. corporations make more difficult the analysis of the income statements of such corporations?
   (c) Defend the lack of inclusion of a company's financial subsidiary in a consolidated statement.
4. Ajax Company owns a 50 percent interest in a nonconsolidated subsidiary, which reported earnings for the year of $400,000. There are 100,000 shares of Ajax Company stock outstanding, and Ajax reports earnings per share for the year of $3.60, including dividends of $100,000 received on the stock of the nonconsolidated subsidiary.
   (a) Discuss the significance of the reported $3.60 per share earnings of Ajax Company and what adjustments should be made by the analyst to reflect "true earnings" per share for Ajax Company shareholders.
   (b) Would it make any difference if the nonconsolidated subsidiary were a foreign operation rather than a domestic operation? Discuss.
5. (a) Should extraordinary items such as a substantial gain (or loss) on the sale of fixed assets no longer needed in the business be reflected in the income statement or should they be treated as direct credits or debits to the retained earnings account? How would you as an analyst handle such items? Discuss.
   (b) How should nonrecurring items be treated by the analyst?
6. Distinguish between a "clean income statement" and an "all-inclusive income statement." Which would you, as an analyst, prefer? Support your position.

7. The Securities and Exchange Commission's Rule 3–17 required companies with a total of $100 million in combined inventories, which comprise 10 percent of their total assets, to include replacement costs in their 10-Ks covering 1976. The commission said it was aware that such costs could not be calculated with precision. Discuss the value of such a requirement.

8. What problems exist in the interpretation of interim reports?

9. Discuss briefly the effect on both the balance sheet and the income statement of using the Lifo method rather than the Fifo method of accounting for inventory during a period of rising prices.

10. What types of items are normally responsible for differences between net income for tax purposes and net income as reported to stockholders? Discuss the problems raised by at least five of these items.

Work-Study Problems

1. Illustrate with a hypothetical example the difference in profit between (a) the flow-through method and (b) the normalizing method of accounting for depreciation, giving figures for sales, expenses, income before depreciation, depreciation, taxable income, tax, net income after tax, and net earnings per share.

2. On June 30, 1977, the Financial Accounting Standards Board issued Statement 16, which required that all items of profit and loss be charged against the current year (affecting fiscal years after October 15, 1977). Only two items can be treated as prior period adjustments. What are they?

3. The following financial data and information pertain to the Temple Corporation for 1981:

	($ Millions)
Sales	200.0
Cost of sales & operating expenses	162.0
Taxes on income (50% rate)	15.2
Earnings available to common	14.4
Common dividends	3.6
Total assets	160.0
Current liabilities	10.0
Long-term debt:	
8% first mortgage bonds	30.0
10% sinking fund debentures	40.0
6% convertible debentures	20.0
Preferred stock, 8%, $25 par	10.0
Common equity (20 million shares)	50.0

The Convertible debentures are convertible into common stock at $12.50 and are considered common stock equivalents.

Required:
(a) Calculate fully diluted earnings per share.
(b) Would primary earnings per share be the same as fully diluted earnings per share in this case? Explain.

21.

Noncash Charges and Cash Flow

Some expenses deducted in the income account represent an accounting charge but not a corresponding cash outlay, thereby causing a company's cash flow that stems from operations to differ from reported profits. Examples of major noncash items that will be discussed below are depreciation, depletion, and the amortization of intangibles. Investment credit, another item to be considered in cash flow analysis, is also discussed.

DEPRECIATION

"Depreciation accounting is a system of accounting which aims to distribute the cost . . . of tangible capital assets, less salvage (if any) over the estimated useful life of the unit (which may be a group of assets) in a systematic and rational manner. It is a process of allocation (of cost), not of valuation. *Depreciation for the year* is the portion of the total charge under such a system that is allocated to the year. Although the allocation may properly take into account occurrences during the year, it is not intended to be a measurement of the effect of all such occurrences."[1]

Because the accounting charge for depreciation does not represent a corresponding outlay of cash, some investors and analysts have at least implied that depreciation is not a real expense by using the terms "cash earnings per share" or "cash flow earnings per share" and have even substituted these terms for "net earnings per share." Strong criticism of this position by the AICPA, the NYSE, and the Financial Analysts Federation has sharply reduced the use of these terms in brokerage houses and annual corporate reports.

---

[1] "Review and Resume," *Accounting Terminology Bulletin No. 1* (New York: American Institute of Certified Public Accountants, 1953), p. 25.

Since fixed assets, particularly plant and equipment, represent such a substantial outlay, it would be impractical to write them off entirely as an expense charged against the income of the year in which they are purchased, especially since benefits from their use will be received over an extended period. Furthermore, as soon as it is purchased, a fixed asset begins to depreciate. To ignore this fact would be to experience a gradual loss of capital without any reflection of the fact on the books of account. Accountants consider the original cost of a fixed asset to be a prepaid expense that must be amortized during the service life of the asset by regular periodic charges to the depreciation expense account. After deduction of the annual charge, the remaining amount is the *unamortized cost;* but in no way, except by coincidence, does this amount represent the *economic value* of the asset at that time.

Basis for Depreciation—Replacement Value vs. Original Cost

Inflation, which has long been a problem, has led many to advocate a policy of substituting replacement cost for original cost as the basis for determining depreciation charges in the income statement. Corporate management has been especially vocal in this regard. The basic function of depreciation charges, as seen by accountants, is to amortize the cost of a capital asset over its useful life. Management is concerned with a second function: providing the funds needed for replacement of assets after they have worn out or become technologically obsolete. Depreciation charges do not in and of themselves provide a company with cash. However, they do not represent a corresponding outlay of cash and, to the extent that they are tax deductible, they do protect cash generated by sales operations from the burden of taxes.

When replacement costs have risen far above original cost, prudent business management must recognize this capital erosion and set aside the additional funds necessary to continue a business in operation. Such funds must presently be provided from retained earnings because the income tax laws do not recognize the inflation situation. In other words, income taxes must be paid on the capital lost through inflation, which makes the problem of maintaining a company's capital doubly difficult.

Of interest to note is that other countries (for example, the Netherlands, Chile, and Brazil) with more rapid inflation than the United States have changed their tax laws in various ways to prevent the gradual liquidation of capital investment through payment of income taxes on capital eroded by inflation; asset values are raised yearly and depreciated on the new values.

A change to replacement cost would change fundamental concepts of accounting, since it would represent a breaking away from the base idea that balance sheet and expense accounts are based on monetary cost and not on economic values. The cost basis of measurement has the advantages of (1) uniformity of interpretation of the values to be entered in the balance sheet and the charges to be entered in the income account and (2) objectivity. Accountants question whether a system based on an attempt to measure replacement values, with its loss of objectivity, has additional advantages that more than offset the advantages of the cost basis. Other questions are raised, such as whether the assets are replaced with like assets or superior ones that justify part of the higher cost, whether the assets will in fact be replaced as technology changes, and whether current or future customers should pay for the replaced equipment.[2]

In June 1969 the AICPA issued APB *Statement No. 3*, "Financial Statement Restated for General Price Level Changes." This statement, which still reflects the AICPA thinking at this writing, is quoted in part as follows:

> The Board believes that general price-level financial statements or pertinent information extracted from them present useful information not available from basic historical-dollar financial statements. General price-level information may be presented in addition to the basic historical statement but should not be presented as the basic statements.[3]

This view was reiterated by the AICPA in its "Fundamental Statement" published in October 1970.

FASB Number 33: Inflation-Adjusted Data

As noted in Chapter 19, *Financial Accounting Standards Bulletin No. 33* now requires the disclosure in annual reports of two types of inflation-adjusted data (in addition to traditional historical cost-based statements) by publicly held corporations with total assets of more than $1 billion, or whose inventories and property, plant, and equipment are valued at more than $125 million dollars. Each of the types of inflation-adjusted data is discussed briefly below.[4]

Constant Dollar Data. Constant dollar data is derived by restating historical accounting data in dollars of current purchasing power. The historical stated accounting value is multiplied by a fraction, the nu-

---

[2] See *Accounting Research Bulletin No. 43*, published in 1953, for both the majority view and the dissenting view of a special committee appointed by the AICPA to study this question.

[3] APB *Statement No. 3*, "Financial Statement Restated for General Price-Level Changes," *Journal of Accountancy* (September, 1969), pp. 62–68.

[4] See Charles T. Horngrew, *Introduction to Management Accounting*, 5th ed. (Englewood Cliffs, N.J.: Prentice-Hall, 1981), chapter 19, for an example of the development of each of the types of inflation-adjusted data from historically cost-based accounting statements.

merator of which is the current consumer price index for urban items and the denominator the index that prevailed at the date related to the amount being restated. For example, assume an asset was acquired for $15,000 on January 1, 1975. It would be restated in terms of December 31, 1980, dollars as follows:

$$\frac{1980 \text{ Index}}{1975 \text{ Index}} \times \$15,000 = \text{Cost of the asset in terms of 1980 dollars;}$$

$$\frac{261.5}{161.2} \times \$15,000 = \$24,333.$$

Raising the value of a depreciable asset affects the income statement as well as the balance sheet since depreciation expense would also be increased, thereby lowering reported profits.

The actual preparation of constant dollar financial statements is more complex than illustrated above. To restate historical statements, one must distinguish between *monetary* and *nonmonetary items*. A *monetary* item is cash or any claim receivable or payable in a specified number of dollars. When the price level rises, each dollar purchases less in terms of real goods and services. A holder of monetary assets, therefore, loses in real terms since the number of dollars will remain fixed. On the other hand, *nonmonetary* assets tend to behave in the opposite manner since the number of dollars that can be obtained through sale of such assets tends to rise during inflation. It is preferable, therefore, to hold nonmonetary assets (fixed assets and inventory) rather than monetary assets during a period of inflation. The value of nonmonetary assets is accordingly raised, as in the illustration above, to recognize the rising value; the purchasing power loss of monetary assets must also be recognized.

One who incurs monetary liabilities (short- or long-term obligations payable in a fixed sum) gains when prices rise since the obligations are repaid with dollars of lesser purchasing power than those acquired when the obligation was assumed. Index adjustments are, therefore, also made to recognize such gains, and the gain on monetary liabilities is offset against the loss on monetary assets to determine whether the firm had a net gain or loss on monetary items.

Constant dollar adjustments do provide objectively determined and consistently determined estimates from company to company of the impact of inflation. This enhances comparability of such data. Unfortunately, however, such estimates can be misleading. Constant dollar data assumes that the impact of inflation falls equally on all firms and all classes of assets and costs, which is just not correct. Using a single index to adjust the historical data of all firms would hide the effects of changing technology, supply and demand shifts that may well be related to the inflation phenomena, and the impact of successful or unsuccessful management in meeting the problems brought on by inflation. In short, one could say that such data are better than nothing, assuming the user understands their limitations. In all cases such data should be used with great caution.

Current Value Data. Proponents of this approach are interested in what the business is worth now rather than historical past accounting values. They argue the value of assets should be stated in terms of the present value of the future receipts these assets can be expected to generate or as the cost of replenishing the assets at today's prices. The latter method is used by most firms to prepare supplementary current value inflation-adjusted data in accordance with requirements of FASB No. 33.

Such estimates seem more useful than index number-adjusted data, but they also suffer serious analytical drawbacks. The differing impact of inflation on firms and classes of assets and costs is estimated. The computation of current value or cost, however, is subjective since many assets do not have a ready market price and might be replaced with a different type of asset or not replaced at all. Accounting rules do allow considerable flexibility in determining current value estimates, and certainly comparing data prepared by different companies will be difficult. In short, the accuracy of current cost estimates is open to serious question. Still, the estimates of management offer possible insights into the impact of inflation on business firms that were not formerly available to analysts.

Tables 21-1, 21-2, and 21-3 offer an illustration of the reporting of inflation-adjusted data by E. I. Du Pont Co. Notice that the income reported after inflation adjustments is less than one-half of the income reported on a historical cost basis. Also note the much higher effective tax rate incurred by the company when inflation-adjusted data are considered. Finally, note that inflation-adjusted earnings per share (constant dollars) did not cover the dollar dividend paid per share in 1980. This has important cash flow implications, as well as showing that profits are significantly overstated on a historical cost basis.

Magnitude of Depreciation

The two major reasons why investors and analysts need to devote so much attention to depreciation are (1) the magnitude of depreciation and (2) the leeway that management can exercise in reporting depreciation—that is, the lack of uniformity in reporting depreciation in published reports. The magnitude of depreciation is evident when it is related to corporate profits as is done in Table 21-4. This table shows that depreciation in absolute terms has risen from $4.7 billion annually

TABLE 21-1. Supplemental Financial Data (dollars in millions, except per share)

| | Consolidated Sales and Net Income by Geographic Area | | | | | | |
| | Sales | | | Net Income | | | |
	1980	1979	1978	1980	1979	1978	
Europe, Middle East, & Africa	$ 2,343	$ 2,060	$ 1,580	$136	$234	$111	
Canada	734	672	523	35	38	22	
Latin America	856	710	534	38	59	32	
Asia/Pacific	713	540	355	38	45	65	
Total International	4,646	3,982	2,992	247	376	230	
United States	9,006	8,590	7,592	469	563	557	
Total	$13,652	$12,572	$10,584	$716	$939	$787	

The above breakdown reflects the destination of the sale rather than the location of the corporate unit making the sale. Net income is determined by charging manufacturing costs and other related expenses directly against sales, regardless of the area in which such expenses were incurred, and by allocating other elements of income and expense to geographic areas.

Sales outside the United States of products manufactured in and exported from the United States totaled $2,175 in 1980, $1,764 in 1979, and $1,266 in 1978.

TABLE 21-1. Supplemental Financial Data (dollars in millions, except per share) (continued)

Other Consolidated Geographic Data

Capital expenditures, investment, and average employment of Du Pont and its consolidated subsidiaries were:

	Capital Expenditures		Investment December 31		Average Employment	
	1980	1979	1980	1979	1980	1979
Europe, Middle East, & Africa	$ 113	$ 81	$ 1,723	$ 1,757	13,300	12,300
Canada	46	21	864	801	6,000	5,600
Latin America	15	11	580	492	7,800	8,000
Asia/Pacific	22	14	309	311	2,600	2,100
Total International	196	127	3,476	3,361	29.700	28,000
United States	1,155	802	13,972	12,866	106,200	106,200
Total	$1,351	$929	$17,448	$16,227	135,900	134,200

Capital expenditures, investment, and average employment are assigned to geographic areas generally based on physical location. Investment is the sum of all assets, before deduction of accumulated depreciation and obsolescence.

TABLE 21-1. Supplemental Financial Data (dollars in millions, except per share) *(continued)*

Affiliated Companies

Sales, net income, and net assets of nonconsolidated affiliates accounted for by the equity method were:

	Sales			Net Income			Net Assets December 31	
	1980	1979	1978	1980	1979	1978	1980	1979
Europe, Middle East, & Africa	$265	$249	$165	$ 58	$ 42	$(58)	$ 70	$ 17
Latin America	242	251	197	26	25	13	141	137
Asia/Pacific	362	364	303	12	8	26	102	100
Total International	869	864	665	96	75	(19)	313	254
United States	71	1	16	(33)	(54)	(9)	191	144
Total	$940	$865	$681	$ 63	$ 21	$(28)	$504	$398
Du Pont Equity in:								
Net Income				$ 19	$ 9	$(10)		
Net Assets							$263	$207
Advances to Affiliates							13	27
Investment in Nonconsolidated Affiliates							$276	$234

Source: 1980 Annual Report of E. I. Du Pont.

TABLE 21-2. Comparative Historical Dollar, Constant Dollar, and Current Cost Income Statements, 1980 (dollars in millions)

	As Reported in the Primary Statements (Historical Dollars)	Adjusted for General Inflation (Average 1980 Constant Dollars)	Adjusted for Changes in Specific Prices (Average 1980 Current Costs)
Sales	$13,652	$13,652	$13,652
Other Income	149	149	149
Total	13,801	13,801	13,801
Cost of Goods Sold and Other Operating Charges	10,293	10,420	10,437
Selling, General, and Administrative Expenses	1,466	1,466	1,466
Depreciation and Obsolescence	804	1,156	1,109
Interest on Borrowings	110	110	110
Total	12,673	13,152	13,122
Earnings Before Income Taxes and Minority Interests	1,128	649	679
Provision for Income Taxes	402	402	402
Earnings Before Minority Interests	726	247	277
Minority Interests in Earnings of Consolidated Subsidiaries	10	10	10
Income from Continuing Operations	$ 716	$ 237	$ 267
Effective Income Tax Rate	36%	62%	59%
Gain Attributable to Holding Net Monetary Liabilities		$ 85	$ 85
Income Including Gain Attributable to Holding Net Monetary Liabilities	$ 716	$ 322	$ 352

TABLE 21-2. Comparative Historical Dollar, Constant Dollar, and Current Cost Income Statements, 1980 (dollars in millions) *(continued)*

	As Reported in the Primary Statements (Historical Dollars)	Adjusted for General Inflation (Average 1980 Constant Dollars)	Adjusted for Changes in Specific Prices (Average 1980 Current Costs)
Increase in Value of Inventories and Net Plants and Properties Held During the Year:			
Measured in Constant Dollars			$ 1,290
Measured by Current Costs*			1,050
Excess of Constant Dollar Over Current Cost Increase			$ 240

*At December 31, 1980, current cost of inventories was $3,300, and current cost of plants and properties, net of accumulated depreciation and obsolescence, was $8,281.

Source: 1980 Annual Report of E. I. Du Pont.

TABLE 21-3. Comparison of Selected Financial Data in Historical Dollars, Constant Dollars, and Current Costs* (dollars in millions, except per share; all constant dollar and current cost data in average 1980 dollars)

	1980	1979	1978	1977	1976
Sales					
Historical Dollars	13,652	12,572	10,584	9,435	8,361
Constant Dollars	13,652	14,272	13,368	12,830	12,103
Income from Continuing Operations					
Historical Dollars	716	939	787	545	459
Constant Dollars	237	620	585	522	421
Current Costs	267	554			
Earnings per Share from Continuing Operations					
Historical Dollars	4.83	6.42	5.39	3.69	3.10
Constant Dollars	1.55	4.21	3.97	3.50	2.81
Current Costs	1.76	3.75			

TABLE 21-3. Comparison of Selected Financial Data in Historical Dollars, Constant Dollars, and Current Costs* (dollars in millions, except per share; all constant dollar and current cost data in average 1980 dollars) *(continued)*

	1980	1979	1978	1977	1976
Effective Income Tax Rate					
Historical Dollars	36%	37%	41%	44%	44%
Constant Dollars	62%	50%	54%	52%	55%
Current Costs	59%	53%			
Gain Attributable to Holding Net Monetary Liabilities	85	102	109	109	77
Earnings per Share Including Gain Attributable to Holding Net Monetary Liabilities					
Historical Dollars	4.83	6.42	5.39	3.69	3.10
Constant Dollars	2.13	4.92	4.73	4.25	3.34
Current Costs	2.34	4.46			
Excess of Constant Dollar Over Current Cost Increase in Value of Inventories and Net Plants and Properties	240	—			
Stockholders' Equity at Year End					
Historical Dollars	5,690	5,312	4,760	4,317	4,030
Constant Dollars	10,251	10,273	9,832	9,491	9,203
Current Costs	10,365	10,585			
Debt Ratio (%) at Year End					
Historical Dollars	21%	20%	22%	26%	27%
Constant Dollars	12%	12%	14%	17%	19%
Current Costs	12%	12%			
Dividends Paid Per Common Share					
Historical Dollars	2.75	2.75	2.42	1.92	1.75
Constant Dollars	2.75	3.12	3.05	2.61	2.53
Market Price per Common Share at Year End					
Historical Dollars	42.00	40.38	42.00	40.13	45.04
Constant Dollars	40.11	43.34	51.09	53.21	63.78
Average CPI-U (1967 = 100)	246.8	217.4	195.4	181.5	170.5

*Current cost data have not been developed for years prior to 1979.

Source: 1980 Annual Report of E. I. Du Pont.

TABLE 21–4. Absolute Importance of Depreciation and Relative Importance to Cash Flow,[a] All U.S. Corporations, 1946–1977
(billions of dollars)

Year	(1) Capital Consumption Allowances (Depreciation Only)	(2) Capital Consumption Adjustment	(3) Capital[b] Consumption Allowances Including Capital Consumption Adjustment	(4) Profits Before Taxes	(5) Profits Tax (Income Tax Liability)	(6) Profits After Taxes	(7) Total Cash Flow I Capital Consumption (Depreciation Only) Plus Net Profits After Taxes (Col. 1 + 6)	(8) Undistributed Profits (Profits After Dividends)	(9) Net Cash Flow II Capital Consumption Allowances (Depreciation Only) Plus Undistributed Profits (Col. 1 + 8)	(10) Capital Consumption Allowances (Depreciation Only) As % of Cash Flow II (Col. 1 ÷ 9)
1946	4.7	2.7	7.4	24.6	9.1	15.5	20.2	9.9	14.6	32.2
1947	5.8	3.4	9.2	31.5	11.3	20.2	26.0	13.9	19.7	29.4
1948	7.0	3.9	10.9	35.2	12.4	22.8	29.7	15.7	22.7	30.8
1949	8.0	3.8	11.8	28.9	10.2	18.7	26.7	11.5	19.5	41.0
1950	8.8	4.0	12.8	42.6	17.9	24.7	33.5	15.9	24.7	35.6
1951	10.3	4.6	14.9	43.9	22.6	21.3	31.6	12.8	23.1	44.6
1952	11.5	4.5	16.0	38.9	19.4	19.5	31.0	10.7	22.2	51.8
1953	13.2	4.1	17.3	40.5	20.3	20.2	33.4	11.5	24.7	53.4
1954	15.0	3.2	18.2	38.1	17.6	20.5	35.5	11.4	26.4	56.8
1955	17.4	2.1	19.5	48.4	22.0	26.4	43.8	16.1	33.5	51.9
1956	18.9	3.0	21.9	48.6	22.0	26.6	45.5	15.5	34.4	54.9
1957	20.9	3.3	24.2	46.9	21.4	25.5	46.4	14.0	34.9	59.9
1958	22.0	3.4	25.4	41.1	19.0	22.1	44.1	10.8	32.8	67.1
1959	23.6	2.9	26.5	51.6	23.6	28.0	51.6	15.8	39.4	59.9

TABLE 21–4. Absolute Importance of Depreciation and Relative Importance to Cash Flow,ᵃ All U.S. Corporations, 1946–1977 (billions of dollars) (continued)

Year	(1) Capital Consumption Allowances (Depreciation Only)	(2) Capital Consumption Adjustment	(3) Capitalᵇ Consumption Allowances Including Capital Consumption Adjustment	(4) Profits Before Taxes	(5) Profits Tax (Income Tax Liability)	(6) Profits After Taxes	(7) Total Cash Flow I Capital Consumption (Depreciation Only) Plus Net Profits After Taxes (Col. 1 + 6)	(8) Undistributed Profits (Profits After Dividends)	(9) Net Cash Flow II Capital Consumption (Depreciation Only) Plus Undistributed Profits (Col. 1 + 8)	(10) Capital Consumption Allowances (Depreciation Only) As % of Cash Flow II (Col. 1 ÷ 9)
1960	25.2	2.3	27.5	48.5	22.7	25.8	51.0	13.0	38.2	66.0
1961	26.6	1.8	28.4	48.6	22.8	25.8	52.4	12.5	39.1	68.0
1962	30.5	-1.2	29.3	53.6	24.0	29.6	60.1	15.2	45.7	66.7
1963	32.5	-2.1	30.4	57.7	26.2	31.5	64.0	16.0	48.5	67.0
1964	34.5	-2.8	31.7	64.7	28.0	36.7	71.2	19.4	53.9	64.0
1965	37.5	-3.8	33.7	75.2	30.9	44.3	81.8	25.2	62.7	59.8
1966	40.6	-3.9	36.7	80.7	33.7	47.0	87.7	27.6	68.2	59.5
1967	44.1	-3.7	40.4	77.3	32.5	44.8	89.0	24.7	68.8	64.1
1968	48.1	-3.7	44.4	85.6	39.3	46.3	94.3	24.2	72.3	66.5
1969	52.9	-3.5	49.4	83.5	39.7	43.8	96.7	21.2	74.1	71.4
1970	56.6	-1.5	55.1	71.5	34.5	37.0	93.6	14.1	70.7	80.1
1971	60.9	-0.3	60.6	82.0	37.7	44.3	105.2	21.3	82.2	74.1
1972	67.9	-2.5	65.4	96.2	41.4	54.8	122.5	30.0	97.9	69.4
1973	73.8	-1.9	71.9	115.8	48.7	67.1	140.9	39.3	113.1	65.3
1974	81.7	2.9	84.6	126.9	52.4	74.5	156.2	43.6	125.3	65.2
1975	88.7	12.2	100.9	123.5	50.2	73.3	162.1	41.0	129.7	68.4

TABLE 21-4. Absolute Importance of Depreciation and Relative Importance to Cash Flow,[a] All U.S. Corporations, 1946-1977 (billions of dollars) (continued)

Year	(1) Capital Consumption Allowances (Depreciation Only)	(2) Capital Consumption Adjustment	(3) Capital[b] Consumption Allowances Including Capital Consumption Adjustment	(4) Profits Before Taxes	(5) Profits Tax (Income Tax Liability)	(6) Profits After Taxes	(7) Total Cash Flow I Capital Consumption (Depreciation Only) Plus Net Profits After Taxes (Col. 1 + 6)	(8) Undistributed Profits (Profits After Dividends)	(9) Net Cash Flow II Capital Consumption Allowances (Depreciation Only) Plus Undistributed Profits (Col. 1 + 8)	(10) Capital Consumption Allowances (Depreciation Only) As % of Cash Flow II (Col. 1 ÷ 9)
1976	97.1	14.7	111.8	156.9	64.7	92.2	189.2	56.4	153.5	63.3
1977	104.7	7.2	111.9	171.7	69.2	102.5	207.2	61.4	166.1	63.0
1978	136.4	13.5	149.9	203.6	83.0	120.6	257.0	86.3	222.7	61.2
1979	155.4	15.9	171.3	225.0	87.6	137.4	292.8	102.5	257.9	60.3
1980	175.4	17.2	192.6	214.4	82.3	132.0	307.4	94.6	270.0	65.0

[a] In 1976 the Bureau of Economic Analysis of the U.S. Department of Commerce completed a benchmark revision of the National Income and Product Accounts. The depreciation measure included in the NIPAs of the revision is based on current-cost valuation and the straight-line depreciation formula. The new measure of depreciation will not be appropriate for all uses. For example, in studies of the effects of tax policies, the old measure probably would be required. Accordingly, in addition to the new series, the NIPAs will continue to show tax return-based depreciation for corporations and non-farm sole proprietorships and partnerships. Also, several variants based on consistent accounting will be provided regularly in the Survey of Current Business so that users can judge the effects of depreciation formulas, service lives, and valuations and, if they desire, substitute an alternative for the NIPA measure.

[b] The adjustment of the previous estimates of capital consumption allowances to the new basis and the associated changes in the profit-type incomes, which are net of capital consumption allowances, is accomplished by a new entry labeled capital consumption adjustment. This entry equals the previous measure of capital consumption (based on tax return information) less the new measure (based on consistent accounting and valued in current prices).

Source: U.S. Department of Commerce, various issues of Survey of Current Business.

in 1946 to $175.4 billion for 1980. Furthermore, in relative terms, depreciation as a percentage of Cash Flow I (depreciation plus net profits) ranged between 46 percent and 58 percent between 1960 and 1980, and depreciation as a percentage of Cash Flow II (depreciation plus undistributed profits after dividends) ranged between 59 percent and 80 percent in the same period. The major uses of cash flow are for

1. Corporate dividends and debt amortization, including sinking fund payments;
2. Required increases in working capital;
3. Capital budget programs, repurchase of company securities, etc.

In broad terms, cash flow (of which net profits are a component) represents the basic protection offered investors for both dividends and debt service requirements, including sinking funds and amortization.

Methods of Reporting Depreciation

Although corporate laws and accounting principles require that corporations make some charge for depreciation (usually based on cost), corporate management is permitted numerous alternatives in the manner in which it amortizes the cost of fixed assets over their useful life on its books and in published reports. Prior to 1954 (the Internal Revenue Code permitted new methods beginning in 1954), corporations were required to use straight-line depreciation for tax purposes except when certificates of necessity had been issued for defense projects permitting rapid amortization. The management of corporations also used straight-line depreciation in their books and published reports.

The *straight-line method* provides for the regular distribution of the original cost of fixed assets, less their estimated salvage value, over their estimated service lives. In addition to the straight-line method of depreciation, the Internal Revenue Code permits two other depreciation methods: the declining-balance method and the sum-of-the-years-digits method.

The *declining-balance method* permits a taxpayer to use a rate of depreciation, not exceeding twice the straight-line rate, on the original cost (unadjusted for salvage value) less accumulated depreciation. Note that the Code permits a taxpayer to change at any time from the declining-balance method to the straight-line method since charging all original cost as depreciation under the declining-balance method is arithmetically impossible. The straight-line rate would be based on a realistic estimate of the remaining life of the property at the time of the switch.

The *sum-of-the-years-digits method* is somewhat more complicated. The annual depreciation deduction is calculated by applying a changing fraction to the original cost of the property less the estimated salvage value. The numerator of the fraction is the number of useful years of life remaining for the property, what it will be in the first year, in the second year, etc. The denominator is the factorial sum of the estimated useful life of the property and may be calculated by using Equation (21.1) below:

$$D = N \left(\frac{N + 1}{2}\right), \tag{21.1}$$

where

    D = the denominator of the fraction used to calculate the annual depreciation charge,

    N = the number of years of useful life of the asset.

For a fixed asset with an estimated life of five years, the fractions used would be $\frac{5}{15}$, $\frac{4}{15}$, $\frac{3}{15}$, $\frac{2}{15}$, and $\frac{1}{15}$.

The annual depreciation charges under the three depreciation methods are contrasted in Table 21-5. Obviously, the reported earnings for a given year would be quite different if companies did not use the same depreciation method, and therefore would not be comparable unless adjustments were made.

    Asset Depreciation Range (ADR) System. In June 1971 the Treasury Department adopted the Asset Depreciation Range System (ADR). When this system was adopted, the department announced that taxpayers not electing it would be able to elect the depreciation guidelines without the reserve ratio test. Congress gave the President authority to prescribe a *class life system*, which is a combination of both ADR and the guidelines for property placed in service after 1970. Thus, taxpayers are able to compute depreciation either under the new class life

TABLE 21-5. Annual Depreciation Charge for a Fixed Asset Costing $1,000 with No Expected Salvage Value and an Estimated Useful Life of Five Years

Year	Straight-Line Method	Declining-Balance Method	Sum-of-the-Years-Digits Method
1	$200	$400	$333.33
2	200	240	266.67
3	200	144	200.00
4	200	108*	133.33
5	200	108*	66.67

*It is assumed that the taxpayer switched to straight-line depreciation in the fourth year.

system or under the general rules using estimated useful lives (old Bulletin F). Many of the elements of the ADR system (including the repeat of the reserve ratio test) are designed to achieve a simpler administration of the depreciation rules. The subsequently adopted Class Life Asset Depreciation system (CLAD) did retain these elements of ADR.

The CLAD assumes broad industry classes of assets. All classes of assets (except buildings and land improvement) are assigned a range of years, the "asset depreciation range," based on the designated class life period (established by asset guidelines); this range extends from 20 percent above to 20 percent below the designated class life period as established by the IRS asset guidelines. For buildings and land improvement a specific class life period, the "asset guideline period," is designated.

While a taxpayer does not need to justify depreciation periods and rates selected, once chosen, the depreciation period may not be changed during the remaining life of the asset.

Flow-Through Method and Normalizing Method of Reporting Depreciation. Since 1954 most corporations have reported publicly on a straight-line basis to stockholders while taking advantage of the rapid amortization permitted under the Code for tax purposes. Until fiscal 1968 income statements in annual reports of numerous corporations reported depreciation by the *flow-through method*, which annually flows through the full tax savings (resulting from rapid amortization for tax reporting) to net income. However, other corporations reported depreciation by the *normalizing method*, making a charge in the income account equivalent to the tax savings and thus washing out the benefits of the tax savings as far as final net income in their published income statements. In published statements the charge for deferred taxes is usually included in the total item entitled "Federal Income Taxes."

In December 1967 the AICPA stated categorically that the *deferred method* of tax allocation should be followed.[5] An exception to insistence on the deferred method would be allowed for regulated companies like public utilities where particular regulatory authorities may require the use of *flow-through* accounting.

Those who favor *normalizing* state that the use of rapid amortization for tax purposes will result in lower taxes being paid in the earlier years of the life of the assets than under the straight-line method because of higher depreciation charges, but that in later years depreciation will be less than straight-line rates; taxes will therefore be higher than in the earlier years. Total taxes for the entire life of the assets should be the same under either straight-line for tax purposes or rapid amortiza-

---

[5] "Accounting for Income Taxes," *Opinions of the Accounting Principles Board No. 11* (New York: American Institute of Certified Public Accountants, 1967).

tion for tax purposes. Therefore, tax savings are merely temporary and deferred until later years of lower depreciation charges. Those holding this viewpoint, including the AICPA and the SEC, therefore wish to eliminate any effect of tax savings on net income in the earlier years of the asset's life.

Those who have advocated the flow-through method, including numerous state public utility commissions (not the SEC), have argued that as long as a company is rather regularly expanding and purchasing fixed assets, the new assets will have the advantage of rapid amortization, therefore offsetting the declining depreciation on older assets. The lower taxes paid in the earlier years, therefore, are not merely deferred to later years, but payment will be deferred indefinitely. Therefore, there will be a constantly increasing "deferred taxes" account on the balance sheet.

Although depreciation is a real expense, it does not involve an outlay of cash in the period charged; therefore, the sales revenues allocated to the depreciation charges do represent a tax-protected source of funds to the business enterprise. While the total depreciation charged over the life of the asset is not affected by the method used, the greater amounts of revenues protected in early years by the declining-balance method and the sum-of-the-years-digits method have a higher present value than funds that might be protected in later years. Rapid amortization is similar to an interest-free loan from the Treasury Department. Generally firms do not have access to other sources of funds with no greater risk or cost than the funds provided by depreciation. Therefore, acquiring an increased amount of funds through depreciation tends to lower the cost of capital to the firm.

Adequacy of Depreciation Charges. Depreciation charges are often substantial, and the estimates made have a material effect on the reported profits or loss of a given year. Profits are overstated when depreciation charges understate the actual using up of assets during the productive process. Depreciation charges can be understated by increasing the estimated life of the asset beyond that over which the asset is economically useful or overstating salvage value. For example, several American airlines extended the depreciable life of their aircraft between 1968 and 1970, thereby reducing annual depreciation expense and increasing reported earnings at a time when airline earnings were generally depressed.

Accountants cannot know in advance how long an asset will last or what its salvage value will be. The depreciation expense charged in the income statement is only a rough estimate of cost and also does not allow for the effects of inflation. Determining the adequacy of depreciation charges is therefore quite difficult. The following tests are suggested:

1. The consistency of the rate of depreciation charged over time can be explored by studying depreciation as a percentage of gross plant assets and sales over an extended period of time.
2. Depreciation rates of a given company should be compared to those utilized by companies similar in nature.

DEPLETION

The depletion allowance, for tax purposes, represents recognition of the fact that operations of companies with wasting assets result in a decrease in the value of their natural resources as these are used up. *Depletion* is the accounting term applied to the amortization of the cost of exhaustible natural resources such as minerals, metals, and standing timber.

Wasting Asset Companies

The majority of wasting asset companies, such as mining companies, depreciate their *fixed assets* through cost depreciation charges to a depreciation expense account. However, for their *wasting assets* they use percentage depletion accounting. Also, these wasting asset companies have large expenditure and development costs. A comparative cash flow analysis, because of heavy depletion charges and encompassing special tax treatment for these development costs, is as essential as net income analysis for wasting asset companies and has been used for such companies for many years.[6]

Percentage Depletion Method

This method[7] differs from normal depreciation methods, and therefore from the cost amortization method, in that allowable depletion charges are based on *gross income* instead of on the cost of reserves. Percentage depletion is calculated by multiplying the allowable percen-

---

[6] On the companies' own books and for public reporting purposes on charges for depletion, they deduct that percentage of the cost of the natural resource property which the mineral (or the resource) extracted bears to the total resource content. This is known as the "units-of-production" method. This method is also applied to calculate the depreciation on equipment, such as cars, where their service life is governed by the same factors.

[7] *Sec. 613. Percentage Depletion—Internal Revenue Code*

General Rule—In the case of mines, wells, and other natural deposits listed in subsection (b) the allowance for depletion under Section 611 shall be the percentage, specified in subsection (b), of the gross income from the property, excluding from such gross income an amount equal to any rents or royalties paid or incurred by the taxpayer in respect of the property. Such allowances shall not exceed 50 percent of the taxpayer's taxable income from the property computed without allowance for depletion. In no case shall the allowance for depletion under Section 611 be less than if computed without reference to this section (i.e., not less than the cost method).

tage for the particular mineral in question by the *gross income* from the property, but it is limited to 50 percent of the taxable or net income from the property. The *gross income* under Treasury regulations is not the same as the *gross income* of the taxpayer as defined in other sections of the Internal Revenue Code. Rather, according to the Treasury, it must be calculated separately. It is the amount for which the mineral is sold if the sale takes place in the vicinity of the property in the form in which the mineral is customarily sold by basic producers; or it is the calculated value at the *basic stage* of production in case it is sold later at a more advanced stage, for example, after processing. The depletion allowance for gas and oil producers was repealed as of January 1, 1975.

Exploration and Related Costs

Under the Internal Revenue Code, the taxpayer *has the choice* of accounting for exploration costs not in excess of $400,000 by either (1) charging them off currently as incurred or (2) considering them as a deferred charge to be deducted proportionately as the extracted minerals that result from the exploration are sold. All such expenditures *may* be capitalized. Any excess exploration costs *must* be capitalized. Such deductions are in addition to depletion allowances, but they must be considered when the taxpayer is calculating net income to determine the 50 percent limitation for percentage depletion.

Mine Development and Exploration Costs. The present code permits the taxpayer *either* to deduct currently *or* to defer costs of mine development sustained in either the development or the production stage, and the amount deductible in any one year is unlimited. Such deductions are in addition to depletion allowances. However, these deductions must be taken into consideration when the taxpayer is calculating net income to determine the 50 percent limitation for percentage depletion.

Exploration and Development Costs—Gas and Oil. Partly due to public resentment against the big oil companies, effective January 1, 1975, the percentage depletion allowance for gas and oil wells (with certain exceptions) was repealed. The repeal affected all tax years after 1974. The 1975 Energy Policy and Conservation Act directed the Securities and Exchange Commission to come up with oil and gas industry accounting standards by December 22, 1977. The Financial Accounting Standards Board held a four-day hearing in New York on March 30, 31, April 1 and 4, 1977, on financial accounting for the extractive industries. There was almost even division between those who wanted the full-cost method (spreading costs out over the years) and those who wished the successful-efforts method (charging costs for unsuccessful attempts against earnings immediately, in this way reducing taxable earnings). On July 19, 1977, the FASB proposed (FASB No.

19) that the successful-efforts method be used "for financial statements for fiscal years beginning after June 15, 1978 . . . (and the standards) to be applied retroactively through the restatement of financial reports for prior periods."[8]

Smaller oil and gas firms objected strongly to FASB No. 19, and the Department of Energy suggested that companies that had been using the full-cost method could reduce their exploration activities because of the unfavorable earnings impact associated with successful-efforts accounting. The SEC then issued three *Accounting Series Releases*, adopting both a form of the successful-efforts approach and a full-costing approach, and suggesting a yet-to-be-developed method (reserve recognition accounting).[9] The SEC will need time to develop the reserve recognition accounting approach. The full-cost or successful-efforts approaches were acceptable at the time of writing this book, although reserve recognition accounting will probably be used once it is developed by the SEC.

Depletion and Depreciation Reserves
Distributed to Stockholders

Unfortunately, the income tax regulations confuse the status of depreciation and depletion reserves that are accumulated. These regulations state that "a distribution made from (charged to) a depletion or depreciation reserve based on the cost or other basis of the property, instead of being charged to retained earnings, will not be considered as having been paid out of the earnings of the property." Therefore, such distributions to stockholders are not taxable as ordinary dividends. However, the regulations clearly state that such reserves are "not a part of surplus out of which *ordinary dividends* may be paid." The intention is clear that such distributions are considered to be *liquidating dividends* because they represent a return of capital and not a distribution of earnings. Numerous tax-exempt dividends result, and prior to 1972 this was the major reason for the tax-exempt status to the recipient of a portion of dividends paid by many public utility companies.

---

[8] Peter B. Roche, "Successful-Efforts Method for Reporting Oil and Gas Search Costs Backed by Panel," *The Wall Street Journal*, July 20, 1977, p. 8.
[9] See "Adoption of Requirements for Financial Accounting and Reporting Practices for Oil- and Gas-Producing Activities," *Accounting Series Release No. 253* (Washington, D.C.: SEC, August, 1978); "Requirements for Financial Accounting and Reporting Practices for Oil- and Gas-Producing Activites," *Accounting Series Release No. 257* (Washington, D.C.: SEC, 1978); and Oil and Gas Producers-Full Cost Accounting Practices," *Accounting Series Release No. 258* (Washington, D.C.: SEC, 1978).

AMORTIZATION OF INTANGIBLES

In addition to the major noncash charges for depreciation and depletion in the income statement, the amortization of intangibles such as goodwill, patents, and trademarks represents noncash charges in the income account.

Intangible Assets

The following statements are pertinent to the classification and amortization of intangible assets:

> Intangible assets are classified in APB *Opinion No. 17*, Par. 12 as follows:
> (a) Those having a term of existence limited by law, regulation, or agreement, or by their nature (such as patents, copyrights, leases, licenses, franchises for a fixed term and *goodwill as to which there is evidence of limited duration*);
> (b) Those having no such limited term of existence and as to which there is, at the time of acquisition, no indication of limited life (such as goodwill generally, going value, trade names, secret processes, subscription lists, perpetual franchises, and organization costs).[10]
>
> When a corporation decides that a type (b) intangible may not continue to have value during the entire life of the enterprise, it may amortize the cost of such intangible by systematic charges against income despite the fact that there are no present indications of limited existence or loss of value which would indicate that it has become type (a) and despite the fact that expenditures are being made to maintain its value.[11]

The problem of determining the time over which the values recognized for intangibles are consumed is a difficult one, and differing judgments can lead to noncomparability of reported income data by different companies.

Goodwill in Business Combinations

As previously noted, there has been a tremendous merger movement in the post–World War II years. Under the *purchase of assets* method of accounting as opposed to the *pooling of interest* method of accounting for mergers, substantial amounts of *goodwill* are frequently added to the balance sheet of the acquiring company when it acquires assets in excess of the book value of the company being acquired. The relationship to the income statement was discussed in Chapter 20.

---

[10] Inventory of Generally Accepted Accounting Principles for Business Enterprises," *Accounting Research Study No. 7* (New York: American Institute of Certified Public Accountants, 1965), p. 54.

[11] *Ibid.*, p. 155.

Pertinent paragraphs in APB *Opinion No. 16*, "Business Combinations," issued by the AICPA in August 1970 are quoted below.

1. A business combination occurs when a corporation and one or more incorporated or unincorporated businesses are brought together into one accounting entity. The single entity carries on the activities of the previously separate, independent enterprises.

2. Two methods of accounting for business combinations—"purchase" and "pooling of interests"—have been accepted in practice and supported in pronouncements of the Board and its predecessor, the Committee on Accounting Procedure. The accounting treatment of a combination may affect significantly the reported financial position and net income of the combined corporation for prior, current, and future periods.[12]

Under the *purchase of assets* method of accounting, the net assets acquired are recorded at cost and are measured in cash on the fair value of securities or other property turned over, or for the fair value of the property acquired, whichever seems more reasonable. Under the *pooling of interests* method of accounting, the combined financial position of the constituent companies is in effect the same as though they had previously been affiliated and therefore *no goodwill* results.

APB *Opinion No. 16* continues:

8. The Board concludes that the purchase method and the pooling of interests method are both acceptable in accounting for business combinations, although not as alternatives in accounting for the same business combination. A business combination which meets specified conditions requires accounting by the pooling of interests method. . . . All other business combinations should be accounted for as an acquisition of one or more companies by a corporation. . . . The cost should then be allocated to the identifiable individual assets acquired and liabilities assumed based on their fair values; the unallocated cost should be recorded as goodwill.

15. The pooling of interests method of accounting is applied only to business combinations affected by an exchange of stock and not to those involving primarily cash, other assets, or liabilities. . . .[13]

As a result of *Opinion No. 16*, the use of the pooling of interests method has been severely restricted since 1970.

In the same month (August 1970) that the AICPA issued APB *Opinion No. 16*, it also issued the related APB *Opinion No. 17*, "Intangible Assets" which stated among other things:

---

[12] APB *Opinion No. 16*, "Business Combinations," *Journal of Accountancy* (October, 1970), pp. 69–85.
[13] *Ibid.*

17. The Board believes that the value of intangible assets at any one date eventually disappears and that the recorded costs of intangible assets should be amortized by systematic charges to income over the periods estimated to be benefited. . . .

28. . . . A reasonable estimate of the useful life may often be based on upper and lower limits even though a fixed existence is not determinable.

29. The period of amortization should not, however, exceed forty years. . . .[14]

CASH FLOW AND FINANCIAL ANALYSIS

Cash flow is not a new concept, but prior to the 1950s it was usually emphasized only in the analysis of wasting asset industries, such as oil companies, for purposes of comparative analysis between companies.

Differing Concepts of Cash Flow

Cash flow is used on Wall Street to designate net earnings after taxes, depreciation, and depletion, with depreciation and depletion added back. This could be designated as "net earnings after taxes but before depreciation." Another concept (retained earnings plus depreciation) implies that dividends are in essence almost like a fixed charge, and those of this opinion think of cash flow as retained earnings plus depreciation. Analysts reject the latter concept because all empirical evidence indicates that before determining dividend payments directors analyze the corporate cash flow and the sources and uses of funds statements—current and projected. However, the truth is that once a dividend rate is established, directors will make every effort to maintain it. The ratio of dividends to cash flow is far more stable than the ratio of dividends to earnings.

The most important point to emphasize is that depreciation (and depletion) is a very real expense, just as important as other operating costs. Any attempt to downgrade the importance of depreciation (or depletion) as an expense can produce an erroneous conception of true corporate earnings power. In most cases, when annual reports shifted to emphasis on cash flow earnings, it was usually an attempt to shift attention from a poor or mediocre earnings record.

In situations in which an investor purchases common stock at a price significantly lower than book value—for example at net current asset book value—and therefore has not in effect paid anything for fixed assets, there is an argument that inasmuch as nothing was paid for

_____

[14] APB *Opinion No. 17*, "Intangible Assets," *Journal of Accountancy* (October, 1970), pp. 85–89.

the fixed assets, depreciation or depletion is not a real cost *to the investor.* The claim, therefore, is that the investor can ignore the factor of depreciation and think in terms of earnings on cost—that is, in terms of cash flow earnings whether reinvested in property or paid out as dividends. Although there is some merit in this argument, such thinking can be dangerous, for inability to generate adequate earnings after depreciation may lead to serious financial problems and inability to replace assets as they depreciate.

Depreciation or depletion can only be considered a source of funds in the sense that funds generated by sales are not siphoned off by depreciation or depletion because these are noncash expenses in the income account. Therefore, funds flow down through the statement and are not diverted by these accounting charges. But a situation where there is no profit before depreciation, or where there is a loss before depreciation, clearly emphasizes that depreciation by and of itself is not a source of funds.

Statement of Changes in Financial Position

In March 1971 the AICPA issued *APB Opinion No. 19*, "Reporting Changes in Financial Position," some important paragraphs of which are cited below:

1. In 1963 the Accounting Principles Board issued *Opinion No. 3*, "The Statement of Source and Application of Funds." Support of that Opinion by the principal stock exchanges and its acceptance by the business community have resulted in a significant increase in the number of companies that present a statement of sources and uses of funds (funds statement) in annual financial reports to shareholders. Several regulatory agencies have acted recently to require funds statements in certain reports filed with them.
2. APB *Opinion No. 3* encouraged but did not require presentation of a funds statement. In view of the present widespread recognition of the usefulness of information on sources and uses of funds, the Board has considered whether presentation of such a statement should be required to complement the income statement and the balance sheet. . . .
3. This Opinion sets forth the Board's conclusions and supersedes APB Opinion No. 3. . . .
7. The Board concludes that information concerning the financing and investing activities of a business enterprise and the changes in its financial position for a period is essential for financial statement users, particularly owners and creditors, in making economic decisions. When financial statements purporting to present both financial position (balance sheet) and results of operations (statement of income and retained earnings) are issued, a statement summarizing changes in financial position should also be presented as a basic financial statement for each period for which an income statement is presented. These conclusions apply to all profit-oriented business entities, whether or not

the reporting entity normally classifies its assets and liabilities as current and noncurrent.

16. This opinion shall be effective for fiscal periods ending after September 30, 1971. . .[15]

Only one member of the APB dissented to *Opinion No. 19.*

INVESTMENT CREDIT

The investment credit is available only for "Section 38 property" (new or used) and must meet all of the following tests:

1. It is tangible personal property (other than inventories) or is nonpersonal tangible property meeting certain qualifications.
2. It is subject to the allowance for depreciation (or amortized in lieu of depreciation, such as leasehold improvements amortized over the remaining term of the lease, when the useful life is longer).
3. It has a useful life of three years or more measured from the time it is placed in service.

To encourage plant modernization and expansion and the purchase of equipment, Congress amended the Internal Revenue Code in 1975 to apply up to 10 percent[16] of the cost of certain property, new and used,[17] in the year of purchase as a direct offset to the taxpayer's tax liability. In general, the full 10 percent credit is available only for the purchase of tangible personal property and other tangible property with a useful life of seven years or more. If credits available in any one year are in excess of the taxes that would otherwise be due in that year, carry-backs and carry-forwards are allowed.

If the useful life of qualified property is seven years or more, 100 percent qualifies; if its useful life is at least five years but less than seven years, $66\frac{2}{3}$ percent qualifies; and if its useful life is at least three years but less than five years, $33\frac{1}{3}$ percent qualifies. This credit was originally introduced in 1962, allowing a 7 percent credit (4 percent for certain public utilities) on qualified investments, suspended between October 10, 1966, and March 9, 1967, and repealed generally on April 18, 1969. The investment credit was restored as of January 1971 and was increased to 10 percent for all taxpayers (including public utilities) begin-

---

[15] APB *Opinion No. 19,* "Reporting Changes in Financial Position," *Journal of Accountancy* (June, 1971), pp. 69–73. Because of the broadened concepts of the "Funds Statement," the APB recommended that the title "Statement of Source and Application of Funds" be changed to "Statement of Changes in Financial Position."

[16] A taxpayer may increase the 10 percent rate to 11 percent if the additional portion is contributed to an employee stock ownership plan.

[17] According to the Tax Reform Act of 1976, the $100,000 limit on the amount of used property eligible for the investment credit was extended for four years (that is, through 1980).

ning January 22, 1975, and scheduled to last through December 31, 1980. The Economic Recovery Tax Act of 1981 continued the allowance of the investment credit, with some changes in calculation rules.

Amendments to the Internal Revenue Code

Under the 1962 law, when the tax credit was taken, it also had to be used to reduce the amount of the cost of the asset that could be depreciated—that is, from 100 percent to 93 percent. Specifically, the taxpayer received an immediate credit equivalent to 7 percent and could then depreciate 93 percent under its usual method of depreciation. However, the taxpayer can now receive the advantage of a 10 percent tax credit in the year of purchase of the depreciable asset and *in addition* can then depreciate 100 percent of the cost of the asset. Assuming a tax rate of 50 percent, a corporation is in effect given the right to depreciate 120 percent of the cost of the asset.

Accounting Treatment for the Investment Credit

When the investment credit was first established in 1962, most companies accounted for the 7 percent credit against taxes by reducing the tax charge shown in the income statement by the full amount of the credit in the year in which the equipment was acquired (in effect, the "flow through" method). The AICPA quickly issued *Opinion No. 2*, concluding that the investment credit "should be reflected in net income (in financial records and published reports) over the productive life of acquired property and not in the year in which it is placed in service."[18] According to this viewpoint, the credit reflected a reduction in the cost of property, and therefore the benefits to income should be recognized over the productive life of the property.

In 1971 the Accounting Principles Board proposed requiring that the investment credit be amortized over the useful life of the asset; the SEC supported this position. Many companies objected to barring the flow-through approach, and U.S. Treasury officials supported this positions feeling that elimination of the flow-through approach would lessen the incentives the credit was intended to offer. Congress set itself above the SEC and the AICPA by including in the Revenue Act of 1971, which restored the investment credit, a clause providing that "no taxpayer shall be required without his consent to use any particular method of accounting for the (investment) credit." Accounting professional bodies and other interested parties objected to Congress legis-

---

[18] "Accounting for the 'Investment Credit,'" *Opinions of the Accounting Principles Board No. 2* (New York: American Institute of Certified Public Accountants, 1962), par. 13, p. 7.

lating accounting requirements, but the law stands. Unfortunately, this creates another area of nonuniformity in financial accounting.

Summary

The material in this chapter supplements the material in the previous chapter on the income statement. The class of items discussed in this present chapter are income statement items, but they are so substantial in amount and so unique in character that they deserve special treatment.

Numerous items that appear as either expenses or income in the income statement do not involve corresponding cash outlays or receipts of funds. Before 1971 these items were incorporated in the so-called "Funds Statement" or the "Statement of Source and Application of Funds," but in March 1971 (APB *Opinion No. 19*) the name of the statement was designated as "Reported Changes in Financial Position."

The internal sources of funds appearing in this statement represent what is usually referred to as cash flow. Cash flow provides the internal sources of funds available for such items as dividends, amortization of debt, additional working capital, additional capital expenditures, and funds for repurchase of the corporation's outstanding securities.

By far the largest amounts of such items are depreciation and depletion that do not represent current outlays of cash. But these items are just as real an expense as salaries and wages, heat, light, etc.

Depreciation is a method of systematically charging off the cost of a fixed asset, but in no way is it a process of valuation of an asset. Neither is depletion accounting a method of valuation.

Because of the heavy impact of inflation, current replacement market values are generally substantially higher than cost, but depreciation accounting only amortizes costs. Concerned with this problem, the AICPA in 1969 issued an APB *Statement No. 3*, "Financial Statements Restated for General Price Level Changes." The SEC has required that beginning with 1976, the largest nonfinancial companies must disclose current-value replacement cost estimates in their 1976 and 1977 statements, along with estimates of natural resource reserves. In 1978 the commission was reviewing the two-year experience to arrive at a feasible rule that would take into account the inflation factor.

Historically (except in World War II and the Korean War) capital assets were required for tax accounting to be depreciated on a straight-line basis. But IRS regulations since 1954 have permitted rapid amortization, which permits depreciation for tax purposes to be higher in the earlier years (and, therefore, lower in the later years) of an asset's life. While most companies take advantage of rapid amortization for tax purposes, many report on a straight-line basis in annual reports, and until

1967 many passed the tax savings through to net income. However, in December 1967 the AICPA stated that the deferred or normalizing method of accounting for depreciation should be used. Of course, the authorized Lifo method of inventory valuation represents an effort to reduce the effect of inflation on the cost of goods sold and, therefore, on profits.

In the case of natural resources—wasting asset companies—the majority use percentage depletion accounting. This method differs from the cost amortization method in that allowable charges for depletion are based on gross income instead of the cost of resources. Percentage depletion is calculated by multiplying the allowable percentage for the particular resource in question by the gross income from the property. However, the depletion allowance for gas and oil producers was repealed as of January 1, 1975.

In addition to the major noncash charges for depreciation and depletion in the income statement, the statement may contain other intangible expenses such as goodwill, patents, and trademarks representing charges in the income account. When a corporation decides that a type (b) intangible may not continue to have value during the entire life of the enterprise, it may amortize the cost of such intangibles by systematic charges against income, despite the fact that there are no indications of limited existence or loss of value which would indicate that it has become a type (a) asset and despite the fact that expenditures are being made to maintain its value.

By far the largest intangible listed on financial statements is goodwill resulting from mergers or acquisitions under the "purchase of assets" method of accounting. If the "pooling of interests" method is used, no goodwill results that needs to be amortized against income. However, the AICPA *Opinion No. 16* issued in August 1970 severely restricts the use of the "pooling of interests" method.

In the same month the AICPA issued *Opinion No. 17*, "Intangible Assets," which stated, "The Board believes that the value of intangible assets at any one date eventually disappears—and that the recorded costs of intangible assets should be amortized by systematic charges to income over the periods estimated to be benefited. . . . The period of amortization should not exceed forty years."

In respect to cash flow, the AICPA in 1971 issued APB *Opinion No. 19*, "Reported Changes in Financial Position." The board concludes that information concerning the financing and investing of a business enterprise and the changes in its financial position for a period is essential for financial statement users. As a result of this opinion, most publicly owned corporations now include such statements in annual reports.

To encourage plant modernization or expansion, Congress has authorized the investment tax credit, although somewhat in an "on and off basis." But as of 1975 the available tax credit was reinstated and has remained in the tax code at this writing.

Questions

1. What is depreciation accounting?
2. Since the depreciation charges of a given period do not represent corresponding cash outlays in that period, are they a real expense of that period? Discuss carefully.
3. In the 1976 benchmark revision of the National Income and Product Accounts, the Bureau of Economic Analysis used a new depreciation measure. On what was it based?
4. Explain the new (1976) capital consumption adjustment figures of the U.S. Department of Commerce.
5. Explain the Class Life Asset Depreciation Range system.
6. How does the percentage depletion method differ from the normal depreciation method? Why was the percentage depletion allowance for oil and gas wells repealed as of January 1, 1975?
7. Generally accepted accounting principles require that the cost of fixed assets be spread over their useful life in such a way as to allocate it as equitably as possible to periods during which services are obtained from the use of the facilities (a paraphrasing of a statement by the Accounting Principles Board).
   (a) What flexibility does the corporation have in determining the annual depreciation charge?
   (b) Of what significance is this flexibility to investment analysts?
   (c) Discuss the merits and shortcomings of the accelerated depreciation techniques. As a stockholder under what circumstances would you prefer that your company (1) use the methods and (2) not use such methods?
   (d) Can the accelerated methods reduce the impact of price-level changes on the firm? Explain.
8. Discuss goodwill under "pooling of interests" vs. "purchase of assets." Do current AICPA rules restrict the use of "pooling of interests" accounting?
9. (a) Explain what is meant by "cash-flow" income.
   (b) Is cash-flow income of more significance to investment analysts than reported earnings per share? Discuss.
10. What is the purpose of investment credit? How has it changed since 1962 and why?

Work-Study Problems

1. (a) Calculate the cash flow of General Motors Corporation for the past five years, submitting with your solution the actual calculations.
   (b) Examine the source and application funds statements of General Motors Corporation for the past five years and present an interpretation of the figures.

2. Assume that Companies A and B each have sales of $100 million, expenses other than depreciation of $60 million, and 5 million shares of common stock outstanding.
   (a) Calculate the first year's depreciation on assets of $100 million that have a ten-year life:
      (1) For Company A on the straight-line basis.
      (2) For Company B on the double-declining-balance basis.
   (b) Assume that the tax rate applicable to both companies is 48 percent and that Company B uses the flow-through technique.
      (1) Prepare an income statement for each company.
      (2) Calculate the net income and the net earnings per share for each company.
   (c) Assume that Company B uses the normalizing technique.
      (1) Prepare the income statement for Company B.
      (2) Calculate the net income and the net earnings per share for Company B.

22.

Analysis of the Balance Sheet

At one time the protection for an investment-grade security was assumed to rest largely on an adequate asset backing of (1) mortgages secured by sufficient real property and (2) book value (or par value) of equity securities backed by sufficient assets as shown by the balance sheet.

In the 1930s fixed-income investors found that assumed asset protection often turned out to be an illusion, while fixed-income securities protected by adequate earning power weathered the storm. This caused the attention of investors to shift to income statement analysis. Investors learned that if earnings and cash flow proved insufficient to meet fixed charges, assumed asset protection just melted away. Liquidation value of assets proved far lower than book value.

Depreciation is only a method of amortizing the cost of fixed assets, and book value is simply original cost less cumulative amortization of that cost. Unamortized cost only coincidentally represents economically realizable values.

It has long been recognized that for most corporations there frequently is little correlation between the earning power value of a stock and its book value and between the economic value of assets and their book value. Most investors and analysts pay little attention to book value except in the case of (1) financial corporations if asset values are assumed to be close to realized market values, (2) public utilities because they are entitled (although not guaranteed) to earn a fair return on the fair value of assets used in the public service, and (3) on occasion, natural resources companies.

Until the 1970s less and less attention had been paid to balance sheet analysis; in many cases analysis rested almost solely on income statement analysis. While it is true that the value of a business and particularly of the owner's equity rests largely on earning power and its quality, this does not preclude balance sheet analysis—especially as the liquidity of corporations in the United States dipped consistently lower in the 1970s.

Figure 22–1 clearly shows that corporate liquidity has been shrinking in the post–World War II period. While the amount of funds received by means of short-term sources declined relatively in 1975, corporations were again raising a larger amount in the short-term markets than the long-term markets by 1977. As a result, two key balance sheet ratios (the ratio of liquid assets to short-term market debt and the ratio of long- to short-term market debt) have dropped to historic lows.

Inflation would encourage a sharp curtailment in liquidity since, as noted in the last chapter, a holder of monetary assets loses during an inflation period while a monetary debtor gains. Still, the dramatic increase in short-term debt and the marked drop in liquidity make corporations more vulnerable to a recession than at any time since the 1930s. Investors should carefully monitor these developments as they apply to companies whose securities they are reviewing for potential purchase.

BALANCE SHEET DISCLOSURE

Investors must understand what balance sheets purport to show. One examines a balance sheet to determine the company's current financial position, the amount and nature of invested capital, the sources of invested capital, the proportionate division of corporate capitalization, and, together with the income statement, the rate of return earned on total assets, on total capitalization, and on stockholders' equity.

Balance Sheet Values[1]

Value is a word of many meanings. The word is used in accounting to describe the figure at which an asset or liability is carried in the accounts, although the amount may represent something quite different than "value" as the word is ordinarily used. Accounting is predominantly based on cost, and assets are usually carried at cost or some modification of cost. For example, accountants report the original cost of fixed assets on the balance sheet, less amortization of that cost over the useful life of the asset. Inventories will reflect the cost to purchase the items included, unless current market value falls below that cost.

_____

[1] This section is a summary of material found in "Inventory of Generally Accepted Accounting Principles for Business Enterprises." *Accounting Research Study No. 7* (New York: American Institute of Certified Public Accountants, 1965), pp. 229–232. See also Paul M. Foster, "Asset Disclosure for Stockholder Decision," *Financial Executive* (January, 1967), and Solomon Fabricant, "Inflation and Current Accounting Practice," *Journal of Accountancy* (December, 1971), pp. 39–44.

a. Cyclical Pattern of Debt Financing

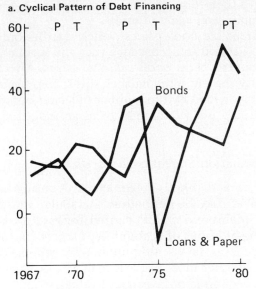

Taxable Bonds vs. Loans and Paper, Annual Net Increases in Amounts Outstanding, $Billions.

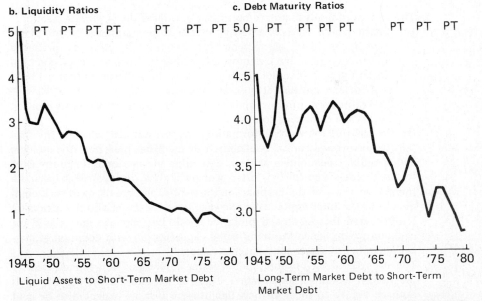

b. Liquidity Ratios

Liquid Assets to Short-Term Market Debt

c. Debt Maturity Ratios

Long-Term Market Debt to Short-Term Market Debt

Note: P (Peak) and T (Trough) Represent N.B.E.R. Reference Cycle Peaks and Troughs.

Source: H. Kaufman, J. McKean, and D. Foster, *1981 Prospects for Financial Markets* (New York: Salomon Brothers, December 8, 1980), p. 7.

FIGURE 22-1. Cyclical Pattern of Debt Financing, Liquidity Ratios, and Debt Maturity Ratios for Nonfinancial Business Corporations.

Accounting values, therefore, are not intended to represent current market value or liquidation value of assets.

Accounting values are *book values*, which signifies only the amount at which an item is stated in accordance with the accounting principles related to the item. The term *book value* is also used to represent the total owners' equity shown in the balance sheet; *book value per share* is that owners' equity divided by the number of shares outstanding. Book value per share should not be thought of as an indicator of economic worth.

Balance Sheet Information Sought by Analysts

Balance sheet is a distinctly technical accounting term. "In this view, a balance sheet may be defined as: A tabular statement or summary of balances (debit and credit) carried forward after an actual or constructive closing of books of account kept according to principles of accounting."[2] This is as far as accountants are willing to go. The investor must expect neither more nor less than this. A balance sheet does not purport to list economic or investment values.

The major types of information that the analyst seeks from the balance sheet are as follows:

1. The sources of funds that have been used to acquire the corporate assets:
   (a) The long-term funds invested by creditors (bondholders, private placement noteholders, equipment trust noteholders, etc.), by preferred stockholders and by common stockholders. In the case of common stockholders, it includes earnings retained in the business (not paid out as dividends) and capital in excess of par.
   (b) The short-term funds supplied by banks, commercial paper houses, factors and trade creditors, etc.
   On the basis of the above information, the investor can calculate the proportion of invested capital contributed by creditors, preferred stockholders and common stockholders and can determine such ratios as long-term debt to stockholders' equity. It is often worthwhile for the investor to calculate the market value of the corporation's securities and the ratios of each component to the total capitalization so calculated. In this calculation par value is often used for bonds and preferred stock, but market value is used for common stock: hence the term "total capitalization with common at market" (number of shares times market value).
2. The strength of the corporation's working capital position as indicated by the various working capital ratios. These ratios indicate the corporation's assumed ability to meet current liabilities, which are expected to be paid with current assets.
3. The assets of the corporation, which indicate the sources of the corporation's income and the manner in which capital was invested.

_____

[2] *Accounting Research Study No. 7*, p. 226.

4. Data for an analysis of the balance sheet combined with an analysis of the income statements to indicate.
   (a) The amount and the rate of return on total long-term capitalization (an excellent test of corporate management).
   (b) The rate of return on total assets.
   (c) The rate of return on the stockholders' equity.
   (d) A check of the retained earnings account in the balance sheet with the earnings reported over a period of years in the income statement. [Retained earnings at the beginning of the period plus earnings (less losses) for the entire period less dividends paid should give the total in the retained earnings account at the end of the period, except for charges or credits made directly to the retained earnings account that may not have been recorded in any income statement but that should have been disclosed in annual reports.]
5. The AICPA requires that a "Statement of Changes in Financial Position" that is related to the balance sheet also be provided. This statement in summary form indicates the major sources and uses of funds by the corporation over the past year.

ASSETS SECTION OF THE BALANCE SHEET

In considering assets in the balance sheet as offsets to the liabilities and capital, the analyst must recognize what asset figures really mean. The analyst should not be under the illusion that these offsets to liabilities and capital represent reliable estimates of economic value, except to some extent in the case of current assets; and, even in this case, book figures may be far removed from economic values, especially in the case of inventories.

Current Assets—Working Capital[3]

Current assets of a business (also called circulating assets or working assets) represent its working capital. The character of a borrower's working capital has always been of prime interest to grantors of credit; and bond indentures, credit agreements, and preferred stock agreements commonly contain provisions restricting corporate actions that would effect a reduction or impairment of working capital (and would impair ability to satisfy debt requirements). Net working capital is represented by the excess of current assets over current liabilities and identifies the relatively liquid portion of total enterprise capital that constitutes a margin or buffer for meeting obligations within the ordinary operating cycle of the business.

---

[3] This section is a shortened version of material found in "Restatement and Revision of Accounting Research Bulletins," *Accounting Research Bulletin No. 43* (New York: American Institute of Certified Public Accountants, 1953), Ch. 3, Sec. A, pp. 19–21.

For accounting purposes the term *current assets* is used to designate cash and other assets or resources commonly identified as those that are reasonably expected to be realized in cash or sold or consumed during the normal operating cycle of the business. Thus, the term comprehends in general the following resources:

1. Cash available for current operations and items that are the equivalent of cash;
2. Inventories of merchandise, raw materials, goods in process, finished goods, operating supplies, and ordinary maintenance material and parts;
3. Trade accounts, notes, and acceptances receivable;
4. Receivables from officers, employees, affiliates, and others, if collectible in the ordinary course of business within a year;
5. Installment or deferred accounts and notes receivable if they conform generally to normal trade practices and terms within the business;
6. Marketable securities representing the investment of cash available for current operations;
7. Prepaid expenses such as insurance, interest, rents, taxes, unused royalties, current paid advertising service not yet received, and operating supplies. (Prepaid expenses are current assets in the sense that if not paid in advance, they would require the use of current assets during the operating cycle.)

The ordinary operations of a business involve a circulation of capital within the current asset group. Expenditures are accumulated as inventory cost. Inventory costs, on sale of the products, are converted into trade receivables and ultimately into cash again. The average time intervening between the acquisition of materials or services entering this process and the final cash realization constitute an *operating cycle.*

Cash and Cash Equivalent Items[4]

Sometimes cash and cash equivalent items are arbitrarily segregated and not included in current assets. If such segregated items have been arbitrarily excluded from current assets and if these items are, in fact, subject to the full control of management and not required to be segregated by regulations or contract agreements, the analyst should add them back to the current assets.

Receivables

In examining receivables the analyst must consider the nature of the receivables in terms of the characteristics of the industry and the company's business. The analyst must determine whether the receivables are proportionately larger than normal in respect to current assets for the type of business and whether the deductions for "estimated doubtful

---

[4] See Paul F. Anderson and Harmon R. D. Boyd, "The Management of Excess Corporate Cash," *Financial Executive* (October, 1964).

accounts" are reasonable and in line with industry averages and firm experience. To the extent possible, the analyst determines the quality of the receivables. Any information on the average age of receivables and trends in this respect is significant. The receivables turnover figure in relation to the industry average is an important analytical tool.

Installment Sales and Receivables

Various methods are used in accounting for installment sales. The following two methods are the most important:

1. Consider each collection on installment sales as both a recovery of cost and a return of profit to the same extent as the ratio of cost and profit at the time the sale was consummated. Such installment sales are only taken up as income and considered as income for tax purposes in the period in which the receivables are *actually collected.*
2. Consider the full amount of installment sales as ordinary sales for the period in which the sales are first consummated, although income taxes will not be paid until the receivables are actually collected. In such cases the analyst should make an estimate of the income taxes to be paid when the receivables are collected and should deduct these taxes from the receivables on the balance sheet.

The estimate for doubtful or uncollectible accounts must be reasonable in relation to receivables in the case of installment sales, and this is especially true if profits on installment sales are taken into income in the period that the sales are accomplished rather than when receivables are collected. If a corporation sells its installment notes to banks or finance companies, it should note whether they have been sold outright or on a "recourse basis." In the latter case the corporation has a contingent liability, which is usually not shown in the balance sheet but is included only as a footnote. The analyst must consider the size of these contingent liabilities and the likelihood of the contingency materializing in the light of industry and company experience and the character of the receivables.

Inventories

The analyst should, where possible, calculate inventory turnover. Unfortunately, a definitive ratio can usually be achieved by outside analysts only through an examination in terms of annual figures, dividing cost of goods sold by average inventory. Ideally, with respect to seasonal business, monthly sales at cost would be the most relevant, but annual figures are often the only ones available to investors.

Recessions, generally characterized as inventory recessions, result from excessive inventory buildups during the previous expansion and require working down. Wide fluctuation in the price structure has heretofore caused severe inventory problems; but the advent of computer controls combined with economic and market analysis has somewhat reduced the inventory problem as opposed to what it was prior to 1945. Still, in certain industries excessive inventories and inventory price fluctuations can cause serious financial problems as in 1974 and 1975. Inventories in the following expansion were more tightly controlled.

The analyst must also consider the implications of Fifo and Lifo inventory accounting as applied to analysis between companies and over a period of years for the same company if company reports do not provide actual figures indicating the effect of a change from Fifo to Lifo or vice versa.[5] One must be careful to make appropriate adjustments when comparing two firms, one of which uses LIFO while the other uses FIFO. The firm using LIFO will report a lower cost of goods sold and inventory than the firm using FIFO, when there are no real differences.

Long-Term Investments—Noncurrent Assets

One of the noncurrent classifications applicable to assets is that of investments. Investments owned by business enterprises include shares of stock, bonds, and other securities, mortgages and contracts receivable, life insurance policies on the lives of officers that designate the company as beneficiary, and special funds to finance plant expansion or to retire long-term debt. Temporary investments are classed as current assets. Only long-term holdings of securities are classified as investments.

A basic accounting position on the reporting of long-term investments and noncurrent assets is quoted below.

> Long-term investments in securities should be carried at the lower of aggregate cost or market. When market quotations are available, the aggregate quoted amounts (and information as to whether aggregate cost or market is the carrying amount) should be disclosed. Investments in affiliates should be segregated from other investments.[6]

Fixed Assets

Fixed assets consist of land, plant, and equipment reported at cost less depreciation, i.e., amortization of cost. The process of depreciation is the process of amortization of cost over the estimated life of the asset and is in no sense a process of valuation, as discussed in Chapter 21.

The economic value of fixed assets is their earning power, which bears no necessary relationship to the amount at which they are carried

---

[5] See Chapter 20 and *APB Opinion No. 20* in the *Journal of Accountancy* (October, 1971), pp. 63–72.
[6] Quoted from *Accounting Research Study No. 7*, pp. 259–260, and *APB Opinion No. 18*, except for changes made by *FASB Statement No. 12* (December, 1975).

in the books. However, in most cases the going-concern value and the replacement value of fixed assets in recent years are well in excess of the amount at which the fixed assets are recorded in the company's books of account.

Since it has been permissible (with a few exceptions) to use one set of accounting rules when reporting to the IRS and another when reporting to stockholders, in the mid 1970s there was overreporting of profits to stockholders. By 1979 underdepreciation is said to have amounted to almost a fourth of pretax profits in reports to stockholders and about half of that in reports to the IRS. Many said that the estimating of replacement costs might have the advantage to corporations of showing the IRS that the corporations' real profits didn't merit present taxes.

Wasting Assets

Natural resources are wasting assets. They are physically exhausted through extraction and, except for timber, they are irreplaceable. Until these resources are extracted from the land, they are classified as fixed assets; once they have been extracted, they are classified as inventories until sold.

Accepted practice in accounting for natural resources is as follows:

> When the presence of a natural resource is discovered *subsequent* to acquisition of the property, or when the extent of the deposit is determined to be materially more extensive than previously assessed, it is accepted practice to reconsider previous allocations of aggregate cost.
>
> The search for new resources is a continuing endeavor. . . . This endeavor necessitates large outlays for exploration, options, lease bonuses, advance royalties, abstract and recording fees, geological and geophysical staff expenses, and so forth. Even when the most advanced geological and geophysical technology is used to predict reserves, there is no assurance that resource deposits in paying quantities will be located, or that once located, the original estimates of the deposit will hold up. The uncertainty characteristic of extractive industries presents difficult problems of cost determination and allocation. It is accepted practice either to capitalize or expense the outlays mentioned above; but the majority practice is to capitalize the costs that are readily identifiable with the successful acquisition of specific resources in paying quantities and to expense the others.[7]

Intangibles

Intangibles that appear in the balance sheet come from two sources: (1) intangible assets purchased outright and (2) intangible assets developed initially in the regular course of business.

---

[7] *Accounting Research Study No. 7*, p. 258.

Intangibles purchased outright are intangibles (such as goodwill) that have been acquired in exchange for an issue of securities, for cash, or for other considerations. The AICPA stated in *APB Opinion No. 17* (1970) that the costs of *all* intangible assets, including those arising from a "purchase" type of business combination, should be recorded as assets and should be amortized by systematic charges to income over estimated benefit periods, the period of amortization not to exceed forty years.[8]

Goodwill has been extremely important in recent years as the result of the multitude of mergers and other acquisitions that have taken place. The acquiring corporation often pays more than the book value of the assets acquired, and the difference is recorded as goodwill under the *purchase of assets method*. As explained earlier, the use of the "pooling of assets" method has been strongly discouraged by AICPA pronouncements.

There may be intangible assets developed in the regular course of the business—for example, as the result of research and development or of advertising and promotion. With respect to research and development, the author of an AICPA-published study has stated that "the most practical treatment is to charge these expenditures to expense currently, for it is usually difficult to determine in advance the benefit that may result in future periods."[9] This position was officially adopted by the AICPA in *Statement of Financial Accounting Standards No. 2*. With respect to advertising costs incident to developing consumer preference for trademarks, trade names, brand names, and brands, this author has also stated: "It is, however, impossible to delineate the portion of advertising costs that have expired in the production of current revenue from the portion that may be applicable to the future. Treatment as current expense is, therefore, accepted practice."[10]

LIABILITIES AND CAPITAL SECTIONS OF THE BALANCE SHEET

The balance sheet furnishes information on the amount of funds raised from creditors, both short- and long-term obligations, and from owners (including retained earnings). Investors should analyze the long-term capitalization of the corporation (long-term debt plus owners' equity), by means of ratios to be discussed later, to indicate the degree of financial leverage being utilized by the corporation and rates of return being earned on capitalization. Short-term obligations should be

---

[8] Also see Dean S. Eiteman, "Critical Problems in Accounting for Goodwill," *Journal of Accountancy* (March, 1971), pp. 46–50.
[9] *Accounting Research Study No. 7*, pp. 265–266.
[10] *Ibid.*, p. 266.

analyzed in terms of the current assets and cash flow factors from which payment must come.

Current Liabilities

Current liabilities designate obligations that must be paid within one year from the date of the balance sheet. The current liability classification, however, is not intended to include a contractual obligation falling due at an early date that is expected to be refunded, or debts to be liquidated by funds that are carried in noncurrent asset accounts.[11] Liquidation of such liabilities could reasonably be expected to require the use of current assets or the creation of other current liabilities, and current liabilities are therefore related to current assets when assessing the possibility that the firm will experience liquidity problems. The ratios used in such an analysis are discussed later in this chapter.

Long-Term Debt

This section consists of long-term obligations such as bonds, private placement notes, equipment obligations, and term and time bank loans, the latter generally with maturities of one to eight years. The amounts that appear on the balance sheet can generally be assumed to state accurately the amount of long-term obligations currently outstanding. Notes to financial statements will furnish additional information about the debt contracts, such as restrictive clauses against charges to retained earnings for dividends and officers' salaries.

Leases

In the post–World War II period, leasing has become a major method of financing the use of property and equipment; annual rentals under leases run into billions of dollars. Leasing differs in technique (although often not in substance) from conventional purchase of assets.

FASB *Statement No. 13* contains guidelines, which became effective January 1, 1977, for classifying leases and accounting and reporting standards for each class of lease.

Before the FASB issued *Statement 13* during 1976, the IRS had ruled on May 5, 1975, that a lessor had to have at least 20 percent equity in the property leased in order to have the owner privilege of the investment credit. At that time the SEC was requiring only footnote disclosure of lease obligations in financial statements. When *Statement 13* called for capitalization on the balance sheet, the debt-to-equity

---

[11] See "Restatement and Revision of Accounting Research Bulletins," *Accounting Research Bulletin No. 43*, pp. 21–23, and amendment by SFAS No. 6 (May, 1975), for a detailed and specific item-by-item discussion of the accounts included as current liabilities.

ratio of companies making use of leasing was greatly affected. For this reason *Statement 13* permitted companies that had leases already in existence four years (until December 31, 1980) before requiring capitalization. However, in the spring of 1977 the SEC proposed requiring immediate retroactive application of FASB *Statement No. 13* to existing leases in reports for fiscal years ending on or after December 1977. This was in the belief "that most of the data will have to be accumulated by the end of this year under other requirements and should be available at that time for restatement purposes."[12] If a company had difficulty resolving its restrictive clause problems, and therefore could not comply with requirements, it was to disclose that fact.

According to FASB *Statement No. 13* leases are classified as (1) capital leases or (2) operating leases. *Operating leases* are those that the lessor will reacquire to lease again. They are to be accounted for as rental expense to the lessee and as rental income to the lessor.

Capital leases are defined under the following criteria:

1. The lease transfers ownership of the property to the lessee by the end of the lease term.
2. The lease contains a bargain purchase option.
3. The lease term is equal to at least 75 percent of the estimated economic life of the leased property. This criterion does not apply if the beginning of the term falls within the last 25 percent of the total estimated life.
4. The present value of the minimum lease payments at the beginning of the lease term equals 90 percent of the fair value of the leased property, less any related investment tax credit retained by the lessor.
5. If the lease meets any of these criteria, it must be capitalized by the lessee on the balance sheet as an asset and an obligation. If it doesn't meet any of these criteria, it is an operating lease and needn't be capitalized, according to the statement.[13]

Unfunded Pension Reserves—Past Service Cost

When a corporation establishes a pension fund, it accepts two costs: (1) past service costs that have not been funded and (2) current pension costs based on current payrolls. Pension costs and especially legislation to require vesting of pensions were discussed in Chapters 16 and 20.

The problem as far as the balance sheet is concerned is that of past service costs—the unfunded pension costs covering the period prior to the inauguration of the pension plan. These funds were not set aside previously but would have been funded if a pension plan had been in

---

[12] See SEC Section of News Report, *Journal of Accountancy* (May, 1977), pp. 20, 22.
[13] Quoted directly from FASB section of News Report, *Journal of Accountancy* (January, 1977), p. 7.

effect. The amount of these unfunded pension costs is often very substantial and in the case of large corporations may amount to several billion dollars.[14] These unfunded pension costs are a liability of the corporation. However, many (perhaps most) pension fund agreements provide that annual payments to amortize unfunded pension costs may be skipped in years of poor earnings, sometimes for as many as three consecutive years.

However, the Accounting Principles Board of the AICPA stated that a major objective of *Opinion No. 8* was to eliminate inappropriate fluctuation in recorded pension costs. It stated that "costs should not be limited to the amounts for which the company has a *legal* liability." The principles involved are that the pension cost accounting method should be *applied consistently from year to year* and that the amount recognized for past pension service costs *should be relatively stable from year to year.*[15] *Opinion No. 8* does not require that certified statements disclose the amount of unfunded or otherwise unprovided for past or prior service costs. However, the SEC does require such disclosure.

It is certainly true that the unfunded cost is to a degree a fluctuating type of liability and therefore should not have to be incorporated as a liability on the balance sheet proper. However, the requirement by the AICPA that the amount of the annual past pension service cost (amortized) should be reasonably stable from year to year should place the analyst on notice that the liability for past service costs is a liability that should be amortized in a relatively stable manner.

Preferred Stock Equity

If the corporation has preferred stock outstanding, the balance sheet will disclose the number of shares, the par or stated value per share, and the total dollar amount of the preferred stock. In the balance sheet preferred stock is listed in the capital section along with the common stock. Although it is essentially an equity security, it is a strictly limited equity security.

The preferred stock is senior to the common stock. The amount shown on the balance sheet should represent the claim of preferred stock coming ahead of the common stock, but this is not always the manner in which it is reported on the balance sheet. If the preferred

_____

[14] See "Unfunded Pension Liabilities: A Growing Worry for Companies," *Business Week* (July 18, 1977), pp. 86–88. The article states that Investors Management Sciences, Inc., recorded, in their survey of 1976 corporate pension liability, that General Motors had $7.3 billion in unfunded past/prior service costs and $3 billion in unfunded vested benefits. IMS's survey covered 1,644 companies.

[15] Julius W. Phoenix, Jr., and William D. Bosse, "Accounting for the Cost of Pension Plans—More Information on APB No. 8," *Journal of Accountancy* (October, 1967); and "Pension Reform," *Journal of Accountancy* (May, 1972), p. 76.

stock has a par value or a stated value relatively close to its legal claim
(for example, liquidating value) ahead of the common stock, then the
balance sheet closely reflects the actual situation. However, if the stated
value is only a nominal amount and is not close to the claim of the preferred stock, then the preferred stock on the balance sheet (number of
shares of preferred stock times the stated value) does not reflect the
true situation. In addition, there may be dividend arrears, which, while
they are not liabilities of the corporation, do represent a claim senior to
the common stock. However, such arrearages are usually not shown on
the balance sheet but are disclosed only as a footnote thereto.

In summary, if the balance sheet does not properly reflect the preferred stock's claim, the analyst should reconstruct the balance sheet so
that it properly reflects the preferred claims that are senior to the common stock.

Common Stock Equity

Because the common stock is the residual claimant to the assets and
the earnings of the corporation, the common stock section of the balance sheet is divided into three separate accounts: capital stock, retained earnings (formerly earned surplus), and capital paid-in in excess
of par (or stated) value (formerly capital surplus).

There is considerable lack of uniformity in the manner in which
common stock (and preferred stock) is reported in the balance sheet.
Many analysis feel that the trend in recent years toward highly condensed statements supported by notes to financial statements has gone
too far—for example, giving only one summary figure for capital stock.
Furthermore, in spite of the opinion[16] that the term "surplus" should
not be used because it has a "money in the bank" connotation that is

_____

[16] *Accounting Research Study No. 7*, pp. 188–190 states:

67. While the terms *capital surplus* and *earned surplus* have been widely used,
they are open to serious objection.
   (1) The term *surplus* has a connotation of excess, overplus, residue, or "that
     which remains when use or need is satisfied" (Webster), whereas no such
     meaning is intended where the term is used in accounting.
   (2) The terms *capital* and *surplus* have established meanings in other fields,
     such as economics and law, which are not in accordance with the concepts
     the accountant seeks to express in using those terms.
   (3) The use of the term *capital surplus* (or, as it is sometimes called, *paid-in
     surplus*) gives rise to confusion. If the word *surplus* is intended to indicate
     capital accumulated by the retention of earnings, i.e., retained income, it is
     not properly used in the term *capital surplus;* and if it is intended to indi-
     cate a portion of the capital, there is an element of redundancy in the term
     capital surplus.
   (4) If the term capital stock (and in some states the term *capital surplus*) be

quite misleading, a few major corporations are still using the term on their balance sheets.

An authoritative writer[17] on accounting has suggested the following breakdown of the capital section of the balance sheet, although stating that "the detail breakdown . . . is not ordinarily shown in financial statements."

Stockholders' equity in capital invested:

Capital stock:

> Preferred stock—5% cumulative; par value $100; authorized _____ shares; issued _____ shares . . . . .

> Class A preferred stock—$2.00 cumulative; no par value, redeemable value $30; authorized and issued _____ shares . . . . .

> Common stock—no par value; stated value $10; authorized _____ shares; issued _____ shares of which _____ are in treasury . . . . .

Capital paid-in in excess of par, redemption and stated values of capital stocks:

> Premium on preferred stock . . . . .
> Arising from treasury stock transactions . . . . .
> Paid-in on common stock . . . . .
> Retained earnings capitalized on stock dividends _ . . . .

---

used to indicate capital which, in the legal sense, is restricted as to withdrawal, there is an implication in the terms *surplus* or *earned surplus* of availability for dividends. This is unfortunate because the status of corporate assets may well be such that they are not, as a practical matter, or as a matter of prudent management, available for dividends.

68. In seeking terms more nearly connotative of the ideas sought to be expressed, consideration should be given primarily to the *sources* from which the proprietary capital was derived. . . .

69. In view of the foregoing the committee in 1949 . . . recommending that, in the balance-sheet presentation of stockholder's equity:

(1) The use of the term *surplus* (whether standing alone or in such combinations as *capital surplus, paid-in surplus, earned surplus, appraisal surplus,* etc.) be discontinued. . . .

(3) The term *earned surplus* be replaced by terms which will indicate source, such as *retained income, retained earnings, accumulated earnings,* or *earnings retained for use in the business.* In the case of a deficit, the amount would be shown as a deduction from contributed capital with appropriate description.

[17] *Ibid.,* pp. 191–192

Retained earnings:

Appropriated in amount equal to restriction under bank loan as to payment of dividends   . . . . .

Unappropriated   . . . .

Total   . . . . .

Deduct cost of _____ shares of treasury stock   . . . . .

Stockholder equity   . . . . .

BALANCE SHEET RATIO ANALYSIS

The purpose of balance sheet ratio analysis is to determine the financial strength of the company, especially its ability to meet its obligations when due, the appropriateness of the capital structure, the potential risk from financial leverage in the capital structure, and the weakness (if any) in the structure as related to the stability or the lack of stability of industry and company earnings. Activity ratios, using data from both the balance sheet and the income statement, are useful in assessing the soundness of current assets and in assessing the effectiveness with which the firm is employing its resources. The analysis should be supplemented by a "funds statement" and cash flow analysis.

Liquidity and Related Ratios

The balance sheet ratios most commonly used in analyzing the liquidity and the related current positions of a company are discussed in the following paragraphs.

Working Capital Position. Current assets represent the working capital or circulating capital, and *net* working capital is the difference between current assets and current liabilities. The major test applied to working capital is aimed at determining (1) the company's ability to meet current liabilities when due and the margin of safety and (2) management's efficiency in its use of working capital. Investors, both in equities and in debt obligations, are vitally interested in measures of the adequacy of a firm's working capital. A complete analysis of working capital requires a thorough analysis of historical cash flows, the "funds statement," and forecasts of cash flows.

Current Ratio. The simplest test is the current ratio—that of current assets to current liabilities. It indicates the company's ability to pay all current liabilities if all current assets were to be converted into cash. For many years the rule was that this ratio should be two dollars of current assets for each dollar of current liabilities. For all U.S. corporations in recent years the ratio has fallen well below 2 to 1 close to 1.8 to 1. Tests of the *composition* of the current assets are much more important than the overall ratio. For example, if the current ratio was only 1.5 to 1 but the ratio of cash and cash items to current liabilities was 1 to 1, there would be no problem in meeting the current obligations. In the case of public utility companies where there is no inventory problem and relatively no receivables collection problem, a current ratio of 1.1 or 1.2 to 1 has generally proved satisfactory. Conversely, if the current ratio for an industrial company was 3 to 1 but slow-moving inventories represented 90 percent of current assets and the ratio of other assets to current liabilities was therefore only 0.3 to 1, the company would be in a weak financial position.[18] The current ratio analysis must be supplemented by other working capital ratios, as well as a careful analysis of the "funds statement." A general standard fails to recognize that an appropriate current ratio is a function of the nature of a company's business.

Acid-Test (Quick) Ratio. Because the problem in meeting current liabilities may rest on slowness or even inability to convert inventories into cash to meet current obligations, the acid-test (quick) ratio is frequently used. This is the ratio of current assets minus inventories (and also usually minus accruals and prepaid expenses) to current liabilities. In effect this is the ratio of cash and cash items plus receivables (sometimes called *quick assets*) to current liabilities. Of course, in some situations receivables may include a substantial amount of accounts that are overdue, raising questions as to their quality. The acid-test ratio assumes that receivables are of good quality and will, in the normal operating cycle, be converted into cash. When receivables can reasonably be assumed to be liquid, in terms of the past record, this ratio provides an excellent test of ability to pay current debts.

Cash Ratio. The cash ratio, which is the ratio of cash and cash items[19] to current liabilities, is the strictest of all tests. Quite obviously, if the cash ratio is 1 to 1, the company can have no problem in meeting its short-term obligations when due, but the ratio will rarely be this high. In fact, such a high ratio would suggest inefficient management of liquid resources because of the potential profits that have been lost

---

[18] For example, a liquor company must age its inventories over much longer than one year, and therefore a large portion of the current assets may not be available for paying current debt.

[19] Cash items usually consist of short-term government securities or certificates of deposit, as well as currency and checking accounts, but they may also include commercial paper and bankers' acceptances.

through holding excess liquidity. The analyst may find that for the industry and the company under review a cash ratio as low as 0.3 or 0.4 or 0.5 to 1 has proved quite satisfactory. For nonfinancial corporations the ratio in recent years has averaged close to 0.15 to 1.

Working Capital Turnover. The working capital turnover is computed by dividing net sales by net working capital. Too low a turnover of working capital indicates inefficient use of current assets, and too high a turnover makes a firm vulnerable to minor reductions in sales. The working capital turnover ratio is a more sensitive indicator than an inventory turnover ratio. Rises or declines in sales may well be accompanied by corresponding movements of inventory so that inventory turnover may remain unchanged. Such inventory changes are usually accompanied by equivalent changes in current liabilities, thus maintaining a stable net working capital. Therefore, while the inventory turnover ratio might remain constant, the working capital turnover ratio would rise with a rise in sales, suggesting more quickly the possibility of overtrading. The working capital turnover ratio shows wide difference from one industry to another.

Accounts Receivable Turnover. Analysis of working capital can include the determination of the time taken to translate receivables into cash. Accounts receivable turnover can be obtained by dividing the net credit sales by the average balances of accounts receivable outstanding. Net credit sales is typically used in the numerator because information is not provided on what portions of the sales were on credit terms. This does tend to overstate the liquidity of receivables when cash sales are significant. Turnover may be converted into the number of days' sales outstanding by dividing the turnover figure into 365. One would usually expect the accounts receivable turnover to be relatively in line with the firm's terms of sale. A high receivables turnover rate tends to offset a low current ratio.

Inventory Turnover. The inventory turnover is computed by dividing the cost of materials used during the year by the average investment in inventories. A low rate indicates that probably the investment in inventory is too high for the sales capacity of the business. A high rate may indicate that inventories maintained are too low. The number of days' sales represented by current inventory holdings can be expressed by dividing the turnover figure into 365. The gross profit per inventory turnover is calculated by dividing the gross profit by the inventory turnover ratio.

The average days' sales outstanding in receivables and in inventory can be combined to obtain an "average age of conversion" of noncash current assets into cash. These figures are useful in the attempt to project cash flows.

Capitalization Ratios

In addition to liquidity ratios, analysts calculate capitalization ratios to determine the extent to which the corporation is trading on its equity and the resulting financial leverage.[20] The analyst relates these capitalization ratios to the stability of industry and company earnings. The general assumption is that the greater the stability of industry and company earnings and cash flow, the more the company can trade on its equity and the higher is the allowable ratio of debt to total capitalization.

In the case of new companies or companies in highly cyclical industries, having any long-term debt may be unsound. Some analysts argue that for certain companies in highly cyclical industries long-term debt may be a sound financial policy if fixed charges for servicing the debt, including debt amortization, are covered by a satisfactory earnings and cash flow margin, even in years of seriously depressed business. In essence, a high proportion of debt in the capital structure means heavy fixed charges.

For companies where earnings stability justifies a leveraged capital structure, the common stockholders can benefit by trading on the equity, with the excess of earnings on funds above the after-tax cost of capital obtained by selling debt obligations (or preferred stock). But for those companies whose lack of earnings stability suggests that using significant amounts of long-term debt is unwise, a leveraged capital structure can be detrimental to the interests of the equity investors. The railroad and air transport industries illustrate the problem. If highly leveraged capital structures have had serious financial consequences, as, for example, the railroads and the airlines in 1960-61, 1970-71, and 1974-75, this will be reflected in exceptionally low prices for the securities of such companies during the period of financial difficulties. However, if an investor believes that the worst has been experienced and that a decided improvement in earnings power can be expected, a commitment in these securities can be very rewarding if expectations prove to be correct.

Summary

Until the 1970s in security analysis less and less attention had been paid to the balance sheet with almost the entire emphasis placed on the income statement. It is true that the value of a business and stockholder's equity and protection for senior securities rest largely on corporate earnings and cash flow and their quality. But this should not

---

[20] Capitalization ratios and interest coverage ratios are discussed carefully in Chapter 24.

preclude balance sheet analysis, especially as the liquidity ratios of corporations in the United States has dipped lower than at any time since the 1930s. Furthermore, the debt leverage factor for many corporations in recent years has become greater as indicated by the debt/equity ratio. These ratios are an important factor in determining the quality of earnings.

Investors must understand what the balance sheet purports to show. One examines the balance sheet to determine the company's current financial position, the amount and nature of invested capital, the sources of invested capital between long-term debt and equity, and the nature of the assets in which capital has been invested. Furthermore, in conjunction with the income statement, the investor can determine the rate of return earned on assets, total invested capital, and equity capital.

The investor should also understand the significance of such terms as "balance sheet values" and "book values" and that these are not values in any economic sense. Accounting values are only book values, which signify only the amount at which an item is stated in accordance with the accounting principles related to the account. This generally means that assets are stated at cost less accounting adjustments, including such adjustments as systematic amortization of costs or less estimated doubtful accounts or adjustments of inventories by applications of the Lifo method of accounting for inventories. The economic value of assets depends on the current earning power, which may have little or no relationship to costs or adjusted costs. Furthermore, replaced values are really replacement costs, which may be far different from economic values based on earning power.

In essence, the analyst is mainly interested in balance sheet data to determine the ability of a company to meet is current and long-term liabilities when due without any difficulty. Together with the income statement, the balance sheet enables the analyst to determine rate of return earned on assets, total invested capital, and equity capital.

Questions

1. Discuss briefly what the balance sheet reveals regarding a corporation.
2. "Depreciation is only a method of amortizing the cost of fixed assets . . . net asset book value is simply cost less amortization of cost." Discuss the significance of this statement for investment analysts in terms of analyzing the balance sheet.
3. (a) What type of assets would likely show book values similar to economic net worth? Why might the values of many assets on the balance sheet be far, far different from economic worth?
   (b) Why may asset values, as expressed in the balance sheet, mislead investors?

4. (a) Define the term "operating cycle" of a corporation in respect to working capital.
   (b) How might the length of the operating cycle affect the amount of working capital required in a business? Explain carefully.
5. Are prepaid items properly current assets? Should an analyst include them as current assets? Discuss.
6. Describe the normal effects of a moderate business recession on the liquidity of corporations.
7. How are current liabilities defined by accountants?
8. (a) What are the more desirable methods of accounting for installment sales?
   (b) Would a liability account appear in the balance sheet of a corporation if it sold its installment notes to banks or finance companies? Should a liability account appear? Discuss.
9. Some claim that the use of the "pooling" method to account for a merger can hide the "true" effects of the merger. What may be "hidden"?
10. (a) What is an intangible asset? Give examples.
    (b) How should the accountant handle research and development costs? Justify your position.
11. What is an "off balance sheet" liability? Where might an analyst gain information about such liabilities?

Work-Study Problems

1. The balance sheet items for two years of a manufacturer of office equipment are given below:
   (a) Arrange the balance sheet in proper order, paying particular attention to arrangement of the current assets and the current liabilities.
   (b) Explain, using at least two ratios for the two years, why the stock of this company might decline on release of the figures for the second year.

Balance Sheet, December 31

	First Year	Following Year
	(000)	
Cash	$ 1,208	$ 700
Plant	9,219	12,410
Short-term notes payable	—	2,095
Accounts receivable	4,368	5,455
Inventories	5,300	8,208
Plant depreciation	2,569	2,788

Miscellaneous liabilities	1,924	1,734
Taxes payable	1,622	638
Investments in subsidiaries	1,044	951
Surplus	9,950	10,016
Accounts payable	2,116	4,351
Miscellaneous assets	174	540
Net property	6,650	9,622
Capital stock	3,132	3,142
Bonded debt	—	3,500
	$18,744	$25,476

2. Critically examine an annual report of a well-known company with reference to the adequacy of the data presented. Particular attention might be given to the following:
   (a) Description of the products.
   (b) Breakdown of sales by products, customers, and geographic areas.
   (c) Affiliations of directors.
   (d) Comparative balance sheets and income accounts with details as to inventory and depreciation policies.
   (e) Capital expenditures.
   (f) Labor costs.
   (g) Research progress and expenditures.
   (h) Lease arrangements and handling of pension costs.
   (i) Comments on competition, industry problems, and outlook.
3. Calculate the capitalization ratios for each of the following and comment on the record:
   (a) For a major electric utility.
   (b) For a major airline.
   (c) For a major railroad.
   (d) For one of the largest steel companies.
   (e) For each of the major automobile companies.
   (Calculate the capitalization ratios based on book capitalization and also based on capitalization using common equity at market value.)

PART 7

Selection and Analysis of
Limited-Income Securities

23.

Bond Selection Strategies

A strategy is a rule for action. A rational investment strategy, therefore, is one that seeks to maximize expected rate of return (or yield) for the degree of risk exposure accepted. To this point in the development of normative theory, portfolio selection strategies have been proposed for applications that assume—by implication—that a risky asset is necessarily a common stock. A bond is also a risky asset, however, and should be thought of as such.

It was shown in Chapter 11 that the introduction of borrowing and lending alternatives to one's strategy for portfolio selection would have important implications for determining the rate at which one could exchange expectation for risk at the margin. The leveraging of a bond portfolio, for example, is sometimes called "speculation." Such terminology is a carry-over from earlier views that failed completely to distinguish certainty and uncertainty analysis, and that viewed the ex-post bond yield (i.e., the yield actually realized after the fact) as something other than a random variable. Modern views, by contrast, as outlined in Chapter 8, regard the purchase of a risky asset—stock or bond—as participation in a variant form of financial lottery.

THE APPLICABILITY AND LIMITS OF MODERN PORTFOLIO THEORY

One assumes that investors are made happy by anticipation of financial gain but are vexed by uncertainty about the flow of future financial benefits. Looked at from this point of view, there seems little reason to suppose that one's attitude toward expectation and risk would be different for bond or stock investment. Nevertheless, these are different financial instruments. One of the major shortcomings of the Markowitz portfolio selection model is that a methodology does not exist for applying it *directly* in the selection of a bond, or mixed bond and stock, portfolio. Needless to say, therefore, we need have no concern—given the state of the art—about what would be the positive implications were all investors to apply a Markowitz approach in bond selection; there is no such game to be played. The capital asset pricing model (see Chapters 12 and 13) is irrelevant to this issue. These points are developed later in this chapter.

When selecting a bond (or mixed bond and stock) portfolio, a different methodology for rational decision must be invoked, but not necessarily a different point of view. In this chapter various strategies for selecting limited income securities are considered. The major precepts of modern risk and analysis developed in Chapters 9 and 10 are not abandoned, but they are found difficult to apply except as providing a framework for reference.

STOCK VS. BOND INVESTMENT

A high-grade bond offers the holder a relatively stable and highly predictable pattern of cash flow over the holding period that is contracted for, assuming that the bond is held to maturity. Each element of cash flow associated with bond investment—both coupon and the return of principal—is fixed in regard to both timing and amount by the contract. This does not guarantee payment, of course, but legal remedies exist in the event of nonpayment. There are no similar remedies—expressed or implied—available to stock investors.

A bond purchaser agrees in principal to accept a fixed return on an investment, and by so doing must forego any claim to a share in the future growth in earnings of the issuer. A common stockholder, by contrast, is entitled to a proportionate share of future net earnings—as may be affected by either success or economic adversity. The holders of variable income securities, therefore, by virtue of their holdings, enjoy potential protection against diminution of capital caused by inflation, but they accept in exchange risk that is inherent in an auction market for variable income securities. A high-grade, long-term bond offers its holder no hedge against inflation, but for the investor who plans to hold the security until maturity some protection is provided against unanticipated variation in either periodic cash flow or the nominal yield.

The average yield on investment quality bonds has been approximately double the average dividend yield on common stocks over the past decade. If one were to project this pattern into the future, then the differential degree of risk exposure associated with a pure investment in common stocks could only be justified by anticipation of substantial capital gains. Such an anticipation would run counter to market behavior at the time of this writing.

Any attempt to compare the determinants of yield on stocks and investment quality bonds is bound to be frustrated by the fact that these are fundamentally different investment mechanisms, with vastly different characteristics and holding periods. At least one logic would suggest that the average yields on on-going pure common stock and pure bond portfolios would not be highly correlated. Stock prices, for example, are highly correlated with shifts in the business cycle and tend to move in the same direction, as where a business cycle peak is approached. Forces set in motion as such a peak is approached, by contrast, cause interest rates to rise and thus the average price of outstanding debt instruments to go down.

The argument is precisely reversed when one contemplates movement toward the trough. There are ample grounds for supposing that the degree of risk reduction that can be achieved by diversification will be higher for a mixed stock and bond portfolio than for a portfolio consisting entirely of either stocks or bonds. Note, however, that at the time of this writing there exists very little empirical or other research support for or against this proposition.

BOND YIELD DIFFERENTIALS

Bond yield, or yield to maturity, is defined in Chapter 7 to be that rate which when used to discount the cash inflows will make their present value precisely equal to the current market price of the bond. At any point in time, and from one point in time to the next, bond yields vary rather markedly. Such bond yield differentials may be explained in terms of a number of different factors:

1. *Bond Quality.* Bonds that are judged to be of higher quality are less risky as regards the prospect that cash flows anticipated in the future will materialize than bonds judged to be of lower quality. The purchaser of a high-quality bond, in effect, trades the higher yield that would be available on a lower-quality bond for safety. The rate at which one may exchange safety for yield, however, is determined neither by the issuer nor purchaser, but by the market for risky investment assets in general.

2. *Maturity.* Yields associated with bonds of short maturity tend to be lower than yields associated with bonds of longer maturity. This follows from the general notion that the shorter the maturity (a) the higher is the probability that one would attach to receiving each of the anticipated cash flows, (b) the higher is the degree of liquidity, and (c) the less sensitive is the current market price to short-term market interest rate variations. During a business cycle upswing, however, as a peak is approached this relationship may be temporarily reversed, for reasons that are explained below.

3. *Coupon Rate.* A strictly intuitive application of the logic of present value discounting would lead to the *mistaken notion* that small variations in the coupon rates on bonds that are otherwise alike would be precisely offset by market discounts or premiums, as the case may be, leaving before-tax yield to maturity unaffected. But capital gains realized on discount bonds are taxed more favorably than the higher coupons offered on premium bonds—

and this has a bearing on market demand relationships. Bonds that offer higher coupon rates, therefore, tend to offer higher before-tax yields as well, and conversely.

4. *Taxation.* A tax-exempt bond clears the market at a lower before-tax yield than a bond of similar quality that is not tax-exempt. Differential yields may be affected directly by taxation in this way, or indirectly as explained under point 3 above.

5. *Call Protection.* A call feature is intended to serve the interests of an issuer and not the investor. High coupon bonds, for example, are more likely to be called than low coupon bonds. All other things being equal, therefore, bonds that are subject to a call provision tend to clear the market at a lower price (i.e., higher yield) than bonds that are not subject to call. The market price (or yield) of a low coupon bond is less sensitive to the existence of a call provision than a high coupon bond, however, as the probability that such a provision would be exercised is lower.

6. *Convertibility.* A bond may be convertible into common stock at some predetermined conversion price. The issuer of such a bond would typically desire and expect the conversion option to be exercised during the conversion period. In general, therefore, issuers set conversion prices at levels that at the time of issue reflect reality. Thus, in most instances a convertible bond will sport a lower yield than a straight bond of similar quality. If the price of the stock into which the bond is convertible, however, should subsequently fall relative to the conversion price, the price of the bond would also fall, assuming it already reflects a value associated with possible conversion. The reverse is true if the price of the stock should rise relative to the conversion price. If the price of the stock were to fall to such a level as to preclude any possibility of eventual conversion, the bond would trade on a par with straight bonds of similar quality and maturity.

These factors interact, individually and in combination, with changing market interest rate patterns in the determination of bond price volatility.

BOND PRICE VOLATILITY

Bond price volatility is a useful measure of bond investment risk for bonds that are not necessarily held to maturity. The sensitivity of bond prices to changing interest rate patterns and other factors are discussed above. These effects may be illustrated in part with the aid of Tables 23-1 and 23-2. The calculations of this illustration assume that bond quality is unaffected by modest fluctuations of the economic variables considered.

Table 23-1 shows that the market price of a bond whose coupon rate is fixed varies inversely with the market interest rate, and that the sensitivity of bond price to changes in the market interest rate is greater the longer the length of time to maturity. A 1 percent change in the market interest rate, for example, would cause the price of the bond of this illustration to fall 7.11 percent assuming that there are ten years to

TABLE 23-1. Price Fluctuation Given a 6 Percent Coupon Rate and Various Maturity Dates and Market Yields

Time to Maturity	Rising Interest Rates (Falling Prices)			Falling Interest Rates (Rising Prices)		
	Price at 6%	Price at 7%	Percent Change	Price at 6%	Price at 5%	Percent Change
1 year	100.00	99.05	- 0.95%	100.00	100.96	+ 0.96%
5 years	100.00	95.84	- 4.16%	100.00	104.38	+ 4.38%
10 years	100.00	92.89	- 7.11%	100.00	107.79	+ 7.79%
20 years	100.00	89.32	-10.68%	100.00	112.55	+12.55%

TABLE 23-2. Price Fluctuations for 3 Percent and 6 Percent Coupon Bonds Maturing in Twenty-Five Years and Assuming a 50 Percent Increase in the Market Interest Rate

Coupon	Price at 4%	Price at 6%	Price at 9%	Percentage Change in Price for 50% Increase in Interest Rates	
				4% to 6%	6% to 9%
3%	84.29	61.41	40.71	-27.14%	-33.71%
6%	131.42	100.00	70.36	-23.91%	-29.64%
				For 50% Decrease in Interest Rates	
				6% to 4%	9% to 6%
3%	84.29	61.41	40.71	+37.26%	+50.85%
6%	131.42	100.00	70.36	+31.42%	+42.13%

maturity, and 10.68 percent assuming that there are twenty years to maturity. This result may be explained in terms of the present value discount equations introduced in Chapter 7.

Evaluated on a before-tax basis, the net present value of a bond's present and future cash flows may be obtained by modification of Equation (7.8):

$$\text{NPV} = A_0 + A_c \sum_{t=1}^{T} (1 + r/2)^{-t} + A_p (1 + r/2)^{-T}, \qquad (23.1)$$

where

A_0 = the purchase price of the bond or negative cash flow,
A_c = the constant interest payment received each period, or one-half of the annual interest payment,
A_p = the principal due upon maturity,
T = the number of interest payments,
r = the yield to maturity currently demanded by the market for bonds of this quality.

Treating A_0 as a variable that fluctuates with the market and NPV as a predetermined constant (say zero as in internal rate of return calculation), we obtain

$$|A_0| = \text{NPV} - [A_c \sum_{t=1}^{T} (1 + r/2)^{-t} + A_p (1 + r/2)^{-T}]. \qquad (23.2)$$

Clearly, $|A_0|$ in Equation (23.2), which represents the absolute value of a negative cash flow, will fall exponentially with each increase in T. That is, the further away the date on which principal is due to be repaid, the smaller the present value of that receipt at any constant rate of discount.

A 0.01 percent (or 1/100 of 1 percent) change in price is called a basis point change. Table 23–2 shows that the sensitivity of bond price volatility to each basis point change in the market interest rate varies *inversely* with the coupon rate and *directly* with the magnitude of the market rate of interest that prevails at the time that a change in market interest rate occurs. Each basis point change in the market interest rate, therefore, will have less of an impact on bond price volatility (a) the higher a bond's coupon rate and (b) the lower the market interest rate from which a change occurs. One important implication of these observations is that all other things being equal, bond price volatility—and thus bond investment risk—will be a maximum for bonds of long maturity, sporting coupon rates that are relatively low at a time when the market interest rate is relatively high. Such conditions are common when a peak in the business cycle is approached.

THE TERM STRUCTURE OF INTEREST RATES

The term structure of interest rates is the name given to positive theory (see Chapter 12) that seeks to explain the interrelationships between yield and maturity. A pattern of yield differentials that exists between securities that differ only in regard to maturity defines a particular yield structure. As explained in the previous section, however, many factors other than maturity that cause yield differentials to exist

are at work. The yield structure on U.S. government securities, on the
other hand, is not affected by contractual provisions other than those
that govern the timing and amount of cash flow, and thus is a useful
and widely used proxy for what the term structure of interest rates is
supposed to represent. Some typical yield curves on U.S. government
debt are shown in Figure 23–1.

The market yield on long-term government debt tends to be higher
for long-term maturities than for short-term maturities, as evidenced by
the yield curves in Figure 23–1. This pattern of variation is due in part
to investor time preference, and in part to the fact that even government debt is not immune from risk of various sorts, such as may be
caused by inflation or market fluctuations. During periods of monetary
contraction, however, such as may be brought about by Federal Reserve policy decisions, the entire yield curve shifts upward. A point is
sometimes reached where the current rate on long-term debt exceeds
the market's expectation for future one-period rates. When this point
is reached, lenders will attempt to lock themselves into long-term commitments that borrowers seek to avoid.

As interest rates rise in tune with a tight money policy, the supply
curve for long-term capital shifts to the right and becomes more elastic,

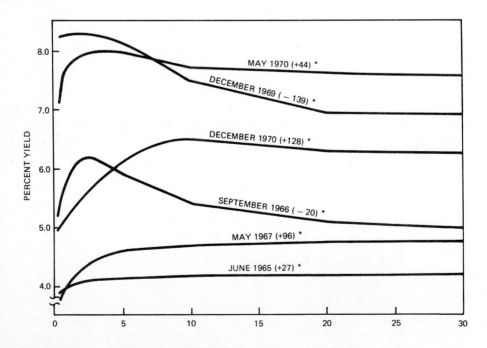

FIGURE 23–1. Yield Structure on U.S. Government Securities

while at the same time the supply curve for short-term loanable funds shifts to the left and becomes more inelastic. The relevant demand curves also pivot and shift, but the primary impact on the term structure is due to variation on the supply side of the market. The yield curve characteristically flattens in the early stages of monetary contraction, as in June 1965, but will eventually become downward sloping, as in December 1969 and September 1966 (see Figure 23–1) if the contractionary policy is continued long enough. Thus, the periodic occurrence of a downward-sloping term structure of interest rates may be explained.

Periodic shifts of the term structure, of course, present bondholders with both opportunity and risk. This type of risk is closely associated with the concept of systematic risk developed in Part 3 of this book.

During a sustained period of an upward sloping and unchanging yield structure, investors tend to "ride the yield curve." Thus, the price of a long-term security paying the market rate would rise as the maturity date is approached. At any point in time, of course, the future rate is subjected to uncertainty. Investors who expect the future one-period rate to rise (i.e., prices to fall) will attempt to exploit this uncertainty to their own advantage by selling long-term debt securities. Each such transaction, of course, takes place between two parties who differ either in circumstance or opinion. Those who fail to predict a rise in the long-term rate may find themselves "locked in" to their long-term securities in the rather limited sense that liquidation might then imply substantial capital loss.

A STRATEGY FOR INVESTMENT DECISION

Bond demand is highly segmented, representing the varied objectives of individuals and financial institutions that make up the market. Each such group is subject to legal and institutional constraints, tax programs, and investment priorities that are unique in various respects. It would be utter nonsense, therefore, to suppose that bond investors are, in general, unconstrained, one-period, mean-variance utility maximizers who trade in perfectly liquid markets where there are no barriers to entrance or exit. Nevertheless, an appropriate strategy for investment decision is one that considers the interrelationships between financial variables and deals rigorously and explicitly with the risk-return trade-offs that are a characteristic of financial markets.

Various Concepts of Risk

Except for the shortest of short-term debt issues of the federal government, a limited-income security—regardless of quality rating—is a risky financial asset and should be regarded as such.

Both from a theoretical and a pragmatic point of view, bond risk is a very complex phenomenon that defies simple categorization according to its various components.[1]

Default Risk. Standard bond ratings allude, somewhat imprecisely, to the unconditional probability of default on or before maturity.[2] The consequence of default, however, is not a direct function of the unconditional probability of default at some point in the life cycle of a bond. What matters is the *conditional probability* of default at each point in time and the remaining consequence of default measured in terms of (1) interest payments and/or the return of principal foregone and (2) the expected proceeds under liquidation or reorganization.

Systematic Risk. The existence of a term structure of interest rates implies that bond prices vary in a systematic fashion over time in tune with market interest rate changes. The resultant investment risk, however, is not a stable function of just one market interest rate, or even of a particular schedule of interest rates, as the characteristics of the term structure vary over time in line with varying business conditions and changes in Federal Reserve policy. The probability of default and the value of a firm under liquidation are affected by business cycle fluctuations that are lead indicators of the market interest rate cycle. As one approaches a peak in the business cycle, for example, default is not common even among lower-quality issues. As one passes the peak and heads for the trough, however, the situation is entirely changed—the probability of default goes up, and the value of assets used to secure a firm's debt (where there are such provisions) goes down. Clearly, aggregate data that are compiled on an ex-post basis (such as that compiled in Hickman's study below) would be of little value in assessing systematic risk on an ex-ante basis. Systematic factors of risk are in any event confounded with factors that are unique to individual firms and the contracts that they enter into.

Nonsystematic Risk. The systematic and nonsystematic components of bond investment risk are not easily and neatly dichotomized as they are in a one-period hold stock market model. Nevertheless, certain factors are unique to individual issues just as certain factors are affected by the market. Where it is appropriate to consider only longer holding periods (i.e., longer than one year), unfortunately, syste-

---

[1] Steven Katz, "The Price Adjustment Process of Bonds to Rating Reclassifications: A Test of Bond Market Efficiency," *Journal of Finance*, Vol. 29 (May, 1974), pp. 551–559. Also see Ronald W. Melicher and David F. Rush, "Systematic Risk, Financial Data and Bond Rating Relationships in a Regulated Industry Environment," *Journal of Finance*, Vol. 29 (May, 1974), pp. 537–544.

[2] George E. Pinches and J. Clay Singleton, "The Adjustment of Stock Prices to Bond Rating Changes," *Journal of Finance*, Vol. 33 (March, 1978), pp. 29–44.

matic and nonsystematic factors of risk interact, rendering it impossible to separate the two. As a long-term bond is a commitment on the part of both lender and borrower for a period longer than a year—typically much longer—the application of a one-period hold logic, such as in the calculation of covariance or beta statistics, would be utter nonsense. A second casualty of the multiperiod nature of bond investment, from the point of view of modern portfolio theory, has to do with the nature and efficacy of diversification. These points are developed in the next section.

The Limited Relevance of Modern Diversification Analysis

The characteristic logic and equations of models that follow the Markowitz ilk do not directly apply to the analysis of portfolios that consist wholly or in part of long-term debt securities. We cannot, for example, describe the precise makeup of the Markowitz efficient frontier in this case. Neither would it be reasonable to assume that for efficient portfolios all but the systematic component of risk will have been diversified away—even in the context of general equilibrium the systematic and nonsystematic components of risk interact. Given the diverse nature and objectives of bond investors, moreover, the assumption that bond investors are, in general, one-period mean-variance utility maximizers would be so much at variance with reality as to lead to no useful implications or conclusions. Nevertheless, if one were willing to accept the more modest proposition that bond investors generally seek the highest after-tax yield given any degree of risk exposure deemed to be appropriate and in light of whatever institutional constraints may apply, then some of the relationships of modern portfolio theory are approximately correct and provide useful insights for bond investors.

Risk-Return Trade-Offs

In Chapter 9 the Markowitz efficient frontier for a portfolio consisting entirely of risky assets was shown to be upward sloping and convex—increasing at a decreasing rate except in the case of perfect correlation. Where market yields in excess of the rate paid on short-term government debt are sought, therefore, a bond or stock investor must be prepared to accept positive levels of risk exposure. It follows from the curvature properties of a Markowitz efficient frontier that, for a portfolio consisting entirely of risky assets, risk will increase at an increasing (and not a constant) rate as higher and higher levels of yield are sought.[3] In a market that is at least reasonably efficient, each unit

---

[3] Even if lending and borrowing were possible at a single, risk-free rate, the restrictive assumptions that lead to the presumption of a capital market line (see Chapter 12) have been cast aside. Thus, expectation and risk cannot in general trade at a constant rate, given a multiperiod investment problem.

increase in yield sought will require a *more* than proportionate increase in risk in order to achieve it. The rate of exchange between expectation and risk, moreover, is *higher* for portfolios that are not well (as distinct from efficiently) diversified than for those that are.

Bond investors should be aware, therefore, that as one attempts to move up the yield curve, each succeeding step will require more than an insignificant change in one's degree of risk exposure. Moreover, institutional investors, by virtue of their large holdings, whether or not efficiently diversified, enjoy a natural advantage over individual investors whose bond holdings tend to be rather limited. The Hickman study[4] found that small investors showed better results by following a policy of safety first and limiting selections to high-quality bonds. Large financial institutions, by contrast, were able to exploit the advantage provided by their large holdings and realized higher yields by investing in lower-quality issues, which they were able to hold through good times and bad. It is natural, therefore, that institutional investors should control the market, especially for lower-quality debt instruments sporting relatively high levels of default risk. Armed with these insights, we are in a better position to deal with the complexity of some real-world phenomena and some basic tenets of traditional analysis that are imprecise at best.

Bond Swaps

The yield and risk characteristics of a bond portfolio can be altered by varying the maturity composition of that portfolio, or by shifting between coupon rates, quality levels, or yields. Three very basic forms of bond swap operations are discussed in this section, but more intricate and complex variations exist.[5]

Substitution Swap. A substitution swap may involve the trade of one bond for another that sells at a lower price but is of equivalent quality, coupon rate, and maturity. The existence of such an opportunity, of course, would indicate a market imperfection; such market imperfections do in fact present themselves from time to time and are available to be exploited. For example, in the case of a new bond offering, the underwriting syndicate supports (or pegs) the price of the new bond during the offering. Once the issue has been sold, the syndicate disbands and thus removes its support. Not infrequently, the price of

---

[4] W. Braddock Hickman, *Corporate Bond Quality and Investor Experience*, National Bureau of Economic Research (Princeton, N.J.: Princeton University Press, 1958).

[5] For a more detailed coverage of the subject, see Sidney Homer and Martin L. Leibowitz, *Inside the Yield Book: New Tools for Bond Market Strategy* (Englewood Cliffs, N.J.: Prentice-Hall, 1972), chapters 6 and 7.

the new bond will fall at this point, perhaps by as much as ten basis points. This is not to say that a new bond's price will always fall in this way, but that such situations do arise from time to time, and may be profitably exploited when they do.

Suppose, for example, that one holds a five-year, AA rated, utility bond that carries an 8 percent coupon and is currently selling at par. Suppose, moreover, that an opportunity comes up to trade the bond for a similar one which is priced at $99.13 per $100.00 of debt to yield 8.10 percent. Disregarding commission costs for the moment, ten basis points may be gained by the trade. Should interest rates fall to, say, 7.5 percent at some future date, moreover, then both bonds would increase in price to $104.29 per $100.00 of debt; that is, given such a fall in the market interest rate, the new bond will gain 5.16 basis points and the one that is presently being held only 4.29.

Securities of Different Coupons. Holding quality and maturity constant, there are two basic motivations for swapping securities bearing different coupon rates. First, one can increase or decrease the effect of anticipated price fluctuations that would result from expected changes in the level of interest rates. For example, if one expects that interest rates will rise in the future, then on an ex-ante basis the expected price decline from such an interest rate change can be reduced by switching from a low to a high coupon issue. Of course, the opposite switch would be suggested, as developed in our discussion of volatility analysis, when interest rates are expected to decline.

Second, one might switch from a low coupon issue to an otherwise similar high coupon issue to increase current income. For example, assume a 30-year, AA rated, 4 percent utility bond is selling at 58.46 to yield 7.5 percent to maturity, and a 30-year, AA rated, 8 percent utility bond is selling at 105.93 to yield 7.5 percent to maturity. The the investor sells the 4 percent bond and buys the 8 percent bond. However, the investor only realizes $584.60 from selling the 4 percent bond. If twenty bonds were sold, $11,962 would be available to invest in 8 percent bonds, allowing the purchase of approximately eleven of these bonds ($11,692 ÷ $1,051). Annual interest income would thereby be increased to $880 (11 × $80) from $800 (20 × $40), and the investor could use $191.77 for immediate spending that was raised through the sale and not reinvested. Of course, the investor will receive only $11,000 at maturity, rather than the $20,000 that would have been received if the 4 percent bonds were held to maturity. The investor is trading future income for current income.

Swaps in Anticipation of Changing Yield Spreads. Assume that the yield spread between high-grade corporate bonds and U.S. government bonds is currently 122 basis points (1.22 percent), and that one expects that this spread will be reduced to just 90 points over a period of time, say the next three months. If this expectation is realized, then the price of high-grade corporate bonds will rise relative to the price of U.S. government bonds. Anticipation of changing yield spreads creates opportunities for swaps involving government and corporate bonds, or corporate bonds of different quality ratings. One's decision to engage in such a swap, of course, is made ex-ante, but the consequences can be known only ex-post. Should expectations not be realized, the investor will lose at least to the extent of the commissions involved to undertake the swap.

Horizon Analysis. Yield differentials vary over time, creating buying and selling opportunities for bond investors. Both sides to each transaction, of course, are faced with various uncertainties, and the rule of randomness that governs the outcome of each transaction (see Chapter 8) is determined by a complex variety of different factors. Sometimes, when performing an analysis that may be preliminary to a bond swap, a single holding period is used as the reference period. Based on analysis and projections, one would then attempt to predict what changes in yield spreads would occur during this period, and what the situation would be at the end of such an *investment horizon*. This sort of analysis is merely a special form of the logical approaches previously outlined, and the importance of this and other mere techniques should be kept in perspective.[6]

Staggered Maturities: Hedging Interest Rate Changes

By spacing the purchase of bond issues more or less evenly over a long period of time, an investor achieves time diversification over the various reinvestment terms offered by the market. The risk of fluctuating annual income is less in a portfolio diversified over time than it would be for a short-maturity portfolio that is constantly rolled over at changing market yields, since only a moderate amount of funds have to be reinvested each year. The risk of a serious decline in the income generated by the portfolio because of declining interest rates is minimized.

Furthermore, the price risk associated with changing levels of interest rates is lessened. A reasonably constant flow of funds is available for reinvestment at periodic intervals, allowing regular review of the desirability of committing the funds to various alternatives, without forced liquidation at a loss in a rising interest rate market. Finally, the staggering of maturities avoids the risk that the entire portfolio will be invested in long-term obligations at rates that later prove to be below average.

---

[6] Martin L. Leibowitz, "Horizon Analysis for Managed Bond Portfolios," *Journal of Portfolio Management*, Vol. 1, No. 3 (Spring, 1975).

In summary, a staggered maturity policy offers a hedge against both rising and falling interest rates. Annual income returns will decrease less for a staggered maturity portfolio when interest rates are falling than for a short-maturity account, while market values will decline less when interest rates are rising than if all funds had been committed to long-term securities. One could modify the degree to which maturities are staggered as the outlook for interest rates changed in an effort to increase returns, but risk is also increased.

Summary

A rational investment strategy is one that seeks to maximize expected rate of return (or yield) for the degree of risk exposure accepted; this is in perfect accord with the view toward rational investment analysis commonly credited to Markowitz. The characteristic setting of the Markowitz portfolio selection framework (see Chapter 9), however, is difficult to exploit directly for the purpose of bond investment decision. Nevertheless, more classical views that attempt to treat the problem deterministically should be more or less abandoned.

The determination of bond yield and yield volatility are easier to explain in terms of economic variables—both for individual securities and groups—than is the case with stocks. However, holding period patterns of stocks and bonds are entirely different. A diversification analysis in the context of bond investment, therefore, cannot be as elegant as in the case of stock investment, but as various important interrelationships are better understood they can be treated effectively in a less elegant setting. The stochastic logic that guided the way through the portfolio selection models of Chapters 8 and 9 need not be abandoned.

Assessing the potential of swap operations in periodic revision of bond investment portfolios is difficult. This area has not received much academic attention, and much of the existing work lacks theoretical foundation. We would hope to see an expanded research effort in this area.

Questions

1. What are the essential disadvantages accruing to the purchaser of fixed-income securities? The major advantages?
2. Would a highly risk-adverse investor be wise to confine bond purchases to issues in the most stable industries in our economy? Discuss.
3. (a) What is a yield curve?
   (b) What is considered to be the normal shape of such a curve, and why is that shape expected?

(c) What conditions are likely to bring about a downward-sloping yield curve?

(d) Of what significance are yield curves to investors? Discuss.

4. (a) What happens to the price sensitivity of a bond for given changes in the general level of interest rates as maturity is lengthened? Why does this occur?

(b) If interest rates are expected to rise, would you prefer longer or shorter maturity bonds? Why?

(c) Relate the forecasting risk to interest rate changes and bond price volatility.

5. (a) Are lower or higher coupon bonds more price sensitive as the general level of interest rates changes?

(b) How is bond price volatility affected as the yield level from which a change in interest rates occurs is increased?

(c) If interest rates are expected to rise, would you prefer lower or higher coupon bond issues? Would the level of interest rates from which the rise is expected to occur influence your answer? Explain carefully.

6. (a) What should be the objectives of a bond investment strategy?

(b) Explain the relevance and applicability of the Markowitz portfolio selection approach.

7. What is a bond swap and what are or might be its objectives?

8. How would staggering the maturities of the bonds included in a bond portfolio provide a hedge against possible changes in the general level of interest rates?

9. The point was made in the chapter that the investment properties of stocks and bonds are difficult to compare. That is, because the holding periods involved and other externalities are quite different, there is no meaningful basis on which to define (let alone calculate) the relevant covariance measures. Moreover, because of differences in the contractual nature of the securities involved, it is not at all clear that a single risk proxy could be appropriate for use in the analysis of both stock and bond portfolios. Discuss.

Work-Study Problem

1. (a) Find two bonds that would currently suggest a potentially desirable substitution swap, holding quality, coupon, and maturity constant. Work out the advantages to be gained through the swap and explain them carefully.

(b) Find two bonds of equivalent maturity and quality that would suggest a potentially desirable swap because of differing coupons. Again, calculate the advantages offered by the swap and explain them carefully.

(c) Would a swap between AAA and BBB corporates seem desirable today? Defend your position.

24.

Analysis of Limited-Income Securities

The relatively high yields offered by bonds in recent markets, both historically and in comparison to dividend yield on common stocks, have made bonds attractive to individual investors. Nonconvertible preferred stocks, by contrast, are not as attractive to individual investors since they typically sell at lower before-tax yields than do equivalent quality bonds. Preferred stocks, on the other hand, are attractive to corporate investors, who benefit from the 85 percent dividend exclusion for income tax purposes.[1] Various standards and analytical techniques useful in judging the quality of bonds and preferred stocks are discussed in this chapter.

BONDS: ORIENTATION OF ANALYSIS

In the previous chapter the sacrifices accepted by purchasers of limited-income securities and the possible advantages offered by investment in limited-income securities were developed. We concluded that individual investors who purchase bonds for long-term yield should emphasize safety of both coupon and principal by confining themselves to high-quality issues. The emphasis in bond analysis is on the adequacy of anticipated cash flows of the issuer to service the debt requirements *under adverse economic conditions*. Therefore, the financial analysis process used in grading bonds in terms of quality tends to have a negative orientation.

The contractual terms included in the indenture and the yield have an important bearing on bond selection. However, contractual terms are usually of less significance than potential profitability of the issuer over the life of a debt issue.

---

[1] See chapter 2 for a discussion and illustration of the advantages of preferred stocks to corporations.

Bond Rating Agencies

Several reporting services[2] compile and publish useful financial data for evaluating companies and also rate bonds in terms of quality. Such ratings represent attempts to rank issues according to the probability of loss due to default. Bond quality ratings are not intended to serve as a guide to the relative attractiveness of an issue in terms of the yield likely to be realized by an investor. The ratings used in these agencies and a brief summary of their meaning are shown in Table 24-1.

According to the Hickman study, "The record of the agencies over the period studied (1900-1943) was remarkably good insofar as their ratings pertain to the risk of default."[3] Defaults and losses were significantly larger during this period for issues rated low-grade (below BBB) than for higher rated issues as indicated below:

Rating Category	Default Rate (% of Par Value)
I (AAA)	5.9%
II (AA)	6.0%
III (A)	13.4%
IV (BBB)	19.1%
V-IX (BB and below)	42.4%

TABLE 24-1. Description of Agency Ratings

Moody's	Standard & Poor's	Quality Indication
Aaa	AAA	Highest quality
Aaa	AA	High quality
A	A	Upper medium grade
Baa	BBB	Medium grade
Ba	BB	Contains speculative elements
B	B	Outright speculative
Caa	CCC & CC	Default definitely possible
Ca	C	Default, only partial recovery likely
C	DDD-D	Default, little recovery likely

_____

[2] The most widely used services are those offered by Standard & Poor's Corporation and Moody's Investor Service, Inc.

[3] W. Braddock Hickman, *Corporate Bond Quality and Investor Experience*, National Bureau of Economic Research (Princeton, N.J.: Princeton University Press, 1958).

Hickman concluded that the high default risk associated with bonds rated below BBB makes them especially unsuited for individual long-term investors who are not in a position to diversify away the default risk. Agency ratings, however, are not an infallible guide. For example, the agencies failed to predict (i.e., by lowering ratings) the difficulties experienced by holders of New York City obligations during the early 1970s. Bond ratings are useful, but the investor must understand their limitations. An independent analysis can help spot the most desirable bonds within a given rating category and may reveal fundamental changes that have not been allowed for in the rating.

Large financial institutions, especially insurance companies, often purchase an entire issue of bonds through a direct placement. Such bonds would not be agency rated unless the lender requested and paid for a rating. A quality rating would have to be established independently for such an issue by the purchaser.

Regulatory Restrictions and Legal Lists

Some states regulate the investment activity of trustees and banks through statutes establishing lists of securities (usually of bonds) considered legal investments for regulated institutions.[4] These statutes establish elaborate tests in respect to assets, earnings, dividends, prior default record, and so forth. Although lists of this sort are frequently criticized as being outmoded, several states continue their use.

TERMS OF THE ISSUE AND STANDARDS
FOR BOND INVESTMENT

Debt instruments may offer different degrees of risk in terms of realized return because of different contractual provisions and quality. While earnings and cash flow of the issuer provide the principal protection from loss for the investor, contractual provisions are important. Some basic and significant contractual provisions are reviewed below.

Provisions Protecting Senior Issues

A senior obligation enjoys a priority of claims over other securities of the same issuer. For such securities there should be reasonable provi-

---

[4] While the statutes, for rated bonds, no longer specifically state that bonds rated investment grade (top four rating categories) are considered eligible investment for national banks by the Comptroller of the Currency, it is generally assumed that bank auditors expect bond investments to be investment quality. Also, bonds rated BBB or better can be carried at book value (amortized cost), while lower-rated securities must be written down to market value when they are below cost and 50 percent of the net depreciation in value has been deducted in computing net capital of the bank. Similar valuation practices are imposed on insurance companies by the National Association of Insurance Commissioners.

sions in the contract to protect the investor's priority financial position and to prevent the issuer from actions that will impair the probability of the issuer's generating cash flows adequate to pay interest and principal.

Provisions Regarding Issuance of an Additional Amount of the Same Issue

Most contracts permit the issuance of additional bonds under the same issue, subsequent to the date of original issue, but subject to two major requirements: (1) that fixed charges on a pro forma basis, including the additional bonds, will be met beyond a reasonable doubt and (2) that the additional obligation will not exceed a given percentage of the value of the new property being acquired, often 75 percent in the case of railroad equipment and 60 percent in the case of public utilities.

Provisions Regarding Subsequent Issues with Prior Liens

Most indentures protecting senior issues provide that no subsequent issues will be given a prior lien over that of the original issue. If a security is a debenture issue, the indenture usually provides that the issue will share "equally and ratably" in any mortgage liens that may subsequently be placed on the issuer's property.

Provisions Regarding Reduction of Debt Principal

The creditor's position is weakened if only interest payments are made while the debt principal remains intact. For this reason, three common methods are used to reduce the debt principal during the life of the issue: (1) sinking funds for publicly issued bonds,[5] (2) amortization for term loans and private placements, and (3) serial maturities for equipment obligations and municipal issues. All debt issues should be protected in one of these three ways.

Provisions Regarding Working Capital

While provisions regarding working capital are rather common in contracts protecting private placements, they are still rather unusual in other bond indentures, in which they are found only in industrial issues. Working capital protection provisions require that net working capital be maintained at a specific dollar level in relation to funded debt or

---

[5] In the case of many public utility issues the indenture provides that instead of placing funds in a sinking fund to retire the issue, funds may be used to acquire new assets. Most utilities are regularly expanding. Protection is provided by requiring that substitution of new property for sinking fund payments will be limited to, say, 75 percent of the value of the property and that charges on a pro forma basis will be covered by a required minimum.

that a given current ratio be exceeded. Frequently payment of dividends is restricted if working capital falls below a designated level. In the case of smaller companies, private placements and term loan agreements frequently include restrictions on officers' salaries if working capital declines below a specified level.

Provisions for Subordinated Convertible Debentures

Since World War II, and especially in the late 1960s, corporations have issued a substantial amount of subordinated debentures. Such issues are usually subordinated specifically to commercial bank term loans and also other senior issues. To make the subordinated issues acceptable to buyers and (especially during the 1960s) to enable them to be sold at lower yields than are straight bonds, such issues were often made convertible into common stock, thereby offering potential protection from inflation and a senior position to equity security holders.

Call Provisions

Most debt issues carry two call provisions, one covering the call of the entire issue and the other covering calls for the sinking fund. The price quoted for sinking fund calls is the lower of the two. The call price covering the entire issue will be noticeably higher but usually will decline in steps as the period to maturity decreases.

A call provision is a negative factor for the investor, as the issuer will not call the entire issue except in periods when market yields are below the contract yield on the issue. In periods of tight money, purchasers of new issues may require that the call date be a minimum of five years, or more, from date of issue. Borrowers may secure lower interest costs at such times by providing ten-year call protection.

Provisions for Leasebacks and Other Leases

Senior issues should be protected from the burden of fixed charges other than interest, such as leases. This can be accomplished by requiring that current operating earnings cover interest and lease payment requirements by a specified multiple, or new obligations cannot be entered into without the permission of holders of senior securities.

OBLIGOR'S DIVIDEND RECORD

Some analysts suggest considering the long-term dividend record of the issuer when evaluating bond quality. Provisions regarding this record are common in statutes governing legal investment. A stable dividend payment record suggests income stability. A corporation may maintain such a record, however, at the expense of sound financial practices. A rapidly growing company, moreover, may follow a "no dividend" or "low dividend" policy to conserve funds for reinvestment. Each case, therefore, must be examined on its own merits, and a dividend payment test, in and of itself, does not seem to offer much analytically.

ASSET PROTECTION

The value of assets offered as collateral for a bond issue tends to be deemphasized when judging bond quality. Experience during the 1930s raises serious questions about the usefulness of asset value tests. For example, large numbers of mortgage bonds were issued in the 1920s, and the falling values of real estate offered little protection for bondholders. The basic protection for limited-income securities is the ability of the issuer to generate adequate cash flows to meet all debt obligations during adverse as well as strong economic periods, not the property pledged as security.

There are cases where the value of the pledged property is highly significant, however. For example, the lowest agency rating usually given to railroad equipment obligations (even when in receivership) is BBB. The reasons for this are (1) the ease with which the equipment can be transferred to, and therefore leased to, other railroads; (2) the need to keep this equipment if the railroad is to operate, and therefore the favorable attitude of the courts when the railroad is in receivership toward paying these obligations promptly and in full; and (3) the fact that the market value of the equipment pledged has usually been 25 percent or more above the outstanding amount of obligations.

STOCK EQUITY TEST FOR LONG-TERM DEBT

The amount invested by the owners in a company serves as a cushion for debtors, since losses are absorbed first by the stockholders. Therefore, all other things being equal, the higher the percentage of total capitalization provided by common equity capital, the safer the position of bondholders, other creditors, and even preferred stockholders. Reliance on the total equity figure shown on a balance sheet may be dangerous and misleading, however, because asset figures that appear on a balance sheet can be highly inflated in terms of earning power value. For this reason an "equity at market" test is considered preferable to a book equity test. The importance of this distinction may be illustrated as follows:

	Book Capitalization		Equity at Market	
Bonds (selling at par value)	$10,000,000	41.7%	$10,000,000	58.8%
Preferred stocks (selling at par value)	2,000,000	8.3%	2,000,000	11.8%
Common stock (1,000,000 shares, par value $10 per share, selling at $5 per share)	10,000,000	41.7%	5,000,000	29.4%
Retained earnings	2,000,000	8.3%		
Total capitalization	$24,000,000	100.0%	$17,000,000	100.0%

Although common stock equity in this example represents 50 percent of total capitalization based on book values, it represents only 29.4 percent based on market values. The market indicates that it considers the equity cushion as much smaller than book figures would indicate.

Various objections can be raised to either test equity at market or book; one's choice involves an element of subjective judgment. The test is at best a crude and general indication of quality, not a final determinant of quality.

Leases and the Stock Equity Test

Many corporations rent buildings and equipment under long-term lease contracts. Required rental payments are obligations similar to bond coupon and repayment of principal obligations in that they are required by a contract. While a footnote to a financial statement will usually indicate that a long-term lease obligation is present, the information contained in such a footnote is usually grossly inadequate for the purpose of judging the risk implications (vis-à-vis an equivalent amount of long-term debt) represented by a long-term lease.

Assets acquired through leasing are often not capitalized and shown in the balance sheet. Thus, two companies might work with the same amount of fixed assets and produce the same profits before interest or rental payments, but the one leasing a high proportion of its productive equipment would show significantly lower debt relative to equity, and lower interest charges relative to reported profit. One must be careful not to be misled by capitalization ratios when comparing firms that follow different leasing policies.

Stock Equity Tests: Standards

Standards can be established, in this regard, only in a general sense. An electric utility, for example, with highly stable income can safely utilize more debt relative to equity than can a company with more cyclical and uncertain earnings. Debt could range from 50 to 65 percent of total capitalization, based on experience, for a public utility without suggesting excessive borrowing and leverage. A railroad bond, on the other hand, would be unlikely to receive a high-quality rating were debt to exceed 50 percent of total capitalization. Caution would be suggested when the debt of a cyclical company, such as a steel company, exceeds 35 percent of its total capitalization.

EARNINGS COVERAGE TESTS

The earnings of a corporation are the basic source of cash flows. Coverage ratios are used to test the adequacy of cash flows from earnings for purposes of meeting debt and lease obligations.

Tests of the adequacy of earnings are typically applied to the past record of the company, although the future record is the one that will determine the soundness of judgment to purchase a security. This approach assumes that the past financial record offers a reasonable indication of future performance. Companies can, however, decline in quality, and coverage ratios are only a surrogate for a full-scale probability analysis of future cash flows.

Calculation of Earnings Available to Cover Fixed Charges

The calculation of a *times fixed charges earned ratio* is simple: earnings available for paying fixed charges are divided by the total fixed charges that must be paid each year. Some disagreement exists, however, regarding whether "earnings available" should be expressed on a before-tax or after-tax basis. Since fixed charges of this sort are tax deductible, the income before taxes is available to pay such charges. Nevertheless, the use of cash to pay taxes in a given year may impair a firm's ability to pay future fixed charges since earnings tend to be overstated in real terms during an inflationary period and inadequate funds may be available for purposes of maintaining the efficiency of productive facilities. A before-tax calculation is technically accurate in terms of determining the funds available in a given year for paying fixed charges, and therefore the following method will be used to calculate the ratio:

$$\frac{E_t + I_t + R_t}{I_t + R_t}, \tag{24.1}$$

where

E_t = earnings before taxes during year t,
I_t = interest charges paid during year t,
R_t = rental payments made under long-term leases during year t.

Financial reporting services uniformly report coverage after taxes but generally also show coverage before taxes. The annual reports prepared by corporations often report the amount available for interest after taxes rather than before and do not consider lease rental payments.

What Should Be Included in Fixed Charges. All interest obligations of a corporation, not just the interest mandated by long-term bonds, plus all rental payments required by long-term leases should be included in determining total fixed charges. Companies typically roll over short-term debt, and failure to pay interest charges, short-term or long-term, can lead to bankruptcy and, at a minimum, inconvenience for bondholders. The rental payments required under long-term leases are as mandatory as the interest payments required by bonds and are therefore included as fixed charges.

Requirements for sinking funds and amortization of debt principal are usually not included as fixed charges. The noninclusion of such items may be justified as follows: (1) creditors are usually willing to waive sinking fund payments for a year or two if a company is temporarily embarrassed and (2) sinking fund payments are presumed to be covered by depreciation charges that have not been added back in the numerator. However, the cash flow coverage of sinking fund payments should be carefully considered where the indenture makes such payments mandatory.

For a holding company, besides interest payments on its own debt, there is the question of interest charges of subsidiaries. The subsidiary cannot pay common dividends until it has met both its debt and preferred stock dividend requirements, and such dividend income may be a significant part of the cash flow available to cover fixed charges of the holding corporation. It would then be appropriate to include the fixed charge obligations of the subsidiary (including preferred dividend requirements) in the determination of total fixed charges for the holding company.

Calculating a Fixed Charges Coverage Ratio. This ratio is calculated by dividing the earnings available to cover fixed charges by the total fixed charges for a given corporation. Separate *interest coverage ratios* for senior and junior bond issues may be desired. When calculating such a ratio, the interest required for each senior issue should be added to that required by the issue for which the calculation is being made, and this total should then be related to the amount available to cover all issues.

To illustrate the importance of considering cumulative interest costs, suppose that a corporation earns $1,000,000 before interest payments and income taxes and has the following bond issues outstanding:

First mortgage, 5 percent bonds, $5,000,000
Second mortgage, 6 percent bonds, $1,000,000
Third mortgage, 6 percent bonds, $500,000

Also assume that the corporation has no lease arrangements. Under the *prior deductions method*, interest charges of senior issues are first deducted from earnings available to pay such charges before calculating the coverage ratio for a junior issue. Table 24-2 shows that when this method is used, earnings coverage for the first mortgage bonds is four times while that of the second mortgage bonds is 12.5 times and that of the third mortgage bonds is 23 times. This logical contradiction points to the inadequacy of the approach since the first mortgage bondholders must be paid in full before anything can be paid to second or third mortgage bondholders.

TABLE 24-2. Calculation of Interest Coverage Ratios Utilizing the Prior Deductions Method

Earnings before interest and taxes (EBIT)	$1,000,000
Interest on first mortgage bonds (5% × $5,000,000)	250,000
Coverage ratio ($1,000,000 ÷ $250,000)	4x
Balance available for second mortgage bonds	$ 750,000
Interest on second mortgage bonds (6% × $1,000,000)	60,000
Coverage ratio ($750,000 ÷ $60,000)	12.5x
Balance available for third mortgage bonds	$ 690,000
Interest on third mortgage bonds (6% × $500,000)	30,000
Coverage ratio ($690,000 ÷ $30,000)	23x

Table 24-3 shows that when earnings coverage ratios are properly calculated using the *cumulative deductions method*, all junior issues show lower coverage than the first mortgage bonds. This method is logically superior to the prior deductions method but is also subject to shortcomings. Since default on any issue could result in delayed or partial payments to senior bondholders, it might be argued that all issues should be judged in terms of the minimum ratio of 2.9 calculated for the third mortgage bonds.

Stability of Earnings. A company's ability to maintain its earnings over time is more important than the adequacy of coverage at a moment

TABLE 24-3. Calculation of Interest Coverage Ratios Utilizing the Cumulative Deductions Method

Earnings before interest and taxes	$1,000,000
Interest on first mortgage bonds (5% × $5,000,000)	250,000
Coverage ratio ($1,000,000 ÷ $250,000)	4x
Interest on second mortgage bonds (6% × $1,000,000)	$ 60,000
Coverage ratio ($1,000,000 ÷ $310,000)	3.2x
Interest on third mortgage bonds (6% × $500,000)	$ 30,000
Coverage ratio ($1,000,000 ÷ $340,000)	2.9x

in time when judging the quality of long-term debt issues. The vulnerability of sales, earnings, and cash flow to cyclical downturns merits serious consideration.

Minimum Standards for Coverage of Fixed Charges. Suggested standards are based on empirical studies relating the incidence of defaults over a number of years to the earnings coverage that prevailed prior to defaults. The Hickman study found a strong relationship between average after-tax earnings protection and bond defaults.[6] Unfortunately, this study did not take into account the varying stability of earnings for different corporations. It is also out of date. The wide diversity of coverage in individual years for various corporations is indicated in Table 24-4. Note the declining average earnings coverage for most of the companies listed in the second half of the decade of the 1970s. The rising debt positions suggested by this decline and the risks created were discussed in Chapter 14.

Different standards are in order for a highly cyclical company than for a stable company, as indicated by the much greater variability of cyclical companies. The data suggest that average coverage over a business cycle should be 8 or better to be classed as higher grade for a cyclical company, while the minimum coverage ratio should not fall below 4 in any year. For stable companies an average coverage of 5 or better and a minimum ratio of 2.5 in any year would suggest high quality. The suggested standards are only rules of thumb based on experience, and quality judgments should be based on complete analysis, not merely coverage ratios.

---

[6] Hickman, *Corporate Bond Quality and Investor Experience*, p. 413.

TABLE 24–4. Earnings Coverage Ratios for Selected Companies (earnings before taxes and interest charges divided by fixed charges)

Selected Companies	S&P Rating 1976–1980		Average Coverage		Mini-mum Cover-age	Year
			1970–1976	1975–1980		
Cyclical companies						
High grade						
Caterpillar Tractor	AA	AA	10.22	9.56	6.22	1979
Deere and Co.	AA	AA	7.00	6.96	2.76	1970
General Motors	AAA	AAA	31.71	27.95	9.08	1975
High medium grade						
Bethlehem Steel	AA	A		6.28	-.45	1977
Borg-Warner	AA	A	5.63	6.43	2.80	1975
Bucyrus-Erie	A	A	17.57	15.96	7.98	1975
Firestone Tire	AA	BBB	5.76	4.64	-.20	1978
Inland Steel	AA	A	6.71	5.97	2.93	1977
Stable companies						
High grade						
American Brands	AA	AA	6.11	6.25	4.92	1975
American Tel. & Tel.	AAA	AAA	6.65	4.55	3.38	1975
Borden Co.	A	AA	7.99	7.34	5.00	1979
Consolidated Natural Gas	AA	AA	3.60	3.77	2.41	1973
Reynolds (R.J.) Ind.	AA	AA	14.80	12.80	9.09	1978
Sears, Roebuck & Co.	AAA	AAA	5.91	5.34	2.64	1979
High medium grade						
Duke Power Co.	A	A	2.40	2.65	2.20	1970
Duquesne Light Co.	AA	A	3.08	3.01	2.79	1978
Florida Power & Light	A	A	3.07	3.20	2.44	1976
Washington Gas Light	A	A	2.41	2.37	1.58	1975

Source: Standard & Poor's Manuals, various years.

Cash Flow Analysis

Cash flow analysis is not as widely used in grading bonds as earnings coverage and other ratios, especially by individual investors, although ratios are, at best, crude approximations as measures of default risk. Internal management of companies and private placement lenders, however, are engaging more and more in probabilistic approaches to cash flow analysis.

Net earnings as reported on a typical accounting income statement do not provide a reliable measure for predicting future net cash flows. The ultimate concern of a bond analyst when grading bonds in terms of quality is with the probability that future cash inflows would not be sufficient to cover fixed charges. The probability of such a state occurring can only be assessed by studying the behavior of each of the components of cash flow under various economic conditions, following the approach developed in Chapter 8 of this text.[7]

Unfortunately, the information at the analyst's disposal is often inadequate for purposes of complete cash flow analysis. Pressure is being brought to bear on corporations to publish more complete sources and uses of funds and cash flow statements, and related information needed to intelligently analyze cash flows over time. Of course, the cost of such analysis does have to be considered and would tend to limit such an extensive approach to situations in what large purchases are involved, such as for institutional investors.

Other Financial Ratios Used in Grading Bonds

Liquidity ratios (such as the current ratio and acid-test ratio), turnover ratios, and profitability ratios used to analyze financial statements also offer useful information for evaluating bond quality. These ratios have been discussed in Chapters 20, 21, and 22.

STANDARDS FOR EVALUATING INVESTMENT QUALITY FOR PREFERRED STOCKS

In discussing the calculation of coverage ratios for bonds, the prior deduction method for junior bonds was rejected. Similarly, the prior deduction method for preferred stock is rejected.

Bonds do have a prior claim on corporate assets over preferred stock, and in terms of potential default, preferred stock is a riskier instrument. For this reason it would seem proper to require higher standards in terms of cash flow protection for a preferred stock than for a bond, and therefore the standards established for preferred stocks should exceed the minimum standards established for bonds.

If coverage for preferred stocks is to be calculated on the basis of earnings available *before* taxes, one must first recognize that bond interest is deductible for tax purposes, but preferred stock dividends are payable from net income remaining after income taxes. The proper method for calculating the coverage of preferred stock dividends is illus-

---

[7]Professor Donaldson has suggested a joint probability tree approach. See Gordon Donaldson, *Corporate Debt Capacity* (Cambridge, Mass.: Harvard University, Graduate School of Business Administration, 1961), chapter 7.

trated in Table 24–5. The amount of income available to pay preferred dividends, other things being equal, would always be less than that available to pay bond interest because of taxes.

TABLE 24–5. Coverage for Bond Interest and Preferred Stock Dividends Based on Before-Tax Earnings

	Corporations with Three Bond Issues and No Preferred Stock	Corporations with Two Bond Issues and One Preferred Stock
First-mortgage 5% bonds	$5,000,000	$5,000,000
Second-mortgage 6% bonds	1,000,000	1,000,000
Third-mortgage 6% bonds	500,000	
Preferred stock, 6% (10,000 shares, $50 par)		500,000
Earnings available *before* taxes for all issues	1,000,000	1,000,000
Interest on first-mortgage bonds	250,000	250,000
Coverage for first-mortgage bonds	$\dfrac{1,000,000}{250,000} = 4.00x$	$\dfrac{1,000,000}{250,000} = 4.00x$
Interest on first- and second-mortgage bonds ($250,000 + $60,000)	310,000	310,000
Coverage for second-mortgage bonds	$\dfrac{1,000,000}{310,000} = 3.23x$	$\dfrac{1,000,000}{310,000} = 3.23x$
Interest on first-, second-, and third-mortgage bonds ($250,000 + $60,000 + $30,000)	340,000	
Coverage for third-mortage bonds	$\dfrac{1,000,000}{340,000} = 2.94x$	
Balance available for preferred stock before taxes ($1,000,000– $310,000)		690,000
Federal income tax at 48%		331,200
Coverage for preferred stock on total deduction basis ($250,000 + $60,000 + $331,200 + $30,000)		$\dfrac{1,000,000}{671,200} = 1.49x$

CONVERTIBLE BONDS AND PREFERRED STOCKS

The holder of a convertible security has the right to exchange that security for common stock in accordance with specific terms set forth in the contract when, and if, the holder finds such an exchange desirable. The privilege of convertibility adds an extra dimension to the bond or preferred stock, allowing participation in corporate growth through the claim on the common stock.

Advantages of Convertible Securities

The investor purchasing a convertible security supposedly receives the advantages of a senior security (safety of principle and income stability) for a bond, or priority for a preferred stock, relative to a common stock. Furthermore, if the common stock of the issuer rises in price, the convertible instrument will also rise in price to reflect the increased value of the underlying stock into which it can be converted. But if the price of the common stock declines, the bond can be expected to decline only to the point where it yields a satisfactory return on its investment or straight bond value. Thus, when bond prices are declining, the price of convertible bonds might rise or drop proportionately less than straight bonds of equivalent quality.

Convertible bonds may have special advantages for financial institutions, notably commercial banks. Commercial banks are not permitted to purchase common stocks for their own account and therefore lose the possibility of capital gains through participation in corporate earnings growth. In 1957 approval was given for the purchase of eligible convertible issues by commercial banks if (1) the yield obtained is reasonably similar to nonconvertible issues of similar quality and maturity and (2) they are not selling at a significant conversion premium. Admittedly, commercial banks hold relatively few convertibles, and convertibles usually do sell at a conversion premium.

Convertible bonds have good marketability, as shown by active trading in larger issues on the New York Stock Exchange, whereas nonconvertible issues of similar quality are sometimes difficult to follow since they are traded over-the-counter.

Disadvantages of Convertible Securities

The investor pays for the conversion privilege by accepting a significantly lower yield than could be obtained by purchasing straight bonds or preferred stocks. The amount of the yield sacrifice will depend on the attractiveness of the underlying common stock and the conversion terms.

Risk can be markedly heightened by purchasing convertibles on margin. Many convertible bonds were bought on margin during the period 1966–1970. Margin requirements were less for convertible bonds than direct purchases of stock at that time, although they are now 50 percent for both instruments. Interest rates rose, bond prices fell, and some convertible bondholders experienced margin calls they could not meet. The bonds had to be sold, depressing the market below a price the purchasers had thought possible based on their estimate of a floor price at which the bonds would sell on a pure yield or straight investment basis.

A call clause can also lessen the potential attractiveness of convertible securities. Conversion can be forced by the corporation by calling the issue when the market value of the common shares that can be acquired in conversion exceeds the call price. This tends to limit the potential gain through growth in the price of the common stock.

The potential advantages noted for convertibles may well cause them to sell at substantial premiums over their straight bond value or the current value of the underlying common stock. If anticipated corporate growth is not realized, the purchaser may have sacrificed yield and may also see the value of the convertible instrument fall in the market. For example, prices of convertibles rose to very high levels in 1965, but in 1966, when both stock and bond markets declined, many convertible issues declined even more than the stocks into which they were convertible. It appears that a speculative premium had been built into the price of convertibles in 1965, and the market no longer felt this premium was justified in 1966.

Calculations for Convertible Securities

The following factors are considered when evaluating convertible securities:

1. What yield sacrifice is required to purchase the convertible?
2. What appreciation in the price of the common stock is required before conversion would become attractive?
3. What are the prospects for growth in the price of the underlying common stock?
4. What is the downside potential in the event that the conversion privilege proves valueless?
5. What is the number of years over which the conversion premium paid to acquire the convertible can be recouped by the favorable income differential of the convertible relative to the underlying common stock? This is called the break-even time.
6. What limitations, if any, exist on the duration of the conversion privilege and the number of shares that will be received?
7. What is the quality of the security being offered?

The discussion that follows will concentrate on calculations useful in evaluating points 1, 2, 4, and 5 above. The grading of bonds and preferred stocks in terms of quality has already been discussed. Tools useful in assessing potential growth of common stock value have already been developed in Chapter 7 and Sections III and IV.

Convertible Bonds: An Illustrative Analysis

In Table 24-6 a $2.80 convertible preferred offered by Atlantic Richfield is contrasted with a $5\frac{3}{4}$ percent convertible debenture of U.S. Steel, which matures in the year 2001. The individual calculations are shown in the table.

Conversion Premium. The conversion premium represents the excess of the cost per share of stock if obtained by conversion over the

TABLE 24-6. Comparison of Two Convertible Securities (as of October 21, 1977)

	Atlantic Richfield $2.80 Convertible Preferred	U.S. Steel $5\frac{3}{4}$'s, 2001 Par $1,000
Known factors		
Conversion ratio[a]	1.20 shares	15.94 shares
Call price	76	105
Duration	life	life
Market price, convertible	$63	$800
Market price, common	$52	$30
Dividend, common	$2.00	$2.20
Yields, equivalent quality		
nonconvertible instruments	7.40%	8.2%
Calculated data		
Market conversion price[b]	$52.50	$50.19
Conversion premium	$.50	$20.19
Conversion premium ratio	0.96%	67.30%
Yield, convertible	4.44%	7.50%
Yield, common stock	3.85%	7.33%
Yield sacrifice on convertible[c]	2.96%	0.70%
Floor price, estimated[d]	$37.84	$744.60

[a]The contract will either state the conversion ratio or a conversion price. When a conversion price is given, the number of common shares that will be obtained by conversion is found by dividing the par value of the convertible instrument by the contractually given conversion price.
[b]Market price of the convertible instrument divided by the conversion ratio.
[c]The yield offered by equivalent quality nonconvertible instruments, less the yield obtained on the convertible instrument.
[d]The price at which the convertible instrument would have to sell to offer the yield then offered by nonconvertible instruments.

cost per common share if the stock were purchased in the market at the prevailing price. The *market conversion price* represents the cost per share of the common stock if obtained by acquiring the convertible instrument. For example, the market conversion price of $52.50 for the Atlantic Richfield preferred stock is obtained by dividing the $63.00 market price of the preferred stock by the 1.20 shares of common stock that could be obtained on conversion. The conversion premium ratio shows the percentage increase necessary to reach the *parity price* (parity is that price relationship between the convertible instrument and the common stock at which neither a profit or loss would be realized by purchasing the convertible, converting it, and selling the common shares that were received in conversion) and is calculated as follows:

$$\text{conversion ratio} = \frac{\text{market price of the convertible}}{\text{market price of the common}}.$$

At the time of this analysis, both instruments were selling at a premium, but the premium on the U.S. Steel bond is substantially greater in both relative and absolute terms. Assuming the appreciation potential on the common stocks of both companies were equal (an unrealistic assumption at the time of this writing), the Atlantic Richfield convertible preferred had a substantial advantage. An increase of less than 1 percent in the common stock of Atlantic Richfield is needed to ensure that further increases will be fully reflected in the value of the convertible instrument. U.S. Steel common stock, on the other hand, would have to increase more than 40 percent before the conversion privilege has an assured value.

There is usually, although not always, some conversion premium present on convertible instruments, which reflects the anticipation of a possible increase in the price of the underlying common. Professional arbitragers are constantly looking for situations in which stock can be obtained more cheaply (allowing for commissions) by buying the convertible instrument and converting rather than buying the stock directly. When such a situation exists, an arbitrager would simultaneously buy the convertible and sell the underlying common stock short, later covering the short sale by delivery of the stock obtained in conversion.

Yield Sacrifice. A yield of 7.4 percent could have been realized by purchasing the $3.75 nonconvertible preferred issue of Atlantic Richfield, rather than the convertible preferred issue, at the time of this analysis. If the primary interest was in maximizing current yield, the investor might have considered the yield sacrificed by acquiring the convertible excessive. On the other hand, negligible yield sacrifice is necessary to acquire the conversion privilege on the U.S. Steel bonds, but a higher conversion premium had to be paid; the prospects for growth in the value of the underlying common were not generally considered as good as for Atlantic Richfield in October of 1977.

Downside Risk Potential. The *floor price* for a convertible is estimated as that value at which the instrument would sell in the market to offer the yield of an equivalent nonconvertible instrument. To calculate this value, the investor must determine the bond's quality and the yield at which similar quality instruments are currently selling. Atlantic Richfield had a nonconvertible preferred outstanding that yielded 7.4 percent in October 1977. Therefore, the floor price for its convertible preferred is calculated by dividing the $2.80 dividend by 7.4 percent, resulting in a value of $37.84. About 40 percent of original capital (63.00 – $37.84/$63.00) could be lost if the investor purchased the convertible preferred, and the market later decided the conversion privilege was worthless; the yield of equivalent quality nonconvertible preferreds remained at 7.4 percent. The loss would be greater if the general level of yields rose in the market after purchase.

The floor price for the U.S. Steel bonds is determined by utilizing bond value tables to find the price the bond would have to sell at in order to offer a yield to maturity of 8.2 percent, such as was available on equivalently rated nonconvertible bonds during October 1977. The downside risk appears to be much smaller on the U.S. Steel bonds, but the upside potential is not impressive.

Break-Even Time. Break-even time represents the number of years it will take for the favorable income differential over the common stock offered by a convertible instrument to equal the conversion premium paid to acquire that convertible instrument. The Atlantic Richfield Convertible Preferred pays $2.80 per share, while the 1.2 common shares that could be obtained in conversion would pay the equivalent of $2.40 per year (1.2 × $2.00 per common share). The break-even time is calculated by dividing the conversion premium per share (.50) by the favorable income differential offered by the preferred (.40), or 1.25 years.

The favorable income differential for each $5\frac{3}{4}$ percent, U.S. Steel, convertible bond is $22.43, calculated as follows:

Interest paid on each $1,000 bond at $5\frac{3}{4}$ percent $57.50
Dividend income offered by 15.94 shares into
    which each bond is convertible   35.07

    $22.43

The favorable income differential per common share is $1.41 ($22.43 ÷ 15.94 shares). The break-even time is 14.3 years ($20.19 ÷ $1.41).

A break-even time exceeding five years is widely regarded as excessive, other things being equal. Therefore, the U.S. Steel bond appears unattractive in terms of break-even time.

Dilution of Convertible Privileges. A large common stock split or stock dividend could markedly dilute the conversion privilege unless adjustment were made. Typically, the conversion privilege is protected by a provision in the bond indenture providing for a pro-rata adjustment of the conversion price and/or conversion ratio, correcting the exchange ratio so that no dilution of the conversion privilege occurs.

When a Convertible Should be Converted or Sold. If the prospects for favorable growth in the underlying common stock or the relative prices and yields of the convertible security and the common stock change significantly, a sale or conversion may be suggested. For example, the dividend obtainable by converting into the common stock of AT&T from the $4 convertible preferred rose to $4.20 a share during 1977. A conversion was then desirable since dividend income could be increased twenty cents per share by conversion.

Summary

Bonds have offered relatively high yields in recent years, both historically and in comparison to common stocks. Individuals and institutional investors have therefore shown increased interest in bonds.

Bond analysis tends to be negatively oriented in the sense that assessment of default risk is emphasized. The focal point of bond analysis is the adequacy of anticipated cash flows of the issuer to service debt requirements *under adverse economic conditions.* Bond ratings offered by rating agencies are useful but have limitations. Independent analysis can help spot the most desirable bonds within a given rating category, and may reveal fundamental changes that have not yet been allowed for in a published rating.

The basic protection for investors in limited-income securities is the ability of the issuer to generate sufficient cash flows for all corporate needs, not the value of pledged assets. Asset values may fall significantly during serious economic recession and are most difficult to liquidate when the corporation is unable to meet debt obligations.

The relation between equity and debt and earnings coverage tests are widely used tools for evaluating bond quality. Liquidity ratios, turnover ratios, and profitability tests are also used. Detailed cash flow forecasts are not as widely used, although the adequacy of cash flow is the focal point of bond quality analysis. Data limitations and cost certainly help explain this. However, probabilistic approaches to cash flow analysis are used by private placement lenders and some large financial institutions.

Some limited-income securities are convertible into common stock, offering the basic advantages of a senior security while allowing the holder to participate in potential corporate growth. The investor pays for the conversion privilege by accepting a significantly lower yield than could be obtained by purchasing nonconvertible bonds or preferred stocks. A convertible usually sells at a premium over the value of the underlying common stock. If the anticipated growth in the value of the common stock is not realized, the purchaser will have sacrificed yield and may well also see the value of the convertible instrument fall sharply. Special calculations useful in assessing the relative attractiveness of the many convertibles available in the market are illustrated and explained in this chapter.

Questions

1. Bond analysis is said to have a "negative orientation." Why?
2. Discuss the usefulness of agency ratings of bonds.
3. (a) Explain the significance of restrictive covenants in long-term debt contracts.
   (b) What type of restrictive covenants might be found?
4. (a) Discuss the significance of a call provision to the investor if
      (1) a decline in interest rates is expected.
      (2) a rise in interest rates is expected.
   (b) What is meant by "call protection"?
5. Why do equipment obligations of railroads have such high standing in the capital markets?
6. "The basic protection for limited-income securities is the ability of of the issuer to generate adequate cash flows to meet all debt obligations during adverse as well as strong economic periods."
   (a) Are stock equity test ratios, as defined in this chapter, then significant? Support your answer carefully.
   (b) Should a stock equity test ratio be calculated in terms of the market value of equity or the book value of equity? Why?
7. Professor Donaldson has stated that "the earnings coverage form of debt capacity is generally intended as a crude approximation of risk measurement in cash flow terms."
   (a) Do you agree? Discuss.
   (b) What practical difficulties stand in the way of developing a more adequate cash flow analysis for the purpose of judging debt capacity?
8. What would you use as the numerator and denominator of an earnings coverage ratio?

9. It can be said that the market price of a convertible bond may reflect either the quality of the instrument relative to nonconvertible instruments or the value of the common stock of the issuer. Explain the circumstances under which each of the two factors mentioned is likely to predominate in determining market price of the convertible bond.

10. Define each of the following terms relative to convertible securities:
    (a) conversion premium
    (b) parity price
    (c) break-even time
    (d) floor price
    In each case, note the significance of the concept to an investor interested in convertible securities.

Work-Study Problems

1. A balance sheet and an income statement for the XYZ Manufacturing Corporation follow.

XYZ Manufacturing Corporation
Balance Sheet
December 31, 19—

Cash		$ 75,000	Accounts Payable	$110,000
Accounts Receivable		250,000	Notes Payable—Bank, 6%	30,000
Inventories		180,000	Other Current Liabilities	30,000
Property and			First-Mortgage Bonds, 4%,	
Equipment	$695,000		due 1985	150,000
Less Accumulated			Second-Mortgage Bonds,	
Depreciation	290,000		5%, due 1995	50,000
		405,000	Preferred Stock, 5%,	
			$100 Par	100,000
			Common Stock, $100 Par	250,000
			Retained Earnings	190,000
			Total Liabilities and	
Total Assets		$910,000	Capital	$910,000

XYZ Manufacturing Corporation
Income Statement
For the Year Ended December 31, 19—

Net Sales	$1,235,000
Less Cost of Sales	860,000
Gross Profit	$ 375,000

Less Selling and Administrative Expenses	320,000
Net Operating Income	$ 55,000
Interest Expense	10,300
Net Income Before Federal Income Taxes	$ 44,700
Federal Income Taxes	16,956
Net Income After Federal Income Taxes	$ 27,744

(a) Calculate the times-interest-covered ratio for the first-mortgage bonds.
(b) Calculate the times-interest-covered ratio for the second-mortgage bonds.
(c) What would be the times-interest-covered ratio for this firm if a total deductions method were used?
(d) Would you consider any or all of this corporation's bonds to be investment-grade? If the information given is inadequate for purposes of rating these bonds, what additional information would you require?
(e) If you had decided to buy the bonds of this corporation (assuming that both first- and second-mortgage bonds were selling at par), which would you buy? Why?

2. The following financial data and information pertains to Saginaw Corporation for 1974:

	($ Millions)
Sales	100.0
Cost of Sales and Operating Expenses	81.0
Taxes on Income—50% rate	7.6
Earnings Available to Common	7.2
Common Dividends	1.8
Assets	80.0
Current Liabilities	5.0
Long-term Debt:	
8% First Mortgage Bonds, 2000	15.0
10% Sinking Fund Debentures, 1995	20.0
6% Convertible Debentures, 1984	10.0
Preferred Stock, 8% ($25 par)	5.0
Common Equity (10 million shares)	25.0

Both the mortgage bonds and the sinking fund debentures are immediately callable at 108. A 2 percent sinking fund on debentures begins in 1980. First mortgage bonds and sinking fund debentures currently sell to yield 9 percent to maturity. The conversion price on the convertible debentures is $12.50.

(a) Calculate the earnings coverage for the preferred stock dividends on a basis comparable to earnings coverage ratios calculated for the debt instruments.

(b) Cite and explain the advantages of holding either the first mortgage bonds or the sinking fund debentures, given the information above.

(c) Calculate fully diluted earnings per share for 1974.
(Adopted from Chartered Financial Analysts Examination I, June 1975, Section 2, Question 1.)

3. (a) Select two current outstanding convertible bonds and determine the following information for these bonds:
Coupon rate for each bond.
Maturity date for each bond.
S & P quality rating for each bond.
Yield on straight bonds of similar quality to each issue.
The conversion price and ratio for each bond.
The current market price of the convertible bonds.
The currently applicable call price of the bonds, if any, and the date at which changes will occur in the call price if they are not constant until maturity of the bonds.
The current dividend yield on the common stock of the issuing companies.

(b) Utilize the above information to calculate the following for each of the bonds you selected:
The conversion premium for each bond.
The yield to maturity for each bond.
The current straight bond value and the potential downside risk suggested.
The call risk, if any, present in each bond.
The relative advantage or disadvantage present, in terms of current yield, by being a holder of the bond rather than a holder of the common stock.

(c) Based on the information you have now developed on each bond, which appears to be the more desirable purchase?

(d) What additional information would you need to evaluate properly the desirability of purchasing either bond?

(e) If the market price of the common stock for the issuing company of each bond were to increase 30 percent over the next two years, what would you expect to be the minimum price at which each convertible bond would sell? Explain your answer.

PART 8
Analysis of Special Classes of Securities

25.

Industrial Securities

Chapter 18 can usefully be reviewed before reading this chapter. Companies included in the industrial group of securities—by far the largest investment group—present a large and dissimilar array to investors. The wide variety and differences make the problem of security analysis difficult and require the analyst to concentrate on the economic characteristics of an industry or industries in which a company operates. Generalizations are less useful here than they are in the public utility field, for example, where both the industry and the companies within the industry have much in common, including standardization of accounts and, usually, relative stability of operations, revenues, and earnings, although economic and rate environments may differ considerably.

In Table 25-1 which shows net income, return on net worth, and net profit margin on sales for leading corporations, the industries through and including "trade" are industrials. The largest group by far in the industrial classification is that of "manufacturing" companies, which account for nearly three-quarters of the net income generated by all industrial companies. The growth rate of earnings and dividends and the volatility of revenues and earnings, and therefore stock market action, vary widely within the industrial group for short, intermediate, and long-term periods.[1]

INDUSTRY ANALYSIS

Industrial companies may suffer severely from competition or, on the other hand, may earn high rates of return on their investments if they enjoy industry leadership. This is true particularly where there is research leadership and especially where a company possesses impor-

---

[1] Table 18-10 contains rates of return on sales and net worth for major manufacturing groups as published quarterly and annually by the Federal Trade Commission.

TABLE 25-1a. Net Income of Leading Manufacturing Corporations for 1976 and 1977 (in millions of dollars)

No. of Cos.	Industry	Reported Net Income After Taxes			Net Worth Beginning of Year 1977-a	Percent Return on Net Worth		Percent Change in Sales-b	Percent Margin on Sales-c	
		1976	1977	Percent Change		1976	1977		1976	1977
8	Baking	$ 116.0	$ 145.3	+25	$ 784.3	16.1	18.5	+ 8	2.8	3.3
7	Dairy products	365.3	402.3	+10	2,720.9	14.7	14.8	+ 5	3.2	3.3
28	Meat packing	294.2	267.1	– 9	2,568.4	12.9	10.4	+ 1	1.5	1.3
18	Sugar	160.2	134.2	–16	1,476.0	11.4	9.1	–2	3.9	3.3
56	Other food products	1,549.0	1,640.7	+ 6	10,710.5	16.1	15.3	+10	4.0	3.9
18	Soft drinks	563.0	642.9	+14	2,829.3	22.4	22.7	+17	6.7	6.6
9	Brewing	205.8	197.9	– 4	1,928.5	11.5	10.3	+ 7	4.4	3.9
6	Distilling	192.2	158.2	–18	1,326.0	16.3	11.9	+ 1	5.0	4.1
9	Tobacco products	904.4	1,132.8	+25	5,876.7	17.2	19.3	+12	5.2	5.5
56	Textile products	401.6	400.9	0	4,453.4	9.6	9.0	+ 7	3.3	3.0
66	Clothing & apparel	429.8	421.2	– 2	3,751.3	12.3	11.2	+ 7	3.4	3.1
19	Shoes, leather, etc.	86.2	86.2	0	633.6	15.0	13.6	+ 7	3.8	3.5
41	Rubber & allied products	485.6	703.6	+45	6,751.1	7.5	10.4	+12	2.5	3.2
35	Lumber & wood products	585.1	673.6	+15	4,183.3	15.5	16.1	+13	6.1	6.2
32	Furniture & fixtures	105.3	101.5	– 4	1,148.8	9.8	8.8	+ 8	3.5	3.1
58	Paper & allied products	1,626.1	1,764.8	+ 9	12,452.5	14.8	14.2	+10	6.0	5.9
67	Printing & publishing	664.3	919.3	+38	5,271.0	13.9	17.4	+14	5.6	6.8
60	Chemical products	3,819.9	3,833.3	0	26,428.8	16.1	14.5	+11	6.7	6.1
11	Paint & allied products	54.8	69.5	+27	554.0	10.9	12.5	+11	2.5	2.8
35	Drugs & medicines	2,131.0	2,266.1	+ 6	12,076.9	20.0	18.8	+11	9.8	9.4
34	Soap, cosmetics	1,007.3	1,180.2	+17	6,079.3	18.3	19.4	+11	5.9	6.2
108	Petroleum production & refining	12,733.1	13,413.8	+ 5	94,806.2	14.8	14.2	+11	5.3	5.0
13	Cement	112.0	153.1	+41	1,216.8	9.8	13.0	+19	5.3	6.3
13	Glass products	579.7	513.4	–11	3,787.3	17.3	13.6	+10	6.4	5.2
29	Other stone & clay products	354.8	413.3	+16	3,562.0	10.6	11.6	+19	4.4	4.3
56	Iron & steel	1,619.4	775.7	–52	20,276.6	8.5	3.8	+10	3.6	1.5

TABLE 25-1a. Net Income of Leading Manufacturing Corporations for 1976 and 1977 (in millions of dollars) *(continued)*

No. of Cos.	Industry	Reported Net Income After Taxes			Net Worth Beginning of Year 1977-a	Percent Return on Net Worth		Percent Change in Sales-b	Percent Margin on Sales-c	
		1976	1977	Percent Change		1976	1977		1976	1977
34	Nonferrous metals	880.8	870.4	− 1	11,114.3	8.5	7.8	+12	4.6	4.1
24	Hardware & tools	275.0	303.6	+10	1,911.7	16.3	15.9	+14	5.3	5.2
13	Building, heating, plumbing equip.	157.4	196.3	+25	877.8	21.0	22.4	+10	5.7	6.5
99	Other metal products	862.0	969.6	+12	6,312.4	15.0	15.4	+11	4.1	4.1
40	Farm, constr., material-hdlg. equip.	1,458.7	1,659.1	+14	9,460.6	17.9	17.5	+12	6.2	6.3
63	Office equipment, computers	3,129.9	3,706.2	+18	20,213.6	17.4	18.3	+11	9.4	10.0
127	Other machinery	1,027.7	1,277.4	+24	8,278.4	13.6	15.4	+13	4.8	5.3
186	Electrical equip. & electronics	3,788.8	4,488.6	+18	26,095.7	16.2	17.2	+14	5.3	5.5
16	Household appliances	384.0	465.9	+21	2,452.6	17.4	19.0	+12	4.5	4.9
15	Autos & trucks	4,604.8	5,624.3	+22	27,729.4	18.3	20.3	+19	4.4	4.5
30	Automotive parts	753.3	888.7	+18	5,427.0	15.3	16.4	+15	4.2	4.3
29	Aerospace	956.5	1,293.6	+35	7,950.7	13.6	16.3	+ 9	3.0	3.7
19	Other transportation equipment	76.8	89.9	+17	590.1	15.1	15.2	+18	3.5	3.5
113	Instruments, photo. goods, etc.	2,284.6	2,631.7	+15	16,197.5	15.7	16.2	+15	7.6	7.6
46	Miscellaneous mfg.	362.4	323.0	−11	2,634.3	15.2	12.3	+11	5.0	4.0
1,746	Total manufacturing	$52,129.9	$57,209.9	+10	$384,899.3	15.0	14.9	+12	5.1	5.0

TABLE 25-1b. Net Income of Leading Nonmanufacturing Corporations for 1976 and 1977 (in millions of dollars)

No. of Cos.	Industry	Reported Net Income After Taxes			Net Worth Beginning of Year 1977-a	Percent Return on Net Worth		Percent Change in Sales-b	Percent Margin on Sales-c	
		1976	1977	Percent Change		1976	1977		1976	1977
10	Metal mining-d	$ 148.6	$ 118.5	− 20	$ 1,289.2	12.5	9.2	+ 5	11.9	9.3
7	Other mining, quarrying-d	187.2	97.3	− 48	986.9	22.1	9.9	− 3	10.2	5.4
17	Total mining-d	335.8	215.7	− 36	2,276.2	16.5	9.5	0	10.9	7.1
40	Food chains	430.1	541.9	+ 26	3,849.6	12.0	14.1	+13	1.0	1.1
54	Variety chains	793.7	893.3	+ 13	5,230.7	17.7	17.1	+16	3.0	2.9
38	Department & specialty	1,330.3	1,596.1	+ 20	11,366.7	13.2	14.0	+11	3.5	3.8
25	Miscellaneous retail	147.8	194.0	+ 31	1,032.9	17.1	18.8	+22	3.6	3.9
149	Wholesale trade	1,144.2	1,199.5	+ 5	7,902.3	16.2	15.2	+12	2.5	2.3
306	Total trade	3,846.1	4,424.8	+ 15	29,382.3	14.7	15.1	+13	2.4	2.5
58	Class I railroads-e,f	320.4	283.5	− 11	15,230.0	2.1	1.9	+ 8	1.7	1.4
45	Trucking-e,j	267.6	315.3	+ 18	1,570.6	20.0	20.1	+22	3.9	3.7
31	Air transport-e	537.3	787.3	+ 47	5,147.0	11.7	15.3	+14	2.8	3.6
15	Miscellaneous transportation	259.8	290.2	+ 12	1,928.1	14.9	15.1	+10	3.8	3.8
149	Total transportation-e	1,385.1	1,676.3	+ 21	23,875.7	6.1	7.0	+13	2.7	2.9
169	Electric power & gas-e	7,698.1	8,744.1	+ 14	74,777.4	11.5	11.7	+19	10.3	9.8
36	Telephone & Communications-e	4,729.3	5,629.3	+ 19	44,296.2	11.5	12.7	+13	11.2	11.8
205	Total public utilities-e	12,427.4	14,373.4	+ 16	119,073.6	11.5	12.1	+17	10.6	10.5
26	Amusements	253.3	356.3	+ 41	1,831.1	15.6	19.5	+14	7.8	9.7
59	Restaurants & hotels	472.0	578.5	+ 23	3,463.4	16.3	16.7	+14	4.6	5.0
152	Other business services	730.1	881.7	+ 21	4,930.3	16.5	17.9	+18	5.2	5.3
40	Construction	815.5	838.4	+ 3	4,314.9	22.5	19.4	+ 6	4.4	4.2
277	Total services	2,270.8	2,654.9	+ 17	14,539.7	18.1	18.3	+12	4.9	5.1
2,700	Total nonfinancial	72,414.1	80,555.5	+ 11	574,046.8	13.9	14.0	+12	5.2	5.2

TABLE 25-1b. Net Income of Leading Nonmanufacturing Corporations for 1976 and 1977 (in millions of dollars) (continued)

No. of Cos.	Industry	Reported Net Income After Taxes			Net Worth Beginning of Year 1977-a	Percent Return on Net Worth		Percent Change in Sales-b	Percent Margin on Sales-c	
		1976	1977	Percent Change		1976	1977		1976	1977
k	Commercial banks & holding cos.	5,919.0	6,576.0	+ 11	56,760.0	10.9	11.6	....	....	....
1,350	Property & liability ins.-g	2,776.4	6,507.5	+134	31,353.4	10.8	20.8	....	....	....
84	Investment funds-h	722.2	827.7	+ 15	18,046.0	4.4	4.6	....	....	....
21	Sales finance	246.3	274.3	+ 11	2,530.1	10.6	10.8	....	....	....
73	Real estate	112.1	345.9	+209	3,734.8	3.2	9.3	....	....	....
37	Miscellaneous finance-i	515.5	580.2	+ 13	3,398.9	17.1	17.1	....	....	....
1,565k	Total financial	10,291.5	15,111.6	+ 47	115,823.2	9.7	13.0	....	....	....
4,265k	Grand Total (incl. manufacturing)	82,705.6	95,666.6	+ 16	689,870.0	13.2	13.9	....	....	....

(a) Net worth is equivalent to shareholders' equity or "book net assets" or "book net assets" or "book net assets" or capital and surplus. (b) Less than 1% of the income do not report sales or revenues. "Sales" include income from investments and other sources as well as from sales. (c) Profit margins are computed for all companies publishing sales or gross revenue figures. (d) Net income is reported before depletion charges in some cases. (e) Due to the large proportion of capital investment in the form of funded debt, rate of return on total property investment would be lower than that shown on net worth only. (f) Association of American Railroads tabulation. (g) Estimated by A. M. Best Co. for all companies on an adjusted basis. (h) Income in most cases excludes capital gains or losses on investments. (i) Includes brokerage firms, savings-and-loan companies, etc. (j) Common carrier trucking, including specialized and household goods carriers as well as general freight. (k) Federal Reserve data for all member banks. Number (5,668) not included in total number of companies.

Source: "Profits '77—Sales Were the Spur," Citibank's Monthly Economic Letter (April, 1978), pp. 6, 7.

tant patents in a growth industry. Mature industrial companies, and most industrial companies are mature, tend to follow the trend of the general economy. Certain industries and companies evidence particularly strong cyclical characteristics such as those providing durable goods for consumers and manufacturers of capital goods. Other industries and companies, notably the growth industries and companies, may show steady fast growth with relatively slight cyclical characteristics until they reach the mature stage.

The record and the success of a company will depend to a great extent on the fortunes of the industry (or industries) in which it operates, and the results will generally be reflected in stock market action.

Industry Categories

Investors tend to place industries in one of three major categories that conform generally to the life-cycle theory discussed in Chapter 18. These categories are discussed in the following paragraphs.

Mature Industries. Some industries, at least in the most recent years, have had a record roughly paralleling the record of GNP, and in the future they are expected to show a continuation of that trend. These *mature* industries and the companies within them are expected to grow at approximately the same rate as the economy and also to reflect cyclical fluctuations in the economy. Business cycles have been relatively mild since 1938, with the most serious contractions occurring mid-1957, mid-1958, and in 1974 and early 1975. Within the industrial groups, producers of such durables as autos and steel, and generally the extractive industries, have suffered severely during these contractions, however.

Growth Industries. To deserve the designation "growth industry," Wall Street has generally required

1. That the threat of obsolescence from technological developments or other changes does not presently appear significant for the industry as a whole.
2. That the demand for the industry's product is growing at a significantly faster rate than the growth of GNP and competing industries, if such exist.
3. That as sales increase, mass production techniques will reduce costs and permit a reduction in sales prices to stimulate additional demand but not enough to reduce profits, thus prolonging the period of rapid growth.
4. That relatively few companies dominate the industry.
5. That earnings are expected to grow at least 12.2 percent per year or double every six years versus an expected 5–6 percent per year for corporate profits overall, averaging through expansions and contractions.

Many investors, at least up to the 1974–75 period, were eager to buy stocks in growth industries. Investments in such industries as business machines, photography, science, aerospace, oceanography and oil service (drilling, etc.), and, more recently, antipollution have provided superior performance for many investors.

However, the majority of investors, individual or institutional, cannot concentrate most of their investment funds on industries characterized as growth industries or stocks characterized as growth stocks. These growth industries represent only a small minority of the industries, the companies, the assets, and the earnings available to investors. Even the concentration of a relatively small proportion of available investment funds has resulted in such stocks selling at relatively high price-earnings ratios and relatively low dividend yields. Attempts to concentrate a major proportion of available investment funds in such stocks would cause them to rise to price-earnings ratios that even the most avid of "growth stock" investors would recognize as completely unreasonable. Those who consistently purchase such stocks regardless of their price and regardless of their high price-earnings ratios are sure to have a poor investment performance record. This was demonstrated in the 1973–74 decline and the 1975–76 recovery of stock price indexes from their 1974 lows. In this respect the reader should examine the stock price record of such "growth stocks" as Eastman Kodak, Xerox, Polaroid, and IBM relative to the market indexes in 1975–76 and in 1977 and 1978.

It is human nature (and both individual investors and the managers of institutional funds have proven to be very human in their emotions and psychology) to desire to get in on the ground floor of what is or appears to be a fast-growing industry. But the higher the projected growth rate and the more investment commitments are based on the expected continuation of such exceptionally high growth rates well into the future, the greater the risk that such projections will not be realized and that stock prices will overdiscount growth.

Industries with a Poorer-Than-Average Record or a Recent Sharp Decline. There have always been industries and companies that, at least for some time, perhaps only a year or two or perhaps for many years, have posted a record in terms of gross revenues and net profits that is inferior to that of the growth of the economy and corporate profits overall. There are also cases when in spite of at least an "average" past record, investors anticipate that the future record will be relatively poor. For the above reasons, at any point of time these industries and companies in these industries are "out of favor" with investors; both individual and institutional investors tend to reject such stocks, at least as far as new investments are concerned.

In many cases, although not all cases, such industries and companies have at least partially recovered favor with investors, providing opportunities for substantial capital gains if their securities were purchased at levels reached when they were distinctly out of favor. Outstanding examples of return to favor in recent years are the coal industry, the motion picture companies for which TV was expected to provide the death knell, the auto industry, which in 1973-74 was heavily out of favor,[2] and even tobacco stocks, which were supposed to enter permanent decline because of the Surgeon General's initial and subsequent report and related pressures.

The automobile industry in 1973-74 provides an excellent illustration of an industry that posted a poor record for a short period, although the long-term record tended to parallel the growth of GNP. For example, General Motors and Ford stocks both declined from about 85 to 28 during the sharp market break in 1973-74. Ford recovered to about 45 in 1975 and 62 in 1976. GM was about 59 in 1975 and rose to 79 in 1976-77. Conversely, the steel, chemical, and ethical drug industries were relatively and distinctly out of favor with investors in 1977.

Industries with a Long Mediocre or Poor Record. Some industries have had a poor record and have been out of favor for some years; they may be expected to do little better in the future than in the past (for example, the cement industries). Such industries may be in the stage of decline. However, in some cases after a long record of deterioration a revival has provided interesting opportunities for investors who projected a significant recovery for a long out-of-favor industry. Again, the coal industry is a real example.

Industries with Difficulties Exaggerated by Performance Pressures. When industries have problems and are out of favor, performance pressures are often so strong that many investors do not take the time to make an industry analysis in depth to determine objectively and unemotionally the longer-term industry prospects. There has been so much emphasis by Wall Street in recent years on short-term performance (even monthly and quarterly) that industries suffering even a temporary setback tend to be sold and/or ignored. They tend to be neglected in terms of objective in-depth analysis to determine the longer term prospects. The pressure for short-term performance on portfolio managers as well as on brokers has been especially strong in

---

[2] The auto industry was again out of favor in early 1982, and some question its ability to regain market share lost to foreign competitors. See "Weak Auto Sales Cause U.S. Firms to Retrench Clouding Their Future," *The Wall Street Journal*, December 3, 1981, pp. 1, 20.

the 1970s following the excellent performance that generally paralleled the market averages in the 1950s and through 1965 to February 1966.

At any point in time those industries that are currently out of favor with investors include some that correctly deserve this judgment, but there are also those that do not deserve the very low rating they are currently receiving. Investors should make a careful industry appraisal in an effort to locate at least one major industry (and major companies in that industry) in which, in their judgment, the current difficulties are only temporary. The investor may decide that, over the longer term, their long-term satisfactory record will continue and that therefore they are distinctly undervalued in the market, offering relatively safe and substantial capital gains potentials. These stocks are usually available at low P/E ratios and high yields, e.g., auto stock in 1974.

Major Emphasis in Industry Analysis

The major emphasis in industry analysis should be on an economic analysis of the demand and supply factors for the industry, including a careful analysis of potential competition and the price prospects for the industry's products or services—all within projected short- and long-term trends for the economy.

Industry Specialists

While industry analysis is often ignored, competent specialists have developed among financial analysts for the large brokerage firms and institutional investors. There are chemical, drug, aerospace, automobile, steel, paper, and many other industry specialists. Many of these specialists are highly competent but tend to have a "constitutional weakness"; i.e., they tend almost always to favor their industry and its prospectus. Of course, in the final analysis the crucial ingredient for success is the *judgment* of the analyst applied to the facts. Techniques in analysis may be taught and learned, but judgment to project satisfactorily is the result of a combination of knowledge, experience, skill, and native ability.

In addition to being concerned primarily with the long-term outlook for the industry, the industry specialist should also be knowledgeable concerning the development of major problems that could adversely affect industry sales and profits over the next one or two years, and therefore stock prices over the short term as well as the intermediate and long term. Investors should use industry specialists' facts and their interpretation of those facts; then, realizing the tendency of industry specialists to favor their industry, investors should make their own interpretations and judgments.

Illustrative Industry Analysis

Part I of a report on "General Motors Corporation in the World Automobile Market"[3] provides an excellent example of an industry analysis. This industry analysis, outlined on page 620, covers the demand side of the automobile industry for both domestic and foreign markets. (The supply side of the industry is given in Part II of this report, outlined on page 623.) An industry analysis is a study of demand and supply forces and their relation to prices of the industry's products and services. Note that the analysis is summarized *only* to suggest an analytical framework, not to offer currently useful material for assessing auto companies.

Demand-Supply Analysis. In the case of the automobile industry, the major emphasis is on demand analysis, that is, industry projections of domestic and worldwide demand for automobiles and trucks.[4] While emphasis on demand is usually the case in most industries, it is

---

[3] "General Motors Corporation in the World Automobile Market," a professional industrial report consisting of 107 printed pages, was included in a Staff Analysis, Subcommittee on Domestic Finance, Committee on Banking and Currency, House of Representatives, 88th Congress, 2nd Session (Washington, D.C.: U.S. Government Printing Office, 1966).

[4] In the report on General Motors, the following industry projections of unit demand and sales were made:

Industry New Car Sales Projections Future Rate of Growth 4%		Industry Projected Annual Truck Demand Future Rate of Growth 3.5%	
Annual Unit Sales		Unit Demand	
1965	7,525,000[a] 7,900,000[b] 8,274,000[c]	1965	1,210,000[d] 1,277,000[e] 1,348,000[f]
1970	9,155,000[a] 9,611,000[b] 10,067,000[c]	1970	1,432,000[d] 1,417,000[e] 1,601,000[f]

[a] Assume scrappage rate of 6.2% of rejected autos   [d] Assuming 5.1% scrappage rate
[b] Assume scrappage rate of 6.7% of rejected autos   [e] Assuming 5.6% scrappage rate
[c] Assume scrappage rate of 7.2% of rejected autos   [f] Assuming 6.1% scrappage rate

	Industry (cars)	G.M. (cars)	G.M.%
Actual 1965 unit sales (millions)	9.3	4.9	53.0%
Actual 1966 unit sales (millions)	8.5	4.4	51.8%
Actual 1967 unit sales (millions)	7.5	4.1	54.7%
Actual 1968 unit sales (millions)	8.6	4.5	52.3%
Actual 1969 unit sales (millions)	8.5	4.4	51.8%
Actual 1970 unit sales (millions)	7.1	3.3	46.5%
Actual 1971 unit sales (millions)	8.7	4.7	54.0%
Actual 1972 unit sales (millions)	9.3	4.8	51.7%
Actual 1976 unit sales (millions)[a]	10.2	4.9	48.0%

[a] Domestic factory sales including exports, not including foreign imports.

especially true in the automobile industry where about 95 percent of domestic sales by U.S. manufacturers are made by only three manufacturers: General Motors, with about 56.6 percent of industry sales; Ford, with about 28 percent; and Chrysler, with about 13.5 percent in 1977.[5] In the case of worldwide sales, General Motors accounts for about 30 percent, Ford about 20 percent, and Chrysler about 10 percent. The other major world automobile manufacturers are Toyota, Datsun, and Honda (Japanese); Volkswagen and Mercedes-Benz (West German); and Volvo, Fiat, Renault, Peugeot, and Simca (other European). By 1968 Japan surpassed West Germany and has become the number two country in world automobile production, exporting significantly to the United States as does West Germany. Foreign car sales represented about 20 percent of total car sales in the United States in 1977.

The supply segment of an industry analysis includes an analysis of the competitive and cost aspects of the industry. In the General Motors report, the supply analysis consisted of a comparison of General Motors' sales with those of its competitors—domestic and worldwide. In other industries, such as steel, the supply side of the analysis is more difficult because of the relatively large number of suppliers, both domestic and foreign, and also because of the importance of foreign imports or exports in the supply picture.[6] In still other industries, the sources of raw materials and their amount, location, and control are very important. The oil industry is a prime example.

---

[5] American Motors accounted for only about 2 percent.
[6] Steel imports represented about 20 percent of industry sales in the U.S. in 1977.

General Motors Corporation
in the World Automobile Market

An Investment Analysis

Part I. The World Automobile and Commercial Vehicle Markets
    A. Future Domestic Automobile Demand
        1. Domestic Demography
            Growth
            Age Structure and Household Formations
            Dispersion
        2. Economic Growth and Living Standards
            Gross National Product
            Personal Disposable Income
        3. Future Modes of Surface Transportation
            The Private Automobile and the Common Carrier
            Highway Improvement

Price Analysis. After completing the supply and demand study, the analyst must determine the past, current, and future price trends for the industry's products and services. While these prices are usually the result of the interaction of the demand and supply schedules, the factor of government intervention in pricing is also of concern. This has been demonstrated in the case of the tobacco, steel, aluminum, copper, and drug industries. Foreign cartel operations approved by foreign governments are a case in point—for example, coffee and oil in the years 1975–76. Taking all factors into consideration, the analyst attempts to project industry product prices (or at least a price range) as well as volume in order to arrive at projections for industry and company dollar sales. The out-of-favor aspects of the aluminum, paper, airline, steel, and food chain industries all reflected pricing problems in the mid-1970s.

COMPANY ANALYSIS

The illustration of a company analysis given below is useful as the basis for a discussion of various aspects of a company analysis that follows a thorough demand-supply-price industry analysis.

Illustrative Company Analysis

Parts II and III of the report on "General Motors Corporation in the World Automobile Market," outlined below, provide a good illustration of a detailed company analysis. The report includes the supply side of the industry by showing General Motors' position in the industry. The report also includes financial data about the company's capitalization, actual earnings, and projected earnings, as well as the market evaluation of General Motors stock. The financial data indicate the types of information that an analyst should require and analyze in a thorough institutional type of company analysis.

Brief History. Most analysts present a brief history of the company to set the stage for an understanding of the company's current operations and its industry prospects. In this case the company history covers a long span but covers only one and a half pages of the 107-page printed report.

Product or Sales Breakdown. The product or sales breakdown was covered in about five printed pages of text in the General Motors report. The report also presented a tabular breakdown as shown below.

Estimated Breakdown of Sales ($)

U.S. Passenger Cars:	
Chevrolet	30.7%
Pontiac	7.2
Oldsmobile	6.9
Buick	6.1
Cadillac	5.7
U.S. Trucks (Chevrolet and GMC)	8.8
Other U.S. Automobile Parts, etc.	2.8
Total U.S. Automotive	68.2%
Canadian Automotive	4.1
Overseas Operations (including nonautomotive)	14.5
Nonautomotive (Domestic)	10.1
Defense Sales	3.1
Total	100.0%

General Motors Corporation
in World Automobile Market

An Investment Analysis—Concluded

Part II. General Motors Corporation
  A. A Brief History
  B. Product Breakdown
    1. Chevrolet
    2. Buick—Oldsmobile—Pontiac
    3. Cadillac
    4. Fisher Body
    5. Other Accessory Divisions
    6. United Motor Service
    7. General Motors of Canada and McKinnon Industries
    8. Overseas Operations
        German—Adam Opel A.G.
        Great Britain—Vauxhall Motors Limited
        Australia—General Motors Holden Pty. Ltd.
        South American Group
        Miscellaneous Overseas Assembly and Distribution Facilities
    9. Nonautomotive Business
    10. Defense Sales
  C. Financial
    1. General Motors Operating Record
    2. Return on Net Worth and Return on Total Capitalization
    3. Capital Expenditures and Sources of Internal Funds
    4. Capital Expenditures for Special Tools
    5. Earnings of Nonconsolidated Subsidiaries
    6. Earnings from Operations Outside the U.S. and Canada
  D. Long-Term Earnings Projections
  E. Industry Position—Supply Situation in the Industry
  F. Research and Development
  G. Organization, Management, and Operating Philosophy
    1. Operating Divisions
    2. Staff Functions
    3. Policy Formulation
    4. The Central Office
    5. Labor Relations
  H. Distribution Organization and Policies
  I. Antitrust—(potential problems for General Motors)

Part III. Market Evaluation of General Motors Common Stock
  A. Stock Price, Earnings, and Price-Earnings Comparisons
  B. Comparative Valuations—(comparison with other automobile
      companies and the DJIA)

The text of the report included one paragraph on each category in the estimated breakdown, except that there were five paragraphs on overseas operations: one each for Germany, Great Britain, Australia, South American Group, and Miscellaneous Overseas and Distribution Facilities.

Sales breakdowns by products, divisions, and subsidiaries are important, but many companies still do not provide sufficient breakdowns in their annual reports. Analysts must then attempt to secure the information directly from the company. Assistance is being provided in this area—especially in the case of conglomerates.[7] The more information an analyst can obtain in this area, the more reliable the analysis and projections. The rate of growth in sales over a reasonably long time period, the persistence of that growth currently, and the causes provide the bases for sales and earnings projections.

Capital Expenditures—Past, Current, and Planned. To secure growth in earnings, corporations must usually increase their total invested capital and their revenues. Therefore, perhaps the most important job of corporate management is the determination under its capital budgeting program of the size and the direction of its capital expenditures. For many companies corporate capital expenditures are simply aimed at maintaining the corporation's position in its industry, rather than toward finding the most profitable investment opportunities. In any case, the analyst must review past capital expenditures and the rate of return accomplished. Then as much information as possible must be secured on capital budgeting plans and expected rate of return on proposed projects. Admittedly such information (especially long-term projections) is difficult to obtain. This type of information helps in assessing the ability of management to meet changing market demands and perhaps government requirements.

Industry Position. In the case of General Motors, the company has had a dominant position in its industry for many years, with sales representing about 50 percent of industry sales. IBM has for many years enjoyed an even more dominant position in its industry, and Xerox and Polaroid have also enjoyed extremely dominant positions. In other industries a major company may have had a declining dominance; for example, U.S. Steel at one time accounted for 33 percent of sales, but in recent years only 22 to 23 percent. Du Pont gradually lost its promi-

---

[7] The AIPCA *Financial Accounting Standard No. 14* requires companies of all sizes, publicly held or not, to report separately segments of their revenues, profits, and losses of a particular segment representing 10 percent or more of revenues, profits, and losses.

nent position in the chemical industry, and Dow Chemical assumed industry leadership.

Determining the trends of the relative position of each company being analyzed as well as those of other competing corporations is important. In the General Motors report, about one page of text and two pages of tables were devoted to the company's relative industry position. This subject came under the heading of supply analysis and competitive analysis.

Research and Development. Research and development expenditures are necessary (1) to develop and produce new and improved products and services and (2) to maintain a company's competitive position within its own industry, as well as cost efficiencies needed to maintain its industry's position relative to competitive industries. Normally the growth of an industry, especially rapid growth, is closely associated with research and development. Research and development expenditures vary widely by industry in absolute amounts and relative to gross revenues. However, the key factor in research and development is not the amount spent or the number of employees in research or research facilities, but the results of research in terms of added revenues. Therefore, the analyst should seek to determine what percentage of current sales have resulted from company research and development and also, if possible, the direction and the potential of current research expenditures. This is the real test of research and also of superior management. Many corporations give such data in annual reports. Research expenditures declined in the 1970s.

In the case of the automobile industry, the major efforts of research and development are aimed at maintaining or improving industry position by improving the product by operating efficiencies and by meeting government safety, antipollution, and gas mileage requirements. However, in other industries, such as electronics and drugs, for example, research and development expenses are aimed at developing completely new, or at least significantly different, products. The industries that have demonstrated the greatest growth have usually done so as a result of research and development. Therefore, this area cannot be overemphasized

Research and Development in the Financial Statements. Research and development in the financial statements of companies should represent research oriented toward technological innovation, not market research or product testing. Unfortunately, management may be tempted to include the cost of such research in reported "research and development." The analyst must try to determine the nature of the charges, trying to obtain a detailed breakdown to provide a judgment as to likely future results as well as current results.

Technological Forecasting. Technological forecasts as a direction for research is an organized way of predicting future scientific and engineering progress based on past developments. Of course, additional research will continue to develop new technology based on key new discoveries that have not been forecast, such as the transistor, integrated circuitry, the laser, desalinization of seawater, and solar heating.

A panel on research and innovation headed by Robert A. Charpie, president of the Carbide Electronics Division of the Union Carbide Corporation, submitted a report to the government. Some of the conclusions in this report are as follows:

1. "Even a casual reading of the business history of this country makes it clear that these innovative enterprises are an important part of the process that differentiates our rate of progress from that of the rest of the world."
2. The panel selected three technological industries and measured their impact on the economy. "In 1945 . . . the television, jet travel, and digital computer industries were commercially nonexistent. In 1965, these industries contributed more than $13 billion to GNP and an estimated 900,000 jobs; and, very important, affected the quality of our lives."
3. The report demonstrated that research and development expenditures were by no means synonymous with innovation. Research and development typically represented less than 10 percent of the total innovative costs of a new product.
4. The panel noted that a handful of large companies (having 5,000 or more employees) *performed almost all of the research and development* conducted in the nation, although *that was not necessarily indicative of innovative performance.* For example, "of 61 important innovations of the twentieth century, over half of them stemmed from independent inventors or small companies. If, however, innovations come from individuals or small companies, the chief problem is first in attracting venture capital, and then in managing the business as it grows and in marketing the product. (Innovators have often proved to be poor managers.)
5. "The challenge is to explore new ways for large companies to work with small technologically based companies to develop within themselves subenvironments that foster the enthusiasm and entrepreneurial spirit of the small firm while benefiting from the overall resources of the total corporate environment."[8]

Certain other factors have come out in studies of innovation. The most important are as follows:

1. It is a continuous process that appears to evolve from the relatively slow accumulation of pertinent facts.

---

[8] National Association of Manufacturers, *Review of 500 Industry Innovations and How They Came About* (New York: National Association of Manufacturers, 1967).

2. It is most often achieved by scientists engaged actively in solving specific research problems.
3. It frequently requires a decade or more to produce 70–90 percent of research that results in a radical innovation and then only a relatively short time to obtain the final results.[9]

Organization, Management, and Operating Philosophy. Any report should at least briefly describe the company's organization and then should analyze the quality of management and its operating philosophy. In the General Motors report there are five subdivisions of this area: (1) operating divisions, (2) staff functions, (3) policy formulation, (4) the central office, and (5) labor relations.

The board of directors sets company policy, and the operating management executes the policy. Obviously, correct policy is highly important to success. In the case of General Motors, some emphasis has been placed on product diversification outside the automobile industry, but overall, the company's policy has been to place heavy emphasis on the automobile business, which produces the major proportion of the company's profits.

The key to nearly any successful business is the management responsible for operating the company. This is especially important for industrial companies. The reason for General Motors' success can be traced directly to its ability to obtain outstanding administrative talents and to place them in an organizational environment conducive to effective operation.

Tests of Corporate Management. The quality of management is difficult to analyze in qualitative terms. Motivation is often as important as competence. The analyst must determine if existing management has a strong desire to excel, to make the company grow at least as fast as the economy, and to stress earnings and dividend growth.

The final tests of the quality of corporate management must largely rest on comparisons with other companies in the same industry. Of course, the industry itself may have such a poor potential that the investor does not wish to make a commitment in that industry. However, there may be some excellent managements in the industry that still find it impossible to earn a satisfactory rate of return on investment.

Comparative Analysis of Management Performance. The major tests of corporate management that are best for comparative tests of competing companies in the same industry are the rate of return on investment and the growth rate of earnings per share. While growth of

---

[9] Department of Defense, *Project Hindsight* (Washington, D.C.: U.S. Government Printing Office, 1967).

revenues and total earnings are important, the key factor is earnings per share. The analyst must always adjust reported earnings where necessary to determine true earning power.

Numerous studies in recent years have shown that, in many cases, salaries of corporate management show a much greater correlation with volume of sales and size of business than with profits and rate of return on investments. The investor should, however, favor those companies where management clearly by the financial record puts most stress on rate of return on investments.

For U.S. corporations as a whole, corporate net profits reached a post–World War II peak in 1959 ($28.5 billion) and then declined slightly in 1960 and 1961 ($26.7 and $27.2 billion, respectively), reaching a quarterly low at an annual rate of $24.4 billion for the first quarter of 1961. They then rose to a peak of $47.1 billion for 1966, or an increase of 65 percent (1959-1966).[10] There was a 93 percent increase from the first quarter of 1961 ($24.4 billion) to the entire year of 1966 ($47.1 billion). During this period, weekly earnings in manufacturing industries rose only from $88.26 in 1959 to $110.00 in January 1966, or $111.92 for the year 1966. This represented an increase of only 27 percent. Labor cost per unit of output (1957–1959 = 100) was 99.9 in February 1966, and the ratio of price (of product sales) to unit labor costs was 105.0 in the first quarter of 1966 (1957–1959 = 100). Labor costs began to rise more rapidly than productivity in 1967–1970.

Most corporations, therefore, in the period 1959–1966 enjoyed a favorable ratio of labor costs to sales. The result was a spectacular increase in profits. The 1966–1971 profits record, however, was horizontal.

The 1972–1978 rise in profits was quite similar in amplitude to the 1961–1966 rise in profits (see Chapter 18). These were the only two satisfactory periods of rising profits in the 1946–1977 period.

Capitalization and Actual Earnings. These financial data about General Motors corporation are presented in the following form:

Capitalization. The data given below are broken down in detail in a more complete table:

---

[10] Using the 1959-60 average as a base (1959 boom year and 1960 recession year), corporate profits after taxes for "All U.S. Corporations" rose 75 percent to the 1966 level ($26.95 billion to $47.1 billion). Then profits were in a horizontal channel: $44.9 billion in 1967, $46.2 billion in 1968, $43.8 billion in 1969, $37.0 billion in 1970, $44.3 billion in 1971, and finally a new high of $54.6 billion in 1972. In 1972 earnings per share of DJIA and S & P indexes were at new historic highs versus previous highs in 1968, and by 1978 profits for all U.S. corporations estimated at about $116 billion were more than double their 1966 and 1972 levels.

	Book Capitalization[11]
Long-term debt	5.7%
Capital stock:	
Preferred	4.4
Common	89.9
Total	100.0%

Operating Record. The data are presented in the form of a ten-year table with the following headings:

Year	Sales	Net Income	Net Income as % of Sales	Net Income Per Share	Dividends Per Share	Price Range	Average P/E Ratio

Return on Net Worth. The data are presented in the form of a ten-year table with the following headings:

General Motors	Automobile Industry	U.S. Industry Average

Capital Expenditures and Sources of Internal Funds. The data are presented in the form of a ten-year table with the following headings:

Year	Capital Expendi-tures	Depreciation, Depletion, and Amortization	Retained Earnings	Total Internal Funds	Excess (Deficit) Internal Funds to Capital Expenditures	Net Working Capital

Equity in Earnings of Subsidiaries Not Consolidated. The data are presented in a six-year table with the following headings:

Year	Total	Per Share

Earnings from Operations Outside the United States and Canada. The data are presented in a ten-year table with the following headings:

Year	Investment Outside U.S. and Canada	Applicable to Foreign Operations	Net Investments Outside U.S. and Canada	Foreign Income	% of GM's Total Net Income	Per 1960 Common Share

Long-Term Earnings Projections. On the subject of long-term earnings projections, the General Motors report states:

> It is well recognized that realistic analysis requires more than a modest degree of caution in preparing future projections. Any long-term appraisal

---

[11] As suggested in the chapters on financial statement analysis, these percentages should also be shown on the basis of market values—that is, capitalization with common stock at market value and debt and preferred stock at book figures, or perhaps only debt at book value.

of General Motors' earnings per share is dependent upon a magnitude of assumptions which make any result so tenuous as to seriously question its validity. Nevertheless, this report attempts to establish some determining industry criteria in the form of demographic estimates, income projections, highway construction plans, and scrappage rates. This form of projection then establishes an expected business environment for the world vehicle industry. Utilizing this industry base, a projected participating range for General Motors is superimposed thereon, which provides high, medium, and low sales projections. Each of these three projections is then subject to a high and low profit margin estimate and a final net income per share range is derived. These results are conceived as *normal earnings power* ranges. It should be emphasized that cyclical effects have not been considered and no attempt has been made to project the timing or shape of future business cycles. The tables providing for earnings estimates are presented below.

Low, medium, and high sales projections are shown in Table 25-2.

Market Evaluation of Common Stock. Part III of the General Motors report presents comparative data concerning stock price, earnings, and price-earnings ratios. In addition to the financial ratios used in Parts II and III of the General Motors report, most of the financial ratios suggested in Chapters 20 and 22 should be included for comprehensive coverage.

The Problem of Conglomerates

Although the investor analyzing industrial companies has always been faced with the problem that many companies do business in a number of industries through divisions and subsidiaries, the problem assumed major proportions in the late 1960s. The SEC acknowledged the problem by requiring corporations to furnish breakdowns by divisions or subsidiaries where sales breakdowns were considered material in registration statements. To some extent the rush to conglomerates in the 1960s appeared to be somewhat of a fad. Heavy cash flow realized by many companies plus a new breed of innovation- and growth-minded managements led to the trend.

Conglomerates are multi-industry companies. By 1970, twenty-four major multi-industry companies had developed, some of the best known of which were the Olin Corporation, W. R. Grace, International Telephone & Telegraph, Litton Industries, Textron, Gulf & Western Industries, Walter Kidde, and Ling-Temco-Vought. Investors in 1966–1969 were demonstrating an almost feverish desire to own these stocks, paying little attention to the severe problem of analysis and especially to the accounting problems involved in determining net income and its sources.

TABLE 25-2. Earnings Projections Based on Assumptions As to Industry Sales

	Low Sales Projection		Medium Sales Projection		High Sales Projection	
	GM% of Market	I $000,000	GM% of Market	II $000,000	GM% of Market	III $000,000
U.S. auto	45%	$ 8,544	50%	$ 9,480	55%	$10,440
U.S. trucks	37.5	1,110	40	1,209	42.5	1,285
Foreign	12.5	2,185	15	2,622	17.5	3,059
Subtotal		$11,839		$13,311		$14,784
Other U.S. auto		400		500		600
Subtotal		$12,239		$13,811		$15,384
Non-auto 10%		1,225		1,381		1,538
Subtotal		$13,464		$15,192		$16,922
Defense		500		750		1,000
Total sales		$13,964		$15,942		$17,922

	Low	High	Low	High	Low	High
Profit margin	16%	17%	18%	19%	19%	20%
Pretax profit	2,235.7	2,375.4	2,870.0	3,029.0	3,215.2	3,384.4
Net income	1,073.1	1,140.2	1,378.0	1,453.9	1,543.3	1,624.5
Per share	$3.70	$3.93	$4.75	$5.01	$5.00	$5.32

Note: Derived industry production levels:

U.S. automobiles	7.7 million units
U.S. trucks	1.3 million units
Foreign (cars & trucks)	10.1 million units

Source "General Motors Corporation in the World Automobile Market," Staff Analysis, Subcommittee on Domestic Finance, Committee on Banking and Currency, House of Representatives, 88th Congress, 2d Session (Washington: U.S. Government Printing Office, 1966).

After 1968–1970 many conglomerates lost their glamour for investors, particularly as a result of SEC pressure for more informative corporate reporting and also as a result of the Justice Department's statement of intentions to study the area in terms of antitrust. The conglomerate stocks declined much more than the market indexes in the bear markets of 1969–1970 and 1973–1974, and many conglomerates began divesting themselves of previously acquired companies.[12] However, a new merger trend occurred during 1977–1979.

While management is highly important in any industrial company, the demands on management reach their zenith with multi-industry companies. On the positive side, top management skills can be applied cross-industry; but on the negative side, if problems develop simultaneously in several industries in which a conglomerate is engaged, even the highest quality of management may be overtaxed. Investors seemed to assume in the late 1960s that the success of conglomerates was assured just by the nature of the phenomena as they "reported" rapid earnings growth.

Investors should appreciate that as the development of multi-industry companies progressed, the following three types emerged:

1. Really homogeneous multi-industry types such as Eastman Kodak, General Precision Equipment, Air Reduction, Rexall, and Chemetron. The distinguishing feature of these amalgamations is that while they are multi-industry, the extension into other industries appeared as logical branches of existing business and was usually accomplished by the parent constructing and closely controlling plants to serve the additional industry to be included. These companies appear to be the most logical forms and the ones that are relatively less difficult to appraise, although lack of financial information on the separate divisions does cause problems.

    General Electric, National Distillers, Pittsburgh Plate Glass, and the Olin Corporation should probably be included in the homogeneous category because they have all emphasized interexpansion much more than acquisitions, but some analysts class them differently because of their rather broad extension into varied industries.

2. Multi-industry companies that have extended as the result of scientific and technological development of the group as a whole in which there is some correlation between the parts. Examples of this type are Litton, Ling-Temco-Vought, and Lear Siegler. Again, the process appears to have de-

---

[12] Several developments negatively affected the conglomerate stocks in 1969–1970. Chairman Mills of the tax-writing House Ways and Means Committee stated that conglomerates "substantially decrease competition, whether or not the mergers occur in similar lines of business, because of the consolidation of financial power that results." Mr. Mills questioned the wisdom of tax laws that make the use of convertible debentures (interest is tax deductible) highly attractive both to the conglomerate and the acquired company. Chairman Mills proposed that interest on such convertibles be excluded as a tax-deductible expense. Mills's other target was a then-current provision in the tax law that permitted capital gains taxes on such exchanges to be deferred until the convertible debentures were paid off, perhaps in twenty years. Thus the tax deferral was equivalent to an interest-free loan from the Treasury. At the same time the antitrust economists in the Federal Trade Commission argued that conglomerates actually decrease competition because profits from some divisions can be used to subsidize losses of others and drive out competition in those industries. The entry of conglomerates into an industry tended to discourage other entrants. They also implied that conglomerates obtain a position to demand reciprocal tie-in sales.

veloped logically, and the closeness of technical and scientific developments and controls justifies the multi-industry company.

3. The true conglomerates consist of multi-industry firms in which the parent merely or largely limits its activity to financial control and support and very broad policy decisions. The relationship between the separate units of the conglomerates is tenuous to say the least. Examples of this type of multi-industry company are Textron, Ogden Corporation, Automatic Sprinkler, and Gulf & Western Industries.

In the middle and later 1960s, some of the multi-industry companies grew so fast through rapid acquisition that even competent analysts found it highly difficult, if not impossible, to develop accurate earnings projections for these groups, especially because of the lack of divisional reporting. In such cases, how could "average" investors hope to cope with the problem? The answer was that they simply bought on faith—faith in a vogue. One Wall Street analyst made the following comments in regard to analyzing conglomerates:

> Under such volatile conditions it is virtually impossible for investors or even trained security analysts to make accurate earnings projections. At the same time, most of these companies do not fit logically into any one specific industry, thus making "normal" P/E ratio ranges unattainable. A less orthodox approach, therefore, must be used in appraising the prospects of many conglomerate companies.
>
> It narrows down to an evaluation of management—the ability of those executives to continue making favorable acquisitions and to control and develop all existing operations, regardless of how diverse. Subjective assessments of management become the determining factors in setting price-earnings ratios, which in turn reflect profit growth rates which are anticipated.
>
> Some of the factors to be considered in an evaluation of management include:
>
> 1. What has been their track record? That is, how many acquisitions have been made that have not worked out? [What is the proportion in dollars?]
> 2. What financing methods have been employed in making acquisitions? Have expansion benefits been watered down by equity dilution?
> 3. Is growth primarily dependent on continuing acquisitions? What percent of sales are contributed by acqusitions made in the past five years?
> 4. In what direction and how quickly are expansion programs moving?
> 5. How susceptible is the company's expansion policy to the possible loss of a key executive?
> 6. Are immediate earnings per share benefits required in acquisitions or is management willing to wait for profits by building up promising but currently unprofitable situations?[13]

---

[13] Abraham J. Briloff, "Dirty Pooling—How to Succeed in Business," *Barron's*, July 15, 1968.

It came to be realized by many investors that the rise in earnings of many conglomerates was partly an illusion resulting from the fact that if a conglomerate's stock sold at a 20 P/E multiple and it could keep acquiring stocks selling at 10 P/E multiples, the parent's earnings could rise at a faster rate than that of company operations, and partly that the rate of growth had been further accelerated by the use of convertible financing, without disclosing before 1968 the potential dilution inherent in the use of convertibles. Until SEC regulations in 1968 and 1969 required financial reports to disclose the effect of potential dilution from conversion of convertibles, such dilution was largely ignored. This was also true of divisional reporting.

FASB Statement No. 14—Financial Reporting for Segments of a Business Enterprise, effective December 16, 1976, has led to increased divisional reporting among the multi-industry companies because of the requirements concerning the inclusion of "information about the operations and export sales, and its major customers."[14]

SUGGESTED OUTLINE FOR AN ANALYSIS OF AN INDUSTRIAL COMPANY

The following is a suggested outline for a comprehensive analysis of an industrial company, including both an industry and company analysis:

ANALYSIS OF AN INDUSTRIAL COMPANY

Part I—Industry Analysis

A. Economic Importance and Characteristics of Industry
  1. Stage and Development of Industry, Its Life-Cycle Position
  2. Degree of Fluctuation in Industry—Sales, Profits, and Earnings per Share in Relation to Economic Cycles and Life Cycles
  3. Regulation and Control of Industry by Government and Related Problems
  4. Labor Problems in Industry, History of Labor Strife, and Costs
  5. Other Industry Problems—Major and Minor

B. Demand Factors
  1. Nature of Demand for Industry's Products
  2. Past Record of Demand—Correlation with GNP, Disposable Personal Income, and Other GNP Components As Have Proved Relevant
  3. Current Demand
  4. Estimated Future Demand—1 year, 3 years, 5 years, 10 years
  5. Foreign Sales Demand if Pertinent

---

[14] "Statement of Financial Accounting Standards No. 14—Financial Reporting for Segments of a Business Enterprise," *Journal of Accountancy* (February, 1977), p. 99.

C. Supply Factors
   1. Nature of Supply and Competition
   2. Concentration of Supply—Breakdown of Supply by Companies
   3. Estimated Present Industry Capacity—Projection of Industry Capacity
   4. Foreign Competition—Importance and Nature of Imports—Current and Projected
   5. Foreign Competition—Tariffs and Quotas
   6. Patents and Trademarks, of Major or Minor Importance

D. Price Factors
   1. Past Relationship of Supply and Demand Factors and Prices and Government Intervention if Any—Types and Degree of Price Competition
   2. Relationship of Demand to Capacity and to Pricing
   3. Importance of Raw Material Costs
   4. Importance of Labor Costs
   5. Current Pricing Situation and Problems
   6. Estimated Future Pricing Situations Considering Supply and Demand Factors for Next 1, 3, 5, and 10 Years

Part II—Company Analysis

(Comparison with at Least Two Competing Companies in Industry)

A. Economic Analysis
   1. History and Business of Company
   2. Relative Position of Company in Industry—Trend in this Regard vs. Major Competition
   3. Breakdown of Company Sales by Divisions, Subsidiaries, and Affiliates
   4. Management—Senior Level, Second Level, and Junior Level—Executive Development Programs
   5. Labor Problems—History of Labor Strife
   6. Research and Development—New Products—Direction
   7. Capital Expenditures (Past and Projected) and Their Nature
   8. Any Special Problems of Company

B. Financial Analysis—Comparative Statement Analysis for Past 10 Years
   1. Balance Sheet Analysis—Determination of Financial Strength
      a. Working Capital Analysis
      b. Analysis of Other Assets—Fixed Assets—Investments
      c. Analysis of Capitalization—At Book but Common at Market
      d. Off-Balance Sheet Liabilities—Leases, Unfunded Pensions, and Other Similar Liabilities
      e. Book Value—Increase for Past 10 Years, Past 5 Years—Basis of Increase

   2. Income Statement Analysis—All-Inclusive Statement
      a. Sales Breakdown by Products, Divisions, and Subsidiaries
      b. Percent Net Increase in Sales—Trends (Since Base Year)
      c. Sales/Gross Plant—Trend Index (Base Year = 100%)
      d. Capital Expenditures/Sales—Growth Index (Base Year = 100%)
      e. Pretax Operating Profit/Sales—Trends (After Depreciation)

  f. Wages and Salaries/Sales—Index (Base Year = 100%)
  g. Research and Development Expenditures/Sales
  h. Depreciation (Depletion) and Rapid Amortization
  i. Cash Flow and Changes in Financial Position
  j. Interest Coverage on Debt—Actual and Trends from Base Year
  k. Adjustment of Reported Earnings for Nonrecurring Earnings—Per-Share Adjusted Earnings—Growth Record (Base Year = 100%)
  l. Cash Flow Per Share—Growth Record (Base Year = 100%)
 m. Projection of Earnings for Next 1, 3, and 5 Years—Estimated Range, High and Low

3. Balance Sheet Ratios[15]
  a. Working Capital
   (1) Current Ratio
   (2) Quick Ratio
   (3) Cash and Cash Items to Current Liabilities
   (4) Net Working Capital Per Dollar of Sales—Actual and Trends vs. Base Year
  b. Capitalization
   (1) Book Capitalization and Market Capitalization (Debt Book)
   (2) Extent of Trading on Equity and Leverage—Effect

4. Income Statement Ratios
  a. Growth Ratios from Base Year or Period
   (1) Dollar Net Sales—Compound Annual % Rate of Growth
   (2) Dollar Net Profit—Compound Annual % Rate of Growth
   (3) Dollar Earnings Per Share—Compound Annual % Rate of Growth
  b. Stability Ratios—Record in Poor Business Years—Volatility
   (1) Dollar Net Sales—Decline %
   (2) Dollar Net Profit—Decline %
   (3) Earnings Per Share—Decline %
   (4) Fixed Charge Coverage on Debt—Actual and Decline % in Years of Poor Business
   (5) Preferred Stock Coverage—Overall Basis—Actual and Decline % in Years of Poor Business
  c. Profit Ratios
   (1) Net Profit After Taxes As Percent of Sales—Actual and Trend
   (2) Net Profit on Total Capital Funds—Actual and Trend
   (3) Net Profit on Stockholders' Equity—Actual and Trend
  d. Payout Ratios
   (1) Dividends Per Share—% of New Income
   (2) Dividends Per Share—% of Cash Flow
  e. Price-Earnings Ratios—Trend vs. Industry and DJIA or S&P 425
  f. Dividend Yields—Trend vs. Industry and DJIA or S&P 425
  g. Earnings Yield—Trend vs. Industry and DJIA or S&P 425

---

[15] Refer to Chapters 20 and 22 for complete balance sheet and income statement ratios to be used.

5. Market Price of Shares—Annual Range Past 10 Years Adjusted for Stock Splits and Stock Dividends and the Effect on Reported Earnings

Summary

The term industrial securities covers the largest group of investment securities and is a large and dissimilar array, not a homogeneous group. In fact, one could say that it includes all types of securities not placed by the investment community in other specific groups such as the transportation securities, utilities, commercial banks, savings and loan associations, and insurance companies. In Chapter 20 we reviewed some of the historical background for industries, including their past record and future plans.

One method of characterizing industries is to place each in one of four groups: (1) mature industries, into which most industries fall, (2) growth industries, (3) industries with a poorer than average record, and (4) industries which have suffered a recent sharp decline. In the post–World War II years investors have favored the growth industries, have tended to neglect the mature industries, and have sharply rejected those industries that have posted a poor record or a recent sharp decline. The result has been a tendency to overvalue in the market industries accepted as growth industries and to undervalue, especially in cyclical market downturns, securities classified in the other groups. In our judgment the latter situation has presented numerous instances of underaction with potentials for significant capital gains. Automobile stocks in 1974 are a primary example of such undervaluation.

Before an analysis is made of a particular company, the investor should carefully analyze in depth the industry in which a company operates to determine whether or not any investment should be made in that industry. It is really a demand, supply, price, cost analysis together with future projections. Once the industry analysis has been completed, including projections of sales and earnings for the industry, then the investor can proceed to analyze companies in that industry, assuming that the industry analysis justifies commitment in that industry.

The company analysis reviews the past record of the company in absolute terms and relative to its industry, its competitors, and also the current situation. The financial statements are reviewed to determine trends, and then an analysis is made of the causes for the trends in terms of such major factors as management, including corporate organization, research and development, and the nature of capital expenditures.

The conclusions of the analysis are projections of revenues and earnings, dividends, and cash flow for a period of five years. The analyst then determines at what price the company's securities would represent a sound value, taking into consideration all of the above factors, especially projections of earnings, dividends and cash flow, and their quality.

Questions

1. (a) How are industrial securities defined?
   (b) What are the major groups of industrial securities?
   (c) Relatively how important are manufacturing corporations in the industrial group?
2. (a) Define a growth industry.
   (b) Could a growth industry possibly be an out-of-favor industry? Discuss.
3. What dangers does an investor face by concentrating on purchasing securities of companies classified as being in rapid-growth industries in the securities markets?
4. (a) Discuss opportunities in low price-earnings ratios in out-of-favor industries.
   (b) Why is the current stress on performance by institutional managers likely to create additional opportunities for the alert investor?
5. (a) Explain the importance of industry demand and supply forces for the security analyst.
   (b) How are these related to industry prices and profits?
6. Discuss the likely effect of a sharp dip in the economy on sales, profits, and the market price of common shares of
   (a) A tobacco company.
   (b) A sugar company.
   (c) A machine tool producer, automobile producer, or steel producer.
   (d) A public utility
7. (a) What should the analyst attempt to learn about the management team?
   (b) How can an analyst evaluate management?
8. (a) How important are research and development expenditures in American industry?
   (b) What are some of the analyst's problems in this area?
   (c) What items in the area of research expenditures should be investigated by the analyst?
9. What special problems do conglomerates pose for the analyst?

Work-Study Problems

1. (a) Select a company showing a growth trend of earnings noticeably higher than the average for all corporations (at least twice the average growth rate) for the DJIA or S&P 400.
   (b) Tabulate the earnings of this company on a *per-share basis* over the last ten years.

(c) Tabulate the annual per-share earnings of Standard & Poor's 400 Industrial Companies for the last ten years and discuss the record.

(d) Calculate the percentage of the earnings of your company in each year to the per-share earnings of Standard & Poor's 400 companies.

(e) Obtain the mean price-earnings ratio of your company. See "Standard & Poor's Year-End (monthly) Stock Guide," or the "Commercial and Financial Chronicle," or "Bank and Quotation Record" for each year.

(f) Divide the annual mean price-earnings ratio of your company by the annual mean price-earnings ratio of Standard & Poor's 400 companies.

2. Assume that you, as a securities broker, are approached by L. W. Jones and asked to buy stock in Jones Food Systems, Inc., which is described to you as follows:

Jones Food Systems, Inc. will be a new company organized to manufacture and sell precooked meals. These meals will be prepared on disposable plates and will be sold at retail for $1 per plate. A variety of foods have been tested for consumer acceptance, including the following:

> Swiss Steak, Gravy
> Filet Mignon, Bordelaise Sauce
> Roast Lamb, Gravy
> Chicken a la King, Sauce

The above plates are ready to serve by heating for a short time. The plan is to sell these precooked meals to airlines, railroads, hotels, restaurants, bus lines, and even institutional buyers. In addition, it is believed that homemakers will constitute an enormous market.

Extensive experiments have been made, and six chemists or food technologists have been employed. The company plans to lease quarters from the Ranger Packing Company at Newark, New Jersey. This location will have the advantage of assuring the supplies of vegetables. The meats will be purchased in the open market.

Estimates are that $4,000,000 will be needed to start this business, as follows:

Plant	$ 700,000
Equipment	700,000
Working capital to finance inventories (including 6 months' supply of vegetables and 43 days' supply of meats) payroll, and other requirements in initial stage of operation	2,000,000
Research, advertising, and sales promotion	600,000
	$4,000,000

To raise this money, 400,000 shares of stock are to be sold at $10 a share. The promoter, L. W. Jones, is to have 50,000 shares for his services to the company.

The management of this enterprise is to be headed by Jones, who is 46 years old. An electrical engineer and a graduate of the United States Naval Academy, Jones founded his own company in 1949 to manufacture a pressure gauge he had invented. His company also manufactures electrical combines and power drives. L. W. Jones & Company's stock was initially sold at $5 a share by well-known investment bankers and is now worth $45 a share and earning $2.03 a share. He desires to expand his interest by manufacturing food processing machines and selling them to Jones Food Systems, Inc. He will be president of this new concern and will receive a $40,000 salary per annum.

Jones will be assisted by Jennifer W. Smith as vice-president and director. Smith is at present vice-president and general manager of a camera company. She will receive a salary of $35,000. Harriet Holt, who is now treasurer of L. W. Jones & Company, will be treasurer and secretary of the new company. The directors will include Gordon A. Stuffer of Stuffer Restaurant Co.; Nancy J. Henderson, a banker; and John Peters, a hotel manager. William Grimes, another director, is a friend of Jones.

(a) Assuming that you or your client can afford to put money into such a venture, list the reasons for and against participating in its financing on the basis of the above description.

(b) What additional information would you require?

(c) How would you obtain this information?

3. (b) Calculate the price-earnings (most recent earnings) ratios of the companies (which you select) for a ten-year period.

(b) Calculate the price-earnings (most recent earnings) ratios of the companies.

(c) Chart the growth rate and the price-earnings ratio to determine the correlation.

Note: Correlation may be determined roughly by drawing a line through the dots or by the following equations:

$$\Sigma(Y) = Na + b\Sigma(X);$$
$$\Sigma(XY) = a\Sigma X + b\Sigma(X)^2 .$$

If the equations are used to determine the estimating equation, the degree of relationship can be measured by determining the coefficient of correlation (r^2).

4. Select for study two companies with markedly disparate price-earnings ratios at a given point in time. Write a report covering each of the following items:

(a) How do you explain the widely different P/E ratios accorded the two companies by investors? That is, why are investors willing to pay so much more for a current reported dollar of earnings of one company than the other?

(b) Forecast earnings per share and dividends paid per share for five years. Determine the present value for each stock using these forecasts and a limited-hold present value model as discussed in Chapter 7.

(c) Which company appears to be the most desirable investment in light of your personal circumstances, including your ability to bear risk?

26.

Regulated Industries: Utilities

The general legal and economic classification of public utilities includes, among others, (1) electric light and power companies, (2) companies supplying natural or manufactured gas, either pipeline companies or direct operating companies, (3) telephone, telegraph, and other companies supplying communication services, (4) companies supplying water, and (5) railroads and other transportation companies.

In the financial community transportation companies are placed in a separate classification for separate analysis, and accordingly they will be discussed in the next chapter. Because electric utilities represent by far the major segment of investor interest in public utilities, they will be emphasized in this chapter. Space limitations permit only limited coverage of other types of utilities, such as gas and communication companies and water companies, that are nonetheless of significant importance in the investment field.

THE PUBLIC UTILITY INDUSTRY

Public utility companies are required to meet the demands for service of all users, irrespective of fluctuation in demand. This, of course, requires maintenance of capacity to meet peak loads, with certain amounts of idle capacity at other times.

Characteristics of Public Utility Companies

Public utility companies can be identified by the following salient features:

1. They are affected with a public interest. Their service is a necessity for a large segment of the economy, and public utilities must meet public demand.
2. They operate under conditions where direct competition is generally not practical, although there may be competition between services, such as electric versus gas service for heating.

3. Because of the above factors, utilities are subject to broad regulation (especially rate regulation) by one or more governmental bodies or agencies.
4. Production of services is simultaneous with customer use and, unlike industrial companies, there is no inventory problem and a minimum of "receivables" problems.

Territory Served. The territory served by a public utility is carefully defined by the franchises and certificates of necessity under which regulated companies operate. The analyst must carefully analyze the economics of the areas served as well as the geographic, physical, and atmospheric environment. Costs of operation, as for example, maintenance for railroads, are generally affected by physical and atmospheric environment.

Capitalization and Securities. Regulators generally must approve the type of capitalization, the type of securities issued, and each sale of securities, including the method of sale and type of securities issued and their specific characteristics, as well as the use to which funds will be put.

Management. Although management of regulated industries operates within a narrower decision scope than does management of industrial companies, management is still important, especially in its relations with the regulators and in the area of operations, such as efficiencies and ability and willingness to provide satisfactory service whenever and wherever needed. Labor relations are another important factor. Perhaps the most serious problem other than in the area of actual operations is public relations and related environmental problems.

Regulation of the Public Utility Industry

An analysis of a utility company should begin with an analysis of the regulatory climate, followed by an economic and financial analysis of the company. Unless the regulatory climate is satisfactory, the analyst should not proceed further. To a major extent, earnings of utility companies are actually determined by regulatory authorities who must approve all rate changes.

Because utility companies are often natural monopolies that supply a necessary service to the public, it is universally recognized that they must be subject to government regulation. Electric utility companies are domiciled in the state in which they operate and are subject to regulation by state public utility commissions. States and local authorities with power delegated to them by their state regulate intrastate utilities.[1]

---

[1] See Moody's *Public Utilities Manual* for information concerning regulating authorities and the National Association of Railroad & Public Utility Commissioners.

Regulation covers a broad area, the most important part of which concerns rates, but also including service rendered, purchase and sale of assets, issuance of securities, and a uniform accounting system. Utilities are required to conform to the uniform system of accounts to which most state utility commissions have subscribed. An excellent utility will make every effort to maintain good relations with its regulatory commission. However, at some point it may have to apply to the courts for approval of rate increases if the commission refuses to sanction equitable rates that would yield a fair return on the fair value of the property and that provide sufficient income to maintain the financial standing of the company's securities in the capital markets. The U.S. Supreme Court has the final decision in rate cases involving the question of fair return.

Franchises and Certificates of Necessity. Contracts between the state (and local subdivisions) and public utilities authorize a particular utility to operate in a particular territory. Contracts may be perpetual, indeterminate, or limited in time. If a utility operates under a definitive term, questions may arise as the terminal date approaches concerning its renewal or at least the characteristics of the new contracts. A utility's bonds should not mature beyond the terminal date. In recent years the trend has been toward indeterminate life franchises continuing as long as service is satisfactory.

Federal Regulation. Several agencies of the federal government are involved in the regulation of utilities as outlined below.

1. The Interstate Commerce Commission regulates the rates, service standards, financing and accounting of railroads, trucking companies and buses engaged in interstate business.
2. The Federal Energy Regulatory Commission regulates those electric utilities that use power from navigable streams as well as other users of these streams and rivers. It also governs utilities regularly transporting electricity and gas across state lines. Regulation includes approval of rates for electric power and gas crossing state lines, approval of mergers and securities acquisitions by such companies and issuance of certificates for construction of interstate natural gas pipelines. Companies must file financial reports with the Energy Information Administration.
3. The Federal Communications Commission determines the rates and controls the accounts and basic practices of telephone and telegraph companies engaged in interstate commerce as they apply to the interstate activities of these companies.
4. The Securities and Exchange Commission, under the Public Utility Act of 1935, regulates public utility electric and gas holding companies that control operating companies in more than one state. Control is exercised over capital structures, financing and accounting of registered public utility hold-

ing companies in conjunction with State Regulation Commissions and their subsidiary operating companies.

5. The Civil Aeronautics Board regulates the air transport industry with authority over routes, schedules, rates, services, safety standards, accounting, mergers and acquisitions, and intercorporate relations.[2]

6. Proposals in connection with the new U.S. Department of Energy were the first attempt by the federal government to regulate overall rates the U.S. charges on both a retail and wholesale basis overriding state and local regulations. (Legislation recommended by House and Senate Conference, Nov.–Dec. 1977.)

The National Association of Railroad and Utility Commissions adopted a revised uniform system of accounts for electric and gas utilities in 1961. The Federal Energy Regulatory Commission requires essentially the same system for hydroelectric companies and utility companies that come under its jurisdiction. Other types of utility companies are also required to use a uniform system of accounting. Uniform accounting is a real aid to financial analysis of utility companies because the analyst can assume that accounts identified by similar names represent identical items as between utilities. However, although there is uniform accounting, there is a considerable divergence in actual accounting practices in published reports—for example, flow-through versus normalizing for depreciation methods, depending on state commissions.

Importance of Regulation to Investors. It has been noted that the regulatory climate in which a utility must operate is of vital importance to the investor, especially because of the effect of regulation on rates and service standards and on rate of return on investment. The rates charged must be approved by the regulatory commission, and the rates charged times the units sold determine the gross income of the utility. The utility has control over its costs but not its revenues. An electric utility company is permitted to earn a fair return on the fair value of its property used in the public service but is not guaranteed such a return.

The *Hope Natural Gas* decision by the U.S. Supreme Court in 1944 has been interpreted as releasing the regulatory commissions from the necessity of adhering to any specific method of determining the rate base. The method used by a commission in determining utility rate base valuation is no longer subject to judicial (U.S. Supreme Court) review. Rather, the overall effect of the rates charged on the company's credit

---

[2] Effective early January 1978, Congress legislated deregulation of rates and routes for air cargo carriers. The Civil Aeronautics Board still has the power to alter "predatory" or "discriminatory" pricing. Deregulation of passenger fares was being proposed as was also deregulation of rates applying to interstate truck and bus companies. In all cases, the industries concerned were fighting deregulation of rates claiming that cutthroat competition would result from deregulation.

standing in the capital markets has become the crucial issue. As most utilities are frequently in the capital markets to secure funds for expansion, the ability to secure their funds at a reasonable competitive cost is crucial and was so recognized by the Court (the cost-of-capital approach).

Methods of determining a fair rate of return vary widely. Some commissions use the accounting and statistical approach, while others have considered the rising cost of new money. There is also evidence in decisions of the recognition of "attrition" in earnings resulting from inflation (or the effect of inflation on the rate base).

Rate of Return on Rate Base. Utilities are permitted to charge rates that will produce the rate of return on their asset rate base approved by the regulatory commission. The allowed rate of return varies among states. In general, the spread ranges from a low in some states of 5 percent, to a high in some states of 10 percent, with an average range of 5 to 7 percent.

The relatively few so-called growth utilities have had two major factors that contributed to growth in earnings greater than that of the industry overall: (1) a favorable regulatory climate—average rate of return of 7.3 percent—on their rate base and (2) the advantage of operating in a rapidly growing economic area, such as Florida and Texas. Both factors need to be present. For example, in spite of the exceptionally rapid population and economic growth in California after World War II, the regulatory climate was not very satisfactory, as the rate of return on the rate base tended to be held to an annual $5\frac{1}{2}$ percent. Therefore, California electric utility companies did not demonstrate nearly as high an earnings growth rate as did the Florida and Texas utilities in the post–World War II years, and this was reflected in stock prices.

In economic growth areas utilities must expand their plants rapidly, which means frequent trips to the capital markets for relatively large sums of capital. Regulatory commissions in states like Florida and Texas wanted to be sure that utilities under their jurisdiction would meet an excellent response to their demands for funds in the capital markets at relatively low costs; therefore, they tended to permit relatively high rates of return on the utility rate base.

The investor must know the rate of return permitted in the state where the utility under analysis operates, as well as whether there has been a trend up or down. The investor should also be familiar with the political climate in the state in regard to the utility commission or the probability of a change in the regulatory climate as a result of a changing political environment.

Of course, the rate base is as important as the allowed rate of return on the rate base. The investor should thus know the principle on which the commission calculates the rate base. For example, a rate base esti-

mated on historical cost would be much lower than one based on repro-
duction cost or one that recognized the effect of inflation on property
values.

Rate of Return on Investment. For electric utilities rates of return
on total invested capital and stockholders' equity were generally satisfactory up to 1970. However, during 1970–1975 a serious lag developed
between inflationary cost increases (particularly costs of fuel, costs of
construction, and interest costs for new financing and refinancing) and
rate increases. As a result, the rates of return on investment and the
amount available to meet fixed charges and provide a return for stockholders fell to unsatisfactory levels from the standpoint of the investor,
and this was reflected in the securities markets. The number of times
fixed charges were earned for the industry overall fell well below two
times, interest costs rose to 9 to 10 percent, and common stocks of
many utilities fell below book values and sold at yields as high as 10
to 11 percent. After 1975 substantial rate relief was granted in a
majority of cases, and the rates of return began to return to satisfactory
levels, which in time was reflected in the securities market (see Table
26-1).

Table 26-1 contrasts key profitability and growth measures for the
utility industry and all corporations covered in the Forbes study. It is
not difficult to understand why utility stocks, on average, have such
low P/E ratios and have shown relatively low, or no growth, in price
over the past decade. They earn less on capital employed and have
shown insignificant earnings per share growth. They are mainly bought
on the basis of the relatively high dividend yield these stocks offer. Util-

TABLE 26-1. Profitability and Growth Measures, 1976–1980

	Profits After Taxes to:		Five-Year Average Growth in:	
	Stockholders' Equity	Total Capital	Sales	Earnings Per Share
Utilities Serving:				
The Northeast	11.5	6.6	12.9	3.3
The Midwest	11.8	6.2	15.1	2.1
The Southeast	12.1	6.6	16.1	2.9
The Southwest	14.0	7.4	19.8	6.0
The West	11.8	6.6	15.8	2.7
All Industry Medians	15.5	10.9	14.0	12.5

Source: "34th Annual Report on American Industry," *Forbes,* January 4, 1982,
pp. 104–108.

ity stock prices are highly sensitive to interest rate changes, and investors can purchase them for capital gain purposes when they believe interest rates will decline significantly.

FINANCIAL ANALYSIS OF ELECTRIC UTILITIES

When valuing corporate securities, the most important element will always be the financial strength of the company, the rate and stability of growth (past, current, and expected) of earnings, cash flow and dividends, and trends of these factors. Tests and standards applied to financial statements and supplementary schedules are all aimed at determining the foregoing factors.

Balance Sheet Analysis

The analysis of important items on the balance sheets of public utility companies is discussed in the following paragraphs.

Working Capital. Current assets include no inventories of finished goods, and the threat of discontinuance of service is sufficient to keep most receivables current. Therefore, the normal current ratios is only about one to one (for example, see the balance sheet for American Electric Power Company in Table 26-2). Current assets are included in a utility's rate base, but the amount is strictly limited to what public utility commissions generally consider to be a reasonable working relationship. Funds obtained in the capital market for construction purposes are not included in current assets for rate base purposes, but a reasonable cost allowance for such funds is permitted to be capitalized and added to the rate base and credited (as a noncash item) to income.

Utility Plant.[3] The great majority of a utility company's assets (82 percent for American Electric Power) are fixed assets: net plant and equipment. The gross plant will generally amount to about four times annual gross revenues and net plant about three and one half times annual revenues for steam plants and six to seven times for hydroelectric plants. Plant capacity should provide reserves at peak loads of at least 15 percent for steam plants and 12 percent for hydroelectric plants.

---

[3] Because of the difficulties of the utilities to earn a fair rate of return in the early 1970s, and the problems with ecologists and uncertainty of the nation's energy program and related energy requirements, the statement in the 1976 American Electric Power Company's annual report is pertinent: "The margin between our power supply and needs of our customers will become increasingly slim towards the latter part of the 1970s or early 1980s. This is a condition generally prevalent across the country and is obviously a matter of great concern."

TABLE 26-2. Consolidated Balance Sheet for American Electric Power Company (dollars in thousands)

	December 31,	1976	1975
Assets and Other Debits			
Utility Plant:			
Production		$3,193,931	$3,168,282
Transmission		1,396,366	1,354,367
Distribution		1,141,032	1,055,124
General and Miscellaneous		346,831	329,213
Construction Work in Progress		1,060,698	737,977
Total Utility Plant		7,138,858	6,644,963
Less Accumulated Provisions for Depreciation and Depletion		1,464,989	1,310,810
Utility Plant, less Provisions		5,673,869	5,334,153
Excess of Cost of Investments in Subsidiaries			
Over Book Value at Dates of Acquisition (not being amortized)		48,428	48,428
Other Property and Investments		224,378	217,388
Current Assets:			
Cash		195,688	166,573
Temporary Cash Investments (at cost which approximates market)		66,637	67,937
Accounts Receivable—Largely from Customers (less provisions for uncollectibles)		155,831	138,834
Materials and Supplies (at average cost or less):			
Fuel		176,279	155,774
Construction and Operation Materials and Supplies		84,789	77,335
Accrued Utility Revenues		59,054	47,482
Prepayments and Other Current Assets		15,143	23,662
Total Current Assets		753,421	677,597

TABLE 26–2. Consolidated Balance Sheet for American Electric Power Company (dollars in thousands) *(continued)*

	December 31,	1976	1975
Deferred Debits:			
Property Taxes		54,429	51,927
Deferred Collection of Fuel Costs		28,802	26,873
Other Deferred Debits		96,132	52,837
Total Deferred Debits		179,363	131,637
Totals		$6,879,459	$6,409,203
Liabilities and Other Credits			
Long-Term Debt (less portion due within one year)		$3,352,207	$3,088,223
Preferred Stocks of Subsidiaries (including premiums)		536,718	536,758
Common Stock of American Electric Power Company, Inc. Par Value $6.50		604,500	539,500
Stock Dividend Declared		—	—
Premium on Common Stock		804,845	637,845
Other Paid-in Capital		581	565
Retained Earnings		554,617	495,311

Current Liabilities:		
Long-term Debt Due Within One Year	121,647	118,331
Short-term Debt (including Sinking Fund Requirements)	254,119	344,520
Accounts Payable	146,790	118,104
Taxes Accrued	118,981	110,460
Interest Accrued	64,424	64,538
Revenue Refunds Accrued	1,856	44,308
Other Current Liabilities	71,936	77,032
Total Current Liabilities	779,753	877,293
Deferred Credits and Operating Reserves:		
Property Taxes	—	12,257
Deferred Income Taxes:		
Accelerated Amortization	59,399	66,284
Liberalized Depreciation	147,067	96,779
(Certain amounts recorded in these accounts, related to reductions in federal income taxes, resulting from accelerated amortization and liberalized depreciation, are invested in the business and are recorded by various subsidiaries in accounts maintained pursuant to state regulatory requirements as restricted earned surplus)		
Other	3,152	2,102
Deferred Investment Tax Credits	17,545	4,597
Other Deferred Credits and Operating Reserves	24,075	15,689
Total Deferred Credits and Operating Reserves	246,238	197,708
Totals	$6,879,459	$6,409,203
* { Authorized Shares	125,000	100,000
{ Outstanding Shares	93,000	83,000

Source: 1976 Annual Report, American Electric Power Company, p. 38.

Capitalization. Because of the historically stable revenues of the electric utilities, a relatively high debt ratio has been acceptable to both commissions and investors, i.e., from 50 to 60 percent, and for long-term debt plus preferred stock, from 60 to 65 percent. Generally, investors and commissions have desired a common stock equity ratio of 35 percent, but at times the ratio has been down to 30 percent, allowing 70 percent for long-term debt plus preferred stock (55 percent debt, 15 percent preferred stock).

Income Statement Analysis

The analyses of pertinent items on the income statements of public utilities are discussed in the following paragraphs.

Gross Revenues. The annual report of a public utility will generally provide in the income statement or in a supplemental statement a breakdown of revenues and KWH's by classes of customer. A utility is to a larger extent the prisoner of its geographic, economic, and political environment, although it may buy and/or sell electricity outside its territory. A reasonable balance between type of customer—residential, industrial, and commercial—is desirable. For example, American Electric Power Company does demonstrate such balance (see Table 26-3).

Residential Load. The residential load for utilities has demonstrated great stability and sustained growth. Years ago lighting was the major load with the peak being in the evening and in December. However, air conditioning has become a major factor for a large proportion of the utilities causing peak loads to be in the summer. Finally, as industrial usage has increased, peak loads occur in the daytime. The analyst should compare average residential loads and rates with other utilities within the state and within the nation.

Commercial Load—Commercial Lighting and Small Power. This load has demonstrated nearly as much stability as the residential load. Customer classification includes stores, restaurants, gasoline stations, garages, hotels, drugstores, theaters, hardware stores, and retail establishments in general. The commercial load consists of lighting, small power, and air conditioners.

Industrial Load—Large Power and Light. The industrial load is less stable than the residential or commercial load in terms of the business cycle. The instability is greatest if the utility services producers of durable consumer or capital goods. The investor should analyze the types of industrial service and the company's past record in this respect, especially during general economic recessions.

TABLE 26-3. American Electric Power Company—Revenues and KWH Sales

	Revenues		KWH Sales	
	Total	Excluding Sales to Other Utilities	Total	Excluding Sales to Other Utilities
Residential	26.2%	34.8%	19.6%	29.0%
Commercial	14.8	19.6	10.7	15.8
Industrial	30.6	40.5	36.4	53.8
To other utilities	24.5	—	32.3	—
Other KWH sales	1.2	3.4	1.0	1.4
Other revenues	3.1	1.7		
Total	100.4%	100.0%	100.0%	100.0%

	Average Annual Bill	Average KWH Price
Residential with electric heating	$559.77	$2.54
Residential without electric heating	234.06	3.21
All residential: AEP	291.06	2.95
Average for all investor owned utilities	298.13	3.75
All customers: AEP		2.13
Average for all investor owned utilities		$3.12

The AEP overall load factor was 67.7 percent in 1976 and 66.7 percent in 1975, and the margin of reserve at time of peak load was 14.8 percent in 1976 and 18.3 percent in 1975.

Source: 1976 Annual Report, American Electric Power Company

Street and Highway Lighting. This load is as stable as the residential load, but political pressures on rates can be serious.

Sales to Other Companies for Resale. Utilities have built up a large network of interconnections and certain utilities consistently sell or purchase power. Such sales may show considerable instability and should be analyzed carefully.

Operating Expenses. The major expense items in the income statement are maintenance, depreciation, federal income taxes, and other taxes (see Table 26-4).

TABLE 26-4. Consolidated Statement of Income for American Electric Power Company (in thousands, except per share figures)

Years Ended December 31	1976	1975
Operating Revenues—98% or More Electric	$1,868,620	$1,637,930
Operating Expenses:		
Operation—Fuel for Electric Generation	752,758	698,244
Operation—Other	192,400	183,706
Maintenance	103,095	81,974
Depreciation	181,542	156,435
Taxes, Other Than Income Taxes:		
Real and Personal Property	47,976	42,401
State Gross Sales, Excise, Franchise and Miscellaneous State and Local	51,096	43,926
Social Security—Federal and State	6,648	5,759
State Income Taxes	618	848
Federal Income Taxes	50,640	13,211
Total Operating Expenses	1,386,773	1,226,504
Operating Income	481,847	411,426
Other Income and Deductions:		
Allowance for Funds Used During Construction	68,690	82,144
Miscellaneous Nonoperating Income Less Deductions	6,247	3,021
Total Other Income and Deductions	74,937	85,165
Income Before Interest Charges	556,784	496,591

Interest Charges:		
Long-term Debt	219,276	250,336
Short-term Debt and Miscellaneous	42,594	20,969
Total Interest Charges	261,870	271,305
Consolidated income before preferred stock dividend requirements of subsidiaries and cumulative effect of accounting changes	234,721	285,479
Deduct preferred stock dividend requirement of subsidiaries	38,459	43,758
Consolidated income before cumulative effect of accounting charges	196,262	241,721
Nonrecurring cumulative effect of accounting changes (net of applicable taxes)	—	—
Consolidated Net Income, Applicable to Common Stock	$ 196,262	$ 241,721
EARNINGS AND DIVIDENDS PER SHARE OF COMMON STOCK:*		
Consolidated income before cumulative effect of accounting changes	$2.44	$2.66
Nonrecurring cumulative effect of accounting changes	—	—
Consolidated Earnings	$2.44	$2.66
Cash Dividends Paid (annual rate at December 31, 1976: $2.06)	$2.00	2.01\frac{1}{2}$
Average Number of Shares Outstanding (in thousands)	80,417	91,005

*Earnings per share for the respective years are based on the average number of shares outstanding, adjusted (where applicable) for a $2\frac{1}{2}$% stock dividend in 1967. Dividends per share are based on the actual number of shares outstanding, adjusted (where applicable) for such stock dividend.

Source: 1976 Annual Report, American Electric Power Company, p. 36.

Operating Ratio.[4] In the early post–World War II years, the operating ratio for electric utilities was generally at the 80 to 85 percent level. It then fell below 80 percent to the 78 to 79 percent level until 1976 when it again rose significantly above 80 percent, reflecting higher costs not balanced by rate increases. Then a large share of utilities received substantial rate relief, and the ratio again fell below 80 percent. If the ratio is below 80 percent, the ratio of operating income is 20 percent or more, which is a satisfactory level.

Other Income and Deductions. The item "Allowance for Funds Used in Construction" is peculiar to utilities and is often a major expense item. The utility borrows funds and pays interest on these funds. The utility is permitted to capitalize a "reasonable" amount of interest (for example, $8\frac{1}{2}$ to $9\frac{1}{2}$ percent in 1975–1978) and to show a noncash credit (income) item in its income statement for the same amount. If the amount is significant, as it was for American Electric Power, the analyst must estimate what it will amount to over the next several years. The item ceases when the plant goes into operation, at which time it is hoped that additional income generated will offset the previous credit item in the income statement "Allowance for Funds Used in Construction."

Income Available for Fixed Charges. In the income statement of regulated companies the income available for fixed charges is "after taxes" because taxes were deducted in operating expenses. If the analyst wishes to calculate the coverage before taxes, income taxes must be added to the "income available for fixed charges." The income coverage should be at least two times. It fell below the level for the industry overall in years such as 1973–1975, but rate increases caused it to recover above two. The analyst recommending utility securities in the years 1973–1975 when they were selling at especially depressed prices and were distinctly out of favor had to feel reasonable assurance that rate relief was forthcoming, which indeed proved to be the case in most areas. The analyst should also calculate the coverage for fixed charges *plus* preferred dividends, allowing for the fact that preferred dividends are not tax deductible as is interest paid.

Amount Available for the Common Stock. This is the amount brought down for the common stock after deducting all expenses including taxes plus fixed charges and preferred dividends. This amount should represent at least 12 percent of operating revenues.

---

[4] For nonregulated industries taxes are not included in operating expenses. Therefore, the operating ratio (operating expenses to operating revenues) also differs.

Financial Statements—Tests—Standards. Financial tests to be applied to the financial statements of electric utilities are listed in Table 26–5, along with the actual rates for AEP for the years 1975–1976 for comparison purposes. In looking at any possible investment, including utilities, one must compare the company's earnings with the DJIA or S&P indexes to assess the performance of the company relative to the performance of other companies in the industry (see Table 26-6).

TABLE 26-5. Financial Statement Tests

	Actual Rates for American Electric Power	
	1976	1977

Balance Sheet

	1976	1977
1. Current assets should be at least 10% of total assets.	11.0%	10.6%
2. Current ratio should be close to 1 to 1 and preferably over 1 to 1.	0.9	0.7
3. Cash and cash items should be close to 4% of total assets.	3.8	3.7
4. Net plant account should be between 82% and 90% of total assets.	82.0	83.0
5. Gross plant should not be over 4 times annual operating revenues for steam plants or 6 times for hydroelectric plants.	3.8	4.1
6. Net plant should not be over $3\frac{1}{2}$ times annual operating revenues.	3.0X	3.3X
7. Plant capacity should provide reserves at peak load of at least 15%.	14.8%	18.3%
8. Long-term debt should not exceed 60% of capitalization.	57.0	58.0
9. Long-term debt plus preferred stock should not exceed 70% of capitalization.	67.0	68.0
10. Common stock equity should represent at least 30% of capitalization. This would mean that debt should not exceed 55% and preferred stock 15% of total capitalization.	33.0	32.0
11. Allowance for accumulated depreciation should be at least 20% of gross plant and 25% of net plant for steam and for hydroelectric 15% of gross plant and 20% of net plant.	20.5	19.7

TABLE 26–5. Financial Statement Tests *(continued)*

	Actual Rates for American Electric Power	
	1976	1977

Income Statement

1. Operating revenues should be well balanced between the various classes of customers
2. Operating ratio (with operating expenses including all taxes) should not exceed 80% for steam plants and 70% for hydroelectric plants.

	74.2	74.9

3. Operating income after taxes should average at least 20% of operating revenues, and at least 7% of net plant.

	25.8	25.1
	8.5	7.7

4. Depreciation plus maintenance should not be less than 15% of revenues for steam plants and 12% for hydroelectric plants.

	15.2	14.6

5. Ratio of fixed charges on long-term debt to operating revenue should be at least 7%.

	7.5	7.5

6. Fixed charge coverage for all debt, short term and long term, should be at least 2 times, and on long-term debt at least 2 times.

	2.22X	2.26X
	2.05X	1.90X

7. Coverage of the total of fixed charges plus preferred dividends should be at least 1.90 times.

	1.89X	1.93X

8. The balance available for common stock should be at least 12% of operating revenues.

	12.9%	12.0%

Utility Industry Diversification. In recent years many utility companies have branched out from their traditional regulated businesses into new areas (primarily nonregulated areas). A multiple regression study by Barry Abramson at Merrill Lynch[5] showed a positive impact on stock price for utilities that so diversified (electric, gas, and telephone). The findings showed that a company that earned more than 10 percent of net income from diversified activities would add 4 percentage points in market to book value ratio because of a higher return on owners' equity and an additional 2 percentage points because of the

---

[5] Barry M. Abramson, "Utility Industry, Does Diversification Affect Utility Stock Prices?" (Pamphlet) (New York: Merrill Lynch, Securities Research Division, January 20, 1982).

TABLE 26–6. Dow Jones Utility Index and DJIA Earnings—Dividends—Market Prices—Price-Earnings Ratios

Year	Earnings DJIA	Earnings Util	Cash Dividends DJIA	Cash Dividends Util	Utility Payout Ratio	Price Close DJIA	Price Close Util	Utility Price as % of DJIA Price	P/E Ratio Close DJIA	P/E Ratio Close Util	P/E Ratio % of DJIA
1952	24.78	3.55	15.43	2.61	74%	292	52.60	18%	11.8	14.8	125
1953	27.23	3.74	16.11	2.63	70	281	52.04	19	10.3	13.9	135
1954	28.18	3.91	17.47	2.66	68	404	62.47	15	14.4	16.0	111
1955	35.78	4.34	21.58	3.57	82	488	64.16	13	13.7	14.8	108
1956	33.34	4.71	22.99	3.33	71	500	63.54	13	15.0	14.6	97
1957	36.08	4.70	21.61	3.39	72	436	68.58	16	12.1	14.6	121
1958	27.95	4.96	20.00	3.49	70	584	91.00	16	20.9	13.3	64
1959	34.31	5.31	20.74	3.66	69	679	87.83	13	19.8	16.5	83
1960	32.21	5.61	21.36	3.98	71	616	100.02	16	19.1	17.8	93
1961	31.91	5.86	20.71	4.31	74	731	129.16	17	22.9	22.0	96
1962	36.43	6.48	23.30	4.14	64	652	129.23	20	17.9	19.9	111
1963	41.21	7.04	23.41	5.14	73	763	138.99	18	18.5	19.7	106
1964	46.43	7.88	31.24	4.94	63	874	155.17	18	18.8	20.3	108
1965	53.67	8.53	28.61	5.19	61	970	152.63[a]	16	18.1	17.9	99
1966	57.68	8.75	31.89	5.84	67	786	136.18	17	13.6	15.6	115
1967	53.87	9.24	30.19	5.87	64	905	127.91	14	16.8	13.8	82
1968	57.89	9.23	31.34	6.11	66	944	137.17	15	16.3	14.9	91
1969	57.02	9.54	33.90	6.21	65	800	110.08	14	14.0	11.5	82
1970	57.02	9.69	31.53	6.37	66	839	121.84	15	16.4	12.6	77
1971	55.09	10.12	30.86	6.56	65	890	117.75	13	16.2	12.6	78
1972	67.11	10.94	32.27	6.73	62	1020	119.50	12	15.2	10.9	72
1973	86.17	10.79	35.33	6.92	64	851	89.37	11	9.9	8.3	84

TABLE 26-6. Dow Jones Utility Index and DJIA Earnings—Dividends—Market Prices—Price-Earnings Ratios (*continued*)

| Year | Earnings | | Cash Dividends | | Utility Payout Ratio | Price | | | Utility Price as % of DJIA Price | P/E Ratio Close | P/E Ratio % of | |
	DJIA	Util	DJIA	Util		Close DJIA	Close Util			DJIA	Util	DJIA
1974	99.04	11.57	37.72	6.91	70	616	68.76[b]		11	6.2	5.9	95
1975	75.66	11.58	37.46	7.20	62	852	83.65		10	6.2	7.2	116
1976	96.72	13.59	41.40	7.55	56	1005	108.		13	10.4	7.9	76
1977	89.10	14.27	45.84	8.23	58	831	111.28		13	9.3	7.8	84
1978	112.79	14.29	48.52	8.79	62	805	98.24		12	7.1	6.9	97

[a]Peak utility 163 in 1965.
[b]Low utility 58 and DJIA 578 in Dec. 1964.
Source: Dow Jones Investor's Handbook, published annually by Dow Jones Books, Princeton, N.J.

favor with which the market looked on a more diversified operating position. It will be interesting to see if more utilities diversify during the next decade.

ANALYSIS OF THE GAS INDUSTRY

There are three segments of the gas industry: (1) pipelines—intrastate and interstate, (2) distribution companies, and (3) integrated companies performing both functions of pipelines and distribution. Initially, most gas consumed, except in areas contiguous to oil-gas wells, was produced near the area of consumption, but such production today is extremely uncommon. In recent years most gas consumed is brought by pipelines to the general area of distribution, such as a state, and then distributed by "distribution companies." Pipeline companies are classified as intrastate pipelines or interstate pipelines. The interstate pipelines may be subdivided into interstate transmission pipelines and interstate and integrated pipelines, the latter being both pipeline companies and distribution companies. Sales to consumers account for 31 percent of volume sales, but about 50 percent of revenues.

Supply of Gas

Proven reserves of natural gas have shown a downward trend since 1970 (see Table 26-7). Significantly, however, additions to reserves

TABLE 26-7. U.S. Natural Gas Production and Reserves, 1970–1979 (in trillions of cubic feet)

Year	Production	Year-end Reserves	Ratio of Reserves to Production	Reserve Additions*	Ratio of Findings to Production
1979	19.9	194.9	9.8	14.3	0.72
1978	19.3	200.3	10.4	10.6	0.55
1977	19.4	208.9	10.7	11.9	0.61
1976	19.5	216.0	11.1	7.6	0.39
1975	19.7	228.2	11.6	10.5	0.53
1974	21.3	237.1	11.1	8.7	0.41
1973	22.6	250.0	11.1	6.8	0.30
1972	22.5	266.1	11.8	9.6	0.43
1971	22.1	278.8	12.6	9.8	0.45
1970	22.0	290.8	13.2	37.2	1.69

*Discoveries, revisions, and extensions. Note: The AGA has ceased preparing its annual gas evaluation survey. The DOE has prepared data for 1980, which are not comparable.

Source: Standard & Poor's Industry Surveys, Utilities-Gas, Basic Analysis, December 24, 1981, Section 2, p. U75.

were sharply higher in the late 1970s, and exploration activity has increased. The passage of the Natural Gas Policy Act in late 1978 stimulated exploration by removing the price disparity between interstate and intrastate natural gas and increasing the price for new gas. Therefore, a reasonable assumption would be to expect a continued narrowing of the gap between production and reserve additions.

Natural gas accounted for about 33 percent of total U.S. energy consumption in 1971, a peak level. This percentage fell to a bit below 26 percent in 1978 and increased to 27 percent in 1980. Analysts expect natural gas to hold a 27 to 30 percent share of total energy use in the 1980s.[6] Imports of natural gas will continue to be significant, with Mexico playing a major role.

Gas Pipelines

Gas pipeline companies have shown strong earnings growth since 1973 (see Table 26–8). "Earnings have increased at a compound annual rate of 13 percent for the ten years through 1980, and at 12 percent annually for the past five years, as measured by the S&P natural gas pipeline index."[7] The earnings growth, however, has not been reflected in higher price-earnings ratios, and there is little reason to anticipate such rises in the near future. The earnings growth has supported rising prices, on average, for common stocks of pipeline companies, as shown by the rise in the price index in Table 26–8.

Pipeline companies have diversified more into nonregulated areas than have distribution companies. Both types of companies are expected to continue diversification efforts in the 1980s to reduce risk and open new growth opportunities. The future of the major pipeline companies will depend to an important extent on the success of their diversification efforts. Diversification has mainly centered in energy-related fields.

Distribution Companies

These companies have also shown favorable earnings growth since 1973 but not at as a high a rate as for the pipeline companies. Earnings have increased at a compound annual rate of 8.6 percent for the ten years through 1980, and at 11 percent annually for the past five years.[8] Distributors have not diversified as much as the pipeline companies, for the most part.

---

[6] *Utilities—Gas: Basic Analysis* (New York: Standard & Poor's Corporation, December 24, 1981), p. U79.
[7] *Ibid*, p. U89.
[8] *Ibid*.

TABLE 26–8. Aggregate Gas Industry Financial Data, 1973–1980 (per share data based on Standard & Poor's group stock price indexes*)

NATURAL GAS—DISTRIBUTORS

The companies used for this series of per-share data are: American Natural Resources; Brooklyn Union Gas; Columbia Gas System; Consolidated Natural Gas; ENSERCH Corp.; ONEOK Inc.; Pacific Lighting; and Peoples Gas Co. Equitable Gas, Houston Natural, Laclede, National Fuel Gas, and Wash. Gas Light were all deleted on 6-30-76.

	1973	1974	1975	1976	1977	1978	1979	1980
Operating Revenues	78.05	91.75	109.97	150.09	184.50	207.95	254.84	312.68
Maintenance	2.70	3.08	3.16	3.44	N.A.	N.A.	N.A.	N.A.
Depreciation	6.16	6.93	7.42	9.64	10.89	11.64	13.19	14.57
Income Taxes	3.77	4.65	5.35	8.26	8.71	9.48	10.44	10.07
Net Operating Income	11.15	12.91	12.98	17.34	18.23	18.00	19.78	21.07
Operating Ratio %	85.71	85.93	88.20	88.45	90.12	91.34	92.26	93.26
Earnings	6.90	7.60	7.89	10.47	11.45	11.71	12.54	13.38
Dividends	3.95	4.12	4.29	5.49	5.96	6.35	6.82	7.35
Earns. as % of Oper. Revs.	8.84	8.28	7.17	6.98	6.21	5.63	4.92	4.28
Dividends as % of Earns.	57.25	54.21	54.37	52.44	52.05	54.23	54.39	54.93
Price (1941-43 - 10)—High	73.61	61.39	66.07	85.06	93.99	86.19	102.72	136.68
—Low	54.14	41.02	55.89	64.16	82.43	76.34	77.83	91.34
Price-Earnings Ratios—High	10.67	8.08	8.37	8.12	8.21	7.36	8.19	10.22
—Low	7.85	5.40	7.08	6.13	7.20	6.52	6.21	6.83
Dividend Yield %—High	7.30	10.04	7.68	8.56	7.23	8.32	8.76	8.05
—Low	5.37	6.71	6.49	6.45	6.34	7.37	6.64	5.38
Long-Term Debt	77.28	81.73	83.83	99.35	93.14	88.31	97.59	95.01
Net Property	139.83	146.34	R145.77	180.88	188.59	196.01	206.81	218.11
% Earned on Net Property	7.97	8.82	8.90	9.51	9.67	9.18	9.56	9.66
Capital Expenditures	19.07	19.94	11.94	18.10	20.01	25.18	32.74	30.95

NATURAL GAS—PIPELINES

The companies used for this series of per-share data are: El Paso Co.; Inter North Inc. (formerly Northern Natural Gas); Panhandle Eastern Pipeline; Southern Natural Resources; Texas Eastern Corp.; and Texas Gas Transmission. Northwest Energy (deleted 6-30-76) & Miss. River Corp. (deleted 9-11-74).

	1973	1974	1975	1976	1977	1978	1979	1980
Operating Revenues	131.37	176.99	200.60	207.40	254.30	286.50	399.71	502.49
Maintenance	N.A.	N.A.	N.A.	N.A.	N.A.	N.A.	N.A.	N.A.
Depreciation	12.32	15.68	16.76	17.20	17.69	19.91	22.81	25.31
Income Taxes	8.00	11.93	13.30	14.55	15.90	15.30	20.08	22.99
Net Operating Income	18.99	21.41	21.80	21.86	27.14	27.87	33.98	33.04
Operating Ratio %	85.54	87.90	89.13	89.46	89.33	90.27	91.50	93.42
Earnings	10.86	15.22	15.81	16.81	18.01	19.77	24.46	27.64
Dividends	4.96	5.43	5.72	6.12	6.87	7.67	8.78	10.23
Earns. as % of Oper. Revs.	8.27	8.60	7.88	8.11	7.08	6.90	6.12	5.50
Dividends as % of Earns.	45.67	35.68	36.18	36.41	38.15	38.80	35.09	37.01
Price (1941-43 - 10)—High	132.71	112.55	112.41	138.62	147.67	146.83	202.25	287.90
—Low	89.01	68.79	89.74	104.44	128.70	118.69	121.50	178.58
Price-Earnings Ratios—High	12.22	7.39	7.11	8.25	8.20	7.43	8.27	10.42
—Low	8.20	4.52	5.68	6.21	7.15	6.00	4.97	6.46
Dividend Yield %—High	5.57	7.89	6.37	5.86	5.34	6.46	7.23	5.73
—Low	3.74	4.82	5.09	4.41	4.65	5.22	4.34	3.55
Long-Term Debt	118.28	137.23	147.31	147.02	134.78	126.61	132.36	141.93
Net Property	203.82	236.21	250.97	250.00	261.09	268.83	298.65	304.00
% Earned on Net Property	9.32	9.06	8.69	8.69	10.39	10.37	11.38	12.48
Capital Expenditures	24.16	26.19	33.42	33.42	37.97	35.33	57.72	64.25

*NOTE: Per-share data are expressed in terms of the S&P Stock Price Index, i.e., stock prices, 1941–43 – 10. Each of the items shown is first computed on a true per-share basis for each company. Totals for each company are then reconstructed using the same number of shares outstanding as was used to compute our stock price index as of December 31st. This is done because the shares used on December 31st, although the latest known at the time, may differ from those reported in the annual reports, which are not available for six or eight weeks after the end of the year. The sum of these reconstructed totals is then related to the base period value used to compute the stock price index. As a double check we relate the various items to the dividends as these are the most stable series. So, for example, if total sales amount to fifteen times the total dividend payments, then, with per-share dividends at 3.50 the indicated per-share sales will be (15 × 3.50) 52.50 in terms of the S&P Stock Price index. For comparability between the various groups, all data are on a calendar year basis, corporate data being posted in the year in which most months fall. Fiscal years ending June 30th are posted in the calendar year in which the fiscal year ends. R-Revised N.A.—Not available.

Source: Standard & Poor's Industry Surveys, Utilities–Gas, Basic Analysis, December 24, 1981, Section 2, p. U91.

663

Regulation

Beginning with the federal Natural Gas Act of 1938, regulation of gas flowing in interstate commerce was placed under the jurisdiction of the Federal Power Commission (FPC). The U.S. Supreme Court in 1954, in the case of *Phillips Petroleum* v. *Wisconsin*, gave the FPC jurisdiction over all sales of natural gas for resale in interstate commerce. Until recently the FPC effectively regulated the price of gas at the wells by establishing area prices at which new gas could be sold in approximately twenty-five areas.[9]

With the establishment of the new Department of Energy in the latter part of 1977, functions of many energy-related agencies were redistributed and new agencies established. The intent was to integrate responsibilities of like nature. The Department of Energy Organization Act of August 4, 1977, transferred to a newly formed Federal Energy Regulatory Commission many of the functions of the Federal Power Commission. Among the functions transferred were "the establishment, review, and enforcement of rates and charges for the transportation and sale of natural gas by a producer or gatherer or by a natural gas pipeline or natural gas company under sections 1, 4, 5, and 7 of the Natural Gas Act."[10]

Up until about 1970, the prices established by the Federal Power Commission were not sufficiently encouraging to attract new funds for new exploration. As a result, U.S. reserves of natural gas decreased because of the lack of opportunities for reasonable earnings growth in the interstate area of the business. In the early 1970s, the transportation of gas through interstate lines actually was declining. This tended to cause all gas pipeline securities to become relatively out of favor with investors. This was reflected in sharply decreasing price-earnings ratios through 1974, falling below price-earnings ratios for the general market averages.

In spite of a decline in earnings for interstate pipeline companies, in the 1970s there was a satisfactory earnings growth rate due to the higher rates of return and higher rate bases approved by the Federal Power Commission.

The energy legislation program that was enacted in 1978 has had a major impact on the pricing and other aspects of pipeline regulation.

Debt Ratios and Bond Quality Rating

Except for El Paso Natural Gas and Transcontinental Gas the debt ratios for the gas companies were lower than those of electric com-

---

[9] *Ibid.*

[10] *Department of Energy Organization Act,* 91 Stat. 565, Public Law 95–91, 95th Congress, August 4, 1977, Section 402. Effective date of provisions of the act was prescribed as October 1, 1977.

panies (see Table 26-9). However, the bond ratings (S&P) for the industry on the average were distinctly lower than for electric and gas operating companies. Of the twenty-one major companies only two (in 1981) had an AA bond rating while seven had a BBB rating. The pretax average for fixed charges coverage for the nineteen companies for which it was given was below three times for six companies and below five times for all but three companies.

Financial Analysis of Gas Pipelines

The most important elements of risk for a gas pipeline company are the heavy debt of the pipelines and the uncertainty of regulation under Washington's 1978 and subsequent energy programs.

TABLE 26-9. Pipeline Bond Quality Measures, 1980

	Quality Rating (S&P)	Long-term Debt Total Cap.	Pretax Interest Coverage
Interstate Transmission Companies:			
El Paso Natural Gas	BBB	67.4	1.64
Northwest Pipeline	BBB	35.1	2.92
Trunkline Gas Company	BBB	56.6	2.08
Southern Natural Gas	A+	35.6	4.80
Tenneco Inc.	A	41.9	3.36
Texas Eastern Corporation	BBB	35.7	5.97
Texas Gas Trans.	A+	39.8	5.70
Transcontinental Gas	BBB	58.4	1.98
United Gas Pipeline	BBB	33.0	3.75
Interstate Integrated Companies:			
Michigan-Wisconsin	A	44.2	2.62
Arkansas-Louisiana	AA	44.4	4.63
Columbia Gas	A	49.3	3.47
Consolidated Natural	AA	41.1	3.64
Florida Gas	BBB	30.2	2.55
Kansas-Nebraska	A+	43.0	3.94
Mountain Fuel	A	42.3	3.87
Internorth Inc.	A+	45.4	4.60
Natural Gas Pipeline	A	45.0	4.33
Intrastate Companies:			
Enserch Corporation	A	39.0	5.01
Houston Natural	A+	33.2	8.34
Pioneer Natural	A+	31.6	8.18

Source: Moody's Public Utility Manual, 1981.

Balance Sheet Analysis. Analysts often use the following rules of thumb, based on experience, when analyzing gas industry balance sheets:

1. Net plant should not exceed two times annual operating revenues and gross plant three times annual operating revenues.
2. Total debt should not exceed 66 percent of total capitalization or about the same percentage of net plant.
3. Long-term debt plus preferred stock should not exceed 70 percent of total capitalization; and if it is 70 percent, long-term debt should not exceed 55 percent of total capitalization, leaving 15 percent for the preferred stock.
4. Common stock equity should represent at least 30 percent of total capitalization.

Income Statement Analysis. The following rules of thumb are suggested as standards when analyzing gas industry income statements.

1. Total operating expenses including taxes and depreciation should not exceed 88 percent of total operating revenues or 70 percent exclusive of depreciation and maintenance.
2. Depreciation plus maintenance should equal at least 10 percent of operating revenues.
3. The average rate of return on common equity should be at least 15 percent.
4. The rate of return on total capitalization should be at least 8 percent.
5. Coverage of fixed charges should be at least 2.75 times.
6. Coverage of fixed charges plus preferred dividends should be at least two times and should not exceed 7 percent of operating revenues.
7. The balance available for the common should be at least 7 percent of operating revenues.

THE TELEPHONE INDUSTRY

The telephone industry in the United States is dominated by the American Telephone and Telegraph Systems (the Bell System), which controls about 80 percent of all telephones through its subsidiaries. It also controls the long-lines interstate system and international cables. Of the remaining telephones the General Telephone and Electric Company controls about 40 percent. There are nearly 1,700 other telephone companies, most of which are very small but some of which are sizable; e.g., Continental Telephone.

In addition to its subsidiary telephone companies, AT&T controls the Western Electric Company, which manufactures most of AT&T's equipment, and the Bell Laboratories research facilities. These research laboratories are very large and are highly respected by scientists throughout the world.

AT&T securities held by the public include the securities of the parent company and also the stocks and bonds issued by the operating telephone subsidiaries of AT&T. Both the parent company and its subsidiaries frequently enter the capital market for the sale of additional securities. Issues of the parent have at numerous times represented the largest single security issues sold in the United States that year. At times AT&T issues convertible securities that it generally assumes will later experience forced conversion into common stock.

Specifics of Analysis of Telephone Company Securities

For the small, and sometimes even tiny, individual telephone company, the following requirements should be considerably stricter than for AT&T subsidiaries because of the risks inherent in their very small size.

Balance Sheet Analysis

1. The current ratio should be above the one to one level.
2. Long-term debt should not exceed 45 percent of total percent capitalization, and debt plus preferred stock, 60 percent.
3. The turnover of net fixed assets (after depreciation) should be at least 2.8 times; i.e., annual revenue should be at least equal to 36 percent of the value of net plant.
4. The account "accumulated depreciation" should be equal to approximately 25 percent of gross plant account.

Income Statement Analysis

1. The operating ratio should not exceed 85 percent (operating expenses including income taxes). If income taxes are excluded from operating expenses, the operating ratio should not exceed approximately 72 percent.
2. The ratio of maintenance plus depreciation to total gross revenue should not exceed approximately 33 to 35 percent.
3. The rate of return on the capital structure (before deduction of fixed charges), i.e., amount available for fixed charges, should be at least 7 to 7.5 percent.
4. The amount available for fixed charges before taxes should show a coverage of at least 3.8 times.

WATER COMPANIES

Most water companies are owned by the municipalities they serve. Some of these have issued revenue bonds that are held by private investors. There are still, however, many privately owned water companies, but the ownership is often closely, even family, held. Some larger privately owned municipal companies are located in Birmingham, Alabama; Indianapolis, Indiana; New Haven, Connecticut; New Rochelle, New York; and San Jose, California. One large privately owned water company, American Water Works, controls about 75 companies operating in 15 states.

The gross revenues of water companies are usually quite stable, and in most areas exhibit relatively consistent growth in revenues and earnings. In fast-growing areas the rate of growth reflects this environment. As with other utilities, fixed assets constitute the bulk of total assets, and the turnover of capital invested in these assets is relatively slow. The operations of water companies are relatively simple resulting in a relatively low operating ratio.

Financial Analysis

The following proportions should be present:

1. Gross fixed assets should not be greater than $5\frac{1}{2}$ to $6\frac{1}{2}$ times annual revenues.
2. The depreciation should be equal to at least 16 percent of gross plant.
3. Long-term debt should not be greater than two-thirds the value of net assets (gross assets less depreciation), and long-term debt plus preferred stock should not exceed three-quarters of total capitalization.
4. The common equity should represent at least one-quarter of the total capitalization.
5. The operating ratio should not exceed 70 percent.
6. The rate of return on the capital structure should at least be in the 5 to 6 percent range.
7. The fixed charge coverage should be at least two and one-half times earnings.
8. Total interest plus preferred dividends should be covered at least one and three-quarter times.
9. The amount of gross revenues carried down to the common equity should be at least 10 percent.

Summary

There are two broad categories of regulated industries: utilities and transportation companies. In general, regulated industries sell services that are affected with the public interest and in many instances, such as electric and gas utilities and telephone companies, enjoy a monopoly position and must be regulated to protect the public from excessive prices and poor service.

In analyzing regulated industries, the first and most important step is to determine the regulatory climate—essentially the attitude of the regulatory commission or agency as to rates and service requirements. The question is, "Is the utility permitted to earn a fair rate of return, fair in the judgment of investors, as expressed in the market yield of its securities compared to similar companies?" If it is determined that the regulatory climate is satisfactory from the investor's viewpoint, then the investor can proceed to analyze specific companies in that jurisdiction.

The financial analysis centers on the major financial statements as is the case with other companies. But each industry has its own special characteristics, and this fact must be given serious consideration in analyzing trends and ratios.

Closely correlated to the financial analysis is the analysis of related statistics that are available to the investor. Most of the larger utility companies furnish financial analysts with statistical booklets to supplement financial statements and other information appearing in annual reports.

The gas industry is subdivided into (1) pipelines—interstate and intrastate, (2) distribution companies, and (3) integrated companies. Each of these types has special characteristics that must be understood if the results of analysis are to be satisfactory.

In the financial analysis of gas companies, especially pipelines, the most serious risk factor is the relatively heavy debt in capitalization—heavy in an overall utility industry in which debt is always a very significant part of capitalization.

The telephone industry is dominated by the American Telephone Company and its subsidiaries. In addition there are several relatively large companies such as General Telephone and Continental Telephone. Finally, while the large companies (except AT&T) have been rapidly absorbing the small companies, there are still a significant number of such companies in operation. Overall, the securities of most of the telephone companies enjoy investment grade ratings because of their record of stability in revenue earnings and dividends, with those of AT&T enjoying the highest rating but with market recognition of the regulatory environment in which AT&T subsidiaries operate.

Most water companies are owned by the municipalities they serve, especially in the large cities. However, there is one large holding company, American Water Works, as well as quite a large number of privately owned water companies, and many of these deserve a favorable investment rating. As with other utilities, fixed assets constitute the majority of total assets, and the turnover of capital invested in these assets is relatively slow. The operations of water companies are relatively simple, resulting in relatively low operating ratios. After October 1, 1977, registrants filing financial reports with other federal agencies have also been required to file annual and quarterly reports with the SEC, and these must follow SEC accounting and auditing rules and regulations.

Questions

1. What are the major characteristics of a public utility?
2. (a) What caused the change in investment status for electric utility stocks that occurred after 1965 and again after 1974?

(b) Is an inflationary environment favorable for utility common stocks? Preferred stocks? Explain.
3. Discuss the importance of the *Hope Natural Gas Company* case to investors.
4. The National Association of Railroad and Utility Commissions adopted a revised uniform system of accounts for electric and gas utilities in 1961. Does this ensure completely comparable accounting reports for electric utility companies? Discuss.
5. Would a current ratio be a particularly significant factor in an analysis of an electric utility security? Discuss.
6. Discuss the capitalization ratios generally considered desirable in the electric utility industry.
7. (a) What are the main breakdowns of utility operating costs that should be studied by the analyst?
   (b) Criticize the breakdown usually given under the uniform system of accounts used by public utilities.
8. What are the major problems of the gas industry?
9. Discuss the problem of the relatively high debt ratios of gas pipelines in relation to industry problems.
10. Discuss the dominance of AT&T in the telephone industry.
11. Explain why stricter financial standards must be applied to small local telephone companies than to AT&T subsidiaries.
12. Discuss the simplicity of operations of water companies and the implications in terms of cost of operations.

Work-Study Problems

1. The following data provide the principal important statistics of two public electric utility companies:

	(dollars in thousands)	
	Company A	Company B
Operating revenue	$ 91,468	$ 133,126
Operating expenses	31,361	56,910
Maintenance	5,411	8,026
Depreciation	11,385	13,447
Taxes	20,367	35,340
Miscellaneous	532	0
Operating revenue deduction	69,056	113,723
Net operating revenue	22,412	19,403
Interest	6,366	4,465
Net income	16,046	14,938
Preferred dividend	2,416	1,960
Common dividend	10,373	8,961

Plant		498,500	492,558
Depreciation		76,591	139,820
Net Plant		421,909	352,738

		Company A	Company B
Debt		$ 211,675	$ 147,889
Preferred		52,500	43,000
Common		88,828	74,676
Surplus		43,636	84,532

		Company A	Company B
Number of shares of common	(100)	$ 10,373	$ 7,467
Customers	1970	277,000	474,000
Customers	1977	295,000	487,000
Capacity	1977	1,340,000	1,051,000
Peak load	1977	1,108,000	1,041,000
Load factor	1977	68.0	58.0
Average residential use	1977	4,081	2,430
Average residential rate	1977	2.70	3.91

Calculate the following for each company:
(a) Depreciation ratio.
(b) Maintenance ratio.
(c) Interest coverage before and after taxes.
(d) Net operating revenue to net plant.
(e) Operating ratio.
(f) Ratio of debt to capitalization.
(g) Overall coverage of preferred dividend.
(h) Per share earned on common.
(i) Per share dividend on common.
(j) Reserve margin.
2. (a) What has been the record of utility companies in your state in securing rate increases since 1974? How does this record compare with that of other states?
(b) What rate of return is permitted for electric utilities in your state? How is it calculated? Do you believe the method used and the rate allowed would be relatively desirable to investors? Discuss.

27.

Regulated Industries: Transportation

The three major components of the transportation industry that will be discussed in this chapter are the railroad industry, the trucking industry, and the airline industry. In a broad legal context these regulated industries are public utilities. The most vital areas of control cover rates of return, mergers, consolidations, and abandonments, with rate of return being the most significant.

In the late 1970s the federal government was acting to decontrol the trucking and air transport industries, but the industries themselves and the unions were opposing decontrol, saying they feared cutthroat competition would develop. Air freight rates were decontrolled in 1978.

THE RAILROADS

Passenger traffic of the railroads has largely been shifted to agencies of the federal government—AMTRAK for long-haul traffic and CONRAIL for commuter traffic. Passenger business quite generally has been a deficit operation for the railroads. Moreover, it has seriously interfered with freight traffic movements.

The share of the railroads in total interstate freight fell from 75 percent in 1929 to 36 percent in 1977, while the share of trucks rose from 3.3 percent to 23.8 percent and oil pipelines from 4.4 to 24 percent (see Table 27-1). However, in terms of revenue, the trucks, while carrying only 24 percent of volume, have had gross revenue in excess of the railroads' revenues in the 1970s. Generally transportation experts assume that the railroads are most efficient for hauls of 400 miles or over while trucks have the advantage for hauls of 400 miles or less. This is the major reason why the eastern roads suffered most severely from truck competition on their relatively short hauls, and accounts largely for the poor record of the eastern roads both in absolute terms and relative to the southern and western roads. Of course, before AMTRAK and CONRAIL, passenger traffic was a heavy loss operation for the northeastern roads. Certain railroads have continually earned a satisfactory rate of return—the coal roads, the Chesapeake and Ohio, the Nor-

TABLE 27-1. Volume of U.S. Intercity Freight and Passenger Traffic

Millions of Revenue Freight Ton-Miles and Percentage of Total (Including Mail and Express)

Year	Railroads[a]	%	Trucks	%	Great Lakes	%	Rivers and Canals	%	Oil Pipelines	%	Air	%	Total
1929	454,800	74.9	19,689	3.3	97,322	16.0	8,661	1.4	26,900	4.4	3	—	607,375
1939	338,850	62.4	52,821	9.7	76,312	14.0	19,937	3.7	55,602	10.2	12	—	543,534
1944	746,912	68.6	58,264	5.4	118,769	10.9	31,386	2.9	132,864	12.2	71	—	1,088,266
1950	596,940	56.2	172,860	16.3	111,687	10.5	51,657	4.9	129,175	12.1	318	—	1,062,637
1960	579,130	44.1	285,483	21.7	99,468	7.6	120,785	9.2	228,626	17.4	778	—	1,314,270
1970	771,168	39.8	412,000	21.3	114,475	5.9	204,085	10.5	431,000	22.3	3,295	0.2	1,936,023
1974	855,582	38.6	495,000	22.3	107,451	4.9	247,431	11.2	506,000	22.8	3,580	0.2	2,215,044
1976[b]	799,000	36.2	510,000	23.1	105,648	4.8	267,217	12.1	523,000	23.6	3,900	0.2	2,208,765
1977[b]	831,000	36.0	549,000	23.8	95,000	4.1	275,000	11.9	556,000	24.0	4,000	0.2	2,310,000

Millions of Revenue Passenger-Miles and Percentage of Total (Except Private)

Year	Railroads[a]	%	Buses	%	Air Carriers	%	Inland Waterways	%	Total (Except Private)	Private Auto-mobiles	%	Private Airplanes	Total (Including Private)
1929	33,965	77.1	6,800	15.4	—	—	3,300	7.5	44,065	175,000		—	219,065
1939	23,669	67.7	9,100	26.0	683	2.0	1,486	4.3	34,938	275,000		—	309,938
1944	97,705	75.7	26,920	20.9	2,177	1.7	2,187	1.7	128,989	181,000		1	309,990
1950	32,481	47.2	26,436	38.4	8,773	12.7	1,190	1.7	68,880	438,293		1,299	508,472
1960	21,574	28.6	19,327	25.7	31,730	42.1	2,688	3.6	75,319	706,079		2,228	783,626
1970	10,903	5.7	25,300	14.3	109,499	77.7	4,000	2.3	149,702	1,026,000		9,101	1,184,803
1974	10,475	5.9	26,700	15.1	135,469	76.7	4,000	2.3	176,644	1,143,440		11,000	1,331,044

TABLE 27-1. Volume of U.S. Intercity Freight and Passenger Traffic (continued)

Millions of Revenue Passenger-Miles and Percentage of Total (Except Private)

Year	Railroads[a]	%	Buses	%	Air Carriers	%	Inland Waterways	%	Total (Except Private)	Private Automobiles	Private Airplanes	Total (Including Private)
1976[b]	10,500	5.5	25,100	13.1	152,300	79.3	4,000	2.1	191,900	1,187,000	11,600	1,390,500
1977[b]	10,450	5.1	25,900	12.7	163,700	80.2	4,000	2.0	204,050	1,237,000	12,100	1,453,150

[a]Railroads of all classes, including electric railways, Amtrak and Auto-Train.
[b]These are preliminary estimates and are subject to frequent subsequent adjustments.
Note: Air carrier data from reports of CAB and TAA; Great Lakes and rivers and canals from Corps of Engineers and TAA; some figures for 1976 and 1977 are partially estimated by AAR and TAA.
Source: Yearbook of Railroad Facts (Washington: Association of American Railroads, 1978), p. 36.

folk and Western, and the long-haul western roads such as the Union
Pacific, the Southern Pacific, and the Atchison, Topeka and Santa Fe.

The investment community considers some railroads to be representative of somewhat higher quality than the industry overall (see Table
27–2). Four are in the western district and own large natural resources
in addition to controlling long-haul traffic. Three are coal shippers, and
two are in the southern district. Except for the very high-density coal
roads, they are long-haul roads or reasonably long-haul roads with reasonable traffic density. If proposals in 1978 for more consolidations
become a fact, the Burlington Northern and Southern Pacific would become transcontinental, which could work out well. But such planned
consolidations usually take a number of years to complete.

Consolidations

Until legislation was passed in the 1950s bringing about railroad
mergers or consolidations was extremely difficult, largely because of
union opposition. However, after helpful 1958 legislation a series of
consolidations began in 1959. Proposals for more consolidations were
continuing in 1978.[1] While a number of consolidations worked out

---

[1]
1. 1959 Norfolk and Western (merger of Norfolk & Western & Virginia into
   Norfolk & Western).
2. 1960 Erie-Lackawanna (Erie and Delaware, Lackawanna & Western into
   Erie-Lackawanna).
3. 1961 Southern Pacific (Southern Pacific and Texas into Southern Pacific).
4. 1963 Southern Pacific (Southern Pacific and Central of Georgia into
   Southern Pacific).
5. 1964 Norfolk & Western (Norfolk & Western and N.Y. Chicago & St.
   Louis into Norfolk & Western).
6. 1967 Seaboard Coast Line (Atlanta Coast Line and Seaboard Airline into
   Seaboard Coast Line).
7. 1968 Penn-Central (Pennsylvania and N.Y. Central into Penn-Central
   with the merged railroad soon going into bankruptcy).
8. 1969 Seaboard Coast Line (Seaboard Coast Line and Piedmont & Northern into Atlanta Coast Line).
9. 1970 Burlington-Northern (Burlington, Great Northern & Northern Pacific into Burlington-Northern).
10. 1971 Illinois Central and Gulf Mobile & Western into Illinois Central Gulf.
11. 1971 Seaboard Coast Line (Seaboard Coast Line & Louisville & Nashville,
    the latter a coal road, into Seaboard Coast Line).
12. Four major carriers in 1978 were planning two lines to span the continent:
    (a) Burlington Northern and St. Louis & San Francisco (Route South-
        east Seaboard to Northern Pacific Coast).
    (b) Southern Pacific and Seaboard Coast Line Industries (Route Wash-
        ington, D.C. and Miami to Los Angeles, San Francisco, and Seattle).
        Merged Nov. 1, 1980.
    As proposed:
    (a) Above would control 10 percent of industry revenues and 10 percent
        industry net investment.
    (b) Above would control 16 percent of industry revenues and 15 percent
        of industry net investment.

TABLE 27–2. Earnings per Share of Eight Average or Better Quality Railroads, 1970–1981

	S&P[a] Quality Ranking	1981E	1980	1979	1978	1977	1976	1975	1973	1970
Burlington Northern (substantial coal reserves)	A–	7.00	7.55	6.55	8.75	5.74	5.69	4.12	4.01	2.00
Santa Fe Industries[b]	A	3.10	3.47	2.69	6.00	5.92	4.61	4.23	4.01	1.96
Southern Pacific	A–	6.10	5.78	6.67	3.75	4.39	4.10	2.81	3.77	2.86
Union Pacific (substantial natural resources)	A+	4.40	4.22	4.01	5.45	4.68	4.02	3.21	2.80	3.56
Southern Railway	A	13.00	11.57	10.39	8.00	7.04	5.85	5.12	4.47	3.78
Kansas City Southern Industries (split 3/1)	B+	3.75	3.17	2.56	3.75	2.47	1.32	1.02	0.53	0.97
Chessie System (coal road)[c]	NR				3.25	4.01	5.38	4.59	3.39	6.09
Norfolk & Western (coal road) (Norfolk & Western & Virginia)	A–	8.25	7.36	6.36	3.55	3.31	4.21	2.80	2.18	6.14
Seaboard Coast Line Industries (includes the coal road Louisville & Nashville)[c]	NR				4.50	7.02	5.84	3.23	5.21	4.36
CSX[c]	NR	8.25	7.13	6.12						

[a]Standard & Poor's ratings: A = high, A– = above average, B+ = average. Note that only the Union Pacific has Standard & Poor's highest-quality rating.
[b]Holding company for Atchison, Topeka, and Santa Fe Railroads (substantial natural resources).
[c]The Chessie System and Seaboard Coast Line were merged to form CSX on November 1, 1980.
Note: Space does not permit footnoting any adjustments made to earnings above by S&P, but the above data generally give a reasonably accurate picture of earnings.
Source: Standard & Poor's Industry Surveys—Railroads, various issues. Class 1 railroads net income ordinary from *Yearbook of Railroad Facts,* various editions.

profitably, the massive Penn-Central bankruptcy proves that consolidation doesn't necessarily work out to the advantage of the security holders.

Cyclical Traffic

Since a substantial portion of railroad traffic is in the area of heavy durable goods, the railroads are particularly subject to contractions in business cycles. High debt/capitalization ratios create high financial leverage. The combination of the cyclical nature of their business and the high financial leverage of most railroads causes their earnings records to be quite volatile over the business cycle (see Table 27-2).

Financial Analysis of Railroads

Table 27-3 shows the major items in the railroad income statement for selected years from 1929–1980. The rate of return on investment is shown in Table 27-4. The gross operating revenue of the railroads stayed in a relatively narrow range from 1950–1969 at $10 to $11 billion, or about 66 percent higher than in 1929. But during that period operating expenses rose about 115 percent. In 1955 and again in 1965–1966, net income from operations of the railroads was temporarily back to about the 1929 level. However, in the 1970s net income has averaged only about one-third of the 1929, 1959, 1965, and 1966 levels. Net income did finally recover to the peak 1929 level in 1980. An examination of Table 27-3 indicates the overall very poor record of the eastern district railroads—railroads most subject to severe truck competition due primarily to relatively short hauls. The eastern district railroads had only nominal net income from 1967–1969 and net losses continuously since that time, until they about broke even in 1980.

Railroad Income Statement Analysis. For analysis purposes the railroad income statement is presented in Tables 27-3, 27-5a, and 27-5b. "Revenues" in railroad accounting terminology always means gross revenues (income) before deducting expenses. "Income" in railroad statements is synonymous with "net income" as used in industrial accounting. Also, while federal income taxes are deductible from net income on industrial company statements, they are included in the same categories as property and excise taxes in railroad accounting. Federal income taxes therefore reduce reported net railway operating income, whereas they would not affect net operating income of an industrial company.

Operating Revenues. The major source (92 to 96 percent) of railroad revenues is freight income (Table 27-5a). The bases for analysis of revenues are therefore: (1) specific sources of revenues (commodity

TABLE 27–3. Condensed Income Statement for All Class I Railroads, Selected Years, 1929–1977 (in millions)

Year	(1) Operating Revenues				(2) Freight Revenues				(3) Operating Expenses			
	U.S.	East	South	West	U.S.	East	South	West	U.S.	East	South	West
1929	6.3	3.1	0.8	2.4	4.8	2.3	0.6	1.9	5.1	2.5	0.6	1.9
1939	4.0	2.0	0.5	1.5	3.3	1.6	0.4	1.3	3.5	1.7	0.4	1.4
1944	9.4	4.1	1.3	4.0	7.0	3.0	1.0	3.0	7.2	3.3	0.9	2.9
1947	8.7	4.0	1.2	3.5	7.0	3.1	1.0	2.9	7.7	3.6	1.1	3.0
1951	10.4	4.6	1.5	4.3	8.6	3.8	1.2	3.7	9.0	4.1	1.2	3.7
1955	10.1	4.4	1.4	4.3	8.5	3.6	1.2	3.7	8.6	3.8	1.2	3.6
1966	10.7	4.2	1.6	4.8	9.3	3.5	1.4	4.3	9.5	3.8	1.4	4.2
1967	10.4	4.1	1.6	4.7	9.1	3.5	1.5	4.2	9.7	3.9	1.5	4.3
1968	10.9	4.2	1.7	4.9	9.7	3.6	1.6	4.5	10.2	4.1	1.5	4.5
1969	11.5	4.4	1.9	5.2	10.3	3.8	1.7	4.8	10.7	4.3	1.7	4.8
1970	12.0	4.5	2.0	5.4	10.9	4.0	1.9	5.1	11.5	4.7	1.8	5.0
1971	12.7	4.7	2.2	5.9	11.8	4.1	2.1	5.6	11.9	4.7	1.9	5.3
1972	13.4	4.8	2.3	6.3	12.6	4.3	2.2	6.1	12.5	4.8	2.0	5.7
1973	14.8	5.2	2.3	7.1	13.8	4.6	2.4	6.8	13.8	5.1	2.2	6.5
1974	16.9	6.0	2.5	8.1	15.8	5.3	2.4	7.7	15.7	5.8	2.6	7.4
1975	16.4	5.8	2.9	7.9	15.4	5.2	2.8	7.6	15.9	6.0	2.5	7.4
1976	18.5	6.4	2.7	9.0	17.4	5.7	2.6	8.7	17.9	6.7	2.9	8.4
1977	20.1	6.7	3.1	9.9	18.9	5.9	3.0	9.6	19.5	7.1	2.5	9.3
1978	21.7	6.9	3.5	11.1	20.2	5.9	3.4	10.7	21.0	7.3	3.2	10.3
1979	25.2	8.2	3.8	12.7	23.4	7.0	3.6	12.2	24.0	8.1	3.4	11.9
1980	28.3	8.5	4.4	14.7	26.3	7.3	4.2	14.2	26.4	8.3	4.0	13.5

Year	(4) Maintenance Ways & Structures	(4) Maintenance Equipment	Transportation Expenses	(5) Net Regular Operating Income U.S.	East	South	West	(6) Net Income Ordinary (in thousands) U.S.	East	South	West
1929	0.9	1.2	2.9	1.3	0.63	0.13	0.48	897	487	73	337
1939	0.5	0.8	1.4	0.6	0.33	0.08	0.18	93	110	12	(29)
1944	1.3	1.6	3.0	1.1	0.46	0.16	0.49	667	266	97	304
1947	1.2	1.6	3.5	0.8	0.30	0.10	0.37	479	161	55	263
1951	1.5	1.9	4.0	0.9	0.38	0.16	0.40	693	235	111	348
1955	1.4	1.8	3.8	1.1	0.48	0.20	0.45	927	349	159	424
1966	1.3	1.8	4.1	1.0	0.38	0.18	0.48	904	285	141	477
1967	1.3	1.9	4.2	0.7	0.17	0.16	0.34	554	94	126	334
1968	1.4	2.9	4.4	0.7	0.14	0.16	0.37	569	67	117	385
1969	1.5	2.0	4.6	0.7	0.12	0.19	0.36	514	21	130	354
1970	1.6	2.2	4.9	0.5	(0.10)*	0.21	0.38	227	(276)	160	343
1971	1.8	2.4	4.9	0.6	(0.06)	0.21	0.44	247	(274)	152	369
1972	1.9	2.4	5.2	0.7	X	0.22	0.42	319	(192)	173	337
1973	2.0	2.5	5.9	0.6	X	0.23	0.41	359	(179)	183	355
1974	2.4	2.8	6.8	0.8	X	0.25	0.48	730	(62)	295	488
1975	2.4	2.9	6.7	0.4	(0.23)	0.22	0.36	144	(345)	189	300
1976	3.0	3.2	7.3	0.5	(0.31)	0.26	0.51	355	(357)	259	454
1977	3.5	3.6	7.9	0.3	(0.49)	0.30	0.54	326	(445)	286	485
1978	4.1	5.4	9.6	0.4	(0.50)	0.30	0.63	307	(454)	226	535
1979	4.6	6.0	11.3	0.8	(0.17)	0.33	0.68	938	(96)	383	652
1980	4.9	6.4	12.7	1.3	(0.01)	0.42	0.91	1130	(10)	392	729

*Parenthesis indicate deficit.
X = Less than $50 million.
Source: Yearbook of Railroad Facts, 1981 Edition (Washington: Association of American Railroads, 1981).

TABLE 27-4. Rate of Return on Investment for Class I Railroads, Selected Years, 1929-1977

Year	All U.S.	Eastern District	Southern District	Western District
1929	5.30%	6.03%	4.27%	4.85%
1939	2.56	3.14	2.77	1.85
1944	4.70	4.37	5.45	4.82
1947	3.44	3.02	3.52	3.84
1951	3.76	3.47	4.74	3.76
1955	4.22	4.19	5.45	3.86
1963	3.12	2.28	4.17	3.15
1964	3.16	2.56	4.04	3.60
1965	3.69	3.32	4.01	3.43
1966	3.90	3.55	4.16	3.87
1967	2.46	1.58	3.86	2.75
1968	2.44	1.27	3.79	3.01
1969	2.36	1.10	4.17	2.81
1970	1.73	def.	4.50	3.02
1971	2.12	def.	4.36	3.51
1972	2.34	0.11	4.61	3.34
1973	2.33	0.07	4.61	3.30
1974	2.70	0.46	4.73	3.66
1975	1.20	def.	3.98	2.65
1976	1.60	def.	4.68	3.57
1977	1.24	def.	5.23	3.71
1978	1.52	def.	5.17	4.22
1979	2.87	def.	5.38	4.38
1980	4.25	0.07	6.33	5.43

Source: Yearbook of Railroad Facts, 1981 Edition (Washington: Association of American Railroads, 1981), p. 20.

classifications) and trends of major components—the analyst has available in annual reports and ICC publications and statistical services complete breakdowns of freight revenues and tonnage by commodity classification and areas; (2) gross revenue carloadings and tonnage analysis and trends; (3) strategic position of traffic, i.e., traffic originated, terminated, and otherwise controlled; (4) trends of traffic between competing systems; (5) trends of traffic density-volume of ton-miles carried; (6) ton-miles carried per dollar of debt; (7) length of average haul; (8) stability of traffic through last two business cycles; and (9) review of trends of revenues over past cycles and estimates for the next five to six years of annual normal revenues by major commodity classification.

TABLE 27-5a. Class 1 Railroads—Income Accounts, All Districts (switching and terminal companies not included)

	1979	% of Total Ry. Oper. Rev.	1978	% of Total Ry. Oper. Rev.	1977	% of Total Ry. Oper. Rev.	1976	% of Total Ry. Oper. Rev.
Freight revenues	23,447,418,000	92.9	20,236,065,000	93.2	19,505,457,000	95.5	17,935,051,000	95.2
Passenger revenues	381,827,000	1.5	355,592,000	1.6	920,322,000	4.5	897,682,000	4.8
Total railway operating revenues	25,219,115,000	100.0	21,721,332,000	100.0	20,429,928,000	100.0	18,836,706,000	100.0
Maintenance of way and structures	4,581,748,000	18.2	4,056,494,000	18.7	3,351,038,000	16.4	3,075,496,000	16.3
Maintenance of equipment	6,018,657,000	24.1	5,437,091,000	25.0	3,846,763,000	18.8	3,406,180,000	18.1
Transportation expenses	11,346,592,000	44.9	9,601,448,000	44.2	8,174,415,000	40.0	7,605,681,000	40.9
Total railway operating expenses	23,994,154,000	95.1	21,043,143,000	96.9	17,132,826,000	83.9	15,573,154,000	82.7
Operating Ratio	95.10%		96.88%		83.86%		82.67%	
Net railway operating revenues	1,224,961,000	4.9	678,189,000	3.1	3,297,103,000	16.1	3,263,552,000	17.3
Federal income taxes	144,149,000	0.6	148,482,000	0.7	60,161,000	0.3	162,956,000	0.9
All other taxes	54,795,000	0.2	....	....	1,916,992,000	9.4	1,758,042,000	9.3
Hire of equipment—net (dr)	....	....	....	....	1,334,560,000	6.5	1,228,779,000	6.5
Joint facility rents—net (dr)	....	....	....	....	19,546,000	0.1	22,175,000	0.1
Net railway operating income	837,232,000	3.3	427,452,000	1.7	d170,765,000	(0.8)	21,429,000	0.1
Other income	1,171,566,000	4.6	945,236,000	4.4	800,391,000	3.9	705,544,000	3.7
Total income	2,396,527,000	9.5	1,623,425,000	7.5	629,626,000	3.1	726,976,000	3.9
Miscellaneous deductions	178,793,000	7.1	185,155,000	0.9	87,449,000	0.4	95,049,000	0.5
Income available for fixed charges	2,217,734,000	8.8	1,438,270,000	6.6	542,177,000	2.7	631,927,000	3.4
Rentals, etc.	....	....	....	....	24,599,000	0.1	32,236,000	0.2
Fixed interest on funded debt	788,723,000	3.1	738,600,000	3.4	653,335,000	3.2	605,504,000	3.2
Interest on unfunded debt	42,859,000	0.2	33,199,000	0.2	58,192,000	0.3	51,926,000	0.3
Amort. discount on funded debt	9,162,000	....	8,897,000	....	9,210,000	....	9,021,000	....
Total fixed charges	840,744,000	3.3	780,696,000	3.6	745,336,000	3.6	898,687,000	4.7
Income after fixed charges	1,376,990,000	5.5	657,574,000	3.0	dr203,159,000	....	dr66,760,000	....
Contingent interest charges	20,110,000	0.1	20,833,000	0.1	20,963,000	0.1	26,033,000	0.1
Net income	938,254,000	3.7	306,786,000	1.4	227,139,000	1.1	dr111,616,000	....
Extraordinary inc.	29,216,000	0.1	dr55,739,000	....	12,998,000	0.1	59,369,000	0.3
Total income	967,470,000	3.8	251,047,000	1.2	dr213,988,000	....	dr52,247,000	....
Inc. appro. to s.f. & oth. res. funds	42,157,000	0.2	44,002,000	0.2	41,445,000	0.2	42,472,000	0.2
Balance	364,370,000	1.4	207,045,000	1.0	dr172,543,000	....	dr9,775,000	....
Times fixed charges earned	....	....	1.84	....	....	....	....	....
Includes:								
Roadway depreciation	168,345,000	0.7	161,841,000	0.7	160,194,000	0.8	165,417,000	0.9
Includes:								
Equipment depreciation	840,180,000	3.3	801,196,000	3.7	741,813,000	3.6	687,300,000	3.6

TABLE 27-5a. Class 1 Railroads—Income Accounts, All Districts (switching and terminal companies not included) *(continued)*

	1975	% of Total Ry. Oper. Rev.	1974	% of Total Ry. Oper. Rev.	1973	% of Total Ry. Oper. Rev.
Freight revenues	$15,893,085,000	95.3	$16,459,475,000	95.7	$14,384,261,000	96.0
Passenger revenues	786,513,000	4.7	744,314,000	4.3	603,187,000	4.0
Total railway operating revenues	16,683,525,000	100.0	17,206,659,000	100.0	14,989,573,000	100.0
Maintenance of way and structures	2,423,924,000	14.5	2,364,873,000	14.5	2,041,539,000	14.4
Maintenance of equipment	2,996,135,000	18.0	2,912,741,000	16.9	2,599,147,000	18.3
Transportation expenses	6,987,008,000	41.9	6,978,683,000	42.8	6,060,704,000	42.6
Total railway operating expenses	13,792,198,000	82.7	13,592,490,000	79.0	11,899,360,000	79.4
Operating Ratio	82.67%		79.00%		79.38%	
Net railway operating revenues	2,891,327,000	17.3	3,614,169,000	22.2	3,090,213,000	20.6
Federal income taxes	58,122,000	0.4	217,723,000	1.3	130,326,000	0.9
All other taxes	1,581,621,000	9.5	1,605,609,000	9.8	1,240,910,000	8.7
Hire of equipment—net (*dr*)	1,089,454,000	6.5	1,028,015,000	6.3	988,197,000	7.0
Joint facility rents—net (*dr*)	26,644,000	0.2	38,396,000	0.2	33,138,000	0.2
Net railway operating income	20,796,000	0.1	513,743,000	3.2	697,642,000	4.9
Other income	630,535,000	3.8	759,344,000	4.7	467,772,000	3.3
Total income	651,331,000	3.9	1,273,087,000	7.8	1,165,414,000	8.2
Miscellaneous deductions	108,501,000	0.7	102,634,000	0.6	108,293,000	0.8
Income available for fixed charges	542,830,000	3.3	1,170,453,000	7.2	1,057,121,000	7.4
Rentals, etc.	59,499,000	0.4	58,020,000	0.4	56,737,000	0.4
Fixed interest on funded debt	623,170,000	3.7	596,824,000	3.7	552,788,000	3.9
Interest on unfunded debt	37,386,000	0.2	25,872,000	0.2	15,350,000	0.1
Amort. discount on funded debt	5,870,000	. . .	6,183,000	. . .	6,575,000	. . .
Total fixed charges	725,925,000	4.4	686,899,000	4.2	631,450,000	4.4
Income after fixed charges	dr183,095,000	. . .	483,554,000	3.0	425,671,000	3.0
Contingent interest charges	24,281,000	0.2	24,997,000	0.2	24,713,000	0.2
Net income	dr207,376,000	. . .	458,557,000	2.8	400,958,000	2.8
Extraordinary inc.	134,456,000	0.8	36,836,000	. . .	49,880,000	. . .
Total income	dr72,920,000	. . .	495,393,000	. . .	450,838,000	. . .
Inc. appro. to s.f. & oth. res. funds	47,645,000	0.3	58,762,000	0.4	29,475,000	0.2
Balance	dr25,275,000	. . .	436,631,000	. . .	371,482,000	. . .
Times fixed charges earned	. . . .		1.70		1.67	
Includes:						
Roadway depreciation	186,697,000	1.1	178,783,000	1.1	172,420,000	1.2
Includes:						
Equipment depreciation	672,022,000	4.0	641,234,000	3.9	629,647,000	4.4

Note: Data for 1980 not available.

Source: Moody's Transportation Manual, 1981, p. a6.

TABLE 27-5b. Distribution of Operating Revenues (millions of dollars)

	1980 Est.	1979	Increase or (Decrease)
Total operating revenues	$28,254	$25,219	$3,035
Wages charged to expenses[a]	10,752	10,203	549
Health and welfare and pensions	731	757	(26)
Payroll taxes	1,648	1,625	23
Total labor costs[a]	13,131	12,585	546
Income taxes on ordinary income[b]	310	144	166
Provision for deferred taxes	283	211	72
Fuel and power-locomotives	3,337	2,402	935
Loss and damage, injuries and insurance	1,000	917	83
Depreciation	1,160	1,020	140
All other expenses[c]	7,696	7,103	593
Total expenses and taxes	26,917	24,382	2,535
Net railway operating income	1,337	837	500

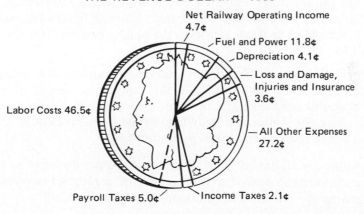

THE REVENUE DOLLAR – 1980

Net Railway Operating Income 4.7¢
Fuel and Power 11.8¢
Depreciation 4.1¢
Loss and Damage, Injuries and Insurance 3.6¢
Labor Costs 46.5¢
All Other Expenses 27.2¢
Payroll Taxes 5.0¢
Income Taxes 2.1¢

[a] Does not include wages charged to investment accounts. Total wages, health and welfare benefits, pensions and payroll taxes applicable to 1980 amounted to 40.5 cents per revenue dollar.
[b] Includes state income taxes.
[c] Includes other materials and supplies, and miscellaneous, equipment and joint facility rents, current taxes (other than payroll taxes and income taxes) and retirement charges and rent for income from leased roads and equipment.

Source: Yearbook of Railroad Facts (Washington, D.C.: Association of American Railroads, 1981), p. 11.

Gross Operating Revenues. The profitability of the railroad will depend on its freight traffic, the composition of the freight, the length of the haul, the traffic density, and the strategic position of the railroad in regard to its freight business. The analyst should study the territory served by the railroad to determine the source and the trends of actual and potential freight tonnage and revenues. Important factors to examine are the natural resources in the area studied, the agricultural situation, the type and trend of industry and commerce in the area, the volume of traffic developed, population trends, and per capita income trends. A study of the major items carried by the railroad will give insight into its earning power, since those carrying higher freight rate commodities will often be in the most advantageous position. However, certain low-rate commodities such as coal, which can be handled with relatively low labor costs, may also be very profitable.

Trend of Revenues. The trend of revenues over a period of years should be studied in relationship to the trend of the railroad industry as a whole, the trend of the region, competing roads within the region, competing modes of transportation such as motor carriers and barge lines, and GNP trends.

Tonnage Analysis. Figures for a qualitative as well as quantitative analysis are provided in "Freight Commodity Loading Statistics," a report published by the ICC. Railway freight tonnage figures for each railroad are segregated in these reports into approximately 160 classes of commodities.

Strategic Position of Traffic. In general, the greater the density of traffic, the greater the net profit. In this connection fairly diversified traffic is desirable, and it should be determined that the major source of traffic is relatively stable and growing. Freight traffic density is measured by the net revenue ton-miles per mile of road.

Ton-Miles per Dollar of Debt. The ton-miles per dollar of mortgage debt is an important ratio for the section of a railroad covered by a specific mortgage. The ratio should generally be at least 40.

Length of Average Haul. Other things being equal, the longer the average haul for freight carried, the less expensive (on an average per-mile basis) it is to move and the more profitable it is to the railroad. Terminal expenses are major expenses because of high wage costs and the amount of labor costs involved; therefore, the longer the haul, the more these expenses can be allocated on a per-mile basis.[2] The railroads

[2] Long-haul railroads are Southern Pacific, Union Pacific, and Atchison, Topeka & Sante Fe. Coal roads, such as Norfolk & Western and Chesapeake & Ohio, are exceptions to the basic long-haul requirements to produce satisfactory ROI.

are at a distinct cost disadvantage for hauls of less than 400 miles in competition with motor carriers.

Operating Expenses. The major operating expenses of the railroads are maintenance, depreciation, transportation expenses, and traffic expenses. Labor costs are the largest individual expense item. The breakdown of major operating expenses is given in Tables 27–5a and 27–5b.

Maintenance. Maintenance is a heavy factor in railroad expenses as is shown in Table 27–5a. In general, a railroad should spend at least 13 to 15 percent of gross revenue for maintenance of ways and structures, 17 to 19 percent for maintenance of equipment, and 38 to 40 percent for transportation expense.

Depreciation. This item has in recent years averaged around 5 percent of gross revenues, or about the same as the amount available for the common stock. Because it is a tax-deductible expense, the effect on net income available for the common stock is readily apparent.

Labor Factors. While railroad management has greatly increased productivity of labor since World War II, reducing the number of workers by half since 1945 while carrying more freight volume, labor costs still represent approximately 50 percent of total revenue. Average earnings of employees have approximately quadrupled. The benefits of capital expenditures and higher labor productivity have often been absorbed by employee wages with little or no benefit for security holders.

In 1929 the number of railroad employees was 1,660,850; in 1944, 1,413,672; and in 1947, 1,351,961. However, productivity so increased that the number of employees was reduced to 780,494 by 1960, to 566,282 in 1970, and to 458,994[3] in 1980. While total compensation was $4.35 billion in 1947 for 1,351,961 employees, it rose to $11.3 billion in 1980 for only 458,994 employees or from $3,218 annually per employee to $24,672 in 1980. Labor costs were 57 percent of operating expenses and 44 percent of total operating revenues in 1947, and 54 percent of operating expenses and 47 percent of total operating revenues in 1980. Therefore, labor costs relative to expenses and revenues were about the same in 1980 as in 1947 in spite of the great increase in labor productivity evidenced by the sharp decrease in the number of employees handling a large volume of freight.

Operating Ratio. The operating ratio is the ratio of operating expenses to operating revenue and consists largely of transportation expenses plus maintenance expenses. It is by far the most important ratio used in railroad analysis. But taken by itself as an indication of

_____
[3] Excludes Amtrak and Auto-Train employees. Including these employees the total is 480,410.

operating efficiency, the operating ratio may give a misleading picture, especially if maintenance is being skimped. Lease rentals, together with maintenance policy, may cause wide differences in operating ratios.

The average operating ratios for Class I railroads are shown in Table 27-6. Note that the operating ratio for all Class I railroads rose to a high of 96.9 in 1978. The historically high ratios recorded in the last three years (through 1980) are discouraging and suggest caution when selecting railroad stocks. In general, the better railroads will have lower operating ratios than the average.

TABLE 27-6. Average Operating Ratios—Class I Railroads

1954-80.2[a]	1961-81.4[a]	1967-79.1	1974-79.0
1955-75.6	1962-78.9	1968-79.0	1975-82.7
1956-77.1	1963-78.1	1969-79.2	1976-82.7
1957-78.5	1964[b]-77.7	1970-80.6[a]	1977-83.9
1958-82.2[a]	1964[b]-78.0	1971-79.3	1978-96.9
1959-77.7	1965-77.8	1972-78.7	1979-95.1
1960-78.5	1966-76.2	1973-79.4[a]	1980-93.3

[a]Business recessions; 1967 was a mini-recession year.
[b]Class I railroads before 1964, revenues of at least $3 million; beginning 1964, at least $5 million.
Source: Yearbook of Railroad Facts (Washington, D.C.: Association of American Railroads, 1981).

Other Income. Most railroads have some income other than that from their normal railroad operations, and for some railroads this other income is very significant. Many investors consider that substantial income from natural resource reserves is a very favorable factor *if normal railway operations are consistently profitable.* Investors considering such railroads should not purchase securities on this basis unless railway operations have been and are expected to be consistently profitable.

Available for Fixed Charges. Railroad fixed charges are regular annual fixed expenses such as interest on debt and rentals on leased properties. The amount available for fixed charges consists of (1) net railway operating income plus (2) other income less other deductions. This is the amount available for all security holders, and it provides the numerator in calculating the number of times fixed charges are earned as published in ICC statistics.

For all Class I railroads the amount available for fixed charges in recent years has averaged about 8 percent of gross operating revenues. The range was from actual deficits to highs of 21 percent, 24 percent, and 36 percent for certain roads.

Times Fixed Charges Earned. The primary test for bonds is the number of times fixed charges are earned. This figure is calculated by dividing the amount available for fixed charges by the fixed charges. There is a wide range for various railroads for the number of times fixed charges are earned. The industry average in years of good business is around 3X. As with other bonds, the test is also the number of times fixed charges have been earned in recession years—the stability or lack of stability of the figures.

The amount of debt that a railroad can bear is of course determined by the traffic and the level of earnings and, as previously discussed, is measured in terms of the times fixed charges are earned and the adequacy of cash flow to meet debt amortization requirements.

Preferred Dividends. Some railroads have preferred stock outstanding, and from the standpoint of the common stock, preferred dividends are a fixed charge. Therefore, the investor should calculate the coverage on an "overall basis," i.e., the number of times fixed charges plus preferred dividends are earned.

Earnings Available for the Common Stock. This is the percentage of gross income after taxes and all prior charges including preferred dividends available for common stock. In good years it has averaged about 8 percent for all Class I railroads. This is a very important figure for the common stock because it indicates the margin of safety—how much all expenses and prior charges could increase before there would be nothing left for the common stock from the gross revenues.

Earnings Available per Share of Common Stock. As with all corporations, this figure is the most important item for common shareholders. The investor must analyze the record and trend over a period of years and make projections for five to six years in the future. The amount and ratio of "other income" to gross and net income are frequently significant.

Economic Recovery Tax Act of 1981. This act contained several provisions that should strengthen the railroad industry's operating and financial position. These are briefly summarized as follows:

1. The expiration period for using up the investment tax credits has been extended to fifteen years from seven years. CSX Corporation, for example, will benefit from this change because it had unused investment tax credits totaling $209 million as of December 31, 1980. Moreover, the law allows transfer of excess investment tax credits through sale to other companies who can use them, without transfer of the asset itself. Such sales will help the cash flow of railroads.
2. Several provisions in the act are expected to drive down the cost of leasing.
3. Accelerated depreciation rules permit a five-year write-off for rail equipment, as contrasted to the fourteen-year write-off allowed under the old rules.

4. Railroads will now be allowed to expense fully the cost of materials for laying track in the year the track is laid rather than capitalizing such costs as required under prior rules.

The changes should significantly increase railroad cash flow and provide financing for needed maintenance and capital growth. Moreover, many railroads will not incur a federal income tax liability for the next several years because of the changes.

Railroad Balance Sheet Analysis. A review of the fluctuations and trends of revenues, costs, and profits (especially the number of times fixed charges are earned, the earnings per share, and the dividends received) as discussed in reference to railroad income statement analysis ordinarily provides a good indication of the prospective quality of a railroad security. However, balance sheet analysis will also provide necessary and useful information.

Working Capital. Railroads have modest working capital requirements because receivables are short term and inventories in the usual sense are not a factor. Working capital for all Class I railroads in recent years has averaged 6 to 7 percent of gross revenues, but the company-to-company range has been broad. Fixed charges must be paid out of working capital. In recent years working capital for Class I roads has averaged 1.6X to 2X fixed charges for Class I railroads, but again a wide range is present among different roads. Net working capital (current assets – current liabilities – inventories) declined sharply until 1975, but has been greatly strengthened in recent years (see Table 27-7).

Property Accounts. The major items on the asset side of a railroad balance sheet are investments in roadways and equipment. These items

TABLE 27-7. Net Working Capital for Class I Railroads—January 1, 1981 (aggregates in millions of dollars)

	1958	1963	1969	1972	1975	1977	1980
United States	995	823	(184.8)*	(60.7)	67.8	570.9	927.7
Eastern district	237	20	(313.9)	(159.7)	13.4	200.8	555.2
Southern district	166	125	64.3	12.9	17.7	105.4	282.8
Western district	593	678	64.7	86.1	36.7	264.8	89.7

*Parentheses indicate deficits.

Note: The association deducts current liabilities, including debt due within one year, from current assets, which include the material and supplies account. If material and supplies were excluded from current assets in 1977, the net working capital would become a $709.1 million deficit.

Source: Yearbook of Railroad Facts (Washington, D.C.: Association of American Railroads, 1981).

should be analyzed to determine the new equipment added annually, as well as the depreciation charged. There has been phenomenal modernization and improvement for the railroad industry as a whole since the end of World War II. The bulk of new capital funds in the railroad industry has gone into equipment, at times stimulated by the "investment credit."

Some analysts question whether railroads can maintain the present volume of capital expenditures, which is needed to exploit and accelerate traffic gains registered in recent years. Expenditures for equipment represent about 70 percent of capital expenditure.

Capital Structure Proportions. Railroad debt has been declining since the 1930s. Generally, debt for an individual railroad should not exceed 40 percent of total capitalization, and the remaining 60 percent should consist of preferred stock, capital stock, and surplus. All additional debt issued to obtain funds since the 1930s has been in the form of equipment obligations.

The amount of debt that a railroad can bear is of course determined by the traffic and the level of earnings and, as previously discussed, is measured in terms of the times fixed charges are earned and the adequacy of cash flow to meet debt amortization requirements.

Combined Statement Analysis. In Table 27–8 we note that for all U.S. Class I railroads the rate of return since World War II never reached 4 percent until 1980, except in one year (1955), because of the poor record of the eastern roads. The rate for the western roads was some-

TABLE 27–8. Rates of Return on Investment by Major Railroad Districts

Year	U.S.	Eastern District	Southern District	Western District
	%	%	%	%
1929	5.30	6.03	4.27	4.85
1939	2.56	3.14	2.77	1.85
1944	4.70	4.37	5.45	4.82
1947	3.44	3.02	3.52	3.84
1951	3.76	3.47	4.74	3.76
1955	4.22	4.19	5.45	3.86
1965	3.69	3.32	4.16	3.87
1966	3.90	3.55	4.45	4.03
1967	2.46	1.58	3.86	2.75
1968	2.44	1.27	3.79	3.01
1969	2.36	1.10	4.17	2.81

TABLE 27-8. Rates of Return on Investment by Major Railroad
Districts *(continued)*

Year	U.S.	Eastern District	Southern District	Western District
1970	1.73	def.	4.50	3.02
1971	2.12	def.	4.36	3.51
1972	2.34	0.11	4.61	3.34
1973	2.33	0.07	4.61	3.30
1974	2.70	0.46	4.73	3.66
1975	1.20	def.	3.98	2.65
1976	1.60	def.	4.68	3.57
1977	1.24	def.	5.23	3.71
1978	1.52	def.	5.17	4.22
1979	2.87	def.	5.38	4.38
1980	4.25	0.07	6.33	5.43

*def. = deficit

Source: Yearbook of Railroad Facts (Washington, D.C.: Association
of American Railroad Facts, various issues).

what less than the rate earned for the southern district. The rate earned
by the southern district reflects to an important extent the good rate
earned by the coal roads, which even in the 1930s posted a good record
and still do. The record for the western roads reflects the advantage of
long-haul traffic versus the short-haul truck competitive traffic of the
eastern district roads.

Regulatory policies that favored competing forms of truck transportation with the economics of the situation have accounted for the fact
that eastern railroads overall operated at deficits in the past. For example, deficits were reported in five of the eight years, 1973–1980, and
near deficits were reported in the other three years. Relatively short
hauls, competition from other modes of transportation, and high local
tax payments caused the eastern roads to do so poorly.

THE TRUCKING INDUSTRY

The trucking industry (motor freight carrier industry) has two
major divisions: private and for hire.[4] The private division comprises
all those businesses that provide their own transportation through

---

[4] The basic source material for this section on trucking is *S&P Basic Analysis—
Trucking.*

owned or leased lines. The for-hire division is subdivided into inter-state, intrastate, and local. Interstate truckers subdivide further into contract and common carriers, with the former operating under con-tinuing contracts with specific shippers. Both common and contract truckers are subject to ICC regulations.

For investment purposes we are concerned with publicly owned interstate ("intercity") common carriers. ICC regulations cover rates, routes, classes of commodities carried, accounting practices, finances, mergers, and acquisitions. ICC requires certificates of necessity that designate the specific routes for each carrier. In 1978 the Carter admini-stration sought to decontrol the carriers but the carriers strenuously objected fearing ruinous competition. The Teamsters Union also voiced strong opposition to deregulation. The Motor Carrier Act of 1980, however, deregulated the trucking industry, throwing it open to fresh competition. The industry did lose a measure of stability that regula-tion had provided but gained the possibility of better control of labor costs. Many smaller carriers have gone out of business, and it seems clear only the most efficient carriers will survive.

The cyclical nature of the trucking industry and its heavy financial leverage are demonstrated by the fact that in the recovery year of 1976 gross freight revenues rose about 15 percent from $22.0 billion to $25.3 billion, but net income doubled from $400 million to $795 million. This data for 1975 and 1976 compares with gross freight reve-nues for railroads of $15.4 billion in 1975 and $17.4 billion in 1976 and net income of $144.4 million in 1975 and $272.5 million in 1976. In 1976 the motor carriers accounted for 54 percent of total revenues of all regulated carriers of freight versus 39 percent for the railroads. In 1960 the motor carriers accounted for 39 percent and the railroads 50 percent. The biggest carriers[5] continue to grow larger through expan-sion of route systems and acquisitions.

The major types of freight carried by motor carriers are as follows:

Refrigerated products	Agricultural commodities
Heavy machinery	Refrigerated liquid products
Motor vehicles	Household goods
Building materials	General freight
Liquid petroleum products	All other

The fastest growing of these classes have been refrigerated products and heavy machinery.

---

[5] For 1976 the largest truckers with gross revenues of over $300 million were (a) Consolidated Freightways, $870.6 million; (b) Roadway Express, $613 million; (c) Yellow Freight, $512.2 million; and (d) McLean Trucking, $371.7 million. Of the sixteen largest publicly owned truckers, only these four had revenues over $300 million, only one between $200 and $300 million (Spector Interstate); five others had revenues of about $100 million and one (Cooper Jarrett) only $64 million.

Competition

In competition with the railroads, the truckers have taken most of the type of freight they desire (such as the less-than-carload business) from the railroads, leaving the latter with the heavy freight that truckers cannot carry economically or the very long-haul traffic. Therefore, the only real competition with the rails remaining is the piggyback freight handled by the railroads which has been growing gradually but has shown very slow growth since 1972. The deregulation of the industry has led to fierce rate discounting, thereby limiting revenue growth in 1981.

Competition therefore is largely intra-industry, but as truck freight rates have risen rather steadily, competition is being felt in the form of freight forwarders using rail piggyback facilities.

While air freight competition is relatively small, it is growing relatively fast and does take the cream of the traffic—the very high-value, high-rate traffic.

The Income Statement of Truck Carriers

As with the railroads, the largest expense items for the truckers are labor costs, which accounted for 62.3 percent of gross revenues in 1976—direct payment costs represented 53.5 percent and fringe benefits 8.8 percent.

The operating ratio for truck carriers generally ranges between 94 and 96 percent for the largest firms, the Class I truckers.

Three items—transportation expenses, terminal costs, and maintenance of equipment—absorb about 73 to 75 percent of total revenue. The balance of revenue is absorbed as follows:

Operating taxes and licenses	$6-6\frac{1}{2}\%$
Depreciation	$3-3\%$
Traffic	$3-3\%$
Insurance and safety	$4-4\frac{1}{2}\%$
General and administration	$6-6\frac{1}{2}\%$
Total	$22-23\frac{1}{2}\%$

The Balance Sheet of Truck Carriers

As with other regulated industries, the current ratio for the trucking industry is at 1.00–1.15 to 1 because there are no inventories (except tires and spare parts), and receivables are generally quite current as most traffic is on a cash basis. The amount of working capital to cover cash operating expense is considered a more significant ratio than the current ratio. For the large, financially strong carriers, the number of days cash operating expenses were covered by working capital worked out to twenty-two days in 1974 and to twenty-six days in

1975. For the industry overall it was as low as sixteen days in 1975 and thirteen days in 1974.

As a measure of the quality of the funded debt, analysts calculate the ratio of all funded debt to total annual cash flow, i.e., how much of the funded debt could be paid off if all annual cash flow was used for that purpose. For the thirty-four largest and publicly owned carriers the rate was 47 percent in 1974 and 59 percent in 1975, versus 73 percent and 76 percent as the average for 1,000 carriers.

Historically, carriers have attempted to purchase new equipment from annual cash flow, but in recent years they have increasingly used revolving credit agreements. The general capital markets are not tapped too frequently for the sale of stocks or bonds; neither are private placements normally used.

Rate of Return

The record of the rate of return on equity for the years 1969–1980 is as follows:

1969	15.50%	1973	21.06%	1977	22.98%
1970	9.04	1974	23.01	1978	21.81
1971	22.52	1975	17.46	1979	17.41
1972	20.47	1976	22.55	1980	13.71

These rates of return (from Standard and Poor's) are for the major, top-quality motor carriers. The companies used in S&P's "Composite Industry Data" are Roadway Express, Consolidated Freightways, McLean Trucking, and Yellow Freight Express.

Accounting Practices in the Industry

In reporting to stockholders, truckers may report either according to AICPA principles or in accordance with ICC procedures. Under AICPA principles, tax reductions resulting from accelerated tax depreciation and tax credits must be recorded as a deferred federal income tax liability charged to net income. But under ICC procedures this tax liability is not recognized, and tax reduction (savings) flows through to net income. Truckers may expense tires and tubes, as well as other prepaid expenses incurred, or may capitalize them and charge them off during their useful life. The method used will affect the current ratio, which normally is only between 1.0 to 1 and 1.2 to 1. Finally, the reported financial condition of the carrier will reflect the proportion of assets that are owned versus leased. An inspection of Figures 27–1 and 27–2 indicates clearly that the stock market action of trucking stocks was noticeably superior to that of the general market overall from 1966-1977, to the S&P 500 Industrial Stock Composite, and also to the index for railroad stocks. When compared with the utility stock in-

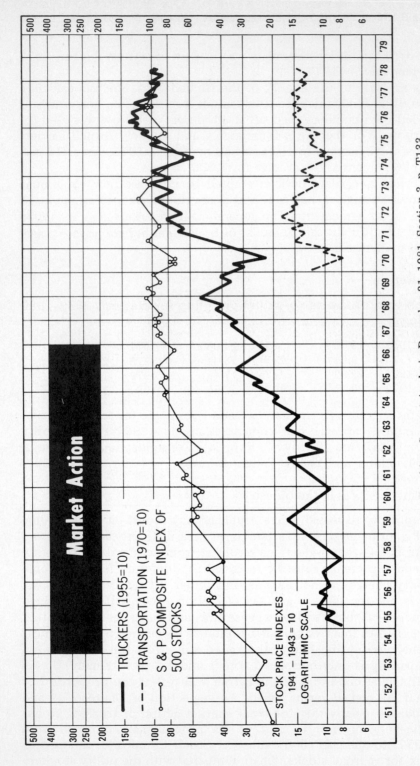

FIGURE 27-1. Market Action of Truckers Measured Against S&P 500 Stock Index, 1977–1981

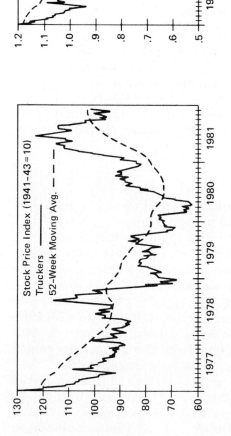

SCOREBOARD

Stock Price Indexes	1-1-81	12-23-81	% Change
500 Composite	135.76	122.31	− 9.9
400 Industrials	154.45	136.80	−11.4
1 Truckers	83.66	98.21	+17.4
2 Transportation	24.79	21.76	−12.2

1 1955 = 10.

2 1970 = 10.

INDUSTRY MARKET INDICATORS

	—Earns. Per Share—			—*P-E Ratios—		
	1979	1980	E1981	1981 High	1981 Low	12-23-81
500 Composite	14.86	14.82	15.43	8.95	7.31	7.93
400 Industrials	16.29	16.11	16.80	9.35	7.50	8.14
Truckers	9.10	8.67	11.07	11.17	7.59	8.87
Transportation	2.38	2.34	2.26	11.76	8.35	9.63

E-Estimated. *Based on est. 1981 earns.

Source: Standard & Poor's Industry Surveys—Trucking, Basic Analysis, June 15, 1981, Section 2, p. A87.

FIGURE 27-2. Market Action of Truckers Measured Against S&P Transportation Index and Composite Index of 500 Stocks

dex, which trended down sharply for much of the period, the index of trucking stocks trended significantly upward.

Summary of Analysis of a Trucking Company

The analyst should determine the economics of the area served, as well as the past and prospective growth trends of the carrier. The analyst should also determine the nature of routes used and the character of restrictions, types of highways, and tax levies. The past financial record should then be analyzed and compared to industry norms and trends in respect to items discussed above. Management's record in respect to the industry norms and management's policies toward mergers and acquisitions should be determined. Finally, the analyst should project revenues and earnings for the next five years, recognizing the cyclical nature of the industry and being especially alert to opportunities in periods of depressed stock markets, discounting general economic recessions.

THE AIR TRANSPORT INDUSTRY

The air transport industry consists of the "trunk carriers," eleven including the domestic traffic of Pan American; the seven regional carriers, including the intrastate carrier PSA; the two all-cargo carriers, Tiger International and Seaboard World; and the four air freight forwarders that bring freight to the airlines, including Emery Air Freight whose volume equals the other three combined. In 1980 operating revenues for "domestic trunk lines" totaled $20.8 billion; for the "regional carriers," $3.7 billion.

Growth Rate of Industry Slowing

During the 1960s traffic growth of the trunk airlines (93 percent of the total) grew at an annual rate of 13 percent. However, 1970 to 1977 growth was both erratic and slow. In the ten years up to January 1977, the annual growth rate slowed to 8.7 percent. In the five years through 1976, growth rate was only 6.1 percent and was quite erratic, with only 2 percent growth in 1974 and 1975 and 10 percent in 1976; and the revenues, of course, reflected the high rate of inflation. The Civil Aeronautics Board estimates that the domestic trunk traffic from 1975–1988 will grow at a 5.3 percent annual rate, international traffic at a 6.5 percent rate, and regional traffic on regional lines at a 6.5 percent annual rate. However, lower fares in 1976 significantly increased traffic.

The growth rate for the all-cargo carriers also slowed from an annual rate of 12.4 percent in the ten years through 1974; the rate from 1970–1974 was only 8.8 percent. In the early 1970s projections ran as high as 19 percent per year, more in line with that of the 1960s. However, in

1977 projections through 1985 were down to about 9 percent per year versus the projections of the early 1970s of about twice that rate, or 19 percent.

The earnings growth of the industry has been nonexistent since 1966-1967, and because of high operating and financial leverage, the earnings record has been erratic (see Table 27-9.) However, growth was strong in 1978.

TABLE 27-9. Domestic Trunk Lines, Net Operating Income, and Net Income (millions of dollars)

Year	Net Operating Income	Net Income	Year	Net Operating Income	Net Income
1966	$454	$239	1973	$415	$257
1967	410	245	1974	679	562
1968	320	127	1975	84	(78)[a]
1969	345	202	1976	472	400[b]
1970	17	(142)	1977	517	422
1971	230	73	1978	839	748
1972	434	269	1979	199	347
			1980	(225)	19

[a]Parentheses indicate deficits.
[b]Includes $112 million of gain on debenture exchanges and other extraordinary items.
Source: Air Transport (Washington, D.C.: Air Transport Association of America, various issues.

Regulation

The air transport industry is regulated by the Civil Aeronautics Board (CAB) which has had authority over routes, schedules, rates, services, safety standards, accounts, mergers, acquisitions, and intercorporate agreements. However, the Federal Aviation Administration (a division of the Department of Transportation) has assumed jurisdiction over traffic control, and airport and airline development and safety. The administration has been seeking deregulation of much of the CAB authority. But an important segment of the industry, fearing cutthroat competition and claiming that many routes to smaller cities would be abandoned, strenuously resisted. As of January 1978, the freight cargo segment of the business was deregulated and opened to free competition.

Load Factors

The most serious problem for airlines has been operational leverage associated with the load factor. Combined with the financial leverage, the heavy debt has resulted in very volatile earnings. Operating costs for specific flights tend to be largely fixed (80 percent). Therefore, once the break-even point is passed, profits rise spectacularly. For example, estimates are that the entire profit for the period 1971 through 1975 for the trunk line industry reflected only 2.3 percent of the load factor. To put it another way, if industry capacity had been 5 percent greater, there would have been no profit, and if capacity had been 5 percent less, profits would have doubled.

The break-even load factor, which had been around 55 percent for the trunk lines for the period prior to 1960, was reduced to around 50 percent in the 1960s, reflecting the increased use of jet aircraft. However, in the 1970s the break-even point again rose to around 55 percent. In 1970, with a load factor of 49.3, there was a net loss for the trunk lines. In 1975, even with a load factor of 54.8, the trunk lines suffered a net loss. In 1977 the CAB projected that for the 1977–1985 period traffic of the trunk lines would rise at an annual rate of 5.3 percent and regional lines at 6.2 percent, and capacity would rise 4.4 percent and 5.8 percent, respectively. On this basis the CAB projected that the load factor for the trunk lines would rise to 60.8 percent and for regional lines to 54.5 percent, but the lower 1978–1979 rates may cause faster growth.

Capital Outlays for New Equipment

In the nine-year period 1967–1975, the trunk lines spent $14 billion for aircraft and related ground equipment, and $4.2 billion for repayment of debt incurred for previous acquisitions or a total of $18.2 billion. The CAB has estimated that over the nine years 1977–1985, the trunk and local service carriers will need to spend $32.5 billion for passenger and all-cargo aircraft and related ground equipment. This reflects the aging of the fleets, the projected growth of traffic, and the newer requirements of the Department of Transportation.

Of the $18.2 billion needed for capital expenditures and debt reduction from 1967–1975, $10.3 billion represented internally generated funds, and $7.9 billion was obtained externally, $6.9 billion by debt financing and $1.0 billion from the sale of stock. For the 1977–1985 period, the CAB estimates that 60 percent of the funds for capital expenditures will be generated internally, largely through depreciation, and 40 percent will need to be raised externally. In the 1970s there was a sharp increase in the lease method of financing. If specific financial institutions could use the investment credits, the effective interest cost to the airlines would be reduced to 3 to 5 percent versus interest costs of 8 to 10 percent if they financed the purchases directly. The lease method was reflected in lower debt on the balance sheet, but we agree with the AICPA that leased rentals should be capitalized and shown on the balance sheet as debt. By the end of 1975, leased properties represented 25 percent of all properties on a cost basis and 27 percent on a net depreciated basis. The efforts of the CAB and Congress to deregulate the airlines and the actual deregulation of freight traffic in January 1978, combined with the poor financial condition of some of the lines, have caused the traditional lenders, especially the insurance companies, to become less anxious to provide funding.

Industry Financial Statements

In reviewing the industry's financial record overall, one must recognize that, just as in the case of railroads, the record of the weaker lines has a strong negative effect. In this respect we can note the variation in the number of years of deficit operation, from 1966-1976, for the trunk lines and the regional carriers:

1. Two carriers—Delta and Northwest—experienced no year of deficit operations.
2. Five carriers—Braniff, Continental, National, Western, and North Central—experienced only one year of deficit operations.
3. Four carriers—American, TWA, UAL, and Piedmont—experienced three years of deficit operations.
4. Two carriers—Eastern and Frontier—experienced four years of deficit operaations.
5. Three carriers—Allegheny, Ozark, and Southern—experienced five years of deficit operations.
6. Pan American experienced deficit operations for eight years beginning with 1969 and lasting through 1976.

Industry Balance Sheet. As of December 31, total U.S. scheduled carriers had $28.8 billion of total assets of which $7.5 billion, or 26 percent, represented current assets and $19.9 billion, or 69 percent, represented net operating plant and equipment.

The current ratio for the carriers ranges as follows:

1966	1.5 to 1	1970	1.0 to 1	1974	1.1 to 1	1978	1.1 to 1
1967	1.5 to 1	1971	1.1 to 1	1975	1.1 to 1	1979	0.9 to 1
1968	1.2 to 1	1972	1.1 to 1	1976	1.1 to 1	1980	0.9 to 1
1969	1.1 to 1	1973	1.1 to 1	1977	1.1 to 1		

The industry has had to rely heavily on debt financing, creating significant financial leverage as is indicated by the following ratios to total capitalization:

	Jan. 1, 1972	Jan. 1, 1974	Jan. 1, 1976	Sept. 30, 1977	Dec. 31, 1980
Long-Term Debt	67%	58%	55.6%	50.4%	59.5%
Equity	33%	42%	44.4%	49.6%	40.5%

The apparent decline in the ratio of debt until 1977 reflects the use of lease-financing without its being capitalized on the balance sheet.[6]

Industry Income Statement. As noted above, the industry record is negatively affected by the poor record of the weaker carriers. Gross revenues of seven[7] companies in the S&P Industry Composite just about doubled from 1966-1976, but earnings per share for this industry gives quite a different picture and indicates the volatile nature of industry earnings, which in turn reflect the high operating leverage (load factor) and financial leverage (high debt) of the industry.

Earnings per Share—S&P Air Transport Industry Composite

1966	$6.38	1970	d$2.89	1974	$2.48	1977	$ 6.56
1967	6.95	1971	d 0.36	1975	d 2.59	1978	11.11
1968	4.03	1972	2.30	1976	3.13	1979	4.26
1969	2.62	1973	1.17				

d = deficit

Rate of Return. The CAB has stated that airlines are entitled to earn 12 percent on investment, but the actual return has been much less and also highly volatile. The rates of return for the airlines are shown in Table 27-10.

Investors and the Airlines

As might be expected, the very sharp decline in profit margins in recent years, the great volatility of earnings, and the deficit operations of some lines have all contributed to disenchantment of investors with airline securities. As Figure 17-3 indicates, since 1968 the market action of the stock of air transport companies has been poor relative to the general market. While the general market has trended horizontally in a broad channel since 1966, the trend of the stock of air transport companies has been both sharply and steadily declining. This is also

---

[6] The 1977 AICPA "Rules on Accounting for Leases and Disclosures" states that leases should be capitalized on the balance sheet.
[7] American, Delta, Pan American, UAL, Eastern, National, and TWA.

TABLE 27–10. Rates of Return on Net Investment—Airlines, 1967–1980

Year	Total U.S. Scheduled Airlines	Domestic Trunk Lines	Local Service Airlines	Intra Hawaiian Airlines	Intra Alaska Airlines	All-Cargo Domestic Airlines	International Territorial Airlines	All-Cargo International Airlines
1967	7.6%	6.9%	2.4%	2.8%	2.9%	5.3%	11.1%	13.6%
1968	4.9	4.9	(0.4)*	(.4)	8.2	(4.9)	7.5	6.2
1969	3.3	4.3	(4.2)	(10.5)	6.0	(0.9)	3.2	6.2
1970 R	1.2	1.4	(3.9)	(6.8)	4.7	(8.3)	2.4	5.9
1971	3.5	3.3	3.7	4.3	5.9	(3.6)	3.2	11.9
1972	4.9	5.1	5.5	17.5	7.1	4.2	3.0	14.8
1973	5.1	4.7	8.9	24.2	9.2	7.9	4.5	12.9
1974	6.4	7.8	10.9	18.1	21.0	4.8	0.6	9.3
1975 R	2.5	2.2	3.5	3.3	17.7	(2.7)	2.2	7.8
1976	8.0	7.4	9.8	11.3	15.2	15.0	7.2	24.3
1977	10.9	9.6	13.7	9.9	8.2	9.3	13.7	16.7
1978	13.0	12.3	12.1	4.0	11.7	11.5	17.7	11.1
1979	7.0	5.4	12.1	11.2	8.5	10.6	7.9	8.6
1980	5.7	6.5	10.9	12.5	13.8	6.9	(1.4)	2.9

*Parentheses indicate deficit.

R = Recession.

Source: Except for "Best Records" all figures are from Air Transport 1981 (Washington, D.C.: Air Transport Association of America).

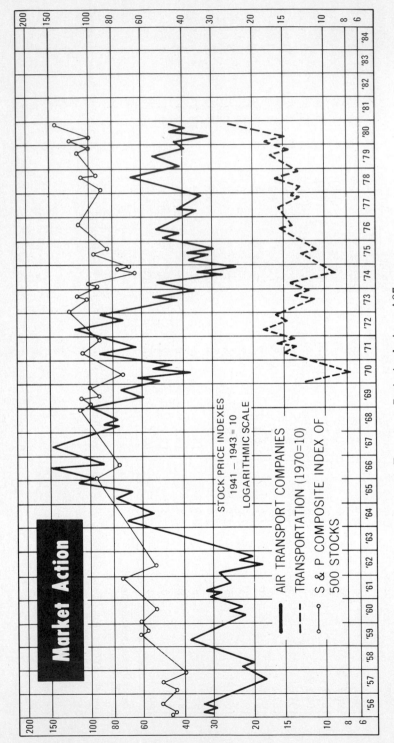

Market Action

STOCK PRICE INDEXES
1941 – 1943 = 10
LOGARITHMIC SCALE

—— AIR TRANSPORT COMPANIES
- - - TRANSPORTATION (1970=10)
—○— S & P COMPOSITE INDEX OF
        500 STOCKS

Source: Standard & Poor's Industry Surveys—Air Transport, Basic Analysis, p. A87.

FIGURE 27–3. Market Action of Air Transport Companies Measured Against S&P Transportation Index and Composite Index of 500 Stocks.

shown in Table 27–11 comparing the S&P 400 to the air transport index. In 1978 there was some renewed enthusiasm for such stocks.

Investors must consider securities in the air transport industry risky as a class because of the high debt and volatility.

TABLE 27–11. Standard & Poor's Comparative Stock Price Indexes, 400 Industrials and Air Transport

Year	S&P 400 Industrials			S&P Air Transport Index		
	High	Low	Mean	High	Low	Mean
1966	100.6	77.9	89.3	145.4	84.93	111.5
1967	106.2	85.3	95.8	143.2	96.20	121.4
1968	118.0	95.1	106.6	97.24	73.92	83.83
1969	116.2	97.8	107.0	98.16	58.02	76.52
1971	115.8	99.4	89.3	61.67	36.50	49.46
1972	133.0	112.2	122.2	112.2	70.49	91.0
1973	134.5	103.4	118.9	75.48	35.31	53.5
1974	111.7	69.5	90.6	51.05	23.06	37.5
1975	107.4	77.7	92.6	38.44	24.10	33.2
1976	120.9	101.6	110.2	51.13	38.89	45.0
1977	118.9	99.9	110.4	44.26	32.68	43.2
1978	118.7	99.5	106.2	65.18	36.38	47.12
1979	124.5	107.1	114.8	52.35	38.54	43.84

Source: Standard & Poor's *The Outlook*, various issues.

Summary

The three major components of the regulated transportation industry covered in this chapter are railroads, truckers, and airlines. In a broad legal context these are all public utilities. The most vital phases of control cover rates of return, mergers, areas of operation, and abandonments with rates of return the most significant.

In the late 1970s the federal government was proceeding toward decontrol of the airlines and trucking industries in spite of rather general opposition from corporate managements and unions in the industry concerned. Some steps toward decontrol of railroads were taken.

Passenger business, unprofitable for the railroads, has essentially been turned over to government agencies. The railroads' share of physical volume of freight traffic has declined from 75 percent to about 37 percent, while the truckers' share has risen from 3 percent to 22 percent and Great Lakes Shippers from about 4 percent to 25 percent. But the trucks have tended to take the cream of the traffic, and by the 1970s their share of freight revenues exceeded the revenues of the railroads even though they carry less tonnage.

Although the railroad industry is quite cyclical and the rate of return for the industry is continuously unsatisfactory, a few railroads such as Union Pacific and Atchison and the "coal" roads have consistently posted a satisfactory earnings record that justifies an investment rating. The securities of most railroads (except equipment trust obligations) must be rated as speculative.

In the financial analysis of a railroad, revenues must be examined to determine the source, nature, and trend of the major segments of revenues and especially the effects of business cycles.

The investment quality railroads are basically either long-haul railroads with satisfactory traffic density or the coal-carrying railroads with heavy traffic density. These roads post the lowest operating ratios and the highest times fixed charges ratios. The next most important ratio is the ratio of revenues carried down to the common stock.

The capital structure of the railroads deserves careful analysis because of the generally high debt. The analyst should determine the preparation of the capital structure according to the corporate books and also based on current market valuations of the company's securities. The analyst should also determine the proportion of equipment abilities to total debt in the capitalization.

Finally, the rate of return earned on investment and on equity must be determined as well as the trends in this respect in absolute terms as well as in terms of the industry.

There are various divisions of the trucking industry, but the potential investor is only concerned with publicly owned interstate (intercity) common carriers. ICC regulations cover rates, routes, classes of commodities carried, accounting practices, mergers, and acquisitions.

Of the roughly 10,000 intercity common carriers, only 64 are publicly owned, and Standard and Poor covers only 16 in their "Basic Analysis-Trucking." These sixteen carriers enjoy the economies of large-scale, computer-controlled operations and other modern management techniques. The larger truckers tend to become even larger through mergers and acquisitions.

The cyclical nature of the industry and the high financial leverage are somewhat similar to the same problems of the railroads, but the problems are somewhat less serious for the large truckers.

The analyst must carefully review the nature, characteristics, proportions and trends of the various sources of revenues and especially the cyclical nature of the components of revenues. The analysis is closely correlated to an analysis of routes. As with the railroads, the largest item of expense is labor costs, which account for nearly two-thirds of all expenses.

Part of the problem of financial analysis of truckers relates to the fact that some carriers report only on the basis of ICC requirements while others also report on GAAP basis (AICPA). There are also variations within these methods so that the analyst making comparative analyses of companies must make sure that comparisons being made are in fact comparable.

The air transport industry consists of eleven "trunk carriers" (including Pan American domestic routes) accounting for 93 percent of the industry traffic, seven regional carriers, two all-cargo carriers, and four air freight forwarders. In the 1970s the annual growth rate was erratic and slow—only about 9 percent versus 13 percent in the 1960s; and the CAB estimates that in the period 1975–1988 the trunk carriers annual growth rate would slow to 5.3 percent, international traffic to 6.5 percent, and regional traffic to 6.5 percent. However, in 1978 the lower fares resulting from the beginning of deregulation resulted in a very considerable increase in traffic. Therefore, it appears that the CAB growth estimates above will probably prove to have been noticeably too conservative. In 1978 air freight was decontrolled.

The break-even load factor for trunk carriers was reduced by the increased use of jets to 50 percent in the 1960s, but it rose to about 55 percent in the 1970s, and the CAB estimated that if growth was as slow as it projected, the break-even load factor could rise to as high as 60 percent.

The financial record of the industry as a whole reflects the negative drag of the weaker lines as in the case of the railroad industry. The current ratio of the industry overall is only slightly above one to one, and the heavy debt in capitalization produces high leverage with very negative effects during economic recessions. The break-even load factor results in fairly high operating leverage. While the CAB has stated that airlines are entitled to earn 12 percent on investment, the results have been much lower as well as volatile.

In recent years the decline in profit margins, the increased break-even load factor, the volatility of earnings, and deficit operations of some of the airlines have combined to cause investors to consider the industry as speculative. However, as is the case with railroads, certain companies in the airline industry do merit an investment rating.

Questions

1. (a) Discuss the relative importance of freight revenues versus passenger revenues in the railroad industry. What is the future of passenger traffic?
   (b) Is capital turnover relatively high or low for railroads? Explain the significance of your answer to this question for investors.
2. Would you recommend a buy-and-hold strategy for railroad securities? Support your position.

3. What has been happening to the relative importance of railroads as a carrier of intercity freight?

4. "The investment community considers that nine railroads represent considerably higher quality than the industry." What factors explain the better-than-average performance of these particular railroads?

5. Discuss recent trends in railroad labor costs and their significance to the investor.

6. What steps might the railroads take to improve future operating results? Do you feel it is likely that significant improvement in operating results will occur? Discuss.

7. (a) What are the important items to examine in an analysis of railroad operating revenues?
   (b) Discuss the importance of (1) length of haul and (2) traffic density in analyzing a particular railroad.

8. (a) What are the major classifications of railway operating expenses? What is the relative importance of each category?
   (b) How might one judge whether or not a railroad is undermaintaining its property? How would undermaintenance affect the income statement?
   (c) What is the operating ratio as applied to railroad income statements? How might this ratio give a misleading indication of operating efficiency?

9. (a) Is the turnover of capital for the trucking industry similar to that of railroads? Of what significance is this comparison to investors?
   (b) The trucking industry is considered quite cyclical in nature. What does this suggest concerning a proper investment approach to this industry? Discuss.

10. Contrast the growth record of airlines to that of the trucking and railroad industries.

11. (a) What factors are mainly responsible for the cyclical volatility of airline earnings that is readily apparent when historical data are reviewed?
    (b) Have airline stock prices reflected this volatility? Discuss.

12. How is "load factor" measured for an airline? What is the significance of this measure?

Work-Study Problems

1. What are the main problems currently confronting each of the three transportation industries discussed in this chapter?

2. Select and contrast a railroad stock, a trucking stock, and an airline stock in terms of

(a) Growth in revenues and operating earnings, earnings after taxes, and earnings per share over a five-year period.
(b) Return on total assets and owners' capital over a five-year period.
(c) Performance of the price of the stock over a five-year period.
(d) Financial strength during a five-year period.

28.
Financial Institutions

In this chapter we cover the two largest financial institutions—commercial banks and insurance companies. These institutions are quite different in their characteristics and in their regulations, and therefore they are treated separately. Commercial banks are covered in the first part of the chapter and insurance companies in the second part.

COMMERCIAL BANKS

The main functions of commercial banks are to receive deposits from other segments of the economy (such as business, individuals, governments, etc.) and to make loans and discounts to industry, commerce, agriculture, and individuals. The nation's commercial banks hold the bulk of the cash assets of individuals, business firms, financial institutions, trust funds, and pension funds, as well as the deposits of federal, state, and local governments.[1]

Banking: A Changing Investment Environment

The banking industry has undergone tremendous change during the past two decades. First, there was the widespread adoption of the one-bank holding company form of organization during the late 1960s and early 1970s. Moreover, bankers realized early in the 1960s that interest-bearing liabilities were likely to become the major source of funds for the support of future asset growth. Banks began to pursue more aggressive asset growth and operating strategies, based on their seeming ability to expand liabilities almost at will. The one-bank holding company

---

[1] Of total financial asset holdings of individuals as of December 31, 1978, of $3,490.8 billion, currency, bank deposits and money market shares ($7,348.9 billion) represented 38.6 percent. See *Flow of Funds Accounts: Assets and Liabilities Outstanding, 1968-78* (Washington, D.C.: Division of Research and Statistics, Board of Governors of the Federal Reserve System), p. 27.

form of organization facilitated the underwriting of a growing variety of assets and led banks into business areas not considered traditional areas of bank operations. Although such changes offered large potential rewards, risks were also present, as some banks have recently learned to their sorrow. Relatively high dependence on borrowed funds to finance expansion, for example, weakened capital structures and made banks more sensitive to interest rate volatility.

Investors greeted the changes with great enthusiasm during the early 1970s, as bank stocks reached all-time highs in terms of price-earnings ratios and the relationship of bank stock price-earnings ratios to the average price-earnings ratio for the stocks included in the Standard & Poor's 400 Industrial Stock Price Index (see Table 28-1). A few bank stocks even sold for higher price-earnings ratios than recorded by the S&P 400 Index during this period, rather than the usual discount.

The growing favor with which investors looked on bank stocks did

TABLE 28-1. Bank Stock Price-Earnings Ratios, 1972–1981

Price-Earnings Multiples for Selected Banks, by Quarters for Years 1972–1981

	1972				1973			
	Mar	Jun	Sep	Dec	Mar	Jun	Sep	Dec
Bankers Tr. NY Corp.	11.9	9.9	11.4	11.6	10.0	8.8	9.5	7.4
Chase Manhattan Corp.	13.1	11.7	14.3	12.0	9.7	9.0	11.6	10.9
Chemical NY	11.5	9.6	10.8	11.3	10.8	9.5	10.0	8.2
Citicorp	16.9	18.3	21.1	21.5	20.9	20.9	22.3	21.3
Irving Bank Corp.	11.8	10.2	10.3	10.3	8.8	8.1	8.3	7.2
Manufacturers Hanover	13.2	12.2	14.5	12.6	11.3	10.1	12.4	10.6
J. P. Morgan	13.9	14.9	16.7	16.0	14.6	16.5	18.1	17.4
Marine Midland	11.2	9.6	10.3	9.2	8.4	8.0	7.4	6.9
FN Boston Corp.	11.8	10.4	13.2	13.0	10.3	9.3	10.9	9.6
Continental Illinois	11.7	12.1	14.4	12.0	9.6	11.1	12.4	10.4
First Chicago	12.8	13.5	14.5	15.1	13.4	13.2	15.9	15.1
Northern Trust	11.1	10.8	12.1	9.8	10.2	9.7	8.8	7.5
Money Center Average	12.6	11.9	13.6	12.9	11.5	11.2	12.3	11.0
First Pennsylvania	16.0	17.7	17.3	16.7	13.3	12.3	12.7	12.1
Philadelphia National	11.0	10.6	12.7	11.5	9.5	8.0	8.5	7.2
Mellon National	11.6	9.9	11.7	10.7	10.1	8.7	8.9	8.2
Pittsburgh National	10.6	9.5	10.8	10.4	10.1	8.5	9.3	7.8
Ameritrust	9.8	9.3	10.4	10.3	9.3	8.1	7.8	6.4
National City, Cleve.	10.6	10.6	11.1	11.0	9.5	8.1	8.1	7.3
Detroitbank	8.6	8.4	8.8	8.4	7.8	6.6	6.4	5.7
NBD Bancorp	8.1	8.0	8.5	8.8	7.9	6.6	7.0	5.5
First Bank System	15.0	15.5	19.3	17.7	16.7	16.1	17.2	16.1
Northwest Bancorp.	13.7	13.5	15.0	16.7	14.8	14.5	15.4	15.1
NCNB Corp.	19.6	25.5	26.4	24.9	25.6	22.2	24.3	24.2
First Atlanta	11.5	11.3	14.7	15.0	12.5	10.9	11.1	8.3
Barnett Banks	18.2	20.9	20.9	22.3	23.2	20.3	21.3	18.1
First International	16.3	17.2	19.5	19.8	19.2	18.4	21.8	21.8
Republic of Texas	15.2	14.9	15.8	16.6	15.2	12.4	13.4	13.6

TABLE 28-1. Bank Stock Price-Earnings Ratios, 1972-1981 *(continued)*

Price-Earnings Multiples for Selected Banks, by Quarters for Years 1972-1981

	1972				1973			
	Mar	Jun	Sep	Dec	Mar	Jun	Sep	Dec
Texas Commerce	13.1	15.7	17.4	16.3	14.5	15.8	19.0	21.2
BankAmerica	15.4	16.7	17.5	17.4	16.2	15.0	15.4	14.5
Crocker National	11.3	10.4	10.6	9.7	8.6	7.6	7.9	7.1
Security Pacific	11.5	10.3	12.9	11.7	9.1	8.7	8.8	7.4
Wells Fargo	12.7	12.0	13.7	13.5	10.5	10.6	10.6	10.4
First Interstate	12.5	10.7	12.8	12.2	10.2	8.7	9.2	7.5
Seafirst	10.7	11.2	12.7	13.0	12.2	10.9	11.7	10.8
U.S. Bancorp	10.9	12.0	13.0	13.3	10.6	9.7	11.7	9.9
Regional Average	12.8	13.1	14.5	14.2	12.9	11.7	12.5	11.6
35 Bank Average	12.7	12.7	14.2	13.8	12.4	11.5	12.4	11.4
S&P 400 Industrials	20.5	19.0	19.0	19.3	17.2	15.0	14.6	12.3
35 Banks Avg. P/E as Percent of Industrials P/E	62.0	66.8	74.7	71.5	72.1	76.7	84.9	92.7

	1974				1975			
	Mar	Jun	Sep	Dec	Mar	Jun	Sep	Dec
Bankers Tr. NY Corp.	8.3	6.4	4.4	4.6	4.8	5.4	4.3	5.0
Chase Manhattan Corp.	9.8	6.7	5.7	4.8	4.9	5.3	4.3	5.6
Chemical NY	8.8	6.3	4.7	4.5	5.0	5.4	3.9	4.4
Citicorp	19.5	14.0	9.3	11.1	12.4	13.8	9.1	10.5
Irving Bank Corp.	7.7	5.4	4.2	4.1	4.7	5.0	4.0	4.2
Manufacturers Hanover	11.1	8.4	5.9	6.0	6.7	8.0	5.0	6.3
J. P. Morgan	16.8	13.0	9.3	11.0	11.7	14.1	9.8	10.8
Marine Midland	7.2	5.5	5.3	4.8	5.9	6.2	5.5	8.6
FN Boston Corp.	10.0	7.0	5.1	5.4	6.1	7.1	5.9	6.5
Continental Illinois	11.1	7.3	4.6	4.8	5.3	6.2	5.1	5.2
First Chicago	16.4	11.6	6.7	6.5	6.3	8.6	6.3	6.8
Northern Trust	8.9	7.3	4.7	6.4	6.5	7.0	5.7	6.4
Money Center Average	11.3	8.2	5.8	6.2	6.7	7.7	5.7	6.7
First Pennsylvania	11.0	6.1	3.8	5.0	6.6	6.6	5.3	10.8
Philadelphia National	7.0	4.8	4.2	4.5	5.4	5.7	4.8	5.0
Mellon National	8.8	6.9	4.9	5.9	7.0	7.7	7.0	7.8
Pittsburgh National	8.1	5.7	4.1	4.8	5.8	6.3	5.6	5.6
Ameritrust	7.6	6.0	4.3	4.9	5.3	6.2	5.3	5.2
National City, Cleve.	7.6	5.8	4.5	5.6	6.2	6.5	6.3	6.4
Detroitbank	5.9	4.8	3.8	3.7	4.1	5.2	4.4	4.8
NBD Bancorp	5.8	4.8	3.6	3.9	4.3	4.9	4.3	4.4
First Bank System	16.0	9.8	7.8	8.7	9.3	11.6	9.3	9.8
Northwest Bancorp	15.4	9.2	6.0	7.7	8.4	9.8	7.8	8.8
NCNB Corp.	20.6	12.4	5.8	7.1	12.0	14.4	9.9	8.9
First Atlanta	8.5	6.2	4.1	4.3	7.3	8.4	8.6	7.4
Barnett Banks	17.1	9.2	7.5	4.9	6.6	8.1	6.6	8.1
First International	20.1	13.8	9.1	11.3	12.8	13.4	11.4	10.5
Republic of Texas	11.9	8.5	4.3	4.7	6.5	8.0	5.9	7.1

	1974				1975			
	Mar	Jun	Sep	Dec	Mar	Jun	Sep	Dec
Texas Commerce	17.9	13.0	9.6	10.3	11.7	13.2	10.8	11.0
BankAmerica	13.9	9.8	6.8	8.6	9.6	11.0	8.9	9.7
Crocker National	8.0	5.9	4.9	6.2	7.4	7.5	6.0	6.0
Security Pacific	8.2	5.2	5.1	5.1	5.7	6.7	5.0	5.2
Wells Fargo	11.7	6.9	4.4	5.3	5.9	7.3	5.4	5.7
First Interstate	8.1	4.9	4.0	4.5	6.1	7.4	5.7	5.6
Seafirst	11.1	7.6	5.5	4.6	6.3	7.1	7.0	6.9
U.S. Bancorp	10.3	7.3	5.0	5.3	7.2	7.5	7.0	6.1
Regional Average	11.3	7.6	5.4	6.0	7.3	8.3	6.9	7.2
35 Bank Average	11.3	7.8	5.5	6.0	7.1	8.1	6.5	7.1
S&P 400 Industrials	11.5	10.2	7.1	7.9	10.2	12.4	11.3	11.8
35 Banks Avg. P/E as Percent of Industrials P/E	98.3	76.4	77.5	75.9	69.6	65.3	57.5	60.2

	1976				1977			
	Mar	Jun	Sep	Dec	Mar	Jun	Sep	Dec
Bankers Tr. NY Corp.	7.1	8.0	7.9	7.9	7.4	8.2	7.6	6.9
Chase Manhattan Corp.	8.1	10.1	9.4	9.3	9.1	10.2	8.8	8.1
Chemical NY	5.9	6.8	6.4	6.7	6.0	6.6	6.0	6.0
Citicorp	12.2	12.1	10.4	10.1	8.8	8.4	7.6	7.5
Irving Bank Corp.	5.3	5.5	5.4	5.8	5.7	5.8	5.6	5.4
Manufacturers Hanover	8.0	9.0	7.4	8.2	7.4	7.2	6.8	6.5
J. P. Morgan	12.3	12.8	11.4	11.2	9.9	9.6	8.8	8.0
Marine Midland	22.3	—	—	13.5	11.3	8.0	9.5	9.3
FN Boston Corp.	8.7	8.5	7.6	8.3	7.6	7.8	7.4	6.5
Continental Illinois	7.2	7.6	6.9	7.8	7.1	7.0	6.8	6.7
First Chicago	8.4	9.0	8.0	9.6	8.4	7.9	7.6	6.6
Northern Trust	7.5	7.3	6.9	7.8	7.1	7.0	6.7	6.3
Money Center Average	9.4	8.8[a]	8.0[a]	8.9	8.0	7.8	7.4	7.0
First Pennsylvania	15.8	25.8	—	10.3	10.1	9.0	8.0	8.0
Philadelphia National	6.7	6.8	6.4	7.4	6.7	6.7	6.0	6.7
Mellon National	9.4	10.0	9.1	8.7	7.7	7.4	7.3	7.0
Pittsburgh National	7.1	7.3	6.9	8.1	6.9	6.9	6.6	6.6
Ameritrust	6.2	6.5	6.7	7.7	6.8	7.5	6.4	6.5
National City, Cleve.	7.3	7.9	7.7	9.0	8.1	8.0	8.0	7.4
Detroitbank	5.8	5.6	6.6	7.0	6.6	6.8	6.6	6.2
NBD Bancorp	5.5	5.5	5.6	6.4	6.3	6.0	5.9	5.6
First Bank System	10.7	11.2	9.7	10.4	8.4	8.1	7.5	7.3
Northwest Bancorp	9.7	10.5	9.7	10.9	9.7	8.7	8.1	7.8
NCNB Corp.	11.8	10.7	9.9	10.1	9.3	8.4	8.1	8.0
First Atlanta	7.7	8.0	7.2	8.2	8.1	9.2	8.0	8.4
Barnett Banks	11.4	10.1	10.2	10.3	10.1	9.4	9.1	9.2
First International	12.6	12.9	10.6	11.4	9.5	10.0	9.7	9.6
Republic of Texas	7.8	9.1	9.2	9.7	9.5	8.7	7.9	8.0
Texas Commerce	11.9	12.9	11.4	11.3	10.3	9.9	9.5	9.5
BankAmerica	11.3	12.2	10.3	12.6	10.3	9.6	9.5	8.4
Crocker National	7.7	8.3	7.9	7.7	7.0	6.6	6.1	5.8

TABLE 28-1. Bank Stock Price-Earnings Ratios, 1972-1981 *(continued)*

Price-Earnings Multiples for Selected Banks, by Quarters for Years 1972-1981

	1976				1977			
	Mar	Jun	Sep	Dec	Mar	Jun	Sep	Dec
Security Pacific	6.7	7.2	6.8	7.4	6.8	6.9	6.8	6.3
Wells Fargo	7.3	8.3	7.3	8.5	8.2	7.7	7.1	6.7
First Interstate	7.3	7.8	7.3	8.0	6.8	6.9	6.5	6.6
Seafirst	8.2	8.8	7.7	8.4	8.0	8.2	8.0	7.7
U.S. Bancorp	7.2	8.6	7.9	8.8	8.2	7.8	7.1	8.1
Regional Average	8.8	9.6	8.3[b]	9.1	8.2	8.0	7.6	7.5
35 Bank Average	9.0	9.4[a]	8.2[c]	9.0	8.2	7.9	7.5	7.3
S&P 400 Industrials	12.4	11.7	11.5	11.2	10.1	9.9	9.3	9.1
35 Banks Avg. P/E as Percent of Industrials P/E	72.6	80.3[a]	71.3[c]	80.4	81.2	79.8	80.6	80.2

	1978				1979			
	Mar	Jun	Sep	Dec	Mar	Jun	Sep	Dec
Bankers Tr. NY Corp.	6.6	6.0	5.6	5.1	4.8	5.2	5.4	4.3
Chase Manhattan Corp.	7.2	6.9	7.0	5.3	4.8	5.1	4.9	4.3
Chemical NY	5.4	5.4	5.6	4.8	4.7	4.7	4.5	4.1
Citicorp	6.5	6.8	7.1	6.1	5.6	6.4	5.9	5.4
Irving Bank Corp.	5.2	5.5	5.5	4.6	4.6	4.8	4.7	4.3
Manufacturers Hanover	6.3	6.6	7.0	5.8	5.8	5.9	5.4	4.9
J. P. Morgan	7.6	7.8	7.8	6.9	6.7	6.9	7.0	6.5
Marine Midland	10.0	9.2	9.2	7.7	6.7	6.8	6.7	5.5
FN Boston Corp.	6.3	6.2	6.2	5.4	4.8	4.9	5.0	4.2
Continental Illinois	5.8	6.5	6.8	5.8	5.5	6.3	5.8	5.9
First Chicago	6.0	6.8	7.4	5.8	5.4	5.6	5.4	5.3
Northern Trust	6.6	7.1	6.8	6.6	5.8	5.9	5.8	5.3
Money Center Average	6.6	6.7	6.8	5.8	5.4	5.7	5.5	5.0
First Pennsylvania	7.0	6.7	7.1	6.2	7.4	7.6	8.4	8.3
Philadelphia National	6.4	6.4	5.9	4.5	4.8	4.6	4.8	4.3
Mellon National	6.8	6.9	6.9	5.9	6.0	6.0	6.2	5.4
Pittsburgh National	6.4	6.6	6.8	5.7	5.9	5.8	5.7	5.2
Ameritrust	6.3	6.6	6.3	5.2	5.8	5.5	5.6	5.2
National City, Cleve.	7.5	7.6	7.3	6.5	6.6	6.5	6.9	6.3
Detroitbank	5.8	5.4	6.1	5.2	4.8	4.6	5.1	4.7
NBD Bancorp	5.8	5.9	5.5	4.7	4.7	4.6	5.2	4.4
First Bank System	7.2	6.6	7.0	6.1	5.7	5.8	6.0	5.7
Northwest Bancorp	7.1	7.4	7.5	6.9	6.2	6.4	6.7	6.0
NCNB Corp.	7.4	7.6	8.0	5.9	5.5	5.9	5.9	5.5
First Atlanta	8.2	7.3	7.3	5.7	5.9	5.7	5.2	4.3
Barnett Banks	9.1	8.9	8.7	6.6	6.1	5.7	6.1	5.1
First International	8.4	9.0	9.6	8.1	7.6	7.9	·8.3	7.8
Republic of Texas	7.2	8.0	7.5	6.8	5.9	6.3	6.9	6.7
Texas Commerce	8.9	9.0	8.8	7.7	8.4	7.7	8.3	7.7
BankAmerica	7.9	7.4	8.3	7.3	6.8	6.8	6.9	6.7
Crocker National	5.5	5.2	5.2	4.1	4.6	4.6	4.6	4.3

	1978				1979			
	Mar	Jun	Sep	Dec	Mar	Jun	Sep	Dec
Security Pacific	6.0	5.7	6.4	4.9	5.1	5.6	5.5	4.7
Wells Fargo	6.0	5.7	6.1	5.3	5.3	5.3	5.3	4.7
First Interstate	6.0	5.9	6.4	5.3	5.2	6.1	5.9	5.5
Seafirst	7.2	7.4	7.9	6.6	6.6	6.8	6.9	6.4
U.S. Bancorp	7.3	7.4	7.9	6.6	6.9	6.9	7.2	6.3
Regional Average	7.0	7.0	7.2	6.0	6.0	6.0	6.2	5.7
35 Bank Average	6.9	6.9	7.0	5.9	5.8	5.9	6.0	5.5
S&P 400 Industrials	8.5	8.9	9.3	8.2	8.0	7.6	7.7	7.5
35 Banks Avg. P/E as Percent of Industrials P/E	81.2	77.5	75.3	72.0	72.5	77.6	77.9	73.3

	1980			
	Mar	Jun	Sep	Dec
Bankers Tr. NY Corp.	3.5	3.5	3.5	4.3
Chase Manhattan Corp.	3.8	4.4	3.8	4.6
Chemical NY	3.8	4.1	3.8	3.8
Citicorp	4.6	5.0	4.4	5.9
Irving Bank Corp.	3.6	4.1	4.0	4.9
Manufacturers Hanover	4.4	5.0	4.6	4.7
J. P. Morgan	6.0	6.2	5.0	5.8
Marine Midland	3.5	3.9	4.7	4.8
FN Boston Corp.	3.7	4.0	3.9	4.3
Continental Illinois	5.1	5.4	5.0	5.5
First Chicago	5.1	6.5	8.1	9.3
Northern Trust	4.8	4.9	5.0	4.8
Money Center Average	4.3	4.8	4.7	5.2
First Pennsylvania	19.1	—	—	—
Philadelphia National	4.1	4.2	4.5	4.7
Mellon National	4.4	5.2	5.3	5.5
Pittsburgh National	4.3	5.0	5.1	5.0
Ameritrust	3.8	4.6	5.3	4.9
National City, Cleve.	4.5	5.8	5.3	5.1
Detroitbank	3.6	4.8	5.2	4.5
NBD Bancorp	3.5	3.8	4.5	3.7
First Bank System	4.9	5.1	5.1	5.4
Northwest Bancorp	4.6	5.6	5.4	6.4
NCNB Corp.	4.5	5.3	5.0	5.2
First Atlanta	3.8	3.8	5.0	5.4
Barnett Banks	4.5	5.9	6.2	6.6
First International	6.7	8.3	7.7	8.5
Republic of Texas	5.2	6.4	6.3	7.0
Texas Commerce	7.0	8.2	8.8	9.2
BankAmerica	5.6	6.1	5.5	6.9
Crocker National	3.8	4.6	5.0	5.5
Security Pacific	4.1	5.0	4.5	5.2
Wells Fargo	4.0	5.0	4.5	5.4
First Interstate	4.5	5.4	5.2	6.1

TABLE 28-1. Bank Stock Price-Earnings Ratios, 1972-1981 *(continued)*

Price-Earnings Multiples for Selected Banks, by Quarters for Years 1972–1981

	1980			
	Mar	Jun	Sep	Dec
Seafirst	5.3	5.7	5.5	6.2
U.S. Bancorp	6.0	6.4	6.4	6.7
Regional Average	5.3	5.5[b]	5.5[b]	5.9[b]
35 Bank Average	5.0	5.2[b]	5.2[b]	5.6[b]
S&P 400 Industrials	6.9	7.8	8.8	9.6
35 Banks Avg. P/E as Percent of Industrials P/E	72.5	66.7	59.1	58.3

	1981 Mar	1981 Jun	Indic. Cash Div.	Earn. 12 Mos. 30 Jun 81	Bid Price 13 Aug 81	Curr. P/E Ratio
Bankers Tr. NY Corp.	4.4	5.3	$1.85	6.25	$32\frac{3}{8}$	5.2
Chase Manhattan Corp.	4.6	5.6	3.10	9.68	$53\frac{3}{4}$	5.6
Chemical NY	4.3	4.6	3.84	12.52	$55\frac{1}{4}$	4.4
Citicorp	5.6	7.5	1.56	3.59	$26\frac{1}{4}$	7.3
Irving Bank Corp.	4.6	4.9	3.04	10.60	$50\frac{1}{2}$	4.8
Manufacturers Hanover	4.6	5.6	2.72	6.94	$35\frac{1}{4}$	5.1
J. P. Morgan	5.5	6.6	3.10	8.99	$57\frac{1}{2}$	6.4
Marine Midland	4.5	5.6	1.05	3.77	$19\frac{1}{2}$	5.2
FN Boston Corp.	4.7	4.7	2.50	9.33	$41\frac{5}{8}$	4.5
Continental Illinois	5.9	7.0	1.80	5.80	$38\frac{1}{2}$	6.6
First Chicago	8.9	10.6	1.20	1.82	$19\frac{1}{4}$	10.6
Northern Trust	4.9	5.7	2.44	7.11	37	5.2
Money Center Average	5.2	6.1	—	—	—	5.9
First Pennsylvania	—	—	—	(2.52)	$4\frac{5}{8}$	—
Philadelphia National	4.8	5.3	2.92	6.37	$32\frac{5}{8}$	5.1
Mellon National	5.9	6.3	2.04	5.99	$35\frac{1}{4}$	5.9
Pittsburgh National	5.2	5.6	3.00	9.24	$48\frac{7}{8}$	5.3
Ameritrust	4.8	5.4	2.72	6.49	$33\frac{3}{4}$	5.2
National City, Cleve.	5.3	5.9	2.75	5.77	31	5.4
Detroitbank	5.0	5.0	2.00	4.32	$22\frac{5}{8}$	5.2
NBD Bancorp	4.2	4.8	2.00	5.92	27	4.6
First Bank System	5.8	6.0	2.44	7.26	$37\frac{3}{4}$	5.2
Northwest Bancorp	6.6	6.9	1.64	4.53	29	6.4
NCNB Corp.	6.3	6.7	.80	2.45	$14\frac{5}{8}$	6.0
First Atlanta	5.8	5.5	1.12	4.71	$24\frac{7}{8}$	5.3
Barnett Banks	7.6	6.3	.96	3.23	24	7.4
First International	8.5	9.0	1.10	3.37	$30\frac{5}{8}$	9.1
Republic of Texas	7.6	7.8	1.40	5.60	42	7.5

	1981 Mar	1981 Jun	Indic. Cash Div.	Earn. 12 Mos. 30 Jun 81	Bid Price 13 Aug 81	Curr. P/E Ratio
Texas Commerce	9.6	9.6	.92	4.09	$38\frac{1}{4}$	9.4
BankAmerica	6.4	6.5	1.52	3.86	$24\frac{1}{8}$	6.3
Crocker National	6.2	6.4	2.40	6.11	$39\frac{3}{4}$	6.5
Security Pacific	5.2	5.7	2.20	7.05	$38\frac{1}{8}$	5.4
Wells Fargo	4.7	5.9	1.92	5.55	$30\frac{3}{4}$	5.5
First Interstate	6.3	7.1	1.84	6.12	$38\frac{1}{2}$	6.3
Seafirst	5.7	6.6	1.28	4.72	$29\frac{5}{8}$	6.3
U.S. Bancorp	7.1	7.5	1.20	4.42	$32\frac{3}{4}$	7.4
Regional Average	6.1^b	6.4^b	—	—	—	6.2^b
35 Bank Average	5.8^b	6.3^b	—	—	—	6.1^b
S&P 400 Industrials	9.8	9.4^E	—	—	—	9.6^E
35 Banks Avg. P/E as Percent of Industrials P/E	59.2	67.0^E	—	—	—	63.5^E

[a]Average P/E for banks excludes Marine Midland.
[b]Average P/E for banks excludes First Pennsylvania.
[c]Average P/E for banks excludes Marine Midland and First Pennsylvania.
[E]Estimate.

Source: T. Hanley, J. Cohn, R. Stewart & L. Christian, "Price Earnings Multiples for Selected Banks by Quarters, for Years 1972–1981" (New York: Salomon Brothers, August 19, 1981).

not, however, last long. The presence of severe problems became evident during 1974–75, and some spectacular failures and near failures occurred for large banking institutions; First Pennsylvania is an example. This led to a reversal in investor attitudes, as exemplified by the sharp decline in price-earnings ratios for bank stocks by 1980–81.

The following six major developments that have altered the face of U.S. banking were outlined in a paper presented at a recent FMA workshop:[2]

1. An increased dependence on purchased money, leading to interest expense becoming a large and volatile number, approximating 50 percent of total expenses.
2. A "growth" philosophy, coupled with the need to cover rapidly rising expenses, led to the liberalization of lending policies and a sharp rise in loan losses.
3. The erosion of bank capital. "In the early 1960s bank net worth generally

_____

[2]*Bank Analysis from External Sources* (New York: Cates, Lyons & Co., Inc., 1979), pp. 3–14.

exceeded 10 percent of total assets, with few exceptions. The growth of assets since that Golden Age has so greatly exceeded the growth of capital that this key ratio now ranges between 4 percent and 8 percent." [3]

4. The growth of overhead resulting from the addition of new headquarters buildings, extensive branching networks to reach depositors and markets, and the addition of computer hardware. Staff compensation also has risen sharply.
5. Competition intensified.
6. The formation of holding companies.

Financial Analysis of Commercial Bank Stocks

As with other industries, an investor is interested in the financial strength and the earning power of a bank. Ratio analysis of bank financial statements is the primary tool used by security analysts, paying attention to both the level and trend of the ratios studied. Any such analysis should, of course, be forward looking. The goal of any security analysis is to use past and present performance characteristics as a basis for assessing future prospects.

Earnings: The Key Variable

Banks must earn competitive rates on their capital if they are to be attractive to investors. The relative importance of various income and expense components for commercial banks is presented in Table 28-2. When analyzing bank operations, one should concentrate on bank earnings—that is, income before security transactions, not net income. One should not lose sight, however, of the fact that net income represents the base from which dividends to stockholders are paid and is the primary source of growth capital generated by bank operations.

Rate Earned on Average Assets. Probably the best indicator of the efficiency of bank operations and earnings performance is the return on average assets. Float can distort the interpretation of this ratio since it is not an indicator of management performance.[4] Also, the portion of earnings derived from nonfunds using sources of income (such as trust services) can vary from bank to bank.

Rate Earned on Average Equity Capital. The rate of return earned on average equity capital by banks is a bit below the average rate earned by manufacturing corporations during the period 1976–1980 (see Table 28-3). This partially explains the lower price-earnings ratios typically

---

[3] *Ibid.*, p. 8.
[4] Checks in the process of collection can be a large or small fraction of total assets at any given time, thereby tending to raise or lower return on assets.

TABLE 28-2. Ratios of Income of Insured Commercial Banks in the United States (States and Other Areas), 1975–1980

Income Item	1975	1976[a]	1977[a]	1978[a]	1979[a]	1980[a]
Amounts per $100 of operating income						
Operating income—total	$100.00	$100.00	$100.00	$100.00	$100.00	$100.00
Interest and fees on loans[b]	68.62	66.49	68.03	70.31	72.08	71.14
Interest on balances with depository institutions[c]	.....	5.56	5.41	5.91	7.10	8.52
Interest on U.S. Treasury securities and on obligations of other U.S. government agencies and corporations	6.67	7.41	7.08	8.26	7.11	7.05
Interest on obligations of states and political subdivisions	7.39	6.37	5.94	5.32	4.63	4.28
Income from all other securities	4.33	4.05	3.80	.96	.80	.75
Income from fiduciary activities	2.41	2.23	2.19	1.88	1.58	1.44
Service charges on deposit accounts in domestic offices	2.34	2.03	2.00	1.80	1.68	1.67
Other service charges, commissions, and fees	2.48	2.71	2.67	2.59	2.42	2.29
Other operating income	5.76	3.16	2.88	2.96	2.60	2.85
Operating expenses—total	86.51	87.71	87.20	86.70	88.09	89.78
Salaries and employee benefits	19.06	18.29	18.09	16.50	14.35	12.93
Interest on deposits in domestic offices	39.43	32.55	31.65	31.39	31.51	33.27
Interest on deposits in foreign offices[e]	.....	10.85	11.31	12.82	16.32	18.32
Interest on demand notes issued to the U.S. Treasury and other borrowed money[d]	6.00	5.36	6.37	8.07	10.66	11.38
Occupancy expense of bank premises net and furniture and equipment expense	5.79	5.56	5.51	4.92	4.18	3.86
Provision for possible loan losses	5.43	4.57	3.65	3.10	2.52	2.35
Other operating expenses	10.80	10.53	10.62	9.90	8.55	7.67

TABLE 28-2. Ratios of Income of Insured Commercial Banks in the United States (States and Other Areas), 1975–1980 (continued)

Income Item	1975	1976[a]	1977[a]	1978[a]	1979[a]	1980[a]
Income before income taxes and securities gains or losses	13.49	12.29	12.80	13.30	11.91	10.22
Amounts per $100 of total assets[e]						
Operating income—total	7.20	7.18	7.23	8.09	9.49	10.87
Operating expenses—total	6.23	6.30	6.30	7.02	8.36	9.76
Income before income taxes and securities gains or losses	.97	.88	.93	1.08	1.13	1.11
Net income	.78	.70	.71	.77	.81	.80
Recoveries credited to allowance	.....	.....	.....	.08	.08	.07
Losses charged to allowance	.....	.....	.....	−.25	−.24	−.28
Provision for possible loan losses	.....	.....	.....	.25	.24	.26
Amounts per $100 of total equity capital[e]						
Net income	11.75	11.41	11.72	12.80	13.89	13.66
Cash dividends declared on common stock	4.91	4.42	4.36	4.42	4.81	4.96
Net change in capital accounts (less cash dividends on common and preferred stock)	6.84	6.99	7.36	14.79[f]	16.53[f]	15.60
Special ratios[a]						
Income on loans per $100 of loans[b]	8.52	8.48	8.66	9.76	11.64	13.29
Income on U.S. Treasury and other U.S. government agency and corporation securities per $100 of those securities	6.73	6.75	6.62	7.12	8.02	9.10

Income on obligations of states and political subdivisions per $100 of those obligations	4.97	5.00	4.95	4.80	5.44	5.86
Service charges on demand deposits in domestic offices per $100 of those deposits	.50	.51	.52	.54	.64	.76
Interest paid on time and savings deposits in domestic offices per $100 of those deposits	5.92	5.53	5.50	6.02	7.48	9.08
Number of banks at end of period	14,384	14,411	14,412	14,391	14,364	14,435

a Based on consolidated (including foreign) reports of income.
b Includes federal funds sold.
c Not available before 1976.
d Includes interest on federal funds purchased, subordinated notes and debentures, and other borrowed money.
e Ratios are based on averages of assets and liabilities.
f Includes all changes: prior to 1978 the ratio represents changes due to net income only.
Source: 1980 Annual Report, Federal Deposit Insurance Corporation, Table 116, p. 277.

TABLE 28-3. Return Earned on Average Equity and all Manufacturing Corporations, 1976–1980

Bank Groups[a]	Year	Return on Average Equity
Peer Group 1 (12 banks: over $20 billion in assets)	1980	15.08%
	1979	15.17
	1978	14.24
	1977	12.48
	1976	12.03
Peer Group 2 (33 banks: $5–20 billion in assets)	1980	13.43%
	1979	14.34
	1978	13.62
	1977	11.93
	1976	11.36
Peer Group 3 (81 banks: $2–5 billion in assets)	1980	14.15%
	1979	13.84
	1978	12.45
	1977	10.83
	1976	9.88
Peer Group 4 (85 banks: $1–2 billion in assets)	1980	14.17%
	1979	13.90
	1978	12.75
	1977	11.19
	1976	9.54
Peer Group 5 (39 banks: $750 million to $1 billion)	1980	13.56%
	1979	14.86
	1978	14.01
	1977	12.42
	1976	11.75
Peer Group 6 (79 banks: $500 million to $750 million)	1980	13.69%
	1979	14.09
	1978	13.09
	1977	11.11
	1976	10.36

TABLE 28-3. Return Earned on Average Equity and all Manufacturing Corporations, 1976–1980 *(continued)*

Bank Groups[a]	Year	Return on Average Equity
Peer Group 7 (80 banks: lender		
$500 million)	1980	13.56%
	1979	14.09
	1978	13.58
	1977	11.53
	1976	10.87
All Manufacturing Companies[b]	1980	13.90%
	1979	16.45
	1978	15.00
	1977	14.18
	1976	13.95

[a]*Source: Keefe Bank Book: 1981* (New York: Keefe, Bryette & Woods, Inc., 1981), p. x.
[b]*Source: Federal Reserve Bulletin*, April, 1981.

accorded bank stocks during this period. Still, the discount at which bank stocks have been selling seems excessive when their earnings performance is reviewed relative to that of manufacturing companies.

Leverage and Rates of Return. Changes in the level of bank earnings from year to year are determined by the rate earned on total bank assets, the rate of growth of those assets, and leverage factors as shown in Table 28-4. A rising return on assets and increased leverage (measured by dividing average total assets by average shareholders' equity) did result in a higher rate of return being earned on stockholders' equity after 1977 than before. Interestingly, bank price-earnings ratios, on average, still fell to a historic low 58.3 percent of the average P/E ratio for the S&P 400 industrial stocks in the fourth quarter of 1980. Bank performance just doesn't seem to explain the disfavor into which their common stocks had fallen by the end of 1980.

Other Key Performance Ratios. Other ratios useful in analyzing bank performance and financial strength are briefly reviewed as follows:

1. The following four ratios should be reviewed to give an indication of possible asset quality problems resulting from the loan decisions of the bank:
   (a) *Period-end reserve for loan losses to period-end loans.*

TABLE 28-4. The Interplay of Asset Leverage and Profit Margins on Return on Equity

	1976			1977		
	Leverage[a] ×	ROA[b] =	ROE	Leverage[a] ×	ROA[b] =	ROE
Citicorp	23.2×	.69%	16.0%	24.5×	.56%	13.7%
BankAmerica	29.9	.52	15.5	28.1	.55	15.5
Chase Manhattan	26.2	.24	6.3	27.3	.26	7.1
J. P. Morgan & Co.	18.9	.78	14.7	19.1	.75	14.3
Manufacturers Hanover	27.7	.50	13.9	26.6	.51	13.6
Continental Illinois	23.6	.63	14.9	23.9	.63	15.1
Western Bancorp.	22.6	.47	10.6	23.0	.58	13.3
Chemical NY	28.9	.37	10.7	29.9	.37	11.1
First Chicago	20.2	.50	10.1	21.1	.53	11.2
Security Pacific	22.8	.49	11.2	23.5	.58	13.6
Bankers Trust NY	28.9	.27	7.8	30.9	.26	8.0
Wells Fargo	23.9	.50	12.0	23.0	.61	14.0
Mellon National	14.6	.69	10.1	14.1	.73	10.3
Northwest Bancorp.	15.5	.86	13.3	16.1	.87	14.0
First Bank System	14.5	.88	12.8	15.2	.89	13.5
Crocker National	25.0	.42	10.5	25.5	.46	11.7
FN Boston	16.2	.51	8.3	18.0	.48	8.6
First International	17.9	.88	15.8	18.2	.88	16.0
National Detroit	16.3	.72	11.7	16.0	.73	11.7
Marine Midland	25.1	.08	2.0	25.7	.16	4.1
Irving Bank Corp.	26.9	.41	11.0	27.6	.40	11.0
Republic of Texas	17.1	.73	12.5	17.3	.70	12.1
Texas Commerce	17.2	.87	15.0	18.0	.88	15.8
Ameritrust	10.4	1.01	10.5	10.3	1.09	11.2
Seafirst	18.5	.76	14.1	19.3	.76	14.7
National City, Cleve.	12.2	1.33	16.2	12.0	1.36	16.3
U.S. Bancorp	16.0	.98	15.7	14.8	1.11	16.4
Pittsburgh National	13.7	.97	13.3	13.2	.97	12.8
Philadelphia National	16.4	.68	11.2	17.0	.56	9.6
NCNB Corp.	18.8	.52	9.8	19.6	.56	11.0
Detroitbank	14.4	.88	12.7	14.9	.90	13.4
Northern Trust	16.3	.75	12.2	17.1	.63	10.8
First Pennsylvania	23.4	.31	7.3	25.7	.35	9.0
Barnett Banks	14.2	.55	7.8	15.0	.60	9.0
First Atlanta	19.8	.46	9.1	19.6	.53	10.4
Composite	22.3×	.54%	12.0%	22.7×	.55%	12.5%

[a]Financial leverage average total assets divided by average shareholders' equity.
[b]Profit margin income before securities transactions divided by average total assets.

Source: T. Hanley, J. Cohn, and R. Stewart, *A Review of Bank Performance: 1981 Edition*

1978				1979				1980			
Leverage[a]	× ROA[b]	=	ROE	Leverage[a]	× ROA[b]	=	ROE	Leverage[a]	× ROA[b]	=	ROE
26.1×	.61%		15.9%	27.9×	.58%		16.2%	28.7×	.47%		13.5%
28.6	.63		18.0	28.9	.64		18.5	28.3	.62		17.5
27.7	.36		10.0	28.6	.52		14.9	27.6	.53		14.6
19.7	.81		16.0	21.7	.71		15.4	23.2	.77		17.9
26.1	.52		13.6	28.0	.51		14.3	29.0	.48		13.9
24.0	.63		15.1	25.7	.58		14.9	27.0	.57		15.4
23.4	.70		16.4	23.8	.79		18.8	23.0	.78		17.9
29.0	.40		11.6	29.9	.42		12.6	30.9	.46		14.2
20.8	.58		12.1	22.1	.45		9.9	23.9	.23		5.5
24.1	.66		15.9	24.1	.70		16.9	24.0	.69		16.6
30.4	.32		9.7	30.5	.42		12.8	29.9	.58		17.3
23.6	.70		16.5	24.4	.68		16.6	25.3	.55		13.9
14.3	.82		11.7	15.6	.81		12.6	17.0	.78		13.3
16.5	.93		15.3	17.0	.95		16.2	17.2	.90		15.5
16.2	.95		15.4	16.5	.95		15.7	16.5	.91		15.0
24.7	.58		14.3	24.5	.60		14.0	24.6	.55		13.5
19.5	.56		10.9	20.7	.66		13.7	22.3	.67		14.9
18.4	.92		16.9	18.9	.95		18.0	18.6	1.01		18.8
15.8	.87		13.7	15.5	.91		14.1	15.8	.80		12.6
29.1	.19		5.5	32.0	.29		9.3	26.5	.35		9.3
29.3	.43		12.6	30.9	.46		14.2	30.4	.52		15.8
18.4	.77		14.2	20.1	.76		15.3	20.1	.81		16.3
18.4	.93		17.1	17.9	1.00		17.9	17.5	1.11		19.4
10.2	1.20		12.2	10.6	1.12		11.9	10.4	1.07		11.1
18.5	.85		15.7	18.8	.86		16.2	18.8	.80		15.0
12.1	1.37		16.6	12.9	1.28		16.5	14.3	1.04		14.9
14.1	1.25		17.6	13.6	1.27		17.3	13.1	1.28		16.8
13.5	1.04		14.0	15.4	1.04		16.0	17.0	.97		16.5
18.5	.66		12.2	18.3	.72		13.2	18.6	.68		12.6
19.3	.74		14.3	19.8	.80		15.8	20.2	.74		14.9
15.9	.98		15.6	15.9	.99		15.7	16.4	.76		12.5
18.3	.63		11.5	19.2	.60		11.5	19.8	.59		11.7
25.5	.37		9.4	23.0	.16		3.7	22.2	-1.12		-24.9
16.1	.84		13.5	16.5	.94		15.5	17.1	.96		16.4
19.8	.57		11.3	19.1	.64		12.2	17.7	.82		14.5
23.2×	.61%		14.2%	24.0×	.63%		15.1%	24.4×	.60%		14.6%

(New York: Salomon Brothers, 1981), pp. 34–35.

(b) *Net loan charge-offs to average total loans.*

(c) *Provision for loan losses to net charge-offs of that period.*

(d) *Nonperforming assets to loans.* This ratio indicates the proportion of total loans that are in default.

2. Financial strength is measured by balance sheet as well as income statement ratios. The following are important ratios to study over time:

(a) *Subordinated debt to total capital accounts.* Although this ratio is low for "all insured commercial banks," it tends to be quite large for large money center banks. While the subordination reduces risk somewhat for the purchaser of such instruments, it does not really reduce bank risk.

(b) *Ratio of capital accounts to assets, deposits, and loans.* In the early 1960s bank capital accounts generally exceeded 10 percent of total assets. Asset growth, financed mainly by adding bank liabilities, has reduced this ratio to 4 to 8 percent by 1980, depending on bank size, location, and management policy. There has been an erosion of bank capital, and the low P/E ratios, already reviewed for bank stocks, make raising new equity capital painful. Bank analysts should and do watch the capital formation rate from internal sources in relation to the rate of asset growth. They also monitor the maturity of debt, as well as the total outstanding.

(c) *Ratio of time and savings deposits to total deposits.* The higher the proportion of time and savings deposits to total deposits for a bank, the greater the interest cost. Time and savings deposits represented only about 22 percent of total deposits for the average bank in 1945. By December 1980 this ratio was about 64 percent. The increased interest expense resulting from this change in deposit makeup has led banks to reach for higher-yielding loans and asset mixes, no doubt, thereby, increasing investor risk.

(d) *Ratio of cash and U.S. government securities to total assets and deposits.* This ratio indicates the immediate liquidity of the bank. Analysts expect the ratio to be at least 12 percent of total assets and 15 percent of deposits.

(e) *Dividends per share divided by earnings per share* (the payout ratio).

The Net Interest Margin. Banks have increasingly depended on purchased money (the incurrence of liabilities) to finance asset growth since 1961. Steadily rising interest rates throughout the 1970s, coupled with the rapidly increasing debt taken on by banks, has resulted in interest expense becoming a large and volatile number. This has led analysts to stress the concept of "net interest margin." Net interest margin is measured by dividing net interest income by average earning assets. This ratio should be considered in terms of the history of the bank being reviewed and the average ratio for similar-sized banks. A net interest margin below the average suggests inefficient use of assets. On the other hand, a ratio that much exceeds the average for similar banks could suggest a bank that has courted high risk loans and investments.

A break-even yield can also be computed for a bank by dividing total interest expense by average gross earning assets. The break-even yield indicates the yield required on earning assets merely to cover interest expense. "For a retail-oriented bank, heavy in demand and savings type deposits, the norm for break-even yield tends to range between 2 and 3 percent, changing little from year to year. For many wholesale banks, which 'buy' most of their investible funds, the break-even yield is not only much higher (5 to 7 percent), but fluctuates according to interest rate movements."[5]

INSURANCE COMPANY STOCKS

Insurance companies can be divided into two major groups: (1) fire and casualty companies and (2) life insurance companies. The characteristics of these two groups are quite different so they will be dealt with separately. One difference is that contracts for property and liability companies are relatively short, usually one, two, or three years, while contracts issued by life insurance companies usually run for many years. Some companies are writing multiline life insurance, health and accident policies, and fire and casualty policies. Insurance companies are also classified as either (1) mutual companies or (2) stock companies, the latter being the only ones in which investors can invest.

Insurance Accounting—Regulatory vs. GAAP Accounting

Historically, until the late 1960s and early 1970s, fire and casualty companies and also life companies reported to stockholders in the manner required by state insurance commissioners. Because statutory accounting differs in significant ways from GAAP accounting, the analyst had to adjust reported statements to conform with GAAP accounting.[6] However, as a result of reports and requirements issued by the AICPA, and also SEC requirements and pressures from the Financial Analysts Federation, most companies whose securities are publicly traded now submit supplementary schedules in addition to statutory reporting. These are necessary for statutory accounting to be reconciled to conform with GAAP accounting. Therefore, analysts operating outside the company are given the reconciliations or can make them with data supplied.[7]

_____

[5] *Bank Analysis from External Sources*, p. 31.

[6] Statutory reporting prorates the income over the life of the policy as under GAAP but, unlike GAAP, does not prorate the expenses of placing policies on the books, but instead burdens the initial fiscal period with all the initial expenses.

[7] (a) Audits of Fire and Casualty Insurance Companies. An AICPA Industry Audit Guide, prepared by the Committee on Insurance Accounting and Auditing of the American Institute of CPA's, New York, 1966. See also, annual editions of Fin-

Fire and Casualty Insurance Companies

The income of insurance companies consists of underwriting premiums collected plus investment income. The expenses consist of underwriting expenses, losses and expenses associated with covered policy losses, and proportionate general and administrative overhead.

Underwriting Tests of Profitability. There are three major tests of underwriting profitability: the loss ratio, the expense ratio, and the combined loss and expense ratio. The historic ratios for the insurance industry are shown in Table 28-5.

Loss Ratio. This ratio is generally taken as the ratio of losses incurred, plus directly related expenses, to premiums earned, although sometimes the ratio is calculated to premiums written. This is a test of the quality of the risks that are underwritten.

Expense Ratio. This ratio is generally taken as the ratio of operating expenses to premiums written but may be taken as a ratio to premiums earned. It is a test of management's efficiency in operations.

Combined Loss and Expense Ratio. This ratio is the sum total of the loss ratio and the expense ratio and, if under 100, indicates the degree of profitability of underwriting and, if over 100, the degree of unprofitability.

Recurring Cycles in Fire and Casualty Business. An examination of Table 28-5 indicates the cyclical nature of underwriting. The business will experience profitability for a period of years and then, especially in years of inflation, the business will become unprofitable. When it is unprofitable, the companies will seek rate increases. Increases in rates for the industry as a whole have always eventually been granted by state insurance commissioners, and the industry has then returned to a period of profitability, which again is followed by a period of unprofitability. These cycles are obvious in Table 28-5. Purchasers of fire and casualty insurance stocks during the unprofitable and out-of-favor phase of the cycle must assume a return to profitability, which to date has always followed. Over the years, until 1975, the loss ratio has gradually increased and the expense ratio gradually decreased. The loss ratio decreased after 1975 while the expense ratio tended to rise.

---

ancial Reporting Trends—Fire and Casualty Insurance, Ernst and Ernst, New York.

(b) Audits of Stock Life Insurance Companies. An Industry Audit Guide prepared by the Committee of Insurance Accounting and Auditing of the American Institute of CPA's, New York, 1972.

(c) See also, annual editions of Financial Reporting Trends—Life Insurance, Ernst and Ernst, New York.

TABLE 28-5. Property and Liability Insurance Companies, Loss and Expense Ratios to Premiums Earned and Written

Year	(1) Loss Ratio to Prem. Earned	(2) Expense Ratio to Prem. Written	(3) Comb. Ratio Cols. 1&2 Stock Companies	(4) Under-writing Profit or Loss to Prem. Earned	(5) Loss Ratio to Prem. Earned	(6) Expense Ratio to Prem. Written	(7) Combined Ratio Cols. 5&6 Mutual Companies	(8) Under-writing Profit or Loss to Prem. Earned
	Stock Companies				Mutual Companies			
1956	63.4	37.1	100.5	-1.7	65.0	26.3	91.3	7.9
1957	66.2	36.7	102.9	-4.3	65.5	25.8	91.3	7.7
1958	63.7	36.3	100.0	-1.0	64.9	25.6	90.5	8.7
1959	62.5	35.3	97.8	0.8	64.7	25.3	90.0	9.1
1960	63.6	34.8	98.4	0.7	64.2	25.6	89.8	9.6
1961	64.4	35.0	99.4	0.3	63.6	25.6	89.2	10.4
1962	64.5	34.5	99.0	0.1	66.7	25.7	92.4	7.6
1963	66.3	34.7	101.0	-1.8	71.4	26.5	97.9	0.8
1964	68.0	33.9	101.9	-2.8	73.4	25.9	99.3	0.1
1965	69.2	32.7	101.9	-3.1	73.1	25.0	98.1	1.1
1966	66.2	31.9	98.1	0.8	70.9	24.2	95.1	4.2
1967	67.2	31.7	98.9	0.2	72.7	24.5	97.2	2.1
1968	68.8	31.2	100.0	-1.1	74.4	24.6	99.0	0.2
1969	70.3	30.3	100.6	-2.0	76.5	24.1	100.6	-1.6

TABLE 28-5. Property and Liability Insurance Companies, Loss and Expense Ratios to Premiums Earned and Written (continued)

Year	(1) Loss Ratio to Prem. Earned	(2) Expense Ratio to Prem. Written	(3) Comb. Ratio Cols. 1&2 Stock Companies	(4) Under-writing Profit or Loss to Prem. Earned	(5) Loss Ratio to Prem. Earned	(6) Expense Ratio to Prem. Written	(7) Combined Ratio Cols. 5&6 Mutual Companies	(8) Under-writing Profit or Loss to Prem. Earned
1970	69.7	29.6	99.3	-0.7	73.3	23.4	96.7	2.4
1971	66.7	29.1	95.8	2.9	69.1	23.1	92.2	7.0
1972	66.0	29.4	95.4	3.5	68.1	23.8	91.9	7.5
1973	68.6	29.6	98.2	0.8	71.2	24.3	95.5	4.2
1974	75.3	29.7	105.0	-5.6	76.4	24.8	101.2	-1.8
1975	78.8	28.7	107.5	-8.4	80.2	24.2	104.4	-5.4
1976	74.6	27.4	102.0	-3.4	77.1	22.5	99.6	-1.1
1977	70.1	26.9	97.0	1.7	72.4	21.5	93.9	5.0
1978	69.0	27.6	96.0	2.4	72.9	21.7	94.6	4.5
1979	71.7	27.9	99.6	-0.6	76.3	21.7	98.0	1.2
1980	73.9	28.5	102.4	-3.0	76.8	22.1	98.9	0.7

Note: All ratios shown in this table are before dividends to policyholders.

Source: Best's Aggregates and Averages, Property and Liability, 1981, published annually by A. M. Best Company, Oldwick, New Jersey.

In the period 1956–1980, for the stock companies, the lowest combined ratios were 95.4 in 1972 and 95.8 in 1971, and the highest ratio was 107.5 in 1975. Investors can expect only slight total profitability when underwriting is unprofitable because the net loss must be absorbed by investment income, which is the source of dividends and the basis for capital gains secured by investors. These ratios represent industry averages. But, of course, certain companies have a better record than the averages and other companies a poorer one.

In general, investors in property and liability insurance companies do not expect much in the way of underwriting profits, only wanting the combined loss and expense ratio to be somewhat below 100 percent, although hopefully in the vicinity of 90 to 95 percent. Their major expectation for income and capital gains centers on investment performance and investment income. Therefore, the investor making an analysis of an insurance company must give major attention to the company's investment portfolio and investment results over a period of years. The comparative investment and underwriting record for 1946–1980 is shown in Table 28–6.

TABLE 28–6. Property and Liability Stock Insurance Companies, Comparative Investment and Underwriting Record

Year	Investment Income		Investment Profit or Loss[a] Dollars (in millions)	Underwriting Profit or Loss[b]	
	Dollars (in millions)	% Earned on Mean Assets		Dollars (in millions)	% of Premiums Earned
1980	8,836	6.02	13,780	-1,956.0	-2.98
1979	7,601	5.97	10,805	-365.0	-0.60
1978	5,724	5.27	7,062	1,335.0	2.41
1977	4,648	5.07	4,720	804.0	1.65
1976	3,629	4.73	6,871	-1,406.0	-3.43
1975	3,143	4.83	6,569	-2,880.2	-8.34
1974	2,891	4.72	-3,251	-1,760.7	-5.60
1973	2,491	4.13	-1,441	225.6	0.78
1972	2,068	3.84	4,724	914.5	3.44
1971	1,785	3.88	3,417	679.2	2.85
1970	1,439	3.57	1,250	-154.0	-0.72
1969	1,238	3.27	-492	-395.8	-2.07
1968	1,101	3.06	2,279	-200.9	-1.17
1967	987	3.03	2,302	10.4	0.07
1966	896	2.87	-552	102.5	0.70

TABLE 28-6. Property and Liability Stock Insurance Companies, Comparative
Investment and Underwriting Record *(continued)*

	Investment Income			Underwriting Profit or Loss[b]	
Year	Dollars (in millions)	% Earned on Mean Assets	Investment Profit or Loss[a] Dollars (in millions)	Dollars (in millions)	% of Premiums Earned
1965	852	2.78	1,466	-424.5	-3.19
1964	782	2.69	1,821	-347.5	-2.81
1963	721	2.69	2,017	-218.7	-1.89
1962	673	2.62	-230	2.5	0.02
1961	621	2.57	2,516	29.8	0.28
1960	592	2.66	655	65.6	0.64
1959	534	2.55	1,021	70.9	0.74
1958	489	2.57	2,074	-92.7	-1.05
1957	461	2.58	-166	-361.3	-4.33
1956	430	2.45	580	-135.8	-1.75
1946	154	2.38	-12	-151.6	-5.78

[a] Includes investment income.
[b] Includes premium balances and miscellaneous underwriting items but before
dividends to policyholders.

Source: Best's Aggregates and Averages, Property and Liability, 1981, published
annually by A. M. Best Company, Oldwick, New Jersey.

Troublesome Underwriting Losses. The stock property-casualty
companies recorded underwriting losses in 1979 and 1980, and another
deficit is expected in 1981. Analysts feel the industry is suffering from
excess capacity brought on by the attraction of relatively high rates of
return on equity capital in recent years. High interest rates, moreover,
encouraged rate cutting to attract funds to invest. Rising inflation rates
further acerbated the problem by causing claim settlements and operating expenses to rise sharply. These trends will have to be closely watched
by investment analysts.

Investment Policy Requirements. Investment policy is based partly
on regulations and partly on management decisions. Regulations governing fire and casualty investments are considerably less restrictive than
regulations controlling investments of life insurance companies. For

fire and casualty companies there is no specific limitation on stock investments.

The minimum capital required must be invested in cash and U.S. government securities, which in recent years has averaged about 8 percent of assets. Unearned premium reserves and required reserves must be invested in cash, government securities, and approved corporate bonds. The balance of funds may be invested in either stocks or bonds as long as the issuers have maintained satisfactory records of interest and dividend payments and are solvent.

Investment Policy. Total investments of property and liability insurance companies increased about 50 percent during the period 1973–1977, but dollar holdings of stocks actually declined (see Table 28–7). The drastic decline that occurred in the stock market from January 1969 to May 1970 (37 percent) and from January 1973 to December 1974 (about 50 percent) discouraged investment in common stocks. Property and casualty companies did begin to again actively acquire common stocks after 1975 and increased the percentage of total assets represented by common stocks from 15.9 to 18.0 percent by year-end 1980.

The dollar growth in state and local securities from 1975 to 1981 is impressive, but these instruments still represented about 46 percent of total assets in 1980 as they did in 1977. Property and liability companies find such securities particularly interesting when the combined ratio is below 100 percent since they then are certain to face a federal income tax on investment earnings.

The higher the ratio of capital and surplus to unearned premium reserves for a company, the more justifiable is a relatively large investment in common stocks. The analyst should always relate the common stock investment to capital funds and determine the effect a given decline in market value of common stocks owned by the company would have on capital and surplus. For this purpose, one can generally anticipate that the rise or decline in a company's common stock portfolio value will coincide fairly closely with the movements of a general market index (such as the S&P 500).

Investment Results. An insurance company's total earnings consist of the adjusted underwriting gain (or loss) plus net investment income. The underwriting earnings tend to be quite variable, fluctuating considerably over the years, and in numerous years companies experience underwriting losses. The pattern is suggested in Table 28–6. But fortunately investment income, largely from debt instruments, tends to be reasonably stable and rising. This means that dividends are paid generally or entirely from investment income. Earnings per share should

TABLE 28-7. Property and Liability Insurance Companies, Annual Amounts Invested in Various Types of Investments and Total Amounts Owned, December 31, 1980 (billions of dollars)

	1975	1976	1977	1978	1979	1980	1981	Amt. Out 31 Dec. 80	Percent-age
U.S. government	1.9	2.6	2.5	0.9	1.2	4.1	4.0	15.8	8.6
Federal agencies	0.6	0.6	0.5	0.4	1.6	1.0	1.0	7.5	4.1
Corporate & foreign bonds	2.2	3.9	3.7	1.6	1.3	3.0	5.5	25.8	14.0
State and local securities	2.6	5.4	10.7	13.1	12.3	9.3	8.0	84.5	46.0
Total credit	7.3	12.5	17.4	16.0	16.4	17.4	18.5	133.6	72.7
Stocks	-0.7	0.9	1.2	2.0	2.4	2.0	1.8	33.0	18.0
Cash and miscellaneous	0.7	1.5	1.5	1.6	1.4	1.1	1.2	17.2	9.4
Total assets	7.3	14.9	20.1	19.6	20.2	20.5	21.5	183.8	100.1

Source: Henry Kaufman, James McKeon and David Foster, 1981 Prospects for Financial Markets (New York: Salomon Brothers, 1980), p. 32.

be calculated after income taxes and their trend and cyclical nature determined.

While companies experience both capital gains and losses in their investment portfolios, security analysts generally do not include portfolio gains or losses in calculating annual earnings. This is in line with the usual accounting practices of excluding nonrecurring gains from income on an annual basis.

Summary of Major Factors to Consider in Analysis of Fire and Casualty Companies. After analyzing the underwriting record and the investment record of a company, the analyst should determine growth in each of several categories. Growth factors for which the compound annual growth should be determined are:

1. Assets	6. Net income from operations after income tax
2. Capital funds	7. Earnings per share
3. Total income	8. Dividends per share
4. Premium income	9. Liquidating value per share (adjusted book value).
5. Other income	

Stability of items 3 through 9 is also of interest. The following analytical tests for fire and casualty insurance companies are suggested:

1. Cash and investment grade bonds (rated in top four grades) should be at least equal to 90 percent of liabilities with cash and U.S. government securities at least equal to 20 percent of total assets and 30 percent of liabilities. The higher the ratio the less concern for market fluctuations in securities, especially common stocks.
2. The ratio of common equity (exclusive of equity in unearned premium reserve) to total assets should be at least 35 percent.
3. The analyst should calculate the effect on capital and surplus if stock prices should decline 50 percent.
4. The loss ratios over both the last *five and ten* years should not average over 72 percent.
5. The expense ratio over the last *five and ten* years should not average over 23 percent.
6. The combined loss and expense ratios should not average over 95 percent for the last *five and ten* years.
7. The rate of return on average assets should have been at least 5 percent over the most recent five years.
8. Investment income should rise on the average *at least as fast* as the growth in assets plus the rate of growth in interest rate on "A" rated bonds.
9. There should be a satisfactory record of at least ten years of growth in assets, net income, earnings per share, and dividends per share.

Life Insurance Companies

The life insurance industry is a major component of the American financial scene. Total assets were $479 billion (investments $391 billion) on December 31, 1980, and the annual gross new loans and investments were $271 billion which, because of "rollovers" of investments, was six times as great as the net increase in assets, $57 billion.

The life insurance industry has traditionally been dominated by mutual companies, which are generally both older and larger than the stockholder-owned companies. In 1976 of the 1,748 companies, 1,605 were stock, but the 143 mutual companies (only 8 percent) controlled nearly half of the assets of all companies.

Financial Reporting. Earlier in this chapter we noted that analysts no longer need to make their own reconciliations of statutory reporting to GAAP because most companies now include in their annual reports, and all must in SEC reports, supplementary schedules that provide these reconciliations.[8]

Growth of Life Insurance Industry. The life insurance industry is well known for its continuous and considerable growth over long periods, including the growth of investment income. This is in sharp contrast to the erratic underwriting record of fire and casualty insurance companies.

In the post–World War II years the life insurance industry has shown a fairly steady growth rate although the rate of growth slowed in the 1955–1970 period only to regain the 1945–1955 growth rate after 1969. The growth rate of major items from 1945–1980 is shown in Table 28–8. The growth rates of group insurance in force and credit insurance have been the fastest-growing segments of the industry while industrial insurance in force has shown little or no net gain after 1955.

New and Discontinuing Companies. Each year many new companies are established (frequently by promoters), and many companies go out of business.[9] Sometimes promoters start companies and accept very

---

[8](a) "Industry Audit Guide—Audits of Stock Life Insurance Companies," prepared by the Committee on Insurance Accounting and Auditing of AICPA, 1972.

(b) "Financial Reporting Trends—Life Insurance, An Annual," Ernst & Ernst, New York.

(c) Statutory reporting prorates income over the life of policies as under GAAP but unlike GAAP, does not prorate the expense of placing policies on the books, but instead burdens the initial fiscal period with all the initial expenses.

[9](a) New and (b) discontinued operation of life insurance companies.

	(a)	(b)		(a)	(b)		(a)	(b)
1955	216	26	1966	156	81	1973	75	62
1960	96	80	1967	90	79	1974	73	82
1961	87	80	1968	112	64	1975	63	74
1962	101	80	1969	74	64	1976	85	89
1963	86	67	1970	73	66	1977	89	42
1964	131	72	1971	49	64	1978	117	66
1965	149	67	1972	76	88	1979	116	61

TABLE 28-8. Growth of U.S. Life Insurance Companies, 1945-1980

	Total Assets	Total Income	Compound Annual Growth In:				
				Insurance In Force			
			Total	Ordinary	Group	Industrial	Credit
1945-1980	7.01%	8.48%	9.42%	8.49%	12.96%	0.75%	19.09%
1975-1980	10.62	11.17	10.60	10.20	11.79	-1.80	8.08
1970-1975	6.90	9.73	8.82	8.01	10.41	0.40	7.68
1965-1970	5.46	8.14	9.26	8.02	12.35	-0.60	7.86
1960-1965	5.85	7.59	8.96	7.88	11.86	0.13	12.75
1955-1960	5.75	6.82	9.51	9.54	11.66	-0.60	14.96
1950-1955	7.15	7.85	9.72	7.77	16.22	3.50	30.40
1945-1950	7.40	8.12	9.06	7.99	16.60	3.84	60.14

Source: Basic data from Life Insurance Fact Book (New York: American Council of Life Insurance, 1981), p. 18. Calculations by author.

low quality risks at low premiums to show a rapid increase in "insurance in force," expecting that the price of their stock will rise rapidly permitting them to sell out at a large profit before the low quality of risks produces poor results. Furthermore, the "insurance in force" figure may rise rapidly without a significant increase in assets if most new policies are term policies. New companies, therefore, usually are of such high risk as not to fit the objectives of most long-term investors.

Financial Statements of Life Insurance Companies. Tables 28–9, 28–10, and 28–11 offer historical balance sheet information for life insurance companies, which should be understood and used for comparative purposes in analyzing particular companies. Table 28–9 presents the major assets and Table 28–10 the major liabilities, reserves, capital, and surplus items. Table 28–11 gives a breakdown of the classification "Government Securities."

Analysis of Assets of Life Insurance Companies. Utilizing the data in Table 28–9, we find that debt instruments (government securities, bonds, mortgages and policy loans) represented 80.4 percent of total assets in 1980. This breakdown is typical for life insurance companies. State regulations governing the investments of insurance companies generally limit investment in equities to 10 percent of total assets, except for pension fund assets, which are set aside in separate accounts.

Pension fund assets are segregated since such assets may be entirely invested in common stock if the insurance company wishes to do so. Insurance companies had actually invested only 49.4 percent of total separate account (pension fund) assets in common stocks at the end of 1980. The rate of return earned is a bit lower when separate accounts are included than when they are excluded, as shown in Table 28–12. This occurs because of the higher proportion of common stocks held in these accounts.

Because liquidity is not a serious problem for life insurance companies, only 1.2 percent of assets are invested in U.S. Treasury securities and only 2.3 percent in federal agency securities, or a total of only 3.6 percent in all U.S. government securities (see Table 28–11). State and local securities represent only 1.4 percent of assets, and investments in foreign government and international agencies 2.0 percent (largely representing securities of Canadian central and local governments).

The largest class of securities is corporate securities, representing 47.4 percent of all assets in 1980 (37.5 percent bonds and 9.9 percent equity). The next largest class is mortgages, representing 27.4 percent of assets, which is among the lowest levels for this category since 1954. Policy loans represent 8.6 percent, real estate 3.1 percent, and miscellaneous assets 6.6 percent in 1980.

TABLE 28-9. Distribution of Assets of U.S. Life Insurance Companies

Millions of Dollars

Year	Government Securities	Corporate Securities		Mortgages	Real Estate	Policy Loans	Misc. Assets	Total
		Bonds	Stocks					
1917	$ 562	$ 1,975	$ 83	$ 2,021	$ 179	$ 810	$ 311	$ 5,941
1920	1,349	1,949	75	2,442	172	859	474	7,320
1925	1,311	3,022	81	4,808	266	1,446	604	11,538
1930	1,502	4,929	519	7,598	548	2,807	977	18,880
1935	4,727	5,314	583	5,357	1,990	3,540	1,705	23,216
1940	8,447	8,645	605	5,972	2,065	3,091	1,977	30,802
1945	22,545	10,060	999	6,636	857	1,962	1,738	44,797
1950	16,118	23,248	2,103	16,102	1,445	2,413	2,591	64,020
1955	11,829	35,912	3,633	29,445	2,581	3,290	3,742	90,432
1960	11,815	46,740	4,981	41,771	3,765	5,231	5,273	119,576
1965	11,908	58,244	9,126	60,013	4,661	7,678	7,234	158,884
1966	11,396	60,819	8,832	64,309	4,885	9,117	7,797	167,455
1967	11,079	64,687	10,877	67,516	5,187	10,059	8,427	177,832
1968	11,096	68,310	13,230	69,973	5,571	11,306	9,150	183,636
1969	10,914	70,859	13,707	72,027	5,912	13,825	9,964	197,203
1970	11,068	73,098	15,420	74,375	6,320	16,064	10,909	207,254
1971	11,000	79,198	20,607	75,496	6,904	17,065	11,832	222,102
1972	11,372	86,140	26,845	76,948	7,295	18,003	13,127	239,730
1973	11,403	91,796	25,919	81,369	7,693	20,199	14,057	252,436
1974	11,965	96,652	21,920	86,234	8,331	22,862	15,385	263,349

PART EIGHT • Analysis of Special Classes of Securities

TABLE 28-9. Distribution of Assets of U.S. Life Insurance Companies (continued)

Millions of Dollars

Year	Government Securities	Corporate Securities Bonds	Corporate Securities Stocks	Mortgages	Real Estate	Policy Loans	Misc. Assets	Total
1975	15,177	105,837	28,061	89,167	9,621	24,467	16,974	289,304
1976	20,260	120,666	34,262	91,552	10,476	25,834	18,502	321,552
1977	23,555	137,889	33,763	96,848	11,060	27,556	21,051	351,722
1978	26,552	156,044	35,518	106,167	11,764	30,146	23,733	389,924
1979	29,719	168,990	39,757	118,421	13,007	34,825	27,563	432,282
1980	33,015	179,603	47,366	131,080	15,033	41,411	31,702	479,210

Percentage of Total Assets

Year	Government Securities	Corporate Securities Bonds	Corporate Securities Stocks	Mortgages	Real Estate	Policy Loans	Misc. Assets	Total
1917	9.6%	33.2%	1.4%	34.0%	3.0%	13.6%	5.2%	100.0%
1920	18.4	26.7	1.0	33.4	2.3	11.7	6.5	100.0
1925	11.3	26.2	.7	41.7	2.3	12.5	5.3	100.0
1930	8.0	26.0	2.8	40.2	2.9	14.9	5.2	100.0
1935	20.4	22.9	2.5	23.1	8.6	15.2	7.3	100.0
1940	27.5	28.1	2.0	19.4	6.7	10.0	6.3	100.0
1945	50.3	22.5	2.2	14.8	1.9	4.4	3.9	100.0
1950	25.2	36.3	3.3	25.1	2.2	3.8	4.1	100.0
1955	13.1	39.7	4.0	32.6	2.9	3.6	4.1	100.0
1960	9.9	39.1	4.2	34.9	3.1	4.4	4.4	100.0
1965	7.5	36.7	5.7	37.8	3.0	4.8	4.5	100.0
1966	6.8	36.3	5.3	38.6	2.9	5.5	4.6	100.0

1967	6.2	36.4	6.1	38.0	2.9	5.7	4.7	100.0
1968	5.9	36.2	7.0	37.1	3.0	6.0	4.8	100.0
1969	5.5	36.0	6.9	36.6	3.0	7.0	5.0	100.0
1970	5.3	35.3	7.4	35.9	3.0	7.8	5.3	100.0
1971	4.9	35.7	9.3	34.0	3.1	7.7	5.3	100.0
1972	4.8	35.9	11.2	32.1	3.0	7.5	5.5	100.0
1973	4.5	36.4	10.3	32.2	3.0	8.0	5.6	100.0
1974	4.5	36.7	8.3	32.8	3.2	8.7	5.8	100.0
1975	5.2	36.6	9.7	30.8	3.3	8.5	5.9	100.0
1976	6.3	37.5	10.7	28.5	3.3	8.0	5.7	100.0
1977	6.7	39.2	9.6	27.5	3.2	7.8	6.0	100.0
1978	6.8	40.0	9.1	27.2	3.0	7.8	6.1	100.0
1979	6.9	39.1	9.2	27.4	3.0	8.1	6.3	100.0
1980	6.9	37.5	9.9	27.4	3.1	8.6	6.6	100.0

Note: Beginning with 1962, these data include the assets of separate accounts.

Source: Life Insurance Fact Book, 1978 (New York: American Council of Life Insurance, 1981), p. 69.

TABLE 28–10. Obligations and Surplus Funds, U.S. Life Insurance Companies (millions of dollars)

Year	Policy Reserves	Policy Dividend Accumu-lations	Funds Set Aside for Policy Dividends	Other Obliga-tions	Surplus Funds	Capital (Stock Companies)	Total
1952	$ 62,579	$ 1,675	$ 841	$ 3,024	$ 4,884	$ 372	$ 73,375
1955	75,359	2,239	1,201	4,625	6,475	533	90,432
1960	98,473	3,381	1,780	6,268	8,827	847	119,576
1965	127,620	4,326	2,647	10,455	12,468	1,368	158,884
1970	167,779	6,068	3,540	12,544	15,651	1,672	207,254
1971	179,649	6,530	3,720	14,364	16,150	1,689	222,102
1972	192,759	7,031	4,030	16,955	17,231	1,724	239,730
1973	204,521	7,552	4,384	16,085	17,995	1,899	252,436
1974	216,507	8,080	4,604	15,517	16,730	1,911	263,349
1975	237,116	8,814	4,875	17,936	18,635	1,928	289,304
1976	262,775	9,633	5,252	21,881	20,077	1,934	321,552
1977	287,932	10,427	5,839	23,907	21,669	1,948	351,722
1978	318,483	11,319	6,380	27,495	24,285	1,962	389,924
1979	351,637	12,112	7,158	31,372	28,023	1,980	432,282
1980	390,339	12,727	7,659	34,127	32,274	2,084	479,210

Source: Life Insurance Fact Book, 1978 (New York: American Council of Life Insurance, 1981), p. 67.

TABLE 28-11. Government Securities, December 31, 1980 (millions of dollars)

	Dollar Amount	Percentage of Total Assets
U.S. Treasury	$ 5,838	1.21
Federal agency	11,144	2.33
Total U.S. government	16,982	3.54
U.S. state and local	6,701	1.40
Total U.S.	23,683	4.94
Foreign government and international agencies (largely Canadian)	9,332	1.95
Total government securities	33,015	6.89

Source: Life Insurance Fact Book, 1981 (New York: American Council of Life Insurance, 1981), p. 76.

TABLE 28-12. Net Rate of Investment Income, U.S. Life Insurance Companies

Year	Rate	Year	Rate
1915	4.77%	1940	3.45%
1920	4.83	1945	3.11
1925	5.11	1950	3.13
1930	5.05	1955	3.51
1935	3.70	1960	4.11

	Rate			Rate	
	Including Separate Accounts	Excluding Separate Accounts		Including Separate Accounts	Excluding Separate Accounts
1965	4.61%	4.61%	1973	5.88%	6.00%
1966	4.73	4.73	1974	6.25	6.31
1967	4.82	4.83	1975	6.36	6.44
1968	4.95	4.97	1976	6.55	6.68
1969	5.12	5.15	1977	6.89	7.00
1970	5.30	5.34	1978	7.31	7.39
1971	5.44	5.52	1979	7.73	7.78
1972	5.56	5.69	1980	8.02	8.06

TABLE 28-12. Net Rate of Investment Income, U.S. Life Insurance Companies *(continued)*

Note: The net rate of investment income is calculated using industry aggregates, and represents the ratio of (1) net investment income to (2) mean invested assets (including cash) less half the net investment income. Before 1940, some federal income taxes were deducted from net investment income; beginning with 1940, the rates are calculated before deducting any federal income taxes.

Source: American Council of Life Insurance.

Earnings Growth, Asset Growth, and Rate of Return. Total assets rose at a 7.0 percent annual rate from 1945-1980, and this is the base for earnings. Not only did earnings growth rise with growth in assets, but because over 90 percent of assets are debt investments, earnings benefited from the rise in interest rates from 1946-1981. Therefore, from the low in interest rates in 1945-1946, rates of return rose from 3.11 percent in 1945 to 8 percent in 1980.

The Income Statement. A typical income statement of a stock life insurance company is presented in Table 28-13. Premium income represents 77.5 percent of total income and net investment income equals 22.5 percent. Benefits and related expenses absorb about 78 percent of income and operating expenses about 16.5 percent, for a total of 94.5 percent of income. Income taxes absorb another 1.5 percent for a total of 96 percent. Dividends amount to 2 percent of income, leaving a balance after deductions of all the above items of 2 percent of gross income.

Sources of Earnings—Underwriting. Normally the investor can take a noninsurance company's sales for a given period and subtract the costs to arrive at the company's profit. In life insurance the sales unit referred to is a promise by the company to pay $1,000 at a future time. The amount received by the company is usually no more than a year's premium, which is a very small fraction of this $1,000. It is the premium payment received each year and not the contract sale that provides income for the insurance company.

Fixing Premiums. In fixing premiums the insurance company will calculate the amount that must be received each year so that, with interest earned, the amounts received will just exactly equal the benefits expected to be paid out over the duration of the contracts. This amount per year is called the *net level premium* and corresponds to the cost of goods sold for an ordinary business. To this net level premium the company then adds an amount that it estimates will cover its costs, including commissions, and give it a small margin of profit. This amount is called the *load* and is the same as the markup for a seller of goods.

TABLE 28-13. A Typical Condensed Income Statement of a Life Insurance Company

Sources of Funds—Income
Premiums and deferred benefits contributions   77.5%
Net Investment Income   22.5

         100.0%

Use of Funds or Distribution of Income
Benefits including surrender benefits   41.5
Annuities and mutual endowment   7.0
Miscellaneous deductions   5.0
Increase in policy and special revenues   24.5

         78.0

Expenses of Operation
Agents' commissions   7.0
General expenses   7.0
Taxes other than income taxes   2.5

         16.5
Total of Above   94.5
   Income taxes   1.5
     Total   96.0

Net Gain After Income Tax, Before Dividends   4.0
Dividends to Policyholders   21.0
Net Gain After Dividends to Policyholders   21.0
         50.0

Changes in Surplus   50.0
   Surplus beginning of fiscal period
   Add: Net gains after income tax   4.0
       Net gain from sale of investments   .5
       Increase in market value of investments   1.0
   Total increase in surplus   5.5
         55.5

   Less: Dividends to policyholders   2.0
       Increase in security valuation reserves   1.0
   Surplus at end of fiscal period   -3.0
         52.5

Conservative Nature of Reported Earnings. In calculating the profit that a life insurance company will make, it must be emphasized that most of the cost factors are estimates and assumptions for long periods of time in the future. The differences between these estimates and the actual costs that occur are the sources of additional possible profit or loss to the company. Since the estimates and assumptions used have generally been conservative (that is, have tended to overstate the costs), these differences have more often been profits than losses.

Determining Companies to Consider. The quantitative measures discussed in the following paragraphs are useful in assessing the quality and potential return for life insurance stocks.

Measures of Efficiency. The tests of management in this area, as in other companies, are such measures as the return on stockholders' equity and the growth of earnings. But it will also be helpful to look at specific indicators, especially in the area of expenses. Renewal expense and investment yield are particularly useful:

1. To calculate renewal expense per $1,000 of old business in force, *renewal expense* must first be estimated. This is done by subtracting from general insurance expense the identifiable first-year expenses that are contained in this item. The renewal expense per $1,000, particularly when calculated separately for ordinary business, provides a measure that is suitable for comparison between companies or with a general standard.
2. *Investment yield* is the ratio of net investment income to mean assets. The trend of a company's investment yield should be rising in line with the general trend for the industry.

Growth in Earnings. Growth in earnings per share is by far the most important factor to be considered in measuring the growth of a company. The rates of growth of both reported and adjusted earnings should be at a satisfactory level. Any divergence of the two over a period of several years should be investigated.

Quality of Business. The investor must attempt to measure the quality of the business. This also indicates the quality of the earnings. The following factors will be of assistance in this effort:

1. *Lapse Ratio.* This is the ratio of voluntary terminations (including both lapses and surrenders) to business in force (average of beginning and ending). The lower the lapse ratio, the longer a company's business is remaining in force on the average and the greater is the profit that can be expected.
2. *Composition of Business in Force.* The proportion of most profitable lines, particularly ordinary life (whole life and endowment), and the trends are extremely important. Investors should prefer life insurance companies that have concentrated on ordinary life rather than group business.
3. *Composition of Premium Income.* As with the composition of business in force, the composition of premium income measure should show a substantial proportion of premium income from ordinary life insurance.

Return on Stockholders' Equity. This is the most important single measure of benefit to stockholders in any line of business. It shows how well management is using the funds provided by stockholders and is used for comparison with other companies. It should be calculated using both reported and adjusted earnings and stockholders' equity. The adjusted figures may be more accurate, but a satisfactory return should be indicated by both calculations.

Standards for Quantitative Measures. Table 28–14 presents standards that should be applied in the analysis of a life insurance company stock.

TABLE 28–14. Suggested Standards for Ratios for Life Insurance Companies

	Minimum	Maximum
Stockholders' equity ratio	8%	
Maximum decline in earnings in a given year:		
Reported		20%
Adjusted		15%
Years of earnings decline in past 10 years		3
Renewal expense per $1,000		$2.50
Yield on investments	4.5%	5.5%
Growth rate of earnings per share	6%	
Lapse ratio		8%
Composition of business in force:		
Ordinary and industrial	50%	
Term		30%
Group		30%
Composition of premium income:		
Ordinary and industrial	50%	
Health insurance		20%
First-year compensation		90%
First-year expense ratio		125%
Return on stockholders' equity	10%	

Performance of Life Insurance Stocks. Life insurance stocks have enjoyed two periods of extreme popularity in the past twenty years. The first of these was 1946-1956; the S&P Monthly Index of Life Insurance Stocks rose nearly ten times from 18.6 to 177.7 while the S&P 500 rose only 2.4 times. In the 1956-1960 period, the life insurance index moved horizontally, reflecting the uncertainty pending action by Congress to increase the impact of the income tax on insurance companies and also the fact that the proportion of personal savings flowing into life insurance was declining.

In the strong 1961 market, life insurance stocks were one of the popular groups. The S&P Monthly Index of Life Insurance Stocks went from 146 in the latter part of 1960 to 304 in 1961 or sixteen times its

1946 high and five times its 1952 high. The index then rose gradually to its all time peak of 365 in 1964. It had bear market lows of 190 in 1966 and 147 in 1970 and in December 1974. The post-1974 recovery high in 1976 was 205. Never after 1964 until this writing has the index come near to recovering to the 1964 high of 365.

Summary

The main functions of commercial banks are to receive deposits from other segments of the economy and to make loans and discounts to industry, commerce, agriculture, and individuals; and to federal, state, and local governments through purchase of their securities. The nation's commercial banks hold the bulk of the cash assets of individuals, business firms, and financial institutions. This means that in total the assets and deposits must grow with the growth of GNP. In fact the growth rates are interrelated.

While management is important with all corporations, it is of special importance in the case of banks because the quality of assets, especially loans, is the most important factor in the determination of the investment status of a bank.

About 90 percent of a bank's assets consist of cash, security investments (currently about evenly divided between U.S. government and agency securities on the one hand and municipals on the other), and loans and discounts, with the latter representing 50 to 60 percent of total assets. Again, the quality of these loans is the crucial factor, and, as the 1970s proved, it is extremely difficult for the analyst or investor outside the bank to accurately determine the quality of loans.

A major factor on the liability side of a bank's statement of condition (balance sheet) has been the continuous increase in the proportion of total deposits in the form of time deposits with a corresponding decrease in the proportion in the form of demand deposits. This has resulted in a substantial increase in costs (interest to be paid on deposits) and lower required reserves to total deposits.

In addition to aggressively seeking time deposits and certificates of deposits, the large banks have actively entered the capital market for funds by selling debentures, which they are permitted to include in the category "capital accounts." Banks have had strong pressure to increase their equity capital because of the substantial increase in deposits, and substantial increases in debentures and other debt outstanding. However, in many cases the fact that market prices of several bank stocks have been below book values has created difficulty in selling more stock in addition to the relatively high cost of equity under such condition.

In the 1970s the growth of bank earnings slowed below that of prior years but still remained above the growth rate for the economy overall. Part of the difficulty was the necessity of many banks to write off substantial losses from real estate loans.

As with other industries, the investor is interested in the financial strength and liquidity of the corporation (bank) and then in the growth rate of earnings past and expected. It must be noted that while earnings may grow satisfactorily for a time based on lower-quality loans, this will eventually result in loan losses that will penalize current and retained earnings.

Insurance companies can be divided into two major groups: (1) fire and casualty and (2) life insurance companies. Historically, insurance companies reported to stockholders in the same form as to regulatory authorities—that is, statutory reporting—and the analyst was forced to attempt to adjust reported earnings to conform with GAAP (generally accepted accounting principles). However, as a result of pressure from financial analysts, the SEC, stock exchanges, and the accounting profession, insurance companies have recently followed the practice of not only reporting on a statutory basis but also on a GAAP basis. This has considerably reduced the problem of analysis.

For fire and casualty insurance companies the three most important ratios are (1) the expense ratio, which measures the operating efficiency of the company, (2) the loss ratio, which measures the quality of the business, and (3) the combined expense and loss ratio, which indicates the operating profit or loss of the business.

Investment policy is based partly on regulations and partly on management decisions. The higher the ratio of capital and surplus to unearned premium reserves (liabilities), the more justification for a relatively large investment in common stock.

Life insurance companies on any basis represent a far larger factor in the overall economy than do fire and casualty companies—in terms of assets, insurance written, premiums earned, and other factors. Insurance written and assets of life insurance companies have shown a continuous growth over the history of the industry and this was reflected in the very high P/E ratios characteristic of the industry up to the mid-1950s. However, after that time the growth rate slowed, reflecting especially such major factors as the larger proportion of new insurance in the form of group insurance and a decrease in the proportion of total savings flowing into life insurance. Again, however, in the 1970s the growth rate of the industry has increased although not returning to the pre-1955 level.

Debt instruments represent about 90 percent of the assets of life insurance companies and equity investments only about 10 percent. Therefore, the almost continuous upward trend of interest rates 1946–1981 was a very favorable factor for the life insurance companies. This was particularly noteworthy in the period after 1966–1968 when the level of common stock prices generally remained in a wider but fairly horizontal channel. Rates of return on investments rose from 3.11 percent in 1946 to 8 percent in 1980. Premium income represents about 75 percent of total income and investment income about 22 $\frac{1}{2}$ percent.

A number of quantitative measures for assessing the quality and potential return for life insurance stocks have been presented. As with other corporations the most significant factors are those that contribute to past and expected growth and stability of earnings. In recent years P/E ratios, having come down from the peaks of earlier years, have contributed to a return of some investment interest in such stocks.

Questions

1. Briefly indicate the changed composition of bank assets in the 1960s and 1970s versus 1945 and explain the changes noted.
2. (a) Distinguish between primary reserves and secondary reserves.
   (b) What has been the trend in these assets since 1946?
3. Discuss the range in maturity distributions of holdings of U.S. government securities of commercial banks.
4. What significant change has occurred in the investment portfolios of commercial banks since 1946? Why has this shift come about?
5. (a) Discuss the factors to consider in the analysis of a bank's basic portfolio.
   (b) Note significant shifts in the composition of loans and discounts that have occurred since 1946. What explanations can you offer to explain these shifts?
6. (a) What is a certificate of deposit? What has made them the significant instrument they have been since 1961?
   (b) What is meant by "disintermediation"?
7. (a) What are the important measures to use in assessing a bank's earnings potential?
   (b) What is the "bottom line" concept of dealing with bank earnings?
8. Discuss the importance of the ratio of capital account to risk assets.
9. (a) Discuss the importance of the ratio of capital accounts to deposits.
   (b) How is the nature of a commercial bank's liabilities and capital structure related to potential return on earning assets?
10. (a) Why is the security analyst interested in the ratio of time deposits to total deposits?
    (b) Of what significance is the increased use of subordinated debt since 1960 by commercial banks to investors in bank stocks?
11. Why should insurance company stocks not be viewed as merely the same as shares of investment companies?
12. (a) Define "statutory underwriting results."

    (b) Define GAAP reporting.

    (c) Discuss current reporting practices.

13. What added difficulties are present in estimating the underwriting results for a property and liability insurance company as contrasted to a life insurance company?

14. Discuss the cyclical and long-run characteristics of fire and casualty insurance stocks.

15. (a) What are the three underwriting tests?

    (b) Explain the meaning and the importance of each test.

16. (a) What factors enter into the calculation of the premium that a life insurance company will charge?

    (b) Why should an investor be wary of using the growth in life insurance companies?

    (c) What are some of the major factors that contributed to the outstanding growth of the life insurance industry?

17. Discuss measures that would be useful to the investor in attempting to assess the quality of business that a particular insurance company has in force and is writing.

Work-Study Problems

1. The following data concern the assets, liabilities, and capital of Bank A and Bank B for a recent year:

	Bank A	Bank B
		(in millions)
Cash	$20	$250
Loans	60	300
U.S. government bonds	10	100
Municipal bonds	5	20
Corporate bonds	1	2
Other assets	3	68
Total	$99	$740
Deposits	$91	$630
Capital stock	3	30
Surplus	2	20
Undivided profits	1	10
Other liabilities	2	50
Total	$99	$740
Shares	300,000[a]	1,000,000[b]
Market average (per share)	$30	$81

[a]Par value, $10 per share.
[b]Par value, $30 per share.

(a) On the basis of the figures given calculate for Bank A and Bank B the following ratios:

(1) Capital funds to deposits.

(2) Capital funds to risk assets.

(3) Loans to deposits.

(4) Cash and government securities to deposits.

(5) Market value to book value.

(b) Comment on the results of your calculations and compare the ratios with those generally accepted.

2. Choose one of the 100 largest commercial banks and prepare a five-year analysis based on the procedures described in the text, using the format suggested below. (See *Moody's Bank and Finance Manual.*) For industry comparisons use tables in the latest annual report of the Federal Deposit Insurance Corporation. Comment on your results.

Bank Analysis

A. Brief history of the bank

Statement of Condition

B. Distribution of assets—trends

    Investments—nonrisk (ratio to deposits)

    Loans and discounts—risk assets and their composition (ratio to deposits)

    Deposits—ratio of time deposits to total deposits

    Capital accounts—ratio to deposits and to risk assets

    Book value—ratio to market value

    Assets and liabilities per $100 of total assets

        Assets—total

            Cash and due from banks

            United States government obligations

            Other securities—total

            Tax-exempt securities

            Other

          Loans and discounts

          All other assets

        Liabilities and capital—total

          Total deposits

            Demand deposits

            Time and savings deposits

Borrowings and other liabilities
Total capital accounts

Income Account

C. (Note: Use the following column headings for data: (1) In Dollars, and (2) Ratios—Amount per $100 of Current Operating Revenues.)

Current operating expenses—total
  Interest on securities
  Interest on loans and discounts
  Service charges, commissions, and fees
  Trust department income
  Other income

Current operating expenses—total
  Salaries, wages, employee benefits
  Interest on time and savings deposits
  Interest on borrowed money
  Taxes other than income taxes
  Depreciation
  Other current expenses
Recoveries, transfers from valuation reserves,
    and profits—total
  On securities and loans
Net income before related taxes
Taxes on income
Net income after taxes
Dividends and interest on capital
Net additions to capital from income

Also calculate:
  Amount per $100 of total assets and amount per $100 of capital account for each of the above items.

3. The following are the important items in the income account and the balance sheets of two fire insurance companies:

	Company A	Company B
	(in millions)	
Net premiums written	$ 201	$ 102
Premiums earned	200	98
Losses incurred	119	63
Underwriting expense	95	42
Gain from underwriting	D4*	D7*

Interest, dividends, & rents, etc.	22	10
Net income	18	3
Number of shares (000)	10,691	1,000
Unearned premium reserve	315	76
Capital	53	10
Voluntary reserves	244	103
Surplus	223	60

*D = Deficit

(a) Calculate for both companies:
    (1) The loss ratio.
    (2) The expense ratio.
    (3) The combined ratio.
    (4) The liquidating value.
    (5) Net earnings per share.
(b) Assuming that Company A stock is selling at 55 a share and Company B stock at 110, comment on the relative merits of the two companies in the light of the ratios you have derived.

4. Select a life insurance company or a property and liability insurance company and analyze it on the basis of the material discussed in this chapter. Prepare statistical data covering a five-year period to aid you in your evaluation, including all pertinent data.

29.

Investment Companies

Investment companies sell shares of stock in their own corporation or trust and then invest the funds thus obtained in a wide variety of securities. There are many forms of investment companies, including management investment companies, face-amount certificate companies, unit investment trusts, collective trust funds, investment partnerships, and "offshore funds." Management investment companies include both open-end (mutual funds) and closed-end companies and exchange, dual-purpose, hedge, and other special purpose funds, venture capital investment companies, and small business investment companies (SBICs).

The two major functions provided by investment companies are wide diversification, which few individuals are able to obtain by direct investment, and professional management, which is expected to be superior to that of most individual nonprofessionals. The record generally shows that the wide diversification obtained, *on the average*, results in performance, especially for the large funds, roughly paralleling but not excluding the major stock averages.[1] Therefore, assumed advantages of professional management, especially for the medium-size or large funds, do not provide results superior to those that could be obtained simply by investing in the "averages." In fact, the introduction of an "index fund" in the mid-1970s, and the later establishment of several such funds by pension funds in 1976–1978, was a tacit admission of this fact.

---

[1] The larger the fund the more results parallel the record of the general stock market indexes. Conversely, those funds that have posted the best performance in recent years have generally been funds with assets of $100 million or less, where selectivity can be practiced because of the size of the fund. Large funds of $500 million and over must be so diversified that their record tends to parallel that of the averages.

INVESTMENT ADVISERS TO FUNDS

The American Institute of Certified Public Accountants' *Industry Audit Guide* describes the nature of fund management organization in this manner:

> Most mutual funds and many closed-end companies, being merely pools of funds, have no employees and are provided services by other entities, such as an investment adviser (manager), a principal underwriter (distributor), a custodian, and a transfer agent. The manager and distributor are usually affiliated, with the distributor function being performed by a separate division or subsidiary company of the manager corporation.[2]

REGULATION OF INVESTMENT COMPANIES

Although investment companies are subject to the statutes of the state in which they are incorporated and to the state "blue sky" laws in states where they sell securities, the major protection for investors is afforded by the regulation of the Securities Acts including the Federal Investment Company Act of 1940 and the Federal Investment Company Amendments Act of 1970.

The 1940 and 1970 acts resulted from a long and thorough study of the industry by the SEC. The final legislation as passed was a combined effort by the SEC and the industry. The 1940 act provided the basis for the tremendous growth of the mutual fund industry after 1940 and especially after World War II.

Under the 1940 act, required information about an investment company must be given in full in a registration statement, in summary form in a prospectus, and in a form regulated by the SEC. The prospectus must be given to any person to whom the security is offered and to every purchaser. The detailed objectives of the 1940 act are listed as follows:[3]

1. Provide investors with complete and accurate information concerning the character of investment company securities and the circumstances, policies, and financial responsibility of investment companies and their management.
2. Assure that investment companies are organized and operated in the interest of all shareholders rather than in the interest of officers, directors, investment advisers, or other special groups or persons.
3. Prevent inequitable provisions in investment company securities and protect the preferences and privileges of outstanding securities.
4. Prevent undue concentration of control through pyramiding or other devices, and discourage management by irresponsible persons.

---

[2] *Audits of Investment Companies, Industry Audit Guide* (New York: AICPA, 1973), p. 5.

[3] *Investment Companies, 1981* (New York: Wiesenberger Financial Services, 1981), p. 26.

5. Assure sound accounting methods.
6. Prevent major changes in organization or business without the consent of shareholders.
7. Require adequate assets or reserves for the conduct of business.

The 1970 amendments to the 1940 act were principally designed to provide for more equitable establishment of fees and sales charges, especially loads (commissions and fees) for contractual plans. The amendments also specifically provided for refunds or cancellations of contracts during the first eighteen months.

SIZE OF FUND ASSETS

The growth record of assets of investment companies is presented in Figure 29-1 and Table 29-1. The total assets for the industry on December 31, 1980, were about $146 billion. Total assets for conventional mutual funds were $138.3 billion; closed-end funds were $8.1 billion.

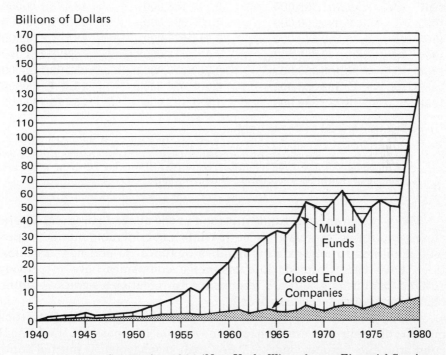

Source: Investment Companies, 1981 (New York: Wiesenberger Financial Services, 1981), p. 12. Reprinted by permission from the *Wiesenberger Investment Companies Service*, 1981 Edition, copyright © 1981, Warren, Gorham & Lamont Inc., 210 South Street, Boston, Mass. All rights reserved.

FIGURE 29-1. Record of Growth of Investment Company Assets

TABLE 29–1. Growth of Investment Company Assets Since 1958

Year	Mutual Funds	Closed-End Companies*	Total
1980	$138,333,100,000	$8,053,201,000	$146,386,301,000
1979	97,053,100,000	6,873,179,000	103,926,279,000
1978	54,144,400,000	6,116,700,000	64,261,100,000
1977	51,479,800,000	6,283,700,000	57,763,500,000
1976	54,174,600,000	6,639,046,000	60,813,646,000
1975	48,706,300,000	5,861,300,000	54,567,600,000
1974	38,545,599,000	5,294,000,000	43,839,599,000
1973	49,310,700,000	6,622,700,000	55,936,700,000
1972	62,456,500,000	6,742,800,000	69,199,300,000
1971	58,159,800,000	5,324,300,000	63,484,100,000
1970	50,654,900,000	5,024,200,000	54,679,100,000
1969	52,621,400,000	4,743,700,000	57,365,100,000
1968	56,953,600,000	5,170,800,000	62,124,400,000
1967	44,701,302,000	3,777,100,000	48,478,402,000
1966	36,294,600,000	3,162,900,000	39,457,500,000
1965	35,220,243,000	3,514,577,000	38,734,820,000
1964	30,370,300,000	3,523,413,000	33,893,713,000
1962	22,408,900,000	2,783,219,000	25,192,119,000
1960	17,383,300,000	2,083,898,000	19,467,198,000
1958	13,242,388,000	1,931,402,000	15,173,790,000

*Including funded debt and bank loans.

Source: Investment Companies, 1981 (New York: Wiesenberger Financial Services, 1981), p. 12. Reprinted by permission from the *Wiesenberger Investment Companies Service*, 1981 Edition, copyright © Warren, Gorham & Lamont Inc., 210 South Street, Boston, Mass. All rights reserved.

Many of the mutual funds included in the above figures and several closed-end funds are relatively new. While a considerable number represent additions to long-existing families of funds, several new organizations have been formed. Life insurance companies have effectively entered the business and are responsible for creating a significant number of funds during the past decade.

Rising interest rates (to historic highs) and a generally flat stock market did spur the creation of a new type of open-end investment company, the "money market" or "cash management" mutual fund. This type of fund grew rapidly in the late 1970s.

CLASSIFICATION OF INVESTMENT COMPANIES

There are various ways of classifying investment companies, but the most comprehensive is (1) open-end or mutual funds and (2) closed-end funds. The major difference is that open-end or mutual funds generally are ready at all times to sell additional shares or redeem outstanding shares, while closed-end funds have a closed capitalization (a stated number of shares) as does the regular business corporation. Like such other corporations the closed-end fund may at times sell additional securities such as stock. As of December 1980 the mutual funds held approximately 95 percent of the total assets of all investment companies.

In 1978 the Association of Closed-End Funds changed its name to the National Association of Publicly Traded Funds in an effort to change its public image and reduce or eliminate the discounts from net asset value at which they have been historically traded. However, in this chapter we will continue to use the term closed-end funds because this is their historic name and the name still generally used in the financial community.

Mutual Funds (Open-End Funds)

The open-end funds are called mutual funds. Mutual funds constantly sell new shares and offer to redeem outstanding shares at all times. The two major classifications of mutual funds are (1) load funds and (2) no-load funds. Load funds make a sales charge when selling their shares, while no-load funds do not.

The prices of mutual fund shares quoted are (1) the "bid" or redemption price, which is the net asset value; and (2) the "asked" price, which for load funds is the net asset value plus a "load" or sales charge ranging from $7\frac{1}{2}$ to $8\frac{1}{2}$ percent of the total payment, or 9.3 percent of the amount invested.[4]

Most no-load funds were started after 1969. There were about 100 by 1973 representing about 10 percent of the assets of all mutual funds. By 1978 there were 232 no-load funds with assets of $14.5 billion representing 21 percent of the total assets of all mutual funds. The 1940 Investment Company Act permits no-load funds to have only one nonaffiliated director versus 40 percent in other types of mutual funds. The sales charges for mutual funds cover both the purchase and the sale with generally no redemption charge. Brokers and dealers have no commission or other incentive to sell no-load funds, and therefore they naturally tend to sell the load funds. No-load funds sell themselves on the basis of no selling charge.

While the Investment Company Act of 1940 requires that, for regulated companies, redemption must be made within seven days of a request, in practice redemption is accomplished the same day. Thus,

---

[4] The sales charge is usually reduced for large orders; for example, to 6 percent on a purchase of $25,000, to 5 percent on a purchase of $50,000, to 3 percent on a purchase of $100,000, and to 1 percent on a purchase of $500,000 or more.

there is no delay such as may occur in the sale of large blocks of other types of securities. Furthermore, the price is fixed at the net asset value at the time. The price is based on NYSE-closing prices for redemption orders received prior to that closing.

Net Asset Value Per Share. The market price of an open-end fund is dependent on and determined by its net asset value per share. Net asset value per share represents stockholders' equity and is calculated as follows:

$$\text{Net Asset Value Per Share} = \frac{\text{Current Market Value of Securities Owned} + \text{Other Assets} - \text{Total Liabilities}}{\text{Number of Shares Outstanding}}.$$

Mutual funds are required by federal law to calculate net asset value per share at least once daily. Many companies actually make the calculation twice daily.

Types of Accounts. There are four types of shareholder accounts: (1) regular accounts, (2) accumulation plans, (3) accounts with automatic reinvestment, and (4) withdrawal accounts. The distribution of these accounts during the period 1970–1980 is shown in Table 29-2. The total number of shareholder accounts has declined significantly since 1970.

Special Services of Mutual Funds—Types of Plans. The mutual fund industry has developed numerous services and devices to increase the convenience, flexibility, and attractiveness of investing in mutual funds. The principal services are discussed in the following paragraphs.

Accumulation Plans. Practically all funds allow an investor, after making an initial investment, to make subsequent investments in regular or irregular amounts by writing a check to the fund's custodian. The investor typically agrees to also have all dividends reinvested into his or her account. Stock certificates are not usually issued, but the shareowner is notified periodically of the balance of shares held in the account.

Accumulation plans may be (1) voluntary, as would be most accounts classified in Table 29-2 as "regular" or "automatic dividend reinvestment," or (2) contractual. Under a *voluntary accumulation plan* fund shares may be purchased whenever the investor desires and in any amount desired. Some mutual funds, however, do have minimum amounts for purchases, such as $50, $100, or $500. A *contractual plan* involves a more formal arrangement (a contract) than the voluntary plan and encourages the investor to follow a specific program

TABLE 29-2. Major Types of Shareholder Accounts, Mutual Funds, 1970–1980

		Number of Accounts (in thousands)		
Year End	Regular Accounts	Accounts with Automatic Dividend Reinvestment	Contractual Single Payment and Accumulation Plans	Withdrawal Plans
1980	1,605	4,879	599	129
1979	1,704	4,901	741	140
1978	1,766	5,314	955	156
1977	2,008	5,387	945	175
1976	2,322	5,325	1,042	190
1975	2,536	5,766	1,155	210
1974	2,783	5,744	1,221	225
1973	2,707	5,992	1,380	252
1972	2,742	6,114	1,499	280
1971	2,866	6,130	1,624	281
1970	2,980	5,826	1,620	264
		Percentage of Total Accounts		
1980	22.2	67.7	8.3	1.8
1979	22.8	65.5	9.9	1.8
1978	21.6	64.9	11.7	1.8
1977	23.6	63.3	11.1	2.0
1976	26.2	60.0	11.7	2.1
1975	26.2	59.7	11.9	2.2
1974	27.9	57.6	12.2	2.3
1973	26.2	58.0	13.4	2.4
1972	25.8	57.5	14.1	2.6
1971	26.3	56.2	14.9	2.6
1970	27.9	54.5	15.1	2.5

Note: Money Market funds are included in totals above; on an annual basis, they numbered: 1974—104,000; 1975—164,000; 1976—155,000; 1977—141,000; 1978—381,000; 1979—1,691,000; 1980—4,746,000.

Source: Investment Companies, 1981 (New York: Wiesenberger Financial Services, (1981), p. 15. Reprinted by permission from the *Wiesenberger Investment Companies Service,* 1981 Edition, Copyright © 1981, Warren, Gorham & Lamont Inc., 210 South Street, Boston, Mass. All rights reserved.

to reach a predetermined goal. A contractual plan calls for periodic purchases (usually monthly) of a fixed dollar amount for a stated period of years—anywhere from five to fifteen years.

The part of the contractual plan that persuades the investor to continue the plan is the procedure for applying the costs—specifically the front-end load. Half of the first year's payments are generally deducted for sales charges. The Investment Company Act provides for a maximum sales charge limit of 8.5 percent and a maximum deduction for these charges of 50 percent of the first year's installment. But under the 1970 act, mutual funds are required to agree to rescind within forty-five days the entire transaction if requested, or to refund all payments less 15 percent commission during the first eighteen months. Alternatively, a plan may charge 20 percent per year for three years, limited to 64 percent over the first four years.

Dividend Reinvestment. Practically all mutual funds make the provision that dividends (both income dividends and capital gains distributions) may be automatically reinvested. In 1980 this represented about 68 percent of all accounts.

Withdrawal Plans. Many mutual funds make provision for investors who are no longer accumulating shares but wish to gradually liquidate their holdings—usually after retirement. Investment income may be divided evenly into twelve monthly payments, or a level monthly payment may consist of investment income plus a certain percentage of capital, or the period payments may fluctuate with the current value of the share in an effort (but not a guarantee) to reduce the risk of exhausting all capital over too short a period of years. These accounts, largely held by retirees, represent about 2 percent of all accounts.

Classification of Investment Companies by Policies. Managements of different investment funds follow a variety of policies in an effort to fit individual needs. Management must spell out its investment policy in its prospectus. Each investor should clearly define investment objectives, select funds whose stated policy conforms to individual policies and goals, and ascertain whether or not the fund in the past has in fact successfully followed its stated policy. Stated policies may be quite broad.

Common Stock Funds. Of the 659 mutual funds covered in *Investment Companies*, 341 or 52 percent were common stock funds as of December 31, 1980 (see Table 29–3). These funds are usually continuously invested 90 to 95 percent in common stocks. The "growth" and "growth and income" policy funds represented 58 percent of all funds and 85 percent of all common stock funds as of December 31, 1976. By December 31, 1980, they held only 26 percent of all funds and 78 percent of all common stock funds.

Balanced Funds. These maintain at all times a diversified portfolio balanced among bonds, preferred stocks, and common stocks with proportions dictated by management's assessment of the probable

TABLE 29-3. Classification of Mutual Funds by Size and Type, December 31, 1980

Size of Fund	No. of Funds	Combined Asset (000)	% of Total
Over $1 billion	30	$ 66,148,100	47.6
$500 million–$1 billion	36	24,575,900	17.7
$300 million–$500 million	33	12,580,400	9.1
$100 million–$300 million	128	22,066,400	16.0
$50 million–$100 million	98	6,961,400	5.1
$10 million–$50 million	205	5,423,300	4.0
$1 million–$10 million	117	571,400	0.5
Under $1 million	12	6,200	0.0
Total	659	$138,333,100	100.0

Type of Fund	No. of Funds	Combined Assets (000)	% of Total
Common Stock:			
Maximum Capital Gain	98	$ 8,252,700	6.0
Growth	139	19,110,100	13.5
Growth and Income	85	16,994,300	12.2
Specialized	19	2,045,400	1.5
Balanced	26	3,502,300	2.6
Income	128	9,875,300	7.2
Bond & pfd stock	11	1,454,400	1.1
Money market	101	71,992,900	52.1
Tax-exempt municipal bonds	43	3,269,100	2.4
Tax-free money markets	9	1,836,600	1.4
Total	659	$138,333,100	100.0

Source: *Investment Companies, 1981* (New York: Wiesenberger Financial Services, 1981), p. 43. Reprinted by permission from the *Wiesenberger Investment Companies Service*, 1981 Edition, Copyright © 1981, Warren, Gorham & Lamont Inc., 210 South Street, Boston, Mass. All rights reserved.

trend of common stock prices and interest rates. At the beginning of 1978 they held about 4 percent of the assets of all funds, but by December 31, 1980, they held only about 2.5 percent. Such funds seem to have significantly dropped in relative importance.

Income Funds. Income funds purchase securities primarily for relatively high income and early in 1977 held about 14 percent of the assets of all funds. By December 31, 1980, they held only about 7 percent.

Bond and Preferred Stock Funds. These funds invest only in bonds and preferred stocks. As of December 31, 1976, they held about 7 percent of the assets of all funds. By December 31, 1980, this figure had fallen to about 1 percent.

Money Market Funds. The very poor stock market record after 1968 and especially in 1969–1970 and 1973–1974 caused heavy redemptions (exceeding sales), and investors became more interested in the relatively high yields of debt instruments. This favored the creation of a new type of fund with investments mainly in short-term government securities, certificates of deposit, commercial paper, and banker's acceptances. Their aim is stability of price and high income. Between 1971 when the first fund was established and 1980, 101 funds were incorporated. Exceptionally high growth was recorded after 1978 when total assets increased from about $4 billion to about $72 billion. Their growth has been at the expense of other types of mutual funds, as indicated in the discussion above. Their sales success depends a great deal on the level of short-term interest rates, as was shown in 1975 when investors started to abandon them as rates began to go down. Money market fund yields need to be above the maximum percentage rate thrift institutions are permitted to pay, as has been true in recent years, in order to attract investors.

Tax-Free Municipal Bond Funds. This is a relatively new type of fund that became popular in 1976. An amendment to the Tax Reform Act of 1976 permitted mutual funds to pass through to their shareholders the tax-exempt aspect of interest earned on municipal bonds. They provide stability of principal and a relatively high yield, long term, when one considers the tax-exempt yield in relation to other fully taxable yields.

Foreign Investments—Canadian and International Funds. Some funds invest only or mainly in foreign securities such as Canadian General Fund, Inc., Canadian Fund, Inc., Japan Fund, and Eurofund.

Option Income Funds. Because of the provisions in the Tax Reform Act of 1976, several mutual funds have been formed that have as their portfolios common stocks on which options can be written. These funds receive as income the dividends on the stocks chosen plus premiums received when the managers sell options against the shares. One fund of this type—the Oppenheimer Option Income Fund—is offering its share-holders a tax shelter feature as well. Shares may be exchanged for a variable annuity contract which would mean that current taxes could be deferred until retirement.

Growth of Mutual Funds. In 1945 total assets of the mutual funds were only $1.3 billion. Ten years later they had risen to $7.8 billion (1955) and in 1968 to $52.7 billion (see Table 29-4).

There was a fairly continuous decline in assets of mutual funds after 1968, reflecting both the trend of stock prices and net redemptions, until 1980. Beginning with 1972, redemptions exceeded sales in each year, except for 1977 and 1980. After the spectacular growth in mutual fund sales and assets, the question naturally arises as to the reason. This decline coincided with the decline in individual shareowners of NYSE stocks as shown by the fact that by 1978 they had declined from 33–34 million to 25–26 million, a decline of nearly 25 percent.

The rise in fund shares and fund assets until 1966-1968 corre-sponded with the rise in the common stock indexes for the DJIA from lows of around 160 in each of the years 1946–1949 to a high of 1000 in February 1966. The DJIA sold higher only in late 1972 and early 1973 when it reached 1052. The S&P indexes continued to rise about 18 percent from February 1966 to December 1968 (after a 1966 de-cline), and then, except for higher prices from mid-1972 to mid-1973, did not exceed their 1968 high through 1981. In December 1976 and January 1977 the averages were back temporarily to their 1968 level but not to their 1973 highs. They then declined again in 1977 and 1978.

Inasmuch as fund asset values and net asset values generally paral-leled the exceptional rise in stock prices in the 1949 to 1966-1968 period, shareowners were enthusiastic about fund performance. As per-formance began to slow after February 1966, a new breed of funds, the "go-go" funds, appeared, and many temporarily did extremely well in 1967 and 1968. However, first the 37 percent decline in the market averages from December 1968 to May 1970 and then the 47 to 50 per-cent decline from January 1973 to December 1974 reduced drastically the value of the funds, and millions of investors became disillusioned not only with these funds but also with common stocks in general. They had come to expect substantial capital gains year after year only temporarily interrupted by market declines. Then during 1966–1976 and through 1981 they witnessed a ten- to fifteen-year period of little or no net capital gains. They developed a negative attitude toward com-mon stocks and especially common stock mutual funds. They found that on the average mutual funds did not outperform the averages and

TABLE 29-4. Growth of Mutual Funds, 1940-1977 (in thousands)

Year	Total Net Assets	Gross Sales	Redemptions	Net Sales	Redemption Rate	Shareholder Accounts	Number of Funds
1940	$ 447,959	NA	NA	NA	NA	296,056	68
1941	401,611	$ 53,312	$ 45,024	$ 8,288	10.6%	293,251	68
1945	1,284,185	292,359	109,978	182,381	10.2	497,875	73
1950	2,530,563	518,811	280,728	238,083	12.5	938,651	98
1951	3,129,629	674,610	321,550	353,060	11.4	1,110,432	103
1952	3,931,407	782,902	196,022	586,880	5.6	1,359,000	110
1953	4,146,061	672,005	238,778	433,227	5.9	1,537,250	110
1954	6,109,390	862,817	399,702	463,115	7.8	1,703,846	115
1955	7,837,524	1,207,458	442,550	764,908	6.4	2,085,325	125
1956	9,046,431	1,346,738	432,750	913,988	5.1	2,518,049	135
1957	8,714,143	1,390,557	406,716	983,841	4.6	3,110,392	143
1958	13,242,388	1,619,768	511,263	1,108,505	4.7	3,630,096	151
1959	15,817,962	2,279,982	785,627	1,494,355	5.4	4,276,077	155
1960	17,025,684	2,097,246	841,815	1,255,431	5.1	4,897,600	161
1961	22,788,812	2,950,860	1,160,357	1,790,503	5.8	5,319,201	170
1962	21,270,735	2,699,049	1,122,695	1,576,354	5.1	5,910,455	169
1963	25,214,436	2,459,105	1,505,335	953,770	6.5	6,151,935	165
1964	29,116,254	3,402,978	1,874,094	1,528,884	6.9	6,301,908	159
1965	35,220,243	4,358,144	1,962,432	2,395,712	6.1	6,709,343	170
1966	34,829,353	4,671,842	2,005,079	2,666,763	5.7	7,701,656	182
1967	44,701,302	4,669,575	2,744,197	1,925,378	6.9	7,904,132	204
1968	52,677,188	6,819,763	3,661,646	2,981,081	7.9	9,080,168	240
1969	48,290,733	6,718,283	3,838,682	3,056,637	7.3	10,391,534	269

1970	47,618,100	4,625,802	2,987,572	1,638,230	6.2	10,690,312	356
1971	55,045,328	5,147,186	4,750,222	396,964	9.3	10,900,952	392
1972	59,830,646	4,892,502	6,562,876	*(1,670,374)	11.4	10,635,287	410
1973	46,518,535	4,359,288	5,651,064	*(1,291,776)	10.6	10,330,862	421
1974	34,061,746	3,091,473	3,380,923	*(289,450)	8.4	9,970,439	416
1975	42,178,683	3,307,213	3,686,343	*(379,130)	9.7	9,712,513	390
1976	47,537,486	4,330,240	6,801,163	*(2,470,923)	15.2	8,879,413	404
1977	45,049,151	6,399,655	6,026,041	373,614	13.0	8,515,079	427
1978	44,979,685	6,705,299	7,232,420	*(527,121)	16.1	8,190,551	444
1979	49,297,058	7,465,400	8,379,500	*(914,000)	17.8	7,485,437	448
1980	58,399,621	9,993,744	8,199,983	1,793,761	15.9	7,212,018	458

Note: Data pertain to conventional fund members of the Investment Company Institute; money market funds not included. Total net assets at the 1977 year-end are 88% of the combined assets of all mutual funds listed in this volume. Institute "gross sales" figures include the proceeds of initial fund underwritings prior to 1970.
*Net redemptions.

Source: Investment Companies, 1981 (New York: Wiesenberger Financial Services, 1981), p. 17. Reprinted by permission from the *Wiesenberger Investment Companies Service,* 1981 Edition, Copyright © 1981, Warren, Gorham & Lamont Inc., 210 South Street, Boston, Mass. All rights reserved.

as the averages during 1966–1968 through 1981 showed poor capital gains performance except in late 1972 and early 1973, the same was true for the mutual funds. However, some funds did materially outperform the averages, and, of course, other funds performed worse; and as might be expected, throughout the period stock dividend yields were only about half of bond yields. Moreover, a new type of fund, the money market fund, offered high yields and quickly attracted significant amounts of funds.

These are the major reasons why net redemptions have generally exceeded net new sales for stock funds beginning with 1972. Only a reoccurrence of the stock market environment of the 1950s and 1960s can be expected to revive broad interest in common stock-oriented mutual funds. There are fundamental reasons why this may possibly reoccur during 1980 to 1990.

The Closed-End Investment Company

The Investment Company Act of 1940 defines all funds that do not redeem their shares as closed-end funds. For years there were few closed-end funds until the advent in 1969 of the newer-type funds. Closed-end funds, because of their closed capitalization, were not competitive with open-end funds. However, between 1969 and 1973, thirty-eight new closed-end funds were incorporated, with most of them stressing low-income funds. There were many new bond funds and others such as leveraged funds investing in convertible bonds and preferred stock. The growth record of closed-end funds was presented in Table 29–1.

Leverage. Modern closed-end funds are typically much different from the highly speculative investment trusts from which many evolved fifty or more years ago. Closed-end funds did raise a substantial amount of funds from the issuance of debt instruments until the late 1940s, thereby magnifying the impact on shareholder profits of price movements in the security market (financial leverage).

As of year-end 1980, only four of the larger closed-end funds provided leverage, "and in every case its effect on the common shares is insignificant."[5] Effective leverage, however, can be obtained through the capital shares of the dual-purpose funds as will be discussed shortly.

Market for Closed-End Shares. When investors sell their shares, the transaction is executed on the market for that fund, such as the NYSE, ASE or the over-the-counter market, in the same manner as a shareowner of an ordinary business corporation.

---

[5] *Investment Companies, 1981*, p. 20.

Discounts of Closed-End Funds. For many years the shares of closed-end companies have generally traded at a discount from their net asset value. For example, at the end of 1980 the average discount for the ten companies in the "Diversified Investment Company Average" was 15.2 percent with a range of 2.9 percent to 31.9 percent. The average discount was near its all time high for the past decade (see Figure 29–2). Clearly if a fund's shares are selling at a discount, the fund, in the eyes of investors, is worth more dead than alive. In any event, if shares sell at a discount, investors are discounting managerial ability in relation to assets under its supervision. Some have commented that the lack of a close and continuing relationship between shareowners and management as contrasted with mutual funds may account in part for the traditional discount in the market.

Dual-Purpose Funds

In 1967 funds of a new type came into existence—dual-purpose funds. These were closed-end funds whose sponsors sought to combine into one fund two classes of securities: (1) income shares and (2) capital shares. Income shares receive all the income generated but do not share in any capital gains; and capital shares, which receive no income, receive all capital gains and share all net losses. The income shares resemble preferred stock having stated cumulative dividends and receiving all additional income. All of the funds started off with two for one leverage. Equal capital was supplied by each class of security. Two funds were created as tax-free exchange funds.

In 1980 there were seven dual-purpose funds[6] with a total asset value approximating $390 million, only 20 percent above the value of the initial seven funds in 1967 ($325 million). On December 31, 1980, the combined value of all shares in the market represented a 10 percent discount from book value. In 1978 the management of closed-end funds hoped that the change in name to "Publicly Traded Funds" would improve their image and reduce or eliminate the discount at which their shares have traditionally been traded.

MAJOR STUDIES OF INVESTMENT COMPANIES

The practices of investment companies have been of considerable interest to various agencies of the government, and several studies have been commissioned as a result. Brief discussions of the most important of these studies follow.

---

[6] Gemini Fund, Hemisphere Fund, Income & Capital Shares Fund, Leverage Fund of Boston, Putnam Duofund, Scudder Duo-Vest Exchange Funds.

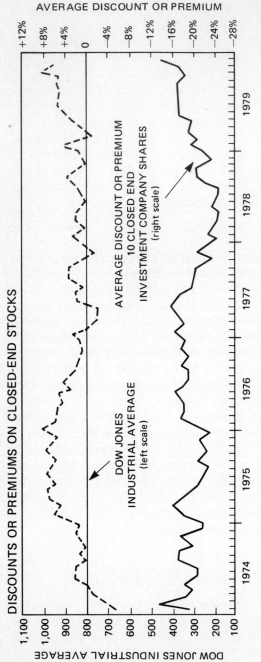

FIGURE 29–2. Discounts or Premiums on Closed-End Stocks Measured Against the DJIA

Wharton Report—1962

In 1958 the SEC commissioned the Wharton School of the University of Pennsylvania to study certain aspects and practices of open-end investment companies. In 1962 the Wharton School made a 539-page report to the SEC, and the report was transmitted to Congress at the same time.[7] This was commonly known as the "Wharton School Report." The study covered the effects of investment company size on investment policies, corporation performance, and the securities markets. It also included an analysis of the activities of investment company advisers and their relationship to the funds. The study found little evidence that the size of the funds was a problem and no instances of violations of legislation or regulation. The report made no specific recommendations for revision of the 1940 act, although it did raise questions as to the relationship between fund managements and investment advisers and potential conflicts of interest between management and shareholders. For example, it raised the problem of "give-ups" of sales commissions by exchange members, a practice that was voluntarily cancelled by exchange members in December 1968.

The SEC stated that the report found that the more important current problems in the mutual fund industry included (1) the potential conflicts of interest between fund management and shareholders already noted and (2) the effect of fund growth and stock purchases on stock prices.

Horowitz and Higgens found a negative relationship between performance and size.[8] A large fund can become so broadly diversified that it cannot hope to show significant better-than-average performance. Also, excessive size can hamper flexibility. A purchase large enough to have a significant impact on total results might drive the price up substantially when buying and drive the price far down when selling. In general, only funds with assets of $100 million or less have demonstrated the possibility of outperforming the averages.

Report on Special Study of the Securities Markets—1962-1963

In 1961 Congress ordered the SEC to make a broad study of the securities markets, which resulted in the publication of the *Special Study of the Securities Markets* in 1962-1963. In addition to the broad

---

[7] "A Study of Mutual Funds," prepared for the Securities and Exchange Commission by the Wharton School of Finance and Commerce, University of Pennsylvania. Report of the Committee on Interstate and Foreign Commerce, Pursuant to Section 136 of the Legislative Reorganization Act of 1946, Public Law 601, 79th Congress, and House Resolution 108, 87th Congress, 2d Session, August 28, 1962.

[8] Ira Horowitz and Harold B. Higgins, "Some Factors Affecting Investment Fund Performance," *Quarterly Review of Economics and Business* (Spring, 1963). The conclusion on large funds is highly significant.

review of the entire securities industry, this study covered aspects of the mutual fund industry beyond the scope of the Wharton Report. It focused its attention on sales of mutual fund shares, industry selling practices, special problems raised by the front-end load in the sale of so-called contractual plans, and allocations of mutual fund portfolio brokerages. Neither the *Special Study of the Securities Markets* nor the Wharton Report was a report *by* the SEC; both were reports made *for* the SEC.

SEC Report on Investment Companies

After the previous reports were published, the SEC evaluated the policy questions that the studies raised and then in 1966 reported its recommendations in a 340-page report.[9] The staff of the SEC drafted legislative proposals, which were submitted to Congress in 1967, at the same time requesting the industry and others to express their views on the proposed legislation. Hearings on the SEC-sponsored bill occupied much of the time of the Senate and House Committee. The bill became law in 1970. The SEC bill contained many amendments to the Investment Company Act of 1940. The 1970 act permits any shareholders to institute legal action for a claimed breach of *fiduciary duty*. The NASD has the responsibility for determining that the initial sales load is not excessive. The act also contains regulations regarding the front-end load of contractual plans and refunds to shareowners and discusses each.

TAXES AND INVESTMENT COMPANIES

Most investment companies are exempt from federal income taxes— those that qualify under Subchapter M of the Internal Revenue Code, i.e., those that distribute their taxable income. The requirements in Subchapter M to meet the definition of "regulated investment company" are given as follows:

---

[9] Report of the Securities and Exchange Commission on the Probable Policy Implications of Investment Company Growth, Report of the Committee on Interstate and Foreign Commerce, 89th Congress, 2d Session, December 2, 1966.

"Other significant reports issued by the SEC included its disclosure policy study of 1969 (The Wheat Report), the "Institutional Investor Study Report," submitted to Congress in 1971, and the "Policy Statement on Future Structure of the Securities Markets," issued in 1972. The Institutional Investor Study Report was an economic study of institutional investors and their effects on the securities markets, issuers of securities, and the investing public. The Policy Statement proposed creation of a "central market system," a system of communication tying together the various elements of the marketplace with a set of rules outlining the relationships of all participants." From *Audits of Investments Companies* (New York: AICPA, 1973), pp. 7–8.

1. It must be a domestic corporation (or domestic entity taxable as a corporation), not a personal holding company.
2. It must be registered at all times during the taxable year under the Investment Company Act of 1940, either as a management company or as a unit investment trust.
3. At least 90 percent of its gross income for any taxable year must be from dividends, interest, and gains from securities.
4. No more than 30 percent of its gross income for any taxable year may be derived from sales of securities held for less than three months.
5. It must distribute as taxable dividends not less than 90 percent of its net income, exclusive of capital gains for any fiscal year. Under a 1950 Amendment, such dividends from the earnings of one year may be paid in the following year provided that they are declared not later than the due date of company's tax return and are paid not later than the first regular dividend date after declaration.
6. At the close of each quarter of the taxable year:
   (a) At least 50 percent of its assets must consist of cash, cash items (including receivables), government securities, securities of other regulated investment companies, and other securities limited to not more than 5 percent of its assets in securities of any one issue and not more than 10 percent of the voting securities of that issue.
   (b) Not more than 15 percent of its assets may be invested in any one company, or in two or more controlled companies engaged in the same or a similar line of business (20 percent of voting power constitutes assumed control).

Practically all mutual funds have complied with these requirements in Subchapter M to ensure exemption from federal income taxes.

Reporting of Income Taxes by Shareowners

When distributing income to shareowners, the fund identifies the portion derived from investment income and the portion derived from capital gains. The shareowner reports the income segment as regular income and the capital gains portion as a long-term capital gain.

Distribution of Capital Gains and Yields

When calculating yield, the investor often includes capital gains distributions. If a fund pays a capital gains distribution equivalent to 20 percent of net asset value, the value of the shares will decline 20 percent immediately after the distribution; thus, in applying dividends paid during the year to net asset value to determine yield, the investor should use only 80 percent of the dividends received. Otherwise, the yield will appear greater than it actually is because of the reduction in the net asset value of the shares after the distribution.

PERFORMANCE EVALUATION

In any undertaking, provision is typically made by those who pay for a service to evaluate the performance of those who perform the service. In this regard the society of professional money managers is not immune.

Starting in the late 1960s and continuing to the present day, a great deal of academic work has concentrated on the performance of no-load and front-load mutual funds. Both Wiesenberger and Forbes offer services that regularly rate the performance of mutual funds in terms of rate-of-return considerations. However, the emphasis of these services and of academic work in the area is markedly different. Moreover, the industry has not been subject to systematic evaluation in accordance with techniques that integrate risk and return considerations, as developed in Section II of this book.

Both Wiesenberger and Forbes proceed along traditional lines, rating funds according to ex-post rates of return with no explicit adjustment for risk, ex-post or ex-ante. Wiesenberger contrasts the performance of funds to that of a broad stock market index for various selected time periods. Such contrasts fail on two accounts, however. First, the contrasts are based on decision horizons of five or more years—a period sufficiently long to mask the variance and covariance effects. Second, most mutual fund portfolios would produce betas less than one. Thus there is an element of mixing apples and oranges in the Wiesenberger contrasts. Forbes, by contrast, does attempt to rate funds on the basis of performance in up and down markets. In the absence of explicit consideration of ex-ante risk objectives, and categorization accordingly, such contrasts and ratings are difficult to use.

The academic work that has been performed in this area, by contrast, has attempted to come to grips with the issue of risk.[10] Although some valid questions may be raised regarding experimental design,[11] on balance the academic work has generally shown that both before and after risk adjustment, the performance of no-load and front-load mutual funds during the periods studied was less than impressive. Indeed, while there were exceptions (though few very significant ones), the ex-post

---

[10] See in particular, Fred Ardatti, "Another Look at Mutual Fund Performance," *Journal of Financial and Quantitative Analysis*, Vol. 6, No. 3 (June, 1971), pp. 909–912; Irwin Friend, Marshall Blume, and Jean Crockett, *Mutual Funds and Other Institutional Investors* (New York: McGraw-Hill, 1970); Michael C. Jensen, "The Performance of Mutual Funds in the Period 1945–1964," *Journal of Finance*, Vol. 23, No. 2 (May, 1968), pp. 389–415; and William F. Sharpe, "Mutual Fund Performance," *Journal of Business*, Vol. 39, No. 1, Part 2 (January, 1966).

[11] See in particular, Eugene Fama and J. MacBeth, "Tests of the Multiperiod Two-Parameter Model," *Journal of Financial Economics*, Vol. 1, No. 1 (May, 1974), pp. 43–66; Richard Roll, "A Critique of the Asset Pricing Theory's Tests; Part 1: On Past and Potential Testability of the Theory," *Journal of Financial Economics*, Vol. 4, No. 2 (March, 1977), pp. 129–176.

rates of return and risk combinations for most "professionally managed" mutual funds would have plotted on or below a line such as that drawn in Figure 29-3, which is a proxy for the capital market line introduced in Chapter 12 and discussed in Chapter 13. In other words, most funds would have done as well or better by indexing, and most investors would have done as well or better by investing a portion of their investment budgets in index funds (which did not appear until the mid 1970s) and a portion in ninety-day treasury certificates.

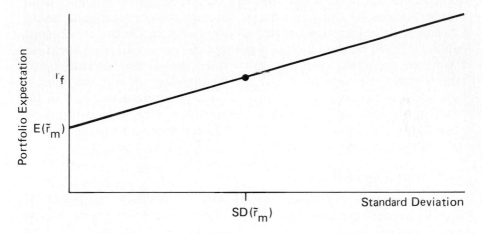

FIGURE 29-3. Proxy: Capital Market Line

In this section we discuss some techniques that have been proposed for evaluating investment performance. It should be understood at the outset that we are dealing with a very complex phenomenon and that each approach is subject to both shortcomings and valid criticism. For this reason an attempt is made to discuss both method and shortcomings side by side. This material is also covered to some extent in Chapter 13 but from a different point of view.

Decision Strategy and Investment Outcome

We pointed out in Chapter 8 that the purchase of a risky asset is tantamount to the purchase of a financial lottery—a gamble. Thus, ex-ante performance should be viewed as a composite of two events: (1) an investment strategy and (2) the interplay of random factors. The following combination of events, therefore, is mutually exclusive but not necessarily collectively exhaustive:

1. Good strategy and good outcome.
2. Good strategy and bad outcome.

3. Bad strategy and good outcome.
4. Bad strategy and bad outcome.

Clearly, ex-post outcomes cannot be classified as good or bad without at least some consideration being given to (1) ex-ante objectives, (2) the constraints imposed on feasible solution to a problem, and (3) purely random factors. As applied to the problem of portfolio management, a number of points should be kept clearly in mind. First, there is always the danger of mixing apples and oranges. The Wiesenberger and Forbes approaches do this to a major extent, but so—to a lesser extent— do each of the approaches that we introduce below. Second, while purely random factors may average out over time, at particular points in time their impacts may dwarf all other effects. On the other hand, control of such random factors is perhaps the essence of diversification. Evaluation contrasts, therefore, must span periods that are sufficiently long to yield valid contrasts, but the methodology of contrast must be dynamic and not static. Finally, it should be realized that risk in the sense of random variation is a two-way street. The market charges a price for risk avoidance, but investors who consent to high degrees of risk exposure must expect from time to time to pay a price also.

Traditional Approach

Wiesenberger's *Investment Companies* follows the traditional approach, measuring performance according to the following rate of return equation:

$$p = \frac{EA + DP + DI}{BA},$$ (29.1)

where

   EA = net assets per share at the end of the period under review,
   DP = distribution per share from profits realized on sale of securities during the period,
   DI = dividends per share from investment income during the period,
   BA = net assets per share at the beginning of the period,
   p = performance index.

Unfortunately, this approach is both incomplete and potentially incorrect. As was stated previously, no account is taken of risk.

From a more technical (in the sense of quantitative analysis) point of view, however, in which the period under consideration spans a period of more than one year, a one-period rate of return model should not be used. Moreover, the terms DP and DI do not necessarily adequately treat or represent the distribution of inflows and outflows that may occur over a period. Thus when used for the purpose of comparing and contrasting the performance of various funds, all of which have (or may have) differing forms of cash inflows and outflows occurring over a period and at different points in time, one inevitably becomes involved in a contrast of apples, oranges, and grapes! Concentration solely on return considerations is not an adequate basis for performance measurement.

Sharpe and Treynor's Reward to Variability Ratios

There are two uniquely different measures of this sort. The first, which is attributed to Sharpe, is based on the logic of the capital market line, as developed in Chapter 12.[12] The second, which is attributed to Treynor, is based on the logic of the security market line.[13] A third measure, which is attributed to Jenson,[14] is not sufficiently different from Treynor's approach to justify separate treatment here.

Under the general equilibrium assumptions of the capital asset pricing model that was introduced in Chapter 12 and discussed in Chapter 13, two uniquely different relationships can be identified:

$$\frac{E(\tilde{r}_m) - r_f}{\text{SD}(\tilde{r}_m)}, \tag{29.2}$$

which is the reward to variability ratio for efficient portfolios as represented by the slope of the CML shown in Figure 26–3 and

$$\frac{E(\tilde{r}_m) - r_f}{\text{Var}(\tilde{r}_m)}, \tag{29.3}$$

which is the reward to variability ratio for undiversified capital assets as represented by the slope of the SML in Figure 29–4. Note that in the context of the capital asset pricing model, the ratios given by equations (29.2) and (29.3) respectively are defined in terms of ex-ante expectations and not in terms of ex-post rates of return.

If we relax our concerns about the equilibrium assumptions that underlie the capital asset pricing model, we may then look at Figures 29–3 and 29–4 from a different point of view—that of descriptive statistics. Specifically, if we substitute the ex-post mean on a broad stock market index

$$\bar{r}_m = \sum_{t=1}^{T} \tilde{r}_{mt}/T \tag{29.4}$$

---

[12] Sharpe, "Mutual Fund Performance."
[13] Jack Treynor, "How to Rate Management of Investment Funds," *Harvard Business Review*, Vol. 43, No. 1 (January/February, 1965), pp. 63–75.
[14] Jensen, "The Performance of Mutual Funds in the Period 1945-1964."

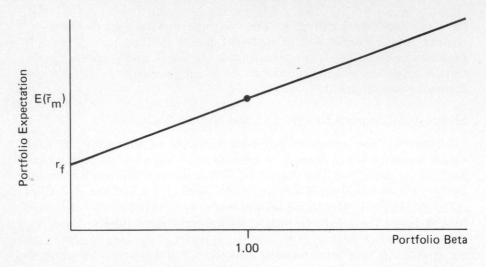

FIGURE 29-4. Proxy: Security Market Line

for the ex-ante expected return that appears in the numerator of equations (29.2) and (29.3) and the corresponding standard deviation and mean in the denominators, respectively, then the following interpretation is possible. Based on such a substitution, the horizontal axis in Figure 29-3 is measured in terms of units that represent total portfolio risk. The horizontal axis in Figure 29-4, by contrast, is measured in terms of units that represent nondiversifiable portfolio risk.

The Sharpe and Treynor portfolio performance measures, therefore, are variations on a single theme. In each case, portfolio performance is measured relative to a standard, according to which risk and return are explicit components. The two measures differ significantly, however, in a different sense.

The Sharpe performance index is simply the ratio of excess rate of return over a measure of total portfolio risk. Such a ratio would plot as a point in the graph shown in Figure 29-3. Funds that plot above the line "beat the market" in a sense, and the other way around for funds that plot below the line. For any point above the line, clearly

$$\frac{\bar{r}_p - r_f}{\mathrm{SD}(\tilde{r}_p)} > \frac{\bar{r}_m - r_f}{\mathrm{SD}(\tilde{r}_m)}. \tag{29.5}$$

Thus, funds that beat the market in this sense can claim to have achieved an above-average reward to variability ratio, measured in terms of total portfolio risk. Note that the relationship represented by equation (29.5) is based on logic that is clearly due to the capital asset pricing model, but does not otherwise depend on the validity of CAPM.

The Treynor measure, by contrast, is defined as the ratio of excess return over systematic risk:

$$\frac{\bar{r}_p - r_f}{\hat{\beta}_p}, \qquad (29.6)$$

where systematic risk is defined according to portfolio beta. This relationship is based not only on the logic of CAPM, but also on the presumption that the model is empirically correct. It is one thing, for example, to suppose that in equilibrium all but the systematic component of risk will have been diversified away. It is quite another thing, however, to suppose either that equilibrium in the sense of CAPM actually exists or that, in any event, portfolio beta is an adequate measure of nondiversifiable risk.

On this basis alone, Sharpe's portfolio performance measure seems less heroic than Treynor's measure and potentially more useful. This view is supported, moreover, by an evaluation of the statistical properties of the ratios and by some recent empirical evidence dealing with the contrast of the two methods.

Statistical Properties of Performance Measures

The traditional measures dealing with rates of return are easily dismissed, in part because risk is not properly considered. A second objection that may be raised to performance measurements such as those available from Wiesenberger or Forbes is that they are based on accounting identities, the mathematical properties of which are unknown. Unfortunately, recognizing the shortcomings of such approaches is one thing, but overcoming them is quite a different matter.

By inspection of equations (29.5) and (29.6), we see that the numerators are the same but that the denominators differ. Assuming that r_f is treated as a constant, $(\bar{r}_p - r_f)$ is a normally distributed random variable. What is not at all clear, however, is that r_f can be regarded as a constant. Indeed, it seems entirely reasonable to suppose that the distribution of $\bar{r}_f$ is very significantly related, in general, to r_f—which is neither a constant nor a mathematically tractible random variable. Moral: the quantity $(\bar{r}_p - r_f)$ is difficult to interpret.

When turning to a consideration of the statistics used to represent risk in the denominator of Equations (29.5) and (29.6), the situation unfortunately becomes even more obscure. The standard deviation is the square root of the variance, whose distribution is chi-square over degrees of freedom. Sample beta, by contrast, is a normal random variable. These points may be of greater interest to statistics majors than finance majors. Both statistics, however, are very sensitive to degrees of freedom—that is, to the number of observations on which an estimate is based. This point is, or should be, of interest to any reader, in that one may, deliberately or inadvertently, affect both the precision and the relevance of these performance measurements by manipulating the periodicity of the data and/or the time span used as a basis for estimation.

By way of further contrast, the Sharpe performance measure is based on total portfolio risk, as represented by portfolio standard deviation. The Treynor performance measure, on the other hand, is based on a measure of systematic risk that is provided by an ex-post beta statistic $\hat{\beta}_p$. Such a statistic is not only subject to random estimation error but also to systematic bias due to model misspecification. In more intuitive terms, $\hat{\beta}_p$ will almost certainly be less faithful than $SD(\tilde{r}_p)$. Thus, on statistical grounds alone, we would expect the Treynor measure to be less reliable than the Sharpe performance measure. A recent study provides empirical evidence that supports this intuition.[15]

Caveat

Modern portfolio theory provides some useful insights and a methodology that is inherently appealing. Application of this methodology must be used with caution, however, and the results interpreted with the greatest care and suspicion. Traditional methodology, for all its faults, has not yet been superseded.

SELECTION OF INVESTMENT COMPANIES

First, the individual must decide whether or not to invest long term, for at least the next five or ten years, in common stocks or to invest in debt instruments only (long term or short term), or to invest in a balanced portfolio of common stocks and bonds. The decision will depend on one's assumption as to whether the record of stocks during the period 1966–1979 is likely to be repeated 1980 to 1985 or 1990. If the 1966–1979 period is expected to be repeated, one should invest in debt instruments (except at relatively low levels for the market averages such as 500–750 DJIA), or one could hedge by having a balanced portfolio of common stocks and bonds. If the investor decides that the 1965–1968 through 1978 stock market history was subnormal and a better market environment is more likely, say from 1980 to 1990, then common stock investments including investments in common stock funds will be favored.

Many investors will have a better record if they use the vehicle of investment funds rather than investing directly. Lack of time or skill

---

[15] The study showed that, from a statistical point of view, "a Sharpe . . . statistic is reasonably well behaved," but "the Treynor measures were not very satisfactory." See J. D. Jobson and Bob M. Korkie, "Performance Hypothesis Testing with the Sharpe and Treynor Measures," *Journal of Finance*, Vol. 36, No. 4 (September, 1981), p. 889.

necessary to supervise their portfolio and inability to achieve effective diversification may well cause individual investors to experience poor returns. This does not mean that they can expect excellent results by using funds but only that they will probably do better than if they invested directly in stocks or bonds selected on their own judgment. Furthermore, by grouping a large number of investors with similar objectives, economics of scale may be realized in terms of administering the account and commissions on transactions. Potential cost savings could be passed on to investors, at least in part, by the fund.

Investors who do decide to invest in funds must examine the record of these funds and decide which stated policy will correspond with the policies that they have selected.[16] They will frequently find major differences between broad stated policies and expected results and actual records. A past record is no guarantee that the future record will be similar. However, this is probably the best way to make the selection once the individual has decided on the investment policy favored.

Summary

Investment companies sell shares of stock in their own corporation or trust and then invest the funds thus obtained in a diversified portfolio of securities. The two major functions provided are wide diversification, which few individuals are able to obtain by direct investment, and professional management, which is expected to be superior to that of most individual professionals. In fact, however, relatively few of the medium or large funds have for any long extended period provided results superior to that of the averages. This is, of course, also true of individuals managing their own portfolios.

Relatively large size and, therefore, relatively wide diversification have generally precluded superior performance. In the period 1946–1966 when the DJIA rose from 160 to 1000, the funds, while generally not out-performing the averages, posted results satisfactory to investors. But the period 1966–1968 through 1978 was far different, as the stock averages largely moved up and down in a horizontal channel, and the resulting record for most funds was quite unsatisfactory in the eyes of most investors. Overall rate of return was below bond yields.

Disenchantment with common stock funds, coupled with the development of bond funds, particularly tax-exempt bond funds and the new money market funds, generally accounted for the only increase posted in total assets of investment companies. The total assets of mutual funds reached their peak in 1968, the second year (1966 was the first year) that the DJIA level was close to 1000. This was also the peak year for the assets of open-end and closed-end fund companies.

----

[16] In this respect the numerous performance tables in Wiesenberger's *Investment Companies* are helpful.

Investment companies are generally classified as open-end, or mutual funds, or closed-end funds. In 1967 a new type of fund was sold—the dual-purpose fund having income shares and capital shares. There were seven funds in 1967. However, in 1977 there were only nine dual-purpose funds with asset values totaling $385 million versus the total assets of the seven funds initiated in 1967 of $325 million.

There are numerous ways of measuring the performance of investment companies. The most important fact to remember is that investment companies often differ widely in their policies and whether comparing performances to the record of other companies or to such indexes as the stock averages, investors must recognize the differences in policies that do have an important effect on performance results. Moreover, performance evaluation must consider risk and return in an integrated, systematic way.

Questions

1. (a) Define investment companies.
   (b) Distinguish between the two major types of investment companies.
   (c) Trace the growth of each major type since 1940 and explain any difference in growth patterns.
2. (a) During the major stock market decline (1929–1932), the net asset values of closed-end funds were generally more severely affected than the net asset values of open-end funds. Why?
   (b) Do the same conditions prevail today? Discuss.
3. (a) What is meant by selling at a discount? Can an open-end fund sell at a discount?
   (b) What possible advantages does the investor gain in purchasing the stock of a closed-end fund at a discount?
4. (a) What problems may be solved for the small investor who invests in mutual funds?
   (b) How does a closed-end investment company differ from an ordinary business corporation?
5. (a) What are the two principal distinguishing characteristics of mutual investment funds?
   (b) What costs does the investor incur in acquiring mutual fund shares? Discuss the reasonableness of these costs.
   (c) Would you prefer to acquire the shares of a large or a small investment company, other things being equal. Discuss.
6. (a) Would it be preferable for investors to invest in no-load rather than load funds? How would you arrive at a judgment concerning a no-load as contrasted to a load fund?
   (b) What are the advantages and the disadvantages of investing in a closed-end fund as opposed to an open-end fund?

7. What are the objections of the SEC to
   (a) Contractual plans for purchasing mutual fund shares?
   (b) The "load" for all funds?
8. What are the highlights of the Investment Company Act of 1940?
9. (a) How are investment companies taxed?
   (b) What is a regulated investment company?
10. (a) What are the major types of policies followed by investment companies?
    (b) What is a dual-purpose fund?
11. (a) Why has the performance of so many mutual funds not been much better than the stock averages?
    (b) Why might it be difficult for a mutual fund manager to concentrate on stock representing out-of-favor, low P/E situations?
    (c) How may size restrict the performance of an investment company?
12. Explain the properties and intent of the performance measures outlined in the chapter.
13. What is wrong with using an ex-ante model as a basis for testing ex-post results?
14. Traditional methods derive their inputs on the basis of accounting numbers and identities. How are we to know the statistical properties of the resulting performance measurements? Why is it important to know the statistical properties of an estimator?
15. The Sharpe measure is a measure of excess return to total portfolio risk. The Treynor measure is a measure of excess return to nondiversifiable risk. In what sense is the Sharpe measure more general than the Treynor measure and why (otherwise) is it likely to be more reliable?

Work-Study Problems

1. Discuss the following Wiesenberger formulas covered in this chapter:
   (a) Capital results alone formula.
   (b) Income results alone formula.
2. Select a stock that you believe would have been a good candidate for NYSE Monthly Investment Plan investing ten years ago. Give reasons why you believe that type of stock, considering the industry and the company characteristics, would have been a good candidate for MIP investing.
3. (a) Select a stock for MIP investing for the next ten years and give reasons for your selection.
   (b) Do you believe that investing in this stock by means of MIP investing would be superior to investing in a mutual fund? Why?

Suggested Readings

Chapter 2

Bildersee, John S. "Some Aspects of the Performance of Non-Convertible Preferred Stocks." *Journal of Finance*, Vol. 28, No. 5 (December, 1973), pp. 1187–1201.

Brittain, John A. *Corporate Dividend Policy, Studies of Government Finance*. Washington, D.C.: The Brookings Institution, 1966.

Donaldson, Gordon. "In Defense of Preferred Stock." *Readings in Finance*. New York: Appleton-Century-Crofts, 1966, pp. 251–274.

Elton, E. J., and M. J. Gruber. "The Cost of Retained Earnings—Implications of Share Repurchase." *Industrial Management Review*, Vol. 9, No. 3 (Spring, 1968), pp. 87–104.

——. "The Effect of Share Repurchases on the Value of the Firm." *Journal of Finance*, Vol. 23, No. 1 (March, 1968), pp. 135–150.

Furst, Richard W. "Does Listing Increase the Market Price of Common Stocks?" *Journal of Business*, Vol. 43, No. 2 (April, 1970), pp. 174–180.

Guthart, Leo A. "Why Companies Buy Their Own Stock." *Financial Analysts Journal*, Vol. 23, No. 2 (March-April, 1967), pp. 105–112.

Stewart, Samual S. "Should a Corporation Repurchase Its Own Stock?" *Journal of Finance*, Vol. 31, No. 3 (June, 1976), pp. 911–921.

Chapter 3

Atkinson, Thomas R. *Trends in Corporate Bond Quality*. National Bureau of Economic Research. New York: Columbia University Press, 1967.

Bullington, Robert A. "How Corporate Debt Issues Are Rated." *Financial Executive*, Vol. 42, No. 9 (September, 1974).

Darst, David M. *The Complete Bond Book*. New York: McGraw-Hill, 1975.

Hickman, W. Braddock. *Corporate Bond Quality and Investor Experience*. National Bureau of Economic Research. Princeton, N.J.: Princeton University Press, 1958.

Homer, Sidney. "The Historical Evaluation of Today's Bond Market." *The Journal of Portfolio Management*, Vol. 1, No. 3 (Spring, 1975).

Jen, **Frank C.**, and **James E. Wert**. "The Effects of Sinking Fund Provisions on Corporate Bond Yields." *Financial Analysts Journal*, Vol. 23, No. 2 (March–April, 1967), pp. 125-133.
———. "The Effects of Call Risk on Corporate Bond Yields." *Journal of Finance*, Vol. 22, No. 4 (December, 1967), pp. 637-651.
Van Horne, James C. *Financial Market Rates and Flows.* Englewood Cliffs, N.J.: Prentice-Hall, 1978.

Chapter 4

Board of Governors of Federal Reserve System. *Federal Reserve Bulletin* (monthly). *The Bond Buyer* (monthly). (Statistics on state and local government finance.)
Handbook of Securities of the United States Government and Federal Agencies. New York: The First Boston Corporation, biennial editions, even years.
Hastie, K. Larry. "Determinants of Municipal Bond Yields." *Journal of Financial and Quantitative Analysis*, (June, 1972), pp. 1729-1748.
Hemple, George H. *Postwar Quality of State and Local Debt.* NBER General Series, No. 94. New York: Columbia University Press, 1971.
Industrial Aid Financing. New York: Goodbody & Co., 1965.
Smith, Warren L. "The Competitive Position of Government Securities." Debt Management in the United States, Study Paper No. 19. Materials prepared in connection with the study of employment, growth, and price levels for consideration by the Joint Economic Committee, 86th Congress, 2d Session, January 28, 1960, pp. 61-72.
"Treasury-Federal Reserve Study of the Government Securities Market, 1959." U.S. Treasury Department. *Treasury Bulletin* (monthly).

Chapter 5

Black, Fischer. "Fact and Fantasy in the Use of Options." *Financial Analysts Journal*, Vol. 31, No. 4 (July/August, 1975), pp. 36-42, 61-72.
———. "The Pricing of Commodity Contracts." *Journal of Financial Economics*, Vol. 3, Nos. 1-2 (January-March, 1976), pp. 167-179.
———, and Myron Scholes. "The Pricing of Options and Corporate Liabilities." *Journal of Political Economy*, Vol. 81, No. 3 (May, 1972), pp. 637-654.
Bookstaber, Richard M. "Observed Option Mispricing and Nonsimultaneity of Stock and Option Quotations." *The Journal of Business*, Vol. 54, No. 1 (January, 1981), pp. 141-155.

Branch, Ben, and Joseph E. Finnerty. "The Impact of Option Listing on the Price and Volume of the Underlying Stock." *The Financial Review*, Vol. 16, No. 2 (Spring, 1981), pp. 1–15.

Cox, John C., and Stephen A. Ross. "The Valuation of Options for Alternative Stochastic Processes." *Journal of Financial Economics*, Vol. 3, Nos. 1–2 (January-March, 1976), pp. 145–166.

Evans, John L., and Stephen H. Archer. "Diversification and the Reduction of Dispersion: An Empirical Analysis." *Journal of Finance*, Vol. 23, No. 5 (December, 1968), pp. 761–767.

Malkiel, Burton G., and Richard E. Quandt. *Strategies and Rational Decisions in the Securities Options Market*. Cambridge, Mass.: MIT Press, 1969.

Merton, Robert E. "The Theory of Rational Option Pricing." *The Bell Journal of Economics and Management Science*, Vol. 4, No. 1 (Spring, 1973), pp. 141–183.

——, Myron S. Scholes, and Matthew L. Gladstein. "The Returns and Risk of Alternative Call Option Portfolio Investment Strategies." *The Journal of Business*, Vol. 51, No. 2 (April, 1978), pp. 183–242.

Prospectus, Options Clearing Corporation. This prospectus is available by writing to any organized exchange, or from any options broker who is registered with an organized options exchange.

Raiffa, Howard, and Robert Schlaifer. *Applied Statistical Decision Theory*. Boston: The Harvard University Press, 1961. Chapter 3.

Reback, Robert. "Risk and Return in CBOE and AMEX Option Trading." *Financial Analysts Journal*, Vol. 31, No. 4 (July/August, 1975), pp. 42–52.

Samuelson, Paul A. "Rational Theory of Warrant Pricing." *Industrial Management Review*, Vol. 6 (Spring, 1965), pp. 13–31.

Understanding Options: A Guide to Puts and Calls. Chicago: The Chicago Board of Options Exchange.

Chapter 6

Federal Tax Course. Chicago, Commerce Clearing House, Inc., revised annually.

Federal Tax Course. (Englewood Cliffs, N.J., Prentice-Hall, revised annually).

U.S. Treasury Department, Internal Revenue Service. *Your Federal Income Tax*, Publication 17. Washington, D.C.: Government Printing Office, revised annually.

U.S. Treasury Department, Internal Revenue Service, *A Guide to Federal Estate and Gift Taxation*. Publication 448. Washington, D.C.: Government Printing Office.

Chapter 7

Bower, Richard S., and Dorothy H. Bower. "Risk and the Valuation of Common Stock." *Journal of Political Economy*, Vol. 77, No. 4 (June, 1969), pp. 349–362.

Brealy, Richard A. *An Introduction to Risk and Return from Common Stocks*. Cambridge, Mass.: MIT Press, 1969.

Foster, Earl M. "The Price-Earnings Ratio and Growth." *Financial Analysts Journal*, Vol. 26, No. 1 (January–February, 1970), pp. 96–103.

Gordon, Myron J. *The Investment Financing and Valuation of the Corporation*. Homewood, Ill.: Richard D. Irwin, 1962.

Homer, Sidney, and M. L. Leibowitz. *Inside the Yield Book*. Englewood Cliffs, N.J.: Prentice-Hall, 1972.

Jaffe, D. M., B. G. Malkiel, and R. E. Quandt. "Predicting Common Stock Prices: Payoffs and Pitfalls." *Journal of Business Research*, Vol. 2, No. 1 (January, 1974), pp. 1–16.

Jen, F. C., and J. E. Wert. "The Effect of Call Risk on Corporate Bond Yields." *The Journal of Finance*, Vol. 22, No. 4 (December, 1967), pp. 637–651.

Malkiel, Burton, G. *A Random Walk Down Wall Street*. New York: W. W. Norton, 1975, Part I.

Malkiel, B. G., and J. G. Cragg. "Expectations and the Structure of Share Prices." *American Economic Review*, Vol. 60, No. 4 (September, 1970), pp. 601–617.

Miller, M., and F. Modigliani, "Dividend Policy, Growth and the Valuation of Shares." *The Journal of Business* (October, 1961), pp. 411–433.

Nicholson, S. F. "Price-Earnings Ratios." *Financial Analysts Journal*, Vol. 26, No. 4 (July–August, 1970), pp. 43ff.

Reilly, Frank K. "The Misdirected Emphasis in Security Valuation." *Financial Analysts Journal*, Vol. 29, No. 1 (January–February, 1973), pp. 54–56, 59–60.

Ross, S. A., "The Determination of Financial Structure: The Incentive-Signaling Approach." *The Bell Journal of Economics* (Spring, 1977), pp. 23–40.

Williamson, J. Peter. *Investments: New Analytic Techniques*. New York: Praeger, 1970, Chapters V-VI-VIII.

Chapter 8

Chernoff, Herman, and Lincoln Moses. *Elementary Decision Theory*. New York: Wiley, 1959.

Markowitz, Harry M. *Portfolio Selection*. New Haven: Yale University Press, 1959.

Mood, Alexander M., Franklin A. Graybill, and Duane C. Boes. *Introduction to the Theory of Statistics.* New York: McGraw-Hill, 1974.

Raiffa, Howard. *Decision Analysis.* Cambridge, Mass.: Harvard University Press, 1968.

Savage, Leonard J. *The Foundations of Statistics.* New York: Wiley, 1954.

Snedecore, George W., and William G. Cochran. *Statistical Methods,* 6th ed. Ames: The Iowa State University Press, 1971.

Chapter 9

Barack, Peter. "The Regulation of Risky Investments." *Harvard Law Review,* Vol. 83 (January, 1970), pp. 603-625.

Evans, John L., and Stephen H. Archer. "Diversification and the Reduction of Dispersion: An Empirical Analysis," *The Journal of Finance,* Vol. 23, No. 5 (December, 1968), pp. 761-767.

Frankfurter, George M., Herbert E. Phillips, and John P. Seagle. "Portfolio Selection: The Effects of Uncertain Means, Variances, and Covariances." *Journal of Financial and Quantitative Analysis,* Vol. 6, No. 5 (December, 1971), pp. 1251-62.

Hicks, J. R. *Value and Capital.* Oxford: The Clarendon Press, 1962, Part III.

Knight, Frank H. *Risk, Uncertainty and Profit.* Boston: Houghton-Mifflin, 1921, Chapter 2.

Markowitz, Harry M. *Portfolio Selection.* New Haven: Yale University Press, 1959.

Raiffa, Howard. *Decision Analysis.* Menlo Park, California: Addison-Wesley, 1970.

Tobin, James. "Liquidity Preference as Behavior Towards Risk," *The Review of Economic Studies,* Vol. 26, No. 1 (February, 1958), pp. 65-86.

Chapter 10

Blume, Marshall E. "On the Assessment of Risk." *Journal of Finance,* Vol. 26, No. 1 (March, 1971), pp. 1-10.

Edwards, Ward, Harold Lindman, and Leonard J. Savage. "Bayesian Statistical Inference for Psychological Research." *Psychological Review,* Vol. 70, No. 3 (March, 1963), pp. 193-242.

Frankfurter, George M., Herbert E. Phillips, and John P. Seagle. "Performance of the Sharpe Portfolio Selection Model: A Comparison." *Journal of Financial and Quantitative Analysis,* Vol. 11, No. 2 (June, 1976), pp. 195-204.

Johnston J. *Econometric Methods*, 2d ed. New York: McGraw-Hill, 1972.

Markowitz, Harry M. "Portfolio Selection." *Journal of Finance*, Vol. 7, No. 1 (March, 1952), pp. 77-91.

———. *Portfolio Selection*. New Haven: Yale University Press, 1959.

Nelson, Charles R. *Applied Time Series Analysis*. San Francisco: Holden-Day, Inc., 1973. Chapter 2.

Pratt, John W. "Risk Aversion in the Small and in the Large." *Econometrica*, Vol. 32, No. 1 (January-April, 1964), pp. 122-136.

Sharpe, William F. "A Simplified Model of Portfolio Analysis," *Management Science*, Vol. 9, No. 2 (January, 1963), pp. 277-293.

Chapter 11

Blume, Marshall E. "On the Assessment of Risk." *Journal of Finance*, Vol. 26, No. 1 (March, 1971), pp. 1-10.

Elton, Edwin J., and Martin J. Gruber. "Improved Forecasting Through the Design of Homogeneous Groups." *Journal of Business*, Vol. 44, No. 4 (October, 1971), pp. 432-450.

Frankfurter, George/M., Herbert E. Phillips, and John P. Seagle. "Portfolio Selection: The Effects of Uncertain Means, Variances, and Covariances." *Journal of Financial and Quantitative Analysis*, Vol. 6, No. 5 (December, 1971), pp. 1251-1262.

———. "Bias in Estimating Portfolio Alpha and Beta Scores." *Review of Economics and Statistics*, Vol. 56, No. 3 (August, 1974), pp. 412-414.

———. "Performance of the Sharpe Portfolio Selection Model: A Comparison." *Journal of Financial and Quantitative Analysis*, Vol. 11, No. 2 (June, 1976), pp. 195-204.

Frankfurter, George M., and Herbert E. Phillips. "Alpha-Beta Theory: A Word of Caution." *Journal of Portfolio Management*, Vol. 3, No. 4 (Summer, 1977), pp. 35-40.

———. "Portfolio Selection: An Analytic Approach for Selection of Securities from a Large Universe." *Journal of Financial and Quantitative Analysis*, Vol. 15, No. 2 (June, 1980), pp. 357-378.

———. "MPT Plus Security Analysis for Better Performance." *The Journal of Portfolio Management*, Vol. 8, No. 4 (Summer, 1982), pp. 29-36.

Friend, Irwin, and Marshall E. Blume. "Measurement of Portfolio Performance Under Uncertainty." *American Economic Review*, Vol. 60, No. 4 (September, 1970), pp. 561-575.

Kalymon, Basil A. "Estimation Risk in the Portfolio Selection Model." *Journal of Financial and Quantitative Analysis*, Vol. 6, No. 1 (January, 1971), pp. 559-582.

Knight, Frank H. *Risk, Uncertainty and Profit.* Boston: Houghton-Mifflin, 1921. Chapter 2.

Morgenstern, Oskar. *On the Accuracy of Economic Observations.* Princeton: Princeton University Press, 1963.

Phillips, Herbert E., and **John P. Seagle.** "Data: A Mixed Blessing in *Journal of Financial and Quantitative Analysis,* Vol. 6, No. 1 (January, 1971), pp. 559–582.

Chapter 12

Allen, R. G. D. *Macro-Economic Theory: A Mathematical Treatment.* New York: St. Martin's Press, 1968. Chapter 5.

Fama, Eugene F. "Risk, Return, and Equilibrium: Some Clarifying Comments." *Journal of Finance,* Vol. 23, No. 1 (March, 1968), pp. 29–40.

_____. "Efficient Capital Markets: A Review of Theory and Empirical Work." *Journal of Finance,* Vol. 25, No. 2 (May, 1970), pp. 383–417.

_____. "Components of Investment Performance." *Journal of Finance,* Vol. 27, No. 3 (June, 1972), pp. 551–568.

Friedman, Milton M. "The Methodology of Positive Economics." *Essays in Positive Economics.* Chicago: The University of Chicago Press, 1953.

Jensen, Michael C. "Risk, the Pricing of Capital Assets, and the Evaluation of Investment Portfolios." *Journal of Business,* Vol. 42, No. 2 (April, 1969), pp. 167–247.

Lintner, John. "Security Prices, Risk, and Maximal Gains from Diversification." *Journal of Finance,* Vol. 20, No. 4 (December, 1965), pp. 587–615.

_____. "The Aggregation of Investor's Diverse Judgments and Preferences in Purely Competitive Security Markets." *Journal of Financial and Quantitative Analysis,* Vol. 4, No. 4 (December, 1969), pp. 347–400.

_____. "The Market Price of Risk, Size of Market and Investor's Risk Aversion." *Review of Economics and Statistics,* Vol. 52, No. 1 (February, 1970), pp. 87–99.

Markowitz, Harry M. "Portfolio Selection." *Journal of Finance,* Vol. 7 No. 1 (March, 1952), pp. 77–91.

Markowitz, Harry M. *Portfolio Selection.* New Haven: Yale University Press, 1959.

Myers, Stewart C. "On the Use of β in Regulatory Proceedings: A Comment." *Bell Journal of Economics and Management Science,* Vol. 3, No. 2 (Autumn, 1972), pp. 622–627.

Phillips, Herbert E. "Capital Asset Pricing Model and Traditional Risk for Capital Budgeting: A Comment." *Financial Review* (Fall, 1977), pp. 91–96.

Roll, Richard. "A Critique of the Asset Pricing Theory's Test" [Part 1: On Past and Potential Testability of the Theory]. *Journal of Financial Economics*, Vol. 4 (March, 1977), pp. 129–176.

Sharpe, William F. "A Simplified Model of Portfolio Analysis." *Management Science*, Vol. 9, No. 2 (January, 1963), pp. 277–293.

——. "Capital Asset Prices: A Theory of Market Equilibrium Under Conditions of Risk." *Journal of Finance*, Vol. 19, No. 3 (September, 1964), pp. 425–442.

——. "Mutual Fund Performance." *Journal of Business*, Vol. 39, No. 1 (January, 1966), pp. 119–138.

——. *Portfolio Theory and Capital Markets*. New York: McGraw-Hill, 1972.

Tobin, James. "Liquidity Preference as Behavior Towards Risk." *Review of Economic Studies*, Vol. 26, No. 1 (February, 1958), pp. 65–86.

Treynor, Jack L. "How to Rate Management of Investment Funds." *Harvard Business Review*, Vol. 43, No. 1 (January–February, 1965), pp. 63–75.

Turnbull, Stuart. "Market Value and Systematic Risk." *Journal of Finance*, Vol. 32, No. 4 (September, 1977), pp. 1125–1142.

Chapter 13

Alexander, Gordon. "An Algorithmic Approach to Deriving the Minimum Variance Zero-Beta Portfolio." *Journal of Financial Economics*, Vol. 4, No. 2 (March, 1977), pp. 231–236.

Black, Fischer, Michael C. Jensen, and Myron Scholes. "The Capital Asset Pricing Model: Some Empirical Tests." *Studies in the Theory of Capital Markets*, edited by Michael C. Jensen. New York: Praeger, 1972, pp. 79–121.

Black, F., and M. Scholes. "The Effects of Dividend Yield and Dividend Policy on Common Stock Prices and Returns." *Journal of Financial Economics*, Vol. 1, No. 1 (May 1974), pp. 1–22.

Blume, Marshall E. "On the Assessment of Risk." *Journal of Finance*, Vol. 26, No. 1 (March, 1971), pp. 1–10.

Elton, Edwin J., and Martin J. Gruber. "Improved Forecasting Through the Design of Homogeneous Groups." *Journal of Business*, Vol. 44, No. 4 (October, 1971), pp. 432–450.

Fama, Eugene F. "Risk, Return, and Equilibrium: Some Clarifying Comments." *Journal of Finance*, Vol. 23, No. 1 (March, 1968), pp. 29–40.

_____. "Efficient Capital Markets: A Review of Theory and Empirical Work." *Journal of Finance*, Vol. 25, No. 2 (May, 1970), pp. 383-417.

Fama, Eugene, and J. Mac Beth. "Risk, Return, and Equilibrium: Empirical Tests." *Journal of Political Economy*, Vol. 71 (May/June, 1973), pp. 607-636.

Frankfurter, George M., and Herbert E. Phillips. "Alpha-Beta Theory: A Word of Caution." *Journal of Portfolio Management*, Vol. 3, No. 4 (Summer, 1977), pp. 35-40.

Frankfurter, George M., Herbert E. Phillips, and John P. Seagle. "Portfolio Selection: The Effects of Uncertain Means, Variances, and Covariances." *Journal of Financial and Quantitative Analysis*, Vol. 6, No. 5 (December, 1971), pp. 1251-1262.

_____. "Bias in Estimating Portfolio Alpha and Beta Scores." *Review of Economics and Statistics*, Vol. 56, No. 3 (August, 1974), pp. 412-414.

_____. "Performance of the Sharpe Portfolio Selection Model: A Comparison." *Journal of Financial and Quantitative Analysis*, Vol. 11, No. 2 (June, 1976), pp. 195-204.

Friend, Irwin, and Marshall E. Blume, "Measurement of Portfolio Performance Under Uncertainty." *American Economic Review*, Vol. 60, No. 4 (September, 1970), pp. 561-575.

Kalymon, Basil A. "Estimation Risk in the Portfolio Selection Model." *Journal of Financial and Quantitative Analysis*, Vol. 6, No. 1 (January, 1971), pp. 559-582.

Koopmans, Tjalling C. "Measurement Without Theory," *Review of Economic Statistics*, Vol. 29, (Ausμst, 1947). Reprinted in Robert A. Gordon and Lowrence R. Klein (eds.). *Readings in Business Cycles*, American Economic Association. Homewood, Ill.: Richard D. Irwin, 1965, pp. 186-203.

Knight, Frank H. *Risk, Uncertainty and Profit.* Boston: Houghton-Mifflin, 1921. Chapter 2.

Kumar, Prem. "Market Equilibrium and Corporation Finance: Some Issues." *Journal of Finance*, Vol. 29, No. 4 (September, 1974), pp. 1175-1188.

Lee, Chang. "Investment Horizon and the Functional Form of the Capital Asset Pricing Model." *Review of Economics and Statistics*, Vol. 58, No. 3 (August, 1976), pp. 356-363.

Lahari, David, and Levy Haim, "The Capital Asset Pricing Model and the Investment Horizon." *Review of Economics and Statistics*, Vol. 59, No. 1 (February, 1977), pp. 92-104.

Lintner, John. "The Aggregation of Investors Diverse Judgments and Preferences in Purely Competitive Markets." *Journal of Financial and Quantitative Analysis*, Vol. 4, No. 4 (December, 1969), pp. 347-400.

Markowitz, Harry M. "Portfolio Selection." *Journal of Finance*, Vol. 7, No. 1 (March, 1952), pp. 77–91.

Miller, M. H., and M. Scholes. "Rates of Return in Relation to Risk: A Re-Examination of Some Recent Findings." *Studies in the Theory of Capital Markets*, edited by Michael C. Jensen. New York: Praeger, 1972.

Morgenstern, Oskar. *On the Accuracy of Economic Observations.* Princeton: Princeton University Press, 1963.

Myers, Stewert C. "On the Use of β in Regulatory Proceedings: A Comment." *Bell Journal of Economics and Management Science*, Vol. 3, No. 2 (Autumn, 1972), pp. 622–627.

Phillips, Herbert E. "Capital Asset Pricing Model and Traditional Risk for Capital Budgeting: A Comment." *Financial Review* (Fall, 1977), pp. 91–96.

Phillips, Herbert E., and John P. Seagle. "Data: A Mixed Blessing in Portfolio Selection?" *Financial Management*, Vol. 4, No. 3 (Autumn, 1975), pp. 50–53.

Pratt, John W. "Risk Aversion in the Small and in the Large." *Econometrica*, Vol. 32, No. 1 (January–April, 1964), pp. 122–136.

Roll, Richard. "A Critique of the Asset Pricing Theory's Tests" [Part 1: On Past and Potential Testability of the Theory]. *Journal of Financial Economics*, Vol. 4 (March, 1977), pp. 129–176.

Ross, Stephen. "The Current Status of the Capital Asset Pricing Model (CAPM)." *Journal of Finance*, Vol. 33, No. 3 (June, 1978), pp. 885–901.

Tobin, James. "Liquidity Preference as Behavior Towards Risk." *Review of Economic Studies*, Vol. 26, No. 1 (February, 1958), pp. 65–86.

Chapter 14

Fischer, Lawrence, and James H. Lorie. "Rates of Return on Investments in Common Stock: The Year-by-Year Record, 1926–1965." *Journal of Business*, Vol. 41, No. 3 (July, 1968), pp. 291–316.

____. "Some Studies of Variability of Returns on Investments in Common Stocks." *Journal of Business*, Vol. 43, No. 2 (April, 1970), pp. 99–134.

Freund, William C., and Edward D. Zinbarg. "Application of Flow of Funds to Interest Rate Forecasting." *Journal of Finance*, Vol. 18, No. 2 (May, 1963), pp. 231–248.

Homer, Sidney. *A History of Interest Rates—2000 B.C. to the Present.* New Brunswick, N.J.: Rutgers University Press, 1963. Parts III and IV.

Packer, Stephen B. "Flow of Funds Analysis—Its Uses and Limitations." *Financial Analysts Journal*, Vol. 20, No. 4 (July–August, 1964), pp. 117–123.

Schott, Frances H. "Forecasting Long-Term Interest Rates." *Business Economics*, Vol. 8, No. 4 (September, 1973), pp. 46–53.

Sprinkel, Beryl W. *Money and Markets: A Monetarist View.*Homewood, Ill.: Richard S. Irwin, 1971.

Terborgh, George, "Inflation and Profits." *Financial Analysts Journal*, Vol. 30, No. 3 (May–June, 1974), pp. 19–23.

Tongue, William W. "How Money Matters." *Business Economics*, Vol. 9, No. 3 (May, 1974), pp. 31–38.

Chapter 15

Baker, Guthrie. "Blueprint for Constructive Reform." *Financial Analysts Journal*, Vol. 27, No. 6 (November–December, 1971), pp. 20–22, 62.

Black, Fisher. "Toward a Fully Computerized Stock Exchange." *Financial Analysts Journal*, Vol. 27, No. 6 (November–December, 1971), pp. 24–28, 86–87.

Farrar, D. E. "Toward a Central Market System: Wall Street's Slow Retreat Into the Future." *Journal of Financial and Quantitative Analysis*, Vol. 9, No. 5 (November, 1974), pp. 815–827.

Freund, W. C. "Issues Confronting the Stock Markets in a Period of Rising Institutionalization." *Journal of Financial and Quantitative Analysis*, Vol. 7, No. 2 (Supp., March, 1972), pp. 1687–1690.

Gillis, J. G. "Securities Law and Regulation." *Financial Analysts Journal* (regular feature).

Kramer, A. "Significance of the Hochfelder Decision." *CPA Journal* (August, 1976), pp. 11–14.

Securities Law—Fraud—SEC Rule 10b-5, Vols. 1 & 2. New York: McGraw-Hill, 1971.

Chapter 16

Bankers Trust Company, 1975 Study of Corporate Pension Plans. Bankers Trust Company, New York City, N.Y.

BNA Pension Reporter, No. 245, June 25, 1979. The Bureau on National Affairs, Inc., Washington, D.C. Pages unnumbered. See in particular, "Labor Department Issues: Final Regulation of Prudent Investment of Plan Assets."

Business Roundtable, "Study of Retirement Benefit Levels, Costs and Issues." Towers, Perrin, Forster & Crosby, Washington, D.C. (August, 1978).

Fama, Eugene F. "Risk, Return, and Equilibrium: Some Clarifying Comments." *Journal of Finance*, Vol. 23, No. 1 (March, 1968), pp. 29–40.

Hamada, Robert S. "Portfolio Analysis, Market Equilibrium and Corporation Finance." *Journal of Finance*, Vol. 24, No. 1, March 1969, pp. 13–31.

Markowitz, Harry M. "Portfolio Selection." *Journal of Finance*, Vol. 7, No. 1 (March 1952), pp. 77–91.

McGill, Danial M. *Fundamentals of Private Pensions*, 3d ed. Homewood, Ill.: Richard D. Irwin, 1975.

Moody's Bond Survey, Vol. 70, No. 8 (February 20, 1978).

Sharpe, William F. "Capital Asset Prices: A Theory of Market Equilibrium Under Conditions of Risk." *Journal of Finance*, Vol. 19, No. 3 (September, 1964), p. 425–42.

Treynor, Jack L., Patrick J. Regan, and William W. Priest, Jr. *The Financial Reality of Pension Funding Under ERISA*. Homewood, Ill.: Dow Jones-Irwin, 1976.

Chapter 17

Chandra, G. "Information Needs of Security Analysts." *Journal of Accountancy* (December, 1975), pp. 65–70.

Falk, Haim, Bruce C. Gobdel, and James H. Naus. "Disclosure for Closely Held Corporations." *Journal of Accountancy* (October, 1976), pp. 85–89.

Linden, John R. "The FASB at Age Three." *Journal of Accountancy* (August, 1976), pp. 75–81.

Mechanic, Sylvia. "Key Reference Sources." Chapter 33 in Levine, Sumner N. *Financial Analyst's Handbook*. Homewood, Ill.: Dow Jones-Irwin, 1975, pp. 859–879.

Nicholson, John W. "Annual and Interim Reporting Under the Securities Exchange Act of 1934." Chapter 37 in Edwards, James Don, and Homer A. Black. *The Modern Accountant's Handbook*. Homewood, Ill.: Dow Jones-Irwin, 1976, pp. 849–874.

Rudd, Alfred S. "Site Visits." Chapter 31 in Levine, Sumner N. *Financial Analyst's Handbook*, Vol. II. Homewood, Ill.: Dow Jones-Irwin, 1975, pp. 849–851.

Sussman, Dorothy Hennessy. "Information Sources: An Overview." Chapter 32 in Levine, Sumner N. *Financial Analyst's Handbook*, Vol. II. Homewood, Ill.: Dow Jones-Irwin, 1975, pp. 852–858.

Chapter 18

Almon, Clopper, Jr., et al. *1985: Interindustry Forecasts of the American Economy.* Lexington, Mass.: D.C. Heath and Co., 1974.

Andrews, John R., Jr. "The Fundamental Case for Investing in Growth." *Financial Analysts Journal* (November–December, 1970), pp. 55–64.

Babcock, Guilford C. "The Concept of Sustainable Growth." *Financial Analysts Journal* (May–June, 1970), pp. 108–114.

Bowman, Charles T., and Terry H. Morlan. "Revised Projections of the United States Economy to 1980 and 1985 (with tables)." *Monthly Labor Review* (March, 1976), pp. 9–21.

Harris, Maury, and Deborah Jamroz. "Evaluating the Leading Indicators." *Monthly Review*, Federal Reserve Bank of New York (June, 1976), pp. 165–171.

Ibbotson, R. G., and R. A. Sinquefield. "Stocks, Bonds, Bills and Inflation: Simulations of the Future (1976–2000)." *Journal of Business* (July, 1976), pp. 313–338.

Klein, Philip A. *Business Cycles in the Postwar World: Some Reflections on Recent Research.* Washington: American Enterprise Institute for Public Policy Research, 1976.

Kutscher, Ronald E. "Revised BLS Projections to 1980 and 1985: An Overview." *Monthly Labor Review* (March, 1976), pp. 3–8.

Mooney, Thomas J., and John H. Tschetter. "Revised Industry Projections to 1985." *Monthly Labor Review* (November, 1976), pp. 3–9.

Moore, Geoffrey H., and Philip A. Klein. "Recovery and Then? New Techniques Are Being Developed to Track the Business Cycle with Precision." *Across the Board*, The Conference Board Magazine (October, 1976), pp. 55–58.

"The National Income and Product Accounts of the United States: Revised Estimates, 1929–74." *Survey of Current Business* (January, 1976), Part I, pp. 1–32. See also, July issues of the *Survey of Current Business* following this.

National Planning Association. *National Economic Projection Series*, Report 75 N–2: "Investment in the Eighties" by Robert Dennis. Washington: National Planning Association, April, 1976.

Partee, J. Charles. "The State of Economic Forecasting." *Business Horizons* (October, 1976), pp. 26–32.

United States Department of Commerce, Domestic and International Business Administration. *U.S. Industrial Outlook, 1976, with Projections to 1985.* Washington: United States Government Printing Office, January, 1976.

United States Department of Commerce, Bureau of Economic Analysis, Social and Economic Statistics Administration. *Questions and Answers about the Revision of the Composite Index of Leading Indicators.* Washington: United States Government Printing Office, May 28, 1975.

United States Department of Labor, Bureau of Labor Statistics. *The Structure of the U.S. Economy in 1980 and 1985, Bulletin 1831.* Washington, D.C.: United States Government Printing Office, 1975.

"United States Economy in 1985." *Monthly Labor Review* (December, 1973), pp. 3-42.

Wheelwright, Steven C., and **Darral G. Clarke.** "Corporate Forecasting: Promise and Reality." *Harvard Business Review* (November-December, 1976), pp. 40-42, 47-48, 52, 60, 64, 198.

Chapter 19

Andrews, Frederick. "Accounting Board Begins to Compose Data 'Constitution.'" *New York Times,* December 9, 1976, pp. 71-82.

Barnes, D. P. "Materiality—An Illusive Concept." *Management Accounting* (October, 1976), pp. 19-20.

Burton, John C. "The Changing Face of Financial Reporting." *Journal of Accountancy* (February, 1976), pp. 60-63.

"Classes of Financial Statement Users." *The CPA* (June, 1975), p. 82.

Hershman, A. "Accounting—More Data for Investors." *Dun's Review* (March, 1976), pp. 56-57.

International Accounting Standards Committee. "Treatment of Changing Prices in Financial Statements: A Summary of Proposals." IASC Discussion Paper (March, 1977).

Kieso, Donald E., and **Jerry J. Weygandt.** *Intermediate Accounting,* 3d ed. New York: Wiley, 1980, Chapter 25.

King, A. M. "Current Value Accounting Comes of Age." *Financial Executive* (January, 1976), pp. 18-24.

Lev, Baruch. *Financial Statement Analysis: A New Approach.* Englewood Cliffs, N.J.: Prentice-Hall, 1974. Part One.

Olson, Wallace E. "Financial Reporting—Fact or Fiction?" *Journal of Accountancy* (July, 1977), pp. 68-71.

Pattillo, J. W. "Materiality: The (Formerly) Elusive Standard," *Financial Executive* (August, 1975), pp. 20-27.

Seminar on the Analysis of Security Prices (Proceedings). Chicago: Graduate School of Business, The University of Chicago, Center for Research in Security Prices. Sponsored by Merrill, Lynch, Pierce, Fenner & Smith, Inc., May, 1976.

Chapter 20

Accounting Trends and Techniques in Published Corporate Annual Reports (Annual). New York: American Institute of Certified Public Accountants.

Bernstein, Leopold A. "Extraordinary Gains and Losses—Their Significance to the Financial Analyst." *Financial Analysts Journal* (November–December, 1972), pp. 49–52, 88–90.

"Consolidated Return Earnings and Profits Regulations." *CPA Journal* (November, 1976), pp. 45–46.

"Complying With ERISA: A Systems Approach" (from Coopers & Lybrand's newsletter). *Journal of Accountancy* (April, 1976), pp. 59–64. Contains a summary of major ERISA reporting and disclosure requirements.

Edwards, James Don, and Homer A. Black (eds.). *The Modern Accountant's Handbook*. Homewood, Ill.: Dow Jones-Irwin, 1976.

Haried, Andrew A., and Ralph E. Smith. "Accounting for Marketable Equity Securities." *Journal of Accountancy* (February, 1977), pp. 54–61.

Lund, Harry A., Walter J. Casey, and Philip K. Chamberlain. "A Financial Analysis of the ESOT." *Financial Analysts Journal* (January–February, 1976), pp. 55–61.

McClure, Melvin T. "Diverse Tax Interpretations of Accounting Concepts." *Journal of Accountancy* (October, 1976), pp. 67–72.

Miller, Martin A. *Comprehensive GAAP Guide*. New York: Harcourt, Brace, Jovanovich, 1979.

O'Malia, Thomas J. *Banker's Guide to Financial Statements*. Boston: Bankers Publishing Company, 1976.

Regan, P. J. "Potential Corporate Liabilities Under ERISA." *Financial Analysts Journal* (March, 1976), pp. 26–32.

Chapter 21

Accounting Trends and Techniques (annual). New York: American Institute of Certified Public Accountants.

"Alternative Estimates of Capital Consumption Allowances and Profits of Nonfinancial Corporations, 1973-75." *Survey of Current Business* (August, 1976), p. 61.

Anthony, Robert N. "A Case For Historical Costs." *Harvard Business Review* (November–December, 1976), pp. 69–79.

APB *Statement No. 4*, "Basic Concepts and Accounting Principles Underlying Financial Statements of Business Enterprises." New York: American Institute of Certified Public Accountants, October, 1970.

Archibald, T. R. "Some Factors Related to the Depreciation Switchback." *Financial Analysts Journal* (September, 1976), pp. 67–73.

Bastable, C. W. "Depreciation in an Inflationary Environment." *Journal of Accountancy* (August, 1976), pp. 58–66.

Crumbley, D. L., and J. R. Hasselback. "Asset Depreciation Range System." *CPA Journal* (January, 1976), pp. 29–33.

Davidson, S., and R. L. Weil. "Inflation Accounting: The SEC Proposal for Replacement Cost Disclosures." *Financial Analysts Journal* (March, 1976), pp. 57–66.

Financial Analysts Federation. Financial Accounting Policy Committee. *Objectives of Financial Accounting and Reporting from the Viewpoint of the Financial Analyst.* New York: FAF, 1972.

Finefrock, J. L. "Opportunities for Increased Investment Credit Found in 1975 Transitional Rules." *Journal of Taxation* (September, 1976), pp. 168–172.

Herring, Hartwell C., III, and Fred A. Jacobs. "The Expected Behavior of Deferred Tax Credits." *Journal of Accountancy* (August, 1976), pp. 52–56.

"Independents Seek IRS Depletion-Rule Changes." *Oil and Gas Journal* (February 2, 1976), p. 43.

Johnson, L. Todd, and Philip W. Bell. "Current Replacement Costs: A Qualified Opinion." *Journal of Accountancy* (November, 1976), pp. 63–70.

Chapter 22

Barstein, L. A. "New Accounting for Foreign Currency Transactions—Some Implications for Financial Analysis." *Journal of Commercial Bank Lending* (October, 1976), pp. 59–63.

Bastable, C. W. "Depreciation in an Inflationary Environment." *Journal of Accounting* (August, 1976), pp. 58–66.

Baxter, John D. "Industry Sells Out Its Future with Underpriced Products," *Iron Age* (July 18, 1977), pp. 20–22.

Bower, Richard S. "Issues in Lease Financing." *Financial Management* (Winter, 1973), pp. 25–34.

Clay, Raymond J., Jr., and William W. Holder. "A Practitioner's Guide to Accounting for Leases" *Journal of Accountancy* (August, 1977), pp. 61–68.

Davidson, Sidney, Clyde P. Stickney, and Roman L. Weil. *Inflation Accounting, a Guide for the Accountant and the Financial Analyst.* New York: McGraw-Hill, 1976.

Deakin, Edward B. "A Discriminant Analysis of Predictors of Business Failure." *Journal of Accounting Research* (Spring, 1972), pp. 167–79.

————. "Distributions of Financial Accounting Rates: Some Empirical Evidence." *Accounting Review* (January, 1976), pp. 90–96.

Edward, James Don, and Homer A. Black. *The Modern Accountant's Handbook.* Homewood, Ill.: Dow Jones-Irwin, 1976.

"Focus on Balance Sheet Reform." *Business Week*, June 7, 1976, pp. 52–56, 58–60.

Goetz, B. E., and J. G. Birnberg. "Comment on the Trueblood Report." *Management Accounting* (April, 1976), pp. 18–20.

Greenstein, Mary, "Keying in on Reference Works (Accounting References Works)." *Journal of Accountancy* (November, 1976), pp. 44–45.

Harwood, Gordon B., and Roger H. Hermanson, "Lease-or-Buy Decisions." *Journal of Accountancy* (September, 1976), pp. 83–87.

Kalata, John J., Dennis G. Campbell, and Ian K. Shumaker. "Lease Financing Reporting." *Financial Executive* (March, 1977), pp. 34–40.

King, A. M. "Current Value Accounting Comes of Age." *Financial Executive* (January, 1976), pp. 18–24.

"The Newest Numbers Game." *Business Week*, June 20, 1977, pp. 85, 88.

O'Connor, Melvin C. "On the Usefulness of Financial Rates to Investors in Common Stock." *Accounting Review* (April, 1973), pp. 1–18.

Parker, C. Reed. "The Trueblood Report: An Analyst's View." *Financial Analysts Journal* (January–February, 1975), pp. 32–41, 56.

Snavely, H. J. "Financial Statement Restatement." *Journal of Accountancy* (October, 1976), pp. 98–100 only.

Chapter 23

Fisher, Lawrence, and Romand L. Weil. "Coping with the Risk of Interest-Rate Fluctuations: Returns to Bondholders from Naive and Optimal Strategies." *Journal of Business*, Vol. 44, No. 4 (October, 1971), pp. 408–431.

Homer, Sidney, and Martin L. Leibowitz. *Inside the Yield Book.* New York: Prentice-Hall, Inc., and New York Institute of Finance, 1972.

Jen, Frank C., and James E. West. "The Deferred Call Provision and Corporate Bond Yields." *Journal of Financial Quantitative Analysis*, Vol. 3, No. 2 (June, 1968), pp. 157–169.

Katz, Steven. "The Price Adjustment Process of Bonds to Rating Reclassifications: A Test of Bond Market Efficiency." *Journal of Finance*, Vol. 29, No. 2 (May, 1974), pp. 551–559.

Lindlow, Wesley. *Inside the Money Market.* New York: Random House, 1972.

Melicher, Ronald W., and David F. Rush. "Systematic Risk, Financial Data and Bond Rating Relationships in a Regulated Industry Environment." *Journal of Finance*, Vol. 29, No. 2 (May, 1974), pp. 537–544.

Nelson, Charles R. *The Term Structure of Interest Rates.* New York: Basic Books, 1972.

Pinches, George E., and J. Clay Singleton. "The Adjustment of Stock Prices to Bond Rating Changes." *Journal of Finance*, Vol. 33, No. 1 (March, 1978) pp. 29–44.

Sharpe, William F. "Bonds Versus Stocks: Some Lessons From Capital Market Theory." *Financial Analysts Journal*, Vol. 29, No. 6 November–December, 1973), pp. 74–80.

Williamson, J. Peter. "Computerized Approaches to Bond Switching." *Financial Analysis Journal*, Vol. 26, No. 4 (July–August, 1970), pp. 65–72.

Chapter 24

Altman, Edward I. "Financial Ratios, Discriminant Analysis and Prediction of Corporate Bankruptcy." *Journal of Finance*, Vol. 23, No. 4 (September, 1968), pp. 589–610.

Atkinson, Thomas R. *Trends in Corporate Bond Quality*, National Bureau of Economic Research. New York: Columbia University Press, 1967.

Donaldson, Gordon. *Corporate Debt Capacity*. Cambridge, Mass.: Harvard University, Graduate School of Business Administration, 1961. Part 2.

Edmister, Robert O. "An Empirical Test of Financial Ratio Analysis for Small Business Failure Prediction." *Journal of Financial and Quantitative Analysis*, Vol. 7, No. 2 (March, 1972), pp. 1477–1494.

Elton, Edward E., and Martin J. Gruber. "The Economic Value of the Call Option." *Journal of Finance*, Vol. 27, No. 4 (September, 1972), pp. 891–902.

Hickman, W. Braddock. *Corporate Bond Quality and Investor Experience*. New York: National Bureau of Economic Research, 1958.

Jennings, Edward H. "An Estimate of Convertible Bond Premiums." *Journal of Financial and Quantitative Analysis*, Vol. 9, No. 1 (January, 1974), pp. 33–56.

Pinches, George E., and Kent A. Mingo. "A Multivariate Analysis of Industrial Bond Ratings." *Journal of Finance*, Vol. 28, No. 1 (March, 1973), pp. 1–18.

____. "The Role of Subordination and Industrial Bond Ratings." *Journal of Finance*, Vol. 30, No. 1 (March, 1975), pp. 201–206.

Walter, J. E., and A. U. Que. "The Valuation of Convertible Bonds." *Journal of Finance*, Vol. 28, No. 3, (June, 1973), pp. 713–732.

West, Richard R. "An Alternative Approach to Predicting Bond Ratings." *Journal of Accounting Research*, Vol. 8, No. 1 (Spring, 1970), pp. 118–125.

Chapter 25

Adams, Walter, ed. *The Structure of American Industry*. New York: Macmillan, 1977.

"Annual Report on American Industry." *Forbes* (first January issue).

Balachandran, M. *A Guide to Trade and Securities Statistics*. Ann Arbor, Mich.: Pierian Press, 1977.

Caves, Richard E. *American Industry: Structure, Conduct, Performance*, 4th ed. Englewood Cliffs, N.J.: Prentice-Hall, 1977.

"How Labor Costs Swung with the Cycle" (Results of Citibank's annual unit-labor-cost survey). Citibank's *Monthly Economic Letter* (August, 1977), pp. 10–15.

Standard & Poor's Basic Industry Surveys (annual survey for each major industry). New York: Standard & Poor's Corporation.

"Survey of Corporate Performance" (Title varies). *Business Week* (one issue each in March, May, August, and November).

U.S. Economic Growth from 1976 to 1986: Prospects, Problems, and Patterns: Studies. Prepared for the use of the Joint Economic Committee, Congress of the United States. Washington, D.C.: U.S. Government Printing Office, 1976–1977.

Chapter 26

American Gas Association. *Annual Report*. Arlington, Va.: American Gas Association.

Edison Electric Institute. Annual reports (industry projections), statistical yearbooks, and weekly and monthly statistical releases. New York: Edison Electric Institute.

Electrical World. (Annual statistical report, Parts I and II.) New York: McGraw-Hill.

Gordon, Myron J., J. S. McCollum, and Michael J. Brennan. "Valuation and the Cost of Capital for Regulated Utilities—Comment." *Journal of Finance* (December, 1972), pp. 1150–1155.

Moody's Public Utility Manual. New York: Moody's Investors Service, Inc., annual.

Public Utilities Fortnightly. Washington: Public Utilities Reports, Inc.

"Regulation: A Look at the Octopus." Citibank's *Monthly Economic Letter* (May, 1977), pp. 9–12.

Standard & Poor's Basic Industry Surveys: Utilities—Electric Utilities—Gas and Telephone. New York: Standard & Poor's Corporation.

Chapter 27

Air Transport 19—, annual report of the U.S. scheduled airline industry. Washington, D.C.: Air Transport Association of America.

American Trucking Trends and Financial Analysis of the Motor Carrier Industry. Washington, D.C.: American Trucking Association, annual.

"The Haulers Brace for a New Age of Competition." *The New York Times,* February 4, 1979, p. E-5. (Haulers = railroads, truckers, barges, and airlines.)

Kane, Robert M., and A. D. Vose. *Air Transportation,* 5th ed. Dubuque, Iowa: Kendall/Hunt Publishing Company, 1976.

MacAvoy, Paul W., and John W. Snow, eds. *Regulation of Passenger Fares and Competition Among the Airlines.* Washington, D.C.: American Enterprise Institute for Public Policy Research, 1977.

Moody's Transportation Manual. Moody's Investors Service, annual, with semiweekly supplements.

"Railroad Decontrol Bill Sighted." *Journal of Commerce* (February 6, 1979), p. 1.

The Secretary's Decision on Concorde Supersonic Transport. Washington, D.C.: U.S. Dept. of Transportation, 1976.

Transport Economics (bi-monthly). Washington, D.C.: U.S. Interstate Commerce Commission, Bureau of Economics.

Wyckoff, Donald D., and David H. Maister. *The Domestic Airline Industry.* Lexington, Mass.: Lexington Books, 1977.

Yearbook of Railroad Facts. Washington, D.C.: Association of American Railroads, annual.

Chapter 28

Banking

Banking 1977 Financial Reporting Trends. New York: Ernst & Ernst, 1977.

Bank Operating Statistics. Washington, D.C.: Federal Deposit Insurance Corporation, annual.

Federal Deposit Insurance Corporation Annual Report, *Federal Reserve Bulletin* (monthly). Board of Governors of the Federal Reserve System.

Heller, Robert, and Norris Willatt. *Can You Trust Your Bank? Sensational Bank Failures of the 1970s.* New York: Charles Scribner's Sons, 1977.

Issues in Bank Regulation, Vol. 1 (Summer, 1977). Park Ridge, Ill.: Bank Administration Institute.

Jessee, Michael A., and S. A. Seelig. *Bank Holding Companies and the Public Interest: An Economic Analysis.* Lexington, Mass.: Lexington Books, 1977.

Kindleberger, Charles P. *America in the World Economy,* Headline Series No. 237. New York: Foreign Policy Association, October, 1977.

Rock, **James M.** *Money, Banking and Macroeconomics: A Guide to Sources.* Detroit: Gale Research Co., 1977.

U.S. Board of Governors of the Federal Reserve System. *Banking and Monetary Statistics, 1941–1970.* Washington, D.C.: Board of Governors of the Federal Reserve System, 1976.

Insurance

Best's Aggregates & Averages: Property-Liability. Oldwick, N.J.: A. M. Best Co., annual.

Best's Flitcraft Compendium. Oldwick, N.J.: A. M. Best Co., annual.

Best's Insurance Reports: Life-Health. Oldwick, N.J.: A. M. Best Co., annual.

Best's Insurance Reports: Property-Liability. Oldwick, N.J.: A. M. Best Co., annual.

Best's Review: Life/Health Insurance Edition. Oldwick, N.J.: A. M. Best Co., monthly.

Best's Review: Property/Liability Insurance Edition. Oldwick, N.J.: A. M. Best Co., monthly.

Bickelhaupt, David L. *General Insurance,* 9th ed. Homewood, Ill.: Richard D. Irwin, 1974.

Fire & Casualty Insurance 1977 Reporting Trends. New York: Ernst & Ernst, 1977.

Greene, Mark R. *Risk and Insurance,* 4th ed. Cincinnati: South-Western Publishing Co., 1977.

Insurance Facts. New York: Insurance Information Institute, annual.

Life Insurance Fact Book. New York: Institute of Life Insurance, annual.

Life Insurance 1977 Financial Reporting Trends. New York: Ernst & Ernst, 1977.

Life Reports: Financial and Operating Results of Life Insurers. Cincinnati: National Underwriter Co., annual.

Chapter 29

"Annual Mutual Fund Survey." *Forbes* (August 15 issues).

Arditti, Fred. "Another Look at Mutual Fund Performance." *Journal of Financial and Quantitative Analysis,* Vol. 6, No. 3 (June, 1971), pp. 909–912.

Fama, Eugene, and **J. MacBeth.** "Tests of the Multiperiod Two-Parameter Model." *Journal of Financial Economics,* Vol. 1, No. 1 (May, 1974), pp. 43–66.

Ferguson, Robert. "Active Portfolio Management: How to Beat the Index Funds." *Financial Analysts Journal* (May-June, 1975), pp. 63–72.

Friend, Irwin, Marshall Blume, and Jean Crockett. *Mutual Funds and Other Institutional Investors.* New York: McGraw-Hill, 1970.

Good, W. R., and others. "Investor's Guide to the Index Fund Controversy." *Financial Analysts Journal* (November-December, 1976), pp. 27–36.

"Independent Appraisals of Listed Stocks." *Financial World* (mutual funds listed as part of this section, usually the last two pages in the first issues of March, June, September, and December).

Investment Companies (annual and supplements). New York: Wiesenberger Financial Services.

Jensen, Michael C. "The Performance of Mutual Funds in the Period 1945–1964." *Journal of Finance,* Vol. 23, No. 2 (May, 1968), pp. 389–415.

Jobson, J. D., and Bob M. Korkie. "Performance Hypothesis Testing with the Sharpe and Treynor Measures." *Journal of Finance,* Vol. 36, No. 4 (September, 1981), pp. 889–907.

Malkiel, Burton G. "Valuation of Closed-End Investment Company Shares." *Journal of Finance* (June, 1977), pp. 847–859.

Mills, Harlan D. "On the Management of Fund Performance." *Journal of Finance* (December, 1970), pp. 1125–1131.

"Mutual Fund Performance." *The Institutional Investor* (monthly).

Mutual Funds Forum. Washington, D.C.: The Investment Company Institute (National Industry Association for Mutual Funds), monthly.

Phalon, Richard. "Closed-End Funds Seek a New Identity" (Personal Investing column). *The New York Times,* June 11, 1977, p. 26. (Article discusses change of name from "closed-end funds" to "publicly traded funds.")

"Quarterly Mutual Fund Record." *Barron's* (weekly).

Roll, Richard, "A Critique of the Asset Pricing Theory's Tests; Part 1: On Past and Potential Testability of the Theory." *Journal of Financial Economics,* Vol. 4, No. 2 (March, 1977), pp. 129–176.

SEC Report on the Public Implications of Investment Company Growth. Washington, D.C.: Securities and Exchange Commission, U.S. Superintendent of Documents.

Sharpe, William F. "Mutual Fund Performance." *Journal of Business,* Vol. 39, No. 1, Part 2 (January, 1966).

Standard & Poor's Basic Industry Surveys. New York: Standard & Poor's Corporation.

"Statement of Position No. 77-1—Financial Accounting and Reporting by Investment Companies." *Journal of Accountancy* (July, 1977), pp. 92–96.

Treynor, Jack. "How to Rate Management of Investment Funds." *Harvard Business Review,* Vol. 43, No. 1 (January/February, 1965), pp. 63–75.

Vickers Associates, Inc. *Vickers' Guide to Investment Company Portfolios* (annual) and periodic reports on individual mutual funds.

Weberman, B. "How to Pick a Municipal Bond Fund." *Forbes*, September 1, 1977, p. 74.

Index

RUSIA

120°

60°

0°

Mar de Beaufort

Alaska (EUA)

Gran Lago del Oso

Bahía de Baffin

Groenlandia (Din.)

Svalbard (Nu

Mar de Groenlandia

Golfo de Alaska

Gran Lago del Esclavo

Jan Mayen (Nor.)

CANADÁ

Bahía de Hudson

Círculo polar ártico

Saskatchewan

Mar del Labrador

Reykjavík

ISLANDIA

Feroe (Din.)

SUECIA

FINLA

Nelson

NORUEGA

He

Lago Winnipeg

Oslo

Estocolmo

ESTON

Missouri

Mar del Norte

GRAN BRETAÑA

DINAMARCA

LETON

Lago Superior

IRLANDA

Copenhague

LITUANIA

Lago Michigan Lago Huron Montreal

Berlín

POLONIA

Bie

ESTADOS UNIDOS

Ottawa San Lorenzo

Londres

P.B.

BÉLG. ALEMANIA

R. CHECA

UC

Chicago

Lago Ontario

LUX.

R. CHECA

ESLOVAQUIA

Lago Erie

Nueva York

PARIS

SUIZA AUSTR. HUNGRIA

Colorado

FRANCIA

ESLOVENIA

RUM

Los Ángeles

Washington

ANDORRA

MÓNACO

CROACIA

H.SERBIA

MADRID

Roma

ITALIA

MONT.

BU

Trópico de Cáncer

Rio Grande

Mississippi

Bermudas (G. B.)

Océano Atlántico

Azores (Port.)

PORTUGAL

Madrid

ALB.

MACED.

Lisboa

ESPAÑA

GRECIA

Atenas

MÉXICO

Golfo de México

Madeira (Port.)

Rabat

Argel

Túnez MALTA

TÚNEZ

Tripoli

El Cai

México

La Habana

CUBA

Nassau

BAHAMAS

Islas Canarias (Esp.)

MARRUECOS

ARGELIA

LIBIA

EGIPT

Sahara Occidental

Sahara

REPÚBLICA DOMINICANA

Puerto Rico (EUA)

JAMAICA HAITÍ

Nouakchott

MAURITANIA

MALÍ

NÍGER

Ja

GUATEMALA

BELICE

Puerto Príncipe

Santo Domingo

SAINT KITTS-NEVIS

ANTIGUA Y BARBUDA

Guadalupe (Fr.)

CABO VERDE

Dakar

Sahel

CHAD

S

Guatemala

HONDURAS

DOMINICA

Martinica (Fr.)

Banjul

SENEGAL

Niamey

San Salvador

NICARAGUA

Mar Caribe

SANTA LUCÍA

SAN VICENTE

GAMBIA

Bamako

BURKINA FASO

N'Djamena

EL SALVADOR

Managua

GRANADA

BARBADOS

GUINEA-BISSAU

Bissau

GUINEA

BENIN

NIGERIA

Isla Clipperton (Fr.)

San José

COSTA RICA

Panamá

TRINIDAD Y TOBAGO

Conakry

COSTA DE MARFIL

TOGO

REPÚBLICA CENTROAFRICANA

PANAMÁ

Caracas

Port of Spain

SIERRA LEONA

Freetown

GHANA

Porto-Novo

Abuja

Bangui

VENEZUELA

Georgetown

Monrovia

Accra

Lomé

CAMERÚN

Ecuador

Bogotá

GUYANA

Paramaribo

LIBERIA

Yamoussoukro

Yaoundé

REP.

Congo

COLOMBIA

SURINAM

Guayana (Fr.)

GUINEA ECUATORIAL

SANTO TOMÉ Y PRÍNCIPE

Libreville

DEL

RUANDA

Galápagos (Ec.)

Quito

Amazonas

GABÓN

CONGO

Kinshasa

BURUND

ECUADOR

Brazzaville

REP. DEM.

DEL CONGO

PERÚ

Amazonia

Ascensión (G. B.)

Luanda

Océano Pacífico

Lima

BRASIL

Santa Elena (G. B.)

ANGOLA

ZAMB

Lusaka

Hara

La Paz

Brasilia

BOLIVIA

NAMIBIA

ZIN

Sucre

Río de Janeiro

Windhoek

BOTSWAN

Trópico de Capricornio

PARAGUAY

São Paulo

Gaborone

Salas y Gómez (Ch.)

Asunción

Tshwane

Isla de Pascua (Ch.)

CHILE

Paraná

Océano Atlántico

REPÚBLICA DE SUDÁFRICA

Juan Fernández (Ch.)

Santiago

Ciudad de Buenos Aires

URUGUAY

Montevideo

Ciudad de El Cabo

Tristán da Cunha (G. B.)

ARGENTINA

Islas Malvinas (Arg.)

Islas Georgias del Sur (Arg.)

Isla Bouvet (Nor.)

Islas Sandwich del Sur (Arg.)

• capital de estado

60°

25°

Círculo po

74°

ANTÁRTIDA ARGENTINA

120°

60°

0°

1. Límite del lecho y subsuelo   2. Límite exterior del Río de la Plata   3. Límite lateral marítimo argentino-uruguayo

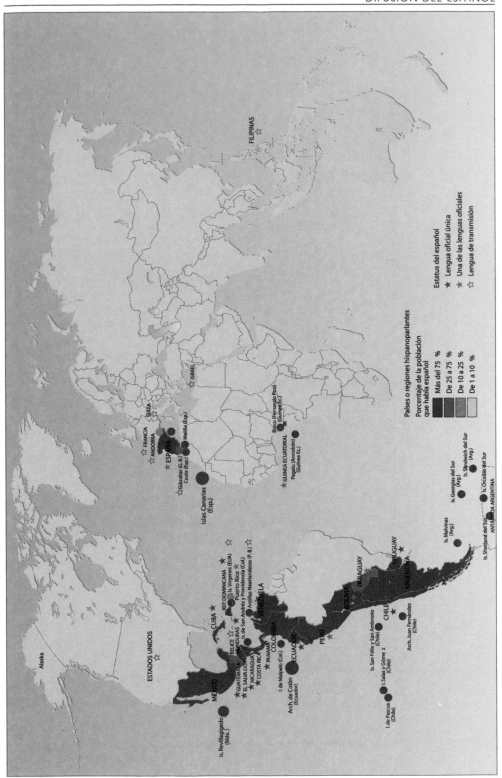

Países o regiones hispanoparlantes

Porcentaje de la población
que habla español

- Más del 75 %
- De 25 a 75 %
- De 10 a 25 %
- De 1 a 10 %

Estatus del español

★ Lengua oficial única
★ Una de las lenguas oficiales
☆ Lengua de transmisión